BHAGAVATA PURANA VOLUME 3

Bibek Debroy is a renowned economist, scholar and translator. He has worked in universities, research institutes, industry and for the government. He has widely published books, papers and articles on economics. As a translator, he is best known for his magnificent rendition of the Mahabharata in ten volumes, the three-volume translation of the Valmiki Ramayana and additionally the *Harivamsha*, published to wide acclaim by Penguin Classics. He is also the author of *Sarama and Her Children*, which splices his interest in Hinduism with his love for dogs.

PRAISE FOR *THE MAHABHARATA*

'The modernization of language is visible, it's easier on the mind, through expressions that are somewhat familiar. The detailing of the story is intact, the varying tempo maintained, with no deviations from the original. The short introduction reflects a brilliant mind. For those who passionately love the Mahabharata and want to explore it to its depths, Debroy's translation offers great promise . . .'—*Hindustan Times*

'[Debroy] has really carved out a niche for himself in crafting and presenting a translation of the Mahabharata . . . The book takes us on a great journey with admirable ease'—*Indian Express*

'The first thing that appeals to one is the simplicity with which Debroy has been able to express himself and infuse the right kind of meanings . . . Considering that Sanskrit is not the simplest of languages to translate a text from, Debroy exhibits his deep understanding and appreciation of the medium'—*The Hindu*

'Debroy's lucid and nuanced retelling of the original makes the masterpiece even more enjoyably accessible'—*Open*

'The quality of translation is excellent. The lucid language makes it a pleasure to read the various stories, digressions and parables'—*Tribune*

'Extremely well-organized, and has a substantial and helpful Introduction, plot summaries and notes. The volume is a beautiful example of a well thought-out layout which makes for much easier reading'—*Book Review*

'The dispassionate vision [Debroy] brings to this endeavour will surely earn him merit in the three worlds'—*Mail Today*

'Debroy's is not the only English translation available in the market, but where he scores and others fail is that his is the closest rendering of the original text in modern English without unduly complicating the readers' understanding of the epic'—*Business Standard*

'The brilliance of Ved Vyasa comes through, ably translated by Bibek Debroy'—*Hindustan Times*

PRAISE FOR *THE VALMIKI RAMAYANA*

'It is a delight to read Bibek Debroy's translation of the Valmiki Ramayana. It's like Lord Ram has blessed Dr Debroy, and through him, blessed us with another vehicle to read His immortal story'—Amish Tripathi

'Bibek Debroy's translation of the Ramayana is easy to navigate . . . It is an effort for which Debroy deserves unqualified praise'—*Business Standard*

'A nuanced translation of a beloved epic . . . There is much to recommend this three volume set that can renew our interest in the Ramayana, surely one of the greatest stories ever told'—*Indian Express*

Translated by Bibek Debroy

THE BHAGAVATA PURANA

3

PENGUIN BOOKS
An imprint of Penguin Random House

PENGUIN BOOKS

USA | Canada | UK | Ireland | Australia
New Zealand | India | South Africa | China

Penguin Books is part of the Penguin Random House group of companies
whose addresses can be found at global.penguinrandomhouse.com

Published by Penguin Random House India Pvt. Ltd
4th Floor, Capital Tower 1, MG Road,
Gurugram 122 002, Haryana, India

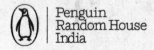

First published in Penguin Books by Penguin Random House India 2018

Translation copyright © Bibek Debroy 2018

All rights reserved

10 9 8 7 6 5 4 3 2

ISBN 9780143428039

Typeset in Sabon by Manipal Digital Systems, Manipal
Printed at Repro India Limited

www.penguin.co.in

For Yudhistir Govinda Das

Contents

Acknowledgements

The corpus of the Puranas is immense, in scope, as well as in length. Taken together, the eighteen Puranas are four times the size of the Mahabharata. If the prospect of translating the Mahabharata seemed challenging, the task of translating the Puranas was/is downright disconcerting and intimidating. After the Mahabharata, the Harivamsha and the Valmiki Ramayana, it was a natural transition, the obvious thing to do. However, it seemed to be an impossible task. Did one dare to start? If so, where? Since there was no 'Critical Edition' of the Puranas, what text should one use? I have now come to believe what should be obvious. Everything one does is determined by destiny. One is merely an instrument, implementing someone else's will. Thus, destiny intervened. It first intervened in the form of my dear friend, Professor Ramesh Kumar Pandey, vice chancellor, Shri Lal Bahadur Shastri Rashtriya Sanskrit Vidyapeetha. He suggested, in the absence of Critical Editions, one should use the Nirnaya Sagar texts. They have much greater acceptance than other versions. In addition, urging me along the road, he gifted me the Nirnaya Sagar texts of eleven of the eighteen Mahapuranas.

That still left a question unanswered. Which Purana should one start with? Destiny intervened yet again, in the form of another friend, Shri Yudhistir Govinda Das of ISKCON. For some time, Yudhistir had been urging us to visit Mayapur. That visit, pending for quite some time, materialized so that it synchronized with the annual Gaura Purnima festival. What better time to visit Mayapur? Yudhistir also gifted us a set of Prabhupada's translation of the

Bhagavata Purana. This determined the answer to the question. The Bhagavata Purana it would have to be. One does indeed deplore the general ignorance about the treasure trove the Puranas are. The dumbed down versions one usually sees or reads are pale shadows of what these texts actually contain. Having said this, the Purana that most people are familiar with is probably the Bhagavata Purana. Therefore, the Bhagavata Purana was a good choice. As a token of appreciation, these three volumes are dedicated to Yudhistir Govinda Das. As Yudhistir well knows, this is nothing more than a token. Dedications are meant for the one who is beyond either of us.

All these translations, ever since the Bhagavad Gita in 2006, have been published by Penguin India. I am indebted to Penguin for believing in the utility of not just the Bhagavata Purana translation, but the entire Purana Project, which still seems to stretch into the interminable horizon of the future. But one step at a time. For the record, with the Bhagavata Purana published, I am now translating Markandeya Purana, the next one in the series. In particular, Meru Gokhale and Ambar Sahil Chatterjee at Penguin India have been exceptionally patient, persevering and encouraging. But for them, the Purana Project might not have taken off. Paloma Dutta has been the editor since the days of the Mahabharata translation. That makes life a whole lot easier. She knows my style and I know hers. There is a Paloma hand in the product, even though it won't be detected and isn't meant to be.

ययोरात्मसमं वित्तं जन्मैश्वर्याकृतिर्भवः। तयोर्विवाहो मैत्री च नोत्तमाधमयोः क्वचित्। (10.60.15) Ever since this translation journey started in 2006, my wife, Suparna Banerjee (Debroy) has been a constant source of support, ensuring the conducive and propitious environment required for the work to continue unimpeded. She has been much more than that. (She was with me in Mayapur too.) In a rich language like Sanskrit, I can think of close to twenty words—all capturing the different nuances of 'wife'. Suparna has been all these and more. अनुकूलकलत्रे यस्तस्य स्वर्ग इहैव हि। प्रतिकूलकलत्रस्य नरको नात्र संशयः॥ This too is destiny.

Introduction

The word '*purana*' means old, ancient. The Puranas are old texts, usually referred to in conjunction with Itihasa (the Ramayana and the Mahabharata).[1] Whether Itihasa originally meant only the Mahabharata—with the Ramayana being added to that expression later—is a proposition on which there has been some discussion. But that's not relevant for our purposes. In the Chandogya Upanishad, there is an instance of the sage Narada approaching the sage Sanatkumara for instruction. When asked about what he already knew, Narada says he knows Itihasa and Purana, the Fifth Veda.[2] In other words, Itihasa–Purana possessed an elevated status. This by no means implies that the word 'purana', as used in these two Upanishads and other texts too, is to be understood in the sense of the word being applied to a set of texts known as the Puranas today. The Valmiki Ramayana is believed to have been composed by Valmiki and the Mahabharata by Krishna Dvaipayana Vedavyasa. After composing the Mahabharata, Krishna Dvaipayana Vedavyasa is believed to have composed the Puranas. The use of the word 'composed' immediately indicates that Itihasa–Purana are *smriti* texts, with a human origin. They are not *shruti* texts, with a divine origin. Composition does not mean these texts were rendered into writing. Instead, there was a process of oral narration, with

---

[1] For example, *shloka*s 2.4.10, 4.1.2 and 4.5.11 of the Brihadaranyaka Upanishad use the two expressions together.
[2] Chandogya Upanishad, 7.1.2.

inevitable noise in the transmission and distribution process. Writing came much later.

Frederick Eden Pargiter's book on the Puranas is still one of the best introductions to this corpus.[3] To explain the composition and transmission process, one can do no better than to quote him:

> The Vayu and Padma Puranas tell us how ancient genealogies, tales and ballads were preserved, namely, by the *suta*s,[4] and they describe the suta's duty . . . The Vayu, Brahmanda and Visnu give an account, how the original Purana came into existence . . . Those three Puranas say— Krsna Dvaipayana divided the single Veda into four and arranged them, and so was called Vyasa. He entrusted them to his four disciples, one to each, namely Paila, Vaisampayana, Jaimini and Sumantu. Then with tales, anecdotes, songs and lore that had come down from the ages he compiled a Purana, and taught it and the Itihasa to his fifth disciple, the suta Romaharsana or Lomaharsana . . .After that he composed the Mahabharata. The epic itself implies that the Purana preceded it . . . As explained above, the sutas had from remote times preserved the genealogies of gods, *rishi*s and kings, and traditions and ballads about celebrated men, that is, exactly the material— tales, songs and ancient lore—out of which the Purana was constructed. Whether or not Vyasa composed the original Purana or superintended its compilation, is immaterial for the present purpose . . . After the original Purana was composed, by Vyasa as is said, his disciple Romaharsana taught it to his son Ugrashravas, and Ugrashravas the *souti*[5] appears as the reciter in some of the present Puranas; and the sutas still retained the right to recite it for their livelihood. But, as stated above, Romaharsana taught it to his six disciples, at least five of whom were brahmans. It thus passed into the hands of brahmans, and their appropriation and development of it increased in the course of time, as the Purana

---

[3] *Ancient Indian Historical Tradition*, F.E. Pargiter, Oxford University Press, London, 1922.

[4] Sutas were bards, minstrels, raconteurs.

[5] Ugrashravas was a suta.

grew into many Puranas, as Sanskrit learning became peculiarly
the province of the brahmans, and as new and frankly sectarian
Puranas were composed.

Pargiter cited reasons for his belief that the Mahabharata was
composed before the original Purana, though that runs contrary
to the popular perception about the Mahabharata having been
composed before the Puranas. That popular and linear perception
is too simplistic, since texts evolved parallelly, not necessarily
sequentially.

In popular perception, Krishna Dvaipayana Vedavyasa
composed the Mahabharata. He then composed the Puranas.
Alternatively, he composed an original core Purana text, which has
been lost, and others embellished it through additions. The adjective
'purana', meaning old account or old text, became a proper noun,
signifying a specific text. To be classified as a Purana, a Purana has
to possess five attributes—*pancha lakshmana*. That is, five topics
must be discussed—*sarga*, *pratisarga*, *vamsha*, *manvantara* and
vamshanucharita. The clearest statement of this is in the Matsya
Purana. A text like the Bhagavata Purana also mentions these five
attributes, but adds another five, making it a total of ten. Unlike
the Ramayana and the Mahabharata, there is no Critical Edition
of the Puranas.[6] Therefore, citing chapter and verse from a Purana
text is somewhat more difficult, since verse, if not chapter, may
vary from text to text. With that caveat, the relevant shloka (verse)
should be in the fifty-third chapter of the Matysa Purana. Sarga
means the original or primary creation. The converse of sarga is
universal destruction, or *pralaya*. That period of sarga lasts for one
of Brahma's days, known as *kalpa*. When Brahma sleeps, during his
night, there is universal destruction.

In measuring time, there is the notion of a *yuga* (era) and there
are four yugas—*satya yuga* (also known as *krita yuga*), *treta yuga*,

---

[6] The Critical Edition of the Valmiki Ramayana was brought out by the
Baroda Oriental Institute, now part of the Maharaja Sayajirao University
of Baroda. The Critical Edition of the Mahabharata was brought out by the
Bhandarkar Oriental Research Institute, Pune.

dvapara yuga and *kali yuga*. Satya yuga lasts for 4,000 years, treta yuga for 3,000 years, dvapara yuga for 2,000 years and kali yuga for 1,000 years. However, all these are not human years. The gods have a different timescale and these are the years of the gods. As one progressively moves from satya yuga to kali yuga, virtue (*dharma*) declines. But at the end of kali yuga, the cycle begins afresh, with satya yuga. An entire cycle, from satya yuga to kali yuga, is known as a *mahayuga* (great era). However, a mahayuga is not just 10,000 years. There is a further complication. At the beginning and the end of every yuga, there are some additional years. These additional years are 400 for satya yuga, 300 for treta yuga, 200 for dvapara yuga and 100 for kali yuga. A mahayuga thus has 12,000 years, adding years both at the beginning and at the end. 1,000 mahayugas make up one kalpa. A kalpa is also divided into fourteen *manvantara*s, a manvantara being a period during which a Manu presides and rules over creation. Therefore, there are 71.4 mahayugas in a manvantara. Our present kalpa is known as the Shveta Varaha Kalpa. Within that, six Manus have come and gone. Their names are (1) Svyambhuva Manu, (2) Svarochisha Manu, (3) Uttama Manu, (4) Tapasa Manu, (5) Raivata Manu and (6) Chakshusha Manu. The present Manu is known as Vaivasvata Manu. Vivasvat, also written as Vivasvan, is the name of Surya, the sun god. Vaivasvata Manu has that name because he is Surya's son. Not only the Manus, but the gods, the ruler of the gods and the seven great sages, known as the *saptarshi*s (seven rishis), change from one manvantara to another. Indra is a title of the ruler of the gods. It is not a proper name. The present Indra is Purandara. However, in a different manvantara, someone else will hold the title. In the present seventh manvantara, known as Vaivasvata manvantara, there will also be 71.4 mahayugas. We are in the twenty-eighth of these. Since a different Vedavyasa performs that task of classifying and collating the Vedas in every mahayuga, Krishna Dvaipayana Vedavyasa is the twenty-eighth in that series. Just so that it is clear, Vedavyasa isn't a proper name. It is a title conferred on someone who collates and classifies the Vedas. There have been twenty-seven who have held the title of Vedavyasa before Krishna Dvaipayana and he is the twenty-eighth.

His proper name is Krishna Dvaipayana—Krishna because he was dark and Dvaipayna because he was born on an island (*dvipa*). This gives us an idea of what the topic of manvantara is about. This still leaves pratisarga, vamsha and vamshanucharita. The two famous dynasties/lineages were the solar dynasty (*survya vamsha*) and lunar dynasty (*chandra vamsha*) and all the famous kings belonged to one or other of these two dynasties. Vamshanucharita is about these lineages and the conduct of these kings. There were the gods and sages (rishis) too, not always born through a process of physical procreation. Their lineages are described under the heading of vamsha. Finally, within that cycle of primary creation and destruction, there are smaller and secondary cycles of creation and destruction. That's the domain of pratisarga. In greater or lesser degree, all the Puranas cover these five topics, some more than the others.

There are Puranas, and there are Puranas. Some are known as Sthala Puranas, describing the greatness and sanctity of a specific geographical place. Some are known as Upa-Puranas, minor Puranas. The listing of Upa-Puranas has regional variations and there is no countrywide consensus about the list of Upa-Puranas, though it is often accepted that there are eighteen of them. The Puranas we have in mind are known as Maha-Puranas, major Puranas. Henceforth, when we use the word Puranas, we mean Maha-Puranas. There is consensus that there are eighteen Maha-Puranas, though it is not obvious that this number of eighteen existed right from the beginning. The names are mentioned in several of these texts, including a shloka that follows the shloka cited from the Matsya Purana. The listing is also included in the last sections of the Bhagavata Purana itself. Thus, the eighteen Puranas are (1) Agni (15,400); (2) Bhagavata (18,000); (3) Brahma (10,000); (4) Brahmanda (12,000); (5) Brahmavaivarta (18,000); (6) Garuda (19,000); (7) Kurma (17,000); (8) Linga (11,000); (9) Markandeya (9,000); (10) Matsya (14,000); (11) Narada (25,000); (12) Padma (55,000); (13) Shiva (24,000); (14) Skanda (81,100); (15) Vamana (10,000); (16) Varaha (24,000); (17) Vayu (24,000) and (18) Vishnu (23,000). A few additional points about this list. First, the Harivamsha is sometimes loosely described as a Purana, but strictly speaking, it is not a Purana. It is more like an addendum to the Mahabharata. Second, Bhavishya (14,500) is sometimes mentioned, with Vayu excised from the list. However, the Vayu Purana exhibits many more Purana characteristics than the Bhavishya Purana does. There are references to a Bhavishyat Purana that existed, but that may not necessarily be the Bhavishya Purana as we know it today. That's true of some other Puranas too. Texts have been completely restructured hundreds of years later. Third, it is not just a question of Bhavishya Purana and Vayu Purana. In the lists given in some Puranas, Vayu is part of the eighteen, but Agni is knocked out. In some others, Narasimha and Vayu are included, but Brahmanda and Garuda are knocked out. Fourth, when a list is given, the order also indicates some notion of priority or importance. Since that varies from text to text, our listing is simply alphabetical, according to the English alphabet.

The numbers within brackets indicate the number of shlokas each of these Puranas has, or is believed to have. The range is from 10,000 in Brahma to a mammoth 81,100 in Skanda. The aggregate is a colossal 409,500 shlokas. To convey a rough idea of the orders of magnitude, the Mahabharata has, or is believed to have, 100,000 shlokas. It's a bit difficult to convert a shloka into word counts in English, especially because Sanskrit words have a slightly different structure. However, as a very crude approximation, one shloka is roughly twenty words. Thus, 100,000 shlokas become two million words and 400,000 shlokas, four times the size of the Mahabharata, amounts to eight million words. There is a reason for using the expression 'is believed to have', as opposed to 'has'. Rendering into writing is of later vintage, the initial process was one of oral transmission. In the process, many texts have been lost, or are retained in imperfect condition. This is true of texts in general and is also specifically true of Itihasa and Puranas. The Critical Edition of the Mahabharata, mentioned earlier, no longer possesses 100,000 shlokas. Including the Harivamsha, there are around 80,000 shlokas. The Critical Edition of the Mahabharata has of course deliberately excised some shlokas. For the Puranas, there is no counterpart of Critical Editions. However, whichever edition of the Puranas one chooses, the number of shlokas in that specific Purana will be smaller than the numbers given above. Either those many shlokas did not originally exist, or they have been lost. This is the right place to mention that a reading of the Puranas assumes a basic degree of familiarity with the Valmiki Ramayana and the Mahabharata, more the latter than the former. Without that familiarity, one will often fail to appreciate the context completely. Specifically for the Bhagavata Purana, more than passing familiarity with the Bhagavad Gita—strictly speaking, a part of the Mahabharata—helps.[7]

Other than the five attributes, the Puranas have a considerable amount of information on geography and even geological changes (changes in courses of rivers) and astronomy. Therefore, those five attributes shouldn't suggest the Puranas have nothing more. They do, and they have therefore been described as encyclopedias. Bharatavarsha is vast and heterogeneous and each Purana may very well have originated in one particular part of the country. Accordingly, within that broad compass of an overall geographical description, the extent of geographical information varies from Purana to Purana. Some are more familiar with one part of the country than with another. Though not explicitly mentioned in the five attributes, the Puranas are also about pursuing dharma, artha, kama and moksha, the four objectives of human existence, and are about the four varnas and the four ashramas. The general understanding and practice of dharma is based much more on the Puranas than on the Vedas. Culture, notions of law, rituals, architecture and iconography are based on the Puranas. There is beautiful poetry too, included in parts of the Bhagavata Purana.

Perhaps one should mention that there are two ways these eighteen Puranas are classified. The trinity has Brahma as the creator, Vishnu as the preserver and Shiva as the destroyer. Therefore, Puranas where creation themes feature prominently are identified

_____

[7] The Bhagavad Gita translation was published in 2006, the translation of the Critical Edition of the Mahabharata in ten volumes between 2010 and 2014 (with a box set in 2015) and the translation of the Critical Edition of the Valmiki Ramayana in 2017. The translations are by Bibek Debroy, and in each case, the publisher is Penguin.

with Brahma (Brahma, Brahmanda, Brahmavaivarta, Markandeya). Puranas where Vishnu features prominently are identified as Vaishnava Puranas (Bhagavata, Garuda, Kurma, Matysa, Narada, Padma, Vamana, Varaha, Vishnu). Puranas where Shiva features prominently are identified as Shaiva Puranas (Agni, Linga, Shiva, Skanda, Vayu). While there is a grain of truth in this, Brahma, Vishnu and Shiva are all important and all three feature in every Purana. Therefore, beyond the relative superiority of Vishnu vis-à-vis Shiva, the taxonomy probably doesn't serve much purpose. The second classification is even more tenuous and is based on the three *guna*s of *sattva* (purity), *rajas* (passion) and *tamas* (ignorance). For example, the Uttara Khanda of the Padma Purana has a few shlokas along these lines, recited by Shiva to Parvati. With a caveat similar to the one mentioned earlier, this should be in the 236th chapter of Uttara Khanda. According to this, the Puranas characterized by sattva are Bhagavata, Garuda, Narada, Padma, Varaha and Vishnu. Those characterized by rajas are Bhavishya, Brahma, Brahmanda, Brahmavaivarta, Markandeya and Vamana, Those characterized by tamas are Agni, Kurma, Linga, Matysa, Skanda and Shiva.

Within a specific Purana text, there are earlier sections, as well as later ones. That makes it difficult to date a Purana, except as a range. Across Purana texts, there are older Puranas, as well as later ones. Extremely speculatively, the dating will be something like the following. (1) Agni (800–1100 CE); (2) Bhagavata (500–1000 CE); (3) Brahma (700–1500 CE); (4) Brahmanda (400–600 CE); (5) Brahmavaivarta (700–1500 CE); (6) Garuda (800–1100 CE); (7) Kurma (600–900 CE); (8) Linga (500–1000 CE); (9) Markandeya (250–700 CE); (10) Matsya (200–500 CE); (11) Narada (900–1600 CE); (12) Padma (400–1600 CE); (13) Shiva (1000–1400 CE); (14) Skanda (600–1200 CE); (15) Vamana (450–900 CE); (16) Varaha (1000–1200 CE); (17) Vayu (350–550 CE); (18) Vishnu (300 BCE to 450 CE); and (19) Bhavishya (500–1900 CE). Reiterating once again that there is no great precision in these ranges, by this reckoning, the Vishnu Purana is the oldest and some parts of the Bhavishya Purana are as recent as the nineteenth century.

As mentioned earlier, there is no Critical Edition for the Puranas. Therefore, one has to choose a Sanskrit text one is going to translate from. If one is going to translate all the Puranas, it is preferable, though not essential, that one opts for a common source for all the Purana texts. The common source for the Bhagavata Purana, and the subsequent Purana translations, is the one brought out by Nag Publishers, with funding from the ministry of human resource development.[8] A transliterated Sanskrit text is available through the University of Gottingen.[9] In Devanagari, the text is available at https://sanskritdocuments.org/doc_purana/bhagpur. html?lang=sa, with the transliterated Sanskrit text at http://www. sanskritweb.net/sansdocs/bhagpur.pdf. The Oxford Centre for Hindu Studies at the University of Oxford has a lot of useful resources under the umbrella of the Bhagavata Purana Research Project.[10] Among other things, this research project has published a book that is a bit like an abridged translation of the Bhagavata Purana.[11] The Bhagavata Purana is divided into twelve *skandha*s. The word skandha means trunk, or largish branch. In this context, it means section or segment. Out of these twelve skandhas, the tenth is the longest and is also the most read. Therefore, there are translations of the Bhagavata Purana that are limited to only the Tenth Skandha. Edwin Bryant's rendering of the Tenth Skandha is almost like such a translation.[12] For the entire Bhagavata Purana, there are unabridged translations in Indian languages. However, to the best of my knowledge, there are only five unabridged translations in English: (1) Manmatha Nath Dutt;[13]

---

[8] *The Bhagavatamahapuranam*, Nag Publishers, Delhi, 1987. This is a reprint of the Kshemaraja Shrikrishnadass, Venkateshvara Press, Bombay, text.

[9] https://web.archive.org/web/20081012022829/http://www.sub. uni-goettingen.de/ebene_1/fiindolo/gretil/1_sanskr/3_purana/bhagp/bhp1-12u.htm

[10] http://www.ochs.org.uk/research/bhagavata-purana-research-project

[11] *The Bhagavata Purana, Selected Readings*, Ravi M. Gupta and Kenneth R. Valpey, Columbia University Press, 2016.

[12] *Krishna: The Beautiful Legend of God (Srimad Bhagavata Purana Book X)*, Edwin Bryant, Penguin Classics, 2004.

[13] *A Prose English Translation of Srimad Bhagavatam*, Manmatha Nath Dutt, H.C. Dass, Calcutta, 1896.

(2) Bhaktivedanta Swami Prabhupada;[14] (3) Ganesh Vasudeo Tagare;[15] (4) Swami Tapasyananda;[16] and (5) C.L. Goswami and M.A. Shastri.[17] In 1901, Purnendu Narayana Sinha published a version that was close to a translation, but fell just short because it followed the path of retelling.[18] The Sanskrit texts used in these five translations vary a bit and the one used in this translation also varies a bit from the ones used in these five. The Bhagavata Purana is believed to have 18,000 shlokas. The table below shows what this particular Sanskrit version has: just over 14,000 spread across 335 chapters. One should not jump to the conclusion that a large number of shlokas are missing. A few are indeed missing. But sometimes, it is also a question of how one counts a shloka. With the content remaining identical, the text may be counted as one shloka in one place and as two shlokas elsewhere. Our numbering is exactly the same as in the Sanskrit text we have followed. Hence, even though there may be no difference in content between our version of the text and, say, that used by Swami Prabhupada, the numbering will vary a bit. (Sometimes, there are minor differences in the Sanskrit text though.) However, there are some shlokas that are indeed missing and Ganesh Vasudeo Tagare is a good source for translations of these missing shlokas, because those missing shlokas have been separately translated there. When we have enumerated all the chapters, there are two identifying numbers that have been provided. The first number refers to the skandha, the second to the number of the chapter within the skandha. Thus, Chapter 4(30) will be the thirtieth chapter in the fourth Skandha.

[14] *Srimad Bhagavatam*, Bhaktivedanta Swami Prabhupada, Bhaktivedanta Book Trust, 1970 to 1977.

[15] *The Bhagavata Purana*, translated and annotated by Ganesh Vasudeo Tagare, Motilal Banarsidass Publishers, Delhi, 1976.

[16] *Srimad Bhagavada*, Swami Tapasyananda, Sri Ramakrishna Math, Chennai, 1980.

[17] *Srimad Bhagavata Mahapurana with Sanskrit Text and English Translation*, C.L. Goswami and M.A. Shastri, Gita Press, 2006.

[18] *A Study of the Bhagavata Purana or Esoteric Hinduism*, Purnendu Narayana Sinha, Freeman and Company, Benares, 1901.

Skandha	Number of chapters	Number of shlokas
1	19	811
2	10	391
3	33	1412
4	31	1450
5	26	738
6	19	855
7	15	752
8	24	929
9	24	962
10	90	3948
11	31	1360
12	13	564
Total	335	14172

In the translations of the Bhagavad Gita, the Mahabharata, the Harivamsha and the Valmiki Ramayana, we followed the principle of not using diacritical marks. The use of diacritical marks (effectively the international alphabet of Sanskrit transliteration) makes the pronunciation and rendering more accurate, but also tends to put off readers who are less academically inclined. Since diacritical marks are not being used, there is a challenge of rendering Sanskrit names in English. Sanskrit is a phonetic language and we have used that principle as a basis. Applied consistently, this means that words are rendered in ways that may seem unfamiliar. Hence, the name of the jewel, often written as Kaustubha, will appear as Koustubha here. This is true of proper names, and, in a few rare cases, of geographical names. The absence of diacritical marks causes some minor problems. How does one distinguish Vasudeva Krishna from Krishna's father, Vasudeva? Often, the context will make the difference clear. If not, we have written the son as Vaasudeva and the father as Vasudeva. In translating, the attempt has been to provide a word-for-word translation, so that if one were to hold up the Sanskrit text, there would be a perfect match.

The intention is also to offer a translation, not an interpretation. That sounds like a simple principle to adopt, and for the most part, is easy to follow. However, there is a thin dividing line between translation and interpretation. In some instances, it is impossible to translate without bringing in a little bit of interpretation. Inevitably, interpretation is subjective. We have tried to minimize the problem by (a) reducing interpretation; (b) relegating interpretation to footnotes and (c) when there are alternative interpretations, pointing this out to the reader through those footnotes. If a Purana text is just about the five attributes mentioned, the task isn't that difficult. Take the Bhagavata Purana as an example. In Chapter 2(10), we are told about the ten characteristics of the Bhagavata Purana and these are sarga, *visarga, sthana, poshana, uti,* manvantara, *isha-anukatha, nirodha, mukti* and *ashraya.* These are (1) gross creation; (2) subtle creation; (3) preservation; (4) sustenance; (5) the addiction to the senses; (6) manvantaras; (7) accounts of the lord; (8) withdrawal; (9) liberation and (10) the ultimate refuge. Therefore, the text has much more than the five attributes cited. The word '*bhagavat*' means the divine one, the illustrious one, the fortunate one, the prosperous one, the blessed one, the sacred one, the holy one. We are often more familiar with the nominative form, *bhagavaan.* Bhagavat/Bhagavaan occur frequently in our text and I have translated the word as 'the illustrious one'. Since this is a Purana devoted to Vishnu, Bhagavat/Bhagavaan typically means Vishnu. But the text is not called Bhagavata Purana; it is in fact called Bhaagavata Purana. What does the word Bhaagavata mean? Taken as an adjective, the word means sacred and Bhaagavata Purana is simply the sacred Purana, a perfectly acceptable meaning. However, taken as a noun, Bhaagavata means a devotee or worshipper of Vishnu—and *bhaagavata dharma* is the dharma of devotion towards Vishnu. Therefore, Bhaagavata Purana is the text that describes this bhaagavata dharma that Vishnu devotees follow.

Hence, it isn't only about stories. As mentioned earlier, the longest Skandha, the tenth, is also the most popular and is read most often. This particular skandha describes Krishna's exploits and pastimes. This includes *rasa lila* and this skandha has some exquisite poetry. The song of the *gopis* is an example of this. As is thus obvious, this skandha has its fair share of stories. But in the other skandhas, the emphasis is more on dharma and moksha and a mix of *bhakti* (devotion), *advaita* (monism), *dvaita* (dualism), *samkhya* and *yoga*,[19] with notions of *avatara*s (Vishnu's incarnations) brought in. There is the influence of *pancharatra* doctrines and texts. Literally, the term pancharatra means five nights, and is a reference to five nights over which sacrifices were performed. However, there were pancharatra doctrines too and these developed a metaphysical philosophy. If we so wish, we can call it a theology. Vaishnava dharma integrated this pancharatra tradition with the other strands that have just been mentioned. Since this is a synthesis of many different strands, there are bound to be nuances and different schools. What does the Bhagavata Purana teach? What is its philosophy? Beyond the obvious tenet of devotion to Vishnu and emphasis on bhakti yoga, this is extremely difficult to answer. As a text that builds a theology, the Bhagavata Purana is much more complicated than the Bhagavad Gita. Indeed, one could say it builds extensively on that Bhagavad Gita foundation. Down the years, there have been several commentaries on and interpretations of the Bhagavata Purana. Depending on the language and the timeline for beginning and ending the cut-off, there must be at least two hundred such commentaries and interpretations. Which of these schools or interpretations should one follow? Should one take cognizance of other possible interpretations? In principle, this dilemma can exist in the course of translating any Purana. But in no other Purana is it as serious, because no other Purana devotes such a large percentage of shlokas to philosophy.

The choice in this translation is conscious and is driven by the objective and the target audience. The target audience is the ordinary reader who desires a faithful rendering of the Sanskrit text. The target reader isn't the academic who desires something like a survey of literature. Nor is the target reader a devotee of one particular Vaishnava school. To state it a bit more explicitly, Bhaktivedanta Swami Prabhupada, Swami Tapasyananda and C.L. Goswami and M.A. Shastri follow one particular line of

[19] Two of the six Indian schools of *darshana* (philosophy).

commentary or interpretation or school. From an academic's perspective, Ganesh Vasudeo Tagare is the best. His translation also includes an excellent introduction and a detailed note on several different commentators of the Bhagavata Purana, certainly covering the major ones. However, apart from the language of the Tagare rendition not being very smooth, that edition is also layered with complexities which can deter the ordinary reader. On the other hand, I have consciously done what is akin to a contemporary Manmatha Nath Dutt translation. Without distorting, I have chosen the simplest possible interpretation or translation that fits. In a few minor instances, this meant choosing an interpretation that was marginally different from those chosen by these preceding translators. It is possible to criticize the avoidance of complexities, but it is a conscious choice and the dissatisfied reader can always go on to read more copious commentaries and annotations. There is plenty in the Bhagavata Purana to immerse oneself in and this translation is not meant to be the final item on that reading list. It can at best be the first.

Tenth Skandha continued . . .

Chapter 10(12)

Shri-Shuka said, 'Once, Hari made up his mind to eat in the forest. He woke up in the morning and used the beautiful tunes of his flute to wake up his friends and the calves. With the calves in front, he then left Vraja. At this sweet sound, thousands of boys went with him, with their pouches,[1] canes,[2] horns and flutes. Each of them placed his own herd, with more than one thousand calves in each, in front. They happily left. They made their own calves mingle in the same herd as Krishna's innumerable calves. They made them graze. Here and there, they engaged in boyish games. They were

---

[1] Filled with food.
[2] For herding the cattle.

adorned with glass beads, *gunja* berries,[3] jewels and gold. But in
spite of being adorned, they ornamented themselves with fruits,
green leaves, bunches of flowers, feathers and minerals. They stole
the pouches from each other. When detected, they flung these far
away. When the owner caught up, they laughed and flung them
further away. When the owner cried, they returned them. Krishna
sometimes went far away, to admire the beauty of the forest. "I
am first. No I am first." Saying this, they touched him and enjoyed
themselves. Some played on flutes. Some blew on horns. Some
buzzed, along with the bees. Others called, along with the cuckoos.
Some rushed towards shadows. Some walked like proud swans.
Some sat down, along with the storks. Some danced with peacocks.
Some tugged the tails of young monkeys seated on braches. Some
climbed those trees. Some made faces at the monkeys. Some leapt on
the branches. Some leapt, along with the frogs. Some got wet from
the water in the river. Some laughed at their own shadows. Some
cursed their echoes. He is the supreme divinity, and the virtuous
who become his servants realize the bliss of the *brahman*[4] through
him. Because of his *maya*, he had assumed the form of a human
child. They enjoyed themselves with him and created stores of merit
for themselves. *Yogi*s who control themselves cannot touch the dust
of his feet after the difficulties of many births. But in this land, he
himself presented himself before them. How can one describe the
good fortune of the residents of Vraja?

'There was a great *asura* named Agha. He saw their happy
pastimes and was incapable of tolerating it. The immortals drank
amrita. But even then, they always waited for an end to his life,
because he disturbed them as long as he was alive. Aghasura saw
the boys, with Krishna at the forefront. He was the younger brother
of Baki[5] and Baka and had been commanded by Kamsa. "This is
the one who has killed both my brother and sister. I will kill him,
along with his followers. When these are offered as sesamum seeds

---

[3] Gunja is a small herb that has red and black berries. Their mothers
had adorned them with these objects.

[4] The supreme soul.

[5] Putana.

and water to my well-wishers,[6] the residents of Vraja are as good
as dead. These children are as dear to them as their breath of life.
When the breath of life is destroyed, why worry about the body?"
Having decided this, he assumed the form of a gigantic python.[7]
It was one *yojana*[8] long, as thick as a large mountain. Having
assumed this extraordinary form, the deceitful one lay on the path,
opening its mouth, which was like a cave, to devour them. The
lower lip was on the ground and the upper lip touched the clouds.
The mouth was like the cave of a mountain. The fangs were like
the peaks of mountains. The inside of the mouth was completely
dark. The tongue was like a broad road. The breathing was like a
harsh storm. The fiery glance was like a forest conflagration. On
seeing it, all of them were of the view that this was a beautiful spot
in Vrindavana, shaped in the form of a python with a gaping jaw.
They looked at it, as if it was a place to play in. "O friends! Tell
us if it is without life, stationed in front of us. Doesn't it resemble
the gaping mouth of a snake that will devour us. Isn't that true?"
"True.[9] The upper lip looks like a cloud tinged red by the rays of
the sun. The lower and reddened lip, on the ground, looks like its
shadow. On the right and the left, the corners of the mouth are like
caves in mountains. Behold. The fangs seem to resemble lofty peaks
of mountains. In length and breadth, the tongue seems to rival a
broad road. The inside of the mouth is as dark as the darkness in
between two peaks. Behold. The fiery breath is like the harsh wind
of a forest conflagration. There is the bad stench of burnt corpses.
There is a smell of flesh emerging from the inside. If we enter, will
it devour us? Or will it be instantly destroyed by this one,[10] like
Baka?" Glancing towards the face of Baka's enemy, they laughed,
clapped their hands and entered. They were ignorant about the
actual truth and thought what was false to be true. The one who
is located inside all creatures knew everything. The illustrious

---

[6] Sesamum seeds and water are offered to dead relatives.
[7] *Ajagara.*
[8] A yojana is a measure of distance, between 8 and 9 miles.
[9] This is a second boy speaking.
[10] Krishna.

one heard and desiring to protect those who were his own, made up his mind to prevent them. However, they entered inside the asura's stomach. But it didn't digest the children or the calves. The *rakshasa* remembered about his beloved relatives being slain and waited for Baka's enemy to enter. Krishna is the one who grants everyone freedom from fear. He saw that they had gone outside his control and were without a protector. They were helpless and were like grass, facing the death from its digestive fire. He was filled with compassion, but also surprised at what destiny had done.[11] "What should be done now? Should one allow the wicked one to live? Or should one prevent injury to the innocent and the virtuous? How can both be achieved?" Thinking in this way, the infinite Hari decided and entered the mouth. The gods who were hidden in the clouds shrieked in fear. Kamsa and others and demons who were Agha's friends rejoiced. The illustrious and undecaying Krishna heard this. It desired to crush him, the children and the calves. However, inside its throat, he swiftly enlarged his size. That gigantic being's breath of life was restricted. Its eyes popped out and rolled around here and there. All the breathing was completely restricted. The breath of life shattered the crown of life and emerged outside. All the breath of life emerged outside. The illustrious one glanced at the calves and his well-wishers, who were dead, and brought them back to life. With them, Mukunda again came out through the mouth. An extraordinary and large radiance rose up from the serpent's body. Through its own resplendence, it illuminated the ten directions. It waited in the sky for the lord to emerge. While all the residents of heaven looked on, it then entered his person. All of them were extremely delighted that their own task had been accomplished. They worshipped him by showering down flowers. Celestial *apsara*s danced. Divine musicians played on musical instruments. *Brahmana*s praised him. Everyone recited chants of victory. There were wonderful prayers and excellent music and singing. There were sounds of victory and festivities, with auspicious tones. Hearing this, Aja soon approached the spot.

[11] Krishna wished to prevent them from entering, but destiny had worked against this.

He saw the lord's glory and was filled with amazement. O king! The wonderful skin of the python was dried. It was kept in Vrindavana and for many days, the residents of Vraja played inside that cave. Hari's exploit of liberating the serpent and bringing them back from the dead happened when he was five years old. However, the astounded boys spoke about it in Vraja when he was six years old. This is not astounding. Using his maya, he assumed the form of a human child. He is cause and effect. He is the supreme creator. Through his touch, even Agha was cleansed of his sins. The wicked find it extremely difficult to obtain him and be identified with him.[12] It is only if one's mind is immersed in him, if one is devoted to him and if one places his form in the core of one's heart, even once, that one attains this state. One then enjoys eternal bliss. He destroys all maya. What need be said of one[13] who is inside him?'

Suta said,[14] 'O brahmanas! Devadatta[15] heard this wonderful account about his own protector, the Yadava. Controlling his mind, he again asked Vyasa's son about the sacred account.'

The king said, 'O brahmana! What explains the gap in time that occurred then? Hari performed his act when he was five years old, but the boys spoke about it in his sixth year. O great yogi! O preceptor! Tell me about this. I have a great curiosity. This must indeed be Hari's maya and nothing else. O preceptor! We are the most fortunate in the world. Though we are kshatra-bandhus,[16] from your mouth, we have repeatedly been drinking the true and sacred account about Krishna's immortal stories.'

Suta said, 'O supreme among devotees of the illustrious one! Badarayana's son was thus asked. As he remembered Ananta in his heart, he lost control of all his senses. With great deal of effort, he slowly regained his external senses and replied.'

---

[12] Agha merged into Krishna.

[13] Agha.

[14] Ugrashrava, the son of Romaharshana or Lomaharshana. A *suta* was a charioteer, but also a bard and raconteur. Here, it is a proper noun, another name for Ugrashrava.

[15] Granted by god, Parikshit.

[16] Worst among kshatriyas, one who is a kshatriya only in name.

Chapter 10(13)

Shri-Shuka said, 'O immensely fortunate one! O supreme among those who are devoted to the illustrious one! You have asked a good question. Hearing repeatedly about the lord's account, you bring new and newer attachment to them. There are those who are virtuous, naturally assimilating the essence and meaning of Achyuta's sacred accounts with their speech, ears and minds at every moment and bringing newer attachment, like dissolute men addicted to women. O king! Hear attentively the secret I will tell you. Preceptors can speak about secret things to disciples they love. The illustrious one saved the calves and their protectors[17] from death in the form of Agha's mouth. He brought them to the sandy banks of the river and spoke to them. "O friends! This sandy bank of the river is extremely beautiful. It is covered with soft and clean sand and has everything required for us to play. There are blooming lotuses and the banks have enchanting trees, the fragrance drawing bees and birds, whose calls are echoing. Let us eat here. Most of the day has passed and we are afflicted by hunger. Let the calves drink water and graze slowly near us, on the grass." The boys agreed. After the calves had drunk, they tethered them, so that they could graze on the green pasture. With the illustrious one, they cheerfully undid their pouches and started to eat. They sat around Krishna in concentric circles and faced him. The boys from Vraja possessed beautiful faces and their eyes were opened wide. They sat with him in that beautiful forest region, just as the stamen of a lotus is surrounded by whorls. For vessels to eat out of, some used bunches of flowers. Others used sprouts, leaves and fruits. Some used their pouches, barks of trees or stones. Showing each other, they separately ate what each of them had brought. They laughed and made the others laugh. With the lord, they ate what others had brought. Those in the world of heaven looked on at the enjoyer of sacrifices enjoying himself in childish pastimes. He[18] tucked in his

---

[17] The boys.
[18] Krishna.

flute between his stomach and the garment at his waist. The horn and the cane were under his left arm. He placed the lovely food and fruits in his hands and picked up mouthfuls with his fingers. He was in their midst, surrounded by his well-wishers. He laughed and played with his own friends. O descendant of the Bharata lineage! With their souls in Achyuta, they and the calves ate. Desiring grass, the calves strayed far away, inside the forest. On seeing this, they were scared. Krishna is the one who causes fright to all kinds of terror. He pacified his friends and said, "Do not stop.[19] I will bring the calves back here." Having said this, with the morsel of food still in his hands, the illustrious Krishna left. He searched for his own calves and those of the others in mountains, caves, bushes and thickets.

'O extender of the Kuru lineage! Earlier, the one born from the lotus[20] had remained in the sky and had witnessed his powers in liberating Agha. He had been filled with great wonder. With his heart immersed in him, he now wished to see the lord's maya and other glory as a child. Therefore, he stole the calves and the cowherd boys. He took them to some other spot, remaining invisible. Krishna couldn't see the calves on the sandy bank or the forest. Nor did he see the cowherd boys. He searched in every direction. The one who knows about everything in the universe couldn't see the calves or the cowherd boys in the forest. He instantly understood that everything had been done by the creator. Krishna, the lord who is the creator of the universe, desired to bring pleasure to him and to the mothers.[21] Therefore, he expanded himself.[22] He became exactly like the cowherd boys and exactly like the small forms of the calves. He became exactly like their sticks, horns, flutes, wreaths and pouches. He became exactly like their ornaments and garments. He assumed their exact forms, conduct, qualities and

[19] Do not stop eating.

[20] Brahma.

[21] To the mothers of the boys and the calves by restoring them, and to Brahma by allowing the boys and the calves to remain hidden.

[22] He assumed the forms of both the boys and the calves.

features, the exact ways they played. Aja[23] assumed all their forms,
their words and their limbs. Everything is permeated by Vishnu.
He is his own *atman* and manifested himself as the calves and
the cowherd boys. The one who is in all atmans thus played and
sported with his own atman and entered Vraja in this way. He took
those separate calves and placed them in their respective pens. O
king! Assuming their forms,[24] he entered their respective homes.
On hearing the respective flutes, the respective mothers quickly
arose. They embraced them in their arms. Without feeling their
weights, they raised them up. Because of the love, milk oozed out of
their breasts, like nectar and *asava*.[25] Taking the supreme brahman
to be their own sons, they fed him. O king! Thereafter, they
massaged them and bathed them, smearing them with unguents.
They decorated them with ornaments and protected them.[26] They
applied *tilaka*[27] and fed them. Thus tended to, Madhava delighted
them with his own conduct. One *yama*[28] passed into another yama
and evening arrived. Soon, the cows reached the pens. With the
sounds of bellowing, they summoned their respective calves and
fed them the milk that flowed from their udders, repeatedly licking
them. As mothers, the love of the cows and the *gopis*[29] increased,
even more than was the case before. Because of Hari's maya, they
didn't realize their sons were missing.[30] For the residents of Vraja,
the affection they had towards their own sons gradually increased
from one day to another day and became limitless. For Krishna, it
was the same as before.[31] This continued for a year. In this way,

[23] Krishna.
[24] Of the cowherds.
[25] Asava is liquor made through distillation, not mere fermentation.
[26] By chanting *mantras*.
[27] A mark made on the forehead.
[28] Day and night are divided into eight yamas, each yama is a period of
three hours.
[29] Wives of cowherds (*gopas*).
[30] This is interpreted in complicated ways. But this is simpler.
[31] There was no reason for Krishna to change his behaviour, even if he
was in the forms of the boys and the calves. However, because Krishna was
in the forms of the boys and the calves, the others became more affectionate.

the one who is his own atman manifested himself in the form of the calves and the cowherd boys. He passed a year in this way, protecting and playing as the cowherd boys in the forest and in the pens.

'Once, along with Rama, Aja entered the forest, tending to the calves. Five or six nights were left for an entire year to be over. Once, the cows were grazing on grass on the summit of Mount Govardhana. From a distance, they saw their calves grazing near Vraja. On seeing them, they were filled with affection and forgot themselves. That herd of cows rushed down difficult paths that were difficult for their protectors to follow. They moved down like bipeds. Their necks were drawn back towards their humps and their tails were raised. They bellowed and with milk flowing from their udders, they swiftly headed down. At the foot of the hill, the cows greeted the calves, as if they had just been born and fed them milk. With milk flowing from their udders, they licked them, as if they would swallow them up. The gopas were unable to prevent their cows from meeting their calves. Frustrated, they were both ashamed and angry. With difficulty, they descended along those impassable paths and saw the cows, the calves and their sons. As soon as they saw their sons, a great affection resulted. They were overwhelmed with love and the rage was gone. They embraced them in their arms and inhaled the fragrances of their heads. They were filled with great delight. The aged gopas were delighted to meet their sons. With great effort, they gradually withdrew from those embraces. They withdrew. However, remembering their sons, they continued to shed tears.[32] Rama witnessed this constant increase in love in Vraja, even among those who had been weaned.[33] He reflected on the possible reason. "What is this extraordinary incident of love towards children increasing in Vraja, just as it does towards Vasudeva, who is in all atmans? I am no exception. This has never happened before. What is this and where has it come from? Has it come from a goddess, a woman or an asura lady? It must be my

[32] Of joy.
[33] Both calves and boys.

master's[34] maya. Who else can confound me?" Dasharha[35] thought
about this. Then, using the wisdom of his vision, he saw that all the
calves and his friends were nothing but Vaikuntha. "O lord! These[36]
are not the lords of the gods or *rishi*s. They are you manifesting
yourself in these different forms. How have you come to appear in
these distinct forms?" Thus asked, the lord explained briefly and
Bala understood.

'The one who created himself[37] returned after one *truti*[38] had
elapsed by his own measurement of time. However, by human
measures, it was one year and he saw that all of them were playing
with Hari. "I made all the boys and all the calves in Gokula go to
sleep on my bed of maya and they have still not woken up. Who
are these and where have they come from? They are not the same
as those who have been confounded by my maya. These are similar
to those in number and have been playing with Vishnu for an
entire year." The one who created himself thought for a long time,
trying to differentiate between the two lots. He tried to distinguish
between the real and the unreal ones, but was unable to. Vishnu can
never be confounded and is the one who confounds the universe.
Yet, having tried to confound him by using his maya, he ended up
being confounded himself. The darkness of mist is absorbed in the
darkness of the night. The light of a firefly disappears in the light of
the day. Like that, a greater maya destroys any attempt by inferior
maya. While Aja[39] looked on, all the cowherd boys were instantly
seen to assume the dark complexion of clouds. They were attired in
yellow silk garments. They were four-armed, holding a conch shell,
a *chakra*, a club and a lotus in their hands. They wore diadems and
earrings and wore necklaces made out of wild flowers. There were
marks of *shrivatsa*, armlets, jewels around their necks and bracelets
on their hands. Like conch shells, their necks were marked with

---

[34] Krishna's.
[35] Balarama.
[36] The cowherd boys.
[37] Brahma.
[38] A small measure of time, equated with half a *kshana* or half a *lava*.
[39] Brahma.

three lines. There were beautiful anklets and bangles, girdles and
rings on the fingers. From the heads to the feet, on all the limbs,
the bodies were decorated with garlands of fresh and delicate *tulasi*
leaves, sacred offerings rendered by large numbers of devotees.
The smiles were as dazzling as the moonlight. There were sidelong
glances from reddened eyes. They seemed to be the creators and
preservers of their own devotees, using *sattva* and *rajas*.[40] All mobile
and immobile embodied forms, beginning with the one who created
himself and ending with a blade of grass, stood around separately
and separately worshipped them with singing, dancing and many
objects of worship. There were *anima* and the other powers.[41] There
were Aja and other personified forms. They were surrounded by
the twenty-four *tattvas*,[42] Mahat and the others. There were time,
nature, *samskaras*,[43] *kama*, *karma* and the *gunas*.[44] With their
own greatness subsumed in his greatness, they worshipped him
in personified forms. All of them were manifestations of the same
single truth and knowledge, the bliss of Ananta. His great glory
could not be comprehended even by those who possessed the insight
of the Upanishads. At the same instant, Aja saw everything in the
paramatman brahman. It is his radiance that illuminates everything,
mobile and immobile.[45] Aja's eleven senses[46] were curious, but were
astounded, stupefied and overwhelmed. He stood there silent, like
the image of a minor divinity in the presence of a greater divinity.
He[47] manifests himself and his own greatness is beyond debate. He

[40] There is the white of sattva in the moonbeams and the red of rajas in
the eyes.

[41] Yoga leads to eight major *siddhi*s or powers. These are anima
(becoming as small as one desires), *mahima* (as large as one desires), *laghima*
(as light as one wants), *garima* (as heavy as one wants), *prapti* (obtaining
what one wants), *prakamya* (travelling where one wants), *vashitvam*
(powers to control creatures) and *ishitvam* (obtaining divine powers).

[42] Of *samkhya*.

[43] Sacraments.

[44] The three qualities (guna) of sattva, rajas and *tamas*.

[45] This is reminiscent of *shloka*s in the Upanishads.

[46] Five senses of action, five senses of perception and the mind.

[47] Vishnu. This is an extremely difficult shloka to translate and we have
taken some liberties.

is beyond all nature and beyond sacred texts that place negative rejection at the forefront.[48] The lord cannot be conceived in this way. On seeing him, the lord of speech[49] was confused and exclaimed, "What is this?" Immediately understanding the state Aja was in, the supreme one removed the curtain from Aja's mind.[50] At this, Kah's[51] external vision was restored. He stood up, like a man who has arisen from the dead. He opened his eyes with great difficulty and saw everything, including himself. He immediately looked around in all the directions and saw Vrindavana standing in front of him, filled with trees and other agreeable objects that people could subsist on. This is a place where men and animals live together, forgetting their natural enmity. Because the unvanquished one resides there, they are like friends. Anger, desire and other vices have immediately left the spot. The supreme Ananta, infinite in his understanding, was acting out a role in a play, as a child born in a family of those who earn a living from animals.[52] Without any sense of duality, Parameshthi Brahma saw him there. As was the case earlier, he was alone, with a morsel of food in his hand, searching everywhere for the calves and his friends. Seeing this, he instantly descended from his mount.[53] He lay down and prostrated his body on the ground, like a golden staff. He touched his two feet with the crests of his four diadems.[54] Bowing down, with tears of joy, he sprinkled his feet. He then arose. But he again fell down at Krishna's feet for a long period of time. He repeatedly remembered the greatness that he had witnessed earlier. Thereafter, he slowly arose and wiped his eyes. With his shoulders bowed, he glanced towards Mukunda. He humbly joined his hands in salutation. He controlled himself. With his body trembling and in a faltering tone, he praised him in these words.'

[48] In the sense of establishing the brahman by the rejection of 'neti, neti', 'not this, not this'.

[49] Brahma.

[50] The curtain of maya.

[51] Brahma's.

[52] The cowherds.

[53] The swan.

[54] Brahma has four heads.

Chapter 10(14)

'Brahma said, "O one who should be worshipped! I bow down before you. Your form is like that of a dark cloud and your garments are like tinges of lightning. You are ornamented with gunja seeds and peacock feathers. Your face is dazzling. You wear a garland made out of wild flowers. You have a morsel of food in your hand and a cane and flute are tucked in. Your gentle feet bear the auspicious marks. I bow down before the son of the herder of animals. O lord! As a favour to me, you have yourself revealed this form of yours, which does not consist of the elements. Even though I am Kah, using all my mental faculties, I am unable to comprehend your measure. How can I comprehend the truth that you are, not to speak of the bliss that you yourself feel? There are virtuous ones who survive, extolling your conduct and your account with their mouths. With all knowledge and efforts, they bow down before you and surrender themselves. They remain in those positions, retaining what they have heard with their bodies, words and minds. You cannot be conquered by the three worlds. However, you are generally conquered by them.[55] O lord! Benefit is ensured along the path of devotion towards you. However, there are those who suffer and deviate from this, seeking to understand only by resorting to knowledge. They are those who pound empty husks from which the grain has been taken out. Nothing but hardship remains for them. O lord! In earlier times, there were many yogis in this world. They offered their efforts and their deeds to you and obtained knowledge through devotion and hearing about your accounts. O Achyuta! They easily obtained the supreme destination with you. O lord! It is possible to understand the greatness of your qualities and your glory if one is unblemished in one's mind and one's atman.[56] You are self-illuminating and beyond any kind of form or illumination. You are without transformations. You can only be comprehended through self-perception and not through any other means. All the

---

[55] Such devotees.
[56] This, and many succeeding shlokas, are interpreted in different ways.

gunas are in you, but who is able to enumerate your qualities? You descend for the sake of ensuring welfare. In the course of time, accomplished people can count the particles of dust on earth, the number of dewdrops in the sky and the number of stellar bodies in the firmament. But who can enumerate you? If a person eagerly waits for your compassion, he can enjoy the fruits of what he has done. He must bow down before you, surrendering his heart, his words and his body. If he lives in this way, he becomes entitled to a status of emancipation. O lord! O Ananta! O original being! O *paramatman*![57] Behold me, the ignoble one. You are full of maya. Yet, desiring to see your powers, I sought to envelope you in my maya. Indeed, what am I? In comparison to an entire fire, I am nothing more than a spark. O Achyuta! Therefore, pardon me. I have been born out of rajas. I did not know. I was insolent and prided myself on being a distinct controller. O Aja! My vision was blinded and I was enveloped in the blinding darkness of ignorance. I think that you are my protector. Therefore, you must show me your compassion. Who am I? I am covered in sheaths of tamas, Mahat, *ahamkara*,[58] space, air, fire, water and earth, in an egg that is the universe and surrounded by seven sheaths. What about someone like you? Like *paramanu*s,[59] innumerable such eggs[60] flow in and out from the pores of your body, like particles of dust. That is your greatness. O Adhokshaja! When a foetus in the womb uses its legs to kick, does the mother take offence? O Ananta! Is there anything, existent or non-existent, that is not inside your stomach? When the three worlds are destroyed, there is a cosmic flood and an ocean of water. Aja emerged from a lotus that sprouted out of Narayana's navel. There is no falsehood in this statement. O lord! Therefore, have I not been generated out of you? You are Narayana. You are in the atmans of all living beings. You are the lord of all the worlds and you are the witness. Narayana is one of your forms.

[57] The supreme soul.
[58] Ego.
[59] A paramanu is an ultimate particle characterized by the trait that it cannot be divided further. It alone is combined with others.
[60] That is, universe.

Everything emerged from the water. It is not true that you lay down on the waters.[61] That too is your maya. O illustrious one! If your form, the refuge of the universe, was lying down in the water, why could I not see it then? Why couldn't I properly see you within my heart then? Why was it the case that I suddenly saw it?[62] O one who dispels maya! In the present *avatara*, you used your maya to manifest to your mother everything that exists outside, inside your stomach.[63] Along with me, everything outside was shown inside your stomach. That is exactly what has occurred now. Without your maya, how is this possible? Today, has your maya not shown me that there is nothing other than you? Initially, you were alone.[64] Later, you were there with all the friends and calves from Vraja. After this, you appeared in all the numerous four-armed forms worshipped by me and all the others. You then appeared as the innumerable universes. You are the ultimate brahman and you do not have a second. To those who are ignorant of your status, you appear in forms other than the atman. However, your atman manifests itself in your extensive maya. In creating, you appear like me. In preserving the universe, you appear like your own self. In destruction, it is you who appear as the three-eyed one.[65] O lord! It is you who appear among the gods, the rishis and men.[66] Though you do not take birth, you appear among inferior species and aquatic creatures. O lord! O creator! You take birth to subdue the insolence of the wicked and to show your compassion towards those you favour. O lord! O illustrious one! O paramatman! O lord of *yoga*! In the three worlds, you spread your *yoga maya* and sport. Who can possibly know where, how, how many times, and when? This entire universe is unreal. It is like a dream, when the intelligence is shrouded. It is

---

[61] Narayana means someone whose resting place (*ayana*) was the water (*nara*).

[62] After performing austerities.

[63] When Krishna showed Yashoda everything inside his mouth.

[64] When Brahma stole the cowherd boys and the calves.

[65] Shiva.

[66] This is a reference to different avataras, as gods (Vamana), rishis (Vyasa), men (Rama, Krishna), inferior species (Varaha), aquatic creatures (Kurma, Matsya).

full of unhappiness and more unhappiness. All of it appears in you.
You are always happiness, knowledge and infinite. Arising out of
your maya, it appears as if it is real. You are the single atman, the
ancient Purusha. You are truth. You are self-luminiscent. You are
infinite. You are the original being. You are eternal and without
decay. You are without birth and unlimited in your bliss. You are
without any blemishes. You are complete, without a second. You
are free from all obstructions. You are immortal. You are in all
atmans. Those who are learned hold this view. They see you as the
atman that is superior to their own atmans. They obtain this insight
from the Upanishads, through preceptors who are like the sun.
Using this, they can cross this ocean of life, which is unreal. There
are those who do not understand the nature of the atman. All
perception of material objects results from this ignorance. Once
there is knowledge, it vanishes. This is like the appearance and
disappearance of a rope and a snake. The bondage of *samsara*[67] and
emancipation are two terms that result from ignorance. This
difference is not true and it results from lack of knowledge. One
should consider only the paramatman, unimpeded in consciousness.
There will no longer be a difference, just as there is no night and day
in the sun. The ignorance of the ignorant is pitiable. You are the
paramatman and they regard you as something distinct from their
own atmans. They thus search for you outside their own selves. O
Ananta! You are inside. Virtuous people reject any sense of
difference and search you out inside. Virtuous people, virtuous in
qualities, must first reject the unreal snake,[68] before identifying the
real. O god! If a person is favoured so that he obtains even a trifling
touch of your two lotus feet, he knows the truth about the illustrious
one's greatness. However, another person, who searches for a very
long time, cannot obtain it. O protector! In this birth and in the
next, even if that is as an inferior species, may I have the great
fortune of being one of your devotees. May I be able to serve at your
tender feet. The cows and women of Vraja are extremely fortunate.
O lord! You have happily drunk the nectar of milk at their breasts,

[67] The wheel of life, the circle of birth and death.
[68] And understand that it is actually a rope.

in the form of calves and their own sons. All the sacrifices undertaken by them till now have not been able to satisfy them as much. How wonderful is the fortune of Nanda and the gopas who reside in Vraja. The eternal and complete brahman,[69] the reservoir of supreme bliss, is their friend. O Achyuta! Though their fortune and glory are great, the eleven of us have also been great in our fortune.[70] Using the senses as cups, Sharva and the others have repeatedly drunk the nectar from your lotus feet and it has been like honey and amrita. The greatest fortune is to be born, as whatever species, in the forest where Gokula is, or to be bathed by dust from the feet of someone from Gokula. For them, their entire lives are nothing but the illustrious Mukunda. Even now, the sacred *shruti* texts search out the dust from his feet. O god! Thinking about any fruit that is superior to you, I am confused. You are the one who confers all the fruits in the universe. O god! By just pretending to be good,[71] Putana and her family were brought to you. For those who reside in this pasture, their homes, wealth, friends, beloved relatives, bodies, children, their breath of life and their minds are devoted to you. What else can you possibly give them? O Krishna! Until people do not become devoted to you, their attachments and other desires are like thieves and make their homes like prisons, where the delusion is like shackles on the feet. O lord! You have nothing to do with the material. But you appear on the surface of the earth and identify with the material, so as to increase different kinds of pleasure among people who seek refuge with you. There are those who think they know you. O lord! Let them know. There is no need for me to say

[69] The supreme soul.

[70] These are the eleven divinities who preside over the eleven senses—the mind (Chandra), intelligence (Brahma), ahamkara (Shiva/Sharva), hearing (the divinities in charge of the directions), touch (Vayu), sight (Surya), taste (Varuna), smell (the two Ashvins), speech (Agni), hands (Indra) and legs (Upendra). There seems to be a sense that the residents of Vraja are more fortunate than these divinities. These divinities have experienced Achutya only through respective senses. However, the residents of Vraja have experienced him with all their senses.

[71] She pretended motherly affection. Her family means Bakasura and Aghasura.

a lot on this. In mind, form and words, your greatness is beyond my comprehension. O Krishna! O omniscient one! O one who witnesses everything! Grant me permission to leave. You are the protector of the universe. Nevertheless, I offer this universe to you. O Shri-Krishna! The lineage of the Vrishnis is like a lotus and you are the one who brings pleasure to it. You are the one who enhances the prosperity of the gods, the earth, brahmanas, animals and the oceans. You are the one who dispels the darkness of *adharma*. You are the enemy of the rakshasas on earth. O one who should be worshipped! O illustrious one! Till the end of the *kalpa*[72] and as long as the sun shines, I bow down to you.”’

Shri-Shuka said, ‘The creator of the universe[73] praised the lord in this way. He bowed down at his feet and circumambulated him thrice. He then returned to his own desired abode. After granting Svayambhu permission, the illustrious one brought the original calves back to the sandy bank, where his friends were, just as they had been before. O king! He was the lord of their lives and in the inner cores of their atmans. Though they had been separated from him for an entire year, because of Krishna’s maya, they thought that it had only been half a kshana. Indeed, if the intelligence is confounded by his maya, what does one not forget in this world? He constantly confounds the entire universe and makes one forget one’s own self. The well-wishers welcomed Krishna and said, “You have returned quickly. We have not eaten a single morsel. It is best that we should eat together.” Hrishikesha laughed and, along with the boys, ate. When they were returning from the forest to Vraja, he showed them the python’s skin. His body was adorned with peacock feathers, flowers and many kinds of minerals from the forest. There was the great sound of flutes, whistles made out of leaves and horns, as if there was a festival. He called out to the calves and they chanted about his sacred deeds. In the midst of the festivities, enhancing the delight of the gopis, he entered the settlement of cowherds. Having gone to Vraja, the boys chanted, “This one, the son of Yashoda and Nanda, has killed a giant serpent today and has saved us.”’

---

[72] A kalpa is the longer cycle of creation and destruction.
[73] Brahma.

The king asked, 'O brahmana! How could there have been this love for Krishna? This is unprecedented. This kind of love doesn't exist for one's own son, not to speak of a person who is someone else's son. Please speak about this.'

Shri-Shuka continued, 'O king! Among all creatures, one's own self is loved the most. Everything else, children, wealth and other things are loved because they belong to one's own self. O Indra among kings! Each embodied being loves his own respective self. Sons, wealth, homes and other things are loved because of the sense of ownership. O supreme among royals! For people who identify with the body, there is nothing that is loved as much as the body and everything else follows. If a person considers the body as "mine" and not as "me", it will not be loved that much. Even when the body decays, the desire to be alive remains strong. Therefore, for all embodied beings, his own atman should be loved the most. All mobile and immobile objects in the universe are for that purpose alone. Know that Krishna is the atman who exists in the atmans of all embodied beings. For the welfare of the universe, he uses his maya and appears in the form of an embodied being. There are those who know all mobile and immobile objects in this world as Krishna. Everything is a form of the illustrious one and there is nothing other than him. For every object that exists, the existence depends on the cause. But the illustrious Krishna is the cause behind all causes. Therefore, there is nothing that is distinct from him. His lotus feet are like a boat. Murari[74] is auspicious and famous. He is the great destination. Those who resort to his feet cross over the ocean of samsara, as if it is a puddle,[75] and reach the supreme destination. At every step, they do not face any dangers. I have thus told you everything that you asked me about this. Hari did this when he was five years old, but it was not talked about until he was six years old. This was Murari's conduct with his well-wishers, his meal on the pasture and his slaying of Agha. His form, superior to the manifest one, was thus extolled and praised by Aja. A man who hears about it, or chants it, obtains everything that he desires. This

[74] Mura's enemy, Krishna.
[75] Vatsapada.

is the way those two[76] played as children. As children, this is the way they spent their time in Vraja. They played hide-and-seek, built bridges and leapt over them like monkeys.'

Chapter 10(15)

Shri-Shuka said, 'Those two attained the age of *pouganda* in Vraja.[77] They were then approved as the tenders of animals.[78] Along with their friends, they herded cows and the marks of their feet made Vrindavana auspicious. On one occasion, along with Bala, Madhava was playing on his flute. He was surrounded by gopas who chanted about his fame. With the animals in front of him, he entered a blossoming forest, to sport there and to find pasture for the animals. It was full of beautiful sounds created by bees, animals and birds. There were pools of water, as clean as the minds of great people. There was a breeze that was fragrant with the scent of lotuses. On seeing this, the illustrious one's mind turned to enjoying himself. He saw the beauty of the red and delicate foliage. The tops of the branches of trees were laden with flowers and fruits and seemed to bend down, wishing to touch his feet. Seeing this, the original being was delighted. He smiled and spoke to his elder brother.

'The illustrious one said, "O supreme among gods! This is wonderful. Your lotus feet are worshipped by the immortals. On their own, the tops of the branches are bowing down at your feet and offering flowers and fruits to you. They will thus destroy the darkness that has led to their being born as trees. O one who is a *tirtha*[79] for all the worlds! The wind is singing about your fame. O

---

[76] Krishna and Balarama.

[77] One moves from *koumara* to pouganda when one becomes six years old. Pouganda lasts until one attains the age of ten.

[78] Before this, Krishna and Balarama only tended to calves. They were now allowed to herd adult cattle.

[79] Place of pilgrimage.

original being! It is following you and worshipping you at every step. They are probably large numbers of sages who are prominent among your devotees. O unblemished one! Even though you have hidden yourself in the forest, you are their divinity and they are not abandoning you. O one who should be worshipped! The peacocks are rejoicing and are worshipping you. With loving glances, like gopis, the does are greeting you. With hymns, large numbers of cuckoos are welcoming your arrival in their homes. These residents of the forest are fortunate. Their nature is like that of virtuous people. The earth is fortunate today and so are the grass and plants, because they have touched your feet. The trees and creepers have been touched by your hands. You have cast compassionate glances towards the rivers, the mountains, the birds and the animals. You have embraced the gopis between your arms, a spot that is desired by Shri.""

Shri-Shuka continued, 'Krishna's mind was delighted at the beauty of Vrindavana and with the animals. Near the mountain,[80] the animals grazed along the banks of the river and with his followers, he himself sported. Sometimes, wearing garlands, he sang along with Samkarshana, when the bees, intoxicated with the honey, buzzed. Sometimes, he imitated the joyous notes of the swans. Sometimes, he danced, mimicking the dancing of the peacocks and causing laughter. His voice rumbled like the deep thunder of the clouds. Sometimes, by name, he cheerfully called out to animals that had strayed far away. This brought pleasure to the minds of the cows and the cowherd boys. He imitated the tones of chakoras, krounchas, chakravakas, bharadvajas, peacocks and other creatures.[81] Sometimes, he seemed to be scared of tigers and lions. Sometimes, he would be exhausted from playing and like a gopa, would lie down, using a gopa's lap as a pillow. When he had himself rested, he would tend to his elder brother by massaging his feet and doing other things. Sometimes, the cowherd boys sang and danced. They moved around, pretending to fight with each other.

[80] Govardhana.

[81] A chakora is a partridge, a krouncha is a curlew/heron, a chakravaka is the ruddy goose or Brahmany duck and a bharadvaja is a skylark.

Holding each other's hands, those two laughed and applauded these activities. Sometimes, he would be exhausted from the wrestling. He would make beds out of tender leaves and lie down near the roots of trees. Like a gopa, he would use another gopa's lap as a pillow. Some massaged the great-souled one's feet. Others, cleansed of all sin, fanned him with fans. O great king! Others gently sang delightful songs that were appropriate for the great-souled one, their minds filled with affection for him. His progress is mysterious and using his own maya, he was born as the son of a gopa and enacted out an appropriate kind of conduct. His tender feet had been attended to by Rama. However, like a villager, he enjoyed himself with other villagers. On some occasions, he acted like the lord.

'There was a cowherd named Sridama and he was Rama and Keshava's friend. Full of affection, he spoke to Subala, Stoka, Krishna and the other gopas. "O Rama! O mighty-armed one! O Rama! O Krishna! O destroyer of the wicked! Not very far from here, there is an extremely large forest and it is full of rows of palm trees. A large number of fruits have fallen down there and continue to fall down. However, those are all seized by the evil-souled Dhenuka. O Rama! O Krishna! He is an asura and has descended here in the form of a donkey. He is surrounded by many of his other relatives, who are exactly like him in strength. O slayer of enemies! He has eaten humans. Therefore, humans are terrified of him. The large number of animals don't go there either and the place is avoided by flocks of birds. There is fragrant fruit there and we have never tasted anything like that earlier. It is that fragrant scent that is spreading everywhere and it can be felt here too. O Krishna! Our minds are tempted because of that fragrance and there is a great desire. Give us those fruits. O Rama! If it so pleases you, let us go there." Hearing the words of their well-wisher, those two wanted to bring pleasure to their well-wishers. Therefore, surrounded by the gopas, those two lords went to the forest of palm trees. Bala entered and started to shake the palm trees with his arms. Like a crazy elephant in his energy, he made the fruits fall down. The asura that was in the form of a donkey heard the sound of the fruits falling down. He rushed towards the spot, making the

surface of the ground and the trees tremble. The powerful one met
Bala and struck him on the chest with his two hind legs. Emitting
sounds of braying, the deceitful one then withdrew a bit. O king!
The donkey approached again and stood there, with his face turned
away. Standing on two legs, he angrily struck out with his hind legs
towards Bala. He seized both of those hind legs in one hand. He
whirled him around and hurled him on the top of a tree, so that he
lost his life. Struck in this way, the large top of that huge palm tree
trembled. It shattered and made another next to it tremble. That
too broke and made an adjoining one tremble. So it went on. As a
result of Bala's playing, the palm tree was struck by the donkey's
dead body. All of them started to tremble, as if they had been struck
by a gigantic storm. Since he is the illustrious Ananta, the lord of
the universe, this is not extraordinary. O dear one! Like the warp
and the woof of a piece of woven cloth, the entire universe is woven
into him. There were other relatives of Dhenuka. With their relative
having been killed, all of them angrily attacked Krishna and Rama.
O king! As they descended, Krishna and Rama toyed with them.
They seized them by their hind legs and flung them on the tops of
the trees. The earth was resplendent, covered with heaps of fallen
fruit, the tops of trees and the dead bodies of *daityas*. It resembled
the sky, covered with clouds. The gods and the others heard about
this extremely great deed. They showered down flowers, played on
musical instruments and uttered words of praise. Thereafter, having
lost their fear, humans ate the fruit of palm trees. With Dhenuka
having been killed, animals grazed on the grass in that forest. The
lotus-eyed Krishna's account is one that is auspicious to hear.
Praised and followed by the gopas, along with his elder brother, he
returned to Vraja.

'The locks of his hair were covered with dust raised by cows
and peacock feathers were stuck to them. He was adorned with wild
flowers. His eyes were beautiful and his smile was enchanting. He
played tunes on his flute, while his companions followed him and
sung about his glory. The gopis wished to see him. They assembled
and came forward to greet him. Their eyes were as dark as bees and
with these, they drank in the nectar of Mukunda's face. During the
day, the women of Vraja suffered from the heat of being separated

from him and this was dissipated in the evening. Accepting all the honours, he entered the settlement of cowherds. The women cast sidelong glances at him, full of bashful and modest smiles. Yashoda and Rohini were devoted to their sons. Appropriate to the occasion, they pronounced the best of desired benedictions on their two sons. They were tired after the journey. They were bathed and massaged. They were attired in beautiful lower garments and decorated with divine garlands and fragrances. They ate the tasty food that was given to them by the two mothers. After being fondled by them, they lay down on the best of beds and happily slept in Vraja.

'In this way, the illustrious Krishna roamed around in Vrindavana. O king! On one occasion, without Rama, but surrounded by his friends, he went to the Kalindi. The cows and the cowherds suffered from the heat of the summer. Afflicted by thirst, they drank the water, though it was contaminated by poison. Because of destiny, they lost their senses and touched that poisoned water. O extender of the Kuru lineage! Losing their lives, all of them fell down at the edge of that water. Krishna, the lord of all the lords of yoga, saw them there in that state. His glance is like a shower of amrita to those whom he protects and they were brought back to life. Regaining their memories, they arose, at the edge of that water. All of them were extremely surprised and looked at each other. O king! They decided that this must have been because of Govinda's compassionate glances. Despite having drunk poison and died, it was as if they had arisen on their own.'

Chapter 10(16)

Shri-Shuka said, 'The lord Krishna saw that the Yamuna[82] had been contaminated by the dark serpent. Desiring to purify it, he exiled the serpent.'

[82] The text uses the word Krishnaa, meaning dark, for the Yamuna. Since the serpent is also dark (krishna), there is a play on words.

The king asked, 'O brahmana! Inside the fathomless waters, how did the illustrious one subdue the serpent? How had it lived there for so many *yuga*s? Tell us. O brahmana! The illustrious lord conducts himself as he wills. The generous one conducted himself as a cowherd. How can one be satisfied with hearing about this *amrita*?'

Shri-Shuka continued, 'There was a pool inside Kalindi.[83] Kaliya resided there and there was fire in its poison. Therefore, the water boiled and even birds flying through the air fell down into it. Drops of that poisonous water mixed with the breeze, and anyone on the banks, mobile or immobile, who touched it, died. The poison was terrible in its energy and power. Krishna had assumed an avatara to subdue the wicked. He saw that the river had been contaminated. He climbed an extremely tall *kadamba* tree. He girded his loins and slapped his arms. He leapt into the poisoned water. The supreme Purusha descended into the serpent's pool with great force. The mass of water, poisoned with the serpent's breath was agitated and overflowed up to an extent of one hundred lengths of a bow. For someone whose valour is unlimited, this wasn't surprising. O dear one! He sported in the pool and made the water swirl with the strength of his arms. His valour was like that of a supreme elephant. There was a roar. Hearing this, it decided that someone had invaded its own abode. Unable to tolerate this, Chakshushrava[84] issued forth. It saw him, delicate and as dazzling as a cloud. He had the shrivatsa mark and was attired in yellow garments. There was a beautiful smile on his face. With feet like the inside of a lotus, he was playing, without any kind of fear. Seeing him, the serpent angrily entwined him in its coils and bit his inner organs. He was enveloped in the serpent's coils and no signs of movement could be seen. On seeing this, his beloved friends, the protectors of the animals, were extremely miserable. They had surrendered themselves, their relatives, their wealth, their wives and their desires to Krishna. Overcome by misery, repentance and fear and their intelligence

---

[83] Kalindi, the river with dark waters, is another name for the Yamuna.
[84] Something that hears with its eyes, a name for Kaliya.

dulled, they fell down. Bulls, cows and heifers[85] were extremely saddened and shrieked. Terrified, they stood there and glanced towards Krishna, as if they were crying. There were three kinds of extremely terrible portents in Vraja—those on earth, those in the firmament and those in the bodies of creatures, announcing impending danger. Noticing this, the gopas, with Nanda at the forefront, were anxious with fear. They learnt that, without Rama, Krishna had taken the cows out to graze. Not knowing about him, from these portents, they formed the view that he had come about his destruction. Their lives and their minds were immersed in him and they were afflicted by grief, sorrow and fear. O dear one! Surrounded by the animals, the young, the aged and the women emerged from Gokula. They were distressed, driven by the desire to see Krishna. The illustrious Madhava Bala saw that they were miserable. He knew about his younger brother's prowess. However, he smiled a little and did not say anything. They looked for their beloved Krishna and searched out his trail. Following the marks of the illustrious one through his footprints, they went to the banks of the Yamuna. O dear one! Here and there, along the path, interspersed with the footprints of cows and other animals, they saw the lord's footprints, with the marks of a lotus, barley, an elephant goad, the *vajra* and a standard. Looking at this, they advanced swiftly. From a distance, they saw Krishna inside the pool, enveloped in the coils of the serpent inside the water. Surrounded by their animals, the gopas lost their senses. Filled with great lassitude and afflicted, they wept. The minds of the gopis were devoted to the illustrious Ananta. They remembered his affectionate smiles, glances and words. Since their beloved had been grasped by the serpent, they were extremely distressed and tormented. Deprived of their beloved, they glanced towards the three worlds as if they were empty. Tears of grief flowed down and they suffered as much as Krishna's mother did. But they held her back from following her son.[86] With their eyes fixed on Krishna's face, they seemed to be dead. They recited to her beloved

[85] Weaned female calves.
[86] Yashoda wanted to follow Krishna into the pool.

accounts from Vraja. The illustrious Rama knew about Krishna's sentiments. He saw that Nanda and the others, whose lives were immersed in Krishna, were entering the pool and restrained them.

'Gokula had no recourse other than him. He saw that it was in this state, with the women and the children extremely miserable on his account. He followed the conduct of mortals and remained in that position for a *muhurta*.[87] Then he rose up from the serpent's bonds. He expanded his own body and crushed the serpent's body with his. The serpent abandoned him and enraged, raised its hood high. It stood there, breathing poison heavily through its nostrils. Its immobile eyes were like two frying pans with torches in them and using these, it looked towards Hari. It licked the corners of its mouth with its forked tongue. Its fiery sight was filled with virulent poison. Like the Indra among the birds,[88] he played with it. It also moved around, waiting for an opportunity to strike. As it kept wheeling around with a raised hood, its energy was exhausted. The original being made it lower its stout hood and climbed atop it. Touching the heap of jewels on its hood, his lotus feet turned coppery red. The original preceptor of all kinds of arts started to dance. The *gandharvas*,[89] the Siddhas, the sages, the *charanas*,[90] the gods and the wives of the gods saw that he was ready to dance. They were delighted and quickly assembled, with flowers and other gifts, sounding drums, kettledrums, tambourines and other musicial instruments, and singing. O dear one! It possessed one hundred and one hoods. Whenever one of these hoods would not bow down, the one who wields a harsh staff would strike it with his feet and make it bend down. As it was whirled around, it started to vomit blood through its mouth and its nostrils. The serpent suffered from great misery. Poisonous waste oozed out of its eyes. Sometimes, an angry hood would rise up, and enraged, breathe heavily. Whenever this happened, he danced and pressed

[87] Though it is sometimes used in the sense of an instant, a muhurta is a measure of time equal to forty-eight minutes.

[88] Garuda.

[89] Gandharvas are celestial musicians and are semi-divine.

[90] Celestial singers.

it down with his feet. The ancient Purusha was worshipped with
flowers that were showered down on him. O king! The hoods
were like umbrellas and that violent dance crushed them. With
its body shattered, it started to vomit copious quantities of blood
from its mouth. It remembered the ancient Purusha, the preceptor
of mobile and immobile objects. In its mind, it went and sought
shelter with Narayana. The universe is inside Krishna's stomach.
Its hoods were like umbrellas and they were shattered from the
blows of his feet and it suffered from his extremely heavy load.
Seeing this, the serpent's wives approached the original being.
Their garments and ornaments were disarrayed and the braids of
their hair were dishevelled. Their minds were extremely anxious
and they placed their sons in front of them. They prostrated their
bodies on the ground and bowed down to the lord of creatures.
Those virtuous wives of a wicked husband joined their hands in
salutation. Desiring to save his life, they sought refuge with the
one who provides shelter.

'The wives of the serpent said, "This one has committed
a crime and this punishment is proper. You assume an avatara
for the subjugation of the wicked. You are impartial in your
outlook, towards enemies and towards your own sons. You
inflict punishment with a view to achieving the fruits. You have
shown us your favours. Indeed, when an evil person is punished,
he is cleansed of sin. This embodied being assumed the form of a
serpent[91] because he was wicked. Your anger should be revered as a
favour. Did he torment himself with extremely difficult austerities
in an earlier life? Did he control his insolence and show respect
towards others? Did he follow dharma? Did he show compassion
towards all beings? You are the source of all living beings and
you are now satisfied with him. O god! We do not know what
this is the result of. What has granted him the right to touch the
dust of your feet? Desiring this, Shri, supreme among women,
performed austerities. Giving up all other desire, she was firm in
her vows for an extremely long period. Those who have obtained
the dust of your lotus feet do not wish for the vault of heaven, the

[91] The text uses the term *dandashuka*.

state of being a universal emperor, the position of Parameshthi, sovereignty over earth, siddhis in yoga, or emancipation from the wheel of life. O protector! What this one has achieved is extremely difficult for others to achieve. This lord of serpents was born in a species characterized by tamas and fell prey to anger. Your glory has manifested itself before him, something that embodied beings who whirl around in the wheel of samsara wish for. O illustrious Purusha! O great-souled one! We bow down before you. You reside in all creatures, but you are the supreme cause behind all creatures. You are the paramatman. You are the reservoir of *jnana* and *vijnana*.[92] You are the brahman, infinite in powers. You are without gunas and without transformations. We bow down before the one who controls Prakriti. You are time. You are the one who is the foundation for time. Time is your form. You are the witness. You are the universe. You are the one who witnesses the universe. You are the one who creates the universe. You are the cause behind the universe. Your atman is in the elements, the objects of the senses, the senses, the breaths of life, the mind, the intelligence and the heart. Because of the three gunas and ahamkara, your atman remains hidden from perception. We bow down before the infinite one. We bow down before the subtle one. We bow down before the mysterious one. We bow down before the omniscient one. We bow done before the one who allows many kinds of debates about himself. We bow down to the power of speech and the power of the one speech describes. We bow down before the one who is the foundation of proof. We bow down before the wise one, the one who is the source of the sacred texts. We bow down before *nivritti* and *pravritti*.[93] We bow down before the one who is the source of *nigama* texts.[94] We bow down to Krishna and Rama, the sons of Vasudeva. We bow down to Pradyumna, Aniruddha and the lord of the Satvatas. We bow down to the one who illuminates the

---

[92] We have translated vijnana as self-knowledge, the transcendental consciousness. We will use jnana for knowledge.

[93] Detachment from fruits and renunciation of action; and action with a desire for the fruits, respectively.

[94] The texts of the Vedas, or related to them.

gunas. We bow down to the one who hides the gunas. We bow down to the one who can be discerned from the functioning of the gunas. We bow down to the one who witnesses the gunas. We bow down to the one who reveals himself to his devotees. Your pastimes and deeds are beyond comprehension. You are the one who can be understood as the cause behind everything. We bow down to Hrishikesha. We bow down to the sage. We bow down to the one who is silent in conduct. You are the one who knows about the progress of everything, superior and inferior. We bow down before the one who is the controller of everything. We bow down to the one who is not the universe. We bow down to the one who is the universe. We bow down to the one who is the witness and is also the cause. O lord! Without being involved and without acting, you use the gunas to ensure the creation, preservation and destruction of the universe. You are the one who upholds the prowess of time. You awaken the latent and innate truth. You are the one who acts. Your pastimes and glances are invincible. You are the one who creates the bodies in the three worlds, serene, turbulent and those born as inferior species. However, those who are serene and virtuous are loved by you and you protect them. The reason for your presence in this world is the protection of *dharma*. If his own servant commits a crime only once, a master should pardon it. You are serene in your atman. You should pardon this foolish one, who has committed a crime out of ignorance. O illustrious one! This serpent is about to give up his life. Please show him your favours. The virtuous should grieve over women. Our husband is our life. Give him back to us. We are your servant-maids. Order us. We will abide by your commands. We will faithfully carry everything out. Free us from all kinds of fear."'

Shri-Shuka continued, 'The illustrious one was properly praised by the wives of the serpent in this way. He was senseless and his hoods were crushed, struck by the blows of the feet. He was allowed to escape. Slowly, Kaliya regained his senses and his breath of life. He breathed with a great deal of difficulty. Miserable, he joined his hands in salutation and spoke to Krishna. "We are wicked because of our birth. We are immersed in tamas and our anger is great. O protector! People find it extremely difficult to give up their innate nature, since it grasps those who are evil. O creator! You have created the universe, with its gunas and different characteristics. There are many kinds of nature, valour, energy, species, seeds, hearts and forms. O illustrious one! We are serpents and we are born angry. How can we abandon your maya? You yourself confound us and make it difficult for us to give it up. You are the cause behind this. You are omniscient and the lord of the universe. Whether it is favour or punishment, do what you think is right for us." Behaving in the form of a human being, the illustrious one heard these words and replied. "O serpent! You must not remain in this place. Without any delay, leave for the ocean, with your relatives, children and wives. Let the river be enjoyed by cattle and men. If a mortal person remembers my instruction to you and recounts this at the time of both the sandhyas,[95] he will not face any fear on your account. If a person bathes at this spot, where I have played, and offers water to gods and others, if he fasts and remembers me and worships me, he will be freed from all sins. Out of fear on account of Suparna,[96] you left Ramanaka dvipa[97] and sought refuge in this pool. However, since you have been marked with my feet, he will not eat you now." O king! The illustrious Krishna, extraordinary in his deeds, freed him in this way. Delighted, the serpent and his wives affectionately worshipped him. They worshipped the protector of the universe with divine garments, garlands, jewels, extremely expensive ornaments, celestial scents and unguents and a large garland of blue lotuses. This pleased the one who has Garuda on his standard. Delighted, they sought his permission, circumambulating and worshipping him. With his wives, well-wishers and sons, he went to the middle of that dvipa.[98] Cleansed of poison, the water of the Yamuna became like amrita. This was because of the favours of the illustrious one, who sported in human form.'

[95] The twilight zones.
[96] Garuda.
[97] Island or region.
[98] Ramanaka dvipa, in the middle of the ocean.

Chapter 10(17)

The king asked, 'Why did Kaliya abandon Ramanaka, the abode of the *nagas*?[99] What did he do so as to make him Suparna's sole enemy?'

Shri-Shuka said, 'O mighty-armed one! Every month, the nagas received a share of offerings from people and it had earlier been agreed that every month, the serpents would leave a share of these at the foot of a large tree. On every new moon day, for the sake of their protection, the nagas would leave a share for the great-souled Suparna.[100] Because of the vigour from his poison, Kaliya, Kadru's son, was filled with insolence. He slighted Garuda by himself eating up the offerings meant for him. O king! Hearing this, the illustrious one, loved by the illustrious one,[101] became angry. Desiring to kill Kaliya, he rushed towards him with an extremely great speed. As he violently descended, he[102] raised his many hoods to strike back, using poison as a weapon. His fangs were his weapons and using these fangs, he bit Suparna. His tongues were terrible. He hissed and his eyes were fierce. Filled with rage, Tarkshya's son repelled him. The one who carried Madhusudana was terrible in his force. Fierce in his valour, he struck Kadru's son with his left wing, which was as dazzling as gold. Struck by Suparna's wing, Kaliya became extremely agitated. He entered Kalindi, which was very difficult to penetrate and he[103] couldn't follow him there. Once, Garuda was hungry and wished to eat an aquatic creature. He was restrained

---

[99] Serpents. Nagas (also known as *uragas*) are different from snakes. They are semi-divine, can assume any form at will and reside in specific locations.

[100] Garuda ate serpents. So that he did not eat serpents, Brahma made this arrangement. The serpents received offerings from those who worshipped snakes. Taking turns, the serpents offered their respective shares to Garuda, so that he would not eat them. Sometimes, it is also suggested that every month, one serpent, and not just the offering, was given to Garuda.

[101] Respectively Garuda and Vishnu.

[102] Kaliya.

[103] Garuda.

by Soubhari.[104] However, rash and hungry, he seized it. On seeing that the king of the fish had been killed, the fish were extremely miserable and distressed. Full of compassion and to ensure the welfare of those who lived there, Soubhari said, "If Garuda enters this place and eats fish, he will instantly be separated from his life. What I have spoken is the truth." Only Kaliya knew about this great secret. The other serpents didn't know. Therefore, scared of Garuda, he resided there, until Krishna banished him.

'Krishna emerged from the pool, adorned in divine garlands, pastes and garments. He was ornamented with large numbers of extremely expensive jewels, polished with gold. On seeing that he arose and that they had got him back, all of them seemed to regain their breaths of life and their senses. The cores of the hearts of the gopas rejoiced. Rejoicing, they embraced him. O Kourava! Yashoda, Rohini, Nanda, the gopas and the gopis had been like dried-up trees. Meeting Krishna, they got everything back. Rama knew about Achyuta's powers. Therefore, he embraced him and laughed. The trees, the cows, the bulls and the calves were filled with great joy. Along with their wives, the brahmana preceptors approached Nanda. They said, "After having been devoured by Kaliya, it is good fortune that your son has escaped. Because Krishna has been freed, give gifts to the brahmanas." O king! Happy in his mind, Nanda gave cows and gold. The immensely fortunate and virtuous Yashoda had lost her son and had got him back. Placing him on her lap, she embraced him and repeatedly released torrents of tears from her eyes. O Indra among kings! The residents of Vraja and the cattle suffered from hunger, thirst and exhaustion. They spent the night there, along the banks of the Kalindi.

'At that time, the forest was dry and a forest conflagration started to blaze everywhere in Vraja. While they were sleeping in the night, it enveloped them from all directions and was about to burn them up. Scorched and scared, the residents of Vraja woke up. They sought refuge with lord Krishna, who had used his maya to appear in human form. "O Krishna! O immensely fortunate one! O Krishna! O infinitely valourous Rama! This extremely terrible fire

---

[104] A sage who was meditating in the water.

will devour us, we who belong to you. This is extremely difficult to cross. Save us from this fire, which is like the fire of destruction. O lord! We are your well-wishers. We are incapable of letting go of your feet. How can there be any fear there?" The lord of the universe witnessed the lassitude his relatives were suffering from. Ananta drank up that terrible fire. He is the one who possesses infinite strength.'

Chapter 10(18)

Shri-Shuka said, 'Krishna was surrounded by his relatives, who were full of joy. They chanted about his glory and entered Vraja, ornamented with herds of cows. The two of them played in Vraja in this way, using their maya to disguise themselves as cowherds. The season known as summer arrived, one that is not liked that much by embodied beings. However, because the illustrious Keshava himself resided there, along with Rama, all the characteristics of spring were seen in Vrindavana. The loud sound of waterfalls surpassed the chirping sound of crickets. The circles of trees were continuously sprayed with drops of water from the waterfalls. A breeze wafted along, above the waves of the rivers, lakes and waterfalls, bearing the fragrance and pollen from white lilies, blue lotuses and other lotuses. The residents of the forest did not suffer from any heat from the summer, forest fires or the sun. There was plenty of green grass. Waves from the fathomless waters of the river beat against the banks and in every direction, moistened the mud along the sandy banks. The fierce rays of the sun, as virulent as poison, didn't exist and didn't rob the earth of its juices and green grass. The beautiful and blossoming forest was filled with many kinds of animals and birds. Peacocks sang and bees buzzed. Cuckoos and cranes called. With Bala, the illustrious Krishna played there. He played on his flute and surrounded by gopas and the wealth of cattle, entered.[105] They decorated themselves with tender leaves, the feathers of peacocks,

[105] The forest.

bunches of flowers, garlands and minerals. Rama, Krishna and the other gopas danced, wrestled and sang. When Krishna danced, some sang and some played on musical instruments. Some used flutes, others clapped with their hands. Some used horns, while others praised him. The gods had assumed the forms of cowherds and disguised themselves as gopa species. O king! They worshipped Krishna and Rama, like actors praising other actors. They whirled around and leapt. They flung and slapped their arms and dragged each other. With sidelocks like a crow's wings,[106] they sometimes played and wrestled. Sometimes, when others danced, those two themselves sang or played on musical instruments. O great king! Sometimes, they applauded, uttering words of praise. Sometimes, they played with *bilva, kumbha* or *amalaka* fruit in their hands.[107] Sometimes, covering their eyes, they played hide-and-seek and tried to touch each other. Sometimes, they pretended to be animals or birds. Sometimes, they leapt like frogs. Sometimes, they joked in many different ways. Sometimes, they swung from swings. Sometimes, they pretended to be kings. In this way, they wandered around in that forest and in rivers, mountains, valleys, groves, woods and lakes, playing games that are known to people.

'Along with the gopas, Rama and Krishna herded animals in that forest. Desiring to capture them, the asura Pralamba came there, assuming the form of a gopa. The illustrious Dasharha, who can see everything, knew about this. However, he accepted him as a friend, thinking about a means of killing him. Krishna, who knew about playing, summoned the gopas and said, "O gopas! Let us play. Let us divide ourselves into two different groups." The two groups of gopas made Rama and Janardana their respective leaders. Some were on Krishna's side and others were on Rama's side. They played many kinds of games, with a member from one team becoming the carrier and a member from the other team becoming the carried. Those who won were carried and those who lost were the carriers. They thus carried and were carried, simultaneously

---

[106] *Kakapaksha* (like a crow's wing) is a description of sidelocks of hair on the temples of boys and young men.

[107] *Kumbha* is a medicinal plant.

herding the cattle. With Krishna at the forefront, they went to a
banyan tree named Bhandiraka. O king! Shridama, Vrishabha and
others from Rama's side became victorious. Having been defeated
in the game, Krishna and the others had to carry them. Defeated,
the illustrious Krishna carried Shridama. Bhadrasena carried
Vrishabha and Pralamba carried Rohini's son. The bull among
the *danavas*[108] thought that Krishna was invincible.[109] Therefore,
very swiftly, he went a great distance away, far beyond where he
was supposed to set the burden down. As he was carried, he[110]
became as heavy as the Indra among mountains.[111] Unable to
proceed, the great asura assumed his own form. He was stationed
there, with golden garments and ornaments. He resembled a cloud
tinged with lightning, carrying the lord of the stars on its back.
The wielder of the plough was slightly distressed and scared to see
him travel swiftly through the sky. His eyes blazed. His eyebrows
were furrowed and his teeth were fierce. His hair was on fire and
he wore a diadem, armlets and earrings. Then Bala remembered
himself and no longer feared the enemy. He was trying to carry
him away from his companions. Like the lord of the gods violently
striking a mountain with his vajra, he angrily struck him on the
head with a firm fist. Thus struck, his hand shattered instantly.
The asura vomited blood from his mouth and fell unconscious.
With a great roar, he lost his life and fell down, like the sound
made by a mountain on being struck by Maghavan's weapon. The
gopas were extremely astounded to see that Pralamba had been
killed by the extremely strong Bala. They uttered words of praise.
They pronounced benedictions over him and worshipped the one
who deserved to be worshipped. Their senses were overwhelmed
with love. They embraced him, as if he had returned from the
dead. When the wicked Pralamba was killed, the gods were greatly
satisfied. They showered down garlands on Bala and uttered
words of praise.'

[108] Demons, progeny of Danu.
[109] But Pralamba didn't think Balarama was invincible.
[110] Balarama.
[111] Meru.

Chapter 10(19)

Shri-Shuka said, 'While the gopas wre engrossed in playing, the cows were attracted by the grass. They grazed around on their own and went far away, entering a dense region. The goats, cows and she-buffaloes wandered from one forest to another forest. They entered a thicket of cane. Suffering from a forest conflagration, they called out loudly. Unable to see the animals, the gopas, Krishna, Rama and the others, were filled with remorse. Not knowing the path the cattle had taken, they started to search. They followed the footprints left by the cattle and the grass their hooves had torn up. At the prospect of their livelihoods being destroyed, they were senseless. All of them followed the trail. They found their respective herds of cattle crying in the thicket of *munja* grass, having strayed from the path. Finding them, they brought them back, but were thirsty and exhausted. In a voice that rumbled like clouds, the illustrious one summoned them.[112] Hearing their own names being uttered, they called back in joy. Suddenly, by chance, a forest fire broke out on all sides and would have destroyed all the residents of the forest. The wind was its charioteer and there were terrible sparks. The large flames licked at mobile and immobile objects. The forest conflagration descended on them from all sides. On seeing it, the gopas and the cattle were terrified. Just as people who are scared of death seek refuge with Hari, they spoke to Krishna and Bala. "O Krishna! O immensely valiant one! O Krishna! O Rama! O one who is invincible in valour! We are being scorched by the forest conflagration and have sought shelter with you. You should save us. O Krishna! Your relatives do not deserve to suffer. O one who knows about all kinds of dharma! You are our protector and we are devoted to you." The illustrious Hari heard the words of his miserable relatives. He said, "Close your eyes. Do not be afraid." They assented and closed their eyes. The illustrious lord of yoga opened his mouth and swallowed up the terrible flames, thus saving them from the calamity. They opened their eyes and

---

[112] The animals.

were surprised to see that they and their cattle had been saved and that they had been brought back to Bhandira again. They witnessed the valour of Krishna's yoga and that they had been saved from the forest conflagration because of the powers of his yoga maya. They thought he was an immortal. It was late in the afternoon. With Rama, Janardana herded the cows back. Praised by the gopas, he played on his flute and returned to the settlement. On seeing Govinda, the gopis were filled with great delight. Even a kshana of separation from him made them feel as if it had been one hundred yugas.'

Chapter 10(20)

S hri-Shuka said, 'The gopas told the women about their[113] wonderful deeds, of freeing them from the forest conflagration and about Pralamba's death. The elders among the gopas and the gopis were astounded to hear this. They thought that two foremost gods, Krishna and Rama, had come to Vraja. The monsoon season commenced, which rejuvenates all living creatures. Lightning flashed in the directions and the sky was agitated by thunder. There were dense blue clouds in the sky, along with lightning and the sound of thunder. The stellar bodies were obscured and shrouded, just as the brahman is by the gunas. For eight months, the sun god had used his rays to drink up juices from the earth. Now that monsoon had arrived, he released that wealth of water. The large clouds flashed with lightning. They trembled because of the terrible winds. Like a shower of compassion, water, the pleasant granter of life, was released. Because of austerities, the earth had become emaciated. She was now nourished by water from the god. It was as if a body that has performed austerities for some purpose has received the fruits. Just as night was about to start, fireflies glowed in the dark, but not the planets. It was like the evil of heretics flourishing in kali yuga, not the Vedas. Hearing the thunder of the clouds, frogs

[113] Krishna and Balarama's.

started to croak, just as brahmanas who have slept silently speak[114] after performing the morning rituals. Smaller rivers had turned dry. They overflowed and deviated from their courses, just like the body, riches and wealth of a man who is not in control of himself. In some parts, the ground was green because of new grass. In other parts, it was red because of *indragopas*.[115] There was shade created by mushrooms. The earth resembled men full of prosperity. The fields were rich with grain and brought delight to farmers. Those who were proud repented, because they did not know that everything is controlled by destiny.[116] All creatures who lived on land or in the water were sprinkled with fresh water. They assumed beautiful forms, like that which is obtained by serving Hari. At confluences of rivers with the ocean, the wind made the waves turbulent. This was just like the mind of an immature yogi who is addicted to desire and is attached to the gunas. The mountains were struck by torrents of rain, but were not distressed. They were like people whose minds are in Adhokshaja and who therefore are not disturbed when assailed by hardships. The roads were overgrown and covered with grass and could not be cleaned. They were like sacred texts not studied by brahmanas and which therefore, suffer from the passage of time. Clouds are the friends of people. However, lightning is fickle in its affection. It did not remain in one place,[117] just as a woman driven by desire does not remain attached to a man with qualities, but moves around. Without a bowstring, the great Indra's bow manifested itself in the sky.[118] It was like Purusha, who is devoid of gunas, but manifests himself in this world, which is a mixture of gunas. The lord of the stars was shrouded and not radiant, its moonlight unable to triumph over the clouds. It was like an embodied being, who possesses his own radiance, but that radiance is shrouded by ahamkara. The peacocks were festive and

[114] Chant their lessons when called by their preceptor, a reference to brahmana disciples. The frogs have also been quiet hitherto.

[115] A reddish insect, sometimes identified with a firefly.

[116] The meaning remains unclear and is subject to interpretation. For example, those who were too proud to farm had to repent.

[117] It moved from cloud to cloud.

[118] Indra's bow is the rainbow.

delighted at the arrival of the clouds and called out. They were like people who were tormented in their homes, but who became happy at Achyuta's arrival. The trees drank up water with their feet and assumed many different kinds of forms.[119] They were like people emaciated and exhausted from austerities, who then start to indulge in desire. O dear one! The cranes were disturbed, but continued to reside along the shores of the lakes. They were like people addicted to sensual pleasures, whose desires cannot be satisfied and who continue to exert in their homes, though they are disturbed. When the lord[120] showered down rain, the torrents of water breached the dams. It was just like the wicked words of heretics breaking down the paths of the Vedas in kali yuga. Goaded by the winds, the clouds released their amrita on living beings. This was just like lords of the earth, who are from time to time urged by brahmanas, and shower their benedictions.[121]

'The forest was thus prosperous with ripe dates and *jambu* fruit. Surrounded by cows and gopas, with Bala, Hari entered it, to sport there. Because of the heavy burden of their udders, the cows moved slowly. Summoned by the illustrious one, they advanced quickly, their affection making milk flow from their udders. The residents of the forest were delighted. There were rows of trees that exuded honey. The waterfalls resounded in the mountains. He saw that there were some caves nearby. When it rained, he sometimes sought refuge in the hollow of a tree or a cave. The illustrious one entered there and sported, eating tubers, roots and fruits. Near the water, he seated himself on a slab of stone and ate curds mixed with rice. He ate and the gopas and Samkarshana also ate with him. He sat on the green grass and saw the satisfied bulls, heifers and cows graze, their eyes closed. Their heavy udders made them tired. He glanced at the prosperity brought by the monsoon. The illustrious one's revered powers, which bring pleasure at all times, were enhanced. In this fashion, Rama and Keshava resided in Vraja.

---

[119] The word *padapa* means tree, signifying something that drinks up water with its feet (the roots).

[120] Indra.

[121] Kings are urged by brahmanas to undertake works of charity.

Autmun arrived. The clouds disappeared. The waters were clear and the wind was no longer harsh. Autmun rejuvenated the lotuses. The waters regained their natural state. It was like minds that have deviated, when they again begin to practice yoga. There were no clouds in the sky. The earth was cleansed of mud and impurities. Creatures no longer suffered from overgrown grass. Just as devotion towards Krishna removes everything inauspicious, autumn cleansed those in every *ashrama*. The clouds gave up everything that they had possessed and their radiance was white and pure. They were like tranquil sages who have given up all desire and have been cleansed of sins. The mountains sometimes released auspicious water, but sometimes did not release it. They were like learned people, who, at the right time, grant the amrita of knowledge, or do not. Aquatic creatures that dwelt in the reducing water levels did not understand that the water was diminishing. They were like foolish men who live with their families and do not understand that that their lifespans are diminishing. Aquatic creatures that resided in the diminishing water suffered from the autumn sun. They were like miserable and distressed people who have not conquered their senses and live with their families. Very gradually, bits of land gave up the parts where there was mud. The plants gave up their state of not being ripe. They were like persevering people, who give up ahamkara, bodies and everything that is not connected with the atman. At the onset of the autumn, the waters of the ocean became silent and tranquil. They were like sages who have properly realized the atman and have therefore given up all rituals associated with the sacred texts. Farmers erect firm dams so that their fields receive an adequate supply of water. In that way, yogis control their breath of life, so that jnana does not get dissipated. The rays of the autumn sun scorched living creatures, but the lord of the stars relieved them of this. This was like the knowledge Mukunda conferred on the women of Vraja, who suffered from pride because of identification with their bodies. Bereft of clouds, the autumn sky was beautiful with sparkling stars. It was like the mind, when it is full of sattva and has insight about the purport of the sacred texts and the meaning of the brahman. The radiant full moon shone in the sky, surrounded by the stars. It was like Krishna, the lord of the Yadus, on earth, surrounded by a circle of Vrishnis. Freed from heat, people embraced the wind fragrant with forest flowers. It was neither hot, nor cold. However, this wasn't true of the gopis. Without Krishna, their minds were distracted. Like rituals performed to the lord for the sake of fruits, cows, does, female birds and women became fertile in the autumn and sought out their own males. With the exception of kumudas,[122] when the sun rose, all the lotuses blossomed. O king! They were like people who are not scared of bandits when a king is present. In cities and villages, there were large agrayani[123] sacrifices that pandered to the senses. Now that the two portions of Hari were present, the earth was ripe and rich with grain. Merchants, sages, kings and snatakas were free to emerge and go out on their respective tasks, which the rainy season had prevented them from doing.[124] They were like Siddhas, who wait for the time for their own funeral rites to arrive.'[125]

Chapter 10(21)

Shri-Shuka said, 'The autumn water was sparkling and the wind was fragrant with the scent of lotuses blooming in the water. Along with the cowherds, Achyuta entered.[126] The blossoming trees, the lakes, the rivers and the mountains resounded with the sound of maddened bees and flocks of birds. With the protectors of the herds and with Bala, the lord of Madhu entered and started to play on his flute. The women of Vraja heard the sound of the flute singing and it ignited desire. In private, some of them started to describe Krishna

---

[122] A lotus that blooms in the night.

[123] Sacrifices at which oblations are offered out of the first harvest after the rainy season.

[124] They couldn't travel during the rainy season. A snataka is a student who has finished studying and is ready to embark on the next phase of life. The word snataka is derived from snana (the act of taking a bath), ritually performed before anything auspicious is undertaken.

[125] Stated simply, they wait for their physical deaths.

[126] Entered Vrindavana forest.

to their own friends. As they started to describe, they remembered Krishna's acts. O king! Since their minds were distracted by the force of desire, they could not continue. His form was like that of the best among dancers, with a crest of peacock feathers. There were *karnikara* flowers on his ears. His dazzling garments were golden yellow. He wore a *vaijayanti* garland. The holes in the flute were filled with nectar that emerged from his lips. He entered the forest of Vrindavana and made it beautiful with his footprints. Gopas surrounded him, chanting about his glories. O king! The sound of the flute stole the minds of all creatures. Hearing it, all the women of Vraja embraced each other[127] and described it to each other.

'The gopis said, "O friends![128] This is the greatest fruit that eyes can have. We do not know of anything superior to those two faces. With their friends, those two are entering, along with the animals. Those two sons of the lord of Vraja possess flutes.[129] We have drunk the loving sidelong glances that they cast around. They are decorated with tender mango leaves, peacock feathers, bunches of flowers and garlands of lotuses and lilies. These touch the wonderful garments that they wear. Those two are indeed resplendent in the midst of the cowherds and the herds. Sometimes, they sing. They are like the best of dancers on a stage. O gopis! The flute must have performed extremely auspicious deeds. It is drinking nectar from Damodara's lips and that only belongs to the gopis.[130] It is enjoying it alone and has only left a little bit of the juice for others. The delighted bodies of the lakes are shedding tears, just as noble trees do.[131] O friend! Vrindavana is enhancing the earth's fame. It has

---

[127] Alternatively, embraced him in their minds.

[128] The text doesn't make it clear whether a single gopi is singing this, whether they are singing this collectively, or whether they take turns. Probably the last is intended. They sometimes address the others in the singular, sometimes in the plural.

[129] Meaning both Krishna and Balarama.

[130] Damodara is one of Krishna's names. He was named Damodara because Yashoda tied a rope (*dama*) around his stomach (*udara*).

[131] The shores of the lakes are where the bamboo grew and the flute was made out of bamboo. The word *arya* means noble, but it also means forefather. The lakes are shedding tears of joy because the flute indirectly

obtained the prosperity that results from the lotus feet of Devaki's
son. Hearing Govinda's flute, the maddened peacocks are dancing.
On seeing this from the top of the mountain, all the other creatures
are standing motionless. Even these does, which have taken birth
as foolish species, are fortunate. They have been able to approach
Nanda's delight, attired in his colourful garb. With the male black
antelopes, they have heard the playing of the flute. With their
affectionate glances, they seem to be offering him worship." Krishna's
form and conduct made it a festival for the women. They saw him.
They heard the clear songs that emanated and vibrated from his
flute. The goddesses, travelling in *vimanas*,[132] came under the spell
of desire. Bunches of flowers were dislodged from the braids of
their hair and they loosened the cords of their garments. The cows
pricked up their ears and used these as receptacles to drink in the
song that emanated from the flute in Krishna's mouth. The calves
were drinking mouthfuls of milk from the udders and stood still.[133]
With tears flowing from their eyes, their atmans seemed to embrace
Govinda with their sight. "O mother![134] The birds in this forest must
generally be like sages. To see Krishna and to hear the melodious
song from his flute, they have climbed on to the branches of trees,[135]
laden with beautiful foliage. With their eyes closed, they have shut
out all other sounds and are listening to this. Hearing Mukunda's
song, it is evident that the minds of the rivers are agitated and the
force of their flow has been impeded.[136] They are stationary and
are embracing Murari with their waves as arms. Clasping his two
feet, they are offering him lotuses. Despite the heat, with Rama
and the gopas, he is herding the animals of Vraja and following
them, playing on his flute. As his friend, the cloud has lovingly
fashioned an umbrella out of its own body and is showering down

---

originated with them. They are like forefathers. The trees shed drops of
dew.
   [132] Celestial vehicles.
   [133] With the milk still in their mouths.
   [134] Meant for senior gopis.
   [135] An allusion to different branches of the sacred texts followed by
sages. Sages meditate with their eyes closed.
   [136] A comparison is being made with the swirling currents in the rivers.

flowers on him.[137] The breasts of the *pulinda* women are smeared with beautiful *kunkuma* applied by their lovers and they are now completely fulfilled with the dust from his lotus feet.[138] Seeing him, they are smitten with desire. The dust is attached to the grass and they smear it on their faces and breasts and are thus freed from all mental anguish. O women! This mountain is the best among Hari's servants. It is rejoicing because it has touched Rama and Krishna's feet. It is respectfully offering them, along with the cattle and the herders, drinking water, tender grass, caves for shelter, tubers and roots. O friends! The two generous ones are following the cattle and the gopas from one forest to another. The melodious tunes of the flute are making the bodies of creatures immobile and they are stopping in their gaits. Even the trees are bristling with joy. Those two, with the wonderful marks, are also carrying ropes and nooses."'[139]

Shri-Shuka continued, 'The illustrious one roamed around Vrindavana. In this way, the gopis described his pastimes to each other and became completely immersed in him.'

Chapter 10(22)

Shri-Shuka said, 'It was the first month of *hemanta*. The *kumarikas* in Nanda's Vraja prepared *havishya* and surviving

---

[137] Krishna is similar in complexion to a cloud and therefore, the cloud is his friend. The cloud is not showering down flowers, but drops of rain that are being compared to flowers.

[138] This shloka has complicated interpretations. We have given a translation that seems to be accurate, but is also simple and not convoluted. There is no reason to take pulinda women to mean women from backward and aboriginal classes, as most interpretations render it. Pulindaka is indeed used for barbaric tribes, usually residing in mountains. But this is along the bank (pulinda) of a river. Therefore, pulinda can simply refer to people who live along the banks of a river.

[139] For tethering the animals, through the nose, or for tying the hindlegs of cows at the time of milking.

only on it, followed the vow of worshipping Katyayani.[140] O king! When the sun was rising at dawn, they bathed in the waters of the Kalindi. On the banks of the river, they fashioned an image of the goddess out of sand and worshipped her with fragrances, garlands, pastes, offerings, incense, laps, tender shoots, fruits, unbroken rice and other superior and ordinary objects. "O Katyayani! O Mahamaya! O Maha-yogini! O Adhishvari![141] O goddess! We bow down to you. Make the son of Nanda gopa my husband."[142] Having chanted this mantra, the maidens worshipped her. With their minds on Krishna, the maidens observed this vow for an entire month. Desiring Nanda's son as a husband, they invoked and worshipped Bhadrakali. They arose at dawn every day and called out to each other by name. Holding each other by the hand, they went to bathe in the Kalindi, chanting about Krishna's glory.

'Once, as they had done earlier, they arrived at the river and left their garments on the bank. Singing about Krishna, they happily sported in the water. The illustrious Krishna, the lord of all the lords of yoga, understood this. Surrounding himself with his friends, he went there, so as to render their rites successful. He quickly gathered up their garments and climbed up a *nipa* tree. Along with the other boys, he laughed. He spoke to them in jest. "O girls! You are suffering from having observed the vow. As you wish, come here and take back your respective garments. I am not joking, but am telling you the truth. I have never uttered a falsehood earlier and these boys know it. O slender-waisted ones! Alone, or

[140] Hemanta is the cold season, the months of Margashirsha (also known as Agrahayana) and Pousha. The first month, Margashirsha, is roughly mid-November to mid-December. Kumarikas are young unmarried maiden girls, less than the ages of ten and twelve. Havishya is food that can be offered as oblations. It is simple and has no seasoning. It is only eaten on special occasions, such as when a vow is being observed. Katyayani is one of Parvati's names and Katyayani *vrata* (vow), also known as Gouri vrata, is performed by maidens to get married, or obtain a groom. Bhadrakali is also one of Parvati's names. These kumarikas may have been even younger, since Krishna was just over six years old then.

[141] Supreme lord, in the feminine.

[142] This prayer is being recited in the singular.

collectively, come here and take your garments back." Seeing that he was teasing them, the gopis were filled with love. Ashamed, they glanced at each other. Though they laughed, not a single one came out. When Govinda spoke to them in this way in jest, their minds were agitated. They were submerged in the cold water, right up to their necks. Trembling, they spoke to him. "Do not be unfair in this way. You are the beloved son of Nanda gopa. O dear one! You are praised by Vraja. We are shivering. Give our garments back to us. O Shyamasundara![143] We will do whatever you ask us to do. O one who knows about dharma! Give our clothes back to us. Otherwise, we will tell the king[144] about this." The illustrious one replied, "O ones with the beautiful smiles! If you are my servant-maids and if you are going to do what I ask you to, then come here and take your own garments back." All the girls were trembling because of the cold. Suffering from the cold, they covered their vulvas with their hands and emerged. The illustrious one saw that they were virgins and was pleased with their pure sentiments.[145] He was pleased. With the garments on his shoulder, he smiled and spoke to them. "You were firm in your vows, but have bathed naked in the water. This is an offence against the gods. To atone for your sins, raise up your hands in salutation above your heads. After this, bow down and accept your lower garments."[146] Achyuta thus instructed the maidens of Vraja. They were also of the view that bathing naked had been a deviation from the vow. However, he is himself the infinite fulfilment of all rites. Therefore, to accomplish their desires, they bowed down before him, so that they might be cleansed of sin. The illustrious one, Devaki's son, saw that they were bowing down in that way. Satisfied and compassionate, he returned their

[143] This can be taken as a proper noun or as an adjective. Shyamasundara is one of Krishna's names, meaning one who has a beautiful dark-blue complexion.

[144] Nanda.

[145] The word used in the text is *anahata*, the opposite of *ahata*. Ahata means struck, injured, impaired. The opposite means virgin, perhaps implying the hymen is intact.

[146] Bathing naked wasn't the only crime. In addition, while observing a vow, the girls had not maintained silence and had sported in the water.

garments to them. They[147] were completely cheated and made to feel ashamed. They were laughed at and he played with them, as if they were puppets. Their garments were stolen. However, they were so content at this association with their beloved that they did not resent this at all. They donned their own garments. They were attached to this association with their beloved. He had captivated their minds. They did not move from that place. Instead, they cast bashful glances towards him. The illustrious one understood that they wished to touch his feet. That is the reason they had resolved to undertake the vow. Damodara spoke to the women. "O virtuous ones! I know that your intention was to worship me. Anything that is approved by me always comes true. Even if something is done out of desire, if the mind is immersed in me, no desire results. This is like grain that has been fried and cooked. Generally, it cannot be made to sprout.[148] O women! Go to Vraja. You will be successful. You will enjoy nights with me. O virtuous ones! That is the reason you observed the vow of worshipping the noble one."[149] Thus instructed by the illustrious one, the kumarikas accomplished their objective. Meditating on his lotus feet, they reluctantly went to Vraja.

'After this, surrounded by the gopas, Devaki's illustrious son went far away from Vrindavana. Along with his elder brother, he herded the cows. At the time of the fierce heat of the summer, the trees spread out their shade like umbrellas, to protect him and his companions. On seeing this, he spoke to the residents of Vraja. "O Stokakrishna![150] O Amshu! On Shridama! O Subala! O Arjuna! O Vishala! O Rishabha! O Tejasvi! O Devaprastha! O Varuthapa! Behold these immensely fortunate ones. Their lives are devoted to the welfare of others. They withstand storms, showers, heat and cold and save us from them. Since they provide subsistence for all kinds of creatures, their birth is most wonderful. Those who desire something are never refused by good people and they are like them. They satisfy desires through leaves, flowers, fruits, shade,

[147] The gopis.
[148] It cannot be used as seed.
[149] Katyayani.
[150] *Stoka* means small, so this can also be translated as Little Krishna.

roots, bark, wood, fragrances, sap, ashes, kernels and tender leaves. An embodied being must always act so as to bring benefit to other creatures through life, wealth, intelligence, words and conducts. It is then that life becomes successful." Saying this, he passed through the midst of lowered branches laden with tender foliage, bunches of flowers and fruits and leaves and arrived at the Yamuna. O king! The gopas made the cows drink the sweet, cool and auspicious water. After this, they satisfied themselves by drinking that sweet water. O king! As they wished, they made the animals graze in a grove there. Suffering from hunger, they approached Krishna and Rama and spoke to them.'

Chapter 10(23)

'The gopas said, "O Rama! O mighty-armed one! O Rama! O Krishna! O destroyer of the wicked! We are suffering from hunger. You should do something to satisfy it."'

Shri-Shuka said, 'The gopas told Devaki's illustrious son this. Desiring to please his devotees, the wives of the brahmanas, he addressed them in these words. "Go to the place where the brahmanas, who know about the brahman, are worshipping the gods through a sacrifice named Angirasa. They are doing this with a desire to attain heaven. O gopas! Go there and announce that you have been sent by the illustrious one and his elder brother, mentioning us by name. Then ask for some cooked rice." Thus instructed by the illustrious one, they went and asked. They joined their hands in salutation before the brahmanas and prostrated themselves on the ground, like rods. "O divinities on earth! Listen to us. We are those who act according to Krishna's instructions. We are gopas who have been urged to come here by Rama. O fortunate ones! Recognize us. Not very far from here, Rama and Achyuta are herding the cows. They are hungry and are asking you for some cooked rice. O brahmanas! O those who are supreme in knowledge of dharma! If you have any faith in them, give them the cooked rice they are asking for. O supreme ones!

With the exception of sacrifices where animals are slaughtered, or *soutramani*, there is no sin attached to eating food that has been given by someone who has consecrated himself for a sacrifice."[151] They heard what the illustrious one desired, but did not listen. They were performing a lot of rites, but were inferior in their wishes. They prided themselves on their age and wisdom, but were foolish. He pervades the time, the place, the separate objects used, the mantras, the *tantras*, the officiating priests, the sacrificial fires, the divinities presiding over sacrifices, the ones performing sacrifices, the *kratus* and dharma. He is himself the supreme brahman. He is the illustrious Adhokshaja. However, their wisdom was tainted. They looked upon him as a mortal human being and did not show him respect. O scorcher of enemies! They did not say "yes", nor did they say "no". Disappointed, the gopas returned to Krishna and Rama and told them what had happened.

'Hearing this, the illustrious lord of the universe laughed. He again spoke to the gopas, intending to demonstrate to them the way people in the world behaved. "Go and tell the wives[152] that I have come here with Samkarshana. They will give you the desired food. They are affectionate and their minds are in me." They went to the place where the wives resided and saw that they were ornamented and seated. The gopas bowed down before the virtuous brahmana ladies and addressed them humbly. "O wives of the brahmanas! We bow down to you. Listen to our words. Krishna is roaming around, not far from here, and he has sent us to you. Herding the cattle, along with the cowherds and Rama, he has come a long distance away. He is hungry. He asks that you should give some food for him and his followers." They were always eager to see him. Their minds were agitated by his accounts. Hearing that Achyuta had arrived, they were filled with

[151] When a person has consecrated himself for a sacrifice, he does not eat until the sacrifice is over, nor does he give food to someone else. What is being said is that this isn't a general rule, but only applies to sacrifices where animals are slaughtered, or soutramani sacrifices. Otherwise, there is no such bar. A soutramani sacrifice is an animal sacrifice in which liquor is also offered.

[152] Of the brahmanas.

excitement. All of them advanced to meet their beloved, like rivers heading for the ocean. They filled vessels with the four kinds of food, with many different qualities.[153] They were restrained by their husbands, brothers, relatives and sons. However, they had heard about the illustrious Uttamashloka for a long period of time and cherished him. Along the banks of the Yamuna, there was a grove of *ashoka* trees, decorated with tender foliage. The women saw him roaming around there, along with his elder brother, and surrounded by the gopas. He was dark blue in complexion and his garments were golden yellow. He was adorned with wild flowers, peacock feathers, minerals and tender foliage. He was in the garb of a dancer and one of his hands rested on a companion's shoulder. He twirled a lotus in his other hand. There were lilies in his ears. The locks of his curly hair dangled over his cheeks. There was a smile on his lotus face. O Indra among men! They had often heard about the glories of their beloved and it had filled their ears. Their minds were submerged in him. He now entered their inner cores through the apertures of their eyes. They embraced him for a very long time and gave up all torment, just as a wise person abandons all sense of ego. They had abandoned all desires and had come there, wishing to see him. The one who is omniscient in his vision knew this. With a smile on his face, he spoke to them. "O immensely fortunate ones! Welcome. Please be seated. What can we do for you? It is most appropriate that you have come here to see me. There are accomplished people who know about what is good for them. They constantly bind themselves to me, without any motive. They are devoted to me and love me like their own atmans. The breath of life, intelligence, the mind, relatives, the body, wives, offspring, riches and other things are loved because of association with the atman. What can be more loved than that? Go to the place where your husbands, the brahmanas, are performing a sacrifice to the gods. You will render their sacrifice successful. Their status as householders is dependent on you." The wives said, "O lord! You should not speak in this harsh way. A promise is made about

---

[153] The four types of food are those that are chewed (*charvya*), sucked (*choshya* or *chushya*), licked (*lehya*) and drunk (*peya*).

resorting to your feet in the sacred texts and you should make that come true.[154] We have obtained your feet. You have kicked away garlands of tulasi leaves and we will wear them in our hair. We will free ourselves from all relationships. Our husbands, fathers, sons, brothers, relatives and well-wishers will not take us back, not to speak of others. Therefore, we have prostrated ourselves at your feet. O destroyer of enemies! There is no refuge other than you. That is what you should grant us." The illustrious one replied, "Your husbands, fathers, brothers, sons and the other people will not be scornful of you. Since you are devoted to me, the gods will also approve of it. Among men in this world, physical association does not contribute to love and affection. Instead, if the mind is united with me, one soon attains me. It doesn't happen through physical contact, but through hearing about me, visualizing me, meditating on me, immersing thoughts in me and by chanting about me. Therefore, return to your houses." Thus instructed, the wives of the brahmanas returned to the sacrificial arena. The women were not reprimanded and the sacrifice was completed. There was one single lady who had been restrained by her husband.[155] When she heard about what had happened with the illustrious one, she clung to him in her heart. She gave up her physical body and the bonds of karma.

'The illustrious Govinda divided up the four kinds of food among the gopas. The lord made them eat and then ate himself. Thus, assuming a human body in his pastimes, he followed the conduct of the world of men. He amused himself with the cows, the gopas and the gopis and delighted them with his form, words and deeds. The brahmanas remembered and repented. "We have committed a sin. We have slighted the two supreme lords of the universe, who had disguised themselves as men." They witnessed the superhuman devotion towards the illustrious Krishna that the women possessed. They thought themselves to be inferior. They repented and censured themselves. "Shame on the three kinds of

[154] About emancipation and liberation from samsara.
[155] From going to meet Krishna.

birth we have had.[156] Shame on our vows. Shame on our extensive
knowledge. Shame on our lineage. Shame on our skill with rituals.
We have withdrawn ourselves from Adhokshaja. Indeed, the
illustrious one's maya is capable of confounding even yogis. We are
brahmanas, the preceptors of men. But we have been confounded
about what is good for us. Look at these women. Their devotion
towards Krishna, the preceptor of the universe, is insurmountable.
For those who are householders, it destroys the noose of death. They
have not gone through the samskaras of brahmanas. They have not
resided in the homes of the preceptors. They have not performed
austerities, nor have they speculated about the nature of the atman.
They have not observed any rites of purification or other auspicious
rites. Nevertheless, their devotion towards Uttamashloka Krishna,
the lord of all lords of yoga, is firm. Despite our samskaras, we have
not developed this. Indeed, we were confounded about what was
good for us. We were intoxicated in our roles as householders. Alas!
Through the words of the gopas, he had reminded us about the path
followed by virtuous people. All desires are satisfied through him.
He is the lord of kaivalya[157] and other benedictions. He is the lord
of everything. Why else would the controller present us with this
pretext? Giving up everything else, Shri serves him, hoping to touch
his feet, casting aside all her taints.[158] His asking us was an attempt
to confound people. He pervades the time, the place, the separate
objects offered, mantras, tantras, officiating priests, sacrificial fires,
the divinities presiding at sacrifices, the ones performing sacrifices,
kratu and dharma. He is the illustrious Vishnu, the lord of all the
lords of yoga, himself. We had heard that he had been born in
the lineage of the Yadus. Even then, we were foolish and failed
to recognize him. We are blessed that we have wives like these.
Their minds are full of unwavering devotion towards Hari and so
is ours. We bow down to the illustrious Krishna, whose intelligence
is unlimited. His maya confounds our intelligence and we are

[156] The physical birth, the investiture of the sacred thread and
consecration for sacrifices.

[157] Emancipation.

[158] Shri is known for being fickle, but not vis-à-vis him.

whirled around along the path of karma. He is the original being. He confounded us through his own maya. We did not understand his powers. Our great transgression should be pardoned." Thus, they remembered their own sins and the slight that they had shown towards Krishna. Though they wished to see the two Achuytas,[159] because they were scared of Kamsa, they did not move.'

Chapter 10(24)

Shri-Shuka said, 'While residing there with Baladeva, the illustrious one saw the gopas making preparations for a sacrifice to Indra. The illustrious one is omniscient and dwells in all atmans. Though he knew, he humbly asked the elders, with Nanda at the forefront. "O father! What are all these great actitivies for? What are the expected fruits? Who is this directed towards? What are the arrangements for this sacrifice? O father! Tell me. I have a great desire to hear about this. Virtuous people who look upon everyone else as their own selves should not keep secrets in this world. They do not distinguish between what belongs to them and what belongs to someone else. They do not distinguish between friends, those who are neutral and enemies. Even if a neutral person is avoided like an enemy, it has been said that a well-wisher is like one's own self. Regardless of whether they understand or don't understand the purposes of rites, they perform them. The learned accomplish the objectives of rites, not those who are ignorant. That being the case, has the purpose of this rite been thought about?[160] Or is it just something that people generally do? It is best that it should be properly explained to those who ask." Nanda replied, "The illustrious Indra is the rain god. The clouds represent his embodied form. They shower down the beloved water, which ensures life and subsistence to creatures. O son! We and others worship the lord and master of the clouds. Men worship him through yajnas and

---

[159] Krishna and Balarama.
[160] Interpreted as—has it been sanctioned by the sacred texts?

kratus,[161] using objects that are ripened through his semen.[162] The remnants of sacrifices are fruits that enable the accomplishment of the three objectives of existence.[163] For enterprising men, Parjanya is the one who determines the fruits. This is the dharma that has come down through tradition. Out of desire, hatred, fear or avarice, if a man rejects this, he does not obtain benefit." Keshava heard the words of Nanda and the other residents of Vraja. With an intention of generating Indra's anger, he spoke to his father.

'The illustrious one said, "Creatures come into being because of karma. It is because of karma that they are destroyed. Happiness, unhappiness, fear and fortune are all the outcome of karma. If there is a lord who confers fruits and other benefits of karma, he becomes dependent on the one who undertakes the karma and has no control over those who do not undertake it.[164] Creatures follow their own respective karma. In this world, what can Indra do to creatures? Men act and are driven by their own natures. What power does he have over this? Each person is under the control of his own nature and follows that nature. Gods, asuras and humans are all based on their own natures. It is because of karma that creatures are born as superior and inferior species and give up those bodies. Karma is the lord and preceptor, the friend, the neutral or the enemy. Therefore, one should worship karma. Based on one's own nature, one must perform one's own karma. Indeed, what can easily be done is the divinity. If one's proclivities are towards one form of subsistence, but he resorts to another, that does not ensure benefit. That is like an unchaste woman indulging with a paramour. A brahmana must devote himself to the brahman.[165]

[161] A yajna and a kratu are both sacrifices. However, the former is performed with a sacrificial post and the latter without one. More specifically, the former is performed with sacrificial animals and the latter without sacrificing animals.

[162] That is, rain.

[163] Dharma, artha and kama.

[164] This has complicated interpretations. The supreme lord cannot be dependent on karma. If he confers fruits according to karma, he becomes dependent on others.

[165] Interpreted as studying and teaching.

Royalty must protect the earth.[166] Vaishyas subsist through trade and shudras by serving dvijas.[167] There are four kinds of means of subsistence—agriculture, trade, tending to cattle and the lending of money. We are continuously engaged in tending to cattle. Sattva, rajas and tamas are the reasons behind creation, preservation and destruction. The universe has been created out of rajas. All the many things on world result from union between one another.[168] It is rajas that urges the clouds and they shower down water in every direction. That is how subjects achieve their purposes. What does the great Indra do? We do not live in cities, habitations, villages or permanent homes. O father! We are residents of the forest. We live in forests and mountains. Therefore, we should organize a sacrifice for cattle, brahmanas and this mountain.[169] Let us use everything that has been brought together for Indra's sacrifice to accomplish that sacrifice. Let many kinds of food be cooked, ending with broth, payasam[170] and other things. Let small cakes be made out of flour and fried. Let cakes be baked.[171] Let all the milk products be taken for that purpose. Let the sacrificial fires be properly kindled by brahmanas who know about the brahman. Let food with many kinds of qualities be given to them. Let them be given cattle as dakshina.[172] Let the appropriate food be given to dogs, shvapakas, chandalas and outcastes.[173] Let grass be given to the cows. Let offerings be rendered to the mountain. After eating,

[166] The text uses the word rajanya. In the present context, this is synonymous with kshatriya.

[167] The three higher varnas.

[168] That is, intercourse.

[169] Govardhana.

[170] A dish made out sweetened milk and rice.

[171] Apupas are small and round cakes made out of flour and fried. Shashkulyas are baked cakes.

[172] Gifts given to brahmanas after the sacrifice.

[173] Shvapakas are sometimes equated with chandalas. Shva means dog and paka means to cook. Thus, shvapaka means someone who cooks dogs (eats dogs) or cooks for dogs (lives with dogs). Chandala has different nuances and a chandala is not necessarily a shudra. A chandala is also of mixed parentage, with a shudra father and a brahmana mother. More generally, chandalas are outcastes, while shudras are within the caste fold.

ornament yourselves. Smear yourselves with pastes and wear excellent garments. After this, circumambulate cows, brahmanas, sacrificial fires and the mountain.[174] O father! This is my view. If it appeals to you, act in accordance with this. A sacrifice for cattle, brahmanas and the mountain will please me a lot."'

Shri-Shuka continued, 'The illustrious one was time himself and he wished to destroy Shakra's pride. Nanda and the others heard him and applauded and accepted his words. All of them acted exactly as Madhusudana had said. They had benedictions pronounced and offered those objects and the offerings that had been collected to brahmanas and the mountain. They gave grass to the cows. Placing the wealth of cattle ahead of them, they circumambulated the mountain. They yoked carts, and gopis ornamented themselves and rode on them, chanting about Krishna's valour. The brahmanas pronounced benedictions. So as to bring about trust in the gopas, Krishna assumed a completely different appearance, with a gigantic form. He said, "I am the mountain" and ate all the offerings.[175] Along with the people of Vraja, he himself bowed down to this form of his and said, "Behold the form of this mountain. It has favoured us by manifesting itself before us. It can assume any form at will and kill residents of the forest who disregard it. For our benefit and that of the cattle, let us bow down before it." Thus, urged by Vasudeva, the gopas undertook a sacrifice to the mountain, cows and cattle, as they had been instructed. Along with Krishna, they then returned to Vraja.'

Chapter 10(25)

Shri-Shuka said, 'O king! Indra got to know that his own worship had been stopped. He became angry with the gopas who had

---

[174] The word used is *pradakshina*, which is much more specific than a mere act of circling. This circling or circumambulation has to be done in a specific way, so that the right side (*dakshina*) always faces what is being circled.

[175] Krishna had two simultaneous forms, his own and that of Govardhana.

accepted Krishna as a protector, with Nanda and the others. There are a host of clouds named *samvartaka*, which bring about universal destruction. Taking himself to be the lord, Indra angrily goaded them in these words. "Because of their prosperity, look at the insolence of greatness that has arisen in the gopas who dwell in the forest. Seeking refuge with a mortal Krishna, they have disregarded a god. They have given up considered knowledge and have resorted to sacrifices full of rites. They wish to cross the ocean of life with these. But since these are broken, they are boats only in name. Krishna talks a lot. He is childish, arrogant and ignorant, but takes himself to be learned. Seeking refuge with a mortal Krishna, the gopas have caused displeasure to me. Their prosperity has maddened them. They take themselves to be protected by Krishna. Destroy their prosperity, insolence and arrogance. Convey their animals to destruction. Astride the elephant Airavata, I will follow you to Vraja. To destroy Nanda's settlement, the large number of extremely forceful Maruts will be with me." The clouds were thus commanded by Maghavan. Freed from their bonds,[176] they used their energy to pour down on Nanda's Gokula and cause suffering. There were flashes of lightning. There were roars of thunder. There were a large number of fierce Maruts. Water and hailstones showered down. The showers were as thick as pillars and the clouds released them incessantly. The torrents of water flooded the earth and high and low ground could no longer be seen. Because of the excessive rain and the strong winds, the animals started to tremble. The gopas and gopis suffered from the cold and went and sought refuge with Govinda. Suffering from the downpour, they covered their heads, and their children with their bodies. Trembling, they sought refuge at the illustrious one's feet. "O Krishna! O immensely fortunate one! O Krishna! O lord! You are Gokula's protector. O one who is devoted to his devotees! You should save us from the god who is angry with us." They were suffering from the shower of hailstones and the extreme storms. Struck by these, they were senseless. On seeing this, the illustrious Hari thought that this was the work of

---

[176] Samvartaka clouds should not have been released until it was the time for universal destruction.

an angry Indra. "This excessive shower and severe storms with hailstones is not characteristic of this season. Since his own sacrifice has been stopped, Indra is showering down, so as to destroy us. I will counter this through an appropriate use of my own yoga. I must take measures. There are those who foolishly pride themselves on being the lords of the worlds. I must destroy the tamas that leads to intoxication at their affluence. The lords of the gods are suffused with sattva. But since they are intoxicated with what is not sattva, this is not surprising in them. I must think of a means to quieten them and shatter their pride. Those in the settlement have sought refuge with me. I am there protector and they are dependent on me. Through my own yoga, I must protect the gopas. That is my vow."

'Saying this, with one hand, though he was still a child, he held up Mount Govardhana. Vishnu held it up easily, as if it was a mushroom. The illustrious one spoke to the gopas. "O mother! O father! O residents of Vraja! As you wish, please enter the cavities in this mountain, along with your wealth of cattle. You should not be scared that the mountain will fall down from my hand. Nor should you be scared of the wind and the rain. This is sufficient to protect you." With their minds assured by Krishna, they comfortably entered those cavities, along with their wealth, their vehicles and their dependents. He abandoned hunger, thirst and all expectations of happiness. As the residents of Vraja looked at him, he held up the mountain for seven days and his feet did not move even a little. On witnessing the power of Krishna's yoga, Indra was extremely astounded. His pride and determination were destroyed and he asked his clouds to withdraw. The sky was clear of clouds and the sun arose. The terrible storm and rain ceased. Seeing this, the one who had held up Govardhana spoke to the gopas. "O gopas! Cast away your fears and emerge, along with your women, wealth and children. The storm and the rain have ceased. The flood in the rivers has almost receded." At this, the gopas emerged, taking their respective wealth of cattle with them. The women, the young and the aged emerged slowly, along with carts loaded with various objects. While all the creatures looked on, the illustrious lord playfully placed the mountain back at the spot where it had been earlier. The residents of Vraja were overwhelmed with a flood of love for him. They came forward, embraced him and did other things.[177] The delighted gopis affectionately worshipped him with curds, unbroken rice and water and pronounced excellent benedictions. Yashoda, Rohini, Nanda and Rama, supreme among strong ones, embraced Krishna. Overwhelmed with affection, they pronounced benedictions. O king! Large number of gods, Siddhas, Sadhyas, gandharvas and charanas praised him from the firmament and showered down flowers. O king! Urged by the gods, conch shells and drums were sounded in heaven. The lords among the gandharvas, Tumbaru being the foremost, sang. The protectors of the animals devotedly surrounded him. O king! With them and with Bala, Hari went to his own settlement. The *gopikas*[178] sang about this and other acts that he had done. He had touched their hearts and they rejoiced.'

Chapter 10(26)

Shri-Shuka said, 'The gopas witnessed this and other things that Krishna did. Since they did not know about his valour, they were extremely surprised. They approached[179] and spoke. "The deeds done by this child are extraordinary. How did he deserve to be born among ordinary people like us? As if he was playing, how could this child hold up a supreme mountain on a single hand for seven days, like a king among elephants does to a lotus? This extremely energetic one had his eyes closed. But like time devours lifespan and the body, he drank from Putana's breast and sucked out her life. When he was only one month old, he was lying down under a cart and crying. He struck it with one foot and made it overturn and fall down. When he was only a year old, he was seated and was carried through the sky

---

[177] This depended on status. For example, seniors inhaled the fragrance of his head, equals and intimate ones embraced him and juniors touched his feet.

[178] Young gopis.

[179] They went to Nanda.

by the daitya[180] Trinavarta. But he seized him by the neck, throttled
him and killed him. On one occasion, because he had stolen butter,
his mother tied him to a mortar. However, crawling on his hands,
he went between two *arjuna* trees and brought them down. With
Rama and surrounded by the children, he was herding calves in the
forest. Baka wished to kill him. However, he tore apart the enemy's
mouth with his arms and killed him. Vatsa[181] wanted to kill him and
penetrated the calves in the form of a calf. However, he playfully
hurled him and killed him, making *kapittha* fruits fall down. With
Bala, he killed the daitya Rasabha[182] and his relatives, thus making
the forest of palm, filled with ripe fruit, safe. He arranged that the
extremely strong Bala should kill Pralamba. He rescued the animals
of Vraja and the gopas from the forest conflagration. In the pool, he
subdued the Indra among serpents who possessed virulent poison.
He forcibly exiled him from Yamuna, freeing the water from the
poison. All of us, the residents of Vraja, have an affection towards
him that is impossible to give up. O Nanda! Your son is also
attached to you and to us. How did this come about? How can
a mere child, who is seven years old, hold up a giant mountain?
Who is he? O lord of Vraja! Therefore, we have a doubt about
your son." Nanda replied, "O gopas! Listen to my words and do
not have any doubts about my son. This is what Garga had told
me about this son.[183] 'According to the yuga, this one has adopted
bodies with three different complexions—white, red and yellow. He
is now dark. Earlier, this son of yours used to belong to Vasudeva.
Therefore, those who know will refer to this prosperous one as
Vasudeva. This son of yours has many kinds of names and forms.
His qualities and deeds are also similar. I know about them, but
other people do not. He will be the delight of Gokula and will
bring welfare to the gopas. It is through him that you will easily
pass over all the difficulties. O lord of Vraja! Earlier, the virtuous

---

[180] Daityas are a specific category of demons, the progeny of Diti.

[181] The name of this demon wasn't given earlier.

[182] Dhenuka, Rasabha means donkey.

[183] Except the last sentence, Garga's quote is a repetition of shlokas
from Chapter 10(8).

suffered from bandits. They were not protected by a king. However, he vanquished the flourishing bandits. Enemies and asuras cannot overcome those who have Vishnu on their side. Those immensely fortunate men bring him pleasure. O Nanda! Therefore, this son of yours is like Narayana in his qualities. Therefore, do not be surprised at his prosperity, powers and deeds.' Garga directly instructed me in this way and returned to his own home. I think that Krishna, unblemished in his deeds, has been born as Narayana's portion." Hearing Nanda's words and what Garga had chanted, the residents of Vraja were filled with joy. Their wonder vanished and they worshipped Nanda and Krishna. The god who showers was angry that his sacrifice had been stopped and showered down thunder, hail stones and winds. Suffering, the protectors of animals and the women sought refuge with him. On seeing this, he was filled with compassion. Though he was only a child, he playfully uprooted the mountain and held it up in a single hand, as if it was a mushroom. He protected the settlement and destroyed the great Indra's pride. May the lord of cows be pleased with us.'

Chapter 10(27)

Shri-Shuka said, 'He held up Mount Govardhana and protected Vraja from the downpour. Surabhi came down to Krishna from Goloka.[184] Shakra was with her. He approached him in a private place. He was ashamed that he had shown him disrespect. He touched his feet with his diadem, which was as radiant as the sun. Indra had seen, and had heard about, Krishna's powers and his infinite energy. His pride at being the lord of the three worlds had been destroyed. He joined his hands in salutation and said the

[184] Surabhi is the divine cow who yields all the objects of desire. She is the mother of all cattle. She is Daksha's daughter and is married to the sage Kashyapa. Goloka is a world meant for cattle and is above all the other worlds. The Mahabharata describes that this was given to Surabhi by Brahma.

following. Indra said, "Your abode is serene and is pure sattva. It is full of austerities and is devoid of anything created by rajas or tamas. This great confluence of gunas is full of maya. It results from the bondage of ignorance and does not exist in you. O lord! Avarice and other things are the signs and symptoms of ignorance. They are the result and the cause.[185] How can these exist in you? For the protection of dharma and for punishing the wicked, you nevertheless wield the rod of chastisement. You are the father. You are the preceptor. You are the controller of the universe. You are time, which is impossible to cross. For the sake of welfare, you wield the rod of chastisement. Out of your own will, you assume forms and perform acts. You destroy the pride of those who take themselves to be lords of the universe. There are ignorant ones like me, priding ourselves on being lords of the universe. On seeing you, fearless in the form of time, we quickly abandon that insolence. We give up our pride and completely follow the path of the noble. This action of yours is only meant to instruct the wicked. As a consequence of my lordship, I was flooded with insolence. Ignorant of your powers, I committed a crime against you. O lord! You should pardon those who are foolish in intelligence. O lord! O supreme one! May I never suffer from such wicked sentiments again. O Adhokshaja! O god! Many leaders of armies have been born. They are a burden on earth and create many difficulties. Your avatara is for their destruction and for the welfare of those who resort to your feet. I bow down to the illustrious one, the great-souled Purusha. I bow down to Vasudeva Krishna, the lord of the Satvatas. According to the wishes of your devotees, you assume a form. Your form is pure knowledge. You are in everything. You are the seed of everything. I bow down to the one who is in the atmans of all creatures. O illustrious one! When my sacrifice was stopped, full of pride, I was filled with fierce rage. I tried to destroy this settlement with showers and terrible winds. O lord! You showed me your favours and destroyed my arrogance and my futile efforts. You are my lord and preceptor. I seek refuge with you." Krishna was thus praised by Maghavan. With a voice that rumbled like that of the clouds, he smiled and

[185] Of maya.

spoke these words. The illustrious one replied, "O Maghavan! It was out of a favour to you that I had your sacrifice stopped, so that you might always remember me. You were intoxicated because of your prosperity as Indra. If a person is blind with the arrogance of prosperity and opulence, he does not see me, with the rod of chastisement in my hand. If I desire to show him a favour, I dislodge him from that prosperity. O Shakra! Leave and act in accordance with my instructions. Remain in the position of responsibility you have been entrusted with, but remain free of insolence." After this, along with her own offspring, the spirited Surabhi approached and spoke to Krishna, the lord who was in the form of a gopa. Surabhi said, "O Krishna! O great yogi! O Krishna! O one whose atman is the universe! O one who is the origin of the universe! O Achyuta! You are the protector of the worlds and you are our protector too. You are our supreme divinity. O lord of the universe! Become our Indra. For the welfare of cattle, brahmanas, gods and virtuous people, become our ruler. Urged by Brahma, we will undertake a consecration ceremony to make you our Indra. O one whose atman is the universe! You have descended so as to reduce the burden of the earth." Thus, Surabhi invited Krishna and consecrated him with her milk. Along with the divine rishis and urged by the mothers of the gods,[186] Indra sprinkled him with water from the celestial Ganga, brought by Airavata's trunk. He gave Dasharha the name of Govinda. "I am the Indra of the gods. You have become the Indra of the cows. In the worlds and on earth, men will chant about you as Govinda."[187] Tumbaru, Narada and the others arrived there— gandharvas, vidyadharas,[188] Siddhas and charanas. They sang about the fame of Hari, the one who cleanses the worlds of impurities. Filled with joy, the celestial women danced. All the prominent ones among the gods praised him. They showered him with wonderful flowers. The three worlds obtained great satisfaction. The cows

---

[186] Such as Aditi.

[187] Govinda = Go + Indra, a slightly convoluted derivation of Govinda. Usually, Govinda = Go + vinda, a person who protects/cherishes/obtains (vinda) cattle (go).

[188] Vidya means knowledge. Thus vidyadhara, one who holds knowledge.

flooded the earth with milk. Floods of many kinds of juices flowed along the rivers. Honey flowed out of the trees. Even without being ploughed, the plants yielded copious crops. The mountains brought out jewels.[189] O extender of the Kuru lineage! All this happened at Krishna's consecration. O son! Even those who are cruel by nature, gave up all enmity. In this way, Shakra instated Govinda as the lord of cows and of Gokula. Surrounded by the gods and others, he then took his leave and returned to heaven.'

Chapter 10(28)

Shri-Shuka said, 'On one occasion, Nanda fasted on the eleventh lunar day. He worshipped Janardana and on the twelfth lunar day, entered the waters of the Kalindi, so as to bathe. He had ignored the time meant for the asuras and had entered the waters in the night. At this, one of Varuna's asura servants seized him and brought him to his presence. Unable to see him, the gopas exclaimed, "O Krishna! O Rama!" The illustrious one heard that his father had been taken away by Varuna. O king! The lord who grants freedom from fear to his own went to his presence. Seeing Hrishikesha, the guardian of the world worshipped him with great offerings, taking the sight of him to be a great festival. Varuna said, "O lord! This is wonderful. My body has become successful today. I have obtained the ultimate objective. O illustrious one! Those who serve at your feet obtain the supreme destination. O illustrious one! I bow down to you. You are the brahman and the paramatman. Maya fashions the creation of the worlds, but it has not been heard to exist in you. My attendant is foolish and ignorant. He does not know about the right tasks. He has brought your father here. You should pardon me. O Krishna! O one who sees everything! You should show me your favours. O Govinda! O one who is devoted to your father! Take your father away from here." The illustrious Krishna, the lord

---

[189] These had remained hidden inside the mountains earlier.

of all the lords, was thus pleased. He took his own father back and his relatives were delighted.

'Nanda was astounded to see the great opulence of the guardian of the world, something that he had not seen before, and also at the honours they[190] had shown Krishna. He told his relatives about this. O king! The gopas formed the view that he was the supreme lord. Their minds were eager and they wondered, "He is the supreme lord. Will he bestow on us his own subtle destination?" The illustrious one witnessed everything and himself discerned what his kin desired. Out of compassion towards them, he started to think about how he might fulfil their wishes. "People in this world circle around as inferior and superior species because of ignorance, desire and karma. They do not know about their own destinations." The extremely compassionate and illustrious Hari thought about it in this way. He showed the gopas his own world, which is beyond tamas. This is truth and infinite knowledge. This is the eternal resplendence of the brahman. After transcending the gunas, controlled sages can see this. They were first conveyed to Brahma's lake. After being submerged there, they were raised up by Krishna. They saw Brahma's world, which Akrura had seen in earlier times.[191] Nanda and the others were extremely surprised to see Krishna being praised there through hymns. They were filled with supreme satisfaction and delight.'

Chapter 10(29)

Shri-Shuka said, 'The illustrious one saw that the autumn nights were beautiful with blossoming *mallika* flowers. He made up his mind to enjoy himself and resorted to his yoga maya.[192] The lord

---

[190] Varuna and his companions.

[191] The tense used requires an explanation. The incident occurs later, in Chapter 10(39). However, at the time when Shuka is recounting all this to Parikshit, the incident belongs to the past tense.

[192] Chapters 10(29) to 10(33) are full of beautiful poetry. They are about *rasa* or *rasa krida/rasa lila*, a circular dance involving Krishna and the gopis. There are various interpretations of Krishna's use of yoga maya.

of the stars arose, smearing the eastern horizon with its cool and red-tinged beams and making it pleasant for those who watched. It was as if a beloved husband had returned after a long time and was wiping away the sorrow from his beloved wife's face.[193] He saw the unbroken full moon, red like newly applied kunkuma and resembling Rama's face. It made the night lotuses bloom. The gentle beams tinged the forest. He played a melodious tune and it stole the hearts of the women with beautiful eyes. The women of Vraja heard the song that increased their desire. Their minds were stolen by Krishna. Not noticed by each other, they went to where their beloved was. Because of their hurry, their earrings swung back and forth. They were eager. Some were milking cows. But without finishing the milking, they went to him. Some had placed vessels of milk,[194] others had placed dishes for cooking. Without removing these, they departed. Some were serving, but left it incomplete. Some were feeding babies milk from their breasts, but left it. Some were feeding their husbands, others were themselves eating. But they forgot the food and left. Some were smearing or cleaning their bodies, others were applying collyrium to their eyes. Some were adorning themselves with garments and ornaments, but left these in disarray. They rushed towards Krishna. They were restrained by their husbands, fathers, brothers and relatives. However, their minds had been stolen by Govinda and, captivated, they did not return. Some gopis were in the inner quarters and couldn't find a means of coming out. Filled with love for Krishna, they closed their eyes and meditated on him. The torment of being separated from their beloved was fierce and impossible to withstand. It cleansed all that was inauspicious. They obtained Achyuta in their meditation and the bliss of that embrace exhausted their auspicious deeds.[195] They united with the paramatman, their minds regarding him as

---

There are also extensive commentaries on these five chapters. We have deliberately kept the translation simple.

[193] The beams of the moon are like a hand, making the wife blush, or smearing kunkuma on her face.

[194] For boiling on stoves, same for the dishes.

[195] That bliss destroys all karma, even if it is auspicious.

a paramour. They gave up their bodies, full of gunas, and were instantly freed of all bondage.'

The king asked, 'O sage! They knew Krishna as a supreme beloved, not as the brahman. Their minds were full of gunas. How could the flow of gunas cease for them?'

Shri-Shuka replied, 'Earlier, it was explained to you how the king of Chedi[196] attained success. This happened for someone who hated Hrishikesha. What needs to be said about those who loved Adhokshaja? O king! He is without decay. He is beyond measurement. Though his atman is behind the gunas, he is devoid of gunas. However, for the purpose of ensuring the welfare of men, the illustrious one manifests himself. Those who constantly harbour desire, anger, fear, identity and affection towards Hari eventually become unified with him. You should not be amazed at this accomplishment on the part of the illustrious Aja. Krishna is the lord of all the lords of yoga. He ensures all emancipation. The illustrious one saw that the women of Vraja had come to his presence.

'The best among speakers spoke to them, his enchanting words bewildering them. The illustrious one said, "O immensely fortunate ones! Welcome. What can I do to please you? Is everything well in Vraja? Tell me the reason why you have come here. O slender-waisted ones! This night is terrible in form and is frequented by beings that are terrible. Go back to Vraja. You should not remain here. On not seeing you, your mothers, fathers, sons, brothers and husbands will begin to search. You should not create anxiety for your relatives. You have seen the blossoming forest, dazzling because of the beams of the lord of the full moon night.[197] The breeze that is blowing from the Yamuna is playing and toying with the beautiful tender foliage. O virtuous ladies! Therefore, return to the settlement without any delay and serve your husbands. The calves and children are crying. Feed them milk and do the milking. On the other hand, your hearts may be completely controlled by

---

[196] Shishupala.

[197] *Raka* means the day/night of the full moon and Rakesha (the moon on such a night) is the lord (*isha*) of raka.

love for me. That is the reason you have come. This is normal on
your part, since creatures are attracted to me. The supreme dharma
for a woman is to faithfully serve her husband, ensure the welfare
of the relatives and take care of the children, without any deceit.
A woman who desires the worlds must not abandon her husband,
even if he is evil in conduct, unfortunate, aged, foolish, diseased or
poor, as long as he is not a great sinner. For women who are from
noble families, illicit intercourse is always condemned, even if it
happens to be a minor one. This does not lead to heaven. It brings
ill fame and hardship. It generates fear. You should therefore not
have any proximity to me, through hearing about me, seeing me,
meditating on me, loving me and chanting about me. Hence, return
to your homes." The gopis heard these disagreeable words spoken
by Govinda. Since their wishes were not met, they were distressed.
They faced an anxiety that was extremely difficult to overcome.
Their faces were downcast and they grieved. They sighed. Their lips
were like *bimba* fruit and those dried up. With the nails on their toes,
they scratched on the ground. The tears smudged and washed away
the collyrium and the kunkuma on their breasts. They stood there,
silently bearing the heavy burden of misery. He was their beloved,
though he had not addressed them in the words of a beloved. They
had given up all other desires for his sake. They wiped their eyes
and controlled their weeping. They were still attached to him. But
somewhat angry, they addressed him in faltering words. The gopis
said, "O lord! You should not speak to us in these cruel words. We
have given up all material objects and have resorted to your feet. We
are devoted to you and you should love us back. You are difficult
to abandon. Do not abandon us. O god! You should be like the
original being, who serves those who seek emancipation. You know
about dharma and you have said that the natural dharma of women
is to serve their husbands, offspring and well-wishers. O dear one!
O lord! This instruction should actually be applied to you. You are
loved by all those who possess bodies. Indeed, as the atman, you
are the relative. Those who are accomplished are attached to you,
as their own atmans. You are the one who is always loved. What
do husbands, sons and the others amount to? They lead to nothing
but hardships. O supreme lord! Be pleased with us and do not cast

us away. O lotus-eyed one! We have cherished you for a very long time. Our minds were cheerfully engaged in our homes. Our hands were engaged in undertaking household tasks. But you took us away. Our feet will not move away from where your feet are. How can we go back to Vraja? What will we do there? O dear one! Pour the amrita from your lips and flood us. Your smiling glances and your melodious songs have ignited a fire in our hearts. O friend! Otherwise, we will give up our bodies in the fire of separation, meditating on your feet and obtaining your state. O lotus-eyed one! When Rama touches your feet, it is like a special occasion for her. You love us, the residents of the forest, and we will also touch them. From this moment onwards, there is no one other than you who will be directly able to stand before us. Indeed, we have been completely fulfilled by you. Along with Tulasi,[198] Shri desires the dust on your lotus feet, which should be enjoyed by devotees, even though she has obtained a position on your chest. Even the gods make efforts to ensure her favourable glances. In that way, we have also approached you for the dust on your feet. O destroyer of all distress! Show us your favours. We have given up our homes and have approached your lotus feet. We hope to worship you. Because of your beautiful smiles and glances, our desire is intense. O ornament among men! Our hearts are tormented. Grant us this servitude. Your face is covered with curly locks of hair. You wear beautiful earrings and your cheeks are shining because of those. There is nectar in your lips and you have smiling glances. We have seen these. We have seen your mighty arms, which grant freedom from fear. Your chest is the source of pleasure for Shri. Grant us this servitude. O dear one! On hearing the melodious and drawn-out rhythm of the music from your flute, which woman in the three worlds will not be captivated and will not deviate from noble and sanctioned conduct? The sight of your form brings fortune to the three worlds. It charms cattle, birds, trees and animals and makes their body hair stand up in delight. It is evident that you have been born to dispel the fear and afflictions of those in Vraja. This is just

[198] The personified form of tulasi.

like the god, the original being,[199] who protected the world of the gods. O friend of those who are afflicted! Therefore, place your lotus hands on the warm breasts and heads of your servant maids." The lord of all the lords of yoga heard their piteous words. He was always satisfied in his own self. Nevertheless, out of compassion, he laughed and proceeded to satisfy the gopis.

'Achyuta was pervasive in his deeds and their faces bloomed when he cast loving glances at them. His broad smile displayed his radiant teeth, which were like *kunda* flowers. They assembled around him and he dazzled, like the moon,[200] when it is surrounded by stars. The leaders among those hundreds of women sang and he sang back. Wearing the vaijayanti garland, he wandered around that forest, rendering it resplendent. With the gopis, he entered the sandy banks of the river. The sand was made cool by the breeze, fragrant with the scent of night lotuses, which blew over the waves. He extended his arms and embraced them, touching their hands, hair, thighs, girdle strings, breasts in sport. He pricked them with the tips of his nails. He glanced at them in jest and laughed with the beauties of Vraja. He gave them pleasure and ignited the god of love[201] in them. Having obtained the great-souled and illustrious Krishna, each of those women became proud, taking herself to be the greatest on earth. Keshava noticed that they were proud and arrogant at their good fortune. Therefore, to pacify this and to show them his favours, he instantly vanished.'

Chapter 10(30)

Shri-Shuka said, 'The illustrious one suddenly disappeared. Unable to see him, the women of Vraja were tormented. They were like female elephants, without the leader of the herd. The

---

[199] Vishnu.

[200] The word used for the moon is *enanka*, meaning the one with the marks of a black antelope.

[201] Ratipati, Rati's consort.

minds of the women were agitated by the movements, loving smiles,
playful glances, delightful conversation, jests and other allurements
of Rama's lord. They took themselves to be him and started to
imitate his pastimes. They were so immersed in him that the
bodies of those beloved ones became like images of their beloved,
in moving, smiling, glancing, speaking and other things. They
identified with him and were bewildered by Krishna's pastimes.
Those women told each other, "I am him." Collectively, they sang
loudly. Like mad women, they searched in one forest and then in
another forest and asked the trees about him. Like the sky, he is the
Purusha who is inside and outside all beings. "O *ashvattha*![202] O
plaksha! O *nyagrodha*! Have you seen Nanda's son? Having stolen
our minds with his loving smiles and his glances, he has vanished.
O *kurubaka*! O ashoka! O *naga*! O *punnaga*! O *champaka*! Has
Rama's younger brother, who destroys the pride of proud women
with his smiles, come here? O fortunate tulasi! You love Govinda's
feet. Achyuta loves you a lot and wears you, along with a swarm of
bees. Have you seen him? O *malati*! O *mallika*! O *jati*! O *yuthika*!
Have you seen Madhava? Has he passed this way, causing you
pleasure with the touch of his hands? O *chuta*! O *priyala*! O *panasa*!
O *asana*! O *kovidara*! O *jambu*! O *arka*! O *bilva*! O *bakula*! O
amra! O kadamba! O nipa! All the others who have been born for
the sake of others and live along the banks of the Yamuna—tell
us about Krishna's trail. We have lost our minds because we are
separated from him. O earth! What austerities have you performed
to merit the touch of Krishna's feet? It has been like a festival and
you are radiant, with your body hair standing up in joy.[203] Has it
been caused now, or is it because his feet touched you earlier, in the

[202] Ashvattha is the holy fig tree, plaksha and nyagrodha are kinds of
fig trees, naga (*nagakesara*) is the Indian rose chestnut, punnaga is nutmeg,
champaka is a tree with yellow and fragrant flowers, malati is a kind of
white jasmine, mallika, jati and yuthika are also kinds of jasmine, chuta is
mango, priyala is the chironji tree, panasa is jackfruit, kovidara is a kind
of orchid, jambu is rose apple, arka is the sun plant, bilva is wood apple,
bakula is a tree with fragrant blossoms, amra is mango and both kadamba
and nipa mean the same kind of tree.

[203] The trees, plants and grass growing on earth.

course of Urukrama's valour?[204] Or is it because he embraced your body in the form of the boar? O wife of the antelope! O friend! Has Achutya passed this way with his beloved? Did his limbs cause delight to your eyes? Was his garland of kunda flowers coloured from the kunkuma on the breasts of his loved, when he engaged with her? The breeze bears the scent of the leader of our lineage. O trees! Did Rama's younger brother pass this way, with one hand resting on his beloved's shoulder and the other holding a lotus? Did crazy bees, blind with intoxication, swarm around his bunch of tulasi leaves and follow him here? When you bowed down at his feet, did he acknowledge that with loving glances? Let us ask these creepers. They are embracing the arms[205] of the trees. Since they are prickling with joy, they must have been touched by the nails of his hand." Maddened and confused while searching for Krishna, the gopis spoke in this way.

'With their hearts immersed in him, they started to imitate the illustrious one's pastimes. One pretended to be Putana, while another pretended to be Krishna and sucked at her breast. One pretended to be a child and cried, while kicking another who was pretending to be the cart. One acted as the daitya[206] and carried away another, who was enacting the role of the infant Krishna. Another crawled, dragging her feet and jingling her anklets. Two imitated Krishna and Rama, while the others pretended to be gopas. One imitated the act of killing Vatsa, while another imitated that of killing Baka. One imitated Krishna calling the cows when they had wandered far away. Another pretended to sport and play on the flute, while the others uttered words of praise. One placed her hand on another one's shoulder and walked. With her mind on him, she said, "I am Krishna. Behold my graceful gait." One sought to raise her upper garment with her hand and said, "Do not be scared of the storm and the rain. I have arranged for you to be saved." O king! Using her feet, one climbed on to another one's head and said, "O wicked serpent! I have been born. Go away from here. I will

[204] As the dwarf incarnation.
[205] The branches.
[206] Trinavarta.

certainly impose the rod of chastisement on those who are wicked."
Another said, "O gopas! Look at this fierce forest conflagration.
Quickly close your eyes. I will easily arrange for your safety."
One tied another to a mortar with a garland of flowers. The one
who had been tied covered her beautiful eyes with her hands and
pretended to be afraid. In this way, they asked the creepers and trees
of Vrindavana about Krishna's whereabouts.

'In one part of the forest, they saw the paramatman's footprints.
"It is evident that these are the footprints of Nanda's great-souled
son. The marks of the standard, lotus, vajra, goad, barley and other
things can be seen." Following and tracing out his footprints along
the trail, those women advanced. However, they were distressed
on seeing that his footprints were mingled with those of a young
woman. They said, "Whose footprints are these? Who has walked
with Nanda's son? He must have rested his forearm on her
shoulder, just as an elephant rests its trunk on a she-elephant. She
must have indeed worshipped the illustrious lord, Hari. Pleased
with her, he has abandoned us and gone with her to a secret place.
O friends! The particles of dust on Govinda's lotus feet are sacred.
For destroying their sins, Brahma, Isha and the goddess Rama place
the dust on their heads. But these footprints of hers have agitated
us a lot. Among all the gopis, she alone has been taken aside and is
enjoying Achyuta's lips in private. However, her footprints can no
longer be seen here. It must indeed be the case that the sharp blades
of grass have caused pain to the delicate soles of her feet. Therefore,
our beloved has raised and carried his beloved. O gopis! Behold. In
this spot, as he has carried the young woman, his footprints have
sunk deeper into the ground. Krishna, full of desire, had a heavy
burden. To collect flowers, the great-souled one placed his beloved
down here. This is where our beloved made efforts to collect flowers
for his beloved. Behold. These footprints are not complete, because
he stood up on the front part of his feet. Filled with desire, this is
where he must have decorated his beloved's hair. It is certainly the
case that he sat down here, so as to fasten them on the braids of his
beloved's hair. He finds pleasure in himself and is always complete.
Nevertheless, this is where he found pleasure with her. He wanted
to demonstrate what happens to those who are filled with desire

and also the state of evil-souled women." Bereft of their senses, the gopis showed each other these and wandered around.

'Leaving the other women in the forest, there was a gopi whom Krishna had taken with him. She now took herself to be the best among all the women. "Abandoning the other gopis, who also desire him, my beloved serves me alone." When they reached a certain spot in the forest, this proud one told Keshava, "I cannot walk any further. Please carry me to wherever you want to go." Thus addressed, he told his beloved, "Climb on to my shoulder." Having said this, Krishna instantly vanished and the young woman was tormented. "O protector! O most beloved one! Where are you? O mighty-armed one! Where are you? Show compassion towards your wretched servant-maid. O friend! Reveal your presence to me." Not very far away, the other gopis were searching out the illustrious one's trail. They saw their bewildered and miserable friend, separated from her beloved. She told them how Madhava had shown her a lot of respect and how she had been humiliated because of her wicked nature. Hearing this, they were filled with great wonder.

'They entered the forest, as far as the moonlight would illuminate it. However, noticing that it was being enveloped in darkness, the women withdrew. Their minds were immersed in him. They conversed about him. They imitated his deeds and they were full of him. They sang about his qualities. They remembered neither themselves, nor their homes. They again returned to the sandy banks of the Kalindi and thought about him. They collectively sang about Krishna and wished that he should return.'

Chapter 10(31)

'The gopis said, "It is because of your birth that Vraja has become even more glorious and Indira[207] resides here constantly. O beloved one! Those who are devoted to you wish to see you. Our lives subsist on you and we have been searching. Show yourself. O

207 Name for Lakshmi.

lord of pleasure! The beauty of your glance surpasses the inside of a perfectly formed lotus in a clear lake of autumn water. O one who bestows boons! Without paying a price, you have obtained us as your female servants. You are killing us. Is that not the same as murder? O powerful one! You have repeatedly protected us from many kinds of fear—drinking poisoned water, the rakshasa in the form of a reptile,[208] rain, storm, lightning, fire, the bull[209] and Maya's son.[210] You are clearly not the son of a gopi. You are the atman, dwelling as a witness inside all creatures. O friend! For the sake of the protection of the universe, Vikhanasa[211] prayed to you. You accordingly appeared in the lineage of the Satvatas. O best among the Vrishni lineage! You created freedom from fear. Those who are scared of samsara approach your feet. O beloved one! Your lotus hand bestows all desire. It is the one you have used to grasp Shri's hand. Please place it on our heads. O brave one! You are the one who destroys the sufferings of the residents of Vraja. Your smile destroys the pride of your own devotees. O friend! We, women, are your servants. Show us your beautiful lotus face. You destroy the sins of embodied creatures who prostrate themselves before you. You follow creatures that graze on grass and they are Shri's abode. You placed your lotus feet on the hoods of the serpent. Please place them on our breasts and quench the desire in our hearts. Your voice is sweet and your words are captivating. You are attractive to the minds of the intelligent. O lotus-eyed one! O brave one! You do what you ask us to and we are bewildered. With the nectar from your lips, please restore life to us. The amrita of your account is described by the wise. It destroys the sins of those who are tormented by life. It brings auspiciousness and prosperity to those who hear. O generous one! People on earth chant about them. O beloved one! Your smiles, your loving glances and your pastimes are auspicious for us to meditate on. O deceiver! The private conversations with you touch our hearts, but also agitate our minds. O protector! O beloved one! When you

---

[208] Aghasura.
[209] Arishta, described in Chapter 10(36).
[210] Vyoma, described in Chapter 10(37).
[211] Being used as a name for Brahma.

leave Vraja to herd the animals, gravel, blades of grass and sprouts
hurt your beautiful lotus feet and make us suffer. Our minds are
disturbed. Dark-blue curls hang over your lotus face. At the close of
the day, it is smeared with thick dust. O brave one! You ignite desire
in our minds. You grant the desires of those who prostrate themselves
before you. The one who has been born from the lotus worships
you. Your lotus feet ornament the earth and must be meditated
on. O beloved! O destroyer of mental anguish! Please satisfy us by
placing them on our breasts. Your beautiful lips repeatedly kiss the
vibrating flute. They enhance desire and destroy grief. They make
men forget attachment and other things. O brave one! Please grant
us the amrita from your lips. During the day, when you wander
around in the forest, a truti without being able to see you seems like
an extended yuga. The curly locks hang over your handsome face.
We look at you. However, the creator must be foolish. He gave us
eyelashes that make us blink. O Achyuta! We have come to you after
ignoring our husbands, sons, followers, brothers and relatives. O
one who knows about movements! We have been confused by your
music. O deceiver! Who but you will abandon women in the night?
The private conversations, your smiling face and the loving glances
stir our hearts. Your broad chest is Shri's residence. On beholding it,
repeated urges of excessive desire confound our minds. O dear one!
Fot the residents of Vraja and the forest, your appearance destroys
all distress and brings what is auspicious to the universe. We are
full of desire for you. Please grant us a little bit of something that
counters this disease in those who are your own devotees. O beloved
one! Please place your beautifully formed lotus feet on our breasts.
We are scared when you roam around the harsh terrain of the forest.
Do small stones and the like not hurt you? Our minds are in a whirl.
Our lives depend on you.'"

Chapter 10(32)

Shri-Shuka said, 'The gopis lamented and chanted in these
colourful ways. O king! Desiring to see Krishna, they wept in

loud voices. Shouri appeared in their midst, a smile on his lotus face. He was attired in yellow garments and wore a garland. He was capable of confounding Manmatha's mind.[212] The women saw that their beloved had arrived. Their eyes dilated in delight. They simultaneously stood up, as if life had returned to all their bodies. One joyfully clasped Shouri's lotus hands in her joined hands. Another placed his arm, smeared with sandalwood paste, on her shoulder. A slender one accepted the betel leaf chewed by him in her cupped palms. Another tormented one placed his lotus feet on her breasts. One was filled with both love and rage and furrowed her eyebrows. She bit her lips with her teeth and cast sidelong glances at him, as if to injure him. Another glanced fixedly at him, savouring his lotus face. She drank it in but was not satisfied, just as virtuous people aren't with his feet. Another placed him in her heart through the apertures in her eyes and closed them. When she embraced him mentally, her body hair stood up, like that of a yogi who is flooded with bliss. Seeing Keshava, all of them were satisfied, as if there were great festivities. They gave up the torment they had suffered from the separation, like people when they attain wisdom.[213] They were free of all misery and the illustrious Achyuta was surrounded by them. O son! He became even more resplendent, like Purusha with his powers. Collecting them, the lord went to the sandy banks of the Kalindi. The breeze bore the fragrance of blooming kunda and *mandara* flowers and attracted bees. The auspicious beams of the autumn moon dispelled the taints of the darkness. There was soft sand, which the river with the dark waters had placed there, using her waves like hands. On seeing him, the joy banished all the grief in their hearts. It was as if the sacred texts had attained their ultimate wishes.[214] Their upper garments were smeared with the kunkuma from their breasts. They spread these out and created a seat for the one who was loved more than their own selves. The

[212] Manmatha is a name for Kama, meaning someone who confounds the mind. There is thus a play on words.

[213] Alternatively, when people meet a wise person.

[214] The gopis are being compared to the sacred texts. Without being able to see Krishna, the rituals of the sacred texts serve no purpose.

illustrious lord, who is in the hearts of all the lords of yoga, seated himself on the seat that had been fashioned. In that assembly of the gopis, his resplendent body, the reservoir of all the prosperity in the three worlds, was worshipped.

'He had ignited love in them and they worshipped him accordingly. They cast smiling and playful glances at him and arched their eyebrows. They pressed his hands and feet and placed them on their laps. They praised him. But they also pretended to be slightly angry and said the following. The gopis said, "Some show favours to those who love them, others act in a contrary way. But there are those who do not do either. Please explain this to us properly." The illustrious one said, "O friends! Those who reciprocate each other's love do it for their own selfish reasons. It has nothing to do with affection or dharma. It is selfishness and nothing else. Those who love those who do not love them back are truly compassionate. They are like parents. O slender-waisted ones! That kind of affection and dharma is without blemish. There are some who do not love those who love them, not to speak of those who do not love them. They are satisfied in their own atmans, have accomplished all their desires, are ungrateful, or hate their superiors. O friends! Even when I am loved by living beings, I do not love them back. That is because I wish to urge their propensities to love me.[215] When a person who is poor obtains some riches and that is destroyed, he can think of nothing else and know nothing else. O women! For my sake, you have given up the commonly held views on the Vedas and your own relatives and have followed me. You loved me even when I vanished and was not in sight. O loved ones! You should not seek to harm someone you love. You have acted out of your own virtuous intentions and you are free of all blemish. Even if I possess the lifespan of the gods, I cannot pay you back.[216] You have loved

[215] Krishna does not belong to the four categories mentioned. But he does not love people back immediately.

[216] One day for a god is one human year, that is, 360 days approximately. The human lifespan is 100 years, so a god's lifespan is 36,000 human years. A few interpretations take the god mentioned in the text as Brahma, which increases the duration further. But that interpretation doesn't seem to be necessary.

me after severing the bonds of the household, which are so very difficult to give up. May that virtuous deed be rewarded.'"

Chapter 10(33)

Shri-Shuka said, 'In this way, the gopis heard his extremely enchanting words. O dear one! They cast aside the torment of separation. Having touched him, their wishes were fulfilled. With those jewels among women, Govinda started the pastime of rasa krida. They happily linked their ams with each other.[217] The festival of rasa commenced and Krishna, the lord of yoga, was in the midst of that circle of gopis, ornamenting it. He entered in between every couple of gopis.[218] He clasped his hands around the neck and each woman took herself to be the closest to him. The minds of the residents of heaven were captivated by the sight. Along with their wives, they assembled to witness it and the firmament was filled with hundreds of vimanas. Kettledrums were sounded and flowers were showered down. The lords among the gandharvas, along with their women, chanted about his blemishless glories. As the women sported with their beloved in that circle of rasa, a tumultuous sound arose from their bangles, anklets and the bells around their waists. Devaki's illustrious son appeared in an extremely resplendent form. He was like a giant emerald, in the midst of gold-encrusted jewels. Krishna's young female companions sang, as radiant as flashes of lightning in a circle of clouds.[219] Their feet moved in measured treads and they moved their hands. They smiled and arched their eyebrows. They bent their waists and their breasts and garments moved. Their earrings swung against their cheeks. Their faces perspired and the braids on their hair and their garments were

[217] They formed a circle, interlocking each other's arms, including that of Krishna's.

[218] He assumed many different forms, so that there was a Krishna between every two gopis.

[219] There were many Krishnas, as dark blue as clouds.

loosened. As they danced, they sang loudly. Loving the pleasure, they clung to his neck. They were delighted at being able to touch Krishna and the sound of their singing permeated everything. One sang along with Mukunda and her pitch did not mingle with his, but rose above it. Pleased at this, he honoured her by uttering words of praise. As her voice vibrated in the introductory words of the song,[220] he showed her even greater honours. One got exhausted from rasa. Her bangles and mallika flowers slipped. The wielder of the club was standing next to her. He clasped her and placed her arm on his shoulder. Krishna's arm was on another one's shoulder and was fragrant with the smell of blue lotus and the anointment of sandalwood paste. She smelt it and kissed it, her body hair standing up. As she danced, another gopi's glittering earrings moved. She placed her cheek alongside his cheek and he gave her the betel leaf that he was chewing. Another sang and danced, her anklets and the bells on her girdle jingling. Achyuta was by her side. When she was exhausted, she placed his auspicious lotus hands on her breasts. The gopis had obtained their beloved Achyuta, dearly loved by Shri alone. With his arms around their necks, they sang about him and rejoiced. Their cheeks were rendered beautiful by the lotus flowers on their ears, the locks that hung down and the perspiration. There was the musical sound from bangles and anklets. The gopis danced with the illustrious one and the garlands dropped from their hair. Swarms of bees joined in as additional singers. In this way, Rama's lord sported himself with the beautiful women of Vraja. He embraced and touched them with his hands. He cast gentle glances at them and laughed enticingly. It was as if a child was playing with its own reflection. O extender of the Kuru lineage! At the physical association with him, they were delighted and their senses were overwhelmed. The women of Vraja could not prevent their hair, garments and coverings on their breasts from becoming dishevelled and loosened. Their garlands and ornaments were scattered. On witnessing Krishna's pastimes, the celestial women in the sky were captivated. They were afflicted by desire. The moon, along with its

---

[220] Dhruva pada.

companions,[221] was amazed. He assumed as many different forms as there were gopa women. Satisfied completely within himself, the illustrious one playfully sported with them. O dear one! When he saw that their faces were exhausted from the pleasures and pastimes, he was full of compassion and lovingly wiped their faces with his hands. The gold earrings worn by the gopis dazzled. The shining locks of curly hair enhanced the beauty of their cheeks. Their glances were full of sweet smiles. They honoured the powerful one and sang about his auspicious deeds. They were delighted at having been touched by his finger nails. He was exhausted from the physical association with them. His garland was crushed and smeared with the kunkuma from their breasts. Along with them, he entered the water, like an elephant that has broken down dams,[222] along with female elephants. He was followed by bees that were like leaders among the gandharvas.[223] O dear one! In the water, the young women splashed him with water. They laughed and cast loving glances at him. Completely satisfied within himself, he played with them, like a king among elephants. Those in vimanas praised him and showered down flowers. Krishna then strolled in a grove along the banks. The breeze was fragrant with the scent of flowers that grew on land and in the water. He was surrounded by bees and by the women. He was like an intoxicated elephant, in the company of female elephants. The night dazzled because of the moon's beams. The one who makes all desires come true was constantly followed by a large number of women. Those autumn nights provide the material for poetic compositions and narrations. He enjoyed them all, but controlled all desire within himself.'[224]

The king asked, 'The illustrious lord of the universe descended in his own portion for the sake of establishing dharma and subduing anything that was contrary. He is the one who enunciated the ordinances of dharma and he is the one who protects them. O

---

[221] The *nakshatras*.

[222] The dams constructed along fields. There is an allusion to Krishna having broken down common social norms.

[223] The bees were buzzing like singing gandharvas.

[224] That is, he was not affected by any of this.

brahmana! By associating with the wives of others, how could he then act in this perverse way? O one who is excellent in vows! The lord of Yadu has accomplished all his desires. Why did he act in this reprehensible manner? What was his intention? Please sever our doubt about this.'

Shri-Shuka replied, 'The best among lords do commit the audacious act of transgressing dharma. Like the fire which devours everything,[225] those who are full of energy are not tainted by this. However, someone who is not a lord should never act in this way, not even in his mind. If a foolish person acts in this way, he will destroy himself, just as a person who is not Rudra will destroy himself if he consumes poison generated from the ocean. The words of the lords are always correct. But that is only sometimes true of their deeds. Therefore, an intelligent person should act in conformity with their words. They are accomplished in conduct and are not driven by selfish motives. O lord! Since they have no sense of ahamkara, it does not lead to any calamity or undesirable effects. He is the controller of all those who are controlled, all creatures, inferior species, mortals and the residents of heaven. Notions of what is pious and what is not pious do not apply to him. Those who have cleansed all the bonds of karma through powers of yoga are satisfied by serving the dust of his lotus feet. Those sages act according to their wishes and are not bound down. How can there be any bondage for the one who has voluntarily assumed a physical body? He is the controller who resides within the gopis, their husbands and all those with bodies. For the sake of his pastimes, he has assumed a body. He assumed a human body to show favour to his devotees. He engages in such pastimes so that those who hear about it become devoted to him. Since they were confounded by Krishna's maya, the residents of Vraja did not become inimical towards him. They thought that their own respective wives were with them, by their sides. When *brahma muhurta*[226] was over, Vasudeva instructed the unwilling gopis, who loved the illustrious

---

[225] And is not polluted.

[226] A muhurta is a period of forty-eight minutes. Brahma muhurta is named after Brahma and is an auspicious time just before dawn, regarded

one, to return to their own homes. In this way, Vishnu sported with
the maidens of Vraja. If a person listens to it faithfully or describes
it, he develops great devotion towards the illustrious one. Within a
short period of time, such a persevering person drives away desire
and all the other ailments of the heart.'

Chapter 10(34)

Shri-Shuka said, 'Once, the cowherds were eager to go on a trip
to visit the god.[227] They yoked bulls to their carts and left for
Ambika's forest. O king! They bathed in the Sarasvati there. With
the appropriate objects, they worshipped the lord and god Pashupati
and the goddess Ambika. They respectfully gave brahmanas cows,
gold, garments, honey and food mixed with honey. All of them said,
"Let the god be pleased with us." The immensely fortunate Nanda,
Sunandaka and others spent the night on the banks of the Sarasvati.
They observed a vow of subsisting only on water. A giant serpent
appeared in that desolate forest. It was extremely hungry. Roaming
around as it willed, the serpent arrived there and started to swallow
Nanda, who was asleep. As he was being devoured by the snake, he
screamed, "O Krishna! O son! O Krishna! This snake is devouring
me. I am seeking refuge with you. Please free me." Hearing his
screams, the cowherds suddenly woke up. They were bewildered to
see him being devoured. They struck the snake with flaming torches.
Though it was scorched by the firebrands, the serpent did not let
him go. The illustrious lord of the Satvatas arrived and touched it
with his foot. The touch of the illustrious and prosperous one's foot
removed everything inauspicious.

'It abandoned the form of a snake and assumed the form of
a worshipped vidyadhara. The resplendent being stood before
him, with his head bowed down. He was adorned with a golden

---

as the last muhurta of the night. The precise hour depends on the time when
the sun rises.

[227] The god in question is Shiva, Ambika is Parvati's name.

necklace. Hrishikesha asked him. "Who are you? You are supreme and radiant in your prosperity, extraordinary to behold. How were you rendered incapable and made to assume this condemned state?" The snake replied, "I am a vidyadhara and used to be known by the name of Sudarshana. I was prosperous, handsome and opulent. I used to roam the directions in my vimana. Proud of my beauty, I laughed at rishis of the Angiras lineage, because they were malformed. Because of my own wicked deed, they made me assume a status as this particular species. They were compassionate by nature and have actually done me a favour through the curse. After all, the preceptor of the worlds has touched me with his foot and has destroyed everything inauspicious. You are the one who dispels fear and those who are scared of samsara seek refuge with you. You are the dispeller of distresses. Through the touch of your feet, I have been freed from the curse. I seek your permission to leave. O great yogi! O great being! O lord of the virtuous! O god! O lord of all the lords of the worlds! Please grant me permission. O Achyuta! As soon as I saw you, I have been instantly freed from the curse of the brahmanas. Chanting your name and hearing it, instantly purifies the reciter and the hearer. What need be said about someone who has been touched by your feet?" Having obtained his permission, Sudarshana honoured and circumambulated Dasharha. He left for heaven. Nanda was also freed from his hardship. The minds of the residents of Vraja were astonished to witness Krishna's great powers. O king! Having completed their rituals, they returned to Vraja, respectfully talking about this along the journey.

'On one occasion, in the midst of the women of Vraja, Govinda and Rama, extraordinary in valour, were sporting in the forest in the night. The women, bound to them in affection, sung about them in enchanting tones. They[228] were ornamented and smeared all over their limbs. They wore garlands and sparkling garments. They applauded the beginning of the night, when the lord of the stars and the stars arose. A gentle breeze blew, bearing the fragrance of jasmine and night lotuses, intoxicating the bees. The two of them sang together, bringing everything auspicious to the minds and

[228] Krishna and Balarama.

the ears of all creatures. Their melody covered the entire scale of all musical notes. O king! Hearing the singing, the gopis lost their senses. They did not realize that their fine garments were slipping and that the garlands on their hair were getting dislodged. As they wished, the two of them sported and sang in this way, as if they were intoxicated. Dhanda had a companion named Shankhachuda and he arrived there. O king! While the two of them looked on, he fearlessly started to drive the screaming women, as if they were without a protector, in a northern direction. They were like cows seized by bandits and screamed, "O Krishna! O Rama!" Seeing that their own followers were being taken away, the two brothers rushed after him. Those two spirited ones grabbed *sala* trees in their hands and shouted, "Do not be afraid." They quickly approached the worst of the *guhyaka*s,[229] who was hurriedly trying to run away. He saw that they were about to reach him, like destiny and death. Therefore, the foolish one became anxious. Wishing to save his own life, he let the women go and started to flee. Wherever he ran, Govinda followed him there. He desired to take away the jewel from his head. Bala remained there, protecting the women. Within a short distance, the lord reached the evil-souled one. He struck him on the head with a blow of his fist and severed his head, along with the jewel that was on it. He killed Shankhachuda and gathered the shining jewel. While the women looked on, he lovingly gave it to his elder brother.'

Chapter 10(35)

Shri-Shuka said, 'When Krishna left for the forest, the minds of the gopis followed him. They spent those days in misery and sang about Krishna's pastimes.

'The gopis said, "He rests his left cheek on his left arm. His eyebrows dance as he places the flute against his lips. He uses

[229] Kubera is the lord of riches/treasure. Guhyakas are a semi-divine species who are Kubera's companions.

his delicate fingers to stop the holes in it. That is how Mukunda makes it vibrate. Along with the Siddhas, there are women who are travelling through the sky in their vehicles. They are amazed and listen to it. Since their minds thus get attracted to the path of desire, they are ashamed. They are filled with lassitude and forget that their girdles are being loosened. O women! Hear this wonderful account. His smile is as dazzling as a necklace. The fickle lightning[230] is fixed on his chest. When Nanda's son plays on his flute, he brings pleasure to people who are afflicted. From a distance, the herds of bulls, deer and cows in Vraja hear the melody of the flute and lose their senses. They hold mouthfuls of grass in their mouths and prick up their ears. They remain stationary there, as if they are asleep, or as if they have been drawn in a painting. Sometimes, he attires himself in the garb of a wrestler and imitates him. He is decorated with peacock feathers, minerals and leaves from a *palasha* tree. O friends! Sometimes, along with Bala and the gopas, he summons the cows. This is what Mukunda does. The rivers lose their currents, as if they want to touch the dust on his lotus feet when it is borne along by the breeze. However, like us, they are limited in their good deeds. They stop their waters and out of love for him, wave their arms around.[231] His valour has been properly described by his followers. He is the original being and his powers do not change. He is the one who always uses his flute to summon the cows that are grazing in the forest, on the slopes of the mountain and along the banks. The creepers and trees in the forest have Vishnu inside them. They display the abundance of their flowers and fruits. The trees bend down with the burden. Their bodies filled with joy and love, they showered forth flows of honey. The tilaka and the garland of flowers is worth seeing. There is the divine scent of tulasi. Maddened by the honey, the swarms of bees sing loudly. He acknowledges this and places the flute against his lips. The beautiful music steals the hearts of the cranes, swans and other birds in the lakes. Their minds wish to worship Hari. They close their eyes and silently meditate

[230] Lakshmi.
[231] The arms of the rivers are the waves, which actually fail to touch him.

on him. He playfully wears a wreath on his head. Along with Bala, he stands on the summits of the mountain. O beautiful ones from Vraja! The one who delights with the sound of his flute brings delight and joy to the entire universe. The cloud is scared of his great prowess and therefore, the response of its thunder is extremely gentle. He is its friend and it showers down flowers on him. Like an umbrella, it casts its shadow over him. O virtuous one![232] Your son is accomplished in all the tasks that gopas undertake. He has himself developed many skills in playing the flute. He places the flute against his lips, which are like bimba fruit, and produces all the different kinds of notes—high, medium and low. When they hear this, the heads and the hearts of the lords among the gods, Shakra, Sharva and Parameshthi as the foremost, bow down. Unable to determine its essence, they are confused. The soles of his lotus feet bear the varied marks of a standard, the vajra, a lotus and an elephant's goad. His footprints on the grounds of Vraja heal the hurt left by the marks of hooves. As he plays on the flute and moves, his stride is like that of a king among elephants. When he walks, he casts playful glances at us and ignites torrents of passion in us. We are filled with lassitude and do not realize that the braids in our hair and our garments have got dishevelled. Sometimes, when he counts the cows, he wears a jewel and a garland of tulasi, especially loved by him. Sometimes, as he sings, he rests an arm on the shoulder of a beloved friend who is following him. Sometimes, with their hearts stolen by the sounds of the flute, female black antelopes, the wives of male black antelopes, follow him. Like gopis, the does follow that ocean of all the qualities and forget their homes and their hopes. He wears wreaths of kunda flowers and colourful attire. Along the Yamuna, he is surrounded by gopas and the wealth of cattle. O unblemished one! He is your son and that of Nanda. He sports and plays with the companions he loves. An agreeable and pleasant breeze blows. It bears the fragrance of sandalwood and honours him with its touch. *Bandis*[233] and many minor divinities surround him, rendering music, singing and other offerings. Compassionate

[232] Meaning Yashoda.
[233] Minstrels and bards who sang the composition of others.

towards Vraja and the cattle, he held up the mountain. At the end of the day, he returns with the entire wealth of cows, playing on the flute. Aged ones stand along the path, worshipping his feet and chanting his deeds. The hooves raise a dust and smudge his garland. His complexion is affected by the exhaustion. Nevertheless, his appearance is like a festival. Desiring to satisfy the wishes of his well-wishers, he is the moon that has arisen from Devaki's womb. His eyes roll a little from the intoxication. Vanamali[234] honours his own well-wishers. His face is pale, like the fruits of a jujube tree. His tender cheeks are rendered radiant by the glitter of his golden earrings. The lord of the Yadus sports like a king among elephants. At the end of the day, his cheerful face is like the lord of the night.[235] It drives away the heat of the day, which the residents of Vraja and the cows find very difficult to tolerate."'

Shri-Shuka continued, 'O king! In this way, the women of Vraja sang about Krishna's pastimes and every day, found pleasure in this. The hearts and minds of those immensely fortunate ones were immersed in him.'

Chapter 10(36)

Shri-Shuka said, 'After this, an asura in the form of a bull, Arishta, arrived in the settlement. It possessed a gigantic hump. It tore up the ground with its hooves and made the earth tremble. It bellowed in an extremely harsh tone and scratched the ground with its hooves. It raised its tail and tore up the embankments with the tips of its horns. It released a little bit of urine. It released a little bit of excrement. It stood there, glaring with its eyes. O dear one! That harsh and cruel sound echoed. Terrified, cows and women miscarried and delivered ahead of their time. Taking its hump to be a mountain, clouds gathered around it. On seeing its sharp horns, gopas and gopis were frightened. O king! The animals were scared

---

[234] Krishna's name, one who wears a garland of wild flowers.
[235] The moon.

and ran away, abandoning Gokula. "O Krishna! O Krishna!"
Exclaiming this, all of them sought refuge with Govinda. The
illustrious one saw that Gokula was scared and was fleeing. "Do
not be scared." Uttering these words of assurance, he challenged
the asura in the form of a bull. "O foolish one! O wicked one!
Why are you scaring the cowherds and the animals? I am here to
chastise wicked and evil-souled ones like you." Saying this, Achyuta
slapped his arms. Hari stood there, extending his arm, which was
like a serpent, on the shoulder of a friend. He clapped his hands and
enraged Arishta with the sound. Arishta was enraged in this way and
scratched on the ground with its hooves. It raised its tail and drove
away the clouds. Then it angrily rushed towards Krishna. It pointed
the tips of its fierce horns in his direction and glared at Achyuta
with blood-shot eyes. It cast sidelong glances and quickly rushed
forward, like the vajra released by Indra. The illustrious one seized
it by the horns and pushed it back eighteen steps, just as an elephant
does against a rival elephant. Thus repulsed by the illustrious one, it
soon arose again. It was breathing heavily and perspiring all over its
body. Senseless with rage, it attacked again. As it rushed forward,
he seized it by the horns and flung it down on the ground. Pressing
down with one foot, he wrung it like a wet piece of cloth. He pulled
out one of the horns and struck it with this, so that it fell down. It
vomited blood and discharged urine and excrement. It kicked its
legs and its eyes rolled around. Suffering all this pain, it then went
to death's abode. Praising Hari, the gods showered down flowers.
When he thus killed the bull, he was praised by the brahmanas. He
entered the settlement with Bala, bringing delight to the eyes of the
gopis.

'When the daitya Arishta was killed, Narada, who possessed
divine sight, went and told Kamsa about Krishna's extraordinary
deeds. "Yashoda's child was a daughter and Krishna is Devaki's
son. Rama is Rohini's son. Scared, Vasudeva entrusted them with
his own friend, Nanda. It is these two who have killed your men."[236]
Hearing this, the lord of Bhoja was filled with rage. His senses were in
a whirl. With a desire to kill Vasudeva, he picked up a sharp sword.

[236] The ones sent by Kamsa to kill Krishna.

Narada restrained him, since it was his two sons who would bring about his death. But knowing this, he bound him[237] and his wife up in iron chains. When the *devarshi*[238] had left, Kamsa summoned Keshi. He despatched him with the order that he should kill Rama and Keshava. He then summoned his advisers, Mushtika, Chanura, Shala, Toshala and others. The king of the Bhojas also summoned the keepers of elephants. He told them, "O brave Mushtika and Chanura! Listen to my words. The sons of Anakadundubhi are residing in Nanda's Vraja. It has been destined that my death will be at the hands of Rama and Krishna. When they have been brought here, you must kill them in a bout of wrestling. Erect a wrestling arena, with many kinds of galleries. Let all the inhabitants of the city and the countryside see and voluntarily participate in the competition. O Mahamatra! O keeper of the elephant! O fortunate one! Convey the elephant Kuvalayapida to the gate of the arena. Let it kill the two who will cause me injury. With all the rites, let everything commence on the fourteenth lunar day with the sacrifice involving the bow. Let animals be offered in sacrifice to the lord of the *bhuta*s, the one who confers benedictions."[239] Having instructed them in this way, he summoned Akrura, the bull among the Yadus, who knew about accomplishing objectives.

'Taking his hand in his hand, he told him, "O lord of generous ones![240] Out of respect, do a good deed for me. Among the Bhojas and the Vrishnis, there is no one else who is as interested in my welfare. O amiable one! Therefore, I am depending on you as a person who can accomplish an important task. This is just as the lord Indra took succour with Vishnu for accomplishing his own objective. Go to Nanda's Vraja. The sons of Anakadundubhi reside there. Without any delay, take this chariot and bring them here. Seeking refuge with Vaikuntha, the gods have sent them here for my death. Bring them here and also bring Nanda and the other gopas,

[237] Vasudeva.

[238] Divine sage.

[239] Meaning Shiva. The idea is that Kamsa offers a sacrifice to Shiva and Shiva's bow as a counter to Krishna.

[240] Akrura was generous in giving gifts and was known as Danapati.

with a tribute of gifts. When they have been brought here, I will have them killed by the elephant, which is like Death. Should they escape, they will be killed by my two wrestlers, who are as quick as lightning. When they have been slain, I will kill their lamenting relatives among the Vrishnis, Bhojas and Dasharhas, with Vasudeva as the foremost. I will also kill my aged father, Ugrasena, who desires the kingdom. I will kill his brother, Devaka, who harbours enmity towards me. O friend! All the thorns will then have been removed from this earth. Jarasandha is my senior[241] and Dvivida is my beloved friend. Shambara, Naraka and Bana have fraternal alliances with me. I will use them to kill all the kings who are allied with the gods and enjoy the earth. Now that you have understood this, quickly go and fetch the two boys, Rama and Krishna. Let them see the sacrifice of the bow and the prosperity of the capital of the Yadus." Akrura replied, "O king! You have thought of a perfect means to ward off your misfortune. However, one must act with indifference towards success or failure. The fruits of any effort depend on destiny. A man may act according to his wishes, but they are thwarted by destiny. He can thus be faced with either joy or misery. But I will do what you have commanded me to." Having instructed Akrura in this way, Kamsa dismissed his ministers. He entered his house and Akrura also went to his own home.'

Chapter 10(37)

Shri-Shuka said, 'Keshi had been sent by Kamsa. It was a gigantic horse, with the speed of thought. It ripped up the ground with its hooves. The hair on its mane drove away the clouds and the multitude of vimanas from the sky. It scared everyone with its neighing. The illustrious one saw that it was terrifying his own Gokula with its neighing. It was dispelling the clouds by the whirling of the hair on its tail. He himself came forward, searching it out. He challenged it and it roared like a lion. On seeing him standing

---

[241] Jarasandha was Kamsa's father-in-law.

in front, it rushed forward in rage. It seemed to swallow up the sky with its mouth. It was impossible to assail, terrible in its speed and impossible to withstand. With its hind legs, it struck out at the lotus-eyed one. Adhokshaja stepped aside and deceived it. He angrily used his arms to seize it by its hind legs. Contemptuously, he flung it away to a distance of one hundred bow-lengths, just as Tarkshya's son[242] would do to a serpent. He then stood there. Once it had regained its senses, Keshi arose again. It angrily opened its mouth and rushed towards Hari. However, he smiled and thrust his left arm into the gaping mouth, just as a serpent enters its hole. As soon as they touched the illustrious one's arm, Keshi's teeth fell out, as if they had touched hot molten iron. Inside its body, the great-souled one's arm extended in size, like a disease that has been neglected. Krishna's arm expanded and stopped its breathing. It flung its legs around. Its body perspired and its eyes rolled around. It fell down lifeless on the ground, releasing excrement. Its body was like *karkatika* fruit.[243] When it was killed, the mighty-armed one withdrew his arm. He was not at all surprised that he had managed to kill his enemy in this way. The gods worshipped him by showering down flowers.

'O king! The devarshi, supreme among devotees of the illustrious one, approached. He privately spoke to Krishna, the performer of unblemished deeds. "O Krishna! O one whose atman is immeasurable! O Krishna! O lord of yoga! O lord of the universe! O Vasudeva, who resides in everything! O foremost among the Satvatas! O lord! You alone are the atman who is in all creatures. You are the creator and you are like the fire in the kindling. You are hidden inside the core of the heart. You are the witness. You are the lord and the great being. You are the refuge of all atmans. Earlier, using your maya, you created the gunas. Your resolution is the truth. You are the lord of creation, preservation and destruction. You have now descended among the creatures on earth, in order to crush the daityas and the rakshasas. You have descended for their destruction and for the protection

---

[242] Garuda.
[243] Cucumber.

of the virtuous. It is good fortune that you toyed with and killed
the daitya that was in the form of a horse. Its neighing was so
terrifying that the gods abandoned their world in heaven. O lord!
Day after tomorrow, during the day, I will see that Chanura,
Mushtika and other wrestlers, the elephant and Kamsa have been
killed by you. After that, you will kill Shankha, Yavana, Mura
and Naraka.[244] After that, you will defeat Indra and steal the
parijata. After that, with the characteristics of *viryashulka*,[245]
you will marry the daughters of the valiant ones. O lord of the
universe! In Dvaraka, you will free Nriga from his curse.[246] You
will get the Syamantaka jewel and a wife. You will restore the
brahmana's dead son to his own abode. After this, there will be
the slaying of Poundraka, the burning down of the city of Kashi
and the slaying of Dantavakra and the king of Chedi in the great
sacrifice. While residing in Dvaraka, there will be many brave
deeds that you will undertake. I will witness what you do and
the poets on earth will sing about them. I will then see you in the
form of the destroyer, time. I will see you as Arjuna's charioteer,
slaughtering the *akshouhinis*.[247] You are full of pure vijnana. You
are based in your own nature. You have already accomplished all
your objectives. Your wishes are always fulfilled. Through your
own energy, you always withdraw from maya and the flow of
the gunas. Let us approach the illustrious one. You are the self-
contained lord. Through your own maya, you have devised all
the different kinds of creation. You have now assumed a human
body to carry out your pastimes. I bow down to the greatest in
the Yadu, Vrishni and Satvata lineages." Thus, the sage who was
supreme among the devotees of the illustrious one bowed down
before Krishna, the lord of Yadu. Delighted at having seen him, he
took his permission and left. The illustrious Govinda killed Keshi

[244] Shankha means Panchajana and Yavana means Kalayavana.
[245] Viryashulka is when the maiden is offered to the suitor who shows
the most valour (*virya*), *shulka* meaning price.
[246] Described in Chapter 10(64).
[247] An akshouhini is an army, consisting of 21,870 chariots, 21,870
elephants, 65,610 horse riders and 109,350 foot soldiers.

in the encounter. Along with the other joyous cowherds, he tended to the animals and brought happiness to Vraja.

'On one occasion, they were herding the animals and wandering around on the slopes of the mountain. They played hide-and-seek. Some of them pretended to be thieves and the others pretended to be guards. O king! Some acted the role of thieves, others the role of guards and still others the role of sheep. They played there, without any fear. Maya's son was Vyoma and he was great in his use of maya. He donned the garb of a cowherd. He stole almost all those who were in the form of sheep and many who were in the form of thieves. The great asura took them away. Having taken them away, he hurled them into a cave in the mountain and blocked the entrance with a boulder. Finally, only four or five were left. Krishna, the refuge of all those who are virtuous, got to know what he had done. While he was taking the gopas away, he seized him, the way an energetic lion seizes a wolf. The powerful one assumed his own form and it was like an Indra among mountains. But though he tried to free himself, he was incapacitated in that grasp and was unable to do so. Achyuta seized him in his arms and flung him down on the ground. While the gods in heaven looked on, he killed him, the way one kills an animal. He smashed the boulder in front of the cave and released the gopas from their hardship. Praised by the gods and the gopas, he entered his own Gokula.'

Chapter 10(38)

Shri-Shuka said, 'The immensely intelligent Akrura spent the night in Madhu's city. He then mounted his chariot and left for Nanda's Gokula. Along the road, he was filled with great devotion towards the illustrious and lotus-eyed one. He thought in the following way. "What auspicious deeds have I done? What supreme austerities have I tormented myself with? What worship or donations have I done? Why will I be able to see Keshava today? I think that being able to see Uttamashloka is extremely difficult for me. It is just like a person born as a shudra, addicted to material objects, being able to chant about the brahman. But enough of this. Even a wicked person like me will be able to see Achyuta. A person who is borne along by the river of time may sometimes be able to reach the bank. Today, all that is inauspicious in me has been destroyed. My birth has yielded results. I will meditate on the illustrious one's lotus feet, contemplated by yogis. Indeed, Kamsa has shown me a favour today. He has sent me to see Hari's lotus feet. He has taken the form of an avatara. Earlier, using the radiance of his circle of toenails, people have crossed the darkness that is so very difficult to cross. They are worshipped by Brahma, Bhava and the other gods, the goddess Shri, the sages and the Satvatas. Using those, along with his followers, he roams around in the forest, herding the cows. They are smeared with kunkuma from the breasts of the gopis. I will certainly see his beautiful cheeks and nose, his smiling glances and his red lotus eyes. Mukunda's face is covered with curly locks of hair. The deer are circumabulating me.[248] As a result of his own wishes, Vishnu has assumed a human form to reduce the burden of the earth. He is the abode of beauty and I will be able to see him today. Therefore, it is not true that my eyes will not be successful.[249] He is the witness of cause and effect, but he is free from ahamkara. Through his own energy, he dispels all tamas and confusion. It can be deduced that using the glances of his own maya, he fashioned the breaths of life, the senses, intelligence and the abodes[250] they reside in. He destroys everything that is a sin. He is extremely auspicious. His qualities, deeds and births ornament and purify the universe and confer life, and varied words describe them. However, if words do not describe them, it is held that they are like decorations on a dead body. He has descended in the lineage of the Satvatas to delight the noble immortals, who are the guardians of the ordinances he has propounded. The lord resides in Vraja and extends his fame. He is the one who brings auspiciousness to everyone and the gods sing about him. He is certainly the greatest

---

[248] As in pradakshina. Since this is a good omen, Akrura will be able to see Krishna.

[249] The text has this double negation.

[250] Bodies.

destination and preceptor. He is loved by the three worlds and is a source of great delight to the eyes. The form that he displays is one that is desired by Shri. Since I have been witnessing extremely good omens since dawn, I will see him. I will immediately descend from my chariot. I will seek out the feet of those two lords, the foremost among beings. For the sake of their own self-realization, yogis fix their intelligences on them. I will certainly bow down before them, along with their friends and the other residents of the forest. When I prostrate myself at the base of his lotus feet, the lord will place his own lotus hand on my head. Men, who are greatly agitated by the powerful serpent that is time, seek refuge with him and he grants freedom from fear. By offering worship to him, Koushika[251] and Bali obtained the status of being Indra over the three worlds. His touch is as fragrant as a *sougandhika* flower[252] and, during pastimes, wipes away the exhaustion of the women of Vraja. Though I have been sent as a messenger by Kamsa, he is the one who sees everything in the universe. Therefore, Achyuta's intelligence will not be such that he regards me as an enemy. He is the *kshetrajna*[253] who is inside and outside every heart. Therefore, he will glance at me with a pure vision. With hands joined in salutation, I will remain at the base of his lotus feet. He will glance at me with smiling and affectionate eyes. All my sins will instantly be destroyed. I will enjoy intense bliss and be bereft of every kind of sorrow. My divinity will think of me as the best among well-wishers and relatives. He will embrace me in his mighty arms. He will immediately make my atman like a tirtha. Consequently, all my bondage of karma will be loosened. Having obtained that physical contact with him, I will join my hands in salutation and prostrate myself. The one who is extensive in his fame will address me as Akrura. At that instant, my taking birth will become glorious. If a person is not honoured in this way, he should be ashamed of his birth. He does not love anyone, nor is

---

[251] Shakra.

[252] Literally, sweet-smelling and fragrant. There is also a plant and a flower by the name of sougandhika.

[253] *Kshetra* is the field, that is, the body. Kshetrajna is one who knows the body, that is, the soul, both human and universal.

anyone best among his well-wishers. There is no one whom he does not love. There is no one whom he hates, or is indifferent towards. However, the tree of the gods yields fruits to those who resort to it. In that way, as they deserve, his devotees receive reciprocal treatment. When I stand before him, hands joined in salutation, and bowed down, his elder brother, supreme among the Yadus, will smile and embrace me. Displaying all signs of respect, he will make me enter the house. He will ask about what Kamsa has done to his own relatives." Thus, Shvaphalka's son[254] thought about Krishna along the journey. O king! On his chariot, he reached Gokula when the sun was atop Mount Asta.

'In the settlement, he saw the earth marked with the wonderful signs of the lotus, the barley, the elephant goad and other marks. These are the footprints and the unblemished dust from the feet that all the guardians of the world bow down their diadems before. On seeing this, his joy and respect was enhanced. Because of his love, his body hair stood up and tears started to flow from his eyes. He got down from the chariot and rolled around on the ground, exclaiming, "This is the dust from my lord's feet." This is the objective of all those who have bodies, to give up pride, fear and grief and see and hear about Hari's signs. Because of the order,[255] he experienced this. He saw Krishna and Rama in Vraja. They had gone to milk the cows. They were respectively dressed in yellow and blue garments and their eyes were like autumn lotuses. They were young[256] and their respective complexions were dark blue and fair. They were the abodes of Shri and were mighty-armed. Their faces were excellent and they were supreme among handsome ones. Their strength and valour was like that of elephants. Their feet were marked with the signs of a standard, a vajra, an elephant goad and a lotus. With compassionate and smiling glances, those two great-souled ones beautified the area. Their pastimes were attractive and generous. They wore garlands and other garlands

[254] Shvaphalka was Akrura's father.
[255] Kamsa's order.
[256] Since the word used is *kishora*, they were older than ten and younger than fifteen.

made out of wild flowers. They were smeared with auspicious pastes. Having bathed, they were dressed in sparkling garments. O lord of the earth! Those two foremost among beings, Bala and Keshava, were the cause behind the universe and had descended in their own portions for the sake of the world. O king! Through their own radiance, they dispelled the darkness of the directions. They were respectively like a mountain made out of emeralds and a mountain made out of silver, both encrusted in gold. Akrura quickly descended from his chariot and was flooded with love. Like a rod, he prostrated himself before the feet of Rama and Krishna. On seeing the illustrious one, he was filled with delight and there were tears in his eyes. O king! The body hair on his limbs stood up. He was so eager that he wasn't even able to explain who he was. The illustrious one recognized him. He was devoted to the ones who loved him. Pleased, he drew him close with a hand that was marked with the sign of the chakra and embraced him. He was bowing down and the great-minded Samkarshana held his hands in his own hands. With his younger brother, he led him home. He asked about his welfare and welcomed him. He offered him an excellent seat. Observing the rites, he washed his feet and respectfully offered him *madhuparka*.[257] He offered the guest a cow and respectfully massaged him, so as to remove his exhaustion. The lord devotedly offered him food that could be offered, with many qualities. Rama knew about supreme dharma. When he had eaten, he happily gave him mouth fresheners and fragrant garlands and made other arrangements, so that he might obtain great delight. When he had been honourably treated, Nanda asked him, "O Dasharha! How have you been? How have you survived under the oppressive Kamsa? You are like sheep being maintained by a butcher. The evil assassin has killed the children of his own sister, while she shrieked. Indeed, you are his subjects. How can we even ask about your welfare?" He was thus honoured by Nanda in these extremely well-spoken words of inquiry. Akrura recovered from the exhaustion of the journey.'

---

[257] A mixture of honey and water, customarily offered to a guest.

Chapter 10(39)

Shri-Shuka said, 'He was happily seated on a couch and greatly honoured by Rama and Krishna. He obtained all the wishes that he had cherished along the journey. O king! The illustrious one is Shri's abode. If he is pleased, what can not be obtained? Therefore, those who are devoted to him do not wish for anything else. When the evening meal was over, Devaki's illustrious son asked about how Kamsa had behaved vis-à-vis the relatives and about what he intended to do.

'The illustrious one said, "O father![258] O fortunate one! Welcome. It is good fortune that you have come. Are our relatives and kin free from physical and mental pain? However, though he goes by the name of maternal uncle, Kamsa is the disease in our family. As long as he prospers, why should we ask about the welfare of our relatives and their offspring?[259] Alas! Because of me, my noble parents had to undergo a lot of suffering. Because of me, their sons had to die. They were also imprisoned because of that reason. O amiable one! It is good fortune that we have seen a relative like you today. O father! Describe how this has come about. Why have you come?"'

Shri-Shuka continued, 'When the illustrious one asked, Madhava[260] described everything—the bond of enmity towards the Yadus and the attempt to kill Vasudeva. He conveyed the message and the reason why he had himself been sent as a messenger, about how Narada had recounted his own birth as Anakadundubhi's son. Hearing Akrura's words, Krishna and Bala, the slayers of enemy heroes, laughed and told their father, Nanda, about the king's command. He[261] commanded the gopas, "Gather all the milk products. Take gifts. Let the carts be yoked. We will leave for Madhu's city tomorrow and give the king the milk products. We will witness the extremely great festival. The residents of the countryside are going." In his own Gokula, Nanda gopa had such

---

[258] Akrura was senior.
[259] Alternatively, instead of offspring, the subjects.
[260] Akrura was also descended from Madhu and was also Madhava.
[261] Nanda.

an announcement made by his governor. When the gopis heard that Akrura had come to Vraja to take Rama and Krishna to the city, they were extremely distressed. Some were tormented in their hearts and sighed, the beauty on their faces faded. For others, their garments were loosened. Their bangles were dislodged and the braids of their hair were dishevelled. Others gave up everything else that they were doing and meditated on him. Like those who have gone to the world of the atman, they did not know what was going on in this world. Others remembered Shouri's affection and smiles. His wonderfully phrased words had touched their hearts and the women lost their senses. They thought about his extremely charming deeds, his gentle and smiling glances, the pastimes that destroyed all misery and his mighty exploits. Immersed in Achyuta and with tears in their eyes, they collectively assembled and spoke.

'The gopis said, "Alas! O creator! There is no compassion in you. You bring embodied beings together, in friendship and love. However, before they have accomplished their objectives, you unnecessarily separate them. This pastime of yours is like a child's game. You have shown us Mukunda's face, framed by curly hair, with excellent cheeks and a tall nose. The slightest bit of his enchanting smile dispels all grief. You are not acting well. You are acting so that we can no longer see it. Under the name of Akrura, you are extremely cruel.[262] Having given us our eyes, like an ignorant person, you are now taking them away. It is with those that we saw the beauty of all your creation, in the form of Madhu's slayer. The affection of Nanda's son is temporary in nature. He does not see us, though we are afflicted on his account. We gave up our homes, our own relatives, our sons and our husbands. However, he is now attached to the gopas, his new loves. The happy morning that follows this night will truly bring benedictions to the women of the city. The lord of Vraja will enter it and they will drink the intoxicating drink of smiling and sidelong glances from his face. Their speech is as sweet as honey. O women! Though Mukunda is devoted to his own, their bashful smiles will entice and confuse him. His mind will be captivated. How can he again return to village women? When they

---

[262] *Krura* means cruel and Akrura means someone who is not cruel.

see him, it is now certain that there will be a great festival for the Dasharhas, Bhojas, Andhakas, Vrishnis and Satvatas. He is Shri's pleasure and is a store of all the qualities. They will see Devaki's son travel along the road. This one may be named Akrura, but he is not compassionate. He is exceedingly cruel. He is not comforting those who are extremely miserable. He is taking away the one whom we love more than everything else, from beyond our range of vision. His heart does not melt. He has ascended the chariot. These insolent gopas are also hurrying after him in their carts. The elders are indifferent. Today, destiny is working against us. Let us approach Madhava and restrain him. What can the elders of the families and the relatives do? It is impossible to tolerate separation from Mukunda for even half a *nimesha*.[263] Destiny has caused this separation and our hearts are distressed. O gopis! He brought us to the rasa in the assembly, with his love, pastimes, charming smiles, sweet conversation, playful glances and embraces. With him, the nights were like a kshana. How can we be separated from him? How will we cross this darkness, which is extremely difficult to surmount? When the day was over, Ananta's friend[264] would enter Vraja, surrounded by the gopas. The dust from the hooves would cover his hair and his garlands. He would play on his flute and look at us with smiling and sidelong glances, captivating our minds. How can we remain without him?"'

Shri-Shuka continued, 'Severely suffering from the separation, the women of Vraja spoke in this way, their minds attached to Krishna. Casting aside all shame, they wept in loud voices. "O Govinda! O Damodara! O Madhava!" While the women were weeping in this way, the sun arose. Having performed the morning rites, Akrura urged the chariot. In their carts, Nanda and the other gopas followed him, having collected milk products in a large number of pitchers. With their minds fixed on their beloved Krishna, the gopis also followed. Then they stood there, wishing that the illustrious one should instruct them. The supreme among Yadus saw that they were tormented at his own departure. Using messengers, he lovingly comforted them, "I will return." When he had left, the gopis

---

[263] The blinking of an eye.
[264] Krishna.

stood there like figures etched on a painting, as long as the standard and the dust of his chariot could be seen. Without any hope that Govinda would return, they then retreated. To dispel their sorrow, they spent the days in singing about their beloved's deeds.

'O king! The chariot moved with the speed of the wind and the illustrious one, Rama and Akrura arrived at the Kalindi, the destroyer of sins. He touched and drank the sweet water, which sparkled like a jewel. Along with Rama, he went to a clump of trees and mounted the chariot.[265] Akrura asked them to be seated on the chariot. Taking their permission, he followed the prescribed rites and went and had a bath in a pool in the Kalindi. He immersed himself in those water and chanted the name of the eternal brahman. Akrura saw that Rama and Krishna were in front of him, together. "Anakadundubhi's two sons were astride the chariot. How can they be here? If they are here, they cannot be on the chariot." Thinking this, he arose from the water. However, he saw them seated there on the chariot, as they had been earlier. "When I saw the two of them in the water, wasn't that true?" Therefore, he submerged himself again and saw the lord of the serpents[266] there, being praised by the Siddhas, the charanas, the gandharvas and the asuras, their heads bowed down. The god possessed one thousand heads and one thousand diademed hoods. He was dressed in a blue garment, which sparkled like a white lotus's fibres. He was stationed there, like a white mountain.[267] There was another being on his lap and he was attired in yellow silk garments. He was serene and four-armed. His red eyes were like the petals of a lotus. His pleasant face was beautiful. His glance was smiling and enchanting. He possessed excellent eyebrows, a tall nose, handsome ears, excellent cheeks and red lips. His long arms were mighty. His shoulders were raised and Shri was on his chest. His neck was like a conch shell and his navel was deep. His stomach was lined, like a leaf. His hips and loins were large and his well-formed thighs were like those of an elephant. He possessed beautiful knees and calves. His raised ankles

[265] The chariot had halted there.
[266] Ananta, Shesha.
[267] Interpreted as Kailasa.

reflected the light from the cirele of his toenails, with delicate toes[268] and lotus feet. He was adorned with extremely expensive jewels, a diadem, bracelets, armlets, a girdle, a sacred thread, a necklace, anklets and earrings. In his hands, his resplendent form held a lotus, a conch shell, a chakra and a mace. The shrivatsa mark was on his chest, as was the radiant Koustubha gem. He wore a garland of wild flowers. Separately, with their own respective sentiments and words and with unblemished souls, he was being worshipped by his attendants, Sunanda and Nanda being the foremost, Sanaka and the others, the lords of the gods like Brahma, Rudra and the others, the nine supreme brahmanas[269] and Prahlada, Narada, Vasu[270] and other foremost ones among the illustrious one's devotees. Divinities like Shri, Pushti, Gira, Kanti, Kirti, Tushti, Ila, Urja, Vidya, Avidya, Shakti and Maya attended upon him.[271] On seeing this, he was greatly delighted and filled with supreme devotion. His body hair stood up in joy and, overwhelmed by the sentiments, his eyes were filled with tears. Satvata[272] regained his composure and controlled himself. He joined his hands in salutation and prostrated himself. In a faltering voice, he slowly uttered words of praise.'

Chapter 10(40)

'Akrura said, "I bow down to you. You are the cause behind all causes. You are Narayana, the original and undecaying

---

[268] Strictly speaking, two big toes and other toes. That is what a literal translation would be.

[269] The number nine means the *saptarshi*s, Marichi, Atri, Angira, Pulastya, Pulaha, Kratu and Vasishtha, and two others who are not in the list, but are important enough. For example, Kashyapa and Jamadagni are possibilities.

[270] Uparichara Vasu.

[271] The personified forms of the goddesses. Pushti is nourishment, Gira is speech/Sarasvati, Kanti is beauty, Kirti is fame, Tushti is contentment, Ila is the earth, Urja is energy, Avidya is the negation of Vidya and Shakti is power.

[272] Akrura.

being. Brahma appeared from the whorl of the lotus that sprouted
from your navel and all the worlds emanated from him. You are
the elements, space, water, fire, wind and the earth and the other,[273]
Mahat, that which is not born and the other,[274] the mind, the senses,
all the objects of the senses and all the divinities who preside over
the senses. You are the cause behind the universe and everything has
originated from your limbs. You are the atman and Aja[275] and the
others do not know your true form. They have been seized by what
is not the atman. Aja is bound by the gunas of that which has not
been born.[276] He does not know your true form, which is beyond
that of the gunas. Virtuous yogis worship you as the lord and great
being, the one who presides over the *adhidaivika, adhibhoutika*
and *adhyatmika*.[277] Some brahmanas follow the rituals of the three
Vedas. Using the rituals of sacrifices, they worship you under many
different forms and names. The learned worship you alone through
the yajna of knowledge, as the personified form of jnana. They
give up all kinds of rites. When these cease, they obtain you. There
are others who follow the injunctions enunciated by you.[278] They
cleanse themselves and are absorbed in you, conceiving of you as
the one who has one form, but manifests himself in many different
forms. There are others who accept you in Shiva's form, following
the path spoken about by Shiva. They worship the illustrious one
in this form, following the different modes stated by many kinds
of preceptors. In this way, all of them worship you, since you
are the lord who is in all the gods. O lord! This is despite their
minds being on others and they being devoted to other gods. O
lord! The rivers are generated from the mountains and are filled
up by rain. However, all of them enter the ocean. Like that, all the
paths end with you. Sattva, rajas and tamas result from the gunas

---

[273] Interpreted as ahamkara.

[274] That which is not born is interpreted as Prakriti and the other is
Purusha.

[275] Brahma.

[276] Prakriti.

[277] Destiny, nature and one's own nature, respectively.

[278] Karma and yoga having been mentioned, this is interpreted as the
pancharatra mode, *agama* texts followed by the Satvatas.

of your Prakriti. Beginning with Brahma and ending with immobile objects, everything is woven into the warf and woof of Prakriti. I bow down before you. Your vision is not attached. You are in all atmans. You are the one who witnesses all kinds of intelligence. You used ignorance to create this flow of gunas that flows through gods, humans and inferior species. The fire is your mouth. Your feet are the earth. The sun is your eye. The sky is your navel. The directions are your ears. Heaven is your head. The Indras among the gods are your arms. The oceans are your stomach. The wind has been thought of as your breath of life and strength. The trees and plants are your body hair. The clouds are the hair on your head. The mountains are the supreme one's bones and nails. The blinking of your eye constitutes night and day. Prajapati is your genital organ and the rain is your semen. You are the undecaying Purusha, the atman. You created the worlds, with many kinds of creatures, and the protectors of these worlds. You can be fathomed through the mind. They are in you, just as aquatic creatures exist in water and insects exist in *udumbara* fruit. For the sake of your pastimes, you manifest yourself in different kinds of forms. Using those, you cleanse impurities from people and delighted, they sing about your fame. I bow down to the original cause. In the form of a fish, you swam around in the ocean of destruction. I bow down to Hayashirsha and to the slayer of Madhu and Kaitabha. I bow down to the giant tortoise that held Mandara up. I bow down to the one who assumed the form of a boar and playfully raised up the earth. I bow down to the one who assumed the extraordinary form of a lion[279] to dispel the fears of virtuous people in the world. I bow down to the dwarf form who strode across the three worlds. I bow down to the lord of the Bhrigus,[280] who severed the forest of insolent kshatriyas. I bow down before the noble Raghu, who brought an end to Ravana. I bow down to Vasudeva. I bow down to Samkarshana. I bow down to Pradyumna and Aniruddha, the lords of the Satvatas. I bow down to the pure Buddha, who will confound daityas and danavas. I bow down to the one who will

[279] Narasimha.
[280] Parashurama.

assume the form of Kalki to destroy kshatriyas who will be almost like *mlechchhas*.[281] O illustrious one! This world of the living is bewildered by your maya. Grasped by notions of 'I' and 'mine', people are whirled around, along the path of karma. O lord! I am also foolish and roam around. I, my sons, my home, my wife, my wealth, my relatives and other things are actually as unreal as a dream, but my intelligence takes them to be real. Obsessed with objects that are temporary, my mind follows a contrary path and creates difficulties for me. I am immersed in the opposite pair of sentiments and do not know that you are the one who my atman loves the most. Because water is covered by weeds, an ignorant person ignores it and chases after a mirage. In that way, I have turned away from you. My intelligence is wretched. My mind is agitated by kama and karma. I cannot check it and am dragged here and there by the powerful senses. Therefore, I have approached your lotus feet, which are extremely difficult for the wicked to approach. O lord! However, I think that because of the compassion you will show me, I can approach them. O one with a lotus in your navel! When a man's mind turns towards the service of virtuous ones, perhaps he deserves to be freed from the cycle of samsara. I bow down before the one who is the embodiment of vijnana, the cause behind all kinds of comprehension. You are Purusha. You are the lord. You are the foremost. You are the brahman. You are infinite in your powers. I bow down to Vasudeva, the refuge of all creatures. O Hrishikesha! O lord! I have surrendered myself to you. Save me.'"

Chapter 10(41)

Shri-Shuka said, 'While he was being praised, the illustrious Krishna, who had displayed his form in the water, withdrew it, just as an actor ends his performance. When he[282] saw the form

---

[281] Barbarians, those who did not speak Sanskrit.
[282] Akrura.

had vanished, he quickly arose from the water. He was amazed. He finished the necessary rites and returned to the chariot. Hrishikesha asked him, "Did you see anything extraordinary in the sky, on land, or in the water? It seems to us that you did." Akrura replied, "You are the atman of the universe. Everything extraordinary in the sky, on land, or in the water exists in you. When I have seen you, what have I not seen? O brahman! Everything extraordinary in the sky, on land, or in the water is in you. How can I have seen anything extraordinary?" Saying this, Gandini's son[283] urged the chariot and at the end of the day, along with Rama and Krishna, reached Mathura. O king! People from the villages assembled along the path. With delight, they glanced at the two sons of Vasudeva and could not withdraw their eyes. Nanda gopa and the other residents of Vraja reached ahead of them. Having reached the city, they waited at a nearby grove for them. The illustrious one, the lord of the universe, met them. As Akrura humbly bowed down, he clasped his hand in his hand. He seemed to smile as he said, "Take the vehicle and, entering before us, go home. We will get down here. After resting, we will see the city." Akrura replied, "O lord! Without the two of you, I will not enter Mathura. O protector! O one who is devoted towards your devotees! You should not abandon me. O Adhokshaja! O best among well-wishers! Come. Let us go. Along with your elder brother, the cowherds and the well-wishers, enter the house along with the master of the house. We are householders. Purify my house with the dust of your feet. Through that purification of sins, the ancestors, the fires and the gods will be satisfied. By washing your feet, the great Bali obtained fame and unlimited prosperity. He obtained the destination meant for those who are devoted to you. The waters that emerged after bathing your feet[284] were cleansed and purified the three worlds. Sharva bore them on his head. By touching them, Sagara's sons went to heaven. O god of the gods! O protector of the universe! Hearing and singing about you is sacred. You are Uttamashloka Narayana. I bow down before you." The illustrious one said,

[283] Akrura.
[284] The Ganga.

"With my revered elder brother, I will indeed come to your house. However, I must first kill the one who hates the circle of the Yadus and bring joy to my well-wishers." When the illustrious one said this, Akrura seemed to be disheartened. He entered the city, told Kamsa that he had accomplished the task, and went home.

'In the late afternoon, along with Samkarshana and surrounded by the gopas, the illustrious one entered Mathura, so as to see the city. He saw the tall turrets made out of crystal, the large gates, the golden doors and arches, storehouses made out of copper and brass, the impenetrable moats, the beautiful gardens and the adornments of groves. There were golden crossroads, mansions and pleasure gardens. There were assembly halls for guilds[285] and other decorated houses. The panels on the windows, the platforms and floors were encrusted with lapis lazuli, crystal, sapphire, coral, pearls and emeralds. Doves and peacocks joyously called, perched on the openings in the windows. The streets, shopping places and quadrangles were sprinkled with water, and flowers, sprouts, parched grain and unhusked rice were strewn there. The doors to the houses were decorated with pitchers filled with curds, sandalwood, flowers, rows of lamps, and fresh sprouts. There were plantain trees and betel nut trees with bunches of fruit. There were festoons of flags. Surrounded by their friends, Vasudeva's two sons entered via the royal road. To see them, the women of the city assembled quickly. O king! Eager to see them, some climbed on to the tops of the mansions. Some donned their garments or ornaments the wrong way round. Others forgot and wore only one ornament and not both.[286] Some wore only one earring on the ear, or only one anklet. Others did one eye,[287] but not the other. Some were eating their meals, but happily abandoned them, without finishing eating. Some did not finish their baths. Hearing the noise, they woke up from their sleep. Mothers were feeding their infants, but cast them aside. His valour was like that of a crazy Indra among elephants. The lotus-eyed one's form is one that brings pleasure

---

[285] Shrenis.
[286] When the ornaments were in pairs.
[287] Applied collyrium.

to Shri. His bold pastimes and smiling glances stole their minds and was like a festival to their eyes. Having heard about him, their hearts had already melted towards him. They saw him now and they were honoured by his smiling glances, which were like nectar. Having seen him, they mentally embraced the embodiment of bliss. O destroyer of enemies! Their body hair stood up in joy and they abandoned the infinite store of mental distress.[288] Their lotus faces bloomed in delight and they climbed on to the tops of the mansions. Happy, they showered down flowers on Bala and Keshava. The happy brahmanas worshipped them with curds, unbroken grain, pots filled with water, garlands, fragrances and other objects of worship. The female citizens exclaimed, "What great austerities did the gopis perform? They were able to see these two, who are like great festivals in the world of men."

'Gada's elder brother[289] saw a washerman-cum-dyer come in their direction. On seeing him, he asked him for some clean and excellent garments. "O dear one! Please give us garments that are worthy of us. If you give us this, there is no doubt that you will obtain supreme prosperity." The illustrious one is complete in every possible way. However, the king's servant was extremely insolent. Thus asked, he angrily replied, "You always roam around in mountains and forests. Do you wear these kinds of garments? You have asked for objects that belong to the king. O foolish ones! Do not ask for these. If you wish to live, quickly leave. If a person is insolent, the king's servants kill him or loot him." When he spoke in this way, Devaki's son became angry. Using the tips of his hands, he severed the washerman's head from his body. All his followers abandoned the bundles of clothes they had. All of them fled along the road and Achyuta took those garments. Krishna and Samkarshana attired themselves in two pieces of cloth that appealed to them. They distributed the remainder among the gopas and flung some away on the ground. There was a weaver who cheerfully attired them in many colourful garments, with ornaments, that were worthy of them. With

[288] This is interpreted as distress due to separation from him.
[289] Krishna.

many kinds of ornamented garments, Krishna and Rama were radiant. Thus decorated, they resembled two young elephants during a festival, one white, the other dark. The illustrious one was pleased with him and granted him supreme prosperity and form that would be like his own.[290] In this world, he gave him strength, prosperity, memory and sharp senses. They then went to the house of a garland maker named Sudamna.[291] On seeing them, he arose and lowered his head down on the ground. He brought seats for them and offered them, and their companions, *padya*, *arghya*[292] and other objects of worship, garlands, betel leaves and pastes. He said, "O lord! Through your arrival, my birth has been successful and my lineage has been purified. The ancestors, the gods and the rishis are satisfied with me. The two of you are indeed the supreme cause behind everything created in this universe. For the sake of welfare and prosperity, the two of you have descended here in your portions. You are the atman of the universe. You are well-wishers who are not partial in your vision. Though you are affectionate towards those who worship you, you are impartial towards all creatures. I am your servant. Command me. What shall I do for you? If you engage a man to do something, you show a favour towards him." O Indra among kings! Discerning their wishes, Sudama was pleased in his mind. He fashioned garlands made out of fresh and fragrant flowers and gave those to them. Thus decorated, along with their companions, Krishna and Rama were pleased. He had sought refuge with them and was bowing down before them. They granted him the best of boons. He sought the boon that he might have unwavering devotion towards the one who is the atman of everything, affection towards his devotees and supreme compassion towards all creatures. He granted him this boon and also prosperity for him and his followers, strength, lifespan, fame and beauty. With his elder brother, he then departed.'

---

[290] After death. Form like his own means *sarupya*.
[291] Later, Sudamna is often referred to as Sudama.
[292] Padya is water to wash the feet, arghya is a gift.

Chapter 10(42)

Shri-Shuka said, 'After this, Madhava proceeded along the royal road. He saw a young woman. Her face was beautiful, but she was hunchbacked. She was carrying a vessel with various unguents for the body. As she was proceeding, the one who grants pleasure smiled and asked her. "O one with the beautiful thighs! Who are you? For whose body are these unguents meant? Tell us truthfully. Give us some of the excellent unguents meant for the body. You will then soon obtain supreme benefit." The *sairandhri*[293] replied, "O handsome one! I am Kamsa's servant-maid and he respects me because of my work with unguents. My name is Trivakra.[294] The lord of Bhoja loves and is attached to what I prepare. However, other than you, who deserves to have these?" She was overwhelmed at their beauty, charm, sweet smiles, conversation and glances. She gave both of them a lot of unguents. When these unguents were smeared on their bodies, they enhanced their own natural complexions.[295] Smeared in this way on the upper parts of their bodies, they were extremely radiant. The illustrious one was pleased with the hunchbacked Trivakra, whose face was beautiful. To demonstrate the fruits of seeing him, he made up his mind to make her straight. He pressed down on the front part of her feet with his feet. He raised his opened palm and held up her chin. In this way, Achyuta straightened her up. Through Mukunda's touch, she instantly became an extremely beautiful woman. Her limbs became straight and beautiful. She possessed wide hips and large breasts. She thus came to have beauty, quality and nobility, and desire was generated in her. She smiled, dragged Keshava by his upper garment and said, "O brave one! Come. Let us go to my house. I cannot leave you here. O bull among men! You have agitated my mind. Please show me your favours." Sought by the woman in this way,

[293] Maidservant.
[294] Literally, bent in three places—neck, breasts and waist.
[295] This has an interpretation that they used contrasting colours to enhance their own natural complexions. Krishna used yellow paste and Balarama used blue paste.

though Rama was looking on, Krishna glanced at the faces of the gopas. He laughed and replied, "O one with the excellent eyebrows! You are the one who destroys the mental distress of men. I will go to your house after I have accomplished my objective. You are the refuge for wayfarers like us." Taking leave from her with these sweet words, he proceeded along the road. The merchants along the road worshipped him and his elder brother with many kinds of offerings, betel leaves, garlands and fragrances. Seeing him, the minds of the women were agitated and they could no longer control themselves. Their garments, braids of hair and bracelets were dislodged. They were like figures etched on a painting.

'Achyuta asked the citizens where the bow was kept. He entered the place and saw the bow, which was as extraordinary as Indra's bow.[296] It was supremely resplendent and was guarded by many men who were worshipping it. Though those men restrained him, Krishna forcibly seized the bow. While the men looked on, in the twinkling of an eye, he playfully raised it up in his left hand, strung it and drew it. Urukrama snapped it in the middle, just as a crazy elephant breaks a stalk of sugar cane. The sound of the bow breaking echoed in the sky, the space between heaven and earth, and in all the directions. When it filled all this up, Kamsa heard it and was terrified. The guards were enraged and wished to seize him and his companions. Those murderers exclaimed, "Let us seize them. Let us kill them." Bala and Keshava discerned their wicked intentions. They angrily picked up the two broken parts of the bow and started to slay them. They also killed an army that had been sent by Kamsa. Emerging through the gate of the arena, they happily wandered around, looking at the riches of the city. The residents of the city witnessed their extraordinary valour, energy, boldness and beauty. They thought these two were supreme gods. As they wandered around as they willed, the sun started to set. Therefore, surrounded by the gopas, Krishna and Rama returned to the place where the carts had camped.

'After Mukunda had left, the gopis suffered because of the separation. They had spoken about the benedictions the city of

[296] The rainbow.

Madhu would enjoy and these came true. They saw that ornament among men, with Lakshmi ornamenting his body. Abandoning others who worshipped her, Shri sought refuge with him. After their feet had been washed, the two of them ate rice sprinkled with milk. They happily slept during the night, knowing what Kamsa desired. Kamsa heard about the breaking of the bow, the slaying of the guards and his own army and about Govinda and Rama's supreme pastimes. The evil-minded one was scared. He remained awake for a long time and in both situations,[297] saw many evil portents, as if they were the messengers of death. Though he could see his own reflection,[298] there was no head. Though no stellar body actually possessed a mirror image, he saw them in pairs. There seemed to be holes in his shadow. He could not hear the sound of his breathing. The trees seemed to be made out of gold. He could not see his own footprints. In his sleep, he saw that he was embraced by *preta*s.[299] He was astride a vehicle drawn by donkeys and was ingesting poison. He was travelling, wearing a garland of *nalada* flowers.[300] He was naked and was smeared in oil. When he was asleep and when he was awake, he saw many other portents. He saw many other signs of death and was terrified. Because of his thoughts, he could not sleep.

'O Kouravya! When night was over and the sun arose from the waters, Kamsa ensured that arrangements were carried out for the great festival of wrestling. The men worshipped the arena and blew on trumpets. The galleries were decorated with garlands, flags, ribbons and arches. With brahmanas and kshatriyas at the forefront, residents of the city and the countryside entered and seated themselves comfortably. Seats were earmarked for kings. Surrounded by his advisers, Kamsa seated himself in the royal gallery. Though he was seated amidst the circle of kings, his heart was trembling. The blare of trumpets was surpassed by the sound

---

[297] When awake and when asleep. When sleeping, he had nightmares.
[298] In a mirror, or in the water.
[299] Ghosts.
[300] Nalada is identified as the Indian spikenard, or as the *Hibiscus rosa*. Here, it probably means the hibiscus, red in colour.

of wrestlers slapping their palms. The proud and ornamented
wrestlers seated themselves, along with their instructors. Pleased
and delighted by the music, Chanura, Mushtika, Kuta, Shala and
Toshala entered the arena. Nanda gopa and the other gopas had
been summoned by the king of the Bhojas. They offered him their
gifts and seated themselves in one of the galleries.'

Chapter 10(43)

Shri-Shuka said, 'O scorcher of enemies! Krishna and Rama
performed their ablutions. They heard the sounds of the wrestlers
and the kettledrums, and approached to see what was happening.
Krishna approached the gate of the arena and saw the elephant
Kuvalayapida stationed there, goaded by the keeper. Shouri girded
up his garments and tied his curly hair. In a voice that rumbled like
the clouds, he spoke to the elephant keeper. "O elephant keeper!
Without any delay, step aside and allow us to pass. O elephant
keeper! If you do not do so, I will send you and your elephant to
Yama's abode." Thus censured, the elephant keeper became angry
and goaded his angry elephant, which was like Yama, the destroyer,
in Krishna's direction. The Indra among elephants rushed forwards
and violently seized him in its trunk. However, he slipped out from
the trunk, struck it and hid under its legs. It was angry and couldn't
see Keshava, though it could smell him. It stretched out and seized
him with the tip of its trunk. However, he forcibly freed himself.
He seized the extremely strong animal by the tail and dragged it
twenty-five bow-lengths away, just as Suparna toys with a serpent.
It moved around, to the left and to the right. However, Achyuta
held on to the tail and also moved around in that way, just as a boy
does with a calf. Krishna then faced the elephant and struck it with
his hand. He ran and it followed. But just as it was about to touch
him, at every step, he made it fall down. As he ran, he playfully
fell down on the ground and instantly arose. However, thinking
that he had fallen down, it angrily struck the ground with its tusks.
When its own valour was countered, the Indra among elephants

became extremely angry. Goaded by the drivers,[301] it angrily rushed towards Krishna. As it was descending, the illustrious Madhusudana approached. He seized its trunk with a hand and flung it down on the ground. When it had fallen down, he pressed down on it with his foot. He played like a lion and uprooted a tusk. Hari used this to slay the elephant and its keepers.

'He left the dead elephant there. With a tusk in his hand, he entered. The tusk was on his shoulder and he was smeared with drops of the elephant's musth. There were drops of his perspiration. His lotus face was radiant. O king! Baladeva and Janardana were surrounded by some gopas. Holding the tusks as excellent weapons, they entered the arena. As he entered the arena with his elder brother, each one regarded him in different ways—the wrestlers as the vajra, men as the best among men, women as the personified form of the god of love, the gopas as their relative, the wicked kings as a chastiser, his parents as their child, the lord of the Bhojas as death, the ignorant as a weak competitor, the yogis as the supreme truth and the Vrishnis as the great divinity. O king! When Kamsa saw that Kuvalayapida had been killed, he thought that they were invincible and became extremely anxious. Having reached the arena, the two mighty-armed ones were resplendent. They were attired in colourful garments, ornaments and garlands. They seemed to have donned the garb of two excellent actors. The minds of those who looked at them were agitated by their dazzle.

'O king! The residents of the city and the country, seated in the galleries, looked at those two excellent men. The outburst of joy was so overwhelming that their eyes dilated. They drank their faces in with their eyes, but were not satisfied. They seemed to drink them in with their eyes, lick them with their tongues, smell them with their noses and embrace them with their arms. They spoke to each other about what they had seen and what they had heard, his form, qualities, sweetness and bravery, as if reminding themselves. "These two are portions of the illustrious Hari Narayana himself. They have descended in Vasudeva's house. This one was born from Devaki and was conveyed to Gokula. All this while, he has secretly

---

[301] The elephant keeper also had assistants. Hence the plural.

resided and grown up in Nanda's house. He conveyed Putana and the danava who was in the form of a whirlwind[302] to their ends. He destroyed the two arjuna trees, the guhyaka,[303] Keshi, Dhenuka[304] and others like that. He freed the cows and the cowherds from the forest conflagration. He subdued the snake Kaliya and destroyed Indra's pride. On one hand, he held up the supreme among mountains for an entire week. He saved Gokula from the showers, storms and thunder. When they looked at his smiling face, the gopis were always delighted. As they looked, they were freed from all the different kinds of torment and exhaustion. It is said that he will make the lineage of the Yadus extremely famous. Protected by him, it will obtain prosperity, fame and greatness. His elder brother is the handsome and lotus-eyed Rama. He is the one who killed Pralamba, Vatsaka, Baka and others."[305] As the people spoke in this way, the trumpets were sounded. Chanura addressed Krishna and Rama in the following words. "O son of Nanda! O Rama! The two of you are respected as brave. Hearing that you were accomplished in wrestling, the king summoned you here, wishing to see for himself. Subjects who do what the king desires, in thoughts, words and deeds, obtain benefit for themselves. It is the contrary for those who do not act accordingly. It is evident that gopas and cowherds always find pleasure in wrestling, playing at such sports as they graze cattle in the forests. Therefore, let you and us do what will bring pleasure to the king. Since all creatures are in the king, all creatures will also be pleased with us." Krishna heard these words. He himself liked to wrestle and welcomed these words. He replied in words that were appropriate to the time and the place. "Though we roam around in the forest, we are the subjects of the lord of the Bhojas. We always do what is agreeable to him. That ensures us his great favours. We are boys and we should sport with those

---

[302] Trinavarta.

[303] Shankhachuda.

[304] Dhenuka was killed by Balarama, but a distinction is not being drawn between Krishna and Balarama. Alternatively, the residents of Mathura may have got some wrong reports.

[305] Here too, Vatsa and Baka were actually killed by Krishna.

who are our equals in strength. Let there be no adharma and let those who have assembled in this wrestling arena be not tainted by that." Chanura replied, "You or Bala aren't children or young boys.[306] You are supreme among strong ones. You playfully killed an elephant that possessed the vigour of a thousand elephants. Therefore, you will have to fight with strong ones and there will be no violation in this. O Varshneya! Exhibit your valour against me and Bala will demonstrate it against Mushtika."'

Chapter 10(44)

Shri-Shuka said, 'When it was decided in this way, the illustrious Madhusudana made up his mind. He was paired against Chanura and Rohini's son against Mushtika. They grasped the opponent's hands with their hands and locked their feet against the opponent's feet. Wishing to be victorious, they powerfully tugged at the opponent. They struck each other—fists against fists, knees agains knees, heads against heads and chests against chests. Each dragged the opponent around in circles, shoved, crushed, flung him down on the ground, withdrew, attacked from the rear and countered the rival's moves. They raised the opponent up, carried him, or remained stationary. In the process of defeating the rival, they harmed themselves. O king! All the assembled women thought the encounter was between the relatively strong and the relatively weak. Filled with compassion, they spoke to each other in groups. "This is not good policy. The members of the royal assembly have sadly followed adharma. While the king looks on, they desire this encounter between the relatively strong and the relatively weak. On one side, there are the two wrestlers, who are like Indras among mountains. All their limbs are as firm as the vajra. On the other side, there are two young boys who have not yet become adults. Their limbs are extremely delicate. It is certain that there has been a violation of dharma in this assembly. One must never remain in a

---

[306] Literally, a boy who is younger than fifteen years.

place where adharma is on the rise. Thinking of the sins committed by an assembly, a wise person should not enter the assembly. Having entered, if a man does not speak, or speaks like an ignorant person,[307] he suffers from sin. Behold Krishna's lotus face as he leaps around on all sides of the enemy. He is perspiring because of the exhaustion and it looks like drops of water on the whorl of a lotus. Are you not looking at Rama's face? His eyes are coppery red. He is full of intolerance towards Mushtika, yet that rage is beautified by his smiles. The land of Vraja is indeed sacred. The ancient Purusha has hidden himself there, disguising himself in human form and wearing a colourful garland of wild flowers. Along with Bala, he has herded the cows and has made his flute vibrate, indulging in pastimes. His feet are worshipped by Shiva and Rama.[308] What austerities have the gopas performed? They have used their eyes to drink up his form, which constantly assumed new expressions. He is the essence of beauty and cannot be equalled or surpassed. There is nothing that can enhance his beauty. He is the only abode of fame, prosperity and opulence. This is a sight that is extremely difficult to obtain. Blessed are the women of Vraja. While milking, threshing, churning, smearing, swinging on swings, taking care of weeping infants, sprinkling, cleaning and performing other activities, their minds have been extremely attached to him and they have sung about him, with tears choking their throats. Their minds have been absorbed in Urukrama. Along with the cows, in the morning, he left Vraja and in the evening, he returned again. They could hear him play on the flute. The women quickly emerged on the road and saw his smiling face and his compassionate glances. Their store of good deeds must be great." O bull among the Bharata lineage! While the women were conversing in this way, the illustrious Hari, the lord of yoga, made up his mind to kill his enemy. Hearing the scared words of the women, the parents, filled with affection towards their sons, were grief-stricken. Since they did not know about the strength of their sons, they suffered from remorse.

[307] Does not speak and remains silent, or defends adharma.
[308] Ramaa, Lakshmi.

'Using many kinds of techniques, Achyuta and his adversary fought against each other. In that way, Bala and Mushtika also fought against each other. The blows from the illustrious one's body descended like cruel and crushing strikes of the vajra on Chanura. They shattered his limbs and he repeatedly fell unconscious. However, he got up with the speed of a hawk. He angrily struck the illustrious Vasudeva on the chest with both of his clenched hands. As a result of that blow, like an elephant that has been struck with a garland, he did not budge. Hari seized Chanura by his arms and whirled him around several times. He powerfully flung him down on the ground, so that his life began to ebb away. His garlands and garments were dishevelled, like Indra's pole when it was brought down.[309] In that way, Mushtika first struck Balabhadra with his own fist. However, he received a blow from the hand and suffered severely. He trembled and, suffering, vomited blood from his mouth. He lost his life and fell down on the ground, like a tree that has been struck by a storm. O king! Rama, supreme among strikers, then faced Kuta. He playfully toyed with him and negligently killed him with a blow of his left fist. In that way, Krishna kicked at Shala's head with the front of his foot. He did the same with Toshalaka. The heads of both were shattered and they fell down on the ground. When Chanura, Mushtika, Kuta, Shala and Toshalaka were killed, all the remaining wrestlers wished to save their lives and fled.

'The two of them then dragged their gopa friends in[310] and they sported together. While the trumpets blared, the two of them danced, their anklets jingling. With the exception of Kamsa, all the people were delighted at Rama and Krishna's deed. With brahmanas at the forefront, they uttered words of praise. When the best among the wrestlers had been killed or had fled, the king of Bhoja stopped the playing of the musical instruments. He spoke these words. "Drive Vasudeva's wicked sons away from the city. Seize the wealth of the gopas and bind up the evil-minded Nanda. Instantly kill the evil-minded Vasudeva, the worst among wicked

---

[309] A pole erected for a sacrifice to Indra is brought down after the sacrifice is over.

[310] In the arena.

ones. Also kill my father, Ugrasena, and all those who are on the side of the enemy." When Kamsa boasted in this way, the undecaying one became angry. He jumped and easily leapt up on to that high gallery.[311] He[312] saw him enter there, like his own death. The spirited one immediately jumped up from his seat and seized a sword and a shield. With that sword in his hand he quickly moved around, to the left and to the right, like a hawk in the sky. However, his fierce strength was irresistible and he powerfully seized him, the way Tarkshya's son seizes a serpent. He seized him by the hair and his diadem was knocked down. From that high gallery, he flung him down on to the arena. The one with the lotus in his navel is the refuge of the universe and controls himself. He flung himself down on top of him. While the world looked on, he seized him by the hair and like a lion dragging an elephant, dragged him along the ground. O Indra among men! Great sounds of lamentation were uttered by all the people. He had always been anxious and his intelligence had been focused on the lord, when he was drinking, eating, moving, sleeping and breathing. He had always seen the one with a chakra as his weapon in front of him. Therefore, he obtained a form just like him, which is so very difficult to obtain.

'He had eight younger brothers, Kanka, Nyagrodhaka and others. They wished to repay their brother's death. Extremely enraged, they attacked. They rushed forward with great force. Rohini's son controlled himself. He raised a club and killed them, the way the lord of deer kills animals. Kettledrums were sounded in the firmament. Brahma, Isha and the others rejoiced and showered down flowers. The women[313] praised them and danced. O great king! His wives and those of his relatives[314] were miserable at their deaths. They approached, beating their heads and with tears in their eyes. The grieving wives embraced them, as they were lying down on a bed meant for heroes. The women lamented in loud tones and repeatedly shed tears. "Alas! O protector! O loved one! O one who

---

[311] The royal gallery.

[312] Kamsa.

[313] Divine ones.

[314] Kamsa's wives and the wives of his brothers.

knew about dharma! O compassionate and kind protector! With
you slain, we, the house and the offspring have also been destroyed.
O bull among men! Without you, the city has lost its lord. Like us,
it is no longer radiant and the festivities and auspicious signs have
ceased. You committed terrible violence against innocent creatures.
That is what has reduced you to this state. How can a person who
causes harm enjoy peace? He is the one behind the creation and
destruction of all creatures. He is the protector too. How can a
person who opposes him ever obtain happiness?" The illustrious
one, the creator of all the worlds, comforted the royal women. He
arranged that the funeral rites of those who had been killed should
be performed. He freed his mother and father from their fetters.
Krishna and Rama bowed down before them, touching their feet
with their heads. Devaki and Vasudeva realized that those two were
the lords of the universe and respectfully honoured them. They were
scared and did not embrace their own sons.'

Chapter 10(45)

Shri-Shuka said, 'Purushottama discerned that his parents had got
to know about his true nature. Since this should not happen, he
cast his maya, which confounds people, over them. With his elder
brother, the bull among the Satvatas approached his parents. He
humbly bowed down and affectionately addressed them as "Father"
and "Mother", pleasing them. He said, "O father! The two of you
have always been anxious about us. During infancy, boyhood and
youth, we were never like sons to you. Suffering from destiny, we
could not reside with you. Boys are nurtured in their father's house
and obtain great joy. The parents give birth and nourish. Even if a
mortal person with a body tries through every possible means and
lives for one hundred years, he cannot repay the debt that is owed
to them. If a capable son does not pay this back himself, using his
riches and means of subsistence, after he dies, he is made to eat his
own flesh. If a capable person does not support his aged mother and
father, his virtuous wife, his infant child, his preceptor, a brahmana

or a person who seeks refuge, even if he breathes, he is as good as dead. We have been incapable because our minds have always been anxious about Kamsa. Since we have not been able to worship you, these days have been spent in futility. O father! O mother! You should pardon us. We were dependent on others. Since we suffered severely from the evil-hearted one, we have not been able to render you service." Hari, the atman of the universe, used his maya to assume human form and said this. Bewildered by his words, they placed him on their laps and embraced him, immensely happy. Bound to him by bonds of affection, they sprinkled him with flows of tears. O king! Their throats choked with tears and confused, they could not say anything. Thus, Devaki's illustrious son comforted his parents. He instated his maternal grandfather, Ugrasena, as the king of the Yadus. He said, "O great king! You should command us and the subjects. Because of the curse inflicted by Yayati, a Yadu should not be seated on a royal throne.[315] Since I am present before you as a servant, the gods, not to speak of kings among men, will humbly bring offerings to you." He then brought back all his kin and relatives who had fled in different directions because of their fear of Kamsa—Yadus, Vrishnis, Andhakas, Madhus, Dasharhas, Kukuras and others. They had suffered from the exile in foreign lands and he respectfully comforted them. The creator of the universe made them dwell in their own houses and satisfied them with wealth. Protected by the arms of Krishna and Samkarshana, they obtained their desires and were successful, finding pleasure in their houses. Their anxieties were removed by Krishna and Rama. Every day, they happily looked at Mukunda's lotus face. They always rejoiced because of his handsome, compassionate and smiling glances. Even the aged ones there became young and extremely energetic. Their eyes repeatedly drank in the nectar from Mukunda's lotus face.

[315] This curse has been described in Chapter 9(19). Yadu and his descendants were barred from inheriting Yayati's kingdom. This doesn't solve the problem, since Ugrasena was also descended from Yadu. The interpretation is that Ugrasena was permitted this deviation because he was so commanded by Krishna.

'Devaki's illustrious son approached Nanda, along with Samkarshana. O Indra among kings! He embraced him and said, "O father! We have been affectionately nourished and loved by the two of you. Parents are more affectionate towards their sons than towards their own selves. Infant children are sometimes abandoned by their relatives because they are incapable of nurturing and protecting them. However, the real father and the real mother are those who nourish them like their own sons. O father! You should now go to Vraja. Because of affection, our relatives here have been miserable. After bestowing happiness on our well-wishers here, we will also go there." In this way, the illustrious Achyuta comforted Nanda and the others from Vraja. He respectfully honoured them with garments, ornaments, utensils and other things. Thus addressed, Nanda embraced him. He was overwhelmed with love. His eyes were full of tears. With the gopas, he left for Vraja.

'O king! After this, Shura's son followed the rites and used a priest and brahmanas to undertake the *dvija samskara* for his two sons.[316] As dakshina, he worshipped and gave them[317] cows ornamented with golden necklaces and their ornamented calves, all of them covered with silken garments. At the time of the birth of Krishna and Rama, the immensely intelligent one had mentally resolved to give some.[318] However, following adharma, Kamsa had seized these. He remembered that and gave those too. With the samskara completed, the two of them attained the status of being a dvija. They followed excellent vows. They also received the vow of *gayatra* from Garga, the priest of the lineage of the Yadus.[319] Those two lords of the universe were the source of all kinds of knowledge and knew everything. No one else could have imparted this unblemished knowledge to them. However, to ensure the welfare of men, they concealed this. Therefore, desiring to reside in their

[316] Shura's son means Vasudeva. Dvija samskara means the second birth and refers to the sacred thread ceremony.

[317] The brahmanas.

[318] Cows and calves.

[319] As long as they were students, they would follow the vow of *brahmacharya*. This was taken by reciting the *gayatri mantra*. Therefore, the vow is known as gayatra.

preceptor's house, they went to the one named Sandipani, who was
from Kashi, but resident of Avantipura.[320] Having obtained him as
a preceptor, those two self-restrained ones served him unwaveringly
and with devotion, setting a yardstick. They revered him like a
god. The supreme among brahmanas was satisfied with their pure
sentiments and humble behaviour. The preceptor spoke to them
about all the Vedas, the Vedangas, the secrets of *dhanurveda*, the
texts of dharma, the paths of *nyaya*, the knowledge of logic and the
six methods of political science.[321] O king! Those two were supreme
among the best of men. All kinds of knowledge originated with
them. Therefore, they assimilated and mastered everything, when it
was uttered only once. O king! They controlled themselves and in
sixty-four days and nights, learnt sixty-four different arts.[322] Having

[320] Avantipura is the city of Avanti, also known as Ujjaini/Ujjain. By
deduction, Sandipani originally hailed from Kashi/Varanasi, though it is
also possible that this refers to his *gotra* being Kashyapa.

[321] Vedanga means a branch of the Vedas and these were six kinds of
learning that were essential to understand the Vedas—*shiksha* (phonetics),
kalpa (rituals), *vyakarana* (grammar), *nirukta* (etymology), *chhanda* (metre)
and *jyotisha* (astronomy). Dhanurveda means the science of warfare. The
six schools of *darshana* or philosophy are nyaya, *vaisheshika*, samkhya,
yoga, *mimamsa* and Vedanta. Samkhya and yoga are not mentioned in
the text and Vedanta is left implicit. The text uses the word *anvikshiki*
knowledge (translated as knowledge of logic), which would naturally
mean mimamsa, closely allied to nyaya. The six methods of political
science (*rajaniti*) are *sandhi* (peace), *vigraha* (war), *yana* (marching), *asana*
(remaining in one place), *dvaidhi* (dividing one's forces into two parts) and
samshraya (seeking refuge).

[322] There are sixty-four types of arts (*kala*)—(1) singing; (2) playing on
musical instruments; (3) dancing; (4) drama; (5) painting; (6) painting the
body; (7) making designs with rice and flowers for offerings; (8) using flowers
to make beds; (9) painting teeth, limbs and garments; (10) ornamenting a
floor with precious stones; (11) preparing a bed; (12) playing music with
water pots; (13) mixing colours; (14) making wreaths and garlands; (15)
ornamenting the head; (16) beautifying the body with garments; (17)
decorating the ears; (18) making fragrances; (19) making ornaments; (20)
jugglery; (21) using disguise; (22) sleight of hand; (23) preparing tasty food;
(24) preparing tasty and colourful drinks; (25) needlework and weaving;
(26) puppetry; (27) making musical instruments; (28) solving puzzles; (29)
making images; (30) speaking cryptically; (31) reciting from books; (32)

satisfied their preceptor, they wished to pay the teacher's dakshina. O king! The brahmana realized their extraordinary greatness and their superhuman intelligence. He consulted his wife and asked for the boon that his son, who had died in the ocean in Prabhasa, might come back.

'The two *maharathas*[323] agreed to this and mounted their chariot. Invincible in their valour, they reached Prabhasa. Having reached the shore, they sat down for a while. The ocean recognized them and respectfully brought them offerings. The illustrious one told him, "You used your giant wave to seize a child here. He is our preceptor's son. Quickly give him back to us." The ocean replied, "O lord! I did not take him away. It was the great daitya, Panchajana. O Krishna! That asura assumes the form of a conch shell and roams around inside the water. He is the one who has really seized him." Hearing this, the lord quickly entered the water and killed him. However, he did not see the child inside his stomach. Taking the conch shell that had been his body, he returned to the chariot and went to Yama's beloved city, known as Samyamani. Along with the one who wields the plough as a weapon,[324] Janardana went there and blew on the conch shell. Yama, the one who controls all subjects, heard the sound of the conch shell being blown. He worshipped them with a lot of offerings and great devotion. He humbly spoke

---

dramaturgy; (33) solving enigmatic verses; (34) cane work and making arrows; (35) spinning; (36) carpentry; (37) architecture; (38) testing silver and jewels; (39) metallurgy; (40) decorating jewels with colours; (41) mineralogy; (42) medicine using herbs; (43) arranging fights between rams, cocks and quails; (44) teaching parrots to speak; (45) driving out (an enemy or a disease); (46) hairdressing; (47) reading letters hidden inside a closed fist; (48) learning mlechchha languages; (49) learning indigenous languages; (50) making toy carts with flowers; (51) constructing magic squares; (52) conversation; (53) mind reading; (54) lexicography; (55) prosody; (56) gambling; (57) controlling evil spirits; (58) attracting remoted objects; (59) playing children's games; (60) using mystical powers; (61) playing tricks; (62) disguising the inferior quality of a cloth; (63) using rituals; and (64) making amulets. Since these are translated from long Sanskrit words, the list of sixty-four varies from one interpretation to another.

[323] A maharatha is a great charioteer.
[324] Balarama.

to Krishna, who resides in the hearts of all creatures. "O Vishnu! In your pastimes, you have assumed human forms. What can I do for you?" The illustrious one said, "Because of the bondage of his own karma, our preceptor's son was brought here. O great king! Give prime importance to my command and bring him here." He agreed and brought the preceptor's son there. The two supreme ones of the Yadu lineage restored him and asked their preceptor to ask for another boon. "O child![325] You have completely fulfilled everything that must be done for a preceptor. With disciples like you, what else can a preceptor desire? O brave ones! Return to your own home. May your deeds purify everything. May you remember the hymns of the Vedas in this world and in the next one." O child! Having taken the permission of the preceptor, they mounted the chariot, which was as swift as the wind. Thundering like a cloud, they returned to their own city. On seeing Rama and Janardana, all the people were delighted. They had not seen them for many days and were like people who had regained lost wealth.'

Chapter 10(46)

Shri-Shuka said, 'The foremost minister of the Vrishnis was Uddhava, Krishna's beloved friend. He was supremely intelligent and was directly Brihaspati's[326] disciple. On one occasion, the illustrious Hari, the refuge of all those who are afflicted, spoke to his beloved devotee in private. He held his hand in his own hand and said, "O Uddhava! O amiable one! Go to Vraja and bring pleasure to our parents. As a result of separation from me, the gopis are suffering. Convey my message and relieve them. Their minds and lives have been immersed in me. For my sake, they have given up everything connected with the body. For my sake, they have cast aside the dharma of the worlds. Therefore, I will nurture them. Though I am far away, for the women of Gokula, I am the most

---

[325] This is Sandipani speaking.
[326] The preceptor of the gods.

loved. O dear one! They remember me and are confounded. Because
of the separation, they are anxious and distracted. Their minds are
on me. It is because I sent them a message about my return that
those cowherd women are managing, somehow or the other, with
a great deal of difficulty, to remain alive." O king! Thus addressed,
Uddhava honoured the words of his master. He brought a chariot
and mounted it, leaving for Nanda's Gokula.

'The prosperous one reached Nanda's Vraja just as the sun
was about to set. His vehicle was covered with dust from the
hooves of the animals that were returning. There was the sound
of excited bulls fighting with each other to have intercourse with
cows that were in heat. Cows with heavy udders rushed here and
there, in search of their own calves. The white calves jumped
around in different directions. There was the sound of cows being
milked, mixed with the notes of flutes. The place was ornamented
with shining gopas and gopis, singing about the auspicious deeds
of Bala and Krishna. The residences of the gopas were beautiful
with fires, the sun, guests, cattle, brahmanas, ancestors and gods
being worshipped with incense, lamps and garlands. There were
blossoming forests in every direction, resounding with the calls of
flocks of birds. The lotus ponds were decorated with swans and
karandavas.[327] As soon as Krishna's beloved companion arrived,
Nanda happily embraced and worshipped him, taking him to be
Vasudeva[328] himself. He ate excellent food and comfortably seated
himself on a mat. His feet were massaged and other things were
done to remove his exhaustion. He[329] then asked him, "O dear
one! O extremely fortunate one! Is our friend, Shura's son,[330] well?
Has he been freed and is he surrounded by his well-wishers? It is
good fortune that the evil Kamsa has been killed, along with his
followers, because of his own sins. He has always hated the virtuous
Yadus, who are devoted to dharma. Does Krishna remember us,
his mother, his well-wishers, his friends and the gopas? He is the

[327] Type of duck.
[328] Krishna.
[329] Nanda.
[330] That is, Vasudeva.

protector of Vraja. Does he remember the cows, Vrindavana and
the mountain? Will Govinda return at least once, to see his own
people? It is only then that we will be able to see his face, with the
excellent nose and the smiling glances. We were saved from the
forest conflagration, the storm, the rain, the bull[331] and the snake,
deadly dangers extremely difficult to cross, by the extremely great-
souled Krishna. O dear one! When we remember Krishna's valour,
his pastimes, sidelong glances, smiles and conversation, all our
activities become slack. When we see the rivers, mountains, forests
and regions that were adorned by his feet and where he played,
our minds become immersed in him. Just as Garga said, I think
that Krishna and Rama are two supreme gods who have come to
this world for some great purpose of the gods. As if playing, like a
king of deer with animals, they killed Kamsa, who possessed the
strength of ten thousand elephants, the two wrestlers and the king
of elephants. Like a king of elephants with a staff, he shattered an
extremely strong bow that was three *tala*s long.[332] With a single
hand, he held the mountain up for seven days. As if he was playing,
he killed Pralamba, Dhenuka, Arishta, Trinavarta, Baka and other
daityas who had defeated the gods and the asuras." Thus, with
his mind devoted to Krishna, Nanda repeatedly remembered this.
Extremely anxious and overwhelmed by the force of his love, he
then fell silent. Yashoda heard the description of her son's conduct.
As she heard, tears flowed and the affection made milk flow from
her breasts.

'Uddhava was delighted to see the great devotion Nanda and
Yashoda had towards the illustrious Krishna. Uddhava said, "O
revered one! The two of you are certainly the most praiseworthy
among all those who have bodies in this world. You possess this
kind of attachment towards Narayana, the preceptor who created
everything. These two, Rama and Mukunda, are Purusha and
Pradhana. They were the seed and the womb of the universe. They
are the two ancient ones, the lords of knowledge, whose signs can
be detected inside all creatures. At the time of death, if a person

---

[331] Arishta.
[332] Thrice the length of a palm tree.

fixes his mind on him even for an instant, his impurities and store of
karma are swiftly destroyed. He obtains the complexion of the sun
and full of the brahman, achieves the supreme objective. Narayana
is the cause behind everything. He has assumed this mortal form for
a specific purpose. You possess greatest devotion towards the great-
souled one. How can there be any other good deeds left for the
two of you to accomplish? Within a short period of time, Achyuta,
the illustrious lord of the Satvatas, will return to Vraja to bring
pleasure to his parents. Krishna told you that he would return after
killing Kamsa, the enemy of all the Satvatas, in the arena and he
will certainly fulfil that pledge. O immensely fortunate ones! Do not
be distressed. You will see Krishna in your presence. Just as fire is
hidden inside kindling, he exists in the hearts of all creatures. He is
beyond attachment. There is no one whom he loves and there is no
one whom he hates. He is impartial towards everyone and no one is
his superior, inferior or equal. He has no mother or father, no wife,
sons, or other relatives. There is no one who is his own. There is
no one who is not his own. He has no body and no birth. He has
no karma. For his pastimes and to protect the virtuous, he assumes
birth in this world as superior, inferior and mixed species.[333] Though
he is devoid of gunas, he assumes the sattva, rajas and tamas gunas.
As part of his pastimes, he uses these gunas to create, preserve
and destroy. If one is being whirled around, to the eye it seems as
if the ground is revolving. In that way, it is said that because of
ahamkara, one takes oneself to be the agent, though the real agent
is consciousness.[334] Indeed, the illustrious Hari is not only your son.
He is the lord and is the son, atman, father and mother of everyone.
Nothing that has been seen, nothing that has been heard, nothing
that has happened, nothing that is happening, nothing that will
happen, the mobile and the immobile, the large and the small—do
not exist without Achyuta. He cannot be described in words. He is
the paramatman, manifested in everything.'

[333] Respectively, human, subhuman and Narasimha avataras.
[334] Depending on the interpretation, this is also translated in a slightly
different way.

Shri-Shuka continued, 'O king! Nanda and Krishna's companion conversed in this way and the night passed. The gopis awoke and lit the lamps. They worshipped the household deities and started to churn the milk. As they pulled on the ropes, the light of the lamps reflected on their shining jewels and the rows of bangles on their hands. Their hips, breasts, necklaces and earrings moved. Their cheeks glowed and their faces were red with kunkuma. The women of Vraja loudly sang about the lotus-eyed one and the sound rose up and touched the sky. This mixed with the sound of the churning, and everything inauspicious in the various directions was dispelled. When the illustrious sun rose, the residents of Vraja noticed the chariot made out of molten gold in front of Nanda's gate. They asked, "Whom does this belong to? Has Akrura, the one who accomplished Kamsa's task of taking away the lotus-eyed Krishna to Madhu's city, arrived? What will he accomplish for his master now? Will he perform funeral rites for us?" While the women were speaking in this way, having finished his morning ablutions, Uddhava arrived there.'

Chapter 10(47)

Shri-Shuka said, 'Krishna's companion possessed long arms and his eyes were like freshly bloomed lotuses. He was attired in yellow garments and adorned with a garland of lotuses. As a result of sparkling earrings, his lotus face was radiant. On seeing him, the women of Vraja were exceedingly surprised. "Who is this, so handsome to behold? Where has he come from? Why are his garments and ornaments like those of Achyuta?" Saying this, all of them, who had sought refuge at Uttamashloka's feet, surrounded him. They humbly bowed down to him and honoured him well, with bashful and smiling glances and delightful words. They understood that he was carrying a message from Rama's lord. Therefore, once he was seated, they asked him in private. "We know that you are an attendant of the Lord of Yadu. You have come here because you have been so instructed by your master, who wishes to bring pleasure to his parents. Otherwise, there is nothing in this Vraja of cattle that is worth remembering. Even for a sage, the bonds of affection towards a relative are extremely difficult to cast aside. The friendship towards others is mockery, because it is driven by a specific purpose and lasts until the objective has been accomplished. It is like the conduct of men towards women, or that of bees towards flowers. Courtesans abandon a person who possesses nothing and subjects an incompetent king. Once they have obtained the knowledge and paid the dakshina, officiating priests abandon their preceptor. When the fruit has been eaten, birds abandon a tree. Once he has eaten, a guest abandons a household. Animals abandon a forest that has been burnt down. After enjoyment, a lover abandons a devoted woman." The words, bodies and minds of the gopis were immersed in Govinda. When Uddhava, Krishna's messenger, arrived, they forgot about worldly norms and met him. They sang about their beloved one's deeds. Forgetting all shame, they wept. They repeatedly remembered his infancy and childhood.

'A gopi thought about her union with Krishna. She saw a bee and thought that it was a messenger sent by her beloved. She addressed it in the following words. The gopis[335] said, "O bee! You are the friend of someone who is deceitful. Do not touch our feet with your beard.[336] It is stained with kunkuma from his garland, when it pressed against the breasts of our rival.[337] Let the lord of Madhu show his favours to those proud women. Why has he sent a messenger like you? In an assembly of the Yadus, this will be looked upon as deceit. He confounded us by making us drink the nectar of his lips only once. After that, he immediately abandoned us, like you abandon a flower. How does Padma[338] serve his lotus feet? Indeed, she must also have lost her mind because of Uttamashloka's conversation. O one with six legs! We are without homes. Why are you singing so much about the lord of the Yadus in front of us? This is old stuff for us. Sing about these

---

[335] The plural is used, but it is clearly a single gopi speaking.
[336] The hair on the bee.
[337] The women from Mathura.
[338] Lakshmi, the one who is seated on a lotus.

topics before the female friends of Vijaya's friend.[339] He is relieving
the wounds in their breasts now. They will give you whatever you
wish for. No woman in heaven, earth or *rasatala*[340] is unavailable
to him. He is deceitful, with a beautiful smile. His eyebrows are
arched. The goddess of prosperity worships the dust of his feet.
Who are we? However, wretched people like us have the words
about Uttamashloka on their side. Remove your head from my feet.
I know you as Mukunda's messenger. Therefore, you are learned
in entreating and flattery. We gave up our husbands, children and
everything else in this world. However, his mind is ungrateful and
he has himself given us up. What reconciliation is possible with
him? Like a hunter, he followed the dharma of a hunter and pierced
the Indra among the apes.[341] He was vanquished by a woman and
disfigured a woman who desired him.[342] Like a crow, he ate Bali's
offerings and thereafter, bound him up. Therefore, even though we
can't give up hearing about him, enough of friendship with that
dark one. Hearing about his pastimes and deeds only once is like
nectar to the ears. It cleanses and destroys the proclivities of the
opposite pair of sentiments. The listeners immediately give up their
homes and miserable families. Behaving like many wretched birds,
they follow the practice of begging for a living. We trusted him and
took his deceitful words to be true. We are like does, the wives of
a black antelope, ignorant about the songs sung by a hunter. On
many occasions, we have seen and felt the fierce pain of desire,
caused by his nails. O messenger! Please speak about something
else. O friend of my beloved! Why have you returned? Has he sent
you again? O dear one! O respected one! Please ask what you wish
for. O amiable one! Union with him is extremely difficult to give
up. But how will you take us to his side? Shri, his consort, is always
with him, right on his chest. Unfortunately, the son of the noble

[339] Vijaya is Arjuna's name. Vijaya's friend is an indirect way of
referring to Krishna.
[340] There are seven nether regions—*atala, vitala, sutala,* rasatala,
talatala, mahatala and *patala.*
[341] As Rama, the Indra among the apes being Vali.
[342] Respectively Sita and Shurpanakha.

one[343] is now in Madhu's city. O amiable one! Does he remember his father's house and his friends, the gopas? Does he ever talk about us, his female servants? When will he rest his hands, fragrant with the scent of aloe, on our heads?" The gopis were anxious to see Krishna. Hearing them, Uddhava comforted them and told them about the message sent by their beloved.

'Uddhava said, "It is certain that you have accomplished your objectives and are worshipped by the worlds. You have dedicated your minds to the illustrious Vasudeva. Devotion towards Krishna is brought about through donations, vows, austerities, oblations, chanting, studying, self-control and many other kinds of superior modes. However, your devotion towards Uttamashloka is supreme. It is through good fortune that you have obtained this devotion, which is extremely difficult for even sages to get. It is through good fortune that you gave up your sons, husbands, bodies, own relatives and houses and sought out the supreme Purusha who is known as Krishna. O immensely fortunate ones! With all your souls, you have obtained this devotion to Adhokshaja as a right, even at a time of separation. You have shown me a favour by displaying it to me. Now listen to the message sent by your beloved. It will bring you pleasure. O fortunate ones! I have come here with my master's private message. The illustrious one said, 'Since I am in all atmans, you can never be separated from me. Just as the elements, space, air, fire, water and the earth exist in all beings, I am present in the mind, the breath of life, the senses and the store of gunas in all beings. Through the maya of my own powers, the elements, the senses and the gunas, I use my own self to create, preserve and destroy within my own self. The atman is full of pure jnana and is distinct from the aggregation of the gunas. It can be perceived in the states of wakefulness, dreaming and deep sleep,[344] created by maya. The objects of the senses are like what one sees in a dream. Even when one is not asleep, one thinks about them and runs after them in vain. Therefore, one should restrain the senses. The learned say that this is the objective of the traditional texts, yoga, samkhya,

[343] Meaning Nanda.
[344] *Sushupti.*

renunciation, austerities, self-control and truth—like rivers heading towards the ocean. I, your beloved, am now far distant from your sight. This is with the objective of attracting your minds towards me, while you desire me and meditate on me. The minds of women are such that when a beloved person is nearby, in front of their eyes, they are not as attracted to him as they are when he is far away. Since your minds are completely immersed in me and you have freed yourself from all other pursuits, since you always remember me, within a short while, you will obtain me. O fortunate ones! There were some who had to remain in Vraja. Consequently, they could not enjoy the rasa pastimes with me in the forest in the night. Nevertheless, because they thought about my valour, they will obtain me.'"

Shri-Shuka continued, 'Thus, the women of Vraja heard the instructions of their beloved. The message revived their memories. Rejoicing, they addressed Uddhava in these words.

'The gopis said, "It is good fortune that Kamsa, who caused injury to the Yadus, has been killed, along with his followers. It is good fortune that Achyuta has accomplished all his objectives and is now happily residing with his relatives. O amiable one! He brought us pleasure and we worshipped him with gentle and bashful smiles. Is Gada's elder brother doing that to the women of the city now and are they casting their generous glances on him? He is accomplished in bringing pleasure and he is loved by the women of the city. Worshipped by their words and bewildering behaviour, how can he not be bound down by them? O virtuous one! In the course of conversations, does Govinda remember us? In the midst of an assembly of urban women, is he free to mention those from the village? Does he remember the nights with his beloved ones in Vrindavana, enchanting with night lotuses, jasmine and the moon? In the midst of the rasa assembly, anklets jingling on the feet, he enjoyed himself with us. There was a time when we glorified his charming accounts. Will Dasharha ever come here? Because of what he has himself done, we are tormented and grieving. Will his limbs bring us back to life, just as Indra's showers do to the forest? But why will Krishna come here? He has won the kingdom and killed those who caused him injury. He has married the daughters of the kings.

Surrounded by all his well-wishers, he is happy. The great-souled one is Shri's lord. He is complete in himself and has accomplished all his desires. What purpose of his can be accomplished by us, who reside in the forest, or by the others? There is supreme bliss when there is no desire left. The *svairini* Pingala said that.[345] Though we know this, it is impossible to give up the hope of seeing Krishna. Who will be interested in giving up conversations with Uttamashloka? Though he does not desire her, rarely does Shri move away from his body. O lord! With Samkarshana, Krishna roamed around here, in these rivers, the mountain, the forest regions, amidst the cows and the sounds of the flute. Indeed, they repeatedly remind us about Nanda gopa's son. The place is marked with his footprints, Shri's refuge. We are incapable of forgetting him. His gait, his charming and generous smiles, his pastimes, his glances and his sweet words have stolen our hearts. How can we forget him? O lord! O Rama's lord! O lord of Vraja! O destroyer of suffering! O Govinda! Gokula is submerged in an ocean of grief. Please raise us up."'

Shri-Shuka continued, 'They were suffering from fever because of the separation, and Krishna's message relieved them. They realized that Uddhava was no different from Adhokshaja and honoured him.[346] He resided there for some months, dispelling the grief of the gopis. Singing about accounts of Krishna's pastimes, he delighted Gokula. For the residents of Vraja, the days that Uddhava lived in Vraja, speaking about Krishna, seemed to pass like an instant.[347] Hari's servant found pleasure in looking at the rivers, forest, mountain, valleys and flowering trees and reminded the residents of Vraja about Krishna. He saw that the gopis were disturbed because of their complete absorption in Krishna. Uddhava was greatly delighted. He bowed down to them and said, "Among all those who possess bodies on earth, the gopa women are supreme.

[345] Svairinis are loose women who have sex with anyone they want, but only with those from the same varna. Here, the word is being used in a broader sense of a courtesan. Pingala's story will be told in the Eleventh Skandha.

[346] There is scope for interpretation. Alternatively, they realized that Adhokshaja was within themselves.

[347] Kshana.

They have perfected their sentiments towards Govinda, who is in all atmans. This is a state desired by sages, and us, who are scared of samsara. If one does not savour the account of the infinite one, what is the point of being born as a brahmana?[348] These women roam around in the forest and are contaminated by their improper conduct.[349] But they have perfected their sentiments towards Krishna, the paramatman. The lord himself certainly confers benefit on those who worship him, even if they are ignorant, just as the king of medicines does,[350] even when it is unwillingly imbibed. In the festival of rasa, the necks of the women of Vraja were embraced by his arms and they obtained this great benediction. Though Shri is on his chest and is constantly associated with him, she does not obtain this favour. Nor do celestial women, whose fragrance and beauty are like those of lotuses. What need be said about others? I desire to be the shrubs, creepers and herbs of Vrindavana, since they have been touched by the dust of their feet.[351] They gave up the noble path and their own relatives, which are so very difficult to cast aside. They worshipped Mukunda's footprints, which the sacred texts seek to search out. The illustrious Krishna's lotus feet are worshipped by Shri, Aja[352] and the lords of yoga, who have accomplished all their desires. In the assembly of rasa, he placed them on their breasts. They embraced these and all their torments were dispelled. I repeatedly bow down to the dust on the feet of the women of Nanda's Vraja. When they sing about Hari's account, they purify the three worlds." After this, Dasharha[353] took his leave of the gopis, Yashoda, Nanda and the gopas. Ready to leave, he mounted his chariot. As he emerged, Nanda and the others affectionately approached him, with many kinds of gifts in their hands. With tears in their eyes, they said, "May our minds and our deeds seek refuge at Krishna's lotus feet. May our words utter

---

[348] Or, what is the point of being born as Brahma?
[349] In the eyes of their husbands and families.
[350] The king of medicines is interpreted as amrita, drunk by the gods.
[351] That of the gopis.
[352] Brahma.
[353] Uddhava.

his names. May our bodies be engaged in bowing down to him. Wherever we are whirled around in our karma, through the wishes of the lord, through our auspicious conduct and gifts, may we be attached to the lord, Krishna." O lord of men! Uddhava was thus honoured by the gopas, who were driven by their devotion towards Krishna. He again returned to Mathura, protected by Krishna. He bowed down before Krishna and told him about the great devotion of the residents of Vraja. He gave Vasudeva, Rama and the king the gifts.'[354]

Chapter 10(48)

Shri-Shuka said, 'The illustrious one could see everything and was in all atmans. He knew that the *sairindhri*[355] was tormented by desire. Desiring to bring her pleasure, he went to her house. It was filled with extremely expensive furnishings. Everything that could be used to satisfy desire was there. There were strings of pearls, flags, canopies, beds and seats. It was decorated with fragrant incense, lamps, garlands and perfumes. Seeing that he was arriving, she was filled with respect and immediately stood up from her seat. With her friends, she came forward to meet Achyuta and respectfully offered him an excellent seat and other objects. As a virtuous person, Uddhava was also honoured. But having touched the seat offered, he sat down on the ground. Krishna followed the conduct observed by people and quickly entered the chamber with an extremely expensive bed. She bathed and anointed herself, attiring herself in garments and ornaments. She prepared garlands, perfumes, betel leaves and fragrant asava and approached Madhava. She glanced at him, with bashful and playful smiles. He summoned the beautiful one, who was bashful and scared because this was a new encounter. He held her by her ornamented hands and made her sit on the bed. Her only good act had been that of offering

---

[354] Here, Vasudeva means Krishna's father and the king is Ugrasena.
[355] Trivakra.

him unguents. However, he enjoyed himself with the beautiful one. Ananga had led to her breasts, chest and eyes being inflamed. But as soon as she inhaled Ananta's feet, those wounds were healed. With both arms, she embraced her beloved one against her breasts. He was the embodiment of bliss and she gave away the torment she had suffered from for a long time. Having offered him unguents, she had obtained the lord of kaivalya, the lord who is so difficult to obtain. The unfortunate one entreated him in these words. "O beloved one! Please spend a few days with me. O lotus-eyed one! Enjoy yourself with me. I cannot bear to give up your companionship." The one who shows honours honoured her and granted her the boon of satisfying desire. With Uddhava, the lord of everything then returned to his own prosperous residence. Vishnu, the lord of all the lords, is extremely difficult to please. Having worshipped him, only an ignorant person will ask for a boon that will please the mind, but is unreal.[356]

'With Uddhava and Rama, the lord Krishna then went to Akrura's house. He desired to bring pleasure to Akrura and also wished to get a task accomplished. From a distance, he saw those best among men, his relatives, approaching. Delighted, he stood up and embraced and honoured them. He bowed down to Krishna and Rama and was honoured by them. Following the recommended rites, when they had seated themselves, he worshipped them. O king! He bathed their feet and sprinkled that water on his head. He gave them expensive garments, divine fragrances, garlands and excellent ornaments. He lowered his head down and worshipped them, taking their feet on his lap and massaging them. Bent down in humility, Akrura spoke to Krishna and Rama. "It is good fortune that you have killed the wicked Kamsa and his followers. You have saved the lineage from endless suffering and have ensured prosperity. The two of you are Pradhana and Purusha. You are the cause behind the universe and you pervade the universe. Without you, neither cause, nor effect, exists. Using your own powers, you have created this universe and have entered it. O brahman! Through

---

[356] This is a reference to the boon asked for by Trivakra.

hearing[357] and direct sight, you are perceived in many kinds of ways. The elements, earth and the others, manifest themselves as different species, mobile and immobile objects. In that way, you alone are the source of everything. You are the atman who controls himself and is manifest in diverse forms. Through your own powers and the gunas of sattva, rajas and tamas, you create, preserve and destroy the universe. But you are not bound down by gunas and karma. Your atman consists of jnana. What can cause you bondage? The body and other such restrictions are not noticed for you. The atman has no birth or differentiation. Therefore, there is no bondage or liberation for you. Perhaps we see you in that way because of our lack of discrimination, or because you desire that it should be like that. For the sake of the welfare of the universe, you expounded the ancient path of the Vedas. Whenever that path is restricted by evil heretics, you manifest yourself in your attribute of sattva. You are that lord and you have now descended in Vasudeva's house in your portion, so as to remove the burden of the earth. You have hence slaughtered one hundred akshouhinis of kings who were the portions of others, and not of the gods. You have done this to extend the fame of the lineage. Today, our homes have indeed been filled with fortune. You are the embodied form of all the gods, ancestors, creatures and kings. The water that washes your feet purifies the three worlds. O Adhokshaja! You are the preceptor of the universe and you have entered our home today. You are affectionate towards your devotees and your words are always true. You are a well-wisher. You are grateful. Which learned person will go to anyone else for refuge? As a well-wisher, you give those who worship you everything that they want, even your own self, which never diminishes, or increases. O Janardana! It is good fortune that you are now manifest before us. This is an objective that the lords of yoga and lords among the gods find very difficult to obtain. Quickly sever the cords of affection towards sons, wives, wealth, homes, bodies and everything else. All this is the result of your maya." The illustrious Hari was thus worshipped and praised by his devotee. He smiled and enchanted Akrura with his words. The illustrious

[357] From the sacred texts.

one said, "You are our preceptor, paternal uncle and a relative who is always praised. We are like your sons, whom you protect and nurture with compassion. Immensely fortunate ones like you are supreme among those who should be worshipped and served. The gods always hanker after what brings them benefit, but virtuous ones are not driven by selfish motives. Unlike the sight of virtuous ones, tirthas with water and gods made out of earth purify after a long period of time.[358] You are our well-wisher. For our benefit and desiring to do benefit to the Pandavas, go to Gajasahvya[359] and ask how they are. When their father passed away, along with their mother, those children were extremely miserable. We have heard that the king[360] brought them to his own city and made them live there. The king, Ambika's son, is inferior in intelligence and is blind. He is under the control of his wicked son and it is certain that he does not treat his brother's sons impartially. Go and ascertain his present conduct, whether it is virtuous or wicked. When we have found out, we will act so as to bring welfare to our well-wishers." The illustrious lord Hari told Akrura this. With Samkarshana and Uddhava, he then left for his own residence.'

Chapter 10(49)

Shri-Shuka said, 'He went to Hastinapura, ornamented by the fame of Indras among the Pourava lineage. He saw Ambika's son, along with Bhishma, Vidura, Pritha, Bahlika and his son,[361] Bharadvaja's descendant,[362] Goutama's descendant,[363] Karna,

[358] The sight of virtuous ones purifies instantly, while tirthas and gods have to be worshipped for a long time.
[359] Hastinapura.
[360] Dhritarashtra. Dhritarashtra's mother was Ambika. While Dhritarashtra was physically blind, the blindness can also be taken to be metaphorical. Dhritarashtra's son was Duryodhana.
[361] Somadatta.
[362] Drona.
[363] Kripa.

Suyodhana,[364] Drona's son,[365] the Pandavas and other well-wishers. Gandini's son[366] met all the relatives in the proper way. He asked the well-wishers about their welfare and in turn, they asked him whether he himself was well. Desiring to find out about the king's conduct, he lived with them for some months. He had wicked sons. His own mind was feeble and he followed the wishes of deceitful ones.[367] The Parthas were powerful, energetic, strong, humble and possessed excellent qualities. They were loved by the subjects and Dhritarashtra's sons could not tolerate this. They gave them poison and committed other unworthy acts. Pritha and Vidura told him everything about all this. Pritha approached her brother Akrura, who had come.[368] She remembered the place where she had been born and spoke to him with tears in her eyes. "O amiable one! Do my parents and brothers remember me? What about my sisters, brother's sons, the women and friends? My brother's son, the illustrious Krishna, is the refuge of all those who are devoted to him. Does he remember his father's sister? What about Rama, whose eyes are like lotus petals? I am grieving amidst my enemies, like a doe in the midst of wolves. Will he comfort me and the fatherless sons with his words? O Krishna! O great yogi! O Krishna! O atman of the universe! O creator of the universe! O Govinda! I am seeking refuge with you. Save me. I, and my children, are suffering. Men are scared of death and samsara and you are the lord who confers emancipation. With the exception of your lotus feet, I do not see any other refuge. I bow down to the pure Krishna, the brahman and the paramatman. O lord of yoga! O embodiment of yoga! I seek refuge with you." In this way, she remembered her own relatives and Krishna, the lord of the universe. O king! Your great grandmother wept in grief. Akrura was indifferent towards joy and misery. He,

[364] Duryodhana is often referred to as Suyodhana.

[365] Ashvatthama.

[366] Akrura.

[367] By deceitful, one presumably means Shakuni, though Shakuni is not named.

[368] Pritha/Kunti and Akrura were cousins.

and the immensely illustrious Vidura, comforted Kunti and told her the reason behind the birth of her sons.

'The king behaved partially because of affection towards his sons. Before leaving, he[369] approached him when he was in the midst of his well-wishers and told him what his relatives and well-wishers[370] had said. Akrura said, "O son of Vichitravirya! O extender of the fame of the Kuru lineage! After your brother, Pandu, died, you have ascended to the throne. Follow dharma and protect the earth. Delight the subjects with your good conduct. If you act impartially, you will ensure your own benefit and obtain fame. However, if you act in a contrary way, you will be condemned in this world and head towards darkness. Therefore, let your conduct towards the Pandavas and your own sons be impartial. O king! In this world, one can never live permanently with anyone else. That is true of one's own body, not to speak of wives, sons and others. Every creature is born alone and dies alone. The fruits of good deeds and wicked deeds are enjoyed alone. If a person with limited intelligence acquires wealth through adharma, this is taken away by others, who go by the false name of those who should be nurtured.[371] This is like water being taken away from an aquatic creature. An ignorant person uses adharma to nurture his breath of life, wealth, sons and other things, taking these to be his own. But all of these abandon him and he is unsuccessful. He does not know what is good for him. Forsaken by them, he has to himself bear his sins. Withdrawing from his own dharma, his objectives remain unfulfilled and he enters blinding darkness. O king! Therefore, look upon this world as a dream, maya or unreal wishes. O lord! Use your atman to control yourself and be impartial and serene." Dhritarashtra replied, "O Danapati![372] The words that you have spoken are beneficial and I am not satisfied with them. I am like a mortal person who has obtained amrita. O amiable one! However, these well-spoken words will not remain fixed in my heart, but are

---

[369] Akrura.
[370] Krishna and the others.
[371] The wealth is enjoyed by sons.
[372] Akrura was generous in giving gifts and was known as Danapati.

as fickle as lightning in a cloud. I am partial because of affection towards my sons. Who can shake off what the lord has determined? Which man can act in a contrary way? To remove the burden of the earth, he has now descended in the lineage of the Yadus. It is impossible to decipher his path. Using his own maya, he creates the gunas, distributes them and enters them. I bow down before the one who cannot be fathomed. Through his pastimes, he controls this wheel of samsara. He is the supreme lord and destination." The Yadava thus ascertained the king's intentions. Taking the permission of the well-wishers, he returned again to the city of the Yadus. O Kouravya! He told Rama and Krishna about Dhritarashtra's behaviour towards the Pandavas. That is the reason why he had been sent.'

Chapter 10(50)

Shri-Shuka said, 'O bull among the Bharata lineage! Kamsa's two queens were Asti and Prapti. When their husband was dead, they were afflicted by grief and went to their father's house. Miserable, they told their father, Jarasandha, the king of Magadha, everything about themselves and about how they had become widows. O king! Hearing this unpleasant news, he was filled with sorrow and intolerance. He made a supreme effort to ensure that no Yadavas would be left on earth. He surrounded himself with twenty-three akshouhinis and from every direction, laid siege to Mathura, the capital of the Yadus. Krishna saw that army, which was like an ocean crossing the limits of the shoreline. It had laid siege to his own city and his own relatives were afflicted by fear. Though the illustrious Hari was the cause behind everything, for a specific purpose, he had assumed the form of a human avatara. Therefore, he thought about what would be appropriate to the time and the place. "To remove the earth's burden, I will destroy the army that has gathered. It has been brought together by the king of Magadha and all the kings are following his command. There are many akshouhinis, consisting of foot soldiers, horses, chariots

and elephants. However, since he will make efforts to raise another
army again, the king of Magadha should not be killed.[373] This is
the reason I assumed this avatara, to remove the earth's burden, to
protect the virtuous and to destroy the others. For the protection of
dharma and to bring an end to adharma, when it becomes powerful
on some occasions, I assume other bodies." While Govinda was
thinking in this way, two chariots instantly descended from the
sky. They were as radiant as the sun and possessed charioteers and
the requisite equipment. On their own, ancient celestial weapons
appeared. Seeing these, Hrishikesha spoke to Samkarshana. "O
lord! Behold the catastrophe that your own Yadus face. This
chariot has arrived, with your beloved weapons. O lord! This is
the reason the two of us have taken birth, to ensure benefit to
the virtuous. Act so as to remove the earth's burden, in the form
of these twenty-three armies." Having consulted in this way, the
two Dasharhas armoured themselves. With their own resplendent
weapons, they emerged from the city on their two chariots. They
were only surrounded by a small army.

'With Daruka as his charioteer, Hari emerged and blew on
his conch shell and this made the hearts of the enemy soldiers
tremble. Magadha[374] looked at them and said, "O Krishna! O worst
among men! I do not wish to fight with you. You are a child and
are alone. That would be a shame. You are evil and the slayer of
relatives. You have hidden yourself.[375] O Rama! If you have faith
and perseverance, muster those and fight. Either kill me, or give up
your body, when it is shattered with my arrows, and go to heaven."
The illustrious one replied, "Those who are really brave do not
boast. Instead, they exhibit their manliness. O king! We do not
accept the words of those who are afflicted[376] and are about to die."

---

[373] Krishna's intention is to kill all the wicked kings, not only the ones
who have assembled at the moment. Therefore, Jarasandha should remain
alive, so that he can raise more armies.

[374] Jarasandha.

[375] As Nanda's son.

[376] This can be interpreted as Jarasandha's affliction because of his son-
in-law's death.

Jara's son[377] advanced towards the two Madhavas. He surrounded
them with an immensely large and powerful army, with soldiers,
vehicles, standards, horses and chariots, just as the sun is covered
with clouds, or a fire is covered with dust particles raised by the
wind. The women of the city were positioned on the tops of houses,
mansions and turrets. They could no longer see the chariots of Hari
and Rama in the battle, with standards of Garuda and the palm
tree.[378] They were afflicted by grief and lost their senses. The army
of the enemy was like a mass of clouds that repeatedly showered
down sharp arrows, like terrible showers of rain. Hari saw that
his own soldiers were suffering as a result of this. He twanged
the excellent Sharnga bow, worshipped by gods and asuras. He
picked up arrows from his quiver and affixed them. He drew his
bow back and released volleys of sharp arrows. Whirling the bow
like a circle of fire, he incessantly slew elephants, horses and foot
soldiers. With their temples shattered, elephants fell down. Their
necks severed by arrows, many horses simultaneously fell down.
Chariots were shattered, their horses, standards, charioteers and
warriors destroyed. The arms, thighs and necks of foot soldiers were
severed. The limbs of bipeds, elephants and horses were mangled
and hundreds of streams of blood started to flow. The arms were
like snakes.[379] The heads of the men were like tortoises. The slain
elephants were like islands. The horses were like crocodiles. The
hands and thighs were like fish. The hair of the men was like moss.
The bows were like waves and the waves were like tangles of weeds.
The wheels[380] were like terrible whirlpools. The extremely expensive
and excellent ornaments were like stones and gravel. In the battle,
these flows caused terror to cowards and caused delight to those
who were spirited. Samkarshana, infinite in his energy, used his
club to slay the indomitable enemies. O dear one! That army was
protected by the Indra among the Magadhas. It was impossible to

[377] Jarasandha was born in two pieces and these were brought together
and revived by the demoness Jara.
[378] Respectively, the chariots of Krishna and Balarama.
[379] The comparison is with a river.
[380] Of the chariots. Alternatively, the shields.

penetrate and terrible. It was like an ocean where the distant shore is impossible to reach. However, Vasudeva's two sons conveyed it to its destruction. Those two supreme lords of the universe toyed with it. He is infinite in his qualities. Through his own pastimes, he brings about the creation, preservation and destruction of the three worlds. Therefore, it was not extraordinary that he should subjugate the enemy's army. However, when he follows the behaviour of a mortal, this is fit to be described.

'The immensely strong Jarasandha was without his chariot and Rama seized him, just as a lion forcibly seizes another lion. His army had been destroyed and he was the only one who was alive. He had killed his enemies in the past and was now bound up with human bonds and those of Varuna. However, Govinda still had a task that he desired to use him for. Therefore, he restrained him.[381] He was freed by the two protectors of the worlds. Revered by brave ones, he was now ashamed. He resolved to perform austerities. But along the way, he was restrained by kings. They used words that achieve purposes of purification, as well as ordinary norms of good policy.[382] "Your defeat at the hands of the Yadus is because of the bondage of your own karma." With all his armies destroyed, the king who was Brihadratha's son returned to Magadha. Having been slighted by the illustrious one, his mind was distressed. Mukunda had crossed the ocean that was the enemy's army with his own forces unharmed. The residents of heaven approved of what he had done and showered down flowers. Delighted and freed from their anxiety, the residents of Mathura approached him. Sutas, magadhas[383] and bandis sang about his victory. As the two lords entered the city, there was the sound from many conch shells, kettledrums, other drums, tambourines, veenas and flutes. The women gazed fondly at him, their eyes widened with love. They showered garlands, curds, unbroken grain and tender shoots. The lord gathered the large number of riches left on the battlefield by

---

[381] Balarama.

[382] Respectively, words from the sacred texts, as well as common maxims. Friendly kings restrained Jarasandha from retiring to the forest.

[383] Minstrels and bards who also composed.

the warriors and the ornaments of the warriors and presented these to the king of the Yadus.

'In this way, the king of the Magadhas and his army of askhouhinis fought against the Yadus seventeen times and was defeated, since they were protected by Krishna. Because of Krishna's energy, the Vrishnis destroyed all those armies. Though his own soldiers were destroyed, the enemy allowed the king to escape. The eighteenth encounter was about to commence. At that time, sent by Narada, the brave Yavana appeared.[384] He arrived and laid siege to Mathura with three crores of mlechchhas. In the world of men, he had heard that the Vrishnis were respected warriors who could fight against him. On seeing him, with Samkarshana as his aide, Krishna started to think. "From two sides, a great difficulty now presents itself before the Yadus. The Yavana has already arrived and has laid siege, with his large army. Either tomorrow, or the day after tomorrow, Magadha will also come here. While we are fighting against him, Jara's powerful son may arrive here and kill our relatives, or capture them and take them to his own city. Hence, we must now construct a fort that bipeds will find impossible to penetrate. When we have settled our relatives there, we will kill Yavana." Having consulted in this way, the illustrious one had a wonderful city constructed.

'Its entire circumference was twelve yojanas and it was inside the ocean. Tvashta's[385] accomplished knowledge of artisanship could be seen there. The roads, quadrangles and avenues were designed in conformity with principles of *vastu*.[386] There were divine trees and creepers in the gardens and there were wonderful groves. The golden summits reached up and touched the sky. The mansions and turrets were made out of crystal. There were treasure houses and stores made out of silver and brass, ornamented with golden pots. The golden houses had jewels on top. The floors were paved with extremely expensive emeralds. The upper floors of the

[384] Kalayavana asked Narada who would be good enough to fight against him and Narada mentioned the Yadavas.

[385] The architect of the gods.

[386] The science of architecture.

houses had shrines meant for the gods. It was full of people from
the four varnas and there were beautiful houses for the lords of the
Yadus. The great Indra gave Hari Sudharma and Parijata.[387] Despite
being a mortal, if one dwelt here, one was no longer subject to the
dharma of mortals.[388] Varuna gave horses that possessed the speed
of thought. These were white, but each possessed one black ear. The
lord of riches gave his store of eight treasures.[389] The guardians of the
worlds presented their own riches. O king! When he descended on
earth, the illustrious one had conferred various kinds of sovereignty
and powers on them. They returned all these to Hari. Through his
powers of yoga, Hari conveyed all the people there. Krishna advised
Rama about protecting the subjects. Wearing a garland of lotuses
and without any weapons, he then emerged through the city's gate.'

Chapter 10(51)

Shri-Shuka said, 'He[390] saw him emerge, like the rising moon.
He was beautiful to behold, dark in complexion and attired in
yellow silk garments. The shrivatsa mark was on his chest and his
neck was decorated with the radiant Koustubha. His arms were
long and mighty and his eyes were red, like a freshly bloomed lotus.
He was always cheerful. His excellent cheeks were beautiful and his
smile was pure. His lotus face shone, due to the sparkling earrings
in the form of makaras.[391] "This being is indeed Vasudeva. He

---

[387] Sudharma is the assembly hall of the gods and Parijata is Indra's
celestial coral tree.

[388] We have taken liberties with the text in this sentence, since the
meaning isn't obvious. Does it mean within Sudharma? Does it mean near
the Parijata tree? We have interpreted it more generally.

[389] Kubera's eight treasures (nidhi) are named Mahapadma (large lotus),
Padma (lotus), Shankha (conch shell), Kurma (tortoise), Nila (sapphire),
Kunda (jasmine), Kumuda (a jewel) and Makara. However, the list varies.

[390] Kalayavana.

[391] A makara is a mythical aquatic creature, but can loosely be
translated as shark or crocodile.

has the shrivatsa mark. He is four-armed and lotus-eyed. With a garland of wild flowers, he is exceedingly handsome. He displays the signs mentioned by Narada. It cannot be anyone else. However, he is without weapons and is walking on foot. Therefore, I will also not use weapons to fight with him." Yavana decided this and ran after him, when he[392] was running away, with his back towards him. He wished to seize the one whom even yogis find it extremely difficult to obtain. At every step, Hari seemed to be within the reach of his hands. He continued to show himself and led the lord of the Yavanas to a mountain cave that was far away. "You have been born in the lineage of the Yadus. It is not proper for you to flee." Since his inauspicious deeds had not yet been exhausted, he abused him in this way and followed him. Abused in this way, the illustrious one entered a cave in a mountain.[393] He[394] also entered and saw another man lying down there. "After having brought me to this distant place, he is now lying down, like a virtuous person." Taking him to be Achyuta, the foolish person struck out with his foot. He had been sleeping for a long period of time and slowly opened his eyes. He looked around in all the directions and saw him standing by his side. O descendant of the Bharata lineage! He glanced at him angrily. A fire was generated from his body and instantly reduced him to ashes.'

The king asked, 'O brahmana! What was the name of this man, the one who destroyed Yavana? Which lineage did he belong to? What was his valour? Why did he enter a cave and sleep there?'

Shri-Shuka replied, 'This great one was born in the lineage of the Ikshvakus and was Mandhata's son. He was known by the name of Muchukunda. He was devoted to brahmanas and to the truth. The large number of gods, led by Indra, were scared of the asuras and requested him to protect them. He protected them for a long period of time. When they obtained Guha[395] as their protector, they told

---

[392] Krishna.

[393] This cave has been identified as a lake near Dhavalapura (Dholapur), ten yojanas from Mathura. There used to be a mountain there earlier.

[394] Kalayavana.

[395] Kartikeya, Kumara.

Muchukunda, "O king! We have been protected by you. But you can now give up this hardship.[396] O brave one! You gave up your kingdom in the world of men, which was free of thorns. You gave up all your wishes and protected us. Your contemporary sons, queens, relatives, advisers, ministers and subjects no longer exist. They have faced the onset of time. The illustrious and undecaying lord, in the form of time, is more powerful than the powerful. Like a herder of animals with animals, time toys with subjects. O fortunate one! Ask for a boon from us, anything but kaivalya. The undecaying and illustrious lord, Vishnu, is alone capable of bestowing that." Thus addressed, the immensely illustrious one honoured the gods. Granted by the gods, he entered the cave and lay down there to sleep.[397] When Yavana was reduced to ashes, the illustrious bull among the Satvatas showed himself to the intelligent Muchukunda. He saw him, as dark as a cloud, attired in yellow silk garments. The shrivatsa mark was on his chest and he dazzled because of the radiant Koustubha. He was four-armed and beautiful, with the vaijayanti garland. His handsome face was pleasant and the earrings, shaped like makaras, were radiant. To the world of men, his affectionate and smiling glances were worth looking at. He was handsome and young. His proud gait was like that of a crazy king of deer. Though he was immensely intelligent, the king was overwhelmed by his indomitable energy. Scared, he asked gently.

'Muchukunda asked, "You have come to this desolate cave in the mountain. Who are you? This place is full of thorns, but you are wandering around on feet that are as tender as the petals of lotuses. Are you the energy that exists in all energetic beings? Are you the illustrious fire god? Are you Surya, Soma, the great Indra, or a guardian of the world? Or are you someone else? Among the three gods among the gods,[398] I think that you are the bull among beings.[399] As if with the radiance of a lamp, you have destroyed the

[396] To protect them, Muchukunda had gone to heaven, though he was unable to enjoy heaven, since he was busy fighting the asuras.

[397] Muchukunda asked for the boon that he might sleep for a long time. If anyone disturbed his sleep, he would instantly be reduced to ashes.

[398] Brahma, Vishnu and Shiva.

[399] That is, you are the most important of these three. Therefore, you are Vishnu.

darkness inside this cave. O bull among men! We wish to hear. If it
pleases you, please tell me truthfully about your own birth, deeds,
gotra and account. O tiger among men! We are from the Ikshvaku
lineage and are kshatra-bandhus. O lord! I am Youvanashva's son
and am known as Muchukunda.[400] After remaining awake for a long
period of time, I was exhausted. My senses were overwhelmed by
sleep. I desired to sleep in a secluded place. But just now, someone
woke me up. Indeed, that person was reduced to ashes because of
his wicked deed. O destroyer of enemies! After that, I noticed your
glorious form. Your energy is extremely difficult to tolerate. We are
incapable of looking at you for long. O immensely fortunate one!
My energy has been destroyed. You deserve to be respected by all
embodied beings."'

Shri-Shuka continued, 'The illustrious one, the creator of all
creatures, was thus addressed by the king. In a deep voice that
rumbled like the clouds, he laughed and replied.

'The illustrious one said, "O dear one! My births, deeds and
names run into thousands. Since they are infinite, even if I try, I
am incapable of enumerating them. Across many births, it may be
possible to count the number of particles of dust on earth. But it is
not possible to do that for my qualities, deeds, names and births.
O king! The supreme rishis enumerate my births and deeds in three
time periods,[401] but cannot reach the end. O dear one! Nevertheless,
listen to my words about the present period. In earlier times,
Virinchi asked to protect dharma and destroy the asuras who were
causing a burden on earth. I descended in the lineage of the Yadus,
in Anakadundubhi's house. Since I am Vasudeva's son, I am referred
to as Vasudeva.[402] I killed Kalanemi, born as Kamsa, and Pralamba
and the others who hated the virtuous. O king! I have ensured that
Yavana was consumed through your fierce glance. I have come
to this cave to show you my favours. I am devoted towards my
devotees and, earlier, you have worshipped me a lot. O royal sage!

[400] Yuvanashva's son was Mandhata. Mandhata's (Youvanashva's)
son was Muchukunda.

[401] Past, present and future.

[402] Vaasudeva.

Seek boons from me. I grant all objects of desire. Those who have satisfied me, never deserve to grieve."'

Shri-Shuka continued, 'Thus addressed, Muchukunda was filled with delight and bowed down to him. He remembered Garga's words and knew him to be the god Narayana.

'Muchukunda said, "O lord! People are confounded by your maya. Not realizing their own benefit, they do not worship you. For the sake of happiness, a man becomes attached to the home and women, which give rise to unhappiness. The state of being a human is extremely difficult to obtain. O unblemished one! Without making efforts, he obtains it and is not disfigured in his limbs. However, evil in his intelligence, he does not worship your lotus feet. Like an animal, he is blind and falls into the pit that is the home. O unvanquished one! This period spent by me has been futile. As a king, I have been intoxicated and have increased the prosperity of the kingdom. My intelligence has taken this mortal body to be the atman and I have been attached, with endless anxiety, to sons, wives, treasures and land. This body of mine is like a pot or a wall.[403] With exaggerated pride at being a lord among men, I have surrounded myself with chariots, elephants, horses, foot soldiers and formations. Ignoring you and extremely indomitable, I have roamed around the earth. An excessively intoxicated person thinks about what needs to be done. He lusts after material objects and his avarice increases. He ignores you and suddenly faces you. Like a hungry snake that licks its tongue and seizes a rat, you appear as a destroyer. Known as a lord of men, earlier, this body roamed around on chariots polished with gold and mad elephants. However, in the form of time, you are impossible to cross and reduce this body to what is known as excrement, worms or ashes.[404] Having wheeled around the directions and conquered them, thus having prevented any future fights, a man seats himself on a supreme throne, worshipped by kings who are his equal. O lord! In the home, he finds pleasure in sexual intercourse with women. But he is led around like a domesticated animal. He performs austerities

---

[403] That is, made of earth.
[404] Through predatory creatures, burial or cremation.

properly and devotes himself to those tasks. He refrains from objects of desire and performs donations in the hope that he might become the king of heaven. In the process, his thirst increases and there is no happiness. O Achyuta! When the material existence ends for such a wanderer, it is only then that there is an association with virtuous people. You are the lord of the superior and the inferior. It is only after association with the virtuous that one obtains the virtuous end of one's intelligence turning towards you. O lord! I think that you have shown me a favour by automatically severing my attachment towards the kingdom. This is what is desired by virtuous ones who worship you and by kings who rule over the entire earth, desiring the solitude of the forest. I desire nothing other than serving at your feet. O lord! Those who desire nothing crave this as a boon. O Hari! You are the one who grants emancipation. Having worshipped you, which noble person will ask for a boon that leads to the bondage of his atman? O lord! Therefore, I completely cast aside all benedictions that lead to the bonds of the gunas and of sattva, rajas and tamas. You are *niranjana*.[405] You are *nirguna*.[406] You are without duality. You are supreme. You are only knowledge. You are Purusha. I will approach you. For a very long time, I have suffered from the travails of this world and have been tormented by remorse. The six enemies[407] are never satiated and I have never obtained peace. O paramatman! I approach you and seek refuge at your lotus feet. O lord! You are freedom from fear. You are immortality. You are freedom from sorrow. I seek refuge with you. Save me."

'The illustrious one replied, "O universal emperor! O great king! Your intelligence is clear and without blemish. I tempted you with boons, but you did not fall prey to desire. Know that I tempted you with boons so that you did not get distracted. Those with single-minded devotion towards me are not distracted by benedictions. O king! Those who are not devotees seek to control their minds

---

[405] Without taints.

[406] The one without qualities or attributes, the brahman.

[407] The five senses and the mind.

with *pranayama*[408] and other techniques. But it is seen that their desire is not destroyed and rises again. With your mind immersed in me, roam the earth as you will. May it always be such that your devotion towards me does not waver. You followed the dharma of kshatriyas. Through hunting and other means, you killed creatures. Therefore, controlling yourself and seeking refuge with me, perform austerities so that those sins are destroyed. O king! In your next life, you will be a supreme brahmana who is a well-wisher towards all creatures. You will only then obtain me.'"

Chapter 10(52)

Shri-Shuka said, 'O dear one! Thus favoured by Krishna, the descendant of the Ikshvaku lineage circumambulated him. He bowed down and emerged through the mouth of the cave. He saw that all mortal beings, animals, plants and trees were small in size. Deducing that kali yuga had arrived, he left for the northern direction.[409] The persevering one was full of devotion and engaged in austerities. He was free of attachment and free of doubts. He fixed his mind on Krishna and entered Gandhamadana. He reached Badarikashrama, the abode of Nara and Narayana. Tolerating all the opposite pairs of sentiments, he was tranquil. He performed austerities and worshipped Hari.

'The illustrious one returned to the city, which was still encircled by *yavanas*.[410] He slew the army of the mlechchhas and took their riches to Dvaraka. Urged by Achyuta, men used oxen to convey those riches. At that time, Jarasandha arrived, as the leader of twenty-three akshouhinis. O king! Seeing the waves of enemy soldiers, the two Madhavas imitated the behaviour of humans and quickly fled. Though they were not scared, they pretended to be

---

[408] Breathing.

[409] Kali yuga hadn't quite arrived, since it would set in after Krishna's death. However, it was imminent.

[410] Kalayavana was only the leader of the yavanas.

frightened and cast away that great store of riches. On feet that
were as tender as lotus petals, they travelled for many yojanas.
On seeing that the two of them were running away, the powerful
Magadha laughed. Not realizing the power of those two lords,
he pursued them with an army of chariots. After having fled for
a long distance, they were exhausted and ascended the summit of
the mountain known as Pravarshana. The illustrious one[411] always
showers down there. O king! Though they were hidden inside the
mountain, he could not discern their trail. Therefore, on every side
of the mountain, he placed kindling and lit a fire. The summit of the
mountain was eleven yojanas high. When the slopes started to burn,
they swiftly leapt up and jumped down on the ground. The two
supreme ones of the Yadu lineage were not noticed by the enemy or
his followers. O king! They again returned to their own city, where
the ocean acted like a moat. Magadha wrongly thought that Bala
and Keshava had been burnt down in the fire. Taking his extremely
large army with him, he returned to Magadha. The prosperous lord
of Anarta was Raivata. Urged by Brahma, he bestowed his daughter,
Revati, on Bala. This has been narrated earlier.[412] O extender of the
Kuru lineage! In a *svayamvara*,[413] the illustrious Govinda married
the daughter of Bhishmaka of Vidarbha. She was born as Shri's
portion. While all the worlds looked on, like Tarkshya's son[414]
taking away the nectar, he used his force to crush the kings, Shalva
and the others who were on Chedi's[415] side, to take her away.'

The king said, 'We have heard that the illustrious one married
the beautiful-faced Rukmini, the daughter of Bhishmaka, through
the rakshasa mode.[416] O illustrious one! I wish to hear how the

[411] Indra.

[412] Revata's son was Kakudmi/Raivata and his daughter was Revati.
This incident has been described in Chapter 9(3).

[413] Svayamvara is a ceremony where the maiden herself (*svayam*)
chooses her husband (*vara*) from assembled suitors.

[414] Garuda.

[415] Shishupala's.

[416] There were eight forms of marriage—some desirable, others less
so. One of these undesirable forms is rakshasa, where the bride is forcibly
abducted by the groom.

infinitely energetic Krishna defeated Magadha, Shalva and others and abducted the maiden. O brahmana! The sweet and sacred account of Krishna removes all impurities from the worlds. After listening to them, who can be satisfied? A person who is accomplished in hearing will always find them to be new.'

Shri-Shuka continued, 'There was a king named Bhishmaka and he was the great lord of Vidarbha. He had five sons, and a daughter with a beautiful face. Rukmi was the eldest and after him were Rukmaratha, Rukmabahu, Rukmakesha and Rukmamali. Their sister was the virtuous Rukmini. Those who came to their home chanted about Mukunda's beauty, valour, qualities and prosperity. Hearing about these, she decided that he was a husband who was her equal. Krishna knew that she was a store of intelligence, auspicious signs, generosity, beauty, good conduct and qualities. He made up his mind that he would marry her, since she was a wife who was his equal. O king! Rukmi hated Krishna. Therefore, though his relatives were willing, he restrained them from bestowing his sister on Krishna. Instead, he wanted to give her to the king of Chedi. Ascertaining this, the dark-eyed princess of Vidarbha became extremely distressed in her mind. Thinking about this, she quickly sent a trustworthy brahmana to Krishna. Having reached Dvaraka, he was brought in by the gatekeepers and saw the original Purusha seated on a golden throne. The lord was devoted to brahmanas. On seeing him, he descended from his own seat and made him sit. He worshipped him, just as he is himself worshipped by the residents of heaven. When he had eaten and rested, the destination of the virtuous approached him. He massaged his feet with his own hands and gently questioned him. "O chief among the best of brahmanas! Is your observance of dharma approved by the elders? Is it undertaken without any difficulty and are you always happy in your mind? If a brahmana is satisfied with whatever comes his way and follows his dharma without any deviation, then everything can be milked so that he gets all the objects of desire. Even if he becomes the lord of the gods, a discontented person wanders around from one world to another. If a person is content with nothing, when he lies down, all his limbs are free from anxiety. I repeatedly bow my head down before virtuous brahmanas who are satisfied with what they have got and are well-wishers towards all creatures. They are without any ego and are tranquil. O brahmana! Is everything well? If a king protects his kingdom so that the subjects reside happily, he is loved by me. Why have you crossed through impassable paths and come to this fortification? What do you wish for? As long as it is not a secret, tell us everything. What can we do for you?" Parameshthi asked the brahmana these questions, since in his pastimes, he had assumed a body. Everything was described to him.

'Rukmini said,[417] "O one who is the beauty of the worlds! I have heard about your qualities. If a person hears about you and if that enters through the apertures in the ears, all the torment of the body is destroyed. If a person with eyes sees your form, all the desired objectives are obtained. O Achuyta! I am shameless and my mind has become immersed in you. O Mukunda! No one but you is your equal in greatness, lineage, good conduct, beauty, learning, youth, prosperity and power. What patient maiden from a noble lineage will not choose you as a husband at the right time? O lion among men! You bring delight to the minds of those in the world of men. O dear one! Therefore, as a wife, I have chosen you as a husband. O lord! I have surrendered myself to you. Please accept me. O lotus-eyed one! Like a jackal, let Chedi not swiftly touch the share of the offering meant for the brave king of animals. If I have sufficiently worshipped the illustrious and supreme lord through sacred works, sacrifices, donations, rituals, vows and other deeds and have honoured gods, brahmanas and seniors, then let Gada's elder brother accept my hand and not Damaghosha's son or anyone else. O unvanquished one! The marriage will take place tomorrow. Come secretly to Vidarbha, surrounded by the leaders of armies. Crush Chedi, the Indra of Magadha and their armies. Use the rakshasa mode to forcibly abduct me and marry me as viryashulka. I will be roaming around in the inner quarters. 'How will I marry you without killing your relatives?' I will tell you about a means. On the preceding day, a great procession to the deity of the lineage, Girija,[418] takes place and the new bride-to-be ventures out. O lotus-

[417] As conveyed by the brahmana.
[418] Daughter of the mountain, Parvati.

eyed one! Great ones like Uma's consort desire to bathe with the dust of your lotus feet, so that their tamas can be destroyed. If I do not obtain your favours, I will emaciate myself through vows and give up my life. I may get what I want after one hundred years."

'The brahmana added, "O lord of the Yadus! This is the secret message I have brought here. Having thought about what needs to be done next, please do it."'

Chapter 10(53)

Shri-Shuka said, 'The descendant of the Yadu lineage heard the message of the princess of Vidarbha. He clasped his[419] hand in his hand, smiled and said the following. The illustrious one said, "My mind is also set on her and I cannot sleep at night. However, I know that because of his hatred, Rukmi has prohibited the marriage. The one with the unblemished limbs has set her mind on me. I will crush those wicked kings in a battle and bring her here, like the flames of a fire rising from kindling."[420] Madhusudana ascertained[421] the nakshatra[422] for Rukmini's wedding. He instructed his charioteer, Daruka, to quickly yoke the chariot. He yoked the horses, Shaibya, Sugriva, Meghapushpa and Balahaka, to the chariot. He brought it there and stood, hands joined in salutation. Shouri ascended the chariot and also made the brahmana mount. With the swift horses, they travelled from Anarta to Vidarbha within a single night.

'The king, the lord of Kundina, was under the subjugation of affection towards his son.[423] To bestow his own daughter on Shishupala, he had all the required arrangements carried out. The city was cleaned and the streets, roads and quadrangles were

---

[419] The brahmana's.

[420] There is the implicit image of those kings being like kindling and Rukmini resembling a fire generated by churning kindling.

[421] From the brahmana.

[422] Constellation.

[423] Kundina was the capital of Vidarbha, identified with Kaundinyapura in Amravati division.

sprinkled with water. It was ornamented with colourful festoons, flags and arches. It was full of men and women decorated with necklaces, fragrances, garlands and radiant garments. The beautiful homes were fragrant with aloe and incense. O king! The gods, the ancestors and the brahmanas were worshipped in the decreed way. They were fed according to the rites and auspicious benedictions were pronounced. The maiden, possessing excellent teeth, was bathed well and went through all the auspicious rites. She was attired in a pair of new silken garments and adorned with excellent ornaments. For the bride's protection, the best of brahmanas chanted mantras from the Rig, Sama and Yajur Vedas. Priests who were skilled in the Atharva Veda offered oblations for pacifying the planets. The king, supreme among those who knew about rituals, gave brahmanas gold, silver, garments, sesamum mixed with molasses and cows. For his son's sake, King Damaghosha, the lord of Chedi, had mantras pronounced and did everything else that was required for prosperity. He travelled to Kundina, surrounded by formations of elephants exuding musth, chariots with golden chains, infantry, horses and other soldiers. The lord of Vidarbha came forward to meet and honour him. Delighted, he made him reside in a residence that had been constructed. Thousands of those who were on Chedi's side arrived—Shalva, Jarasandha, Dantavakra, Viduratha, Poundraka and others. They hated Krishna and Rama and wanted to ensure that Chedi got the maiden. "Surrounded by the Yadus, if Krishna, Rama and the others come here to abduct her, we will collectively fight against them." Making up their minds in this way, all those kings on earth arrived, complete with armies and mounts.

'The illustrious Rama heard about the arrangements made by the enemy kings. Since Krishna had gone alone to abduct the maiden, he suspected that there might be an encounter. He was overcome with affection towards his brother. With a large army consisting of elephants, horses, chariots and foot soldiers, he quickly went to Kundina. Bhishmaka's beautiful daughter wished for Hari's arrival. But since she did not see the brahmana return, she started to think. "Alas! My fortune is limited. Only a night[424] remains before my

[424] *Triyama*, three yamas, nine hours.

wedding. The lotus-eyed one has not arrived and I do not know the reason. The brahmana who went with my message has also not returned so far. Perhaps the one with the unblemished atman noticed something reprehensible in me. Why has he not made efforts to come and accept my hand? I am unfortunate. The creator[425] and Maheshvara are not favourably disposed towards me. The virtuous goddess, Gouri, Rudrani, Girija, is also unfavourable." With her mind stolen by Govinda, the maiden thought in this way. Though she knew that there was time, her eyes were filled with tears and she did not open them. O king! In this way, the bride waited for Govinda's arrival. Her left thigh, arm and eye started to twitch, indicating something pleasant. Instructed by Krishna, that excellent brahmana came and saw the divine princess in the inner quarters, where she was confined. The virtuous one with the beautiful smile knew about the signs and could see his cheerful face and confident stride. She asked. He told her that the descendant of the Yadu lineage had arrived and that he had uttered truthful words about taking her away. Hearing that he had arrived, the princess of Vidarbha was delighted in her mind. Since she could not see anything agreeable to offer to the brahmana, she bowed down before him.[426]

'Hearing that Rama and Krishna had arrived, eager to witness his daughter's marriage, to the sound of the blaring of trumpets, he[427] went forward to receive them, bearing appropriate gifts. He presented them with madhuparka, drinks, sparkling garments and other desired gifts, worshipping them in the decreed way. The immensely intelligent one arranged a handsome place for them to reside in. As is appropriate, he arranged for the hospitality of the soldiers and the companions. He also honoured the assembled kings with all the objects of desire, according to valour, age, strength and wealth. The residents of the city of Vidarbha heard that Krishna had arrived. They came and drank in his lotus face, using their eyes like cupped hands. "Rukmini deserves to be his wife and

---

[425] Brahma.

[426] An interpretation is added. Since Rukmini was born from Shri's portion, the brahmana would be blessed with prosperity.

[427] Bhishmaka.

not anyone else's.[428] His form is without any blemish. He is the appropriate husband for Bhishmaka's daughter. May the creator of the three worlds be satisfied with whatever little good deeds we have performed. May Achyuta show us his favours and may he accept the hand of the princess of Vidarbha." Bound to her in their love, the citizens of the city spoke in this way. Protected by soldiers, the maiden left the inner quarters to go to Ambika's shrine. Meditating entirely on Mukunda's lotus feet, she went out on foot to see Bhavani's tender feet. She was silent and was accompanied by her mothers and surrounded by her female friends. The king's brave and armoured guards protected her, their weapons upraised. Drums, conch shells, kettledrums, trumpets and other drums were sounded. There were thousands of foremost courtesans, bearing many kinds of gifts and offerings. The wives of brahmanas were decorated with garlands, fragrances, garments and ornaments. Sutas, magadhas and bandis also advanced, surrounding the bride. Reaching the shrine of the goddess, she washed her lotus hands and feet. She touched water and purified herself. Tranquil, she entered and approached Ambika. Aged wives of brahmanas were accomplished in the rituals and showed her how to worship Bhavani, Bhava's wife, and Bhava himself. "O Ambika![429] O Shiva's wife! I constantly bow down before you and your children. Please allow the illustrious Krishna to become my husband." She separately used water, fragrances, unbroken grain, incense, garments, necklaces, garlands, ornaments and many kinds of presents, offerings and rays of lamps for the worship. The married wives[430] of the brahmanas also worshipped her with salt, fried cakes, betel leaf, kanthasutras,[431] fruits and sugar cane. The women gave her[432] what remained of their offerings and pronounced benedictions over her. The bride bowed down to them and to the queens and accepted the remnants of the offerings.

[428] This is the citizens speaking with each other.

[429] This is Rukmini praying.

[430] Those whose husbands were alive.

[431] Literally, a kanthasutra is a thread worn around the neck. It can be interpreted as the mangalasutra worn by married women.

[432] Rukmini. They gave her prasada.

'Completing the vow of silence, she emerged from Ambika's shrine. She held on to a female servant's hand with her hand, ornamented with jewels. She was like the god's maya and confounded those who were patient. She was slender of waist and her face was ornamented with earrings. She was *shyama*[433] and a bejewelled girdle encircled her hips. She had budding breasts and her darting eyes seemed to be scared of her own hair. Her smile was sweet and her red lips were like bimba fruit, glowing against teeth that were like jasmine buds. She walked with the stride of a supreme swan. Jingling and well-crafted anklets beautified her feet. On seeing her, all the brave and famous kings who had assembled lost their senses. Their hearts were afflicted at the sight of her. The kings looked at her broad smiles and bashful looks. The desire for her made them lose their senses. Bewildered, they fell down on the ground from their elephants, chariots and horses. Using the guise of the procession, she displayed her own beauty to Hari alone. She advanced slowly on feet that were like lotus buds. She was waiting for the arrival of the illustrious one and used the nails of her left hand to brush away her hair. As she cast bashful and sidelong glances towards the kings, she saw Achyuta. The princess was eager to mount his chariot and while the enemies looked on, Krishna abducted her. He raised her up on to his chariot, marked with the signs of Suparna. Madhava repulsed that circle of kings. With Rama at the forefront, he slowly left, like a lion seizing his share from the midst of jackals. The proud enemies, with Jarasandha at the forefront, could not tolerate their own defeat and the destruction of their fame. "Alas! Shame on our fame. We are armed with bows. Yet, the gopas have taken her away, like deer taking something away from lions."'

---

[433] We have deliberately not translated shyama. Usually, this means dark. But shyama also means a woman who has not had children and it is this second meaning, in the sense of virgin, which is intended here. More specifically, shyama is used for a maiden who is not yet sixteen years old.

Chapter 10(54)

Shri-Shuka said, 'All of them were greatly enraged. Armouring themselves, they ascended their vehicles, each of them surrounded by his own respective army. Holding aloft raised bows, they followed. The leaders of the Yadava army saw them descend. O king! They stood there and faced them, twanging their own bows. They[434] were accomplished in the use of weapons. Mounted on the backs of horses and elephants and astride chariots, they released showers of arrow, like clouds pouring down water on mountains. The slender-waisted one saw that her lord's army was enveloped with arrows and her eyes were agitated with fear. Ashamed, she glanced at his face. The illustrious one laughed and said, "O one with the beautiful eyes! Do not be scared. Those on your side will instantly destroy the enemy's forces." The brave ones, Gada, Samkarshana and the others, could not tolerate this display of valour. They used iron arrows to slaughter the horses, elephants and chariots. The heads of crores of charioteers, horses and elephants fell down on the ground, along with earrings, diadems and headdresses. Hands with swords, clubs, bows and arrows, arms, thighs, legs and the heads of horses, donkeys, elephants, camels, asses and mortals were strewn around. The Vrishnis desired victory. Seeing that their soldiers and forces were slaughtered, the kings, with Jarasandha at the forefront, were disheartened and left. They approached Shishupala, who was afflicted at his promised wife having been abducted. His colour had faded. His enterprise was gone and his face was dry. They spoke to him. "O tiger among men! Give up this distress in your mind. O king! Among embodied beings, the agreeable and the disagreeable are not seen to be permanent. This is like the wooden image of a woman being made to dance according to the wishes of the puppeteer. In that way, happiness and misery in this world are under the control of the lord." "In encounters with Shouri, with twenty-three akshouhinis, I have been defeated seventeen times and have

---

[434] The enemy.

been victorious only once.[435] Nevertheless, I never rejoice or grieve. I know that everything in this world is driven by time and destiny. All of us are lords of leaders of valiant ones. However, we have now been defeated by a small number of Yadus who are protected by Krishna. The enemy has triumphed because destiny favours them now. Like that, when time turns and becomes favourable towards us, we will be victorious." Thus comforted by his friends, Chedi and his followers returned to his city. The remaining kings also left for their own respective cities.

'Rukmi hated Krishna and could not tolerate that Krishna had married his sister through the rakshasa mode. Surrounding himself with an akshouhini, the powerful one followed Krishna from the rear. The intolerant Rukmi was armoured. In the hearing of all the kings, the mighty-armed one had armoured himself. With a bow and an arrow, he had taken a pledge. "I will kill Krishna in a battle and bring Rukmini back. Otherwise, I will not enter Kundina. I am stating this truthfully." Having said this, he mounted his chariot and told the charioteer, "Quickly urge the horses towards the spot where Krishna is, so that there can be an encounter with him. Today, using sharp arrows, I will take away the pride that the evil-minded cowherd has about his valour. He has used violence to abduct my sister." The boastful and evil-minded one did not know about the measure of the lord's prowess. Govinda was alone on his chariot and he challenged him, "Wait. Stay." He drew his bow back extremely firmly and struck Krishna with three arrows. He said, "O worst of the Yadu lineage! Wait for a while. You are stealing my sister, like a crow taking away oblations. O wicked one! O one who uses maya! O one who fights using deceit! Today, I will rob you of your pride. Before you are struck with my arrows and forced to lie down, release the maiden." Krishna smiled and used six arrows to pierce and shatter Rukmi's bow. He struck the four horses with eight arrows, the charioteer with two and the standard with three. Picking up another bow, he pierced Krishna with five arrows. Despite being struck with floods of arrows, Achyuta severed his bow again. He

[435] This is Jarasandha speaking.

picked up another one, but the undecaying one severed that too. Whatever be the weapon he chose to pick up, club, spear, trident, shield, sword, lance, javelin—Hari severed all these. At this, he angrily leapt down from his chariot. Wishing to kill him, with a sword in his hand, he rushed towards Krishna, like an insect towards a fire. As he descended, he[436] used arrows to shatter the sword and the shield into fragments that were like sesamum seeds. He seized a sharp sword and got ready to kill Rukmi. On seeing that he was getting ready to kill her brother, Rukmini became agitated with fear. The virtuous one fell down at her husband's feet and piteously spoke these words. "O lord of yoga! O one whose atman is immeasurable! O god of the gods! O lord of the universe! O fortunate one! O mighty-armed one! You should not kill my brother." Because of her fear, her limbs trembled. The grief made her mouth dry up and tears choked her throat. Because of her fright, her necklace, made out of molten gold, was dislodged. She seized his feet and out of compassion, he desisted. He tied up that evil-acting person with a piece of cloth. He disfigured him by shaving him, but left some of his beard and hair untouched.

'Like elephants destroying lotuses, the foremost and valiant ones among the Yadus crushed the extraordinary enemy soldiers. Having approached Krishna's presence, they saw Rukmi there. He was in a condition that was close to having been killed.[437] The lord, Samkarshana, was filled with compassion and freed the one who had been bound. He told the illustrious Krishna, "O Krishna! What you have done is wicked. It is contemptible. He is a relative and you have disfigured him by shaving off his hair and beard. This is tantamount to killing him. O virtuous lady![438] Concerned and thinking about your brother's disfigurement, you should not hate us. A man enjoys the fruits of what he himself has done and no one else is responsible for his happiness or unhappiness. Even if a relative commits a crime that deserves his being killed,

---

[436] Krishna.

[437] The shame contributing to this.

[438] Addressed to Rukmini. His words are partly addressed to Rukmini and partly to Krishna.

a relative should not be killed. Instead, he should be cast aside. Since he has been killed because of his own sin, what is the need to kill him again? Prajapati[439] determined a dharma for kshatriyas, following which, a brother must kill his own brother. Nothing is more terrible than this. Those who are proud and blind because of their prosperity and intoxication disrespect others because of kingdoms, land, wealth, women, honour, power, or other reasons. Your perception is not level-headed.[440] He has harboured ill intentions towards all creatures. He has always acted against your well-wishers. Yet, like an ignorant person, you are thinking of behaving kindly towards him. Fashioned by the god's maya, men are bewildered about the atman. Taking the body to be the atman, they think of friends, enemies and neutral parties. There is only one supreme atman, existent in all bodies. However, like the illumination in the sky, foolish people perceive them as many.[441] Composed of material elements, the breath of life and gunas, the body has a beginning and an end. The body does not know about the atman, and samsara is imposed on it. O virtuous lady! Since nothing else is real, the atman has no association or disassociation with anything else. It is the cause of its own perception, just as the sun gives perception to its form through the sense of vision.[442] The body goes through birth and other transformations, but this is not true of the atman. This is like the waxing and the waning of the moon through its kalas[443] and its death during *kuhu*.[444] When a man is asleep, he sees himself and enjoys objects and the fruits of these, though these are not real. In that way, an ignorant person experiences material existence. The grief that is drying you up and confounding you arises out of ignorance. O one with the sweet smiles! Destroy it with true knowledge and regain your

---

[439] Brahma.

[440] This is addressed to Rukmini.

[441] Such as the sun or the moon, reflected in different images in different vessels of water.

[442] One perceives the sun through the eye.

[443] A small measure of time.

[444] Kuhu is the deity (and the day) for the night of the new moon. The moon disappears (dies), but this is not real.

natural self." The illustrious and slender one was thus enlightened by Rama. She cast aside her distress and used her intelligence to steady her mind.

'The adversaries only left him[445] his life. His forces and radiance were destroyed. His own wishes were frustrated and he remembered his disfigurement. He constructed a great city named Bhojapura,[446] so that he could live there. "I will not enter Kundina until I have killed the evil-minded Krishna and brought back my younger sister." Having pledged this, he angrily resided there. O extender of the Kuru lineage! Defeating the lords of the earth, the illustrious one brought Bhishmaka's daughter back to the city. He followed the rites and married her. At that time, in every house in the city of the Yadus, men observed great festivities. O king! Their minds were only devoted to Krishna, the lord of the Yadus. Men and women rejoiced, adorned in earrings studded with jewels and brought many kinds of gifts to the bride and the groom, who were attired in excellent garments. Flags to Indra were raised in the city of the Vrishnis. There were colourful garlands, garments and arches encrusted with gems. The city was beautiful. Auspicious arrangements were made at every door. There were pots filled with water, aloe, incense and lamps. The roads were sprinkled with musth from elephants belonging to the beloved kings who had been invited. The elephants were used to decorate the entrances with areca nut and plantain trees. The Kurus, Srinjayas, Kaikeyas, Vidarbhas, Yadus and Kuntis roamed around here and there, happily meeting each other. Here and there, they heard the account of Rukmini's abduction being sung and the kings and the princesses were extremely amazed. O king! The residents of the city of Dvaraka were extremely delighted to see Krishna, Shri's consort, united with Rukmini, who was Rama[447] herself.'

[445] Rukmi.
[446] Identified as a village near Vidisha, in Bhopal district.
[447] Ramaa, Shri/Lakshmi.

Chapter 10(55)

Shri-Shuka said, 'Kama was part of Vasudeva's portion and was earlier, burnt down by Rudra in his rage.[448] So that he might get his body back, he resorted to him.[449] Through Krishna's seed, he was born as the son of the princess of Vidarbha. He was known as Pradyumna and he was not inferior to his father in any way. Shambara recognized him to be his enemy.[450] He could assume any form at will and abducted the child when he was not ten days old. Having hurled him into the sea, he returned to his own house. An extremely powerful fish swallowed him. Along with others, this fish was caught in a large net cast by fishermen. The fishermen brought the extraordinary fish as a gift to Shambara. The cooks took it to the kitchen and started to cut it up with a knife. Finding the child in the stomach, they took him to Mayavati.[451] Her mind was suspicious, but Narada arrived and told her everything, about the boy's birth and about how he had entered the stomach of the fish. She was Kama's illustrious wife, known by the name of Rati. When her husband's body had been burnt down, she had been waiting for him to get back his body. Shambara had entrusted her with the task of preparing rice in the kitchen. Knowing that the infant was Kamadeva, she started to feel love towards the child. Within a short period of time, Krishna's son became a youth. All the women who looked at him were captivated. O dear one! His eyes were as large as the petals of a lotus and his arms were long. He was the most handsome in the world of men. Rati glanced at him with bashful and loving glances, with her eyebrows arched. She lovingly approached him, desiring intercourse. Krishna's illustrious son told her, "O mother! Your mind is perverse. You have transgressed the

[448] Kama is the god of love. When he disturbed Shiva, the fire in Shiva's third eye reduced him to ashes. Kama thus became Ananga (the one without a body).

[449] Kama resorted to Vasudeva.

[450] Pradyumna would kill the asura Shambara.

[451] Mayavati used to work in the kitchen. She was Rati, Kama's wife, and had taken birth so that she might be reunited with her husband.

sentiments of a mother and are behaving like a lover." Rati replied, "You are Narayana's son. Shambara abducted you from your home. O lord! You are Kama and I am Rati, your rightful wife. When you were not even ten days old, the asura Shambara hurled you into the ocean. You were swallowed by a fish. O lord! I have got you back from its stomach. This enemy of yours is invincible. He knows one hundred different kinds of maya and is impossible to defeat. However, using maya, stupefaction and other techniques, you will slay him. With her son gone, your mother is grieving like a female curlew. Overwhelmed with affection towards her son, she is distressed, like a cow afflicted on account of its calf." Mayavati knew about *mahamaya*,[452] which was capable of destroying all other kinds of maya. She bestowed this knowledge on the great-souled Pradyumna.

'He approached Shambara and challenged him to an encounter. He hurled all kinds of abuses at him, using this abuse to generate a conflict. He was provoked by these demeaning words, like a serpent struck with the foot. He emerged, with a club in his hand. His eyes were coppery red with rage. He swiftly whirled his club around and hurled it at the great-souled Pradyumna, roaring and making a sound that was like the bolt of thunder. As it descended, the illustrious Pradyumna repulsed the club with his own club. O king! Then, filled with anger, he hurled his club towards the enemy. The asura resorted to the maya of the daityas that had been taught to him by Maya. He took to the sky and showered down weapons on Krishna's son. Obstructed by this shower of weapons, Rukmini's maharatha son used the great knowledge, full of sattva, which could crush all kinds of maya. The daitya used hundreds of modes used by guhyakas, gandharvas, *pishacha*s,[453] serpents and rakshasas. However, Krishna's son destroyed all of these. He raised his sharp sword and used force to severe Shambara's head, with a copper-coloured beard, diadem and earrings, from his body. The residents of heaven praised him and showered down flowers. His

---

[452] Great maya.
[453] A malevolent being that survives on human flesh.

wife could travel through the sky. Through the sky, she took him back to the city.[454]

'O king! The excellent inner quarters were filled with hundreds of excellent women. With his wife, he entered there through the sky, like a cloud accompanied by lightning. The women saw him, with a complexion that was as dark as the cloud. He was attired in a yellow silken garment. His arms were long and his eyes were coppery red. He possessed a handsome and smiling lotus face, ornamented with blue and curly hair. They took him to be Krishna and, ashamed, hid themselves here and there. Slowly, the women noticed slight differences in the signs.[455] They were extremely surprised and happily approached him and the one who was a jewel among women. The black-eyed princess of Vidarbha, sweet in speech, remembered her own son, who had been destroyed, and love oozed out of her breasts. "Who is this lotus-eyed jewel among men? Whom does he belong to? Who has borne her in her womb? Who is the one[456] who has been obtained by him? My son was lost and was taken away from the delivery chamber. If he is alive somewhere, his age and beauty will be like this one's. The one who has come here is similar in form to the wielder of the Sharnga bow. How is this possible? His structure, limbs, gait, voice, smiles and glances are like his. He must certainly be the son I bore in my womb. That is the reason I feel this great love for him. My left arm is throbbing."[457] While the princess of Vidarbha was speculating in this way, Uttamashloka, Devaki's son, arrived there, along with Devaki and Anankadundubhi. Though he knew the truth, the illustrious Janardana remained silent. It was Narada who recounted everything, about the abduction by Shambara and everything else. The women in Krishna's inner quarters heard this extremely wonderful account. They welcomed the one who had returned after many years, as if he had come back from the dead. Devaki, Vasudeva, Krishna, Rama, the women and Rukmini embraced the

---

[454] Dvaraka.

[455] For example, the shrivatsa mark and Koustubha were missing.

[456] The wife.

[457] An auspicious sign.

couple and were filled with joy. Hearing that Pradyumna, who had been destroyed, had returned, the residents of Dvaraka exclaimed, "Wonderful. It is good fortune that the child has returned, as if from the dead." His form was exactly like that of his father's and in private, his mothers repeatedly worshipped him and were attracted to him, taking him to be their lord. Indeed, this is not at all surprising. His form was like a reflection of the form of the one who is Rama's refuge. What need be said of other women? They remembered Kama, when he came within range of their vision.'

Chapter 10(56)

Shri-Shuka said, 'Satrajit caused an offence to Krishna. Therefore, he made efforts to give him the Syamantaka jewel and bestow his own daughter on him.'

The king asked, 'O brahmana! What offence did Satrajit cause to Krishna? Where did the Syamantaka jewel come from? Why did he bestow his daughter on Hari?'

Shri-Shuka replied, 'Surya was a great friend of Satrajit, his devotee. He was satisfied with him and happily gave him the Syamantaka jewel. O king! Wearing the radiant gem around his neck, he entered Dvaraka, as resplendent as the sun. Such was its brilliance, that he was himself almost unnoticed. When people looked at him from a distance, their eyes were blinded by the radiance. They suspected that he was Surya. They went and told the illustrious one, who was playing with dice. "O Narayana! O wielder of the conch shell, chakra and mace! O Damodara! O lotus-eyed one! O Govinda! O delight of the Yadu lineage! We bow down before you. O lord of the universe! To see you, the sun god is coming here. The circle of his fierce rays is robbing men of their sight. The bulls among the gods are seeking to search out your progress in the three worlds. O lord! Having now realized that you have hidden yourself among the Yadus, Aja[458] has come here."

---

[458] The one without birth. Here, it means Surya.

Hearing these childish words, the lotus-eyed one laughed. He smiled and said, "This is not the sun god. It is Satrajit, with his blazing jewel." Satrajit entered his prosperous house. He made brahmanas perform the auspicious rites. He entered the house meant for the gods and made them instate the jewel there. O lord! Every day, the jewel produced eight *bharas*[459] of gold. In the place where the jewel was kept and was worshipped, there was no famine, untimely death from calamities and snakes, mental or physical disease. There was nothing inauspicious from those who were deceitful. On one occasion, Shouri desired the jewel, so that it could be given to the king of the Yadus.[460] However, he was so greedy about wealth that he refused to give it, oblivious of the transgression involved in this.

'On one occasion, wearing the extremely radiant jewel around his neck, Prasena[461] mounted a horse. He went to the forest on a hunt and wandered around. A maned lion killed Prasena and his horse and took the jewel away. When it entered a mountain, it was killed by Jambavat, who desired the jewel. In his cave, he gave his son the jewel, to play with. Unable to see his brother, Satrajit was tormented on account of his brother. "He went to the forest, wearing the jewel around his neck. Perhaps Krishna has killed my brother." The people heard this and it was passed around, from one ear to another ear. The illustrious one heard this and wished to wipe away the ill fame that was being attributed to him. With some citizens, he followed Prasena's footsteps. In the forest, they saw Prasena and his horse, slain by the lion. The people saw it on the slope of the mountain, killed by the bear.[462] The terrible cave of the king of the bears was covered in darkness. Leaving the subjects outside, the illustrious one entered it alone. There, he saw that the excellent jewel had been made into a child's toy. Making up his mind to take it away, he stationed himself near the child. Not having seen a man before, as if in fear, the nurse maid cried out. Hearing this, Jambavat, supreme among strong

[459] A bhara is a measure of weight. It can roughly be taken to be almost 100 kgs.

[460] Ugrasena.

[461] Satrajit's brother.

[462] Jambavat.

ones, angrily rushed forward. He did not realize that the illustrious
one was his own master. Taking himself to be an ordinary man, he
angrily started to fight with him. Both of them wished to triumph
against the other and there was a tumultuous duel in the course of
the fight. Like hawks fighting over a piece of meat, they fought with
weapons, stones and trees. It continued for twenty-eight days and
nights. Incessantly, they struck each other with hard blows of the fists
that were like strikes of the vajra. As he was struck by blows from
Krishna's fists, the strong joints in his limbs were crushed. His spirit
started to diminish. He started to perspire all over his body. Amazed,
he exclaimed, "I know you. You are the breath of life, energy and
strength of all living creatures. You are Vishnu, the ancient being.
You are the powerful Vishnu, the lord of everything. You are the
creator of all the creators of the universe. You are the reality behind
creation. You are time. You are the lord of all subjugators. Among
all atmans, you are the supreme atman. The slight rage in your
sidelong glance agitated the ocean, full of crocodiles and *timingilas*.[463]
It parted and granted you passage. As a mark of your own fame,
you constructed a bridge and set Lanka on fire. Using arrows, you
brought down the heads of the rakshasas on the ground." O great
king! Ascertaining that he had got to know, the illustrious Achyuta,
Devaki's son, spoke to the king of the bears. He was filled with great
compassion towards his devotee. The lotus-eyed one touched him
with his auspicious hand. In a voice that rumbled like the clouds, he
said, "O lord of the bears! I have come to this cave for the sake of
the jewel. I intend to use this jewel to wipe away the false accusation
that has been levelled against me." Addressed in this way, as a mark
of his worship, he happily bestowed the jewel and his own daughter,
Jambavati, on Krishna.

'The people saw Shouri enter the cave and did not see him emerge
again. They waited for twelve days. Then, miserable, they returned to
their own city. Devaki, Queen Rukmini, Anankadundubhi and other
well-wishers and kin heard that Krishna had not emerged from the
cave. They grieved. Grieving, the residents of Dvaraka abused Satrajit.

---

[463] Timingila is a fish that devours whales (*timi*). The reference is to
Rama in the Ramayana. Jambavat was Rama's ally and devotee.

They presented themselves before Mahamaya Durga and prayed for Krishna's return. The goddess pronounced her benedictions on them. Successful in his objective, Hari manifested himself, along with his wife, and caused them delight. They got Hrishikesha back, as if he had returned from the dead. He had his wife with him and the jewel was around his neck. All of them engaged in great festivities. The illustrious one summoned Satrajit to the assembly. In the king's presence, he told him how he had got the jewel back and gave it to him. Ashamed, he[464] accepted the jewel, hanging his head down in embarrassment. Tormented because of his wicked behaviour, he returned to his own residence. He thought about this sin of his and was anxious because of a conflict with those who were more powerful. "How will I wipe away the stain on me? How will I placate Achyuta? What will be good for me? How will people no longer condemn me as short-sighted, inferior and foolish, and as one who is greedy for riches? I will bestow the jewel, and my daughter, who is a jewel among women, on him. That is the appropriate way. There is no other means for me to find peace." Having used his intelligence, he arrived at this course of action. Satrajit himself made arrangements to gift the jewel, and his own auspicious daughter, to Krishna. Following the proper rites, the illustrious one married Satyabhama. She possessed good conduct, beauty, generosity and other qualities and there were many who had sought her hand. O king! The illustrious one said, "We will not accept the jewel. You are the god's[465] devotee. Thereby, we will also enjoy a share in the fruits.""

Chapter 10(57)

Shri-Shuka said, 'Though he knew the truth, Govinda heard that the Pandavas and Kunti had been burnt down.[466] To do

---

[464] Satrajit.

[465] Surya's.

[466] In an attempt made by Duryodhana at Varanavata, a story told in the Mahabharata. Kunti and the Pandavas escaped.

what needed to be done for the lineage, along with Rama, he went to the land of the Kurus. They met Bhishma, Kripa, Vidura, Gandhari and Drona. Sharing in their grief, they exclaimed, "Alas! What a great misery!" O king! Finding this opportunity, Akrura and Kritavarma told Shatadhanva,[467] "Why should we not seize the jewel? Satrajit promised each of us his daughter, who is like a jewel. But neglecting us, he gave her to Krishna. Why should he not follow his brother?"[468] Urged by them and goaded by his avarice, he killed Satrajit while he was asleep. In this way, the evil one, worst among the wicked, shortened his own lifespan. While the women shrieked and screamed, like those without a protector, he killed him, the way a butcher slays an animal. Seizing the jewel, he left. Satyabhama saw that her father had been killed and was immersed in grief. She lamented, "Alas, father! I have been slain." She lost her senses. She placed the dead body in a vat filled with oil and went to Gajasahvya.[469] Though Krishna already knew the truth, she was tormented and wanted to tell him about her father's death. O king! When those two lords[470] heard this, they imitated the behaviour of the world of men. "Alas! What a great misery for us." With tears in their eyes, they grieved.

'With his elder brother and his wife, the illustrious one returned to the city. He prepared to kill Shatadhanva and seize the jewel back. Learning that these efforts were being made, he was scared and wished to save his own life. He approached Kritavarma for help, but was told, "I will not show disrespect to the two lords, Rama and Krishna. If a person commits an offence against them, how can he hope to obtain peace? Because of their enmity, Kamsa and his followers lost their lives and their prosperity. After fighting against them in seventeen encounters, Jarasandha lost his own chariot." Refused in this way, he went to Akrura and sought his help. However, he also said, "If a person knows about the strengths

---

[467] Kritavarma's brother and Hridika's son.

[468] That is, why should he not be killed?

[469] Hastinapura.

[470] Krishna and Balarama. They already knew, but followed human norms.

of those two lords, how can he oppose them? In his pastimes, the unvanquished one creates, preserves and destroys the universe. The creators of the universe are bewildered and do not know about his endeavours. When he was seven years old, he uprooted a mountain and held it up on a single hand. Though he was a child, he playfully held it up, like an infant holding up a mushroom. I bow down before the illustrious Krishna, the performer of extraordinary deeds. He is infinite. He is the original cause. He is the one who is inside all atmans. I bow down before him." Refused by him too, Shatadhanva entrusted the great jewel in his care. Ascending a horse that could travel for one hundred yojanas, he left. O king! Rama and Janardana ascended the chariot that had Garuda on its standard. On extremely swift horses, they pursued the one who had caused harm to their senior. In a grove on the outskirts of Mithila, the horse fell down and died. Abandoning it, the terrified one fled on foot and Krishna angrily pursued him. He fled on foot and the illustrious one also pursued him on foot. With the chakra that was sharp at the edges, he severed his head. He searched his upper and lower garment for the jewel. Unable to find the jewel, Krishna went to his elder brother's presence and said, "Shatadhanva has been killed in vain. The jewel isn't here." Bala replied, "It is evident that Shatadhanva has entrusted the jewel to some other man. Return to the city and search him out. I wish to see the king of Videha. I love him a great deal." O king! Saying this, the descendant of the Yadu lineage entered Mithila. On seeing him, the lord of Mithila was delighted in his mind and immediately stood up. He worshipped him with all the objects of worship, following the prescribed rites. The lord remained in Mithila for some years. Filled with affection, the great-souled Janaka honoured him. It is at this time that Dhritarashtra's son, Suyodhana, learnt how to fight with the club.[471]

'Keshava returned to Dvaraka. He wished to do what would bring pleasure to his beloved. He told her about Shatadhanva's

---

[471] There were several kings of Mithila named Janaka. Indeed, they were all known as Janaka, descended from the Janaka lineage. This Janaka is not the Janaka who was Sita's father. Balarama taught Duryodhana/Suyodhana how to fight with the club.

death and about his inability to find the jewel. Since his relative[472] had been killed, he had the funeral rites performed. Along with his well-wishers, the illustrious one attended all these funeral rites. Akrura and Kritavarma heard about Shatandhanva's death. Those two instigators were filled with dread. In their fear, they fled from Dvaraka. When Akrura went on exile, the residents of Dvaraka suffered from calamities of adhidaivika and adhibhoutika kinds.[473] They were tormented by physical and mental ailments. O dear one! Some forget what I have said before. The sages find an abode in him. How could calamities manifest themselves when he resided there?[474] When the god did not shower down, the lord of Kashi bestowed his own daughter, Gandini, on Shvaphalaka,[475] who had arrived there. It then rained in the kingdom of Kashi. His son, Akrura, possessed similar powers. The god showered down wherever he was. There were no calamities or epidemics. Janardana heard the words of the elders, but decided that this was not the only reason.[476] He summoned Akrura and spoke to him. He honoured and greeted him and engaged him in delightful conversation. He knew what is in all hearts and knew the truth. He smiled and said, "O Danapati! Shatadhanva must have left the prosperous Syamantaka jewel in your care. We already knew that. Since Satrajit had no son, his daughter's sons should accept his inheritance.[477] After performing the water rites, they should repay his debts and accept whatever is left. O one who is excellent in vows! However, others will find it

[472] Satrajit.

[473] Respectively linked to destiny and nature.

[474] How could there be calamities when Krishna resided in Dvaraka? This shloka is interpreted in various ways. For instance, the residents of Dvaraka had forgotten about Krishna's glory. One must however bear in mind Shri-Shuka's statement about his having explained it before. Therefore, this probably means that Krishna was simply behaving like an ordinary human.

[475] Also written as Shvaphalka. Shvaphalaka was Akrura's father. He possessed the power to cause showers and Akrura inherited these powers. In exile, Akrura went to his maternal grandfather's house, in Kashi.

[476] Over and above Akrura's powers, there was the power of the Syamantaka jewel and its presence or absence.

[477] That is, Satyabhama's sons.

impossible to bear. Therefore, let the jewel remain with you. But my
elder brother does not completely believe this about the jewel.[478] O
immensely fortunate one! Hence, show it to my relatives and bring
them peace of mind. You are now incessantly performing sacrifices
on golden altars."[479] Shvaphalaka's son was reassured with these
words. He brought the jewel, as radiant as the sun and wrapped in
a piece of cloth, and handed it over. The lord showed Syamantaka
to his relatives and removed the stain ascribed to him. He then
returned the jewel again. If a person reads, hears or remembers
this extremely auspicious account of the illustrious lord Vishnu's
glorious valour, all his sins are destroyed. His ill fame and wicked
deeds are driven away and he obtains peace.'

Chapter 10(58)

Shri-Shuka said, 'Once, to see the Pandavas, the prosperous
Purushottama went and presented himself in Indraprastha.[480] He
was surrounded by Yuyudhana[481] and others. On seeing Mukunda,
the lord of everything, arrive, all the brave Parthas[482] simultaneously
stood up, as if the foremost breath of life had arrived.[483] The brave
ones embraced Achyuta and all their sins were destroyed from the
touch of his limbs. Glancing at his affectionate and smiling face, they
were filled with delight. He bowed down at the feet of Yudhishthira
and Bhima and greeted them.[484] He embraced Phalguna[485] and was
honoured by the twins.[486] When Krishna was seated on an excellent

---

[478] That it is with Akrura and not with Krishna.

[479] Thus, it is obvious that you possess the jewel.

[480] It was now known that the Pandavas had not perished in Varanavata.

[481] Satyaki.

[482] Technically, Nakula and Sahadeva are not Parthas. They were the
sons of Madri, not of Kunti/Pritha.

[483] The image is that of the senses greeting the breath of life.

[484] They were older to him.

[485] Arjuna.

[486] Nakula and Sahadeva.

seat, the newly married and unblemished Krishna[487] approached him slowly and bashfully and honoured him. In that way, Satyaki was honoured and welcomed, by the Parthas. The others were also honoured and welcomed and sat down on different seats. He met Pritha and showed her his respects. Her eyes were wet with tears of affection and she embraced him. He asked his father's sister, and her daughter-in-law, about their welfare and they asked him about his relatives. She[488] was overwhelmed by her love. Her voice choked and her eyes were full of tears. She remembered the many kinds of hardships. She spoke to the one who shows himself so as to remove hardships. "O Krishna! You are our protector. Ever since you remembered your relatives and sent my brother[489] as a messenger, we have been well. You are our well-wisher and are the atman of the universe. You do not have any delusions about 'mine' and 'someone else's'. Nevertheless, you reside in the hearts of those who constantly remember you and remove their hardships." Yudhishthira said, "O lord! We are inferior in intelligence. The lords of yoga find it extremely difficult to see you. I do not know what good deeds we have done that we should see you." Requested by the king,[490] the lord happily resided there during the months of the rainy season, generating delight in the eyes of the residents of Indraprastha.

'One day, Vijaya, with the ape on his banner, mounted his chariot. He grasped the Gandiva bow and the two inexhaustible quivers and armoured himself.[491] Along with Krishna, he went to a large and desolate forest that was full of many predatory beasts and deer. To hunt, the destroyer of enemy heroes entered it. Using his arrows, he pierced tigers, boar, buffaloes, *ruru* antelopes,

---

[487] Krishnaa, Droupadi.

[488] Kunti.

[489] Akrura.

[490] Yudhishthira.

[491] Vijaya is Arjuna's name. After Khandava forest was burnt down, Agni gave Arjuna Gandiva, two inexhaustible quivers and a chariot with an ape on the standard.

sharabhas, gavayas, rhinos, deer, hares and porcupines.[492] Since
there was a special auspicious occasion, the servants took the
ones that were appropriate as sacrificial offerings to the king.[493]
After this, thirsty and exhausted, Bibhatsu[494] went to the Yamuna.
The two maharathas touched the sparkling water and drank it.
The two Krishnas[495] saw a maiden, beautiful to behold, roaming
around. Her hips were beautiful. Her teeth were excellent and her
face was lovely. Sent by his friend, Phalguna[496] approached that
excellent woman and asked her. "O one with the beautiful hips!
Who are you? Whom do you belong to? Where have you come
from? What do you wish to do? O beautiful one! I think that you
wish for a husband. Tell me everything." Kalindi replied, "I am the
sun god's daughter. Vishnu is the granter of boons and deserves to be
worshipped. Desiring him as a husband, I have resorted to supreme
austerities. O brave one! Other than the one who is Shri's abode,
I will not accept anyone as a husband. The illustrious Mukunda is
the refuge of those without a protector. May he be pleased with
me. I am known as Kalindi and I will reside in the waters of the
Yamuna, until I see Achyuta. My father has constructed a residence
for me there." Gudakesha[497] reported this exactly to Vasudeva,
though he already knew about this. He[498] placed her on his chariot
and went to Dharmaraja. Requested by Krishna, Vishvakarma had
earlier constructed a colourful and supremely wonderful city for the
Parthas.[499] Desiring to bring pleasure to those who were his own,
the illustrious one resided there. So that Khandava forest could be
given to Agni, he became Arjuna's charioteer. O king! Satisfied,
Agni gave Arjuna a bow, a chariot yoked to white horses, two

---

[492] Sharabha has many meanings—young elephant, camel. It is also a
mythical animal with eight legs, believed to be stronger than a lion. Gavaya
is a kind of wild ox.

[493] Yudhishthira.

[494] Arjuna's name.

[495] Krishna is also one of Arjuna's names.

[496] Arjuna.

[497] One who has conquered sleep, Arjuna's name.

[498] Krishna.

[499] That is, Indraprastha.

inexhaustible quivers and armour that weapons could not pierce.[500] Maya was freed from the fire and built an assembly hall for his friend.[501] It is there that Duryodhana's vision got confused and he mixed up water and ground. After having sought and obtained leave from his well-wishers, surrounded by Satyaki and other foremost ones, he[502] returned to Dvaraka again. When an extremely auspicious nakshatra was in the ascendant and the conjunctions were favourable, he married Kalindi. He spread great delight and brought everything auspicious to those who were his own.

'Vinda and Anuvinda from Avanti were Duryodhana's followers. Their own sister was attracted to Krishna, but they forbade her from choosing him at a svayamvara. O king! Mitravinda was the daughter of Rajadhidevi, his father's sister.[503] While all the kings looked on, Krishna forcibly abducted her.

'O king! King Nagnajit of Kosala was extremely devoted to dharma. He had the princess Satya, also known as Nagnajiti, as his daughter. Kings were not allowed to marry her until they had vanquished seven bulls with sharp horns.[504] These were vicious and extremely difficult to vanquish. They could not tolerate the smell of brave ones. The illustrious lord of the Satvatas heard that she could be won by vanquishing the bulls. Surrounded by an extremely large army, he went to the capital of Kosala.[505] The lord of Kosala was delighted. He rose from his seat and offered him a seat and many other valuable gifts of worship. He was honoured back in turn. On seeing all the assembled suitors, the king's daughter desired Rama's

---

[500] There is an obvious consistency, since we have been told Arjuna already possessed these.

[501] Maya is the architect of the asuras. Since Arjuna allowed him to escape from the fire, he built this assembly hall for Arjuna. Duryodhana took a pool of water to be the floor and fell into it. He also took the floor to be a waterbody and tripped.

[502] Krishna.

[503] In Chapter 9(24), Rajadhidevi has been mentioned as Anakadundubhi's sister. Rajadhidevi's sons have also been described as the kings of Avanti.

[504] A suitor would have to tame these seven wild bulls.

[505] Ayodhya.

consort. "If I have been firm in my vows, may my unblemished wishes come true and may I get him as a husband. The dust of his lotus feet is borne on their heads by Shri, the one born from the lotus,[506] Girisha and the guardians of the worlds. In his pastimes, in the course of time, he assumes bodies to protect the ordinances he himself has created. How can the illustrious one be satisfied with me?" Having worshipped him again, he[507] said, "O Narayana! O lord of the universe! You are complete in your own bliss. What can an insignificant person like me do for you?" O descendant of the Kuru lineage! Delighted, the illustrious one accepted the offered seat. In a voice that rumbled like the clouds, he smiled and said, "O Indra among men! If kings follow their own dharma and are bound by it, wise people condemn asking anything from them. Nevertheless, out of affection towards you, I am asking you for your daughter, but we will not pay any price in return."[508] The king replied, "O protector! In this world, who can be superior to you as a groom for my daughter? You are a reservoir of all the qualities. Shri resides on your body and never leaves you. O bull among the Satvatas! However, we have already taken a pledge to test the valour of the men who desire to be a possible groom for my daughter. O brave one! These seven bulls are impossible to restrain and impossible to control. They have broken and shattered the limbs of an extremely large number of princes. O descendant of the Yadu lineage! O Shri's lord! If you control them, you will become the sanctioned groom for my daughter." Hearing about the vow, the lord girded his loins. He divided himself into seven parts. As if he was playing, he controlled them. With their pride shattered and their energy gone, Shouri tied them up with ropes. As if playing, he tied and dragged them along, like a child does with a wooden figure.[509] Amazed and delighted, the king bestowed his daughter on Krishna. Following the prescribed

[506] Brahma.

[507] Nagnajit.

[508] Viryashulka is when the maiden is offered to the suitor who shows the most valour (virya), shulka meaning price. In this case, the valour is that of taming the bulls.

[509] The image is of wooden bulls used as toys. The bulls were dragged along with ropes through their noses.

rites, the illustrious lord accepted her. The king's wife was extremely delighted that her daughter had obtained Krishna as her beloved husband. There were great festivities. Conch shells, drums and trumpets were sounded. There was singing and the playing of musical instruments. Brahmanas pronounced benedictions. Happy men and women adorned themselves with excellent garments and garlands. As a wedding gift, the lord[510] gave ten thousand cows, three thousand maidens attired with excellent garments and with golden necklaces[511] around their necks, nine thousand elephants, chariots that were one hundred times the number of elephants, horses that were one hundred times the number of chariots and male servants who were one hundred times the number of horses. The lord of Kosala made the couple ascend a chariot, surrounded by a large army. His heart melting with affection, he sent them on their way. The valour of those extremely intolerant kings had been shattered by the bulls among the Yadus earlier. Nevertheless, hearing that the maiden was being taken away, they obstructed the path. They showered down torrents of arrows. However, desiring to bring pleasure to his friend, Arjuna used his Gandiva to drive them away, just as a lion drives away inferior animals. Devaki's illustrious son accepted the gifts and went to Dvaraka with Satya. The bull among the Yadus found happiness there.

'Krishna married Bhadra from Kekaya, the daughter of his father's sister, Shrutakirti, when her brothers, Santardana and others, bestowed her on him.[512] Lakshmana, the daughter of the king of Madra, possessed all the auspicious signs. Like Suparna[513] taking away the nectar, he single-handedly took her away from her svayamvara ceremony. Krishna had thousands of many other wives. They were beautiful to behold. Bhouma had imprisoned them. But he killed him and rescued them.'[514]

[510] Nagnajit.

[511] Strictly speaking, necklaces made out of gold coins.

[512] Chapter 9(24) states that Shrutakirti was Anankadundubhi's sister and that her sons ruled over Kekaya.

[513] Garuda.

[514] Bhouma is Narakasura. There were sixteen thousand such women. Krishna killed Narakasura and married them.

Chapter 10(59)

The king asked, 'How did the illustrious one kill Bhouma, who had imprisoned those women? Tell me about this brave act of the wielder of the Sharnga bow.'

Shri-Shuka replied, 'He stole his umbrella. He stole the earrings of his relative. He took away his place from the mountain of the immortals. He was informed by Indra about all of Bhouma's deeds.[515] With his wife, he mounted Garuda and went to Pragjyotishapura, which had fortifications made out of mountains, weapons, water, fire and wind. There were terrible and firm obstructions fashioned by Mura.[516] He used his club to shatter the fortifications made of mountains and his arrows to shatter those made out of weapons. He used his chakra to sever the fortifications made out of fire, water and wind. He used his sword to sever Mura's nooses. He shattered the machines with the blare of his conch shell and also the hearts of those spirited ones. The wielder of the mace used his heavy mace to shatter the ramparts. The sound of Panchajanya[517] was like the terrible clap of thunder at the end of a yuga. Hearing this, the five-headed daitya Mura, who was asleep in the waters, arose. He raised a trident and was impossible to look at. His terrible radiance was like that of the sun or the fire at the end of a yuga. With his five mouths, he seemed to devour the three worlds. Like a serpent, he descended and attacked Tarkshya's son.[518] He roared with his five mouths. He whirled the trident and forcefully hurled it towards Garuda. The loud roar filled earth, heaven, the space in between, all

---

[515] Narakasura stole Varuna's umbrella, not Indra's. He stole the earrings of Aditi, the mother of the gods. He dislodged Indra from the summit of Mandara, the mountain of the immortals. Narakasura's capital was Pragjyotishapura, Kamarupa/Kamakhya near Guwahati. Why did Krishna take Satyabhama with him? This gives rise to speculative interpretations. Perhaps Indra related the misdeeds in Satyabhama's presence and she wanted to come along. Perhaps because Narakasura was the earth's son and Satyabhama was born from the earth's portion.

[516] A demon.

[517] Krishna's conch shell.

[518] Garuda.

the directions and the sky and filled the space inside the cosmic egg.
As the trident descended towards Garuda, Hari used two powerful
arrows to splinter it into three fragments and struck him in the face
with arrows. At this, he[519] angrily released a club towards him. As
the club descended towards him in the battle, Gada's elder brother
used his own mace to shatter it into one thousand fragments. As
he rushed towards him with upraised arms, the unvanquished one
playfully used his chakra to slice off his head. Devoid of life, he
fell down in the water, like a mountain whose summit has been
severed by Indra's energy. His seven sons were distressed at their
father's death. Filled with rage, they exerted themselves to exact
revenge. Urged by Bhouma, they emerged, wielding weapons—
Tamra, Antariksha, Shravana, Vibhavasu, Vasu, Nabhasvan
and Aruna as the seventh. In the battle, they placed Pitha, the
commander, at the forefront. Fierce and angry, they used arrows,
swords, clubs, spears, double-edged swords and javelins against
the unvanquished one. However, the illustrious one was invincible
in his valour and used his own arrows to shatter that mountain
of weapons into fragments that were as small as sesamum. He
severed the heads, thighs, arms, legs and armour and dispatched
them, with Pitha as the foremost, to Yama's eternal abode. His
own army was thus repulsed by Achuyta's chakra and arrows.
On seeing this, Naraka, the earth's son, became intolerant. He
emerged on elephants, originating in the ocean of milk, exuding
musth.[520] He saw Krishna seated astride Garuda, along with his
wife, resembling a cloud tinged with lightning above the sun. He
hurled a *shataghni* towards him.[521] All the warriors also struck
him simultaneously. Gada's illustrious elder brother used sharp
arrows whetted on stone, with colourful feathers. He severed the
arms, thighs, heads, necks and bodies of Bhouma's soldiers. At
the same time, he killed the horses and the elephants. O extender
of the Kuru lineage! Whenever a warrior used a *shastra* or an

[519] Mura.
[520] The elephants were descended from Airavata.
[521] A shataghni was a weapon that could kill one hundred at the same
time and could have been a giant catapult.

astra[522] against him, Hari used one sharp arrow to splinter it into three fragments. He was astride Suparna, who used his wings to strike at the elephants. Garuda used his beak, wings and talons to slaughter the elephants. Suffering in the battle, Naraka continued to fight, but entered his city. He saw that his own soldiers were routed and made to suffer by Garuda. Bhouma struck him with a javelin that had once repulsed the vajra. But though pierced by it, he did not waver, like an elephant struck by a garland. Frustrated in his efforts, Bhouma, seated on an elephant, seized a javelin, so as to kill Achyuta. However, before he could release it, Hari used his chakra, sharp at the edges, to sever his head. With earrings, a beautiful diadem and ornaments, it blazed as it fell down on the ground. "Alas! This is excellent!" exclaimed the rishis. The lords of the gods showered down flowers on Mukunda and worshipped him.

'The earth approached Krishna and presented the radiant earrings to him. They were made out of molten gold and were studded with jewels. She gave him a vaijayanti garland and a garland made out of wild flowers. She gave him the umbrella belonging to Prachetas and the great jewel.[523] O king! The goddess praised the lord of the universe, worshipped by the supreme among the gods. With her mind full of devotion, she bowed down, her hands joined in salutation. The earth said, "O lord of the gods! I bow down before you. O wielder of the conch shell, the chakra and the mace! O one who assumes forms that devotees desire! O paramatman! I bow down before you. I bow down to the one who has a lotus in his navel. I bow down to the one who wears a garland of lotus flowers. I bow down to the one whose eyes are like lotuses. I bow down to the one whose feet bear the marks of lotuses![524] O illustrious Vasudeva Vishnu! I bow down to you. I bow down to Purusha,

---

[522] These are both weapons and the words are often used synonymously. However, an astra is a weapon that is hurled or released, while a shastra is held in the hand.

[523] Prachetas means Varuna. Mahamani (the great jewel) is the summit of Mandara, known as Maniparvata.

[524] Or, whose feet are like lotuses.

the original seed. I bow down to the one who is complete in his understanding. O one without birth! O one who gives birth! O brahman! O one who is infinite in powers! O atman of the superior and the inferior! O one who exists in the atmans of all beings! O paramatman! I bow down before you. O unborn lord! When you wish to create, you assume the powerful form of rajas.[525] For destroying and withdrawing, you assume the form of tamas.[526] O lord of the universe! For the preservation of the universe, you resort to sattva.[527] You are time, Pradhana[528] and Purusha, but you are also distinct from them. You are the illustrious one who is without a second. I, water, fire, wind, space, the *tanmatras*,[529] the gods, the mind, the senses, ahamkara, Mahat and all these mobile and immobile objects are only illusions. His son[530] is approaching your lotus feet. He is terrified. You are the refuge of those who are afflicted. Show him your favours. You should protect him. Place your lotus hand on his hand and cleanse him of all his sins." Humble and full of devotion, the earth entreated him in these words. Granting her freedom from fear, he entered Bhouma's residence, which was filled with all kinds of prosperity.

'Hari saw sixteen thousand princesses there. Using his valour, Bhouma had abducted them from kings. When they saw that noble man enter, those women were captivated. In their minds, they accepted him as their husband, brought there by destiny. Each one of them separately set their hearts on Krishna. "May he be my husband. May the creator sanction this." He had them attired in clean and sparkling garments and sent them to Dvaravati on vehicles borne by men.[531] He also sent a large treasure consisting of chariots, horses and immense wealth. Keshava also sent sixty-four white elephants. They were spirited and four-tusked, born in

[525] As Brahma. The text uses the word *utkata*. Instead of powerful, this can also be translated as fierce.

[526] As Rudra.

[527] As Vishnu.

[528] Interpreted as Prakriti.

[529] Five tanmatras or subtle elements.

[530] Narakasura's son, Bhagadatta.

[531] Palanquins.

Airavata's lineage. He went to the abode of Indra of the gods and returned Aditi's earrings to her. He was affectionately worshipped by Indra of the gods and his beloved and great Indrani.[532] Urged by his wife,[533] he uprooted Parijata and placed it on Garuda. Having defeated Indra and the gods, he took it to his city. He placed it in the garden in Satyabhama's house and it beautified the place. Greedy for its fragrance and intoxicating honey, bees followed it all the way from heaven. He[534] touched Achyuta's feet so that his objective could be accomplished, bowing down with the tips of his crown and entreating him. However, after his task had been accomplished, he slighted the great one. Such is the darkness the gods are in. Shame on their opulence. At the same muhurta, the illustrious and undecaying one simultaneously assumed different forms and married those women in different mansions. Those houses had no parallel and were superior to all others. The one whose deeds are inconceivable remained in those houses.[535] Completely satisfied in his own bliss, he enjoyed himself with those women, like an ordinary householder engaged in his tasks. Those women obtained Rama's consort as their husband, even though Brahma and the others do not know about his course. They happily enjoyed themselves, their love constantly increasing. Every engagement with him was like a new one and they exchanged smiling glances and bashful speech. Though each of them possessed hundreds of maidservants, they themselves undertook to serve the lord. They approached him. Offering him a seat, they worshipped him with excellent objects, washing his feet, offering betel leaves, removing his exhaustion by fanning him, applying fragrances, ornamenting him with garlands, dressing his hair, preparing his bed, bathing him and presenting him with gifts.'

---

[532] Shachi.

[533] Satyabhama. There is a contradiction with what has been stated in Chapter 10(50), about Indra voluntarily parting with Parijata when Dvaraka was established.

[534] Indra.

[535] Simultaneously.

Chapter 10(60)

Shri-Shuka said, 'On one occasion, the preceptor of the universe was happily lying down on his bed. The princess of Bhishma[536] was serving her husband, while her friends were fanning them. Following his pastimes, the lord who is the creator, preserver and destroyer of the universe was born in the lineage of the Yadus, so as to protect his own ordinances. The inner part of that house was radiant. Strings of pearls hung down. There was a dazzling canopy and the lamps were studded with jewels. There were garlands of jasmine flowers, with the sound of bees buzzing. The sparkling beams of the moon entered through apertures in the lattice work. From the grove, the breeze carried the fragrance of parijata blossoms. O king! The smell of incense and aloe emerged through the holes in the lattice work. Her husband, the lord of the universe, was happily lying down on a bed that was as white as the froth on milk, on an excellent pillow. She was serving him. The fan was made out of yak hair, with a bejewelled handle. The queen took it from her friend's hand and began to serve the lord by fanning him. As she stood near Achyuta with the whisk in her hand, there was a sound from her bejewelled anklets and her beautiful rings and bangles. The ends of her garment hid her breasts, red and decorated with kunkuma. Wearing her necklace, she looked dazzling. An extremely expensive girdle was wound around her hips. She was Shri personified and he alone was her objective. She had assumed a form that was similar to the form he had assumed in his pastimes. Pleased, he looked at her, with her locks of hair, earrings, a golden necklace around her neck and a delighted and smiling face that was like honey. Hari smiled and spoke to her.

'The illustrious one said, "O princess! You were desired by kings who were as powerful as the guardians of the worlds. They were great in their powers, prosperous, handsome, generous, strong and energetic. Chedi and the others were smitten by love, impossible to control, and were your suitors. Your brother and your own

[536] Rukmini.

father wanted to bestow you on them. Ignoring them, why did you choose me? I am not their equal. O one with the excellent brows! Terrified of the kings, we have sought shelter in the ocean.[537] We have engendered an enmity with the strong. We have almost had to give up the king's seat. O one with the excellent brows! If women follow men whose ways are unclear and who do not follow paths that are usually traversed by men, they generally tend to suffer. We possess nothing. We are always loved by people who possess nothing. O slender-waisted one! That is the reason affluent people do not generally worship me. Marriage and friendship must take place between those who are equal in wealth, birth, prosperity, form and prospects, never between a superior and an inferior. O princess of Vidarbha! You did not know this. You were not far-sighted. You have chosen us, devoid of gunas.[538] We are only praised by confused beggars.[539] Therefore, you should choose a bull among kshatriyas who is similar to you. You will then truly obtain your wishes, in this world and in the next. O one with the beautiful thighs! Kings— Chedi, Shalva, Jarasandha, Dantavakra and others—hate me. So does your elder brother, Rukmi. They were blind because of their valour and intoxication. O fortunate one! I only abducted you to destroy their insolence and arrogance, so as to destroy the energy of the wicked. Indeed, we are indifferent and do not hanker after wives, children and wealth. We are completely satisfied within our own selves and are indifferent towards a body or a home. Like a light,[540] we are not engaged in any action."

Shri-Shuka continued, 'She regarded herself as extremely loved by him, because he was always with her. So as to destroy her pride, the illustrious one said this and stopped. The queen had never heard such disagreeable words from her beloved, who was the lord of all the lords in the three worlds. Hearing this, she was scared. Her

---

[537] Retreated to Dvaraka.

[538] This has a double meaning, as in devoid of qualities, or devoid of gunas.

[539] With another double meaning, of mendicants, as opposed to beggars.

[540] Which is a mere witness.

heart shuddered and she trembled. Overcome by great anxiety, she started to weep. Her well-formed feet were beautiful, with red nails. She scratched on the ground with these. Tears flowed from her dark eyes, decorated with collyrium, and sprinkled her breasts, red with kunkuma. She stood there, with her face cast downwards. The grief made her words choke. The great misery, fear and sorrow made her lose her mind. The bangles slipped from her hand and the fan fell down. She lost control over her body and her senses were suddenly confounded. With her hair dishevelled, she fell down, like a plantain tree uprooted by the wind. His beloved was bound to him by bonds of love and was unable to understand the purport of his jesting. Seeing this, the illustrious and merciful Krishna was filled with compassion for her. He swiftly got down from the bed and raised her in his four arms.[541] He gathered up her hair and wiped her face with his lotus hand. The tears of grief had flowed from her eyes and had stained her breasts. He wiped them. O king! She was virtuous and devoted to no one but him. He embraced her in his arms. The lord was compassionate towards those who were distressed. The destination of devotees knew how to comfort people and assured her. She did not understand the purpose of his jesting and did not deserve to suffer in this way.

'The illustrious one said, "O princess of Vidarbha! Do not be displeased with me. I know that you are devoted towards me. O dear one! I jokingly spoke those words with a desire to hear what you would say. I wished to see your loving face, with your lower lip quivering in rage, while you furrowed your beautiful eyebrows and cast sidelong and angry glances at me. O timid one! O beautiful lady! This is the greatest gain for householders in a home, spending time in joking with the beloved."'

Shri-Shuka continued, 'O king! Thus, the princess of Vidarbha was consoled by the illustrious one. She understood that the words had been spoken in jest and gave up all fear of her beloved abandoning her. She glanced bashfully towards the face of the illustrious one, bull among men. O descendant of the Bharata lineage! Her smile was beautiful and gentle. Rukmini said, "O lotus-eyed one! What

[541] He manifested four arms for the purpose.

you have said is indeed true. You are the illustrious one and I am not your equal in might. You find pleasure in your own greatness. You are the lord of the three lords.[542] I am Prakriti, characterized by gunas. It is the ignorant who grasp my feet. O Urukrama! It is true that you lie down on the ocean, as if you are afraid of the gunas. As atman, you are only awareness. You are always against the wicked aggregation of the senses and are engaged in fighting against them. Your servants give up the status of being kings, rejecting the blinding darkness.[543] Sages enjoy the honey of your lotus feet. Your path is not evident to men who are like animals. It is indeed impossible to comprehend. O lord! The lord's activities are superhuman. Therefore, this must also be true of those who follow you.[544] You possess nothing because there is nothing superior to you. That is the reason Aja[545] and the others, those who enjoy offerings, bring you their offerings. Those who are satisfied with their bodies and blinded by their affluence do not know you as the Destroyer. You are loved by those who enjoy offerings and they are also loved by you. You are the embodiment of all the objectives of human existence. You are the fruits. Because they are intelligent, those who desire you give up everything else. O lord! They are the right people for you to associate with. This is not like intercourse between a man and a woman, which brings both happiness and misery. Sages who have given up the staff[546] have spoken about your glory. You are the atman of the universe and you give your atman away.[547] That is the reason I have chosen you, rejecting the one born from the lotus, Bhava and the lords in the vault of heaven, not to speak of others. Their hopes are destroyed by the force of time, which is generated from the movement of your eyebrows. O Gada's elder brother! You drove away the kings through the roar of your Sharnga bow, like a lion driving away animals from its

[542] Brahma, Vishnu and Shiva.
[543] Therefore, why should you want to be a king?
[544] That is, they cannot possibly suffer.
[545] Brahma.
[546] The staff is only an external manifestation of renunciation.
[547] To your devotees.

own share, and abducted me, your own share. O lord! Therefore, your words that you sought refuge in the ocean because you were scared of them is false. Desiring you, jewels among kings like Anga, Vainya,[548] Jayanti's son,[549] Nahusha's son,[550] Gaya and others gave up their universal sovereignty. O lotus-eyed one! They cast aside their kingdoms and entered the forest. They followed you. Did they suffer in this world? Virtuous ones have described the scent of your lotus feet as something that confers liberation on people. It is Lakshmi's abode. Having smelt these, which mortal woman who knows what is good for herself will ignore you and resort to someone else who always suffers from fear? You are the lord of the universe and I have chosen you because you are appropriate for me. You are my atman and will satisfy my desires in this world and in the next. May the shelter of your feet protect me from wandering around,[551] just as they grant freedom from all that is false to those who approach them and worship you. O Achyuta! O afflicter of enemies! Your glories have been chanted in assembles of Mrida[552] and Virinchi. You mentioned some kings. Let them be servants in the houses of women who have not heard about you and where the servants are asses, cows, dogs and cats.[553] A woman who has not smelt the fragrance of your lotus feet is confused in her intelligence. She will love and serve a living corpse with skin, whiskers, body hair, nails and filled from the inside with flesh, bones, blood, worms, excrement, phlegm, bile and wind. O lotus-eyed one! May I be devoted to your feet. You are satisfied within yourself and do not glance too much towards me. However, when there is an excessive increase in rajas, you do look at me.[554] That itself is great compassion towards me. O Madhusudana! I do not think that your words are false. Like Amba, unmarried maidens often develop

[548] Vena's son, Prithu.
[549] Bharata, the son of Rishabha and Jayanti.
[550] Yayati.
[551] In the cycle of samsara.
[552] Shiva.
[553] This is interpreted as those kings being married to such women.
[554] As Prakriti, for creation of the world.

love.[555] Even if she is married, a *pumshchali*[556] always looks for new and newer lovers. An intelligent person should not maintain such a wicked woman. She has deviated in both worlds."

'The illustrious one said, "O virtuous lady! O princess! We deceived you only because we wished to hear you speak. Everything that you have said in reply is true. O beautiful lady! O fortunate one! You are always single-minded in your devotion towards me. Everything that you desire will happen, but you will also obtain freedom from desire. O unblemished one! I have experienced love towards the husband and devotion to the husband. Though I tried to disturb you with my words, your mind was attached to me and did not deviate. I am the lord of emancipation. But confounded by my maya, there are those who perform austerities and observe vows with the objective of obtaining happiness as couples. O proud one! I am the lord of emancipation and I am also the lord of prosperity. But having obtained me, there are unfortunate men who desire prosperity, which can also be obtained in hell. They are addicted to material objects and hell is the most appropriate place for them. It is good fortune that you are the mistress of my household. You are constantly engaged in faithful service towards me and that liberates from the cycle of samsara. The deceitful find this very difficult to accomplish, especially those whose intentions are also wicked. This is an extremely heavy burden to bear for a woman who is deceitful. O proud one! Among all the houses and all the wives, I have not seen such a loving one as you. At the time of your own marriage, there were kings who had arrived. But disregarding them, simply because you had heard true accounts about me, you secretly sent a brahmana to me with a message. Your brother was defeated and disfigured in the encounter. At the time of the marriage, he was killed during a gambling match.[557] You experienced this intolerable suffering. However, because you were scared of being separated

[555] Amba, the princess of Kashi, who was in love with Shalva.

[556] Wanton or unchaste woman.

[557] This is an inconsistency. It hasn't yet happened and the story will be told in the next chapter. The marriage is of Aniruddha, Rukmini's grandson.

from me, you did not utter a word. We have been conquered by you. To obtain me, you sent a messenger with secret counsel. When I took a long time, you thought that everything was empty. Unwilling to be united with anyone else, you wished to give up your body. We rejoice in this affection and may it always remain with you.'"

Shri-Shuka continued, 'Thus, the illustrious lord of the universe found his own pleasure with Rama and indulged in this conjugal conversation. He was imitating the conduct in the world of men. Similarly, in the other houses, the lord also behaved like a householder. Hari, the preceptor of the worlds, was engaged in following the dharma of a householder.'

Chapter 10(61)

Shri-Shuka said, 'Each of Krishna's women gave birth to ten sons each. They possessed all his prosperity and in no way were they inferior to their father. The princesses saw that Achyuta was always in their house. Not knowing about his true nature, each of those women thought that she was the most loved by him. They were captivated by his beautiful face, which was like the whorl of a lotus, his large eyes, his long arms, his loving and smiling glances and his attractive conversation. The women tried to conquer the lord's mind with their own allurements, but were incapable of doing so. They cast bashful and smiling glances at him and indicated their desires by arching their eyebrows and sending other strong messages of intercourse. However, though those sixteen thousand wives used such arrows of the god of love, they were incapable of agitating his senses. The women obtained Rama's consort as their husband. Not even Brahma and the others know the means to obtain him. They constantly enjoyed the pleasure of that increased love towards him and his smiling and sidelong glances. Their desire for union with him was always new. Though each possessed hundreds of servant-maids, they themselves took up the task of serving the lord. They approached him and offered him a seat and other objects of worship. They washed his feet. They offered him betel leaves. They dispelled his exhaustion by fanning him and gave him fragrances and garlands. They dressed his hair, prepared his bed, bathed him and gave him presents. Each of Krishna's wives had ten sons. Earlier, I have mentioned eight queens. I will now recount the names of their sons, Pradyumna and the others. With Pradyumna as the eldest, those born from Rukmini were Charudeshna, Sudeshna, the valiant Charudeha, Sucharu, Charugupta, Bhadracharu, Charuchandra, Vicharu and Charu as the tenth. Not a single one of these sons of Hari was inferior to his father. Satyabhama's ten sons were Bhanu, Subhanu, Svarbhanu, Prabhanu, Bhanuman, Chandrabhanu, Brihadbhanu, Atibhanu as the eighth, Shribhanu and Pratibhanu. Jambavati's sons were Samba, Sumitra, Purujit, Shatajit, Sahasrajit, Vijaya, Chitraketu, Vasuman, Dravida and Kratu. Samba and the others were dear to their father. The sons of Nagnajiti were Vira, Chandra, Ashvasena, Chitragu, Vegavan, Vrisha, Ama, Shanku, Vasu and the prosperous Kunti. The sons of Kalindi were Shruta, Kavivrisha, Vira, Subahu, Bhadra, Ekala, Shanti, Dasha, Purnamasa and Somaka as the youngest. Madra's[558] sons were Praghosha, Gatravan, Simha, Bala, Prabala, Urdhvaga, Mahashakti, Saha, Oja and Aparajita. The sons of Mitravinda were Vrika, Harsha, Anila, Gridhra, Vardhana, Annada, Mahamsha, Pavana, Vahni and Kshudhi. Bhadra's sons were Sangramajit, Brihatsena, Shura, Praharana, Arijit, Jaya, Subhadra, Vama, Ayus and Satyaka. Through Hari, Rohini's sons were Diptiman, Tamratapta and others. O king! When they lived in the city of Bhojakata, through Rukmavati, Rukmi's daughter, Pradyumna had an immensely powerful son named Aniruddha. O king! Sixteen thousand mothers gave birth to those who descended from Krishna and their sons and grandsons numbered hundreds of crores.'

The king asked, 'Rukmi had been defeated by Krishna in an encounter and was waiting for an opportunity to kill him. O learned one! How did he bestow his daughter on his enemy's son? Tell me how two enemies entered into a matrimonial alliance. Yogis can properly see everything in the past, the present and the future, even

---

[558] Madra is also known as Lakshmana.

if it is beyond the senses and distant and even if it is obstructed from vision.'

Shri-Shuka continued, 'He[559] was the embodiment of Ananga himself and when she chose him at her svayamvara, on a single chariot, he defeated the assembled kings and abducted her. Rukmi remembered the enemy and the disrespect shown by Krishna. However, since he wished to please his sister, he bestowed his daughter on his nephew. O king! Kritavarma's powerful son married Rukmini's large-eyed daughter, Charumati. Rukmi bestowed Rochana, his granddaughter, on his daughter's son, Aniruddha. Despite his being bound in enmity towards Hari, he wished to bring pleasure to his sister. Though he knew this marriage was adharma, he was bound by bonds of affection.[560] O king! At the time of the marriage, Rukmini, Rama, Keshava, Samba, Pradyumna and the others went to the city of Bhojakata.

'When the marriage was over, insolent kings, headed by the king of Kalinga,[561] told Rukmi, "Defeat Bala in a game of dice. O king! Though he does not know how to play with dice, he is extremely addicted to it." Thus addressed, he challenged Bala and a match of gambling with the dice commenced. Rama placed stakes of one hundred, one thousand and ten thousand.[562] Rukmi won them all. Kalinga displayed his teeth and laughed loudly at Bala. The wielder of the plough could not tolerate this. After this, Rukmi placed a bet of one lakh and Bala won this. However, resorting to deceit, Rukmi exclaimed, "I have won." The prosperous one became turbulent with rage, like the ocean on the day of the full moon. His eyes turned red because of his great rage and he placed a bet of ten crores. According to dharma, Rama won this. However, resorting to deceit, Rukmi said, "I have won. Let the referees make their decision." A voice was heard from the firmament, "According to dharma, Bala has won the bet. What Rukmi has spoken is false."

[559] Pradyumna.
[560] This adharma is about a matrimonial alliance with an enemy and not about marriages between cousins.
[561] Dantavakra.
[562] Progressively. Obviously, this means coins.

Urged on by the wicked kings, the one from Vidarbha did not pay heed to this. Goaded by destiny, he laughed at Samkarshana and said, "You cowherds roam around in the forests. You are not accomplished in playing with the dice. Playing with dice and playing with arrows are for kings, not for the likes of you." Abused by Rukmi and laughed at by the kings, he was enraged. In that assembly of kings, he raised a club and slew him. The king of Kalinga, who had displayed his teeth and laughed, tried to flee. But he angrily seized him at the tenth step and knocked out his teeth with force. Other kings suffered from Bala's club. Their arms, thighs and heads were crushed and covered with blood. They ran away in fear. O king! Hari was scared that his relationship of love with Rukmini would suffer. Therefore, when his brother-in-law, Rukmi, was killed by Bala, he did not say anything—praising it, or condemning it. Rama and the other Dasharhas placed Aniruddha and his bride on an excellent chariot and went to Kushasthali[563] from Bhojakata. Having sought refuge with Madhusudana, they had accomplished all their objectives.'

Chapter 10(62)

The king said, 'O great yogi! The best of the Yadus[564] married Bana's daughter, Usha. As a result, there was a terrible battle between Hari and Shankara. You should tell me everything about this.'

Shri-Shuka replied, 'The great-souled Bali, who had given the earth to Hari in his form as a dwarf, had one hundred sons and Bana was the eldest. His[565] biological son was Bana and he was always devoted to Shiva. The intelligent one was revered and generous. He was firm in his vows and did not waver from the truth. Earlier, he used to rule over his kingdom from the beautiful city known

---

[563] Dvaraka.
[564] Aniruddha.
[565] Bali's.

as Shonita. Because of Shambhu's favours, the immortals behaved as if they were his servants. When Mrida engaged in his *tandava* dance, he pleased him by using his own one thousand arms to play on musical instruments. The illustrious lord of all creatures is one who should be worshipped. He was devoted towards his devotees and asked him to choose a boon. He requested him to be the lord of the city. He became intoxicated with his valour. On one occasion, Girisha was standing next to him. He touched his lotus feet with his diadem, which had the complexion of the sun. He said, "O Mahadeva! I bow down to you. You are the lord and preceptor of the worlds. You are like the tree from heaven that satisfies all the unfulfilled desires of men. The one thousand arms you have given me have become a great burden. Other than you, I do not find anyone in the three worlds that I can fight with. O original being! My arms were itching to have a fight. I advanced against the elephants who are the guardians of the directions, pulverizing mountains with my arms. However, they were terrified and fled." Hearing this, the illustrious one became angry. "O foolish one! When you fight against someone who is my equal, your standard will be shattered. That is when your insolence will be broken." Thus addressed, because of his wicked intelligence, he was delighted and entered his own residence. Evil in his intelligence, he waited for Girisha's instructions, so that his own valour might be destroyed.

'He had a daughter named Usha. In a dream, she had intercourse with Pradyumna. The maiden obtained him as his beloved, though she had never seen him or heard of him. Unable to see him,[566] she arose in the midst of her friends and exclaimed, "O beloved! Where are you?" At this, she was disturbed and greatly ashamed. Bana's minister was Kumbhanda and his daughter, Chitralekha, was her friend. Filled with curiosity, she asked her friend, Usha. "O one with the excellent brows! Whom are you searching for? What is this wish of yours? O princess! I have not yet seen anyone accept your hand." Usha replied, "I saw a man in my dream. He was lotus-eyed and dark in complexion. His arms were long and he was attired in yellow garments. He was one who touches the hearts of women.

[566] When she woke up.

He is the beloved one I am searching for. Having made me drink the nectar of his lips, he has gone somewhere. I am craving after him. He has abandoned me in this ocean of misery." Chitralekha said, "I will dispel your misery. As long as he exists anywhere in the three worlds, I will bring your groom to you. Please indicate the one who has stolen your heart." Having said this, she drew portraits of gods, gandharvas, Siddhas, charanas, serpents, daityas, vidyadharas, *yakshas* and men. Among men, she drew portraits of Vrishnis, Shura, Anakadundubhi, Rama and Krishna. On seeing Pradyumna, she was ashamed.[567] O lord of the earth! Seeing Aniruddha's portrait, she cast her face downwards in shame. She smiled and said, "This is he. It is him." Chitralekha was a *yogini* and recognized him as Krishna's grandson. O king! Travelling through the sky, she went to Dvaraka, protected by Krishna. Pradyumna's son was sleeping on an excellent couch. Using powers of yoga, she seized him. She took him to Shonitapura and showed her friend her beloved. Seeing that most handsome of men, her face filled with joy. She took Pradyumna's son to her own house, which was impossible for men to see. There, she enjoyed herself with him. She served and worshipped him with extremely expensive garments, garlands, fragrances, incense, lamps, seats, other objects, drinks, food, other eatables and pleasant words. He was secreted in the maiden's house and his affection towards her constantly increased. Since his senses were overwhelmed by the enjoyment, he did not realize the number of days that had passed.

'As she enjoyed herself happily with the brave Yadu, her vow was broken.[568] It was impossible to conceal the signs. The female servants went and said, "O king! We have noticed signs of behaviour in your daughter that will taint the lineage. O lord! She has been guarded by us in the house and she couldn't be approached. It was impossible for men to see her. We do not understand how your daughter could have been polluted." Hearing about his maiden being polluted, Bana was distressed. He swiftly went to his daughter's room. There,

---

[567] Because Pradyumna was her father-in-law.
[568] Of being a virgin.

he saw the supreme one of the Yadu lineage. He was Kama's[569] son and the most beautiful person on earth. He was dark in complexion and his garment was yellow. His eyes were like lotuses. His arms were long and his earrings and locks of hair made his face beautiful. His glances were full of smiles. He sat there, in front of his beloved and auspicious daughter, playing with dice. Since it was spring, a garland of jasmine flowers hung between his arms and because he had embraced his beloved, it was smeared with kunkuma from her breasts. Seeing this, he[570] was amazed. Madhava saw him enter, surrounded by several soldiers who were like assassins. He raised an iron club and stood there, like the Destroyer[571] wielding his rod, ready to strike. As they approached and surrounded him, desiring to seize him, he struck, like a leader of boars at dogs. Struck by him, their heads, thighs and arms were shattered and they left the residence and fled. When he struck and killed his own soldiers, Bali's powerful son became angry and tied him in bonds made out of serpents.[572] When she heard about his bondage, Usha was overwhelmed with great grief and misery. Tears flowed from her eyes.'

Chapter 10(63)

Shri-Shuka said, 'O descendant of the Bharata lineage! The four months of the rainy season passed. Aniruddha's relatives could not see him and grieved. The Vrishnis, for whom Krishna was a divinity, heard from Narada about what he had done and his bondage. They went to Shonitapura. Assembling twelve akshouhinis, the bulls among the Satvatas laid siege to Bana's city from all directions. They were Pradyumna, Yuyudhana, Gada, Samba, Sarana, Nanda, Upananda, Bhadra and others—all Rama and

[569] Pradyumna's.
[570] Bana.
[571] Yama.
[572] *Nagapasha.*

Krishna's followers. The groves, ramparts, mansions and arches of the city were shattered. Seeing this, he[573] became angry and emerged with an army that was equally large. For Bana's sake, along with his son,[574] Shiva surrounded him with *pramathas*.[575] Astride the bull Nandi, he fought with Rama and Krishna. O king! There was a tumultuous encounter that made the body hair stand up, between Krishna and Shankara and between Pradyumna and Guha.[576] Bala fought with Kumbhanda and Kupakarna, Samba with Bana's son and Satyaki with Bana. On their vimanas, Brahma and the other lords among the gods, sages, Siddhas, charanas, gandharvas, apsaras and yakshas arrived to witness it. With sharp-tipped arrows shot from his Sharnga bow, Shouri drove away Shankara's followers—bhutas, pramathas, guhyakas, *dakinis*, *yatudhanas*, *vetalas*, *vinayakas*, pretas, *matris*, pishachas, *kushmandas* and *brahma-rakshasas*. The wielder of the Pinaka used many different kinds of weapons against the wielder of Sharnga. Without being surprised at all, with the Sharnga bow in his hand, he pacified all these with counter-weapons. He countered *brahmastra* with brahmastra, *vayavyastra* with *parvatastra*, *agneyastra* with *parjanyastra* and *pashupata* with his own weapon.[577] Using *jrimbhanastra*, he confounded Girisha by making him yawn. Shouri used swords, a club and arrows to kill Bana's soldiers. From every direction, Skanda was struck by Pradyumna's showers of weapons. With blood flowing from his limbs, astride the peacock, he fled from the battle. Kumbhanda and Kupakarna suffered from the club[578] and fell down. With these leaders slain, the soldiers fled in different directions. Seeing that his own army had been routed, Bana was filled with great intolerance. He abandoned his duel with Satyaki, and on his chariot, attacked Krishna in the battle. Indomitable in the battle, Bana simultaneously drew back the strings on five thousand bows and on each string,

---

[573] Bana.

[574] Skanda.

[575] Beings that torment, Shiva's companions.

[576] Skanda.

[577] These are names of various divine weapons. Pashupata is Shiva's weapon, while Krishna's own weapon means Narayanastra.

[578] Wielded by Balarama.

affixed two arrows.[579] The illustrious Hari simultaneously severed
all these arrows and killing the charioteer and horses and destroying
the chariot, blew on his conch shell. His mother was named Kotara.
Wishing to save her son's life, she appeared before Krishna, naked,
and with her hair loose.[580] Gada's elder brother turned his face
away, so that he would not have to look at the naked one. At
that time, devoid of his chariot and with his bow severed, Bana
entered the city. When the large number of bhutas had run away,
Jvara[581] attacked Dasharha. He possessed three heads and three feet
and seemed to burn down the ten directions. Seeing this, the god
Narayana released his own Jvara. The two Jvaras, Maheshvara and
Vaishnava, fought against each other. Suffering from Vaishnava's
strength, Maheshvara started to cry. Maheshvara Jvara was
frightened and could not find freedom from fear anywhere else.
Therefore, he sought refuge with Hrishikesha. He joined his hands
in salutation and praised him.

'Jvara said, "I bow down before you. You are infinite in your
powers. You are the supreme lord. You are in all atmans. You are
pure consciousness and absolute. You are the cause behind the
creation, preservation and destruction of the universe. You are
the brahman. You are the signs of the brahman. You are serene.
You are time, destiny, karma, *jivatman*,[582] nature, objects, kshetra,
prana,[583] atman and transformations. You are the seed that leads to
the constant interaction between these. It is your maya and I seek
refuge with you to counter that maya. In many forms, you indulge
in pastimes to protect the gods, virtuous people and the ordinances
of the worlds. You kill those who deviate from the path and subsist
through violence. This birth of yours is for the sake of removing the
earth's burden. I am scorched by your energy, which is impossible

[579] He possessed one thousand arms.
[580] Kotara should not be taken as the name of Bana's biological mother.
Bana's biological mother was Ashana. This is the family deity, identified
with Durga. Kotara means someone who dwells in a cave or in the hollow
of a tree.
[581] Fever, this is Shiva's *jvara*.
[582] The individual soul.
[583] Prana is the breath of life or the life force.

to withstand. This Jvara is extremely fierce in its energy and is extremely cold. As long as they do not serve at the soles of your feet and as long as they are bound to desire, embodied creatures are tormented by it."

'The illustrious one replied, "O three-headed one! I am pleased with you. Let the fever on account of my Jvara go away. If a person remembers this conversation, may he not suffer fear on account of this."'

Shri-Shuka continued, 'Thus addressed, Maheshvara Jvara took Achyuta's permission and left. However, astride his chariot, Bana advanced against Janardana. The asura wielded many kinds of weapons in his one thousand arms. O king! Extremely angry, he released arrows at the one who wields the chakra as a weapon. He repeatedly hurled weapons at him. The illustrious one used his chakra, sharp at the edges, to lop off his arms, as if they were the branches of a tree. When Bana's arms were being severed, the illustrious Bhava was filled with compassion towards his devotee. Approaching the one who wields the chakra as a weapon, he spoke to him.

'The illustrious Rudra said, "You are the brahman. You are the supreme illumination. You are concealed in words about the brahman.[584] You are as unpolluted as the sky and those with spotless atmans can see you. The sky is your navel. The fire is your mouth. The water is your semen. The firmament is your head. The directions are your ears. Your feet are the earth. The moon is your mind. Your eyes are the sun. I am your ahamkara. The ocean is your stomach. Your arms are Indra. The herbs and plants are your body hair. The clouds are your hair. Virinchi is your intelligence. Prajapati is your genital organ. Dharma is your heart. You are Purusha, the creator of the worlds. O one who is infinite in powers! For the welfare of the universe, you have assumed this avatara to protect dharma. All of us are dependent on you and maintain the seven worlds. You alone are the original being. You are without a second. You are transcendental and self-manifesting. You are without cause, but you are the lord

[584] Interpreted as the Vedas.

behind all causes. Nevertheless, you can be perceived through the transformations. You use your own maya for the manifestation of all the gunas. When covered under its own shadow,[585] the sun illuminates its own shadow and all the forms. In that way, your attributes are hidden behind the gunas. O lord! But you are like a lamp to those who possess those gunas. Your maya confounds and causes immersion in sons, wives, homes and other things. Thus attached, they are immersed in this ocean of misery, rise up and are submerged again. A man obtains birth in this world of men through the god's favours. However, if he does not conquer his senses and does not honour his feet, one should grieve over him. He is deceiving himself. For the sake of the objects of the senses, which are calamities, if a mortal person abandons you, the beloved lord who is his own atman, he gives up amrita for the sake of poison. You are the lord who is most loved by our atmans. I, Brahma, the gods and sages who are pure in their consciousness have sought refuge in you with all our souls. You are the reason behind the creation, preservation and destruction of the universe. You are impartial and tranquil. You are our well-wisher and divinity. You are unique and without a second. The universe is in your atman. We worship this god for the sake of liberation from samsara. This one[586] is loved by me and follows me. O god! I have bestowed freedom from fear on him. Through your favours, let that be granted to him, just as the lord of the daityas[587] obtained your favours."

'The illustrious one replied, "O illustrious one! I will do what you have said and give you pleasure. We will act accordingly. I find this virtuous and approve of it. This asura, the son of Virochana's son, will not be killed by me. I granted Prahlada the boon that I would not kill any of his descendants. I lopped off his arms so that I could destroy his insolence. His large army has been killed because it was a burden on earth. Four arms still remain and he will be immortal, without suffering from old age. This asura will be the

---

[585] Clouds, which are created by the sun.
[586] Banasura.
[587] Prahlada.

foremost among your attendants and will not suffer from fear from any source.'"

Shri-Shuka continued, 'Having thus obtained freedom from fear from Krishna, the asura bowed his head down. He placed Pradyumna's son and his bride on a chariot and brought them there. Taking Rudra's leave, he departed, placing him and his wife, in front, with excellent garments and ornaments. They were surrounded by an akshouhini. He entered his own capital, which was ornamented with flags and arches. The roads and quadrangles were sprinkled with water. There were the sounds of conch shells, drums and kettledrums. He was welcomed by citizens, well-wishers and brahmanas. Thus did Krishna triumph over Shankara in the encounter. If a person wakes up and remembers it, he is never defeated.'

Chapter 10(64)

Shri-Shuka said, 'O king! On one occasion, Samba, Pradyumna, Charu, Bhanu, Gada and other young ones from the Yadu lineage went to a grove to amuse themselves. After playing there for a very long time, they became thirsty. They searched around for water and found a well without any water in it. They saw an extraordinary creature there. It was a lizard that was as large as a mountain. On seeing it, their minds were astonished. Full of compassion, they made great efforts to raise it up. It had fallen down there. The boys tied it up with leather thongs and ropes. However, they were unable to raise it. Anxious, they went and told Krishna about this. The illustrious lotus-eyed creator of the universe went there and saw it. Effortlessly, he used his left hand to raise it up. Touched by Uttamashloka's hand, it immediately abandoned its form as a lizard. His beautiful complexion was like that of molten gold. His amazing form was like that of a resident of heaven, with ornaments, garments and garlands. Though he knew, with a view to making it known among people, Mukunda questioned him. "O immensely fortunate one! Who are you? Your form is excellent. Indeed, I must count you as a supreme among the gods. What karma reduced you to this state? O extremely fortunate one! You do not seem to deserve it. We are eager to know. Tell us about yourself. If you think it to be appropriate, tell us." The king was thus asked by Krishna, who has an infinite number of forms. Wearing a diadem that was as radiant as the sun, he bowed down before Madhava.

'Nriga replied, "O lord! I am a king among men, named Nriga. I am descended from the lineage of Ikshvaku. When the list of generous ones is recounted, it is possible that you may have heard of me. O protector! There is nothing that is not known to you. You are the witness in the atmans of all creatures. Your vision is not affected by time. Nevertheless, because of your command, I will speak. In charity, I gave away as many cows as there are grains of sand on earth, as many stars as there are in the firmament and as many drops of rain as there are in showers. They yielded milk and were young. They were excellent in conduct and form. They were full of attributes. They were brown and their horns were encrusted in gold. They had been obtained in the proper way.[588] Their hooves were plated with silver and they were with their calves. They were covered with garments, garlands and ornaments and I gave them away. I gave them to young bulls among brahmanas who had ornamented themselves with their qualities and good conduct. They were from families that were suffering. They were devoted to truth and the vows. They were known for their austerities, learning, knowledge about the brahman and virtue. I gave them cows, land, gold, houses, horses, elephants, maidens,[589] female servants, sesamum, silver, beds, garments, jewels, furnishings and chariots. I performed rites, sacrifices and auspicious works. There was a cow that belonged to a foremost brahmana. It got lost and entered my own herd of cattle, getting mixed up in the process. Not knowing about this, I gave it to a different brahmana. Seeing it being taken away, its owner spoke these words. 'This belongs to me.' The one who had received it said, 'This belongs to me. It was given to me by Nriga.' The two brahmanas debated in this way. Seeking to accomplish

[588] By paying a price for them.
[589] In marriage.

their own respective objectives, they came and spoke to me. 'You gave it to me.' 'You took it away from me.' Hearing them, I was filled with confusion. Because of dharma, I faced a difficult situation and entreated both the brahmanas. 'In exchange for this cow, I will give one hundred thousand excellent cows. You should show me your favours. I am your servant and have done this unwittingly. Please save me from this calamity. Otherwise, I will descend into an impure hell.' The owner said, 'O king! I do not want that.' Saying this, he left. The other one said, 'I do not desire ten thousand cows in exchange for this cow.' Saying this, he too left. O god of the gods! O lord of the universe! At this time, Yama's messengers arrived and conveyed me to Yama's eternal abode, where Yama questioned me. 'O king! Do you first want to experience the consequence of your wicked deed, or the consequence of your good deeds? I do not see any end to the generous deeds of dharma you have performed. You have obtained radiant worlds.' I replied, 'O god! I first want to experience the consequences of my wicked deed.' He said, 'Then, fall.' O lord! I saw myself fall down and I have become this lizard. O Keshava! I was generous and I was devoted to brahmanas. I am your servant. Since I have always desired to meet you, my memory has still not been extinguished. O lord! O paramatman! How is it that you are yourself before my eyes now? O Adhokshaja! I am blind in my intelligence and am suffering severely from this hardship. You are perceived by lords of yoga who meditate in their hearts, using the unblemished insight of the sacred texts. You are the one who liberates from the cycle of samsara. Perhaps that is the reason you have shown yourself to me. O god of the gods! O protector of the universe! O Purushottama! O Narayana! O Hrishikesha! O one of auspicious fame! O Achyuta! O undecaying one! O Krishna! O lord! Give me leave to return to my state as a god. Wherever I may be, may you remain in my consciousness and may I seek shelter at your feet. I bow down before the source of all creation. O brahman! O one who is infinite in powers! O Krishna! O Vasudeva! O lord of yoga! I bow down before you.'"

Shri-Shuka said, 'Saying this, he circumambulated him, touching his feet with his diadem. Having taken his permission, while all the men looked on, he mounted his vimana. The illustrious Krishna,

Devaki's son, spoke to his own people. He regarded brahmanas as divinities and possessed dharma in his soul. He wished to instruct those born in royal lineages. "Indeed, the property of a brahmana, however little, is as difficult to digest as a fire that has been consumed. In fact, it is more powerful. What need be said about kings who pride themselves on being lords? I do not think that *halahala* is a poison, since it has an antidote.[590] It has been said that the property of a brahmana is a poison for which there is no antidote on earth. If a brahmana's property is used without his permission, it ruins three generations. However, if it is seized and enjoyed by force, it destroys ten generations of ancestors and ten generations of successors. Kings are blinded by the prosperity of their kingdom and do not see their own downfall. Foolish, they regard it as virtuous to take a brahmana's property and head for hell. If a king from a royal lineage loses control and takes away the means of subsistence of a generous brahmana with a family, he takes away the brahmana's share, which is then stained with the tears of weeping. He is then cooked in *kumbhipaka* for as many years as there are particles of dust.[591] Whether it has been given to him by the brahmana himself or whether it has been given by someone else, if a person takes away his property, for sixty thousand years, he is born as a worm in excrement. May a brahmana's wealth never come to me. Men who hanker after it are limited in their lifespans. They are defeated and dislodged from their kingdoms. They become snakes that cause anxiety. O those who are my own! Do not injure a brahmana, even if he has caused offence. Even if he strikes you a lot and curses you, always bow down before him. I control myself and always bow down before brahmanas. You should always bow down in a similar way. Otherwise, you will face punishment from me. Even if a brahmana's possession has been taken away ignorantly, the taker will fall downwards, just as it was with Nriga, who took away the brahmana's cow." In this way, the illustrious

---

[590] The deadly poison that arose from the churning of the ocean. Interestingly, the word also means a lizard.
[591] Kumbhipaka is the name of a specific hell. There, sinners are baked (*pacha*) like a clay pot (*kumbha*).

Mukunda made the residents of Dvaraka listen. The purifier of all the worlds then entered his own residence.'

Chapter 10(65)

Shri-Shuka said, 'O best among the Kuru lineage! The illustrious Balabhadra[592] mounted his chariot. Eager to see his well-wishers, he went to Nanda's Gokula. The gopas and gopis had been anxious for a very long time and they embraced him. Rama greeted his parents.[593] They welcomed him and pronounced their benedictions over him. "O Dasharha! May you and your younger brother, the lord of the universe, protect us for a very long time." Saying this, they placed him on their laps and embraced him, their eyes wet with tears. In the proper way, according to age, friendship and the relationship with himself, he bowed down before the elders among the gopas and those who were younger bowed down to him. He then went to the cowherds and smilingly clasped their hands. After he had rested and was happily seated, they surrounded him and questioned him. In words that faltered because of their affection, they asked about the welfare of their relatives. They had given up everything they possessed for the sake of the lotus-eyed Krishna. "O Rama! Are all our relatives well? O Rama! With your wives and sons, do you still remember us? It is good fortune that the wicked Kamsa has been killed. It is good fortune that our well-wishers have been freed. It is good fortune that they have killed and vanquished their enemies and have found shelter inside a fortification." The gopis approached Rama and welcomed him, questioning him with smiles. "Is Krishna, the darling of the women of the city, happy? Does he remember his relatives and his father and his mother? Do you think he himself will come back and see his mother even once? Does the mighty-armed one remember the service we rendered him? O Dasharha! O lord! For his sake, we abandoned our mothers,

[592] Balarama.
[593] Nanda and Yashoda.

fathers, brothers, husbands, sons and sisters. These are extremely difficult to give up. He is ungrateful. How can the intelligent women of the city accept the words of someone who is so fickle? Perhaps they accept them because his words are colourful and charming. Perhaps they are agitated by his smiling glances and desire is ignited in them. O gopis! Why are we talking about him? Let us talk about something else. If he spends his time without us, we should also behave in a similar way." But the women remembered Shouri's smiles, conversation, beautiful glances, gait and loving embraces. They started to weep. The illustrious Samkarshna was accomplished in comforting. He assured them by conveying Krishna's message and calmed their minds.

'The illustrious Rama resided there for the two months of Madhu and Madhava.[594] During the nights, he brought the gopis the pleasure of intercourse. Surrounded by large numbers of women, Rama frequented a grove on the banks of the Yamuna. It was bathed by the beams of the full moon and the breeze bore the fragrance of night lotuses. Sent by Varuna, the goddess Varuni[595] emerged from the hollow of a tree. She flowed everywhere in that forest and made it more fragrant with her own aroma. The wind conveyed the smell of that flow of honey to Bala. He inhaled it and approached. Together, he and the women drank it. As the women sang about his conduct, the wielder of the plough roamed around in the forests with them. Intoxicated by the liquor, his eyes started to roll. He wore a garland and a single earring, with the vaijayanti garland. His smiling lotus face was radiant, decorated with beads of perspiration. Inebriated, the lord wanted to sport in the water and summoned Yamuna there. In the state of intoxication, he took it that the river had slighted his words. Since it had not come, he became angry. He used the tip of his plough to drag it there. "O wicked one! You have shown me disrespect. You go where you want. Though I have summoned you, you have not come here. Therefore, with the tip of my plough, I will fetch one hundred of your flows here."

[594] The first two months of spring. Respectively, Chaitra and Vaishakha.
[595] The goddess of liquor. *Varuni* was the liquor born from the churning of the ocean, accepted by the asuras.

Thus censured by the descendant of the Yadu lineage, Yamuna was terrified. O king! She fell down at his feet. She trembled and spoke these words. "O Rama! O mighty-armed one! O Rama! I did not know about your valour. O lord of the universe! With only one of your portions,[596] you hold up the universe. O illustrious one! I did not know about your supreme powers. O atman of the universe! You are compassionate towards your devotees. O illustrious one! I have sought refuge with you. You should free me." Asked in this way, the illustrious Bala released Yamuna. With the women, he entered the water, like a king of elephant with female elephants. As he wished, he sported in the waters. When he emerged, Kanti gave him two blue garments, extremely expensive garments and a sparkling garland.[597] He attired himself in those blue garments and adorned himself with the golden garlands. With those excellent ornaments and pastes, he was radiant, like the great Indra's elephant. O king! Even today, the course of the Yamuna being dragged away by the infinitely valiant Bala can be seen, indicating his valour. Rama's mind was agitated by the sweetness of the women of Vraja. Therefore, as he sported in Vraja, all those nights seemed to be like a single night.'

Chapter 10(66)

Shri-Shuka said, 'O king! When Rama had gone to Nanda's Vraja, the ignorant lord of Karusha thought, "I am Vasudeva."[598] Accordingly, he sent a messenger to Krishna. He was flattered by foolish people. "You are the illustrious Vasudeva. You are the lord

[596] Shesha.

[597] Kanti is the goddess Lakshmi, or her manifestation. The text says the garments were not white. This is interpreted as blue, because of what follows.

[598] The kingdom normally referred to as Karusha is in Datia district of Madhya Pradesh. At that time, the king of Karusha was Dantavakra, killed by Krishna. This Karusha is actually the kingdom of Pundra, in broader Bengal, especially the northern parts. The king of Pundra called himself Poundra Vasudeva and imitated and wore all of Vasudeva's signs.

of the universe who has descended." Therefore, he took himself to be Achyuta. The foolish and ignorant one was like a king chosen by children.[599] The evil-minded one sent a messenger to Krishna, whose paths are inconceivable, in Dvaraka. Arriving in Dvaraka, the messenger went to the lord Krishna when he was in his assembly hall. He conveyed the king's message to the lotus-eyed one and said, "I alone am the Vasudeva who has descended for the sake of showing compassion to beings. There is no other. Therefore, give up your false title. O Satvata! It is out of confusion that you sport my signs.[600] Abandon them and seek refuge with me. Alternatively, fight with me." Hearing the boasting of Poundraka, limited in his intelligence, Ugrasena and the others in the assembly laughed loudly. After the jocular conversation, the illustrious one spoke to the messenger. "O foolish one! Just as you have boasted, I will hurl those signs away.[601] O ignorant one! When you are killed and lie down, your mouth will be shut and you will be surrounded by kites and vultures. Dogs will find a refuge in you." The messenger conveyed all this abuse to his lord.

'Krishna mounted his chariot and went to Kashi.[602] Maharatha Poundraka noticed his efforts and quickly emerged from the city, along with two akshouhinis. O king! His friend, the king of Kashi, followed him, guarding his rear with three akshouhinis. Hari saw Poundraka bearing the signs—conch shell, sword, mace, Sharnga bow, shrivatsa mark, Koustubha jewel, garland of wild flowers, yellow silken garments, Garuda on the standard, expensive diadem and ornaments and shining earrings shaped like makaras.[603] Hari saw him in that artificial attire, an exact imitation of his own, just like an actor on a stage, and laughed loudly. Hari's enemies attacked him with spears, clubs, bludgeons, javelins, double-edged

[599] In their playing.

[600] Conch shell, chakra, mace, garland of wild flowers, etc.

[601] This probably means that Krishna will hurl Poundraka's false signs away, though it is possible that in an encounter, Krishna will hurl his signs (club, chakra) towards Poundraka. In a subsequent shloka, the latter meaning seems to be intended.

[602] Poundraka was with his friend, the king of Kashi.

[603] These were imitations.

swords, spikes, lances, swords, battleaxes and arrows. The armies of Poundraka and the king of Kashi had elephants, chariots, horses and foot soldiers and Krishna severely afflicted them with his mace, sword, chakra and arrows, like the fire of destruction separately afflicts subjects at the end of a yuga. His chakra severed and littered the field of battle with chariots, horses, elephants, bipeds, donkeys and camels. This brought pleasure to the hearts of the spirited. It resembled the terrible pleasure ground of the lord of bhutas.[604] Shouri spoke to Poundraka. "O Poundraka! You used your messenger's words to speak to me about weapons. I will now release them towards you. O ignorant one! Give up my title, which you have assumed falsely. If I do not wish to fight against you, I will certainly seek refuge with you today." Having abused him in this way, he used his sharp arrows to deprive Poundraka of his chariot. Using his chakra, he severed his head, like Indra using his vajra to slice off the peak of a mountain. In similar fashion, he used his arrows to sever the head of the king of Kashi and, as if it was a lotus bud borne by the wind, made it fall inside the city of Kashi. Having thus killed the ones who were jealous of him, Poundraka and his friend, Hari entered Dvaraka. The Siddhas chanted about his immortal accounts. O king! By always thinking about the illustrious one, he[605] severed all his bonds. By assuming Hari's form, he himself became immersed in him.

'The head, decorated with earrings, fell down at the gate of the palace. Bewildered, people asked, "What is this? Whom does this head belong to?" O king! The queens, sons and relatives recognized that it belonged to the king, the lord of Kashi. Along with the citizens, they lamented and wept, "Alas! Our protector has been killed." His son, Sudakshina, performed the funeral rites for his father. "I will slay my father's slayer and exact vengeance for my father." Having made up his mind in this way, accompanied by his priest, he worshipped Maheshvara, performing supreme meditation. The illustrious lord, the granter of boons, was pleased and appeared in

[604] Shiva/Rudra.
[605] Poundraka.

Avimukta.[606] As a boon, he asked, "I wish for a means so that my father's killer can be slain." "Along with brahmanas and officiating priests, worship *dakshinagni*.[607] Follow the rites of *abhichara*.[608] Surrounded by pramathas, like a brahmana who is used for a specific purpose, that fire will accomplish your objective." Thus instructed, he followed the abhichara vow and directed it towards Krishna. The fire arose in personified form from the sacrificial pit, extremely terrible in form. His tuft of hair, moustache and beard had the complexion of molten copper. His eyes were like burning coal. There were tusks as his teeth and his eyebrows were furrowed and arched. His face was harsh and he licked the corners of his mouth with his tongue. He was naked and he brandished a blazing trident. On feet that were as large as palm trees, he made the earth tremble. Surrounded by bhutas, he rushed towards Dvaraka, setting the directions ablaze. The residents of Dvaraka saw him advance towards them, burning everything. All of them were terrified, like animals at a forest conflagration. The illustrious one was playing with dice in an assembly hall. Afflicted by fear, they screamed, "Save us. O lord of the three worlds! Save us. The fire is burning down the city." He heard about it from the people and saw that those who were his own were suffering. The granter of refuge laughed and said, "Do not be scared. I will grant you protection." The lord is a witness who is inside and outside everything. He knew that this demoness[609] had been unleashed by Maheshvara. The chakra was by his side and he commanded it to destroy her. Sudarshana blazed like one crore suns. It was as resplendent and dazzling as the fire of universal destruction. Mukunda's chakra radiated the sky, the directions, heaven and earth with its own energy and made the fire suffer. O king! The fire created by the demoness was repulsed by the energy of the weapon of the one who holds a chakra in his hand. Its face shattered, it retreated and approached Varanasi. Though Sudakshina had created it through abhichara for his own

---

[606] A specific place inside Kashi.
[607] The fire that is towards the south. This is Shiva speaking.
[608] Magical mantras used for malevolent purposes.
[609] The feminine gender is used, *kritya* or demoness.

purpose, it burnt him, his officiating priests and his relatives down. Commanded by Vishnu, the chakra followed and burnt down Varanasi, with its towers, assembly halls, residences, shops, arches, mansions, treasuries, storehouses, kitchens and buildings for housing elephants, horses and chariots. Having burnt down everything in Varanasi, Vishnu's Sudarshana chakra again presented itself by the side of Krishna, whose deeds are unblemished. If a mortal person controls himself and hears about Uttamashloka's valour, or makes it heard, he is cleansed of all sins.'

Chapter 10(67)

The king asked, 'I again wish to hear about Rama's extraordinary deeds. The lord is infinite and immeasurable. What else did he do?'

Shri-Shuka replied, 'There was an ape named Dvivida and he was Naraka's friend. The valiant one was Mainda's brother and was Sugriva's adviser. As an act of vengeance for his friend, the ape created havoc in the kingdom. He set cities, villages, mines and cowherd settlements on fire by igniting flames. On one occasion, he uprooted a mountain and pulverized all the regions, especially of Anarta. That is where Hari, his friend's killer, dwelt. He possessed the strength of ten thousand elephants. On another occasion, he used his arms to agitate the ocean. He hurled that water at regions and submerged the areas around the coast. He shattered the trees in the hermitages of the foremost rishis. The wicked one used urine and excrement to defile the sacrificial fires. Like a wasp sealing up insects,[610] the insolent one hurled men and women inside caves in the valley of a mountain and sealed them up with boulders.

'Once, he was thus engaged in devastating kingdoms and polluting the women of noble families. Hearing an extremely melodious song emanating from Mount Raivataka, he went there. There, he saw Rama, the lord of the Yadus, wearing a garland made

[610] In a wasp's nest as food.

out of lotuses. All his limbs were exceedingly handsome. He was in the midst of a crowd of beautiful women and he was singing. Since he had drunk varuni, his eyes rolled with intoxication. His body was radiant and he was like an elephant that was in musth. The wicked ape climbed a tree and shook the branches. He made a *kilakila* sound,[611] so that he might be noticed. When they noticed the ape's insolence, Baladeva's wives started to laugh. They were young women, naturally given to joking. They loved to laugh. While Rama looked on, the ape slighted them by twisting his eyebrows and making faces at them. He displayed his anus to them. Bala, supreme among strikers, became angry. He picked up a rock and hurled it. Avoiding the rock, the ape seized the pot of liquor. Showing more disrespect, the wily one laughed, angering him even more. The wicked one broke the pot and tugged at their garments.[612] The powerful one, inflated by his own insolence, slighted and showed greater disrespect towards Bala. He saw his arrogance and the devastation he had wrought in the kingdoms. So as to kill the enemy, he angrily picked up his club and his plough. The greatly valiant Dvivida picked up a *shala* tree in his hand. He rushed forward towards Bala and powerfully struck him on the head with this. However, Samkarshana was as immobile as a mountain. As it descended, the powerful one seized it. He used Sunanda[613] to strike back. Struck by the club on his head, he was radiant and streams of blood started to flow. He was like a mountain from which red minerals were flowing. However, he did not even think about the blow. He again uprooted a tree and used his strength to strip it off its leaves. Extremely angry, he struck again, but Bala shattered it into one hundred fragments. He angrily struck with another tree. But this too was shattered into one hundred fragments. Thus, he repeatedly fought against the illustrious one and the trees were repeatedly shattered. He uprooted trees in every direction and the forest became bereft of trees. Intolerant, he showered down a mass of rocks on Bala. But playfully, the one whose weapon is the club,

---

[611] A chattering sound expressing pleasure.
[612] Of the women.
[613] The name of Balarama's club.

shattered all of these. The lord of the apes now clenched his arms, which were like palm trees, into fists. He approached Rohini's son and struck him on the chest with these. The Indra among the Yadavas flung aside his club and his plough. He angrily struck him on the collarbone with his two hands. He[614] started to vomit blood and fell down. O tiger among the Kuru lineage! When he fell down, the mountain,[615] with its summits and trees, trembled, like a boat tossed around on the water by the wind. Gods, Siddhas and Indras among sages showered down flowers from the firmament and exclaimed, "Victory to you! We bow down to you! This is wonderful! This is praiseworthy!" In this way, Dvivida, who had caused devastation in the world, was killed. Praised by the people, the illustrious one entered his own city.'

Chapter 10(68)

Shri-Shuka said, 'O king! Samba, Jambavati's son, who was victorious in assemblies, abducted Duryodhana's daughter, Lakshmana, from her svayamvara ceremony. The angry Kouravas said, "This boy is insolent and has shown us disrespect. Against her wishes, he has forcibly abducted the maiden. Let us imprison this insolent one. What can the Vrishnis do? We showed them our favours by bestowing this land on them. That is what they are enjoying. On hearing that their son has been captured, if the Vrishnis come here, we will shatter their insolence. Like the breath of life when it is controlled, they will be pacified." Sanctioned by the elders of the Kuru lineage, Karna, Shala, Bhuri, Yajna, Ketu and Suyodhana set out to fight against Samba. Seeing that he was being followed by those on Dhritarashtra's side, maharatha Samba picked up his bow. He stood alone, like a lion. They wished to capture him and angrily said, "Stay. Wait." With Karna at the forefront, those archers approached him and showered him with arrows. O

[614] Dvivida.
[615] Raivataka.

best among the Kuru lineage! Though he was assailed by them, the descendant of the Yadu lineage, the son of the inconceivable one, did not tolerate it. He was like a lion against inferior animals. He stretched his beautiful bow and pierced all of them with arrows. The valiant one simultaneously pierced the six charioteers, Karna and the others, with separate arrows. He struck each of the four horses with four arrows and each of the charioteers and chariot drivers with one arrow. At this, all those great archers applauded him. However, they deprived him of his chariot. Four of them killed his four horses, one killed his charioteer and another broke his bow. When he had been deprived of his chariot, with a great deal of difficulty, the Kourava warriors bound him. Having triumphed, they took the boy and their own daughter and entered their own city.

'O king! Hearing about this from Narada, they[616] were filled with intolerance. Urged by Ugrasena, they made attempts to act against the Kurus. However, Rama pacified the armoured bulls among the Vrishnis. He did not wish for dissension between the Kurus and the Vrishnis. He wished to dispel the contamination that would result from conflict. Instead, on a chariot that was as resplendent as the sun, he went to Hastinapura. Brahmanas and aged ones of the lineage surrounded him, like the planets around the moon. Having gone there, Rama remained in a grove that was outside Gajasahvya.[617] He sent Uddhava to Dhritarashtra to ascertain their intentions. Honouring Ambika's son,[618] Bhishma, Drona, Bahlika and Duryodhana in the proper way, he told them about Rama's arrival. Hearing that Rama, the best among their well-wishers, had come, they were extremely happy. Having honoured him,[619] all of them went forward, with auspicious objects in their hands. As is proper, they met him and offered him a cow and arghya.[620] Knowing about Bala's powers, they bowed

---

[616] The Yadavas.

[617] Hastinapura.

[618] Dhritarashtra.

[619] Uddhava.

[620] Gift given to a guest.

their heads down. After hearing that their relatives were well, they were asked about their own welfare and health. Once they had respectively conversed with each other, Rama addressed them in these fearless words. "Ugrasena is the lord of all the lords on earth. Hear about what the lord has commanded. You should listen to this attentively. After that, without any delay, you should act accordingly. Following adharma, many of you fought against a single person who was observing dharma. You bound him up. Nevertheless, with a desire to ensure unity amongst relatives, I am tolerating this." Baladeva's words were full of bravery, valour and strength and were full of his own powers. Nevertheless, hearing this, the Kurus became angry. They said, "This is a great wonder. The progress of destiny is certainly impossible to cross. A piece of footwear now wants to step on a head that wears the crown. Since the Vrishnis are bound to us through matrimonial alliances, we allow them to share our couches, our seats and our food. We have granted them equality and it is because of us that they have obtained royal thrones. It is because we ignored them that they enjoyed whisks, fans, conch shells, white umbrellas, crowns, seats and couches.[621] But enough of granting the Yadus signs of royalty. Like hooded serpents that are fed amrita, they turn against their benefactors. The Yadavas have been made prosperous because of our favours. But like those who have lost all sense of shame, they are now ordering us. Even Indra will not dare to appropriate something that Kurus like Bhishma, Drona, Arjuna and the others have not given him. Does a ram desire something a lion has seized?" O bull among the Bharata lineage! They were insolent because of their birth, relatives and great prosperity. Having made Rama hear these wicked words, those uncivilized ones entered the city.

'Witnessing the evil conduct of the Kurus and hearing those wicked words, Achyuta[622] became filled with wrath and intolerance and he was impossible to behold. He laughed repeatedly and said, "It is evident that these wicked ones are so insolent that they do not wish for peace. Like a stick is used against an animal, let them

[621] All these represent royal insignia.
[622] Balarama.

then be chastened with punishment. I gently appeased the intolerant Yadus and the angry Krishna. I came here, desiring peace with them. But these ones are evil in intelligence. They are deceitful and love conflict. They have repeatedly slighted me. They have insulted me by using wicked words against me. Shakra and the other guardians of the world followed Ugrasena's command. He is the lord of the Bhojas, Vrishnis and Andhakas. Yet they say he is not a lord. He[623] is seated in Sudharma. He brought and enjoys parijata, the tree of the immortals. Yet they say he is not fit to sit on a throne. Shri, the goddess of everything, herself worships his feet. Yet, Shri's lord does not deserve the insignia of a king of men. The dust of his lotus feet is borne on the heads of all the guardians of the worlds. Among tirthas, he is worshipped as the greatest tirtha. Brahma, Bhava, I and Shri are only portions of his various portions. We too bear that dust for a long time. He does not deserve a king's throne. We, Vrishnis, only enjoy that bit of the earth that has been given to us by the Kurus. We are only footwear, while the Kurus are themselves the head. Alas! They are intoxicated and insolent because of their prosperity, like those who are inebriated. These words are incoherent and harsh. Which person, capable of chastising, will tolerate them? Today, I will remove all Kouravas from the earth." Extremely angry, he seized his plough. He stood up, as if he was going to burn down the three worlds. Using the tip of his plough, he raised the city of Gajasahvya. Angry, he dragged it towards the Ganga, ready to fling it in. The Kouravas were filled with terror. Their city was being whirled around like a raft. It was about to descend into the Ganga. They saw that it was being dragged in that direction. Wishing to save themselves and their families, they sought refuge with him, placing Samba and Lakshmana at the forefront. They joined their hands in salutation before the lord. "O Rama! O foundation of everything! O Rama! We do not know your powers. We are foolish and wicked in intelligence. You should pardon our transgression. You alone are responsible for creation, preservation and destruction. There is no cause other than you. O lord! It is said that the worlds are your playthings and that you play with them. O

[623] Krishna.

Ananta! In your pastimes, you alone hold up the entire earth on your one thousand hoods. At the end, you are the one who withdraws the entire universe into your own atman. You lie down, without any second entity existing. Your anger is for the sake of instructing everyone, not because of hatred or envy. O illustrious one! Basing yourself on sattva, you are intent on protecting and preserving. We bow down before the one who is in the atman of all creatures. O one who possesses all the potencies! O one without decay! We bow down before the one who is the creator of the universe. We have sought refuge with you." Since their habitation was trembling, anxious, they sought refuge with Bala. Extremely pleased, he showed them his favours and granted them freedom from fear. Affectionate towards his daughter, as a wedding gift, Duryodhana gave twelve hundred elephants that were sixty years old, ten thousand horses, six thousand golden chariots that were as radiant as the sun and one thousand female servants with golden necklaces.[624] The illustrious bull among the Satvatas accepted everything. He left with his son[625] and his daughter-in-law, honoured by his well-wishers. After this, the wielder of the plough entered his own city and met his relatives, whose hearts were attached to him. In the midst of an assembly, he told all the bulls among the Yadus about what he had done vis-à-vis the Kurus. Even today, that city[626] displays signs of Rama's valour. An elevation can be seen along the southern side, along the banks of the Ganga.'

Chapter 10(69)

Shri-Shuka said, 'Narada heard about Naraka's death and that Krishna had alone married several women. He wished to see him. It was extraordinary that though he possessed a single body, he simultaneously and separately married sixteen thousand

[624] Necklaces made out of gold coins.
[625] Son by extension.
[626] Hastinapura.

women. Though alone, he dwelt in all their houses. Eager to witness this, the devarshi went to Dvaravati, which was beautiful because of blossoming groves and pleasure gardens, filled with sounds of birds and bees. The lakes were full of blooming blue lotuses, lotuses that blossomed during the day, white lotuses, lotuses that blossomed during the night and water lilies. They were filled with the loud sounds of swans and cranes calling. There were nine hundred thousand palaces, made out of crystal and silver. These were ornamented with the best of emeralds, gold, jewels and furnishings. The city was laid out with main roads, smaller roads, quadrangles, markets, assembly halls and shrines for the gods, and was beautiful. The roads, courtyards, avenues and gates were sprinkled with water. Fluttering flags and pennants warded off the heat of the sun. Hari's beautiful inner quarters were worshipped by all the lords. In constructing it, Tvashta had exhibited all his skills. It was ornamented with sixteen thousand residences, for each of Shouri's wives. He[627] entered one of these great residences. It was supported by coral pillars, studded with excellent lapis lazuli. The walls were made out of sapphire and so were the floors, which sparkled continuously. Tvashta had constructed canopies, with nets of pearls that hung down. The couches and seats were fashioned out of ivory and were studded with excellent jewels. There were female servants with necklaces made out of gold coins, ornamented and attired in excellent garments. The men wore jackets, headdresses, excellent garments and earrings made out of jewels. The darkness was dispelled by the illumination created by bejewelled lamps. O dear one! Colourful peacocks danced there. As the smell of aloe and incense flowed out through apertures in the lattice, they called out loudly, taking these to be clouds.

'The brahmana saw the lord of the Satvatas there. One of his wives was fanning him with a whisk made out of yak hair, with a golden handle. In turn, she was served by one thousand female servants, who were identical in qualities, beauty, youth and excellent attire. The illustrious one is the best among all

[627] Narada.

those who uphold dharma. On seeing him, he quickly arose from Rukmini's bed.[628] He bowed his diademed head down at his feet. He joined his hands in salutation and made him sit on his own seat. He was the preceptor of the universe and the lord of the virtuous. Nevertheless, he washed his feet and placed that water on his own head. His qualities were appropriate for the appellation *brahmanya-deva*.[629] The waters that wash his feet are the ultimate tirtha.[630] Having worshipped the devarshi according to the rites, Narayana, the ancient rishi who was Nara's friend, conversed with him in measured words that were as sweet as amrita. He asked, "O lord! What can we do for you?" Narada replied, "O lord! You are the protector of all the worlds. You are friendly towards all people and chastise the deceitful. O one who is praised! For benefit and for the preservation and protection of the universe, you assume your own avataras. We know this well and, therefore, this behaviour on your part isn't extraordinary. I have seen your feet, which bring liberation to creatures. Brahma and the others, unfathomable in their intelligence, think about them in their hearts. Those who have fallen into the well of samsara seek them out for support. Please grant me the favour that I remember your feet and meditate on them." After this, Narada entered the residence of another one of Krishna's wives. He desired to see the yoga maya of the lord of all the lords of yoga.

'There, he saw him playing with dice with his beloved[631] and Uddhava. He stood up, worshipped him with supreme devotion and gave him a seat and other objects. As if he did not know, he asked him, "When did you arrive? We are incomplete people. What can we do for a complete person like you? O brahmana! Tell us and make our births auspicious." Astonished, he[632] stood up. Silent, he went to another house. He saw Govinda there,

---

[628] The text uses the word Shri. In this context, it means Rukmini. Narada first entered Rukmini's residence.

[629] For whom, a brahmana is a divinity.

[630] Nevertheless, Krishna washed Narada's feet.

[631] This is interpreted as Satyabhama, but there is nothing in the text to suggest this. This was simply another one of Krishna's wives.

[632] Narada.

fondling his infant sons. In another house, he saw him making arrangements to have a bath. In one house, he was offering oblations into the fire and performing the five sacrifices.[633] In one place, he found him feeding brahmanas. In another, he was eating the food that was left. In one place, he was seated, performing the sandhya rituals. In another, he had controlled his speech and was chanting about the brahman. In one place, he was practising movements with a sword and a shield. In another place, Gada's elder brother was roaming around on horses, elephants or chariots. In some places, he was resting on a couch, praised by bandis. In one place, he was consulting with his ministers, Uddhava and the others. In another place, he was playing in the water, surrounded by the best of courtesans. In some places, he was donating ornamented cows to the best among brahmanas. In other places, he was listening to auspicious accounts from the Itihasa[634] and the Puranas. In one house, he was laughing with his beloved, having recounted an amusing story. In some places, he was serving dharma. In other places, he was pursuing artha and kama. In some places, he was seated alone, meditating on Purusha, superior to Prakriti. In some places, he was serving the seniors, offering them objects of pleasure and worshipping them. In some places, Keshava was planning for war. In others, he was planning for alliances. In some places, with Rama, he was discussing the welfare of the virtuous. In some places, he was following the ordinances and at the right age, getting his sons and daughters married to wives and husbands who were equal in prosperity. He was arranging for great festivities, sending his children off and receiving them[635] and all the people were amazed to see what the lord of yoga did. In some places, he worshipped all the gods through kratus. In other places, he performed *purta dharma*[636] by

[633] Known as the five *mahayajna*s performed every day by a householder—offerings to gods, offerings to ancestors, tending to guests, offerings to humans and offerings to non-human species.

[634] The Ramayana and the Mahabharata.

[635] When they went off after marriage and returned thereafter.

[636] The dharma of undertaking civil works.

digging wells and constructing pleasure grounds and *matha*s.[637] In some places, astride horses from the Sindhu region,[638] he was engaged in hunting. Surrounded by the bulls among the Yadus, he was killing animals meant for sacrifices. In some places, without any signs of who he was, the lord of yoga was roaming around in the inner quarters and homes as an ordinary person, wishing to know what people were thinking.

'Having witnessed Hrishikesha's yoga maya and his assumption of human conduct, Narada smiled and spoke to him. "We know about your yoga maya, having served at your feet. Even those who know about maya find this impossible to comprehend. O lord of yoga! O atman! O god! Grant me leave. I will travel around the worlds, which are flooded with your fame, chanting about your pastimes, which purify the world." The illustrious one replied, "O brahmana! I am the one who speaks about dharma. I am the one who performs it and I am the one who sanctions it. O son! Do not be distressed. I have come to this world so that I can instruct."[639] Thus, in all the houses, he saw the same one present, observing the dharma of the virtuous, meant to purify householders. Krishna is infinite in his valour. The rishi had been curious about his pervasive yoga maya. Having repeatedly witnessed it, he was astounded. In this way, Krishna exhibited his own faith in artha, kama and dharma and honoured him properly. Delighted and remembering him, he departed. O dear one! He followed the conduct of humans. Narayana, the creator of everything, used his powers in this fashion. He amused himself with sixteen thousand beautiful women. Casting their bashful, affectionate and smiling glances at him, they were satisfied. He is the cause behind the creation, preservation and destruction of the universe. Hari's deeds were impossible for anyone else to perform. O dear one! If a person sings about them, hears them or approves of them, he has devotion towards the illustrious one, which is the path for liberation.'

[637] Temples or monasteries.
[638] Famous for horses.
[639] By setting an example.

Chapter 10(70)

Shri-Shuka said, 'When dawn approached, the cocks started to crow and clinging to the neck of their husband, Madhava's wives, afflicted by the prospect of separation from him, cursed them. The birds called loudly and woke Krishna up from his sleep. Bandis sang about him and the breeze bore the scent from mandara groves.[640] Though this was an extremely auspicious time, the princess of Vidarbha[641] did not like it, since she would be deprived of the embrace of her beloved's arms. Madhava arose at brahma muhurta. He touched water, cleansed himself and meditated on the atman, which is beyond darkness, which is alone and self-illuminating and is infinite and without decay. It is always established in his own nature and destroys all impurities. It is his own powers, the cause behind the creation, preservation and destruction of the world, that is known as the brahman. In this way, he manifests his existence and bliss. Following the rites, he bathed in sparkling water. He performed the rituals and wore his two garments. The excellent one performed the sandhya rituals and offered oblations into the fire. Silently, he chanted on the brahman.[642] Every day, he worshipped the rising sun, which was a manifestation of his own atman. In control of his atman, he worshipped gods, rishis, ancestors, the aged and brahmanas. He gave brahmanas cows that were well behaved, with gold-encased horns, ornamented with necklaces made out of pearls. They yielded milk and had calved only once. He covered them with excellent coverings and donated them along with their calves. Their hooves were plated with silver. Along with them, he also gave linen garments, deerskin and sesamum seeds. Every day, he gave brahmanas large numbers[643] of such ornamented cows. He worshipped all the cattle, brahmanas, the aged, seniors and creatures, which were manifestations of his

[640] The coral tree.
[641] Rukmini.
[642] Interpreted as a recital of the gayatri mantra.
[643] The word used is *badva*. This means a large number, but is also taken to be 13,084.

own self. He then touched auspicious objects. Though he was an ornament in the world of men, he ornamented himself with his own garments, ornaments, divine garlands and pastes. He looked at *ghee*, a mirror, cows, bulls, brahmanas and gods.[644] He gave all the varnas, the residents of the city and those who were in the inner quarters and the ministers the objects of desire they wished for. He honoured and satisfied them. He first distributed garlands, betel leaves and pastes to brahmanas. He gave them to his well-wishers, his ministers and his wives. It is only after this that he himself accepted them. The charioteer brought his extremely wonderful chariot, yoked to Sugriva and the other horses. He bowed down and stood in front of him. Along with Satyaki and Uddhava, he held the charioteer's hand in his hand and mounted the chariot, resembling the sun atop the eastern mountain. With bashful glances full of affection, the women of the inner quarters looked at him. They let go of him with great difficulty. He departed, stealing their hearts with his smiles.

'O dear one! Surrounded by all the Vrishnis, he entered the assembly hall known as Sudharma. Those who enter it do not suffer from the six hardships.[645] There, the lord seated himself on a supreme seat. His own radiance illuminated all the directions. Surrounded by the Yadus, lions among men, the best of the Yadus resembled the lord of the stars in the firmament, surrounded by large numbers of stars. O king! There, the jesters amused the lord with diverse jokes. Those who were masters of dancing presented themselves, along with female dancers. Each separately performed tandava dances.[646] There were the sounds of *mridanga*s, veenas, flutes, *tala*s and conch shells.[647] Sutas, magadhas and bandis danced and sang and praised him. Some brahmanas seated there knew about the brahman and chanted about it. Others recounted the stories of former kings, famous for their piety.

[644] All these are auspicious.

[645] Hunger, thirst, sorrow, delusion, old age and death.

[646] In this context, this simply means energetic dances performed by male dancers.

[647] Mridanga is a kind of drum, tala is a cymbal.

'O king! Once, a man arrived there. He had never been seen before. The gatekeepers told the illustrious one that he had come and made him enter. He joined his hands in salutation and bowed down before Krishna, the supreme lord. He told him about the misery of the kings who had been imprisoned by Jarasandha. When he was engaged in his conquest, twenty thousand kings did not submit to him. They were forcibly imprisoned in Girivraja.[648] "O Krishna![649] O one whose atman is immeasurable! O Krishna! O one who destroys fear! We seek refuge with you. Despite our intelligence being separate,[650] we are terrified of material existence and seek shelter with you. Because they are distracted, people are always accomplished in performing perverse deeds. For their own benefit, you have spoken about the karma of worshipping you. In the hope of remaining alive, which is extremely powerful in this world, we are bowing down before you. You are the one who instantly severs that hope in a nimesha. You are the controller of the universe. For the welfare of this world, you have descended so as to protect it, and to restrain those who are deceitful. O lord! How can someone transgress your commands? How can such a person do what he himself wills and still obtain the fruits?[651] We do not understand this. O lord! We are under the control of someone else and royal happiness is like a dream. We are constantly afraid and are bearing this burden, like those who are dead. We have given up the happiness for our atmans, which is only available in this world from you. We are suffering a lot. Because of your maya, we are miserable in this world. Your two feet destroy the grief of those who prostrate themselves before you. Please remove this bondage of our karma, which goes by the name of what Magadha has done. He alone wields the power of ten thousand elephants. Therefore, he has imprisoned us in his residence, like a king of animals does to sheep.

[648] Known as Rajagriha (Rajgir) now.

[649] This is the message of the imprisoned kings, being relayed by the messenger.

[650] That is, suffering from a sense of duality and not realizing unity. In broad terms, their intelligence was inferior.

[651] The apparent beneficial consequences.

O wielder of the chakra! You are infinite in your valour. On eighteen occasions, you routed the deceitful one in battles. Since you have followed the conduct of the world of men, he has defeated you only once. However, his insolence has become firm. He torments your subjects. O invincible one! Please do something." The messenger added, "In this way, those who have been imprisoned by Magadha desire to see you. They are distressed and seek the shelter of your feet. Please do something for their benefit." While the messenger of the kings was speaking in this way, the extremely resplendent devarshi appeared. With the mass of golden and matted hair on his head, he was radiant, as if the sun had appeared. On seeing him, the lord of all the lords of the worlds, the illustrious Krishna, was delighted. He stood up and, with those in the assembly hall and his followers, bowed his head down and worshipped him.

'After the sage had been honoured in the proper way and had taken a seat, he satisfied him by addressing him in these well-articulated and reverent words. "Are the three worlds now free from fear from all the directions? O illustrious one! We know that you possess the quality of roaming around the worlds. Among everything that the lord has created in the worlds, there is nothing that is unknown to you. Hence, we are asking you. What do the Pandavas wish to do?" Narada replied, "O lord! On many occasions, I have witnessed your maya, which is impossible to transgress. It confounds even the creator of the world.[652] Despite your own powers, you roam around among creatures on earth, like the flames of a concealed fire.[653] Therefore, this is not extraordinary. Who can completely comprehend what you do? Using your maya, you create and you destroy. Everything that exists is because of your atman, though your own atman cannot be detected. I bow down to you. The living being is caught in the midst of undesirable things in samsara and does not know how to free himself. In your pastimes, you assume avataras and use your own fame as a lamp that blazes. Therefore, I surrender myself to you. O brahman! However, you

[652] Brahma.
[653] A fire concealed inside kindling. Therefore, it is not surprising that Krishna should ask, though he knows.

are imitating the world of men. Hence, I will tell you. I will tell
you what the king,[654] your father's sister's son who is devoted to
you, wishes to do. The Pandava will worship you by performing
rajasuya, foremost among sacrifices. The king wishes for complete
sovereignty. You should approve of the idea. O god! Wishing to
see you, all the gods, others and the famous kings will assemble at
that excellent sacrifice. Even those who live at the periphery[655] are
purified by hearing about you, chanting about you and meditating
on you. You are the lord who is full of the brahman. What needs to
be said about those who see you and touch you? Your unblemished
fame has spread like a canopy through heaven, the earth, rasatala
and the directions. It brings all that is auspicious to the world. The
waters, Mandakini in heaven, Bhogavati in the nether regions and
Ganga in this world,[656] wash your feet and purify the universe."
Those on his side did not agree to this, because they wanted to
be victorious.[657] Keshava smiled at his servant, Uddhava, and
spoke these gentle words. The illustrious one said, "You are our
supreme eye and well-wisher. You know about counselling and
accomplishing the objective. Therefore, tell us what should be done
now. We will trust you and act accordingly." Thus instructed by
his master, though he knew everything, Uddhava seemed to be
confused. With his head bowed down, he accepted the command
and replied.'

Chapter 10(71)

Shri-Shuka said, 'Having heard what the devarshi had said and
having ascertained the views of the assembly and Krishna, the
immensely intelligent Uddhava spoke. Uddhava said, "O god! As

[654] Yudhishthira.

[655] Outcasts, not outcastes.

[656] The names of the three flows of the Ganga.

[657] Instead of going to the rajasuya sacrifice, the Yadavas wanted to
fight against Jarasandha and defeat him.

stated by the rishi, you must assist the sacrifice of your father's sister's son, but you must also protect those who have sought refuge. O lord! The rajasuya sacrifice can only be performed after a person's wheel has conquered all the directions. Therefore, Jara's son must be defeated. In my view, both tasks can be accomplished. Through this, a great objective will be accomplished by us. O Govinda! The kings will be freed from their bondage. Thereby, your fame will increase. That king possesses the strength of ten thousand elephants and is impossible to withstand. He is strong. Other than Bhima, there is no one who is his equal in strength. He can be defeated in a duel, not when he is with one hundred akshouhinis. He is so devoted to brahmanas that he never refuses a request made by a brahmana. Vrikodara[658] should go to him in the garb of a brahmana and request him. In your presence, there is no doubt that he will kill him in a duel. You are the supreme lord. You are time. Hiranyagarbha and Sharva,[659] responsible for the creation and destruction of the universe, are but your forms. In their homes, the queens will sing about your extensive deed of killing the common enemy of the kings and about freeing them, just as the gopis did.[660] Sages who seek refuge with you will sing about setting free of the king of elephants, Janaka's daughter and your parents.[661] O Krishna! The slaying of Jarasandha will accomplish several objectives. It will cook what has not been cooked.[662] Hence, you should approve of the sacrifice." O king! These words were welcome and infallible in every possible way. The devarshi, the aged among the Yadus and Krishna applauded them. Devaki's illustrious

---

[658] Bhima.

[659] Brahma and Shiva respectively.

[660] About being freed from Shankhachuda, described in Chapter 10(34).

[661] The king of the elephants refers to the incident of the elephant being freed from the crocodile, Janaka's daughter means Sita in the Ramayana and Krishna's parents had been imprisoned by Kamsa.

[662] The single word in Sanskrit requires expansion. It will accomplish the good deed (cook) of freeing the kings. It will also accomplish the objective of bringing to a fruition (cook) Jarasandha's evil deeds (what should not have been cooked).

son instructed the servants, Daruka, Jaitra and the others, to make preparations for the journey. The lord took the permission of the seniors.'

'O destroyer of enemies! He arranged for the departure of his wives, his sons and their attendants. He took the permission of Samkarshana and the king of the Yadus.[663] He then mounted his own chariot, brought there by the charioteer, with Garuda on the standard. He was surrounded by a fearful army of chariots, elephants, soldiers, horse riders and their leaders. Drums, larger drums, kettledrums, conch shells and trumpets were sounded, resounding in the directions. He emerged. Excellent in their vows, along with their sons, Achuyta's wives followed their husband, astride golden palanquins borne by men. They were adorned with the best of garments, ornaments, pastes and garlands. On all sides, they were surrounded by men with swords and shields in their hands. The ornamented attendants[664] and courtesans were borne by men,[665] camels, buffaloes, donkeys, mules, carts and female elephants. Everything required, huts made of grass, blankets, clothing and other equipment, was loaded. It resembled an ocean agitated by timinigilas and waves. There was the large army, with its standards, banners, umbrellas, whisks and the best of weapons, ornaments, diadems[666] and armour. There was a tumultuous sound and it was brilliant, as the sun's rays reflected off it. Honoured by the lord of the Yadus, the sage[667] bowed down. Placing him in his heart, he left through the sky. He had been honoured and had heard the decision. Having met Mukunda, all his senses had been gratified. The illustrious one addressed the messenger of the kings in pleasant words. "O messenger! O fortunate one! Do not be scared. I will arrange for Magadha to be slain." Thus addressed, the messenger left and reported it accurately to the kings. Desiring to be freed, the kings waited to meet Shouri. Hari passed through Anarta,

[663] Ugrasena.
[664] The female attendants of the queens.
[665] On palanquins.
[666] Or helmets.
[667] Narada.

Souvira, Maru, Vinashana, mountains, rivers, cities, villages, settlements of cowherds and mines. Mukunda crossed Drishadvati and Sarasvati. Having crossed Panchala and Matsya, he arrived at Shakraprastha.[668]

'Men find it extremely difficult to see him. Hearing that he had arrived, Ajatashatru[669] was delighted. He emerged with his priests and well-wishers. There was the sound of singing and the playing of musical instruments. Sounds of the brahman were chanted. He approached Hrishikesha, just as the senses welcome the breath of life. Seeing Krishna, Pandava's heart melted with affection. He had seen his loved one after a long time and he repeatedly embraced him. With his arms, he embraced Rama's unblemished abode. From the touch of Mukunda's body, everything inauspicious was removed from the king. There were tears in his eyes and he obtained supreme satisfaction. His body was exhilarated and he forgot the delusion of this world. Bhima smiled and embraced his maternal uncle's son. He was satisfied. His eyes filled with tear and his senses were overwhelmed with affection. The twins and Kiriti[670] were delighted. Shedding profuse tears, they embraced Achyuta, the most loved among their well-wishers. Arjuna embraced him and the twins worshipped him. As was befitting, he worshipped the brahmanas and the aged. He was honoured by the Kurus, Srinjayas and Kekayas and honoured them back. Sutas, magadhas, gandharvas, bandis, jesters and brahmanas praised the lotus-eyed one. There was singing and dancing. Drums, conch shells, tabors, veenas, kettledrums and trumpets were sounded. Thus surrounded by his well-wishers, the illustrious Uttamashloka,[671] the crest among jewels, was praised and entered the ornamented city. The roads were sprinkled with water mixed with the scent from the musth of elephants. It was decorated with colourful flags, golden arches and pots filled with water. Men and young women were resplendent, decorating themselves with

---

[668] Indraprastha.

[669] Yudhishthira.

[670] Arjuna.

[671] The text uses the word Punyashloka. Though the nuance is slightly different, the two words can be taken to be almost identical.

excellent garments, ornaments, garlands and fragrances. He saw the ornamented residences in the abode of the king of the Kurus. Arrays of lamps were lit. There were offerings. The fragrant smell of incense emerged through the apertures in the lattice work. Banners fluttered. The tops of the houses had golden pots, with bases made out of silver. He was like a vessel from which the eyes of men drank. Hearing that he had arrived, the young women were eager to see him and emerged on the royal road. In their haste, their hair was dishevelled and the knots of their garments were loosened. They immediately left their household tasks and the beds of their husbands. But the roads were crowded with elephants, horses, chariots and bipeds. To see Krishna and his wives, the women climbed on the tops of their houses. Embracing him in their minds, they showered down flowers. They welcomed him with their smiling glances. Along the road, the women saw Mukunda's wives, like the stars with the lord of the stars. They exclaimed, "What deeds have they performed? Their eyes can see this jewel among men, with his generous smiles and playful glances. Even a bit of that is like a festivity." Here and there, the citizens approached with auspicious objects in their hands. They worshipped Krishna. So did the leaders of the shrenis and their sins were cleansed.

'Their eyes full of delight, those in the inner quarters hurried and approached Mukunda, as he entered the king's residence. Pritha saw Krishna, her brother's son, the lord of the three worlds. Along with her daughter-in-law,[672] she happily arose from her couch and embraced him. The king welcomed Govinda, the lord of the gods, to his house and welcomed him. He was so overwhelmed with joy that he did not know how to worship him. O king! Krishna bowed down before his father's sister and the wives of the elders. Krishnaa and his own sister bowed down to him.[673] Urged by her mother-in-law, Krishnaa worshipped all of Krishna's wives—Rukmini, Satya, Bhadra, Jambavati, Kalindi, Mitravinda, Shaibya and the virtuous Nagnajiti, as well as the others who had arrived, with

[672] Droupadi.
[673] Krishnaa means Droupadi. Krishna's sister means Subhadra. She was married to Arjuna, but that incident is described in Chapter 10(86).

garments, garlands and ornaments. Dharmaraja made comfortable arrangements for Janardana to reside in. Every day, he made new arrangements for him, his soldiers, his followers and his wives. Along with Phalguna, he satisfied the fire god with Khandava. When Maya was freed, he constructed a divine assembly hall for the king.[674] So as to bring pleasure to the king, he[675] resided there for a few months. Surrounded by soldiers and with Phalguna on a chariot, he would amuse himself.'

Chapter 10(72)

Shri-Shuka said, 'Once, Yudhishthira was seated in his assembly hall, surrounded by sages, brahmanas, kshatriyas, vaishyas, his brothers, preceptors, elders of the lineage, relatives, matrimonial allies and kin. While all of them heard, he spoke the following words. Yudhishthira said, "O Govinda! O lord! I wish to perform the purifying rajasuya sacrifice, the king of sacrifices, and worship your potencies. Please help us to accomplish it. O lord! Those who constantly serve your footwear, meditate on them and sing about them are purified and everything that is inauspicious is destroyed for them. O one with the lotus in your navel! They obtain emancipation from samsara. If they have wishes, those are satisfied. But this is not true of others.[676] O god of the gods! Let the worlds witness the power that comes from serving your lotus feet, the difference in status between those who worship you and those who do not worship you. O lord! Display this to the Kurus and the Srinjayas. You are the brahman and your mind does not distinguish between those who are your own and those who are not your own. You are in all atmans. You are impartial in your outlook. You experience bliss within your own self. You are like

[674] That is to say, this incident of Krishna and Arjuna burning down Khandava forest and satisfying Agni occurred at this time.
[675] Krishna.
[676] Those who do not worship you.

the tree of the gods.[677] Those who serve you obtain favours that are proportionate to the service they render. There is no violation of this." The illustrious one replied, "O king! O afflicter of enemies! This decision of yours is appropriate. Through this, the worlds will witness your auspicious fame. O lord! This king of sacrifices is not only desired by us, your well-wishers, but also by the rishis, the gods and all creatures. Defeat all the kings and bring the entire earth under your subjugation. Collect all the necessary objects and perform this great sacrifice. O king! These brothers of yours have been born as portions of the guardians of the worlds. Those who have not cleansed their atmans find it impossible to conquer me. But I have been conquered by you. If a person is devoted to me, no one in the worlds is capable of overcoming him in energy, fame, prosperity and powers, not even a god. What need one say about a king?" Hearing what the illustrious one had said, his[678] face was delighted and resembled a blooming lotus.

'He engaged his brothers, who were imbued with Vishnu's energy, in conquering the directions. Along with the Srinjayas, Sahadeva was sent to the south. Nakula was sent to the west and Savyasachi[679] to the north. Along with the Matsyas, Kekayas and Madras, Vrikodara[680] was sent to the east. O king! Those brave ones used their energy to defeat the kings. From the directions, they brought a lot of wealth for Ajatashatru to perform the sacrifice. However, on hearing that Jarasandha had not been defeated, the king thought about this. Hari told him about the means that Uddhava had earlier spoken about. Bhimasena, Arjuna and Krishna, assumed the disguise of three brahmanas. O son! They went to Girivraja, where Brihadratha's son was. The king was devoted to brahmanas and observed the rites of a householder. They reached at the time meant for receiving guests.[681] Disguised as brahmanas, they begged him.

---

[677] Which grants all the objects of desire.

[678] Yudhishthira's.

[679] Arjuna.

[680] Bhima.

[681] The word used is *atithi*. An atithi is an unannounced guest, arriving unexpectedly. The householder reserves a time of the day for receiving unexpected guests.

"O king! Know us as atithis who have come from a long distance away for a specific purpose. O fortunate one! Therefore, grant us what we wish for.[682] For those who have fortitude, there is nothing that is intolerable. There is nothing that the wicked will not do. There is nothing that a generous person will not give. For those who are impartial in vision, there is no one who is a stranger. This body is impermanent. Despite being able to do so, if a person does not use it to acquire the eternal fame that is sung about by the virtuous, he is contemptible and one should grieve about him. Harishchandra, Rantideva, Unchhavritti, Shibi, Bali, the hunter, the pigeon—there are many who used the impermanent to obtain an eternal state."[683] From their voices, their forms and the marks left on their forearms by bowstrings, he discerned that they were related to royal families. He thought about whether he had seen them earlier. "Though they are in the disguise of brahmanas, they are certainly related to royal families. However, I must give them what they beg for, even if it is my body, which is so very difficult to give up. Bali's sparkling and pervasive fame is heard about in all the directions, despite his being dislodged from his prosperity by Vishnu in the form of a brahmana. The king of the daityas knew that in the form of a brahmana, for Indra's sake, Vishnu wished to rob him of his prosperity. Despite being restrained,[684] he gave him the earth. Life is for the sake of brahmanas. For a kshatra-bandhu, it has no other purpose. Even if

[682] The following statements pre-empt Jarasandha from stating that he needs to know their wish first, before agreeing to it.

[683] They gave up their bodies to obtain eternal fame. Harishchandra gave up everything to pay Vishvamitra's debt. After fasting for forty-eight days, Rantideva obtained some food and water, but gave that away to those who asked for it. To protect a pigeon from a hawk, Shibi gave up his own flesh. Bali gave everything away to Vishnu in his form as the *vamana* avatara. Unchhavritti is really an adjective, not a proper noun. There are grains left after a crop has been harvested, or after grain has been milled. If one subsists on these leftovers, this is known as *unchhavritti*. Here, it is being used as proper name for Mudgala, who subsisted in this way, but gave whatever he had to guests. When there was a hungry hunter, the pigeon gave up its body to satisfy his hunger. Seeing this, the hunter also gave up his body.

[684] By Shukracharya, Bali's preceptor.

the body falls down, one must strive for eternal fame." Generous in his intelligence, he spoke to Krishna, Arjuna and Vrikodara, "O brahmanas! I will give you what you ask for, even if it happens to be my own head." The illustrious one replied, "O Indra among kings! Fight with us. If you find it proper, grant us a duel. We belong to royal lineages. We have come here for a fight and we desire nothing else. This is Vrikodara, Pritha's son. This is his brother, Arjuna. Know me as Krishna, your enemy. They are the sons of my father's sister." Thus addressed, the king of Magadha laughed loudly. Full of intolerance, he said, "O foolish ones! In that case, I will grant you a fight. I will not fight with you. You are a coward and your energy deserted you in a battle. You abandoned Mathura, your own city, and sought shelter in the ocean. This Arjuna is not my equal in age. Nor is he my equal in strength. He is not a proper adversary. Bhima is my equal in strength." Having said this, he gave Bhimasena a large club. Seizing a second one himself, he went outside the city.

'On level ground, those two brave ones engaged with each other. Both of them were indomitable in the encounter and struck each other with clubs that were like the vajra. Following wonderful modes, they wheeled to the left and to the right. As they moved around in that encounter, they were as beautiful as actors on a stage. O king! As they hurled their clubs at each other, like two tusked elephants, there was a clapping sound, like that of thunder. Using the force of their arms, they brought the clubs down on each other, on shoulders, hips, feet, hands, thighs and collarbones. With their rage ignited, they fought against each other like two elephants and like branches of arka trees,[685] the weapons were fragmented. When the two clubs were fragmented, those two brave men angrily struck each other with their fists, which were like iron to the touch. As they struck each other like two elephants and slapped each other with their palms, the sound that arose was like the harsh clap of thunder. The two fighters were equal to each other in training, strength and energy. O king! Their energy was undiminished and the encounter did not come to any conclusions. O great king! In this way, the

[685] Arka is the sun-plant, actually a small tree. The imagery is probably that of arka trees being crushed when two elephants fight.

fight between them continued for twenty-seven days. They fought each other during the day, but were like friends at night. O king! Once, Vrikodara spoke to his maternal uncle's son. "O Madhava! I am incapable of defeating Jarasandha in this encounter." Hari knew about the adversary's birth and death and about how he had been brought to life by Jara. He told Partha[686] about this and gave him his own energy. He thought about it. Having thought about it, infallible in his insight, he thought about a means of ensuring the death. He indicated this to Bhima by breaking the branch of a tree.[687] Bhima, supreme among strikers and great in his spirit, understood this. He seized the enemy by the feet and brought him down on the ground. He pressed down on one foot and seized the other one with his arms. Starting with the anus, he tore him apart into two parts, like a large elephant does to the branch of a tree. The subjects saw two parts, each with one foot, thigh, one testicle, one hip, one part of the back, one part of the chest, one collarbone, one arm, one eye, one eyebrow and one ear. When the lord of Magadha was killed, great sounds of lamentation arose. Jaya[688] and Achyuta embraced Bhima and honoured him. The illustrious lord, the creator of all creatures, is immeasurable in his atman. He instated his[689] son, Sahadeva, as the king of Magadha. He freed the kings who had been imprisoned by the king of Magadha.'

Chapter 10(73)

Shri-Shuka said, 'Twenty thousand and eight hundred had been defeated in battles and imprisoned. They emerged from the valley of the mountain. They were dirty and their clothes were filthy. They were thin from hunger. Their mouths were dry. Having been imprisoned, they were suffering. They saw Hari, dark blue like

[686] Bhima.
[687] While the duel between Bhima and Jarasandha was going on.
[688] Arjuna.
[689] Jarasandha's.

a cloud, dressed in yellow silken garments. He bore the shrivatsa mark and was four-armed. His eyes were red, like the inside of a lotus flower. His beautiful face was pleasant. Earrings in the shape of makaras sparkled. He held a lotus in one hand and a mace, a conch shell and the chakra in the others. He possessed all the signs. He was ornamented with a diadem, a necklace, a belt around his waist and armlets. He was radiant, with the jewel[690] around his neck and with a garland of wild flowers hanging. They seemed to drink him in with their eyes and lick him with their tongues. They seemed to smell him with their noses and embrace him with their arms. They bowed their heads down before his feet and were cleansed of their sins. They were so delighted to see Krishna that all the exhaustion from imprisonment was destroyed. The kings joined their hands in salutation and praised Hrishikesha in these words. The king said, "O god! O lord of the gods! O undecaying one! You remove the afflictions of those who seek refuge with you. O Krishna! We are desperate because of this terrible samsara and have sought shelter with you. O protector! O Madhusudana! We do not censure Magadha. O lord! It is because of your favours that kings are dislodged from their kingdoms. Intoxicated by the prosperity of the kingdom, a king is not restrained and does not know what is good for him. He is confounded by your maya and takes impermanent riches to be permanent. This is like foolish people taking a mirage to be a store of water. Without a sense of discrimination, he takes *vaikarika maya*[691] to possess substance. Earlier, because of prosperity and intoxication, we did not possess sight. Desiring to conquer, we challenged each other. O lord! We were extremely cruel and killed our own subjects. We were indomitable and did not pay heed to your form as death, standing in front of us. O Krishna! Time, your form, is mysterious in its ways and its force is impossible to cross. It dislodged us from our prosperity. Your favours have destroyed our insolence. May we remember your feet. We do not want kingdoms. They are like mirages. They are enjoyed by physical bodies and are always the source of hardships on earth.

[690] Koustubha.
[691] Associated with rajas.

O lord! After death, nor do we wish to enjoy the fruits of our rituals. Those only sound pleasing to the ear. As we go through samsara on this earth, teach us methods whereby we constantly remember your lotus feet. O Krishna! O Vasudeva! O Hari! O paramatman! O one who destroys the hardships of those who bow down! O Govinda! We bow down before you." The kings, freed from bondage, praised the illustrious one.

'O son! The granter of refuge addressed them in these gentle and compassionate words. The illustrious one said, "O kings! As you have wished, from now on, there will certainly be unflinching devotion in me, the atman who is the lord of everything. O king! It is good fortune that you have arrived at this conclusion and your words are true. I have seen how the intoxication of prosperity and opulence can make men mad. Because of their intoxication, Haihaya,[692] Nahusha, Vena, Naraka and many other lords among gods, daityas and men have been dislodged from their positions of prosperity. Having understood that everything like the body has a beginning and an end, worship me through sacrifices. Use dharma to protect the subjects. You will generate offspring. You will experience happiness and unhappiness, birth and death. Accept whatever comes and conduct yourselves with your minds on me. Be detached towards everything connected with the body. Find pleasure in your own atmans and be firm in your vows. Immerse your minds completely in me. At the end, you will obtain me, the brahman." Having instructed the kings in this way, the illustrious Krishna, the lord of the universe, employed male and female servants in the task of bathing the kings. O descendant of the Bharata lineage! He made Sahadeva honour the kings and give them appropriate garments, ornaments, garlands and pastes. They were bathed well and ornamented well. They ate excellent food. The kings were honoured with many objects of pleasure, betel leaves and other things. Thus honoured by Mukunda, the kings were resplendent, with dazzling earrings. Released from their hardships, they gleamed like planets at the end of the rainy season. They were mounted on chariots drawn by well-trained horses. They were ornamented with jewels

[692] Kartavirya Arjuna.

and gold. Thus gratified, with pleasant words, they were sent off
to their own countries. They were thus freed from their hardships
by the extremely great-souled Krishna. They left, meditating on
the lord of the universe and on what he had done. They told their
ministers what the great being had done. Attentively, they followed
the instructions of the illustrious one.

'Keshava used Bhimasena to kill Jarasandha. Worshipped
by Sahadeva, he then left with the two Parthas. Having defeated
the enemy, they went to Khandavaprastha[693] and blew on
their conch shells. They thus delighted their well-wishers and
caused misery to their ill-wishers. Hearing this, the residents of
Indraprastha were delighted in their minds. They thought that
Magadha had been pacified. The king[694] thought that his wishes
had been accomplished. Bhima, Arjuna and Janardana greeted
the king. They told him everything about what they had done.
Dharmaraja heard about the compassion that Keshava had shown
him. He shed tears of joy and because of his love, he was unable
to say anything.'

Chapter 10(74)

Shri-Shuka said, 'Thus, King Yudhishthira heard about
Jarasandha's death and about the lord Krishna's powers.
Rejoicing, he spoke these words. Yudhishthira said, "All the
preceptors of the three worlds and all the lords of the worlds bear
your instructions on their heads, though it is extremely rare to obtain.
O lotus-eyed one! O lord! That you should follow the instructions of
miserable ones who pride themselves on being lords is a travesty.[695]
You are alone, without a second. You are the brahman. You are
the paramatman. Like the sun, your energy is neither increased, nor

[693] Indraprastha.
[694] Yudhishthira.
[695] Yudhishthira is referring to Krishna listening to Yudhishthira's
request.

diminished, by these acts. O invincible one! O Madhava! Those who are devoted to you do not think of 'I', 'mine', 'you' or 'yours'. These differences are perversions of intelligence and are like those of animals." After saying this, when it was time for the sacrifice, with Krishna's permission, Partha[696] engaged brahmanas who knew about the brahman as officiating priests. There were Dvaipayana, Bharadvaja, Sumantu, Goutama, Asita, Vasishtha, Chyavana, Kanva, Maitreya, Kavasha, Trita, Vishvamitra, Vamadeva, Sumati, Jaimini, Kratu, Paila, Parashara, Garga, Vaishampayana, Atharvan, Kashyapa, Dhoumya, Bhargava Rama,[697] Asuri, Vitihotra, Madhuchhanda, Virasena and Akritavarna.

'O king! There were others who were invited—Drona, Bhishma, Kripa and others, Dhritarashtra with his sons and the immensely intelligent Vidura. Brahmanas, kshatriyas, vaishyas, shudras, all the kings and the ministers of the kings came there to witness the sacrifice. At the place where the sacrifice to the gods was to be performed, the brahmanas followed the ordinances and ploughed the ground with golden ploughs. They consecrated the king. As was the case with Varuna's sacrifice in ancient times, all the objects used were made out of gold. Indra and the other guardians of the worlds, Virinchi, Bhava, large numbers of Siddhas, gandharvas, vidyadharas, giant serpents, sages, yakshas, rakshasas, birds, kinnaras, charanas, kings and all the wives of the kings were invited and came to the rajasuya of the king who was Pandu's son. They were not surprised, because they thought that this was worthy of someone who was Krishna's devotee. The officiating priests who performed the great king's sacrifice were as radiant as the gods. The rajasuya was performed with the proper rites, just as the immortals had done it for Prachetas.[698] On the day of sutya,[699] the lord of the earth controlled himself and in the proper way, worshipped the officiating priests and the immensely fortunate lords present at the assembly.

[696] Yudhishthira.
[697] Parashurama.
[698] Varuna.
[699] The day when soma juice is extracted.

'The members in the assembly wondered about who in the assembly should be worshipped first. However, since there were many deserving ones, they could not arrive at a unanimous decision. At this, Sahadeva spoke. "The illustrious lord of the Satvatas is the foremost among those who should be worshipped. He represents all the gods, all the regions, time, wealth and everything else. This universe is his atman. Sacrifices are his atman. Oblations in the fire, mantras, samkhya and yoga are meant for him. He is absolute, without a second. This universe has his atman as its foundation. O those in the assembly! He uses his atman to create, preserve and destroy. It is his favours that give rise to many kinds of tasks—everything beneficial undertaken in this world, characterized as dharma and the others. Therefore, the supreme offering must be given to the great Krishna. Thereby, we will show worship to all creatures and to our own selves. He is in the atman of all creatures and sees himself as no different from them. He is tranquil and complete. If a person desires infinite fruits from his donation, he should give it to Krishna." Sahadeva knew about Krishna's powers. Having said this, he was silent. Hearing this, all the virtuous and excellent people who were present praised these words. The king heard what the brahmanas had said and knew what was in the hearts of those present in the assembly. Delighted and overwhelmed with love, he worshipped Hrishikesha. He bathed his feet. Along with his wife, younger brothers, advisers and members of the family, he happily bore that water, capable of purifying the world, on his head. He offered him yellow silken garments and extremely expensive ornaments. Since his eyes were full of tears, he was incapable of looking at him. When the people saw that he had been honoured, all of them joined their hands in salutation. They prostrated themselves, exclaiming, "We bow down. Victory to you." Flowers were showered down.

'Hearing this, Damaghosha's son[700] arose from his seat. Hearing the description of Krishna's qualities, his anger was aroused. He waved his arms around. While the illustrious one heard, he fearlessly addressed the assembly in these harsh words. "The sacred

[700] Shishupala.

texts state that the lord who is time cannot be countered. This is indeed true. The intelligence of the elders has been confused by a child's[701] words. O lords of the assembly! You know who is the most worthy recipient. Do not pay attention to what a child has spoken. All of you have agreed that Krishna should be worshipped. There are lords in the assembly who possess austerities and learning and observe vows. Their knowledge has destroyed their sins. There are supreme rishis who base themselves in the brahman. They are honoured even by the guardians of the worlds. Passing over all of them, how can a cowherd, the worst of his lineage, be offered this honour? This is like giving a cake to a crow. He doesn't possess a varna, an ashrama, or noble lineage. He is outside the pale of all dharma. He does what he wants and is devoid of qualities. How can such a person deserve to be worshipped? Yayati cursed this lineage and since then, all virtuous people have shunned them. They are always engaged in the futile pursuit of drinking. How can such a person deserve to be worshipped? They have abandoned the regions frequented by *brahmana rishis*. They are in a place where the radiance of brahmanas does not exist. They have resorted to a fortification in the ocean. Like bandits, they oppress the subjects." Since his store of everything auspicious had been destroyed, he uttered many other inauspicious words. However, just as a lion does not react to the cries of a female jackal, the illustrious one said nothing.

'The ones present in the assembly found it impossible to listen to the condemnation of the illustrious one. They covered their ears and left, angrily cursing the king of Chedi. If a person hears criticism of the illustrious one or his devotees, he certainly falls downwards and is deprived of all his good deeds. Pandu's sons became angry. Along with the Matsyas, the Kekayas and the Srinjayas, they stood up and raised their weapons, desiring to kill Shishupala. However, Chedi wasn't scared. He seized a sword and a shield. O descendant of the Bharata lineage! In that assembly, he reprimanded the kings who were on Krishna's side. Himself angry, the illustrious one arose and restrained them. Using his sharp-edged chakra, he severed the

---

[701] Sahadeva's.

head of the enemy who was descending on him. When Shishupala was killed, a great uproar arose. Desiring to save their lives, the kings who were on his side fled. As all the creatures looked on, a radiance that was like a meteor dislodged from the firmament, arose from Chedi's body and entered Vasudeva. Extending across three births,[702] because his intelligence had been firm in enmity towards him, he meditated on him and obtained union with him. One's sentiments are responsible for what one becomes.

'Following the prescribed rites, the universal emperor[703] gave copious amounts of dakshina to the officiating priests and the assistant priests. Having honoured everyone, he bathed.[704] Krishna, the lord of all the lords of yoga, ensured that the king's sacrifice was successfully accomplished. Requested by his well-wishers, he resided there for a few months. Thereafter, though the king did not wish this, he took his leave. With his wives and advisers, Devaki's son returned to his own city. In great detail, I have described to you the account of the two residents of Vaikuntha.[705] Because of the curse of the brahmanas, they had to be repeatedly born. When King Yudhishthira bathed himself at the end of rajasuya, in the assembly of the brahmanas and the kshatriyas, he was as resplendent as the king of the gods. All the gods, humans and those who roamed around in the sky were honoured by the king. Praising Krishna and the sacrifice, they happily returned to their own abodes. The only exception was the wicked Duryodhana, the bane in the lineage of the Kurus. He was like Kali.[706] Witnessing the increased opulence of Pandu's son, he could not tolerate it. If a person chants about Vishnu's deed, the slaying of Chedi and the others,[707] the freeing of the kings and the sacrifice, he is freed from all his sins.'

---

[702] Shishupala and Dantavakra were first born as Hiranyaksha and Hiranyakashipu, then as Ravana and Kumbhakarna, and finally as Shishupala and Dantavakra.

[703] Yudhishthira.

[704] The *avabhritha*. Avabhritha is the most important final component of a sacrifice, characterized by the taking of a bath.

[705] Jaya and Vijaya. This story has been stated in the Seventh Skandha.

[706] The personification of evil, as in *kali*, or in kali yuga.

[707] Such as Jarasandha.

Chapter 10(75)

The king said, 'Witnessing the great festivities at King Ajatashatru's rajasuya sacrifice, all the assembled kings, rishis and gods rejoiced. O brahmana! Duryodhana was the exception there. O illustrious one! That is what we have heard. Please explain the reason for this.'

Shri-Shuka replied, 'At your great-souled grandfather's rajasuya sacrifice, all the relatives were bound to him by love and served him. Bhima was in charge of the kitchen, Suyodhana was in charge of the treasury, Sahadeva was given the task of welcoming people and Nakula was engaged in procuring the required objects. Jishnu[708] served the seniors, while Krishna washed the feet. Drupada's daughter served food and the great-minded Karna gave the gifts. In that great sacrifice, Yuyudhana, Vikarna, Hardikya, Vidura and others, Bhuri and other sons of Bahlika and Santardana and the others had specific tasks earmarked for them. O Indra among kings! Wishing to bring pleasure to the king, they did all this. The officiating priests, the assistant priests, learned ones and well-wishers were honoured with pleasant words, objects of worship and dakshina. When Chedi entered the feet of the lord of the Satvatas, the avabhritha bath was performed in the heavenly river.[709] At the festivities connected with avabhritha, many kinds of musical instruments were sounded—drums, conch shells, kettledrums, tabors, larger drums and trumpets. Cheerful female dancers danced. Groups of singers sang. The sound of veenas, flutes and clapping of the hands touched the firmament. Wearing golden necklaces and with well-ornamented soldiers, the kings emerged.[710] They had colourful flags and standards, with large elephants, chariots and horses. Placing the one performing the sacrifice[711] at the forefront, the Yadu, Srinjaya, Kamboja, Kuru, Kekaya and Kosala soldiers made the earth tremble. The assistant priests, the officiating

---

[708] Arjuna.
[709] Yamuna.
[710] Headed towards the Yamuna.
[711] Yudhishthira.

priests and the best among brahmanas repeatedly chanted about the brahman. The gods, rishis, ancestors and gandharvas uttered words of praise and showered down flowers. There were men and women, ornamented well with fragrances, garlands, ornaments and garments. They sported, smeared each other and sprinkled each other with many kinds of liquids. The men smeared the courtesans with oil, curds, fragrances, turmeric and thick layers of kunkuma. They were smeared back in turn. To directly witness, the wives of the kings emerged, protected by male guards.[712] They were like goddesses in the sky, astride the best of vimanas. When their maternal cousins[713] and friends sprinkled them, their radiant faces bloomed and they smiled bashfully. Using syringes,[714] they also sprinkled their brothers-in-law and friends. Their clothes got wet, revealing their limbs, breasts, thighs and waists. In their eagerness, their hair was dishevelled and the garlands were dislodged from the braids of their hair. Through these charming pastimes, they agitated the minds of those who were impure. The king was astride a chariot yoked to well-trained horses with golden harnesses. Along with his wives, he was as radiant as the king of sacrifices,[715] surrounded by various rituals. The officiating priests made him perform *patni-samyaja*[716] and avabhritha. Along with the drums of humans, the drums of the gods were sounded. Gods, rishis, ancestors and humans showered down flowers. Thereafter, men from all the varnas and ashramas bathed there. They were instantly cleansed of all their sins, including great sins. The king donned two new silk garments and ornamented himself. He honoured officiating priests, assistant priests, brahmanas and the distressed with garments and ornaments. The king was always devoted to Narayana. He honoured relatives, kin, kings, friends, well-wishers and all the others. With jewels,

[712] This probably means that they were on palanquins borne by male guards.

[713] The Yadavas.

[714] For want of a better word. The word used is *driti*, meaning a leather bag used for holding water or other liquids.

[715] The rajasuya sacrifice.

[716] Ritual where the performer of the sacrifice and his wife offer oblations together.

earrings, garlands, headdresses, jackets, girdles and extremely expensive necklaces, all the people were as radiant as gods. The beautiful faces of the women were resplendent because of earrings and their shining locks of hair. They were attired in golden girdles. O king! The extremely virtuous officiating priests, assistant priests who knew about the brahman, brahmanas, kshatriyas, vaishyas, shudras, the assembled kings, gods, rishis, creatures and guardians of the worlds, along with their followers, were honoured. After this, they sought leave and returned to their own abodes. Just as a mortal person is not satisfied with drinking amrita, they praised the great rajasuya sacrifice of the royal sage who was Hari's servant and were not satisfied.

'King Yudhishthira was afflicted at the prospect of being separated from his well-wishers, matrimonial allies, relatives and Krishna. Out of his love, he restrained them. O dear one! To do what would bring him pleasure, the illustrious one resided there for some time. However, he sent the Yadu heroes, Samba and the others, to Kushasthali.[717] In this way, the king who was Dharma's son accomplished his desires through Krishna's help. He lost all his anxiety. It was as if he had crossed a great ocean that was extremely difficult to cross.

'On one occasion, Duryodhana witnessed the prosperity of the inner quarters. He was tormented by this and by the greatness of the rajasuya performed by the one who had Achyuta in his soul. There,[718] the creator of the universe[719] had fashioned all the many kinds of resplendent prosperity of Indras among men, Indras among daityas and Indras among the gods. The daughter of King Drupada served her husbands. The king of the Kurus[720] was attracted to her and his heart was tormented. At that time, the thousands of wives of the lord of Madhu[721] also resided there. Because of their heavy hips, they walked slowly. Charming anklets tinkled on their

---

[717] Dvaraka.
[718] The inner quarters.
[719] Meaning Maya.
[720] Duryodhana.
[721] Krishna.

legs. They possessed beautiful waists. Their necklaces were red because of the kunkuma from their breasts. Their earrings moved and their thick locks of hair enhanced the beauty of their faces. On one occasion, the emperor who was Dharma's son was seated in the assembly hall constructed by Maya. He was surrounded by his followers and relatives and by Krishna, who was like his own eye. With Parameshthi's[722] prosperity, he was praised by the bandis. O king! Surrounded by his brothers, the proud Duryodhana would not be restrained. With a diadem on his head and a sword in his hand, he angrily abused them[723] and entered. He was confounded by Maya's maya. Taking the floor to be water, he gathered up the ends of his garments. In another place, taking the water to be the floor, he was bewildered and fell into the water. Seeing this, Bhima, the women and other kings laughed at him. O dear one! This was despite the king[724] trying to restrain them. However, it was sanctioned by Krishna. He was ashamed and his face blazed with rage. Though he was silent, he exited and left for Gajasahvya. The virtuous ones raised great lamentations of "Alas!" Ajatashatru's mind was dejected. Since the illustrious one wished to remove the earth's burden, he was silent. It was his glance that had led to the delusion.[725] O king! I have thus described to you what you had asked me about, about how Suyodhana's evil intentions increased in the course of the great rajasuya sacrifice.'

Chapter 10(76)

Shri-Shuka said, 'O king! Now hear about another one of Krishna's extraordinary deeds. In his pastimes, he assumed a human form and killed the lord of Soubha. Shalva was Shishupala's

---

[722] Brahma.

[723] The guards who tried to restrain him.

[724] Yudhishthira.

[725] That is, Krishna had ensured that Duryodhana would be confounded, leading to the eventual war.

friend. When he came for Rukmini's marriage, he, Jarasandha and the others were defeated by the Yadus in the encounter. In the hearing of all the kings, Shalva took a pledge. "Behold my manliness. I will make the earth empty of Yadavas." Having taken this pledge, the foolish one worshipped the lord and god, Pashupati.[726] Every day, the king only subsisted on a fistful of dust.[727] Uma's illustrious consort is easily pleased.[728] Shalva had sought refuge with him and at the end of a year, he asked him to choose a boon. He asked for a vehicle that would be able to go anywhere at will and would be impenetrable by gods, asuras, humans, gandharvas and rakshasas. The Vrishnis would find it terrifying. Girisha agreed and instructed Maya, the conqueror of enemy cities. He[729] constructed such a city, made out of iron, and gave it to Shalva. He obtained that vehicle, which was enveloped in darkness. It could travel anywhere at will and was impossible to assail. Remembering the enmity that the Vrishnis had engendered, Shalva used it to go to Dvaravati.

'O bull among the Bharata lineage! With an extremely large army, Shalva laid siege. He destroyed all the groves and gardens in the city. He showered down weapons from that supreme vimana on the turrets, gates, palaces, mansions, terraces and pleasure gardens. Rocks, trees, bolts of thunder, snakes and hailstones rained down. There were fierce whirlwinds and the directions were enveloped in dust. O king! Krishna's city was thus severely afflicted by Soubha. There was no peace. It was as if the earth had been attacked by Tripura.[730] The illustrious Pradyumna saw how his own subjects were suffering and told them, "Do not be scared." The brave and immensely illustrious one mounted a chariot. Satyaki, Charudeshna, Samba, Akrura and his younger brothers, Hardikya, Bhanuvinda, Gada, Shuka, Sarana and other

[726] Shiva.

[727] The word *pamshu* means dust. However, Pamshu is also one of Shiva's names. So perhaps this simply means that he ate a handful, after having offered it to Shiva.

[728] The word being Ashutosha, easily pleased. We have translated Ashutosha as an adjective. But Ashutosha is also one of Shiva's names.

[729] Maya. The city could fly through the sky and was known as Soubha.

[730] The three cities of the daityas, destroyed by Shiva.

great archers, leaders of arrays of charioteers, emerged. They were
armoured and protected by chariots, elephants, horses and infantry.
A battle ensued between Shalva's forces and the Yadus. It was
tumultuous, like that between the asuras and the gods, and it made
the body hair stand up. With his divine weapons, Rukmini's son[731]
destroyed the maya of the lord of Soubha, just as the hot rays of the
sun destroy the darkness of the night in an instant. He used twenty-
five gold-tufted, iron-tipped and well-jointed arrows to pierce the
one who was protecting Shalva's standard. He struck Shalva with
one hundred arrows and pierced each of his soldiers with one each.
He pierced each leader with ten arrows and the mounts with three
arrows each. Witnessing the great-souled Pradyumna's great and
wonderful deed, all the soldiers, on one's own side and on the
adversary's side, applauded. However, it[732] had been fashioned by
Maya and was full of maya. It would appear as one and as many.
It would be visible and would not be visible. The enemy found it
impossible to determine where it was. It was sometimes on the
ground and sometimes, it was in the sky. Sometimes it was on the
summit of a mountain and sometimes it floated on water. Soubha
whirled around like a circle of fire and was never in a single spot.
Wherever, Soubha, Shalva and his soldiers appeared, the leaders of
the Satvatas directed their arrows at those spots. Shalva, his city
and his soldiers were thus confounded by the enemy and suffered.
The arrows were like the fire or the sun to the touch. They were as
invincible as virulent serpents. The valiant ones among the Vrishnis
were also severely afflicted by the floods of weapons released by
Shalva's army. However, desiring to conquer both the worlds,[733]
they did not abandon the field of battle and remained in their
respective positions. Shalva's adviser, named Dyuman, had earlier
suffered at Pradyumna's hands. The powerful one struck him with
a heavy iron club and roared loudly. Pradyumna was a scorcher of
enemies, but his chest was shattered by the club. His charioteer,

[731] Pradyumna.

[732] Soubha.

[733] This world in the case of victory and the next world in the case of
death.

Daruka's son,[734] knew about dharma and took him away from the field of battle. Krishna's son recovered his senses in an instant and told the charioteer, "Alas! O charioteer! Taking me away from the field of battle is a contemptible act. With my exception, it has never been heard that a person born in the lineage of the Yadus has withdrawn from the field of battle. I have now been tainted by a charioteer whose intelligence is like that of a eunuch. When I meet my fathers, Rama and Keshava, what will I tell them? When they ask me about myself, will I ask them to pardon me because I withdrew from the field of battle? It is evident that my sisters-in-law will laugh at me and say, 'O brave one! Tell us. Tell us about how the enemy turned you into a eunuch in the battle. Please tell us how this happened.'" The charioteer replied, "O lord! O one with a long life! I did this because I knew about dharma. In times of difficulty, the charioteer must protect the warrior and the warrior must protect the charioteer. Knowing about this, I took you away from the field of battle. You were struck by the enemy's club. You were hurt and lost your consciousness."'

Chapter 10(77)

Shri-Shuka said, 'He[735] touched water, armoured himself and picked up his bow. He told the charioteer, "Please take me to the brave Dyuman's side." Dyuman was slaughtering his soldiers. However, Rukmini's son smiled and repulsed him, piercing him back with eight iron arrows. He struck the four horses with four arrows and his charioteer with one. With two arrows, he severed his bow and standard. With one more arrow, he severed his head. Gada, Satyaki, Samba and the others killed the soldiers of the lord of Soubha. With their heads severed, the torsos of all those in Soubha fell down into the ocean. Thus, the Yadus and those on Shalva's

---

[734] Daruka was Krishna's charioteer and Daruka's son was Pradyumna's charioteer.

[735] Pradyumna.

side slew each other. The tumultuous and fierce battle continued for twenty-seven nights.[736]

'Invited by Dharma's son, Krishna had gone to Indraprastha. The rajasuya had been concluded and Shishupala had been killed. He took his leave from the aged ones in the Kuru lineage, the sages and Pritha and her sons. As he left for Dvaravati, he witnessed terrible portents. "I have come here with my noble elder brother. The kings who are on Chedi's side must certainly have attacked my city." He arrived and saw the carnage caused among those on his own side. He arranged for the protection of the city and saw Soubha and King Shalva. Keshava told Daruka, "O charioteer! Quickly take my chariot to Shalva's presence. The king of Soubha resorts to maya, but you need not be scared on that account." Thus addressed and urged, Daruka drove the chariot and entered. Everyone, on one's own side and on the adversary's side, saw the standard with Aruna's younger brother.[737] With his forces almost exhausted, the lord Shalva noticed Krishna. In the encounter, he hurled a javelin towards Krishna's charioteer and it emitted a terrible roar. It swiftly descended from the sky, like a giant meteor blazing the directions. With his arrows, Shouri shattered it into one hundred fragments. He pierced him with sixteen arrows. As Soubha roamed around in the sky, he struck it with torrents of arrows, like the rays of the sun filling up the sky. Shalva struck Shouri, the wielder of the Sharnga bow, on his left arm, holding the Sharnga bow. Thus pierced, the Sharnga bow fell down from his hand and this was extraordinary. Seeing this, great sounds of lamentation arose from the beings who were there. The lord of Soubha roared and spoke to Janardana. "O foolish one! While we looked on, you abducted the wife of a friend who was like a brother.[738] While he was distracted in the middle of the assembly, you killed my friend. You pride yourself on being invincible. If you remain in front of me today, with my sharp arrows, I will convey you to the region from where there is no

---

[736] Meaning, it continued for twenty-seven days and nights continuously, without stopping during the night.

[737] Garuda. Aruna is Garuda's older brother.

[738] That is, Shishupala.

return." The illustrious one replied, "O wicked one! Why are you boasting in vain? You do not see Death, standing near you. Brave ones exhibit their manliness. They do not speak a lot." Saying this, the illustrious one struck Shalva on the collarbone with a club that was terrible in its force. He wavered and started to vomit blood. As soon as the club was withdrawn, Shalva instantly vanished from the spot. At that instant, a man arrived and bowed his head down before Achyuta. Bowing down and weeping, he spoke these words. "I have been sent by Devaki. O Krishna! O mighty-armed one! You are devoted to your parents. O Krishna! Like an animal bound by a butcher, your father has been bound and has been taken away by Shalva." Krishna heard this unpleasant news. Since he was following the conduct of a human, his mind was filled with distress and compassion. Because of his love, he spoke like an ordinary person. "The fearless Rama is invincible and cannot be defeated by the gods or the asuras. How could the insignificant Shalva have defeated him and taken my father away? Destiny is powerful." When Govinda said this, the king of Soubha presented himself again. Apparently leading Vasudeva, he addressed Krishna in these words. "This is your father, who gave birth to you. It is because of him that you are alive. While you look on, I will kill him. O foolish one! Save him if you can." Full of maya, he abused him in this way and used his sword to sever Anakadundubhi's head. Taking it, he entered Soubha, which was stationed in the sky.

'He[739] is full of knowledge. However, because of affection towards his own relative, for an instant, he was overwhelmed by ordinary feelings. But the great one comprehended that this was the maya of asuras. Developed by Maya, Shalva was merely using it. Now alert, Achyuta did not see the messenger, or his father's body, on the field of battle, as if he had woken up from a dream. He saw his enemy roaming around in the sky and got ready to destroy Soubha. O royal sage! There are some rishis who are inconsistent in their reasoning. Indeed, they do not remember what they themselves have said and are contradictory in their statements. Sorrow, delusion, affection and fear are created by ignorance. How can these exist in him? His

[739] Krishna.

jnana and vijnana are infinite. His powers are infinite. By serving at his feet, people earn for themselves knowledge about the atman. They thereby destroy the mistaken identification of the atman,[740] which has existed right from the beginning. They obtain union with the infinite lord. He is the supreme destination of the virtuous. How can he suffer from delusion?[741] Shalva energetically struck him with torrents of weapons. However, invincible in his valour, Shouri struck him back with arrows. He pierced and shattered his armour, his bow and the jewel on his head. Using a club, he shattered the enemy's Soubha. The club wielded by Krishna's hand shattered it into one thousand fragments and it fell down. Abandoning it, Shalva descended on the ground. Raising a club, he quickly rushed towards Achyuta. As he rushed forward, he[742] used a broad-headed arrow to sever his arm, along with the club. To slay Shalva, he then raised his wonderful chakra, which resembled the sun at the time of universal destruction. He was resplendent and dazzled like the sun atop Mount Udaya.[743] He was full of maya, but Hari severed his head with that, along with the earrings and the diadem, exactly as Purandara had done to Vritra with the vajra. Great sounds of lamentation arose from amidst the men.[744] The wicked one fell down and the club destroyed Soubha. O king! Large numbers of gods sounded their drums in the firmament. Desiring to avenge the deaths of his friends, Dantavakra angrily attacked.'

Chapter 10(78)

Shri-Shuka said, 'Shishupala, Shalva and the evil-minded Poundraka had left for the world hereafter. He[745] wished to

[740] With the body.

[741] There is no such contradiction, because Krishna was behaving like an ordinary human being.

[742] Krishna.

[743] The sun rises from behind Mount Udaya.

[744] Shalva's followers.

[745] Dantavakra.

display his affection towards those who had died. O great king! He advanced angrily on foot, with a club in his hand. He was alone and the earth trembled from his strides. The great being showed himself. On seeing him advance, Krishna quickly got down from his chariot and seized a club. He countered him, just as the shoreline holds the ocean back. The indomitable Karusha[746] raised his club and spoke to Mukunda. "This is good fortune. It is fortunate that you have come within the range of my vision today. O Krishna! You are the son of my maternal uncle.[747] But you have injured my friends and wish to kill me too. O foolish one! Therefore, I will slay you with this club, which is like the vajra. O ignorant one! I am devoted to my friends. In this way, I will repay my debt towards my friends. I will kill you, because you are like an enemy in the form a relative. You are like a disease that is roaming around in the body." He afflicted Krishna with these harsh words. Then, like an elephant that has been urged with a goad, he struck him on the head with the club and roared loudly, like a lion. Though he was struck in the field of battle with the club, the extender of the Yadu lineage did not waver. With his large and heavy Koumadaki[748] club, he struck him between the breasts. His heart was shattered from the blow of the club and he began to vomit blood from his mouth. His hair was dishevelled. With his arms and legs stretched out, he fell down on the ground, having lost his life. O king! While all the creatures looked on, an extraordinary and subtle light arose and entered Krishna, just as it had done at the time of Chedi's death. Viduratha was his brother and he was overwhelmed with grief on account of his brother. Sighing heavily, he advanced to kill him, holding a sword and a shield. O Indra among kings! As he descended, Krishna used his chakra, sharp at the edges, to sever his head, along with his diadem and his earrings. Thus, he destroyed Soubha, Shalva, Dantavakra and his younger brother, who were invincible to others, gods and humans alike. Sages, Siddhas, gandharvas, vidyadharas, giant serpents, apsaras, large numbers of ancestors, yakshas, kinnaras

---

[746] The king of Karusha, Dantavakra.

[747] Dantavakra was the son of Shrutadevi, Vasudeva's sister.

[748] Also spelt Koumadoki. The name of Krishna's club.

and charanas sang about his victory and showered down flowers. Surrounded by the brave ones among the Vrishnis, he entered the ornamented city. The illustrious Krishna, the lord of the universe and the lord of yoga, is victorious in this fashion. Only those with the vision of animals think that he has sometimes been defeated.

'Rama heard that preparations were under way for a battle between the Kurus and the Pandavas. Since he was truly neutral, he left, intending to bathe at the tirthas. He bathed in Prabhasa[749] and satisfied gods, rishis and humans. Along with brahmanas, he followed the course of the Sarasvati from its mouth to its origin. O descendant of the Bharata lineage! He went to Prithudaka,[750] Bindusaras,[751]   Tritakupa,[752]   Sudarshana,[753]   Vishala,[754] Brahmatirtha,[755] Chakratirtha,[756] and the place where the Sarasvati flows in an eastward direction. O descendant of the Bharata lineage! He travelled along the banks of the Yamuna and the Ganga. He then went to Naimisha, where the rishis were performing a sacrifice. The sages had been performing this sacrifice for a long time. On seeing him, as is proper, they honoured him. They stood up, bowed and worshipped him. Thus worshipped, along with his companions, he accepted a seat. However, he noticed that Romaharshana, the

[749] Somanath.

[750] Prithudaka is named after King Prithu. It is believed that Vishvamitra became a brahmarshi in the Sarasvati temple there. This is identified as Pehowa in Karnal district.

[751] Siddhapura (Sitpur) in Gujarat.

[752] The sage Trita fell into a kupa (well) here, somewhere along the banks of the Sarasvati.

[753] Identified with Ramahrada, somewhere near Kurukshetra.

[754] Probably Vaishali. But there were seven (sapta) tributaries or different names for the Sarasvati in different places—Suprabha in Pushkara, Kanchanakshi in Naimisha, Vishala in Gaya, Manasahrada in Uttara Kosala, Suvenu in Kedara, Vimaloda in Gangadvara and Sarasvati in Kurukshetra.

[755] On the banks of the Sarasvati. It is impossible to be more specific than that.

[756] On the banks of the Sarasvati. It is impossible to be more specific than that.

great rishi's[757] disciple, remained seated. This son of a suta did not stand up. He did not bow down and join his hands in salutation. He remained seated on a seat that was higher than that of the brahmanas. On seeing this, Madhava was enraged. "He has been born from a *pratiloma* marriage.[758] However, this evil-minded person seats himself above brahmanas and above all of us who are protectors of dharma. Having been a disciple of the illustrious rishi,[759] he has studied a lot—Itihasa, the Puranas and all the texts of dharma. However, he is not self-controlled. Nor is he humble. He prides himself on being learned, but in vain. There are no qualities in him. He is like an actor who has been unable to control his mind. This is the reason why I have assumed an avatara in this world. I will kill the ones who bear aloft the banner of dharma, since they are greater sinners."[760] Having said this, the illustrious one refrained from killing the wicked.[761] With a blade of *kusha* grass in his hand, the lord struck him. However, destiny took over and he was killed.

'Distressed in their minds, all the sages lamented, "Alas! Alas!" They told Samkarshana, "O god! O lord! You have performed an act of adharma. O descendant of the Yadu lineage! Until the sacrifice was over, it is we who gave him the seat meant for a brahmana, a long life and freedom from physical harm. What you have unwittingly done is like the killing of a brahmana. But you are the lord of yoga and the controller. Therefore, the injunction doesn't apply to you. O purifier of the worlds! Nevertheless, without being urged by others, you must perform an act of atonement for the sin of killing a brahmana. This must be done as an example to the world." The illustrious one replied, "Desiring to show compassion to people, I will perform an act of atonement for the killing. But

---

[757] Vedavyasa's.

[758] Pratiloma means against the natural order and applies to progeny where the mother is superior in varna to the father. A suta has a kshatriya father and a brahmana mother.

[759] Vedavyasa.

[760] Those who pretend to follow dharma are greater sinners than those who follow adharma.

[761] Since he was visiting the tirthas. He only struck Romaharshana with the blade of grass, not intending to kill him. But destiny took over.

first tell me about the recommended ritual that has to be performed. Tell me what you have wished for him—a long lifespan, strength of the senses and so on. I will ensure that through my yoga maya." The rishis said, "O Rama! Arrange it so that the valour of your weapon, the inevitability of death and our pledge, all remain true." The illustrious one replied, "The instruction of the Vedas is that one's own self is born as a son. Therefore, let his son be the one who expounds.[762] As you have promised, let him possess a long lifespan and strength of the senses. O best among the sages! Tell me what else you wish for. I will accomplish it. O learned ones! Please think about the atonement for something I have done unwittingly." The rishis said, "There is a terrible danava named Balvala and he is the son of Ilvala. He comes here on the day of the new moon and the full moon and pollutes our sacrifice. O Dasharha! Kill that wicked one. It will be a great service. He showers down pus, blood, excrement, urine, liquor and meat. After that, you must control yourself and travel around Bharatavarsha for twelve months, bathing in the tirthas. You will then be purified."'

Chapter 10(79)

Shri-Shuka said, 'When the next day of the full moon arrived, there was a terrible dust storm. O king! There was a fierce wind and a foul stench in every direction. Balvala devised and showered down inauspicious objects on the sacrificial arena. He then appeared, wielding a trident. He was gigantic in form, like a mass of black collyrium. His hair, beard and moustache were like hot copper. His face had terrible teeth and furrowed eyebrows. On seeing him, Rama remembered his club, which was capable of shattering the soldiers of the enemy, and his plough, used to chastise daityas. These immediately presented themselves. Balvala was roaming around in the sky and with the tip of his plough, Bala dragged him, angrily striking the one who injured brahmanas on the

---

[762] The Puranas. Romaharshana's son was Ugrashrava.

head with the club. His forehead was shattered and blood started to flow out. Emitting a roar of agony, he fell down on the ground, like a red mountain that had been struck by the vajra.[763] The sages praised Rama and pronounced their infallible benedictions over him. They sprinkled water on him, just as the gods had done to the slayer of Vritra. They gave Rama divine garments, other celestial ornaments and a vaijayanti garland made out of lotuses that did not fade, Shri's abode.

'With their permission and along with the brahmanas, he went to Koushiki[764] and bathed there. He then went to the lake where the Sarayu originates.[765] He followed the course of the Sarayu and reached Prayaga. He bathed there and satisfied gods and others. He then went to Pulaha's hermitage.[766] He bathed in Gomati and Gandaki and bathed in Vipasha and Shona. He went to Gaya and worshipped the ancestors there. He next went to the confluence of the Ganga with the ocean. He touched the water in Mount Mahendra. Having seen Rama,[767] he honoured him. He went to the seven tributaries of the Godavari, Vena, Pampa and Bhimarathi. Having seen Skanda, Rama went to Shrishaila, where Girisha resides. The lord saw the extremely sacred Mount Venkata, in the Dravida region. He went to Kamakoshni, the city of Kanchi and the River Kaveri. He went to the extremely sacred place known as Shriranga, where Hari resides. He went to Mount Rishabha, Hari's region. This is like the Mathura of the south. He went to the bridge across the ocean,[768] the place that destroys the greatest of sins. There, the one who wields the plough as a weapon gave brahmanas

---

[763] The blood made him resemble a mountain with red minerals and ores flowing out.

[764] The name of a river, Koshi in Bihar.

[765] This is believed to be Lake Manasa.

[766] *Shalagrama* is a sacred stone that is Vishnu's personification. According to legend, Vishnu promised that he would be present as this stone in the River Gandaki. River Gandaki is therefore famous for its shalagrama stones. Specifically, Pulaha's hermitage is believed to be a place known as Shalagrama, near the source of the Gandaki.

[767] Parashurama.

[768] Constructed by Rama.

ten thousand cows. He went to Kritamala, Tamraparni and the *kulachala*, Malaya.[769] Agastya was seated there and he bowed down to him and honoured him. After receiving his benedictions and taking his leave, he went to the southern ocean. There, he saw the goddess Durga, known as Kanya.[770] After this, he went to Phalguna and the excellent lake known as Panchapsara, where Vishnu is present.[771] Having touched the water and bathed there, he gave away ten thousand cows. The illustrious one then travelled through the lands of Kerala and Trigarta.[772] He went to Shiva's kshetra, known as Gokarna. Dhurjati[773] is present there. Bala saw Arya, who resides on an island, and went to Shurparaka.[774] Having touched the waters of the rivers Tapi, Payoshni and Nirvindya, he went to Dandaka.[775] Entering, he went to the Reva, where the city of Mahishmati is.[776] He touched the water in Manutirtha and returned to Prabhasa again.

'He heard the brahmanas conversing about the battle between the Kurus and the Pandavas, in which, all the kings had been killed. He thought that the earth's burden had been removed. The descendant of the Yadu lineage desired to stop Bhima and Duryodhana from fighting with clubs on that battlefield of destruction. He went there. Seeing him, Yudhishthira, Krishna, Arjuna and the twins honoured him. They wanted to ask, "Why have you come here?" But were silent. He saw that those two were angrily roaming around, executing wonderful motions, with clubs in their hands, wishing to be victorious. He told them, "O king!

[769] A kulachala is a great mountain.

[770] In Kanyakumari.

[771] The tirtha known as Phalguna is identified with Anantapur, near Bellary. Panchapsara means five (*pancha*) apsaras.

[772] Trigarta is identified as North Canara.

[773] Shiva.

[774] Arya means Parvati. Shurparaka is Sopara in Maharashtra. Shurparaka is also identified as the region near the origins of the Narmada, that is, what is the southern part of Gujarat now.

[775] Payoshni is the river Purna, while Nirvindhya is the Newaz/Newaj, in Madhya Pradesh.

[776] Reva is Narmada and Mahishmati is Maheshwar.

O Vrikodara! Both of you are brave and equal in strength. I think that one of you is superior in strength, while the other is superior in learning.[777] Both of you are equal to each other in valour. Therefore, I do not see either of you as being victorious. Stop this futile encounter." O king! Though his words were full of meaning, because they were firm in enmity, they did not accept his words. They remembered the evil acts that they had done to each other and they wicked words they had used against each other. Deciding that this was because of destiny, Rama went to Dvaravati. Ugrasena and his other relatives were delighted that he had returned. He again went to Naimisha, where the rishis were engaged in performing a sacrifice. Since he was himself the embodiment of all sacrifices, they rejoiced. He renounced everything to do with the conflict. The illustrious lord bestowed pure vijnana on them. Through this, they saw him, the atman of the universe, in their own atmans, and saw the universe in their own selves. Along with his relatives and well-wishers and with his wife,[778] he had the avabhritha bath. He attired himself in excellent garments and ornamented himself well. Radiant in his own resplendence, he was like the moon. Bala was full of strength and performed such innumerable feats. He is infinite and immeasurable. It is because of maya that he appears as mortal. If a person chants Rama's extraordinary feats and deeds in the morning and in the evening, he is loved by the infinite Vishnu.'

Chapter 10(80)

The king said, 'O illustrious one! O lord! The great-souled Mukunda is infinite in his valour. We wish to hear about his other acts of valour. O brahmana! Uttamashloka's account is excellent. If a person is accomplished and is dissatisfied with the path of desire, how can he cease to be interested in repeatedly hearing about these? If words chant about his qualities, they represent true

---

[777] Bhima in strength and Duryodhana in learning.
[778] Revati.

speech. If hands undertake his work, they are true hands. If the mind remembers him, it is a true mind. He is present in mobile and immobile objects. If the ears hear about this sacred accounts, they are true ears. If a head bows down to both his forms,[779] it is a true head. If they see the god, they are true eyes. If limbs always honour the water that has washed the feet of Vishnu's devotees, those are true limbs.'

Suta said, 'Badarayana's illustrious son was thus asked by Vishnurata.[780] With his heart immersed in the illustrious Vasudeva, he replied.'

Shri-Shuka replied, 'Krishna had a brahmana friend and he was excellent in his knowledge about the brahman. He was not interested in pursuing the objects of the senses. He had conquered his senses and was tranquil in his atman. Voluntarily, he followed the conduct of a householder. He could not dress well and was hungry and lean. His wife also suffered in that way. She was devoted to her husband, but her face was wan. She was suffering from poverty. Trembling, she went to her husband and said, "O brahmana! Isn't it true that the illustrious one is your friend? He is the consort of Shri herself. The illustrious bull among Satvatas is the refuge of brahmanas. O immensely fortunate one! He provides shelter to all those who are virtuous. Your family is suffering. Go to him and he will give you plenty of riches. The lord of Bhojas, Vrishnis and Andhakas is now in Dvaravati. If a person remembers his lotus feet, he gives his own self away. He is the preceptor of the universe. Why will he not confer the desired artha and kama on someone who worships him?" The wife repeatedly entreated the brahmana in many kinds of ways. He thought, "To see Uttamashloka is itself a great gain." Thinking this, he made up his mind to go. He asked, "O fortunate one! Is there anything in the house that can be given to him as a gift?" From brahmanas, she begged four handfuls of parched and flattened rice. She tied this up in a piece of cloth and gave it to her husband as a gift. Accepting this, the foremost among brahmanas left for Dvaraka. He kept thinking, "How will I be able

---

[779] Mobile and immobile.
[780] Parikshit.

to meet Krishna?" With other brahmanas, he passed through three checkpoints and three gates, which are difficult to cross. He passed in front of the houses of the Andhakas and the Vrishnis, who were devoted to dharma.

'The brahmana then entered an opulent house of one of Hari's sixteen thousand queens. When he entered it, it was as if he had obtained the bliss of attaining the brahman. Achyuta was seated on his beloved's couch and saw him from a distance. Rejoicing, he immediately stood up and embraced him in his two arms. He was extremely delighted at having been able to touch the body of his beloved friend, the brahmana rishi. The lotus-eyed one shed tears of joy from his eyes. He made him sit on his own couch and gave him objects of worship. O king! The illustrious one, the purifier of the worlds, brought water for washing his feet and sprinkled that water on his own head. He smeared him with divine fragrances, sandalwood, aloe and kunkuma. Having honoured him, he gave him betel leaf and a cow and spoke words of welcome. The brahmana's garments were dirty. He was emaciated and his veins protruded. The queen[781] herself served him and fanned him with a whisk. The people in the inner quarters witnessed Krishna's unblemished deed. They were astounded at the great honour and affection that was being shown towards an *avadhuta*.[782] "What are the auspicious acts that this beggar avadhhuta has performed? He is devoid of prosperity. In this world, he is condemned as someone who is inferior. This one is revered as the preceptor of the three worlds. He is Shri's abode. He has abandoned Shri on her couch and has embraced him, like an elder brother." O king! They grasped each other by the hand and conversed about the charming incidents, when they had resided in their teacher's household together.[783]

---

[781] Interpreted as Rukmini because of the reference to Shri later.

[782] An avadhuta is an ascetic who has renounced all worldly attachments. Here, it has the sense of someone who is poor and has no worldly possessions.

[783] So far, we have not been told the brahmana's name. From Chapter 10(41), we can deduce this was Sudamna/Sudama. Krishna and Sudama studied together, in Sandipani's hermitage.

'The illustrious one asked, "O brahmana! You know about dharma. After having received the instruction from the preceptor and giving him the dakshina, did you return and marry a wife who is your equal? Even though you are generally engaged in household affairs, your intelligence is not agitated by desire. O learned one! You do not find any pleasure in wealth. That is known to me. There are some who are like me. They give up all desire from their minds and perform action. For the sake of being an example to people, they abandon all the natural propensities that have a divine origin. O brahmana! Do you remember our residence in our preceptor's house? It is in this way that a dvija[784] learns what is there to know and achieves that which is beyond darkness. O dear one! The first guru is the one from whom one obtains birth in this world.[785] Next is the one through whom one becomes a dvija.[786] Last is the one through whom a person in different ashramas obtains knowledge and he is like my own self. O brahmana! In this world, in different varnas and ashramas, those who accept my words as a guru are the ones who know what is good for them. They cross the ocean of life easily. I am in the atmans of all beings. I am not as satisfied through sacrifices, noble birth, austerities and self-control as I am through service towards the guru. O brahmana! Do you remember what happened when we resided with our guru? On one occasion, we were urged by our guru's wife to go and fetch some kindling. O brahmana! We entered a large forest and there was an extremely large and unseasonal storm. It was fierce and harsh and there was thunder. With the sun having set, all the directions were enveloped in darkness. Since everything was covered in water, nothing could be discerned, the high ground or the low. We were there, struck repeatedly by the fierce wind and water. There was a deluge of water everywhere. In the forest, we could not determine the directions. Suffering, we wandered around, holding each other by the hand.

---

[784] We have deliberately left this as dvija, since it doesn't necessarily mean a brahmana.

[785] The father. Generally, the parents.

[786] The one through whom the investiture of the sacred thread ceremony occurs.

Our guru, Sandipani, got to know. When the sun arose, he searched for us and found us, his disciples, in that distressed state. "Alas, my sons! You have suffered from a great deal of misery for our sake. All beings love their own selves the most. However, devoted to me, you ignored that. This is the task of all good disciples, repaying the debt due to the guru. With pure sentiments, everything, including one's own self, must be surrendered to the guru. O best among dvijas! I am satisfied with you. May all your desires come true. In this world and in the next, may the mantras never leave you."[787] While we resided in our guru's house, there were many other incidents. It is through a guru's favours that a man becomes complete and obtains tranquility.

'The brahmana replied, "O god of the gods! O preceptor of the universe! You are one who accomplishes all desires. Since my residence with the guru was with you, what could we possibly not accomplish? O lord! In the form of the mantras, your body is the brahman. You are the field where everything beneficial is sown. That you resided with the guru is itself a matter of great wonder."'

Chapter 10(81)

Shri-Shuka said, 'In this way, Hari conversed with that best of brahmanas. He knew about what was in the minds of all creatures. He smiled and spoke to him. The illustrious Krishna was devoted to brahmanas. He joked with his dearest brahmana. The one who is truly the destination of all virtuous people glanced at him with affectionate eyes.

'The illustrious one said, "O brahmana! What gift have you brought me from your house? A trifling gift offered by a devotee satisfies me, but not a great deal of gifts by a person who is not devoted to me. If a person devotedly controls himself and offers me a leaf, a flower, a fruit or some water, I accept it."'[788]

---

[787] That is, may you never forget them.
[788] This shloka is identical with 9.26 in the Bhagavad Gita.

Shri-Shuka continued, 'O king! Though the brahmana was addressed in this way by Shri's lord, he was ashamed and did not give the parched and flattened rice. His face was cast downwards. He is the direct witness in the atmans of all creatures. He knew the reason for his coming there. He thought, "Desiring riches, this one has never served me earlier. My friend wants to do what will bring pleasure to his wife, who is devoted to her husband. That is the reason he has come to me. I will grant him riches that even the immortals find extremely difficult to obtain." The parched and flattened rice was tied up in a rag inside the brahmana's clothes. Thinking this, he himself snatched it and asked, "What is this? O friend! You have brought me this. O dear one! I love this a lot. This parched and flattened rice will satisfy me and the entire universe." Saying this, he ate a handful. As he was about to eat the second handful, devoted to Parameshthi, Shri seized him by the hand.[789] "O atman of the universe! This is sufficient to grant him all kinds of wealth in this world and in the next. You are the reason behind a man's satisfaction." After eating and drinking, the brahmana happily spent the night in Achyuta's house. He thought that he had gone to heaven. O son! Next morning, he left for his own house. He was delighted. For a part of the way, he was followed by the creator of the universe, the one who is his own source of bliss. He had not obtained riches from Krishna. Nor had he asked for them himself. He was satisfied with only having met him. However, as he returned to his own home, he was embarrassed. "He treats brahmanas like divinities. I have seen how devoted he is to brahmanas. The one who has the radiant Lakshmi on his chest has embraced a person like me, the poorest of the poor. Who am I? I am poor and wicked. Krishna is Shri's abode. I am a *brahma-bandhu*.[790] Nevertheless, he has embraced me in his arms. Like a brother, he made me sit on his couch, where his beloved had sat. Since I was exhausted, the queen fanned with a whisk made of yak

---

[789] As has been mentioned earlier, Shri is Rukmini. There are interpretations about why Rukmini prevented Krishna from eating a second handful. Since they differ quite a bit, we will not get into that.

[790] One who is a brahmana only in name, worst among brahmanas.

hair in her hand. He served me in a supreme way, massaging my feet and doing other things. He treats brahmanas like divinities. Like a god, I was worshipped by that god of gods. Worshipping his feet is the cause behind obtaining heaven, emancipation for men, the prosperity of earth and rasatala and all the kinds of siddhi.[791] 'If this person without riches obtains riches, he will become intoxicated and not remember me.' That must be the reason why he did not give me even a little bit of riches." Thinking in this way, he came close to his own house.

'In every direction, it was surrounded by palaces that were like the sun, the fire and the moon. There were wonderful groves and gardens and many flocks of birds called out from them. There were bodies of water with blooming night lotuses, day lotuses, white lotuses and water lilies. It was surrounded by ornamented men and women whose eyes were like those of deer. "What is this place? Whom does this belong to? Where did all this come from?" While he was debating in this way, those men and women, who were as radiant as immortals, came forward to welcome the immensely fortunate one. They sang and played on many musical instruments. Hearing that her husband had come, his wife was excited and delighted. She quickly emerged from her house, in a form that was like that of Shri coming out of her residence. She was devoted to her husband. When she saw her husband, her eyes filled with tears of love and eagerness. She closed her eyes. In her heart, she embraced him with her mind. He glanced at his radiant wife, resembling a goddess in a vimana. She was resplendent in the midst of female servants wearing golden necklaces[792] and he was astounded. He was himself delighted and entered his own house with her. It was full of hundreds of bejewelled pillars, like the great Indra's residence. The beds were as white as the froth on milk. They were made out of ivory and were covered with golden spreads. There were couches with golden legs and fans and whisks. There were golden seats, with soft cushions on them. Nets of pearls hung from the dazzling canopies. The walls were made out

---

[791] Yoga leads to eight major siddhis or powers.
[792] Literally, necklaces made out of gold coins.

of sparkling crystal and inlaid with extremely expensive emeralds. There were women ornamented with gems, holding dazzling lamps studded with jewels. The brahmana saw the opulence there, with every kind of prosperity. Without any agitation, he debated about the reason behind his prosperity. "I am certainly unfortunate. Since childhood, I have suffered from penury. The reason for my prosperity is nothing but the one who confers great opulence through his glances. That is none other than the best among the Yadus. He is the one who enjoys all kinds of prosperity. Though I did not speak, he gave me plenty of what I wanted to ask for, like Parjanya showering down. My friend is a bull among the Dasharhas and he himself saw. He regards what he himself has given as a trifle. However, if a well-wisher does something that is insignificant, he regards it as a lot. I only took him handfuls of parched and flattened rice. However, filled with joy, the great-souled one accepted it. From one life to another life, may I possess goodwill, friendship, affection and servitude towards him. The great being is a reservoir of qualities. May I be attached to those who are devoted to that Purusha. For his devotees, the wonderful and illustrious one is himself a treasure. The one without birth is capable of bestowing kingdoms and prosperity. However, he is himself wise and can see that for those who lack foresight, wealth is the cause of intoxication and downfall." He was extremely devoted to Janardana and he used his intelligence to decide in this way. Though he wished to give up all these objects, with his wife, he enjoyed them. However, he did not lust after them excessively. The lord Hari is the god of the gods. He is the lord of sacrifices. Though he is powerful, he accepts brahmanas as divinities. He does not know of anything that is superior to them. The brahmana was the illustrious one's well-wisher. He saw that the unvanquished one is conquered by those who are his own servants. He meditated on him and the force of this loosened his own bonds. Within a short period of time, he obtained the abode that is the destination of the virtuous. He regards brahmanas as divinities. If a person hears about his devotion to brahmanas, his sentiments turn towards devotion towards the illustrious one and he is freed from all the bondage of karma.'

Chapter 10(82)

Shri-Shuka said, 'Once, while Rama and Krishna were residing in Dvaravati, there was a great eclipse of the sun, as if the end of the kalpa had arrived. O king! Having got to know about it in advance, people from all directions went to the region known as Samantapanchaka, so as to ensure benefit for themselves.[793] Rama,[794] supreme among the wielders of weapons, made the earth empty of kshatriyas at that spot. The floods of blood from the kings created large lakes there. The illustrious Rama was untouched by this deed. However, so as to instruct people, the lord performed a sacrifice there, as if to dispel any sin he might have been tainted with. It was a great tirtha and all the subjects of Bharatavarsha went there on a pilgrimage. O descendant of the Bharata linage! The Vrishnis, Akrura, Vasudeva,[795] Ahuka and others, went there, wishing to cleanse themselves of their own sins. So did Gada, Pradyumna, Samba and others. Suchandra, Shuka, Sarana and Aniruddha, along with the leader, Kritavarma, stayed back, for protection.[796] Along the road, those greatly energetic ones, wearing golden necklaces, were resplendent. Their chariots were like the vehicles of the gods. The movement of the horses was as light as that of waves. The elephants trumpeted like clouds. The men were as dazzling as vidyadharas. Along with their wives, they were adorned in divine garlands and garments and were armoured. They seemed to be travelling through the sky. The immensely fortunate ones bathed there. They controlled themselves and bathed. They gave brahmanas cows, garments, garlands and golden necklaces. After this,[797] following the rites, the Vrishnis again bathed in Rama's lakes. They gave the best of food to the best of brahmanas

---

[793] They got to know about it astronomically. Samantapanchaka is the area around Kurukshetra. At the time of an eclipse, it is auspicious to bathe in such a sacred place.

[794] Parashurama.

[795] Krishna's father.

[796] For protecting Dvaraka.

[797] After the eclipse was over.

and said, "May our devotion to Krishna remain." Having taken
the permission of those who were divinities to Krishna,[798] as they
chose, the Vrishnis seated themselves under the cool shade of trees
and ate.[799]

'Wishing to see them, the kings who were their well-wishers and
matrimonial allies arrived there—Matsyas, Ushinaras, Koushalya,
Vidarbhas, Kurus, Srinjaya, Kambojas, Kekayas, Madras, Kuntis,
Anartas and Keralas. O king! There were hundreds of others, from
their own side, as well as adversaries. Their well-wishers, the gopas
and the gopis, Nanda and the others, had been anxious for a long
time. They were overwhelmed with joy at seeing each other. Their
hearts and faces resembled radiant and newly bloomed lotuses.
With tears flowing from their eyes, they embraced each other
firmly. Their body hair stood up. Since they were overwhelmed
with joy, their voices choked. With a great deal of affection, the
women glanced at each other. Casting smiling and sidelong glances,
they embraced each other. The kunkuma from one person's breast
smeared against that of another's. With tears of love in their eyes,
they engulfed each other in their arms. They honoured the elders
and were honoured by those who were younger. They welcomed
each other and asked about each other's welfare. They then spoke
to each other about Krishna's accounts.

'Pritha met her brothers, sisters and their sons, and her parents
too. She met Mukunda and the wives of her brothers. While
conversing with them, she forgot her sorrow. Kunti said, "O noble
elder brother![800] I think that there have been no benedictions for
me. When I was afflicted because of the hardships, you excellent
ones did not remember me. When destiny is unfavourable, a
person's own relatives, well-wishers, kin, sons, brothers and even
the parents, no longer remember the person." Vasudeva replied,
"O mother![801] Do not censure us. Men are puppets in the hands of

---

[798] The brahmanas.

[799] They broke their fast.

[800] She is addressing Vasudeva, Krishna's father.

[801] Kunti is being addressed as a mother, not as Vasudeva's mother.
The word used is *amba*.

destiny. Whether one does something, or is made to do something, people are under the lord's subjugation. Tormented by Kamsa, all of us fled in different directions. O sister! It is destiny that has again brought us back to our proper places." Vasudeva, Ugrasena and the other Yadus honoured the kings. On seeing Achyuta, they were filled with supreme bliss. Bhishma, Drona, Ambika's son,[802] Gandhari and her sons, the Pandavas and their wives, Kunti, Sanjaya, Vidura, Kripa, Kuntibhoja, Virata, Bhishmaka, the great Nagnajit, Purujit, Drupada, Shalya, Dhrishtaketu, Damaghosha, Vishalaksha, Maithila, Madra, Kekaya, Yudhamanyu, Susharma, Bahlika and others, along with their sons, were present. O Indra among kings! The kings who followed Yudhishthira were amazed to see Shouri's form, the residence of Shri, along with his wives. Rama and Krishna honoured those who had arrived in the proper way. Filled with joy, they praised the Vrishnis, who were Krishna's companions. "O lord of Bhoja![803] Among men in this world, your birth has been successful. Yogis find it impossible to constantly see Krishna. But you have seen him in that way. The sacred texts speak about his glory, which purifies all contamination, as do the water that has washed his feet and the words he speaks through the sacred texts. The touch of his lotus feet revived the powers of the earth, which had been ravaged by time, and she showers down all the objects of desire. The householder's path is one that leads to hell. However, Vishnu himself, the source of heaven, emancipation and cessation,[804] has resided there with you. You can see him. You can touch him. You can walk with him. You can converse with him. You can lie down with him. You can be seated with him. You can eat with him. You can have matrimonial alliances with him. You can have blood relationships with him."[805]

---

[802] Dhritarashtra. Clearly, this incident occurred before the war in Kurukshetra and many other events that have been mentioned earlier.

[803] This is addressed to Ugrasena.

[804] The cessation of samsara.

[805] The word used is *sapinda*, connoting the same lineage as one's mother.

'Hearing that the Yadus, with Krishna at the forefront, had come there, Nanda arrived there, wishing to see them. He was surrounded by gopas, who had many objects on their carts. Seeing him, the Vrishnis were delighted, as if life had returned to their bodies. Not having seen him for a long time, they had suffered. They stood up and firmly embraced him. Delighted and overwhelmed with love, Vasudeva[806] embraced him. He remembered how he had suffered because of what Kamsa had done and how he had left his son in Gokula. Krishna and Rama embraced and honoured their parents.[807] O extender of the Kuru lineage! Their throats choked with love and they were unable to say anything. The immensely fortunate Yashoda embraced her two sons in her arms and placed them on her lap, forgetting her sorrow. Remembering the friendship that she had shown towards them, Rohini and Devaki embraced the queen of Vraja.[808] With tears choking their voices, they said, "O queen of Vraja! Who can forget the constant friendship the two of you have shown us? There is nothing in this world that is enough to pay you back, even if one possessed Indra's riches. When these two had not seen their parents, you were their parents. You tended to them, reared them, nourished them and protected them. They resided with you and you protected them, just as the eyelids protect the eyes. There was no fear from any quarter. The virtuous do not distinguish between someone who is theirs and someone who is someone else's." The gopis had obtained their desired Krishna after a long time. Glancing at him with their eyes, they cursed the creator of eyelids.[809] Using their eyes, all of them completely embraced him in their hearts. This state of immersion is one that is impossible to achieve, even for those who are constantly engaged.[810]

'When they were in such a state, the illustrious one met them in a secluded place. He embraced each of them and asked about their welfare. He smiled and spoke to them. "O friends! Do you

---

[806] Krishna's father.
[807] The foster parents.
[808] That is, Yashoda.
[809] Since these led to blinking and a pause in the vision.
[810] Such as in meditation and yoga.

remember me? It was to accomplish the objective of my relatives that I have been away for such a long time. My mind was engaged in destroying the side of the adversary. Do you reprimand me? Do you suspect me of being ungrateful? Indeed, it is the illustrious one who brings creatures together and separates them. The wind brings together and separates masses of clouds, grass, cotton and dust. This is exactly what the creator of beings does with beings. Devotion towards me certainly leads to immortality. It is good fortune that you possess this kind of affection towards me. That leads to obtaining me. I am the beginning and the end of all beings. O beautiful ladies! I am inside and outside, just like the elements—space, water, earth, wind and fire. It is these that exist in beings. The atman is in beings.[811] Both of these are manifest in me. But behold the supreme and the imperishable, manifest in me." The gopis were thus instructed by Krishna about the knowledge of *adhyatma*.[812] Through constantly remembering him, they destroyed their living sheaths and were immersed in him. They said, "O one with the lotus in the navel! Lords of yoga, those who are unfathomable in their understanding, think about your lotus feet in their hearts. They are the support for deliverance from the well of samsara into which, those who are engaged in household pursuits have fallen. May our minds be always enlightened.'"

Chapter 10(83)

Shri-Shuka said, 'The illustrious one, who was the preceptor as well as the destination, favoured the gopis in this way. He next asked Yudhishthira and all the other well-wishers about their welfare. They were asked by the protector of the world and honoured extremely well. Delighted, they replied. On seeing his feet, all their sins were destroyed. "O lord! How can there be anything

---

[811] The elements constitute and exist in physical beings, but the elements neither constitute, nor exist, in the atman.

[812] Spiritual truth.

inauspicious for those who have drunk the nectar from your lotus feet? Sometimes, those great minds articulate this through their mouths and using the ears as cups, it can be drunk. Those with bodies suffer from amnesia about who created the bodies and this destroys that loss of memory. The radiance of your atman destroys the three kinds of states created in ourselves.[813] You are a deluge of bliss. Your knowledge is absolute and without limits. Time has ravaged the sacred texts and using your yoga maya, you have assumed a form so as to save them. You are the destination of *paramahamsa*s.[814] We bow down before you." The people spoke in this way about Uttamashloka, who is like a jewel on the crest, and praised him. The Andhaka and Kourava women met and spoke to each other about Govinda's account, which is sung about in the three worlds. Listen. I will describe it to you.

'Droupadi said, "O princess of Vidarbha,[815] who is never separated from him! O Bhadra![816] O Jambavati! O Koushala! O Satyabhama! O Kalindi! O Shaibya! O Rohini![817] O Lakshmana! O wives of Krishna! The illustrious one uses his maya to follow the conduct of ordinary people. Tell us. How did he himself marry you?"

'Rukmini replied, "When I was to be bestowed on Chedi, all the invincible kings and their soldiers raised their bows. However, he placed the dust of his feet on their heads. Like a lord of deer, he took his share away from a herd of sheep. His feet are Shri's abode. May they always be mine to worship."

'Satyabhama replied, "My father's heart was tormented because of his brother's[818] death. He defeated the king of bears to remove the

---

[813] We have kept it simple, but there are complicated interpretations. The contact with material objects creates the three states. The contact with the mind creates the three states. The three states result from sattva, rajas and tamas. Alternatively, the three states are wakefulness, dreaming and dreamless sleep.

[814] A paramahamsa is a person who has reached the supreme state.

[815] Rukmini.

[816] Satyabhama.

[817] Not to be confused with Balarama's mother.

[818] Prasena's.

stain on his reputation. He took away the jewel.[819] Because of his powers, my father was terrified and bestowed me on him, though I had been promised to another."[820]

'Jambavati replied, "My father[821] did not know that his own protector and divinity, Sita's consort, had assumed a body. He fought against him for twenty-seven days. When he had tested him and got to know, he respectfully offered me as a gift, along with the jewel, clasping his feet. I am his female servant."

'Kalindi replied, "He knew that I was performing austerities with the hope of touching his feet. He sent his friend[822] and accepted my hand. I am the one who sweeps his house."

'Mitravinda replied, "He came to my svayamvara and defeated all the kings and my brothers, who insulted him. He took me away, like a lion taking away its share from a pack of dogs. The abode of Shri brought me to his own city. In one life after another, may I have the fortune of washing his feet."

'Satya replied, "My father arranged for seven bulls that were extremely strong. They were energetic and possessed extremely sharp horns. He wished to test the bravery of the kings. They destroyed the pride of those brave ones. However, he swiftly subdued them. Toying with them, he bound them up, the way a child does with a kid goat. In this way, he won me and my female servants as viryashulka. With four kinds of forces,[823] kings tried to obstruct his path. But he defeated them and brought me away. May I be able to serve him."

'Bhadra replied, "O Krishna![824] My heart was devoted to Krishna, my maternal cousin. My father himself invited him and bestowed me on him, along with my female friends and one akshouhini. From one life to another life, as I am whirled around in my bonds of karma, may I be able to touch his feet. That will be best for me."

---

[819] Syamantaka.
[820] Akrura. Satyabhama's father was Satrajit.
[821] Jambavat.
[822] Arjuna.
[823] Chariots, elephants, horses and infantry.
[824] Krishnaa, Droupadi.

'Lakshmana replied, "O queen! I repeatedly heard Narada chant about Achyuta's birth and deeds. My mind was fixed on Mukunda. Indeed, the one with the lotus in her hand[825] thought about it carefully and chose him, rejecting the guardians of the worlds. O virtuous lady! My father is known as Brihatsena and he is devoted to his daughter. Ascertaining my intentions, he devised a means of bringing this about. O queen! In your svayamvara, a fish was devised for Partha's[826] sake. It was the same with mine, except that the fish was covered from all sides and could not be seen. There was only a reflection in the water. Hearing about this, all the kings arrived in my father's city. They knew the truth about all astras and shastras and were accompanied by thousands of instructors. According to valour and according to age, my father honoured all of them. With their minds on me, they took up the bow and arrow kept in the assembly and tried to pierce it. Some picked up the bow, but unable to string it, put it aside. Some lords were only able to string it up to the elbow.[827] They were hurled back and fell down. There were other brave ones, Magadha,[828] Ambashta, Chedi, Bhima, Duryodhana and Karna, who could string it. But they could not determine the location.[829] Partha looked at the reflection of the fish in the water and could determine its location. However, when he released the arrow, it only touched the target from the side and did not pierce it. The kings withdrew, their pride shattered. As if toying, the illustrious one picked up the bow and strung it. He fixed the arrow and looked at the fish's reflection only once. He pierced it with the arrow and it fell down. At that time, the sun was in Abhijit nakshatra.[830] Drums were sounded in heaven and shouts of 'victory' were raised on earth. The gods were filled with joy and repeatedly showered down flowers. At this, I entered the arena

[825] Lakshmi.

[826] Arjuna's. In Droupadi's svayamvara, the artificial fish had not been completely covered.

[827] They could string the bow on one side, but not on the other.

[828] Jarasandha.

[829] Of the fish.

[830] An auspicious moment.

on my feet, anklets tinkling. I held a brilliant garland that was
made out of gold and jewels. I was wearing new lower and upper
garments made out of silk. A wreath of flowers was braided into
my hair. I smiled bashfully. I raised my face, with its thick locks of
hair. The shine of the earrings illuminated my cheeks. With a gentle
smile, I cast a sidelong glance at the kings who were all around.
With my heart devoted to Murari, I slowly placed the garland
around his neck. There were the sounds of drums, tabors, conch
shells, larger drums, kettledrums and other instruments. Male and
female dancers started to dance. The singers started to sing. O
Yajnaseni![831] In this way, I chose the lord. However, the leaders
among the kings could not tolerate my choosing the illustrious
one. With their hearts full of desire for me, they challenged him.
He placed me on the chariot, yoked to four jewels among horses.
He raised the Sharnga bow and armoured himself. The four-armed
one stood there, ready to fight. O queen! Daruka drove the chariot
that was plated with gold. The kings looked on, just as deer looked
at a king of deer. Trying to restrain him, for some distance, the
kings followed him from the rear. Some were ready and raised
their bows. But they were like village dogs after a lion. Torrents
of arrows were released from Sharnga and some fell down on
the field of battle, with their arms, thighs and necks severed. The
others gave up and fled. The lord of Yadu entered his decorated
city of Kushasthali, which is praised in heaven and on earth. There
were colourful flags, pennants and arches that blocked out even
the sun. He entered, as if the sun was entering its own abode. My
father honoured his well-wishers, matrimonial allies and relatives
with extremely expensive garments, ornaments, couches, seats and
other furnishings. Though he[832] is complete, he gave him female
servants, all kinds of riches, soldiers, elephant riders, chariots,
horse riders and extremely expensive weapons. He finds bliss in
his own self and there are maids in his home. Abandoning all
attachment, we must have undertaken austerities."[833]

---

[831] Droupadi.

[832] Krishna.

[833] Earlier, that is the reason we are fortunate now.

'The queens[834] replied, "He killed Bhouma[835] and his companions in the battle and found us imprisoned there. He got to know that we were the daughters of kings whom he had defeated in the course of his conquest. He freed us. However, in a desire to be free of samsara, we had been remembering his lotus feet. Therefore, though he has already achieved all his desires, he married us. O virtuous lady! We do not desire a kingdom on earth, a kingdom in heaven, unlimited objects of pleasure, supernatural powers, the status of Parameshthi,[836] anything infinite, or Hari as a destination. We desire only this much, that we should bear the dust of his handsome feet on our heads. He is the wielder of the mace and the dust has been enriched by the fragrance of the kunkuma from Shri's breasts. We desire what the women of Vraja, the gopas who herd the cows and the plants and grass along the banks desire—the touch of the great-souled one's feet.'

Chapter 10(84)

Shri-Shuka said, 'Pritha, Subala's daughter,[837] Yajnaseni, Madhavi,[838] the wives of the kings and his own gopis were bound to Hari in bonds of love. Krishna is in the atmans of everything. Hearing all this, all of them were extremely amazed and their eyes filled with tears. In this way, the conversation occurred, men with men and women with women. At that time, wishing to see Krishna and Rama, the sages arrived there—Dvaipayana, Narada, Chyavana, Devala, Asita, Vishvamitra, Shatananda, Bharadvaja, Goutama, Rama[839] and his disciples, the illustrious Vasishtha, Galava, Bhrigu, Pulastya, Kashyapa, Atri, Markandeya, Brihaspati, Dvita, Trita,

[834] The other queens. This is interpreted as Rohini speaking on behalf of the other queens.

[835] Narakasura.

[836] Brahma.

[837] Gandhari.

[838] Subhadra.

[839] Parashurama.

Ekata, Brahma's sons,[840] Angiras, Agastya, Yajnavalkya, Vamadeva and others. The kings, the Pandavas, Krishna and Rama, and the others had been seated earlier. They quickly arose and bowed down to the ones who are respected throughout the universe. All of them, along with Rama and Achyuta, honoured them and gave them many kinds of offerings—words of welcome, seats, water to wash the feet, arghya, garlands, incense and pastes.

'When they were happily seated, the illustrious one, whose body protects dharma, addressed them in these words. In the midst of that great assembly, they heard. The illustrious one said, "Wonderful! We have now obtained all the fruits of being born. We have seen the lords of yoga, whom even the gods find it extremely difficult to behold. How can men who are limited in austerities and whose perception of god is limited to those who are worshipped,[841] get an opportunity of seeing you, touching you, questioning you, bowing down to you and worshipping your feet? Water does not constitute tirthas. Gods are not made out of clay and stone. These purify after a long period of time, but the sight of virtuous ones purifies instantly. Agni, Surya, Chandra, the stars, earth, water, space, breath, speech and mind may be worshipped. But these are created by a sense of duality and do not take away sin. However, the service of the learned destroys it instantly. This body is like a corpse, consisting of the three elements.[842] A person whose intelligence is such that he takes this body to be his self, wife and others to be his own, if his intelligence is such that he takes objects made of earth as objects of worship, and if his intelligence is such that he takes water to be a tirtha, then people who know never regard him as wise. He is like a cow or a donkey." They heard the words of the illustrious Krishna, whose intelligence was unlimited. They were extremely difficult to comprehend. The brahmanas remained seated and silent. Their minds were in a whirl. The sages thought for a long time and decided that since he was the lord who controlled everything, he must have said this for the sake of instructing people.

---

[840] Sanaka, Sananda, Sanatana and Sanatkumara.
[841] Such as images of gods worshipped in temples.
[842] Bile, phlegm and air.

They smiled and spoke to the preceptor of the universe. "We are the best among those who know the truth and we are the foremost among those who have created the universe. However, we are confounded by your maya. The lord's conduct is hidden in what he does in this world. How wonderful is the illustrious one's conduct. How wonderful is the lord's imitated conduct.[843] He makes no efforts, but appears in many kinds of forms. He creates, preserves and destroys, but is not bound down by that. He is like the earth, since the transformations of the earth appear in many names and forms. From time to time, to protect those who are your devotees and to chastise the wicked, you assume the form of sattva.[844] In your own pastimes, you are the eternal path of the Vedas and the atman of varnas and ashramas. You are the supreme Purusha. The brahman is your pure heart. Through austerities, studying and self-control, one can perceive the truth that is beyond the manifest and the unmanifest. O brahman! Those who are born in the lineages of brahmanas use the sacred texts to realize your atman. You are the true abode. You are foremost among those who are devoted to brahmanas and you worship them. Today, our birth, learning, austerities and vision has been rendered successful. You are the destination of the virtuous and the supreme and ultimate benefit and we have met you. O illustrious Krishna! O one who is unlimited in intelligence! We bow down to you. You are the paramatman, but you have shrouded your glory through your own yoga maya. The kings and the Vrishnis find pleasure with you, but they do not know you. You are the lord. You are time. Their atmans are covered in the curtain of maya. A sleeping person's perception of the reality about his self is coloured by the attributes of the names and forms he sees. He does not know what is distinct from this.[845] In that way, the senses of someone who is confounded by maya takes the names and forms of material objects to be real. His memory is confused. Today, we have seen your feet. They are the source of the tirtha that

[843] Imitating human behaviour.

[844] Though you are nirguna.

[845] This is a difficult shloka to translate. A sleeping person sees various things in a dream. They seem to be real, but aren't. Reality is different.

washes away floods of sins.[846] Extremely perfected yogis hold them in their hearts. However, only those who possess extreme devotion towards you can destroy the sheath of the living body and attain you as a destination. Therefore, show compassion towards your devotees." O royal sage! Having said this, the sages made up their minds to leave for their own hermitages and sought the permission of Dasharha, Dhritarashtra and Yudhishthira.

'Seeing that they were about to leave, the immensely illustrious Vasudeva[847] bowed down and clasped their feet. He controlled himself and spoke to them. Vasudeva said, "I bow down to the rishis. All the gods are in them. You should listen to what I have to say. You should explain what karma one should undertake, so that one can counter the effects of karma." Narada replied, "O brahmanas! It is not surprising that Vasudeva should desire to know this. Thinking Krishna to be his child, he has asked us about what is good for his own atman.[848] In the mortal world, familiarity is the root cause of disregard. Those who live on the banks of the Ganga ignore it and go elsewhere to be purified. His[849] wisdom is not affected by time, creation, destruction and other things. His attributes are his own and there is nothing else that can disrupt them. He is not affected by material hardships, the consequences of karma and the gunas. The lord's consciousness is not affected. He is absolute, without a second. However, his own powers are enveloped in prana and other things and others take him to be ordinary, just like the sun, when it is shrouded in clouds, mist and eclipses." O king! After this, while all the kings and Achyuta and Rama heard, the sages addressed Anakadundubhi. "The virtuous have determined the karma that must be undertaken to counter the effect of karmas. One must faithfully perform a sacrifice to Vishnu, the lord of all sacrifices. Wise ones, who possess the insight of the sacred texts, have said that this leads to tranquility of mind. This has been shown to be an easy path of yoga and a pursuit of dharma

---

[846] The Ganga originates there.
[847] Krishna's father.
[848] The sense is, why does he need to ask us?
[849] Krishna's.

that delights the mind. For a dvija who is in the householder stage,
this is the route to obtain benedictions. With wealth one has oneself
earned, one must perform devoted and pure worship to Purusha.
The desire for riches is curbed by giving donations at sacrifices.
The desire for homes, wives and sons is curbed. O supreme one!
In this way, a learned person casts aside all the hardships that are
caused to him by the ravages of time. That is the reason patient
people have given up the desire for household life and have left for
hermitages. O lord! Dvijas have three kinds of debts, to gods, rishis
and ancestors. If he gives up his body without first repaying these
through sacrifices, studying and sons,[850] his downfall is certain. O
immensely intelligent one! You have already been freed from two
of those, to rishis and ancestors. Perform a sacrifice to free yourself
of the debt to the gods. Having repaid that, you can be without a
shelter.[851] O Vasudeva! You must certainly have worshipped Hari,
the lord of the universe, with supreme and great devotion. That
is the reason he has become your son." Hearing their words, the
great-minded Vasudeva bowed his head down and gratified them.

'He asked those rishis to be the officiating priests. O king! He
was devoted to dharma and the rishis were requested according
to the principles of dharma. In that place,[852] they prepared for a
supreme sacrifice. O king! When he was about to be consecrated,
the Vrishnis and the kings bathed and attired themselves in excellent
garments. They wore garlands of lotuses and decorated themselves
with excellent ornaments. The delighted queens wore necklaces
made out of gold[853] and wore excellent garments. They smeared
themselves with pastes and with objects in their hands, approached
the arena marked for the consecration. Drums, tabors, conch shells,
larger drums and kettledrums were sounded. Male and female
dancers danced. The sutas and magadhas sang words of praise. Along
with their husbands, gandharva ladies sang in extremely melodious

---

[850] Sacrifices repay the debt to gods, studying to rishis and sons to
ancestors.

[851] That is, you can cease to be a householder.

[852] Kurukshetra.

[853] Made out of golden coins.

voices. Following the prescribed ordinances, the officiating priests sprinkled and consecrated him. Surrounded by his eighteen wives, he looked like King Soma, surrounded by the stars. They wore girdles, bangles, necklaces, anklets and earrings. Ornamented and clad in deerskin, he was radiant. O great king! The officiating priests wore silk garments and jewels. The assistant priests were radiant, like at the sacrifice of Vritra's slayer.[854] Along with their own relatives, sons and wives, Rama and Krishna, the two lords of all living creatures, dazzled because of their own powers. Each part of the sacrifice was performed according to the ordinances. *Agnihotra* and other aspects were observed. The lord was worshipped through *prakrita, vaikrita, dravya* and jnana rituals.[855] At the appropriate time, as has been recommended, he gave dakshina to the officiating priests. Though they were ornamented, he gave them ornaments, cows, maidens and extremely expensive gifts. The *maharshi*s made him execute the patni-samjaya and avabhritha parts. With the performer of the sacrifice[856] at the forefront, the brahmanas bathed in Rama's[857] lake. After having bathed, along with his wives, he gave ornaments and garments to the bandis. Wearing ornaments, he worshipped all the varnas and dogs with food. With a lot of gifts, he honoured his relatives, along with their wives and sons, Vidarbha, Kosala, Kuru, Kashi, Kekaya, Srinjaya, the officiating priests, the assistant priests, the large number of gods, men, bhutas, ancestors and charanas. All of them praised the sacrifice and taking the leave of the one who was Shri's abode, departed.

'The hearts of Dhritarashtra, his younger brother,[858] the Parthas, Bhishma, Drona, Pritha, the twins, Narada, the illustrious Vyasa, the well-wishers, the matrimonial allies and the relatives were filled with affection and they embraced their relatives, the Yadus. Suffering because of the separation, together with the other

---

[854] Indra.

[855] Prakrita is the primary sacrifice, vaikrita means secondary sacrifices, dravya stands for objects used/offered and jnana stands for mantras.

[856] Vasudeva.

[857] Parashurama's.

[858] Vidura.

people, they left for their own countries. Nanda and the cowherds were worshipped with a great deal of gifts, given by Krishna, Rama, Ugrasena and the others. Devoted to their relatives, they resided for some more time. Thus, Vasudeva easily crossed the great ocean, represented by his wishes. Surrounded by his well-wishers and delighted in his mind, he held Nanda by the hand and spoke to him. Vasudeva said, "O brother! This bond, known as affection among men, has been created by the lord. I think that it is extremely difficult to sever, even for brave ones and yogis. Hence, despite us being ungrateful and undeserving, you supreme ones have shown us this friendship. It has not been reciprocated and can never be repaid. O brother! Earlier, we were incapable of doing anything good towards you. Now, we are blinded by the intoxication of prosperity and do not see that you are right in front of us. O one who deserves to be honoured! The prosperity of a kingdom is not meant for a person who desires benefit for himself. His vision becomes like that of a blind man and he does not see his own relatives and friends." Thus, Anakadundubhi's heart was softened by love. He wept. As he remembered the act of friendship that had been done towards him, his eyes filled with tears. Nanda desired to do what would bring pleasure to his friend. He also loved Govinda and Rama. Therefore, he said, "I will leave today" or "I will leave tomorrow". However, honoured by the Yadus, he resided with them for three months. Along with the residents of Vraja and along with his relatives, all his desires were satisfied. He was given extremely expensive ornaments, silken garments, priceless gifts and furnishings. Thereafter, with the gifts given by Vasudeva, Ugrasena, Krishna, Uddhava, Bala and the others, he left, along with the Yadus.[859] The minds of Nanda, the gopas and the gopis were fixed on the lord Govinda's lotus feet and they were incapable of withdrawing. They left for Mathura. Krishna was like a divinity to the Vrishnis. When the relatives had departed, on seeing that the monsoon was about to set in, they again returned to Dvaravati. They told the people about the great festivities

[859] Some Yadus accompanied Nanda and his people on their return journey, perhaps to protect them.

performed by the lord of the Yadus,[860] about how they had met their well-wishers and about everything else that occurred in the course of their visit to the tirthas.'

Chapter 10(87)

Parikshit asked, 'O brahmana! The brahman cannot be described and is without gunas. It is supreme and is beyond manifestations and their causes. How can the shruti texts, which are about the conduct of the gunas, be used to directly describe it?'[861]

Shri-Shuka replied, 'For living beings, the lord created intelligence, senses, mind and prana for material gratification, and samsara so that the atman can be realized. This is what the Upanishads say about the brahman, and the ancestors of our ancestors meditated on this. If a person meditates on this, he is freed from material association and attains success. In this connection, I will describe to you an account connected with Narayana. This is about a conversation between Narada and the rishi Narayana. Once, Narada, loved by the illustrious one, was roaming around the worlds. To meet the ancient rishi, he went to Narayana's hermitage. From the beginning of the kalpa, he has been there, in this Bharatavarsha, performing austerities with dharma, jnana, self-control and tranquility. He has done this for the welfare of men in this world and in the next one. He was seated there, surrounded by rishis and residents of the village of Kalapa. O extender of the Kuru lineage! He bowed down and asked him exactly this. While the rishis heard, the illustrious one[862] told him about an ancient

---

[860] Vasudeva.

[861] This chapter is known as Shruti-Gita. The shlokas are subject to numerous and complicated interpretations and we have chosen the simplest interpretation possible. Essentially, Parikshit's question is a simple one. How can shruti texts (the Vedas and the Upanishads), which use words, be used to describe the brahman?

[862] Narayana.

conversation that had taken place among the residents of Janaloka about the nature of the brahman.

'The illustrious one[863] said, "O one born from Svayambhu! In ancient times, in Janaloka, there was a sacrifice. There were sages born through mental powers there, those who held up their seed, and they spoke about the brahman. At that time, you had gone to Shvetadvipa to see the lord, who was lying down.[864] There was an extremely well-conducted discussion about the brahman and the shruti texts. What you asked me is exactly the question that was raised there. They were all equal in learning, austerities and good conduct, and they were all impartial in their treatment of their own enemies and neutral parties. Nevertheless, they chose one to speak and the others listened."

'Sanandana said, "After swallowing up his own creation,[865] the supreme one lay down, along with his potencies. The shrutis awoke him, describing his signs.[866] This was like a sleeping king being woken at dawn by bandis, his servants, who approach him and use excellent shlokas to praise his valour."

'The shrutis said, "Victory to you. O unvanquished one! Victory to you. You are the one who is complete in his atman, with all your potencies. You are the one who awakens the energies of everything, mobile and immobile. Destroy the taints of those who have accepted the gunas. As you engage, the sacred texts can sometimes appreciate your unvanquished atman. The supreme is the foundation of creation and destruction and is pervasive. Like clay, it generates transformations, but is not subject to transformations itself.[867] Therefore, the perceived world is identified with the supreme. The minds, words and conduct of the rishis were immersed in you.[868] The feet of men are placed on earth. How can they ignore the earth

---

[863] Rishi Narayana.

[864] This is Vishnu in his form of Aniruddha, lying down after the universal destruction.

[865] At the time of universal destruction.

[866] At the time of the next creation.

[867] Just as pots are made out of clay, but when they are destroyed, become clay again.

[868] And not on the transformations.

on which they dwell?[869] O lord of the three![870] The wise submerge themselves in the ocean of amrita that your accounts are, and cast aside their torments. These destroy all impurities from the worlds. What need be said about those who have used their own powers to cleanse their minds of gunas and the effects of time? O supreme one! They worship your true nature and experience infinite and uninterrupted bliss. Only those who follow you truly breathe, the others are like bellows. It is through your favours that Mahat, ahamkara and the others were created from the cosmic egg. You are the ultimate Purusha who enters and animates the forms, *annamaya* and the others.[871] You are supreme and distinct from the gross and the subtle. You are the underlying reality. Among those who follow the paths of the rishis, those with gross vision worship you in the stomach.[872] The followers of Aruni are more subtle and worship you in the cavity of the heart.[873] O infinite one! Their consciousness rises up to your supreme abode in the crown of the head.[874] A person who reaches that spot no longer falls down into this world, into the mouth of death. You enter the many wonderful species you have yourself created, as if you are their cause. Like the fire, you imitate the forms, superior and inferior, that you yourself have created.[875] Those who are spotless in their intelligence and do not desire anything material comprehend your undifferentiated, unchanging

[869] Like the earth, you are the foundation. If the shrutis describe your transformations, they describe part of you, though not the whole.

[870] This probably means sattva, rajas and tamas, not the three worlds.

[871] Five sheaths cover the atman and are annamaya (related to food), *pranamaya* (related to energy), *manomaya* (related to the mind), *vijnanamaya* (related to knowledge) and *anandamaya* (related to bliss).

[872] A reference to the *manipura chakra*, located above the navel and below the solar plexus. In ascending order along the spinal column, the seven chakras are *muladhara*, *svadhishthana*, manipura, anahata, *vishuddhi*, *ajna* and *sahasrara*.

[873] The cavity of the heart is *anahata chakra*. Aruni must mean Uddalaka Aruni, referred to in the Upanishads.

[874] The *kundalini* rises up the *sushumna nadi* and reaches the crown of the head (*sahasrara chakra*).

[875] Fire is latent in kindling. Fire has no form, but assumes the form of whatever it is burning.

and true manifestation among all these unreal forms. The individual entity resides in these forms because of his own karma, but is covered by the gross and the subtle. You are spoken of[876] as the Purusha who possesses all the powers and these manifestations are your own portions. Thus, wise men have ascertained in the sacred texts that the human state is the field into which the seed is sown. They therefore worship your feet on earth.[877] Faith in you is the means of escaping from samsara. O lord! The truth about the atman is extremely difficult to comprehend. You assume forms to elucidate this. There are those who destroy their exhaustion by submerging themselves into the ocean of amrita represented by your great deeds. Some such people do not desire anything, not even emancipation. They renounce their homes and associate with your devotees, who gather at your lotus feet like swans. When the nest[878] follows the path that leads to you, it behaves like a beloved friend to the atman. You are always eager to help and friendly towards those who seek to ensure for themselves. But alas! There are those who do not find pleasure in you. They worship the unreal and this is like killing their own selves. Because of their desires, they wander around in this fearful existence, in evil physical bodies. There are sages who controlled their breath, mind and senses, firm in their practice of yoga. Thereby, they worshipped you and obtained your state. However, that state was also obtained by your enemies, who constantly remembered you. So did the women, whose minds were attached to your sturdy arms, which were like the coils of the Indra among serpents. You look upon us in the same way. We see you in everything and we will also obtain the nectar of your lotus feet. Indeed, how can anyone who has been born or died after the universal destruction know about someone who existed before all this? The rishi[879] and the large number of gods of both categories[880] who followed him came after that. At that time, the gross and the

---

[876] In the sacred texts.

[877] Through the rites of the sacred texts.

[878] The physical body.

[879] Brahma.

[880] Those in heaven and those who preside over the senses.

subtle, the composition of the two,[881] the flow of time and the sacred texts did not exist, since you were lying down and had withdrawn everything. Those who teach that creation results from the unreal, or those who say that the permanent atman dies, or those who posit duality, or those who declare that the material is permanent, base themselves on illusions. Those who believe that Purusha results from the three gunas, or from modifications,[882] say this because of ignorance. This has no basis in you. You are pure knowledge and absolute consciousness. That the real is based on the three modes[883] is a projection of the mind on you. To human beings, the unreal appears in this way. Those who realize the atman consider this universe as real only because it is a projection of the atman. Transformations of gold need not be rejected, because their essence consists of gold. In that way, what you have created and entered can be ascertained to be no different from your atman. Those who worship you as the entity that exists within all beings disregard death and place their feet on its head. However, those who turn away from you are bound down by your words,[884] like animals. Indeed, only those who are devoted to you are purified. Though you possess no material senses, you are self-luminous and the one who wields power over all the senses. Material nature and the gods[885] accept offerings offered to them and worship you. This is like lords of territories offering tribute to the lord of the entire earth. The creators of the universe faithfully execute the tasks that have been assigned to them by you. O liberated one! You are supreme and in your pastimes, when you cast your glances, the energy and motivation of the species know as mobile and immobile objects is awakened. There is nothing that is alien to you. Nor is there anything that is your own. You are like the sky, which has no attributes but resembles the void that it fills. O one who is

[881] Physical bodies resulting from composition of gross and subtle matter.

[882] That is, from Prakriti.

[883] The three gunas.

[884] Through the injunctions of the sacred texts.

[885] Literally, the ones who do not blink.

permanent! If the numerous embodied entities were permanent and could go everywhere, there would be no one to control and rule them.[886] Therefore, it must be otherwise. That which is created is controlled by the creator, since the created is never distinct from its cause.[887] Though you are equally present in all your manifestations, those who profess to know you do not know. You are beyond knowledge and that view is itself defective. Creation does not result from Prakriti, Purusha, or their combination.[888] Like bubbles come into existence through the combination of water and air, living entities are only apparently generated from that combination. All these, with different names and attributes, merge back into you, the supreme. This is like rivers merging into the ocean, or juices[889] merging into honey. Among men who are whirled around in your maya, there are some who are wise and greatly devoted to you and render service to you, the potent one who delivers from samsara. How can those who follow you suffer from fear of samsara? The three rims[890] are caused by the furrowing of your eyebrows and lead to fear among those who do not seek shelter with you. Even those who conquer their senses and their breath of life cannot control the mind, which is like an unrestrained horse. O one without birth! In this world, they attempt to regulate it through unsteady means that only lead to hardships. They abandon the preceptor's feet and are beset by hundreds of difficulties. They are like merchants, who have not engaged a helmsman, on the ocean. For those men who seek refuge with you, you are the atman, the embodiment of all pleasures. What use do they have for own relatives, sons, bodies, wives, wealth, homes, immobile property, chariots and even life itself? Those who do not know this truth are engaged in the pursuit of sexual pleasure. What happiness can this world give? Its nature is such that it is destroyed. It has no more than transient substance.

[886] The individual jivatmans must have an entity that is superior.

[887] The paramatman is the controller and creator of the individual jivatman.

[888] Parkriti is inert and cannot create an animate jivatman. Purusha, or its combination with Prakriti, makes Purusha subject to transformations.

[889] From different flowers.

[890] Of time, as in the past, the present and the future.

There are rishis who are devoid of pride. They bear your lotus feet and the water that washed your feet in their hearts. They visit sacred places and tirthas on earth. They find eternal bliss in the atman. If a man turns his mind towards you, he no longer serves anything connected with the home, since those only rob him of his qualities. Since this universe arose from the real, it must be real. This logic is subject to refutation. In some ordinary cases, this is not true.[891] In other cases, perceptions about both can be illusory.[892] A traditional succession of blind people desire to establish the imaginary as permanent reality. They are bewildered by numerous words and are dulled by repeated mentions of rituals. This universe did not exist before its creation. Nor will it exist after its destruction. Hence, it is false. But it can be deduced that in the interim, it appears within the absolute you as your manifestation. Therefore, it can be compared to the various kinds of transformations that material objects undergo. It is a figment of the mind and is not real. Those who take it to be real are ignorant. Under the influence of material energy, the jivatman lies down next to maya and embraces her qualities. It serves those assumed forms and, deprived of its prosperity, follows the cycle of birth and death. But just as a snake casts aside its skin, you cast aside material energy. You are immeasurable in your greatness and glory. You possess the eight potencies[893] and opulence. If those who have renounced do not exterminate the roots of desire from their hearts, though you exist in their hearts, they find it impossible to obtain you. You remain like a jewel around the throat, forgotten by the wearer. O illustrious one! Those yogis who gratify their senses find miseries both in this world and in the next. Death does not let them go and they do not obtain you. Because of you, a person who obtains you does not know the auspicious or the inauspicious, the consequences of good deeds or wicked ones. O

[891] The effect is not similar to the cause. For example, a son may be distinct from the father.

[892] Both means the real and the unreal. Perceptions about the real can be illusory, just as a rope can be taken to be a snake. Therefore, perceptions about the world are clouded by the illusion that shrouds that perception.

[893] Compassion, forgiveness, cleanliness, lack of jealousy, altruism, lack of greed, purity and self-control.

one with the qualities! Nor is such an embodied entity aware of the words recommended every day, for every yuga.[894] He hears about you, chanted from one generation to another generation. Through this, men obtain the goal of emancipation. Since you are infinite, the lords of heaven have not been able to reach you. Since you are infinite, nor have you yourself done that. You are indeed inside innumerable cosmic eggs, along with their sheaths. The wheel of time whirls them around inside you, like particles of dust in the sky. The shrutis find their ultimate fruit in you. But their conclusion is indirect, negating every assertion about you."

'The illustrious one[895] said, "Brahma's sons heard this instruction about the atman. Having been successful and having known the destination of the atman, they worshipped Sanandana. In this way, great-souled ones who were born earlier and travelled through the sky[896] distilled out all the essence of the Vedas, the Puranas and the Upanishads. O Brahma's son![897] Faithfully uphold in your heart this instruction about the atman, capable of burning up the desires of men. As you will, travel anywhere on earth."

Shri-Shuka continued, 'O king! When he was commanded by the rishi in this way, the sage, who knew about the atman, faithfully accepted it. His vow was like that of a valiant one. He could remember everything, after hearing it only once. Having entirely accomplished his purpose, he spoke. Narada said, "I bow down to the illustrious Krishna. His deeds are spotless. So that all living creatures do not have to go through samsara, he uses his portions to manifest himself in charming forms." Having said this, he bowed down before the original rishi and his great-souled disciples. He then directly went to the hermitage of my father, Dvaipayana. O king! I have thus described to you the answer to the question you posed before me, about how the mind can reach the nirguna and undefinable brahman.[898] He is the one who watches over the

---

[894] The injunctions. These don't matter to him.
[895] Narayana.
[896] Sanandana and the others.
[897] Narada.
[898] Through the sacred texts.

beginning, the middle and the destruction of the universe. The lord
of jivatmans is not manifest. He creates the universe and enters it,
along with the jivatmans, controlling them. Just as a sleeping person
loses all sense of his body, by resorting to the one who is without
origin, one abandons maya. If a person desires kaivalya and desires
to avoid the fear of birth, he should constantly meditate on Hari.'

Chapter 10(88)

The king said, 'Gods, asuras and humans who worship the
auspicious Shiva generally obtain wealth and enjoy objects of
pleasure, but not those who worship Hari, Lakshmi's consort. We
have a great doubt about this and want to know. The two lords
have contrary kinds of conduct and the states obtained by those
who worship them are also contrary.'

Shri-Shuka replied, 'Shiva is always with Shakti and is united
with the three signs of the gunas. He is the divinity for the three
kinds of ahamkara—*vaikarika, taijasa* and *tamasa*. The sixteen
transformations resulted from these.[899] When a person worships
one of these potencies, he enjoys all the resultant states. Hari is
nirguna. He is the supreme Purusha, beyond Prakriti. He is
omniscient and is witness to everything. A person who worships
him becomes devoid of gunas. When the horse sacrifice was over,
your grandfather, King Yudhishthira, heard about dharma from
the illustrious one and asked Achyuta this question. The illustrious
lord was pleased with the one who desired to hear. For bestowing
benefit on the lineage of men, he had descended in the lineage of the
Yadus. He spoke to him. The illustrious one said, "When I show
favours on a person, I slowly rob him of his wealth. When he is
without riches, his own relatives desert him and he moves from one
misery to another misery. All his attempts to get wealth become

[899] The mind from *vaikarika ahamkara*, the five senses of perception
and the five senses of action from *taijasa ahamkara* and the five elements
from *tamasa ahamkara*.

futile and he is frustrated. He then contracts friendship with those who are devoted to me and I bestow my favours on him. He realizes the supreme and subtle brahman, the pure consciousness that is the infinite reality. Realizing the nature of the atman, the person is freed from samsara. Therefore, I am extremely difficult to worship. People ignore me and worship others who are easy to satisfy.[900] Having obtained kingdoms and prosperity, they become insolent, maddened and distracted. They are so rash as to slight the ones who conferred boons on them." Brahma, Vishnu, Shiva and other lords can confer boons and also curse. O dear one! Shiva and Brahma curse and bestow favours instantly, but not Achyuta. There is an ancient account about this, about how Girisha bestowed a boon on Vrikasura and brought about a calamity.

'There was an asura named Vrika and he was Shakuni's son. He met Narada on the road. On seeing him, the evil-minded one asked him which of the three gods was quickly satisfied. He said, "If you worship the god Girisha, you will obtain success swiftly. He is easily satisfied with the smallest qualities and is easily enraged with the slightest bit of wickedness. Like bandis, when they praised him, he was satisfied with the ten-headed one[901] and with Bana. He granted them a great deal of prosperity, but in each case, this resulted in a grave danger." Thus instructed, the asura started to worship Hara in Kedara.[902] He sliced off bits of flesh from his own body and offered these as oblations into the mouth of the fire. He was frustrated at being unable to see the god. On the seventh day, he bathed his head in the waters of the tirtha and was about to slice off his head with an extremely sharp weapon. At this, the greatly compassionate Dhurjati[903] arose from the fire, like Agni. Just as we would do, he seized his arms with his own arms and restrained him. Through that touch, his wounds were healed and he regained his original form. He said, "O dear one! Enough of this. Ask for a boon from me. I

[900] Quickly (ashu) satisfied (tosha), or Ashutosha, is also one of Shiva's names.
[901] Ravana.
[902] Kedaranatha.
[903] Shiva.

will give you the boon that you desire. I am pleased if men worship
me with some water and you have unnecessarily made your body
suffer excessively." The wicked one asked the god for a boon that
would bring fear to all creatures. "If I touch anyone on the head
with my hand, let him die." O descendant of the Bharata lineage!
Hearing this, the illustrious Rudra was disturbed in his mind. He
said, "*Oum*"[904] and smiled. Like giving amrita to a serpent, he
granted it to him. To test the efficacy of the boon, the asura tried to
place his own hand on Shambhu's head. Shiva was terrified at what
he had himself brought about. Scared and trembling at the prospect
of being touched, he fled from that northern direction and was
pursued. He fled everywhere on earth and heaven and to the ends of
the directions. The lords of the gods were silent, not knowing how
to counter this. He then went to radiant Vaikuntha, which is beyond
darkness. Narayana was himself there, the supreme destination for
those who have renounced everything, those who are serene and
have cast aside their staffs.[905] If one goes there, one never returns.[906]

'The illustrious one, the destroyer of afflictions, had perceived
the hardship. Using his yoga maya, he assumed the form of a small
boy.[907] He wore a girdle[908] and deerskin and held a staff and *aksha*
beads. He blazed like the fire. He held kusha grass in his hand. He
approached from a distance and greeted him, as if in humility. The
illustrious one said, "O Shakuni's son! It is evident that you are
exhausted. Why have you travelled such a long distance? Please rest
for a while. It is a person's body that yields all the objects of desire.
O lord! If it is appropriate for us to hear, please tell us what you
intend to do. Usually, a person accomplishes his purpose with the
help of others." The illustrious one asked him in words that seemed
to be a shower of amrita. All his exhaustion was gone and he[909]
told him everything that he had already done. The illustrious one

---

[904] As a sign of assent.

[905] They have renounced violence.

[906] To samsara.

[907] A boy who is observing brahmacharya as a student, *batuka*.

[908] Made out of grass.

[909] Vrika.

said, "If that is the case, we do not believe in his words. He became
a pishacha because of Daksha's curse and is the king of pretas
and pishachas. O Indra among the danavas! If you trust him as a
preceptor of the universe, you can quickly test his words by
placing your hand on your own head. O bull among the danavas!
If Shambhu has not spoken the truth in any way, you can then
kill the liar, so that he doesn't utter a falsehood ever again." The
wonderful and well-articulated words spoken by the illustrious one
confounded the evil-minded one. Without realizing what he was
doing, he placed his own hand on his head. He instantly fell down,
his head shattered, as if he had been struck by the vajra. Words
of "victory", "salutations" and "excellent" were heard in heaven.
When the wicked Vrikasura was slain, Shiva was saved from the
calamity and gods, rishis, ancestors and gandharvas showered
down flowers. The illustrious Purushottama spoke to Girisha, who
had been saved. "O god! O Mahadeva! This wicked one has been
killed because of his own sins. O Isha! After causing offence to great
beings and creatures, who can obtain peace, not to speak of a person
who causes offence to the lord of the universe and the preceptor of
the universe?" Hari is the paramatman himself. He is supreme. He
is an inconceivable ocean of powers. If a person hears or recites the
account of Girisha's liberation, he is freed from enemies and from
samsara.'

Chapter 10(89)

Shri-Shuka said, 'O king! The rishis performed a sacrifice on
the banks of the Sarasvati. A debate started among them about
who among the three lords[910] was the greatest. O king! Wishing to
know and find out, they sent Bhrigu, Brahma's son, to Brahma's
assembly. Desiring to test his sattva, he did not bow down to him,
or chant any hymns in his praise. Enraged at this, the illustrious one
blazed in his own energy. Though rage was surging within himself,

[910] Brahma, Vishnu and Shiva.

since it was his son, the lord used his intelligence to pacify it, just as fire is extinguished with water, which is created from it.[911] After this, he went to Kailasa. The god Maheshvara was happy to see his brother.[912] He arose and came forward to embrace him. But he did not desire this and said, "You deviate from the path."[913] At this, the god became angry. He raised his trident and with fiery eyes, got ready to kill him. But the goddess[914] fell down at his feet and comforted him with her words. After this, he[915] went to Vaikuntha, where the god Janardana was. He was lying down on Shri's lap and he kicked him on the chest with his foot. The illustrious one, the destination of the virtuous, stood up, along with Lakshmi. He got down from his own couch and bowed his head down before the sage. He said, "O brahmana rishi! Welcome. Rest on this seat for a while. O lord! You should pardon us. We did not know that you were going to come. Please purify me, my world and the guardians of the world who are with me with the water that has washed your feet. It is like a tirtha that purifies the tirthas. O father! O great sage! Your feet are exceedingly soft." Saying this, he massaged the brahmana's feet with his hands. "Till today, the illustrious Lakshmi has single-mindedly served me. Now that your foot has purified my chest, the goddess of prosperity will reside there."[916] The lord of Vaikuntha addressed Bhrigu in these solemn words. He[917] was delighted, satisfied and silent. He was overwhelmed with devotion and tears flowed from his eyes. O king! He again returned to the sacrifice being conducted by the sages who knew about the brahman. In detail, Bhrigu described the experience he had been through. Hearing this, the sages were amazed and their doubts were dispelled. They developed a great deal of devotion towards Vishnu, the one who confers tranquility and freedom from fear. Dharma, jnana and non-attachment emanate directly from him and so do

[911] In the original creation, water was created from fire.
[912] Both were born from Brahma.
[913] That is, Shiva does not follow the sanctioned path.
[914] Parvati.
[915] Bhrigu.
[916] This is the spot known as shrivatsa, where Shri resides.
[917] Bhrigu.

the eight kinds of siddhis that cleanse the atman of impurities. He is said to be the supreme destination for virtuous ones and sages who desire nothing, tranquil and impartial in outlook, having cast aside their staffs.[918] His beloved form is made out of sattva and he worships brahmanas as divinities. Tranquil ones, accomplished in intelligence, worship him, wishing for no benedictions. Through his maya, based on the gunas, he creates three kinds of forms—rakshasa, asura and *sura*.[919] Of these, sattva is the means for attaining success and purification. To remove the doubts of men, the brahmanas along the banks of the Sarasvati came to this conclusion. They served Purusha's lotus feet and found a destination with him.'

Suta said, 'This account about the supreme being emanated from the fragrant lotus mouth of the sage's son.[920] It is glorious nectar that destroys the fear of samsara. If a traveller[921] constantly drinks it in, using his ears as cups, all the exhaustion from his journey is destroyed.'

Shri-Shuka continued, 'O descendant of the Bharata lineage! On one occasion, in Dvaravati, a brahmana's wife gave birth to a son. However, as soon as he was born and touched the ground, he died. The brahmana took the dead infant and came to the king's[922] gate. Distressed in his mind and suffering, he lamented in these words. "My child has died and left because of the evil deeds of a kshatra-bandhu.[923] He hates brahmanas. He is deceitful in his intelligence. He is greedy and is attached to material objects. He sports and indulges in violence. He has not been able to conquer his senses and his conduct is wicked. Subjects who serve him will suffer. They will always be poor and miserable." In this way, the brahmana rishi went through a similar suffering for a second and a third child. He left them at the king's gate and chanted the same lamentation. On one occasion, when he was in Keshava's presence,

[918] That is, those who have abjured violence.

[919] The rakshasa form is based on tamas, the asura form on rajas and the sura form on sattva.

[920] Meaning Shuka.

[921] Travelling along the road of samsara.

[922] Ugrasena's.

[923] Ugrasena.

Arjuna heard the brahmana, when his ninth child had died. He asked him, "O brahmana! Is there no one in your residence who can wield a bow? These kshatra-bandhus are like brahmanas undertaking a sacrifice.[924] If brahmanas have to grieve because they lose their wealth, wives and sons, these are actors who are seeking to subsist in the garb of royalty. O illustrious one! You are suffering and I will protect your offspring. If I am unable to accomplish my pledge, I will enter the fire and atone for my sins." The brahmana replied, "Samkarshana, Vasudeva, the supreme archer Pradyumna and the unrivalled charioteer, Aniruddha, have been unable to save me. The lords of the world have found this task to be impossible. You are foolishly speaking about this feat. We do not believe you." Arjuna said, "O brahmana! I am not Samkarshana, Krishna, or Krishna's son. My name is Arjuna and my bow is Gandiva. O brahmana! Do not slight my valour, which has satisfied the three-eyed one.[925] O lord! I will defeat Death in a battle and bring your sons back." O scorcher of enemies! The brahmana was thus assured by Phalguna. Having heard about Partha's valour, he was happy and returned to his own house.

'When the time for his wife's delivery arrived, the excellent and suffering brahmana told Arjuna, "Save my child from Death." He touched water and purified himself, bowing down to Maheshvara. He strung Gandiva and remembered the divine weapons. He invoked arrows with many weapons and covered the delivery chamber from all sides. Above, below and diagonally, Partha created a cage made out of arrows. The brahmana's wife gave birth to a son who cried repeatedly. However, he suddenly vanished into the sky, along with his body. In Krishna's presence, the brahmana reprimanded Vijaya.[926] "Behold. I was a fool to trust you. You boasted, but are impotent. When Pradyumna, Aniruddha, Rama and Keshava are unable to save a person, who else is capable of protecting him? Shame on Arjuna. Shame on that boastful one's bow. When touched by destiny, it is only a foolish

[924] They are as powerless. Arjuna is referring to the Yadavas.
[925] Shiva.
[926] Arjuna.

and evil-minded person who thinks of bringing someone back."
The brahmana rishi cursed him in this way. Phalguna resorted
to his learning and instantly went to Samyamani,[927] where the
illustrious Yama was. Unable to see the brahmana's son there,
with his weapons raised, he went to the cities of other lords—
Indra, Agni, Nairrita, Soma, Vayu, Varuna, rasatala and the
vault of heaven. However, not having obtained the brahmana's
son anywhere, he was unable to fulfil his promise. Therefore, he
got ready to enter the fire. However, Krishna restrained him and
addressed him in these words. "Do not degrade yourself in this
way. I will show you the brahmana's sons. We will soon establish
our spotless deeds among men." The illustrious lord addressed
Arjuna in this way. Along with him, he ascended his divine chariot
and left for the western direction.

'It crossed the seven dvipas, the seven rivers and the seven
ranges of mountains that separate them. It then crossed Lokaloka[928]
and entered extremely great darkness. O bull among the Bharata
lineage! The horses, Shaibya, Sugriva, Meghapushpa and Balahaka,
lost their sense of direction in that darkness and could not proceed.
Seeing this, the illustrious Krishna, the great yogi and the lord of all
the lords of yoga, sent his own chakra on ahead, blazing like one
thousand suns. With its great and radiant energy, it cut through that
extremely terrible, dense and great darkness. Just as Rama's arrows
released from the bow cut through the enemy army, Sudarshana
penetrated with the speed of thought. Through the path created by
the chakra through the darkness, beyond all this, Phalguna saw a
pervasive, infinite and dazzling light. His eyes were pained by this
and he closed them. After this, he entered water that was buffeted by
extremely powerful winds. The resultant waves were like ornaments.
He saw a supremely resplendent and wonderful mansion there.
There were thousands of pillars, radiant with gems. The great and
wonderful serpent, Ananta, was there. There were brilliant gems
on each of his one thousand hoods. This radiance reflected on his

[927] Yama's capital.
[928] The mountain that separates the region illuminated by the sun from
the region not illuminated by the sun.

two thousand fiery eyes. He was white, like the white mountain,[929] but his neck and tongues were dark. He saw the lord, the great and supreme being, Purushottama, reclining happily on the coils of the serpent. His beautiful complexion was like that of a cloud. His beautiful garment was yellow. His face was pleasant and his eyes were long and beautiful. His diadem and earrings were studded with many clusters of precious gems. The illumination from this reflected off his dense locks of hair, with thousands of strands. His eight handsome arms were long. He wore the Koustubha gem and the shrivatsa mark was on his chest. He was adorned with a garland of wild flowers. The lord was served by his own attendants, Sunanda and Nanda being the foremost. His own weapons, chakra and the others, stood around him in personified form. *Pushti, shri, kirti, ajaya*[930] and all the other potencies served the supreme Parameshthi. Achyuta bowed down to himself, in the form of Ananta. Jishnu[931] was astonished at the sight. Both of them[932] stood there, their hands joined in salutation. The lord, the controller of all the other Parameshthis,[933] smiled and addressed them in a deep voice. "I brought the brahmana's sons here because I wished to see the two of you. You are my portions, born on earth to protect dharma. When you have killed the asuras and the earth has been divested of her burden, you will again return into me. The two of you are the rishis Nara and Narayana and have already accomplished all your wishes. O bulls among rishis! However, for the sake of instructing people, you are there, observing dharma." The two Krishnas[934] were thus instructed by the illustrious Parameshthi. They uttered "Oum"[935] and bowed down before the lord. They took the brahmana's sons with them and rejoicing, returned to their own abode along the route they had come by. They gave the brahmana his sons, in the

[929] Himalayas.

[930] Pushti, shri and kirti respectively stand for grace, splendour and fame. Ajaya means unvanquished and stands for the powers of maya.

[931] Arjuna.

[932] Krishna and Arjuna.

[933] The various other lords, Brahma and the others.

[934] Krishna and Arjuna, one of Arjuna's names is Krishna.

[935] Signifying assent.

same age and the same appearance that they had been lost. Having
seen Vishnu's abode, Partha was greatly surprised. He decided that
a man can only exhibit that much of manliness that Krishna seeks
to favour him with. There are many other such deeds of valour that
he[936] exhibited in this world. Like an ordinary person, he enjoyed
material objects and undertook potent sacrifices. The illustrious one
resorted to his own supremacy and showered down all the objects of
desire on subjects, brahmanas and others, just like Indra showering
down at the appropriate time. He slew the kings who were addicted
to adharma and had the others killed through Arjuna and the
others. Through Dharma's son[937] and others, he easily established
the path of dharma.'

Chapter 10(90)

Shri-Shuka said, 'Shri's consort was residing happily in his
own city of Dvaraka. It was full of every kind of prosperity
and wealth and the bulls among the Vrishnis. The women were
attired in excellent garments. They were beautiful because of newly
bloomed youth. As they played with balls in their mansions, they
were like flashes of lightning. The roads were always crowded with
crazy elephants exuding musth, ornamented soldiers and horses and
chariots that blazed with gold. The gardens and groves were filled
with large numbers of blossoming trees. From every side, the sounds
of bees humming and birds calling could be heard. He was the sole
beloved of sixteen thousand wives and enjoyed himself with them
in their extremely expensive houses, assuming as many wonderful
forms. The pure water in those homes was fragrant with pollen
from blooming water lilies, white lotuses, night lotuses and day
lotuses. Flocks of birds called. The powerful one immersed himself
in the waters of those pools and amused himself. When the women
embraced him, his body was smeared with the kunkuma from their

[936] Krishna.
[937] Yudhishthira. The 'others' means other kings.

breasts. Accompanied by the sound of drums, kettledrums and larger drums, gandharvas sang his praises. Delighted, sutas, magadhas and bandis played on veenas and other musical instruments. The women laughed and used syringes to sprinkle Achyuta with water. Like a king of yakshas with female yakshas, he sprinkled them back and played with them. Because their garments were wet, the region around their thighs and breasts became exposed. Wishing to take away the syringe and sprinkle him, they embraced their beloved and flowers were loosened from the braids in their hair. Desire was ignited in them and because of their smiling faces, they were resplendent. Krishna's garland was smeared with the kunkuma from their breasts. Since he was engaged in sporting, his locks of hair were dishevelled. He repeatedly sprinkled the young women and they sprinkled him back. He sported with them, like a king of elephants with female elephants. Krishna and the women gave the ornaments and garments used in sporting,[938] to the male and female performers who earned a living from singing and the playing of musical instruments. While Krishna was engaged in sporting in this way, his gait, conversation, glances, smiles, jesting, joking and embraces stole the hearts of the women. With their minds on Mukunda, they were like those who were mad and dumb. Their thoughts were on the lotus-eyed one. I will tell you about the words they spoke. Listen.

'The queens said, "O female osprey! Why are you lamenting? Why are you without sleep and why can't you rest? It is night in the world. The lord has covered his understanding and has gone to sleep. O friend! Like us, has your heart also been pierced deeply by the generous and smiling glances of the one whose eyes are like lotuses? O female chakravaka! You close your eyes in the night, but cannot see your beloved. Therefore, you are weeping piteously. Like us, have you obtained Achutya's servitude? Do you want to wear the garland that touched his feet in the braids of your hair? O ocean! You are always roaring. You do not get to sleep in the night and suffer from insomnia. Is that because Mukunda has taken away your signs?[939]

[938] After the sporting was over.
[939] Such as the Koustubha jewel.

Have you been reduced to a state from which it is impossible to recover? O moon! You have been seized by the powerful disease of consumption. You have become so emaciated that your beams can no longer dispel the darkness. Like us, can you no longer remember what Mukunda told you? It seems to us that your power of speech has been numbed. O wind that blows from the Malaya mountain! What disagreeable act have we performed towards you? Our hearts have been shattered by Govinda's glances. Why are you igniting desire in them? O handsome cloud! You are indeed loved by the Indra among the Yadavas, adorned with the shrivatsa mark. Like us, bound to him in bonds of love, you are meditating. Like us, your heart must be distraught and extremely anxious. Repeatedly remembering this, you are shedding profuse tears. Association with him leads to misery. O cuckoo! Your notes are sweet. Your voice can revive those who are dead. You are uttering sounds that have been spoken by our beloved.[940] What can I do now to please you? Tell me. O mountain! O one who is extensive in intelligence! You do not move or speak. You must be thinking about something of great import. Or perhaps, just like us, you desire to hold the feet of Vasudeva's son against your breasts?[941] O wives of the ocean![942] Your lakes have dried up now and the beauty of your lotuses has been lost, just as we are completely dried up now. We can no longer obtain the beloved glances of our husband, the lord of Madhu. Our hearts have been deceived. O swan! Welcome. Please be seated here and drink some milk. O dear one! Tell us about Shouri's account. Indeed, we know that you are his messenger. Is the unvanquished one well? Does he remember what he told us long ago? His affections are fickle. Why should we worship him? O inferior servant of the one who satisfies desires! Tell him to come here without Shri. Is she the only woman who can serve him faithfully?"'

Shri-Shuka continued, 'Krishna is the lord of the lords of yoga and behaving with such sentiments, Madhava's wives attained the supreme destination. His numerous deeds are sung about and he attracts the mind of women who have only heard about him. What

[940] The cuckoo is imitating those sounds.
[941] The breasts are the mountain's peaks.
[942] The rivers.

need be said about those who have seen him? He is the preceptor of
the universe. Taking him to be a husband, they lovingly served him,
by massaging his feet and doing other things. How can one describe
the austerities they must have performed? He is the destination
of the virtuous and he observed the dharma spoken about in the
Vedas. He repeatedly demonstrated how dharma, artha and kama
can be pursued, even in the state of a householder. In his status of
a householder, Krishna performed supreme dharma. He had more
than sixteen thousand and one hundred queens. O king! Among
these jewels among women, eight were the chief, Rukmini and the
others. I have already described them progressively, along with
their sons. Through each of the wives, Krishna had ten sons, who
were exactly like him. The lord's progress is invincible. Among
these large numbers of valiant sons, eighteen were maharathas.
Their fame was pervasive. Hear about their names from me. They
were Pradyumna, Aniruddha, Diptiman, Bhanu, Samba, Madhu,
Brihadbhanu, Chitrabhanu, Vrika, Aruna, Pushkara, Vedabahu,
Shrutadeva, Sunandana, Chitrabahu, Virupa, Kavi and Nyagrodha.
O Indra among kings! These were the sons of Madhu's enemy.
Among them, the first was Pradyumna, Rukmini's son, and he was
like his father. The maharatha married Rukmi's daughter.[943] Her
son was Aniruddha, who possessed the strength of ten thousand
elephants. He[944] was the son of Rukmi's daughter and he married
the daughter of Rukmi's son.[945] Their son was Vajra and he was the
only one who was left after the clash with the clubs.[946] Vajra's son
was Pratibahu and Pratibahu's son was Subahu. Subahu's son was
Shantasena and Shantasena's son was Shatasena. No one born in
this lineage was poor and there was no one who did not have many
children. There was no one who was limited in lifespan. There was
no one who was limited in valour. No one was born who was not
devoted to brahmanas. Many men born in the Yadu lineage were

[943] Rukmavati.

[944] Aniruddha.

[945] That is, Rochana.

[946] When the Yadavas fought against each other and destroyed
themselves.

famous for their deeds. O king! Even in tens of thousands of years, one is incapable of enumerating them. It has been heard that three crores, eighty eight thousand and eight hundred teachers were employed to teach the sons of the Yadu lineage. Who is capable of enumerating the great-souled Yadavas? Ahuka had ten thousand times ten thousand lakhs.[947] There were extremely terrible daityas who were killed in the battle between the gods and the asuras. They were born as humans and were insolent, making the subjects suffer. O king! To chatise them, Hari asked the gods to be born in Yadu's lineage. There were more than one hundred and one branches in the lineage. The illustrious and powerful lord, Hari, was their authority. Among all the Yadavas, those who followed him flourished. The minds of the Vrishnis were so immersed in Krishna that they were not conscious of their own selves when sleeping, seating, walking, conversing, playing, bathing and performing other deeds. O king! The divine river[948] is a tirtha because it washed his feet. However, when he was born in the lineage of the Yadus, her fame was diminished. Those who hated him and those who loved him attained union with him. He is unvanquished and supreme. Others make efforts to obtain Shri, but she is only his. Whenever his name is heard or spoken about, it destroys everything inauspicious. Krishna created the dharma for different gotras. It is wonderful that he wields the wheel of time as a chakra to remove the burdens of the earth. Though he is spoken about as the one who was born from Devaki, the victorious one resides in all people. Though he was served by the best among the Yadu lineage, it was his own arms that destroyed adharma. For everything mobile and immobile, he destroys sins. His handsome and smiling face ignited the god of love among the women in the city of Vraja. For the sake of protecting his own path,[949] in his pastimes, he assumes different forms and imitates conduct that is appropriate to those. The deeds of the supreme one among the Yadus destroy all the consequences of

[947] Ahuka is Ugrasena. It is not clear whether this means sons or attendants, probably the latter.

[948] Ganga.

[949] Of dharma.

karma. If a person desires to follow in his footsteps, he should hear about these. Through constant hearing, chanting and meditating on Mukunda's beautiful account, with increasing devotion, a mortal person obtains his abode. Death, which is irresistible, loses its force there. For the sake of obtaining him, from ordinary homes people went to the forest, and so did kings.'

This ends the Tenth Skandha.

Eleventh Skandha

Chapter 11(1)

Shri-Shuka said, 'With Rama, and surrounded by the Yadus, Krishna killed daityas. To reduce the burden of the earth, he suddenly ignited the rising dissension. On several occasions, the sons of Pandu were angered by their rivals—the deceitful gambling,

313

insults, the seizing of the hair[950] and other things. Using these as triggers, the lord removed the earth's burden by destroying the kings who had assembled on either side. The Yadus were protected by his own arms and they were used to destroy the armies of the kings, a burden on earth. The immeasurable one then thought, "Some may say that the earth's burden has gone, but I do not think so. The intolerable lineage of the Yadavas still remains. No one else can ever defeat them, through any means. Because they seek shelter with me, their powers have always been unrestricted. I will engender conflict within the lineage of the Yadus and they will be destroyed, like a bamboo grove consumed by the fire. I can then peacefully return to my abode." O king! The lord's resolutions always came true and he decided in this way. Using the pretext of the curse pronounced by brahmanas, the lord withdrew his own family. His own form brought beauty to the world and stole the eyes of men away from everything else. The minds of those who heard his words remembered them. His gaits and acts attracted people. His glory spread through excellent shlokas. These allowed people to easily cross over the darkness. The lord thought that he would return to his own abode.'

The king asked, 'The minds of the Vrishnis were immersed in Krishna. They were generous and devoted to brahmanas. They always served the aged. Why did the brahmanas curse them? O supreme among brahmanas! What was the reason for the curse and what was its nature? They were united. How could there have been dissension among them? Please tell me everything.'

Shri-Shuka continued, 'His radiant form was an accumulation of all that was beautiful. Having performed extremely auspicious deeds on earth, his wishes were accomplished. The one who was pervasive in his deeds enjoyed himself in his abode.[951] He remained there because a small task still needed to be completed. He desired to destroy his lineage. He accomplished extremely auspicious and sacred deeds in this world. Chanting about these deeds takes away the impurities of kali yuga. In his form as the Destroyer, he resided

---

[950] Droupadi was dragged by the hair into the assembly hall.
[951] Meaning Dvaravati.

in the house of the lord of the Yadus.[952] The sages took his leave and went to Pindaraka.[953] They were Vishvamitra, Asita, Kanva, Durvasa, Bhrigu, Angiras, Kashyapa, Vamadeva, Atri, Vasishtha, Narada and others. While playing, young boys born in the Yadu lineage approached them. They clasped their feet and asked them a question in mock humility. They attired Samba, Jambavati's son, in a woman's garments and asked, "O brahmanas! This black-eyed lady is expecting and wants to ask you. O ones infallible in vision! However, she is ashamed of asking you directly. She will deliver soon and desires to have a son. Can you tell us about the delivery?"[954] O king! Thus deceived, the sages became angry and replied, "O foolish ones! She will give birth to a club that will destroy the lineage." Hearing these words, they were extremely terrified. They uncovered Samba's stomach and saw that there was indeed a club made out of iron. "We are unfortunate. What have we done? What are people going to say?" Completely confused, they returned to their homes, taking the club with them. The radiance had vanished from their faces. They took it to the king's assembly and in the presence of all the Yadavas,[955] reported what had happened. O king! The residents of Dvaraka heard about the invincible curse of the brahmanas and saw the club. They were astounded, scared and terrified. Ahuka,[956] the king of the Yadus, had the club pulverized. He had the fragments, along with a small bit of iron that remained, flung into the ocean. A fish swallowed that bit of iron. The fragments were carried to the shore by the waves. Stuck there, they grew into *eraka* reeds. Along with other fish caught by fishermen from the ocean, that fish was also caught. A hunter[957] used that bit of iron to fashion his arrowhead. The illustrious lord knew everything, but he did not wish to counter the curse of the brahmanas. In his form as the Destroyer, he sanctioned it.'

[952] Vasudeva, Krishna's father.
[953] A tirtha near Dvaravati.
[954] Whether the child will be male or female.
[955] However, Krishna was not present.
[956] Ugrasena.
[957] The hunter's name was Jara. The word also means old age.

Chapter 11(2)

Shri-Shuka said, 'O extender of the Kuru lineage! Dvaravati was protected by Govinda's arms. Constantly eager to worship Krishna, Narada resided there for some time. O king! Mukunda's lotus feet are worshipped by the best among the immortals. Which person with senses, always confronted by death, will not worship them? Once, the devarshi went to Vasudeva's[958] house. He was worshipped. When he was comfortably seated, he[959] greeted him and addressed him in these words. Vasudeva said, "O illustrious one! Your visits are for the welfare of all embodied beings who are distressed. You are like a father for those who follow Uttamashloka's path. The activities of the gods bring happiness and unhappiness to beings. However, virtuous ones like you, who have their atmans in Achyuta, only bring happiness. The gods are like shadows. The gods reciprocate according to the acts used to worship them.[960] However, virtuous ones are always compassionate towards the distressed. O brahmana! I wish to ask you about *bhagavata dharma*.[961] On faithfully listening to this, a mortal person is freed from all kinds of fear. The infinite one bestows emancipation. In an earlier birth on earth, I worshipped him. However, confounded by the god's maya, I did not ask for emancipation, but for offspring. O one excellent in vows! There are many kinds of hardships. Instruct me, so that I can directly and easily be freed from fears from every direction." O king! The devarshi was thus questioned by the intelligent Vasudeva. He remembered Hari's qualities and, delighted, spoke to him.

'Narada said, "O bull among the Satvatas! You have correctly asked about bhagavata dharma, which purifies the universe. If this dharma is heard, recited, meditated on, accepted or praised, it instantly purifies those who hate the gods or creatures in the universe. The illustrious one is supremely auspicious. Hearing about him or chanting about him is sacred. You have now reminded me about my

---

[958] Krishna's father.
[959] Vasudeva.
[960] There is a proportionate quid pro quo.
[961] The dharma of devotion to the illustrious one.

god, Narayana. In this connection, an ancient history is recounted, about a conversation between the great-souled Videha and the sons of Rishabha. Svayambhuva Manu had a son named Priyavrata. His son was Agnidhra, Agnidhra's son was Nabhi and Nabhi's son was known as Rishabha, spoken of as a portion of Vasudeva. He descended on earth to teach about *moksha dharma*. He had one hundred sons and all of them possessed knowledge about the brahman. The eldest among them was Bharata and he was devoted to Narayana. It is after him that this wonderful *varsha* goes by the name of Bharata. Having enjoyed objects of pleasure, he gave them up. He left home and performed austerities for Hari. After having worshipped him, he obtained his state after three births. Nine[962] became lords of the nine dvipas that were all around. Eighty-one were brahmanas and initiated the various rituals. The remaining nine were extremely fortunate sages and explained the ultimate objective. They were accomplished in knowledge about the atman. They were mendicants who exerted themselves, using the wind as a garment.[963] They were Kavi, Hari, Antariksha, Prabhuddha, Pippalayana, Avirhotra, Drumila, Chamasa and Karabhajana. They visualized the form of the universe, cause and effect, gross and subtle, as no different from the atman of the illustrious one and roamed around earth. They were unrestricted in their movements and went to the worlds of the gods, the Siddhas, the Sadhyas, the gandharvas, the yakshas, men, the kinnaras and serpents. They roamed around freely, as they willed, in the worlds of sages, charanas, the lords among the bhutas, vidyadharas, brahmanas and cattle. Once, the great-souled Nimi[964] was performing a sacrifice in Ajanabha,[965] following the instructions of the rishis. Wandering around as they willed, they went there. O king! Those great devotees of the illustrious one were like the sun. On seeing them, everyone, the performer of the sacrifice, the sacrificial fires and the brahmanas,

---

[962] Out of Rishabha's one hundred sons.

[963] That is, they were naked.

[964] The king of Videha.

[965] Named after Nabhi, this varsha was initially known as Ajanabha. It came to be known as Bharatavarsha later.

stood up. The king of Videha knew that they were devoted to the illustrious one. Delighted, he offered them appropriate seats and worshipped them. Those nine blazed in their own radiance and were like Brahma's sons.[966] Extremely happy, the king bowed down in humility and asked them."

'Videha asked, "I think that you are the direct attendants of the illustrious one, Madhu's enemy. Those with Vishnu inside them roam around, purifying the worlds. Among embodied beings, the status of a human is extremely difficult to obtain, though it is also fragile. But even among those, I think it is extremely difficult to find those who manage to see those loved by Vaikuntha. O supremely fortunate ones! O ones without blemish! Therefore, I am asking you. For men in this world, even half a kshana's[967] association with the virtuous is a treasure. If you think that we are capable of listening to bhagavata dharma, please tell us about it. He is devoted to those who seek shelter with him and is ready to give up his own self."

'Narada continued, "O Vasudeva! Those great ones were thus asked by Nimi. Happy, they honoured the king, the officiating priests and the assistant priests and spoke.

"'Kavi said, 'He is the atman of the universe. In this world, one's intelligence is constantly agitated, because one identifies the atman with the transient. Achyuta's lotus feet grant freedom from fear. If one constantly worships them, I think there can be no fear. The means and techniques for easily realizing the atman and obtaining the illustrious one have been described, even by ignorant men. Know that as bhagavata dharma. O king! A man who resorts to this is never distracted. Even if he runs with his eyes closed, he will never trip or fall down.[968] Everything done with the body, words, mind, senses, intelligence, the atman and by following one's own nature,[969] must be offered to the supreme Narayana.[970] Because

---

[966] Sanaka, Sananda, Sanatana and Sanatkumara.

[967] A kshana is a small measure of time.

[968] There is the symbolism of the shrutis and *smritis* constituting the eyes of knowledge and of falling down into samsara.

[969] As a consequence of past karma.

[970] This echoes Bhagavad Gita 9.27.

of loss of memory, there is misidentification and one turns away from the direction of the lord, becoming absorbed in the second.[971] That leads to fear. An intelligent person knows that this is maya. He devotedly worships the absolute lord, the guru and divinity for his atman. This manifestation of duality has no real existence. The intelligence experiences it like the wishes confronted in dreams. The mind leads to doubts about what should be done and what should not be done. An intelligent person brings the mind under control and fearlessness results from that. One must hear about the extremely auspicious birth and deeds in this world of the one who wields a chakra in his hand. One must sing about those names and their significances. One should roam around unattached and without any embarrassment, sing about these. If one follows this vow, his names and deeds come to be loved. Attachment develops and his heart melts. He laughs loudly. He cries, or becomes agitated. He sings and dances like a mad person. He does not care about the external world. The devotee bows down to everything, taking everything to be no different from Hari's body—the sky, the air, the fire, water, the earth, the stellar bodies, living creatures, the directions, trees and others, rivers and oceans—all that exists. For a person who surrenders himself, three things occur simultaneously: devotion to the supreme lord, experiencing him and non-attachment towards everything else. It is like a person who is in the process of eating. With every mouthful, there is satisfaction, nourishment and elimination of hunger. Thus, the devotee constantly worships Achyuta's feet. There is devotion, non-attachment towards everything else and awareness about the illustrious one. O king! In this way, a person who is devoted to the illustrious one directly experiences supreme serenity.'

'"The king[972] asked, 'Tell me more about the kind of man who follows bhagavata dharma. How does he behave? How does he speak? What are the signs of a person loved by the illustrious one?'

'"Hari said, 'If a person is suffused with the illustrious one, he sees the illustrious one in all creatures and all creatures in the atman

[971] The notion of 'I', which is second, Narayana being primary.
[972] Nimi.

of the illustrious one. He is superior among those who are devoted
to the illustrious one. A person who is devoted to the illustrious
one, friendly towards his devotees, compassionate towards foolish
ones[973] and indifferent towards those who hate him,[974] is a medium
kind of devotee. A person who worships Hari's image faithfully,[975]
but does not honour his devotees or others, is said to be an ordinary
kind of devotee. The senses come in contact with the objects of the
senses. If a person is not delighted or unhappy with this, recognizing
this to be Vishnu's maya, he is supreme among devotees of the
illustrious one. If a person remembers Hari and is not confounded
by the body, the senses, prana, the mind, the intelligence, birth,
death, hunger, fear, thirst and other hardships associated with the
dharma of samsara, he is the foremost devotee of the illustrious one.
If Vasudeva is the supreme shelter for someone, the desire for the
seeds of karma do not arise in his mind. Such a person is supreme
among devotees of the illustrious one. Hari loves a person who has
no sense of ahamkara and is not attached to notions of noble birth,
karma, varna, ashrama and other things associated with the body
in this world. If a person does not have any sense of differentiation
between "mine" and "someone else's", vis-à-vis the body or
possessions, and is serene and impartial towards all creatures, he
is a supreme devotee of the illustrious one. Gods and others, and
those who have not conquered their atmans, seek out the illustrious
one's lotus feet. If a person's memory is not disturbed and if he does
not waver from those feet for a lava[976] or half a nimesha, even for
the sake of lordship of the three worlds, he is Vishnu's foremost
devotee. The illustrious one's strides have accomplished deeds of
valour. The radiance from the jewels of nails on his feet are like
cool moonbeams and destroy the torment in the heart. How can a
person who worships him suffer? This is like the power of the rising
moon dispelling the sun's heat. A person is said to be a foremost
devotee of the illustrious one if Hari does not leave his heart, his

---

[973] Those who ignore Krishna.

[974] Those who hate Krishna.

[975] His interpretation of devotion is limited to worshipping the image.

[976] A very small measure of time.

lotus feet firmly and directly bound there by bonds of love. Even if he is called accidentally, he destroys the mass of sins.'"'

Chapter 11(3)

"'"The king[977] said, 'The supreme lord Vishnu's maya confounds. O illustrious ones! We wish to know about this maya. Please tell us. I am tormented by the miseries of samsara. I am not satisfied from hearing from you about Hari's account, which is like amrita. It is like medication for the sufferings of a mortal being.'

"'"Antariksha said, 'O mighty-armed one! He is the atman in all creatures. He is the original being. From his own parts, he has created these creatures, superior and inferior, out of the gross elements, so that they can enjoy objects of the senses or realize the atman.[978] The beings are created out of the five elements and having created them, he enters them. He is one, but divides himself into ten, and makes them engage with the gunas.[979] Goaded by the lord, the jivatman uses the senses to enjoy the objects of the senses. He identifies his atman with what has been created and thereby becomes attached. The embodied being is an instrument and uses the senses of action to engage in karma. Accepting the fruits of past karma, he whirls around, in joy and misery. Thus, the being follows towards many inauspicious destinations determined by karma. From the creation of the universe to its end, he helplessly experiences many births and deaths. When the end of the elements is imminent, the one without a beginning and without an end assumes the form of time and withdraws the manifest objects and gunas into his unmanifest atman. At that time, the earth is ravaged by a terrible drought that lasts for one hundred years. At that time, the sun's

---

[977] Nimi.

[978] Depending on their inclinations.

[979] The five senses of perception and the five senses of action add up to ten.

heat is heightened by time and scorches the three worlds. From Samkarshana's[980] mouth, a fire is initiated from the bottom of patala. Aided by the wind, the flames rise upwards and, increasing, burn down the directions. Large masses of clouds known as samvartaka shower down for one hundred years. The flow of the downpour is as thick as the trunks of elephants. The entire universe is deluged in water. O king! Vairaja Purusha[981] abandons the universe and enters the subtle and the unmanifest, like fire, when the kindling has been consumed.[982] The wind robs the earth of its property of smell, which is then transformed into water. The wind also robs water of its liquid nature and it is transformed into fire. The darkness robs fire of its form and it merges into the wind. Space robs wind of its attribute of touch and the wind merges into space. In the form of time, the atman robs space of its attribute and it merges into tamasika ahamkara.[983] O king! The senses and intelligence merge into rajasika ahamkara. The mind and divinities of the senses merge into sattvika ahamkara. Ahamkara, along with its attributes,[984] merges into Mahat.[985] This is the maya of the illustrious one, which leads to creation, preservation and destruction. It has three hues.[986] I have described it to you. What else do you wish to hear?'

'"The king[987] asked, 'O maharshi! Those who have not cleansed their atmans find it impossible to overcome the lord's maya. How can those with gross intelligence[988] easily tide over it? Please describe that.'

'"Prabuddha said, 'Men engaged in sexual intercourse[989] start acts with the objective of destroying unhappiness and enjoying

---

[980] In the form of Shesha.

[981] That is, Brahma.

[982] When the kindling has been consumed, fire enters into the principle of the fire.

[983] There is a bit of interpretation in these shlokas. A straight translation wouldn't have been clear.

[984] Tamasika ahamkara, rajasika ahamkara and sattvika ahamkara.

[985] It is left implicit that Mahat merges into Prakriti.

[986] Sattva, rajas and tamas.

[987] Nimi.

[988] Those who are attached to material objects.

[989] That is, couples who live together in the householder stage.

happiness. They should note that the consequences can be quite contrary. Wealth is always the cause of hardship. It is extremely difficult to obtain and is like death for one's own self. What happiness is ensured from fickle objects like homes, children, relatives and animals? In that way, one should know that worlds hereafter, obtained as a result of karma, are also destructible. Like vassals to an emperor, these are characterized by rivalry among equals and jealousy towards superiors. Therefore, a curious person who desires the greatest benefit must resort to a guru who is accomplished in explaining the supreme, is detached, and has realized the brahman. Treating the guru as a divinity and like one's own self, bhagavata dharma must be learnt. Without any deceit, one must serve him. When Hari, the paramatman, is satisfied, he will bestow realization about the atman. In the beginning, the mind must be detached from everything and one must associate with the virtuous. As is appropriate, he must be compassionate, friendly and respectful towards all creatures. There must be purity, austerities, forbearance, silence, studying, uprightness, brahmacharya, non-violence and equanimity when one is faced with the opposites.[990] He must look on everything as a manifestation of the lord's atman. He must dwell in solitude, without a fixed place of residence. He must be detached, wearing tattered rags[991] as garments. He must be satisfied with whatever is obtained. He must be faithful towards texts that are about the illustrious one, but must not be contemptuous of others. He must control his mind, speech and deeds, observing truthfulness, control of the mind and control of the senses. He must hear, chant and meditate on Hari's extraordinary deeds and his birth, deeds and qualities. All his activities, sacrifices, donations, meditation, conduct and everything that his mind loves, wives, sons, homes and life, must be dedicated to the supreme. He must be friendly towards men who have accepted Krishna as their atman and protector. He must serve both[992] and great and virtuous men. He must converse with others about the illustrious one's purifying

---

[990] Joy and misery, heat and cold and so on.
[991] Or bark.
[992] Mobile and immobile objects as representing Krishna.

glory. Through mutual love, they will find mutual satisfaction and their mutual atmans will find detachment. He must remember and remind others about Hari, the one who dispels the flood of sins. Devotion leads to the awakening of further devotion and because of the ecstasy, the body hair stands up. Immersed in thoughts about Achyuta, sometimes, he cries. Sometimes, he laughs. Sometimes, delighted, he speaks in superhuman ways. Sometimes, he dances. Sometimes, he sings. Sometimes, he imitates the one without birth. Sometimes, withdrawn and immersed in the supreme, he is silent. In this way, by learning about bhagavata dharma, devotion is awakened. Submerged in Narayana, he crosses over the maya, which is impossible to overcome.'

'"The king[993] asked, 'O supreme among those who know about the brahman! The brahman and the paramatman is also known by the name of Narayana. Do they represent the same transcendental being? You should tell us about this.'

'"Pippalayana said, 'O Indra among men! He is without cause, but is the cause of creation, preservation and destruction. He is the truth who exists in the states of sleeping, being awake and sushupti, and also in the state beyond them.[994] Know him to be the supreme one who animates the body, the senses, the breath of life and the mind and makes them carry out their functions. Sparks cannot illuminate the fire. Like that, the mind, speech, sight, intelligence, the breath of life and the senses cannot penetrate him. The words of the Vedas can only describe the atman indirectly, not directly.[995] But in its absence, even that negative description would not have been possible. In the beginning, there was only one. But it assumed the three modes of sattva, rajas and tamas. With rajas, it became Sutratma. With sattva, it became Mahat. With tamas, it became ahamkara,

---

[993] Nimi.

[994] This is a reference to the four states of consciousness—wakefulness (jagrata), dreaming (svapna), deep sleep (sushupti) and pure consciousness (turiya).

[995] This is a difficult shloka, with alternative interpretations. The description is as 'neti', not this.

enveloping the jivatman.[996] The brahman, with diverse forms and powers, is radiant in jnana,[997] the senses, the objects of the senses and the fruits. It is manifest in the gross and the subtle and in everything that is beyond both of these. The atman was not born. Nor will it die. It does not grow, or decay. It is the witness to the progress of time in bodies.[998] It is everywhere. It is eternal. It is the pure consciousness that does not disappear. It is like prana in the body. Because of the power of the senses, this appears to be many, but is one. In whatever state the jivatman is born in, from an egg, from wombs, from seeds or from sweat, prana follows accordingly. When the aggregate of the senses and ahamkara are in a state of deep sleep, it exists and can be remembered on waking up. If, with intense devotion, a person desires to seek the feet of the one with a lotus in his navel, he cleanses all the impurities that are in his heart as a result of gunas and karma. In that purified state, he perceives the truth about the atman. He directly experiences it, just as the sunlight is visible to a person with clear vision.'

'"The king said, 'Tell us about karma yoga, through which, a man can cleanse himself. He can quickly eliminate the effects of karma and attain a supreme state of *naishkarma*.[999] In my father's[1000] presence, I had earlier asked the rishis who are Brahma's sons. However, they did not reply. Please tell me the reason for that.'

'"Avirhotra said, 'Karma, *akarma* and *vikarma* are spoken about in the Vedas and are beyond the purview of ordinary discourse.[1001] The Vedas emanate from the lord's atman and even

---

[996] This is more than a word for word translation, since the text is cryptic. Rajas brought about the power of creation and Sutratma is the same as Hiranyagarbha. Tamas is the ignorance that envelops the jivatman.

[997] Interpreted as gods who embody knowledge, or the divinities who preside over the senses.

[998] Such as birth, youth, old age and death.

[999] Cessation of karma.

[1000] Ikshvaku's.

[1001] Karma stands for acts sanctioned by the Vedas, akarma for failure to perform those acts. Vikarma stands for the commission of prohibited acts.

wise people are confused about these.[1002] Like instructing a child,
the Vedas speak about something other than what they are taken
to imply.[1003] Like the medicine, the objective of karma is to free
oneself from karma. If an ignorant person has not conquered his
senses and does not act in accordance with what the Vedas have
said, he follows adharma. By engaging in vikarma, he goes from
one death to another death. The acts spoken about in the Vedas
must be performed without attachment and offered to the lord. It is
through this that one obtains the success of naishkarma. The fruits
spoken about in the sacred texts are only for purposes of making it
attractive. If a person wants to swiftly sever the bonds of the heart,
he should follow the rituals[1004] or what is spoken about in tantra,
and worship the god Keshava, the paramatman. Having obtained
the preceptor's favours and having been instructed about agama,
he must worship the great being in a form that he himself finds
attractive.[1005] He must purify himself and be seated, facing the deity.
He must cleanse himself through pranayama and other techniques.
He must purify the gross body through *nyasa*.[1006] Having protected
himself in this way, he must worship Hari. He must first purify
whatever objects of worship have been obtained, the physical
objects that are to be offered, the ground, his own self, his mind,
the image and the seat, sprinkling them with water. He must control
himself and keep padya and the other objects of worship nearby.
He must perform nyasa in the heart and other parts of the body

---

[1002] The answer to the question is left implicit. The sages did not tell
you, because you were not ready for the knowledge.

[1003] For instance, a child may have an illness that needs to be cured
through ingesting a bitter medicine. The objective is the curing of the
illness, not the medicine. Since the medicine is bitter, it is hidden inside
something sweet, or the child is tempted with the offer of something sweet
after the bitter medicine has been taken.

[1004] Mentioned in the Vedas.

[1005] Agamas are texts other than the Vedas, such as the tantra texts.
Having obtained the preceptor's favours means having been initiated by
the guru. The devotee chooses a personal form of the lord that appeals to
himself.

[1006] This is known as *anga-nyasa*, the mental appropriation (nyasa) of
different limbs of the body (*anga*) to different divinities.

and worship, using the seed mantra. He must worship the limbs of the image, the emblems,[1007] the attendants[1008] and their personified forms, using their respective mantras, offering padya, arghya and *achamaniya*.[1009] The image must be bathed and adorned with garments and ornaments. Following the recommended methods, he must worship the image with fragrances, garlands, unbroken grain, flowers, incense, lamps and other offerings. Having worshipped in this way, he must prostrate himself before Hari. He must immerse himself and meditate on Hari's form, worshipping him. He must place the remainder of the offerings on his head and respectfully restore the image to the proper place. In this way, if a person worships the lord in the form of the sun, water, the guest and within his own heart, he is swiftly liberated."'

Chapter 11(4)

' " The king[1010] said, 'According to his own wishes, Hari takes different births and undertakes many kinds of deeds. He has performed them, is performing them and will perform them. Please tell us about those.'

"'Drumila replied, 'Ananta's qualities are infinite. A person who seeks to enumerate them is childish in his intelligence. In the course of time, it may be possible to count all the particles of dust on earth. However, it is impossible to count all the potencies of that reservoir. He himself created the five elements out of his own self. Having created this universe, which is like his own body, he entered it, using a portion of his own self. Narayana, the original divinity, thus came to be known as Purusha. The arrangement of the three worlds is based on his body. It is his senses that make both

---

[1007] Such as Sudarshana chakra.
[1008] Such as Sunanda.
[1009] Padya is water to wash the feet, arghya is a gift, achamaniya is water to rinse the mouth.
[1010] Nimi.

kinds of senses[1011] of embodied beings function. Jnana comes from him. Physical strength, the strength of the senses and their activities flow from his breathing. Through sattva and the others, he is the original agent behind creation, preservation and destruction. In the beginning, for the sake of creation, he used rajas to manifest himself as Brahma. For preservation, as the lord of sacrifices who protects brahmanas and the ordinances of dharma, he is there as Vishnu.[1012] Using tamas, he is Rudra for purposes of destruction. For creation, preservation and destruction, the original Purusha is thus always there among subjects.

'"'The serene and supreme rishi, Nara-Narayana, was born as the son of Dharma and Murti, Daksha's daughter. He practised karma and spoke about the signs of naishkarma. He exists even today and noble rishis serve at his feet. Indra suspected that he[1013] might covet his abode. Therefore, he engaged Kama and his companions. Along with large numbers of apsaras, the spring and an extremely gentle breeze, he[1014] went to the place known as Badari. Not knowing about his greatness, he pierced him with arrows, in the form of the glances of the women. The original being knew that the crime had been committed by Shakra. He laughed. Without any sense of pride, he laughed and spoke to those trembling ones. "O Madana! O Maruts! O wives of the gods! Do not be scared. Please accept these gifts and do not make this place non-existent."[1015] When the divinity, Nara, spoke in this way, the gods lost their fear. Ashamed, they bowed their heads down and asked him to be compassionate. They said, "O lord! This act on your part is not surprising. You are supreme and unchanging. Large numbers of patient ones who seek bliss bow down before your lotus feet. The gods create many kinds of impediments for those who serve you. Those who are your

---

[1011] Of perception and action.

[1012] Based on sattva.

[1013] Nara-Narayana.

[1014] Kama.

[1015] A hermitage exists so that it can offer hospitality to guests. The idea is: 'Please accept the offerings as hospitality due to a guest.' Otherwise, the hermitage becomes non-existent in a figurative sense.

own transcend those and reach your supreme feet. They[1016] do not wish to give others a share from their share of offerings. However, protected by you, your devotees place their feet on the heads of such impediments. There are some who manage to cross over the ocean of impediments created by us in the form of hunger, thirst, the three seasons of time,[1017] the wind, taste[1018] and the genital organs.[1019] However, they succumb to rage and fail to reach your feet. Having traversed an extremely difficult path of austerities, they throw it away in vain.[1020] This is like drowning in a *goshpada*."[1021] While he was being praised in this way, the lord showed them women who were extraordinary to behold. They were beautifully adorned and were serving him. The companions of the gods saw those women, who were as beautiful as Shri. Their fragrance bewildered them and their own beauty faded because of their magnificent beauty. They bowed down before him. The lord of the lord of the gods[1022] seemed to laugh. He said, "From among these, choose any one who is appropriate. She will be an ornament in heaven." Uttering "Oum", the bandis of the gods bowed down and accepted this order. Placing Urvashi, the best among apsaras, at the forefront, they returned to heaven. They bowed down before Indra in his assembly. While all the residents of heaven heard, they spoke about Narayana's strength. Shakra was both amazed and terrified.

"'Achyuta assumed his own form of a swan and spoke about *atma yoga*.[1023] He assumed the forms of Datta,[1024] the Kumaras[1025] and our illustrious father, Rishabha. For the welfare of the worlds,

---

[1016] The gods.

[1017] Extreme weather during the three seasons of summer, rain and winter. Extreme austerities are performed to overcome these impediments.

[1018] And other senses of perception.

[1019] And other senses of action.

[1020] As a result of rage, they utter curses and fritter the fruits away.

[1021] This literally means the mark of a cow's foot in the soil and the small puddle of water that fills up such a mark, that is, a trifle.

[1022] Narayana.

[1023] As a swan, he taught *jnana yoga* to Brahma.

[1024] Dattatreya.

[1025] Sanaka, Sananda, Sanatana and Sanatkumara.

Vishnu descended in his portions. As Hayagriva, he is the one who killed Madhu, recovering the shrutis that had been stolen. As a fish, at the time of the deluge, he protected Manu, the earth and all the herbs. As a boar, he slew Diti's son and raised up the earth from inside the water. As a tortoise, at the time of the churning of the ocean for amrita, he supported the mountain on his own back. When the distressed king of the elephants sought refuge with him, he freed it from the crocodile. He saved the ascetic rishis who fell down and prayed to him.[1026] When Shakra entered darkness consequent to killing Vritra, he saved him. The divine women were imprisoned in the house of the asura and were without a protector. As Nrisimha, he killed the Indra among the asuras and granted the virtuous freedom from fear. In battles between the gods and the asuras, for the sake of the gods, he slays the lords of the daityas. In various *manvantaras*, in different portions, he saves the worlds. He became vamana and took the earth away from Bali. Under the pretext of asking for alms, he handed it over to Aditi's sons. As Rama, he was a fire in the lineage of the Bhargavas. He destroyed the Haihaya lineage and rid the earth of kshatriyas twenty-one times. As Sita's consort, he is the victorious one whose deeds cleanse the world of all impurities. He bound the ocean and destroyed the one with ten heads, along with Lanka. To remove the burden of the earth, he will be born in the Yadu lineage and will perform tasks that are extremely difficult even for the gods.[1027] Through arguments, he[1028] will confuse unworthy ones who will be engaged in performing sacrifices. At the end of kali yuga, he[1029] will slay the shudra kings. The births and deeds of the lord of the universe

---

[1026] These were the minute *valakhilya rishi*s, who fell into a goshpada and were about to drown.

[1027] There is a tense problem. This part of the text is in the future tense, which is fine because this is being told to King Nimi. However, the bit about Rama has a bit in the past tense and a bit in the present tense. The only logical conclusion possible is that this entire conversation took place while Rama was still alive.

[1028] As Buddha.

[1029] As Kalki.

are like this. O mighty-armed one! There are many others, full of glorious fame, similar to the ones I have described.'"

Chapter 11(5)

" "The king[1030] asked, 'O supreme among those who know about the atman! There are those who generally do not worship Hari. Their desires are not quenched and they have not conquered their atmans? What destination do they obtain?'

"'Chamasa said, 'The four varnas, brahmanas and others, along with the ashramas, were separately born from Purusha's mouth, arms, thighs and feet, through combinations of the gunas. Their origin is directly the result of Purusha's powers. If any one of them does not worship, or neglects, the lord, he is dislodged from his state and falls downwards. There are some who are far away from hearing about Hari's account. There are others who are far away from chanting about Achyuta. Women, shudras and others like that deserve the compassion of people like you. After having received their second birth of initiation, brahmanas, kshatriyas and vaishyas are allowed to approach Hari's feet. However, they may be confused and may not follow the sacred texts properly. They do not know about karma. They are insolent and foolish, taking false pride in their learning. They are eager to hear sweet words and foolishly, speak sweet words.[1031] Because of rajas, their resolutions are terrible. They are lascivious and their anger is like that of snakes. Insolent, proud and wicked, they laugh at the ones who are loved by Achyuta. They worship women. The benedictions in their homes are only in the form of sexual intercourse and they speak to each other about this. They perform sacrifices without following the injunctions and without distributing food and dakshina. Ignorant of the consequences, they slaughter animals only for their own subsistence. The intelligence of these deceitful

---

[1030] Nimi.
[1031] They distort the meanings of the Vedas.

people is blinded by their wealth, powers, noble birth, learning, renunciation, beauty, strength and deeds. The resultant insolence leads them to show disrespect to the lord Hari and to virtuous ones who are loved by him. He is eternally inside embodied beings, like the sky. The desired lord is in their atmans. He is chanted about in the Vedas, but the ignorant ones do not listen to this. Instead, they converse about topics that further their desires. In this world, living beings are always addicted to sexual intercourse, flesh and liquor and no sanction[1032] is required for this. There are prescribed sanctions for intercourse through marriage and flesh and liquor through sacrifices. However, the objective behind these is ultimate renunciation. The sole fruit of wealth is dharma. Through this, jnana, vijnana and serenity result. However, those who are householders use it for the sake of the body and do not see death, which is invincible in its force. It is sanctioned that inhaling liquor is as good as imbibing it. While killing of animals is sanctioned, that is not sanction for violence. In that way, sexual intercourse is for the sake of offspring, not for pleasure. But people do not understand that this is the pure state of one's own dharma. There are wicked people who do not know this. They are obstinate and pride themselves on being virtuous. They cause violence to trusting animals and after death, are devoured by these creatures. They hate lord Hari, who is present in their own atmans, just as he is in the bodies of others. Their addiction is bound to this mortal body and its associations. Therefore, they descend downwards. There are foolish people who may have crossed the threshold of folly, but have not achieved kaivalya. Moving beyond the momentary, they pursue the three objectives,[1033] but also destroy their own atmans. Those who kill their own atmans are not serene. Though they are ignorant, they pride themselves on being learned. Since they cannot accomplish their objectives, they suffer. All their wishes are frustrated by time. Because of the maya fashioned by Vasudeva, they turn away from him. They have to abandon their homes, offspring, well-wishers and prosperity and enter darkness.'

[1032] From the sacred texts.
[1033] Dharma, artha and kama.

'"The king[1034] asked, 'At different periods of time, under what names is the illustrious one worshipped by men? What are his complexions and forms? What are the rituals? Please tell us that.'

'"Karabhajana replied, 'In *krita*, *treta*, *dvapara* and kali, Keshava has different complexions and names. There are different rituals for worshipping him. In krita, he is fair and four-armed, with matted hair. His garments are made out of bark and black antelope skin. He has a sacred thread and holds a string of *rudraksha* beads, a staff and a *kamandalu*.[1035] The men are then serene, without enmity. They are impartial and friendly towards everyone. They worship the divinity through austerities, control of the mind and control of the senses. The lord is glorified as Hamsa, Suparna, Vaikuntha, Dharma, Yogeshvara, Amala, Ishvara, Purusha, Avyakta and Paramatman. In treta, his complexion is red. He is four-armed and his girdle has three strands.[1036] His hair is golden and his atman has the signs mentioned in the three Vedas—the wooden ladle, the wooden spoon and other equipment for sacrifices.[1037] Men are then immersed in the divinity Hari, who has all the gods in him. They follow dharma, know about the brahman and worship him through the rituals of the three Vedas. He is glorified by the names Vishnu, Yajna, Prishnigarbha, Sarvadeva, Urukrama, Vrishakapi, Jayanta and Urugaya. In dvapara, the illustrious one is dark blue in complexion. His garments are yellow and he wields his own weapons. He is characterized by signs like shrivatsa and other signs on his body. O king! Mortal men who wish to know about the supreme Purusha worship him through Vedas and tantras, worshipping him like a great king. "I bow down to Vasudeva. I bow down to Samkarshana. I bow down to Pradyumna and Aniruddha. I bow down to the illustrious one. I bow down to the rishi Narayana, the great-souled Purusha, Vishveshara, Vishva, the one who is in all atmans." O lord of the earth! In dvapara, this is the way they praise the lord of the universe. Now hear about the

---

[1034] Nimi.

[1035] A water pot.

[1036] Standing for the three Vedas.

[1037] That is, he is personified in sacrifices.

diverse tantras and rituals of kali. He is dark in complexion, but his lustre is brilliant. Those who are excellent in intelligence generally worship him through sacrifices and collective chanting, worshipping his limbs, his ornaments, his weapons and his associates. "O great Purusha! I worship your lotus feet. You must always be meditated on. You satisfy all wishes and destroy all the humiliations of material existence. You are the refuge of all the tirthas. Shiva and Virinchi bow down and seek refuge with you. You are the protector of all those who prostrate themselves before you. You destroy the afflictions of your servants. You are the boat for crossing samsara. O great Purusha! I worship your lotus feet. You are devoted to dharma. Because of the words of your father, you have given up the prosperity of the kingdom, which even the gods find difficult to relinquish, and left for the forest.[1038] To accomplish the desires of your beloved, you pursued a deer fashioned out of maya." O king! Hari is the lord who bestows everything beneficial. In this way, as is appropriate to the yuga, men who follow the conduct of that particular yuga worship the illustrious one in different forms. Noble ones who know about qualities and can pick up the true essence, praise kali. During this era, all the objectives can be accomplished only through chanting his name. This is the greatest gain for those who are wandering around in this world. This is the way they will obtain supreme serenity and destroy samsara. O king! Subjects from krita and the others wish to be born in kali. It is indeed in kali that those who are devoted to Narayana will be born. O great king! Some will be born here and there, but a large number will be born in the Dravida region, where the rivers Tamraparni, Kritamala, Payasvini, the immensely sacred Kaveri and the western part[1039] of the Mahanadi flow. O lord of men! Men who drink these waters are generally spotless in heart and are devoted to the illustrious

[1038] Though not mentioned by name, this seems to be addressed to Rama. In fairness, interpretations have also tried to identify this with Krishna and Chaitanya.

[1039] The word used is *pratichi*, meaning west. It is not clear whether the word is being used as an adjective or a proper noun. Given the Mahanadi's course, adjective is probably more natural.

Vasudeva. O king! With all his soul, if a person goes to Mukunda, the refuge, for shelter, all his tasks[1040] can be discarded. He is not a servant of gods, rishis, creatures, men, relatives or ancestors. Nor is he indebted to any of them. Hari, the supreme lord, loves those who abandon all other sentiments and worship his feet. He resides in their hearts. Even if such a devotee commits a perverse act by chance, he destroys all such sins.'"

'Narada said, "Thus, the lord of Mithila heard about the dharma of being devoted to the illustrious one. Delighted, along with his priests, he worshipped the sages who were the sons of Jayanti. After this, while everyone looked on, the Siddhas vanished. The king followed dharma and obtained the supreme destination. O immensely fortunate one! You have heard about the dharma of being devoted to the illustrious one and you should faithfully resort to it. Free of attachment, you will then obtain the supreme end. The world has been filled with the fame of the two of you, husband and wife,[1041] since the illustrious lord Hari has come to you as a son. You have acted affectionately towards Krishna, treating him like a son. You have seen him, embraced him, conversed with him, slept with him, shared seats with him and eaten with him. Through this, your atmans have been purified. Kings who bore him enmity, Shishupala, Poundra, Shalva and others, thought about him while they slept and were seated. Their minds were fixed on his stride, his glances, his pastimes and other things. Thereby, they attained a state of union with him. What need be said about those whose minds are attached to him? Krishna is the lord who is in all atmans. In vain, do not think of him as a son. Using his maya, the supreme and undecaying one has hidden his potencies and has followed the conduct of a human. He did this to protect the virtuous and to slay the kings, who are asuras, who were a burden to the earth. His fame pervades the worlds and he descended to confer liberation."'

Shri-Shuka continued, 'Hearing this, the immensely fortunate Vasudeva was greatly surprised. He, and the immensely fortunate Devaki, gave up the delusion that was there in their atmans. If a

---

[1040] As sanctioned by the sacred texts.
[1041] Vasudeva and Devaki.

person controls himself and meditates on this sacred history, all
his impurities are cleansed in this world and he becomes worthy of
realizing the brahman.'

Chapter 11(6)

Shri-Shuka said, 'Along with his sons, Brahma, surrounded by the
gods and the Prajapatis, went there.[1042] Surrounded by a large
number of bhutas, Bhava, who brings welfare to creatures, also
went there. Indra, the Maruts, the illustrious Adityas, the Vasus,
the two Ashvins, the Ribhus, Angiras, the Rudras, the Vishvadevas,
Sadhyas, other divinities, the gandharvas, the apsaras, the nagas,
the Siddhas, the charanas, the guhyakas, the rishis, the ancestors,
the vidyadharas and the kinnaras—all of them went to Dvaraka.
Through his form, the illustrious one charmed the world of men.
His fame spread throughout the worlds and destroyed all impurities
from the worlds. They saw the dazzling prosperity and great
opulence there. They saw Krishna, wonderful to behold, and their
eyes were not satisfied. They covered the supreme one among the
Yadus with garlands of flowers from celestial gardens. They praised
the lord of the universe in colourful words that were deep with
meaning.

'The gods said, "O protector! With our intelligence, senses,
prana, mind and speech, we prostrate ourselves at your lotus
feet.[1043] Those who wish to be liberated from the great bondage of
karma are filled with devotion towards you and meditate on you in
their hearts. Because of your maya, consisting of the three gunas,
you are impossible to conceive. Resorting to those gunas, you
create, preserve and destroy all that is manifest. O unvanquished
one! However, you are not affected by any of these acts. You are
unimpeded and completely absorbed in your own bliss. You are

[1042] To Dvaraka.

[1043] Since there are five senses, this is *sashtanga namaskara*, with eight
(*ashta*) limbs (*anga*).

beyond reproach. O one who should be praised! Men who are contaminated by desires cannot be purified only through worship, knowledge, studying, donations, austerities and rituals, unlike those whose atmans are based in sattva. O supreme one! It can only happen through increasing faith and devotion, resulting from listening to your glories. The hearts of sages melt towards you and for their benefit, they bear in their hearts your lotus feet. Like a consuming fire, let those feet burn down everything inauspicious in us. For the sake of an opulence like yours, those who are in control of their atmans and are devoted to you worship the manifestations[1044] which take them beyond the world of heaven, thrice a day.[1045] O lord! Those who follow the rituals of the three Vedas and nirukta, take oblations in their cupped hands and when they offer oblations into the sacrificial fire, think about your feet. There are devotees who are superior to these. They are yogis who engage in *adhyatma yoga* and wish to know about the illustrious one's maya. For their supreme benefit, they too meditate on your feet. O lord! You cheerfully accept all the offerings that are properly rendered to you, even this garland of faded wild flowers, which the illustrious Shri rivals, like a co-wife. May your feet be a fire that destroys all the impure wishes in our hearts. Your feet caused fear in the army of the asuras and granted the army of the gods freedom from fear. The valour in your three strides was like a flagpole, from which, like banners, was strung the one with the three streams.[1046] O powerful one! This ensured heaven for the virtuous and drove the deceitful away from there. O illustrious one! We worship your feet. May they cleanse us of our sins. Like cattle tethered through the nose, Brahma and the others, and those with bodies, are under your subjugation, in your form as time. They struggle against each other. You are beyond Purusha and Prakriti. O Purushottama! May your feet spread benefit among us. You are the cause behind creation,

[1044] Vasudeva, Samkarshana, Pradyumna and Aniruddha.

[1045] Morning, noon and evening.

[1046] This is a reference to the vamana incarnation and Vishnu covering the three worlds in three strides (the three flagpoles) and the Ganga flowing (like a streamer) in the three worlds.

preservation and destruction of the unmanifest, the jivatman and even Mahat. You are spoken of as time, with three naves.[1047] As time, your movements are imperceptible, but you are engaged in diminishing everything. You are the supreme being. It is from you that Purusha obtains the seed of creation, invincible in its energy, and impregnates, like an embryo, the principle of Mahat. Thus joined, from within itself, it creates this golden cosmic egg, with the external sheaths that cover it. You are the lord of everything mobile and immobile. You are the lord of the senses.[1048] The objects of the senses arose from the transformation of the gunas, which are the result of your maya. However, even though you enjoy the objects of the senses, you are never attached to them. Others may themselves renounce the objects of the senses, but are scared of them. You have sixteen thousand wives. They exhibit their smiling glances and alluring feelings by arching their eyebrows. They send impudent messages of engaging in intercourse, using Ananga's arrows. However, they have not been able to agitate your senses even for an instant. There are streams of amrita in the form of your accounts and there are also rivers that have flowed after washing your feet. Both can destroy all the impurities of the worlds. Those who desire purification for themselves approach either of these two tirthas—hearing your accounts from the sacred texts, or bathing their limbs in waters that have flowed from your feet.'"

Badarayana's son said, 'Along with the gods and Isha, the performer of one hundred sacrifices[1049] praised Hari. Stationed in the sky, he bowed down and addressed Govinda in these words.

'Brahma said, "O lord! Earlier, you were requested by us to relieve the earth of her burden. O one who exists in the atmans of everything! All that we asked for has been accomplished. You have established dharma among virtuous ones who are devoted to the truth. Your fame has been spread in all the directions and it destroys all the impurities of the world. Descending in the lineage

---

[1047] This is invariably interpreted as four-monthly periods of summer, monsoon and winter. But past, present and future also seems feasible.

[1048] That is, Hrishikesha.

[1049] Brahma.

of the Yadus, you have manifested your supreme form. For the welfare of the world, you have performed wonderfully powerful deeds. O lord! During kali yuga, virtuous people who hear about your conduct and chant it will easily cross over the darkness. O Purushottama! O lord! Since you descended in the lineage of the Yadus, one hundred and twenty-five autumns have passed. O one who holds up everything! So far as the task of the gods is concerned, nothing remains now. Because of the curse of the brahmanas, it is as if your lineage has already been destroyed. Therefore, if you so desire, please enter your supreme abode again. O Vaikuntha! We are your servants. Save us, the guardians of the worlds, and their worlds."

'The illustrious one replied, "O lord of the gods! I have understood what you have said. All your tasks have been accomplished and the earth's burden has been reduced. Through their valour, courage and prosperity, this lineage of the Yadus wished to devour the world. But I have checked it, just as the shoreline holds back the great ocean. If I leave without destroying this insolent lineage of the Yadus, the world will be destroyed by their surging flow. Because of the curse of the brahmanas, the destruction of the lineage has now started. O Brahma! O unblemished one! When it is over, I will visit you in your residence."'[1050]

Shri-Shuka continued, 'Thus addressed by the protector of the worlds, Svayambhu bowed down before him. Along with the large number of gods, the divinity returned to his own abode. After this, terrible portents arose in Dvaravati. Witnessing these, the illustrious one spoke to all the assembled elders among the Yadus. The illustrious one said, "These terrible portents have arisen all around us. This is because of the curse imposed on our lineage by the brahmanas and it is impossible to counter it. O revered ones! If we wish to live, we should no longer reside here. Prabhasa is an extremely sacred place. Without any delay, let us go there today. Because of Daksha's curse, the lord of the stars was seized by consumption.[1051] After bathing

[1050] On the way to Vaikuntha.
[1051] Chandra was married to the nakshatras, Daksha's daughters. But since he loved Rohini more than the others, he was cursed by Daksha.

there, he was instantly cleansed of the sin and resumed waxing again. Let us also bathe there and satisfy the gods and the ancestors. Let us feed the revered brahmanas with food that possesses all the qualities. They are worthy recipients and with a great deal of respect, let us give them gifts. Using these donations like boats, we will easily cross over this ocean of hardships." O descendant of the Kuru lineage! The illustrious one instructed the Yadavas in this way. Making up their minds to go to that tirtha, they started to yoke their chariots.

'O king! Uddhava saw this and heard what the illustrious one had said. He was always devoted to Krishna and he too saw the terrible portents. He approached the lord of all the lords of the worlds in private. He bowed his head down at his feet. Joining his hands in salutation, he spoke to him. Uddhava said, "O god! O lord of the gods! O lord of yoga! Hearing and chanting about you is sacred. O lord! You are capable and you could have countered the curse of the brahmanas. But you have decided to destroy the lineage and give up the world. O Keshava! O protector! Even for half a kshana, I cannot tolerate being separated from your lotus feet. Also take me to your own abode. O Krishna! Your pastimes are extremely auspicious for men and are like nectar to the ears. As soon as they hear it, people give up all other desires. Whether we are lying down, seated, standing, bathing, playing or eating, we are always devoted to you. We love you like our own selves. How can you abandon us? By being servants to you, we are capable of defeating your maya—eating the remnants of your food and ornamenting ourselves with garlands, fragrances, garments and ornaments that you have already enjoyed. There are rishis who use the wind as a garment. They are mendicants and hold up their seed. They are serene and unblemished *sannyasis*. They go to your abode, known as the brahman. O great yogi! But we wander around in this world, following the path of karma. By conversing about you with those who are devoted to you, we will cross over this insurmountable darkness. We will remember you and chant about what you have done and said, your strides, your generous smiles, your glances and your playful pastimes. You followed the conduct of the human world and did all this." O king! Devaki's illustrious son was addressed in this way. In that extremely private place, he spoke to his beloved servant, Uddhava.'

Chapter 11(7)

'The illustrious one said, "O immensely fortunate one! You have correctly described what I wish to do. Brahma, Bhava and the guardians of the worlds desire that I should return to my own abode. In this world, I have completely accomplished the task of the gods. Requested by Brahma, that is the reason why I descended, along with my portion.[1052] The lineage has already been burnt by the curse and will be destroyed by fighting with each other. On the seventh day, the ocean will overflow and submerge this city. As soon as I abandon this world, it will certainly lose everything that is auspicious in it. O virtuous one! It will soon be overtaken by kali. When I leave, you should no longer reside on earth. You are without sin. However, in kali yuga, people will be full of sin. Therefore, give up all attachment towards your own relatives and friends. You must completely immerse your mind in me and, impartial in vision, wander around the earth. Everything that is perceived through the mind, words, eyes, ears and other senses is perishable. Know that these are thought because of maya. A person who is separated from the truth roams around, pursuing many objectives and suffering from good and bad consequences. Because of a sense of differentiation in his intelligence, he thinks of good and bad karma, akarma and vikarma.[1053] Therefore, control the aggregate of the senses. Control your mind and visualize this universe within your own atman. See your atman spread out within me, the lord. With jnana and vijnana, realize that your atman is one with all embodied beings. You will realize the atman and be content in the atman. There will be no impediments in your progress. A

[1052] Balarama.
[1053] Henceforth, throughout this discourse to Uddhava, the shlokas are subject to different interpretations.

person who is beyond perceptions of good and bad is like a child. He does not refrain from what is prohibited because it is prohibited, or because he uses his intelligence to judge what is good or bad. He is serene and friendly towards all beings. Fixed in jnana and vijnana, he sees that the universe is pervaded by my atman and does not face hardships again."[1054]

Shri Shuka continued, 'O king! The great devotee of the illustrious one was thus instructed by the illustrious one. Uddhava was eager to know the truth. He prostrated himself before Achyuta and said the following.

'Uddhava said, "O lord of yoga! O one who spreads yoga! O one whose atman is yoga! O one from whom yoga results! For my benefit, you have said that renunciation is the sign of sannyasa. O lord! Renunciation is extremely difficult for those who desire objects of pleasure for themselves. O one whose atman is in everything. This is especially true of those who are not devoted to you. That is my view. O illustrious one! Because of foolish intelligence, I am immersed in notions of 'I' and 'mine'. Your maya has created this bondage for me. Therefore, instruct your servant, so that I can easily follow those instructions. You are the self-illuminating atman. You are the truth. O lord! Barring you, I do not see anyone, even among the gods, who can do this. The minds of Brahma and all the others with bodies are confounded by your maya and conceive the external as the truth. You are perfect. You are without limits. You are the omniscient lord. You are without agitation. You are the one who resides in Vaikuntha. Though my mind has renounced, I am tormented by material hardships. O Narayana! O Nara's friend! I seek refuge with you."

'The illustrious one continued, "There are men in this world who are often accomplished in discerning the truth about the world. Using their own intelligence, they raise their atmans above inauspicious desires. Especially for humans, the atman is one's preceptor. Through direct perception and inference, a person can realize what is best for himself. There are patient people who are accomplished in samkhya and yoga. With this, they can directly see

---

[1054] Of samsara.

me, along with all my potencies. Many kinds of bodies have been created—with one foot, with two feet, with four feet, with many feet, or with no feet. Among all these, humans are dear to me. In this form, they can search for me, the lord, through signs. I cannot be perceived through the qualities,[1055] but can be inferred through the signs.[1056] In this connection, an ancient history is recounted. This is a conversation between the infinitely energetic Yadu and an avadhuta. There was a young and wise brahmana who was an avadhuta. On seeing him wander around, without any fear, Yadu, who knew about dharma, questioned him.

'"Yadu asked, 'O brahmana! Though you do not do anything, how did you come to possess this greatly developed intelligence? Having acquired this knowledge, you are roaming around in this world, like a child. In general, men pursue dharma, artha and kama and for this purpose, try to obtain lifespan, fame and prosperity. You are capable, wise and accomplished. You are extremely handsome and your speech is like amrita. However, you do not desire to do anything. You are like a dumb or crazy person, like a pishacha. People are scorched in the fire of desire and avarice. However, you are not burnt by that fire. You are free, like an elephant standing in the waters of the Ganga.[1057] O brahmana! What is the reason for your finding bliss in your own atman? We are asking you. Please tell us. How are you devoid of touch and the other senses? You are alone in your atman.'"

'The illustrious one continued, "The immensely fortunate Yadu asked the immensely intelligent brahmana. Asked respectfully, the brahmana spoke to the one who was bent down in humility.

'"The brahmana replied,[1058]'O king! Using my intelligence, I have had many preceptors. Having obtained my intelligence from them, I have become free and roam around this world. Listen. O king! I have accepted twenty-four as my preceptors—the earth, the air, space, water, fire, the moon, the sun, the pigeon, the python, the

---

[1055] Intelligence, mind or senses.
[1056] There are interpretations on what is being inferred.
[1057] Thus escaping the forest conflagration.
[1058] The brahmana is identified as Dattatreya.

ocean, the moth, the bee, the elephant, the gatherer of honey, the
deer, the fish, Pingala, the osprey, the child, the maiden, the maker
of arrows, the snake, the spider and the wasp. My knowledge and
conduct are derived from whatever I have learnt from them. O
Yayati's son! O tiger among men! I will tell you exactly what I
have learnt from each of them. Listen to what I have to say. Even
if a person is attacked by creatures, he must be patient and realize
that they are under the control of destiny. Having grasped this, a
person must not deviate from his path. I have learnt this conduct
from the earth. Everything in this world must be for the sake of
others. The benefit of others is the reason for one's birth. As a
student of the mountain and as a student of the tree,[1059] a virtuous
person learns about living for others. A sage must be satisfied with
whatever is necessary for physical subsistence and must not seek
gratification of the senses.[1060] Knowledge must not be destroyed.
Nor must speech and the mind be agitated. A yogi comes into
contact with objects that possess many kinds of characteristics.
However, like the air, his atman must not be attached to the good
or the bad. In this world, one enters a body that is made out of the
elements and thereby assumes their attributes. But just as the air
bears scents, but is not attached to them, a yogi who has realized
the atman must not be attached to these attributes. Space is present
within all mobile and immobile objects. But though it pervades,
it is unlimited and unattached. A sage must meditate and behave
like the pervasive sky. Despite association, he must be unattached,
with his atman immersed in the brahman. Space is not touched
by clouds and other things that are borne along by the wind. In
that way, like space, a man must not be touched by fire, water
and food and other qualities that are created by time. Water is
naturally pure, gentle and sweet. At tirthas, its purifying qualities
are chanted about. In that way, a sage must be friendly towards
men and must purify them. Like the fire, a person who is united
with his atman blazes because of his austerities. He is unshakeable

---

[1059] These have not been specifically mentioned as instructors. Both the
mountain and the tree are parts of the earth.

[1060] The breath of life, that is the air, behaves in this way.

and uses his stomach as a vessel.[1061] He eats everything. But like
the fire, he does not accept anything that is impure. Like the fire,
he is sometimes hidden and sometimes noticed. He is worshipped
by those who desire their benefit. He eats everything that donors
give him and burns down everything inauspicious that they have
done or will do. Through his maya, the lord created everything
with the attributes of the superior or the inferior, and entered. Like
the fire in kindling, he entered and assumed the respective forms
of each one. Beginning with birth and ending at the cremation
ground, time, whose progress is indiscernible, brings about stages
in the physical body, but not in the atman. This is like the apparent
waxing and waning of the moon. The swift flow of time brings
about the creation and destruction of beings. Though it is constant,
it is not noticed by the atman, just as the fire is not affected by what
happens to its flames. At the right time, the sun sucks up water
through its rays and releases them. Like that, a yogi experiences
qualities and the lack of qualities, but is not attached to them.
The sun is one, but is apparently different when it is reflected in
different objects. Like the sun, those with gross intelligence perceive
the atman as identified with whatever it occupies. There must
never be excessive attachment or association. Otherwise, one will
experience torment, like the male pigeon, inferior in intelligence.
There was a male pigeon in a forest. Along with a female pigeon,
his wife, he had built a nest in a tree. Along with her, he lived
there for some years. Since they were following the dharma of
householders, the hearts of the two pigeons were bound to each
other in love. Their eyes, limbs and intelligence were bound to each
other. They slept, sat, walked, stood, conversed, played and ate
together. They were a couple and fearlessly roamed around among
the trees. O king! She gave him whatever he wished and satisfied
him. Compassionately, he brought her whatever she wished for,
even if it meant a great deal of effort. He was unable to conquer
his senses. When the time arrived, the female pigeon conceived for
the first time. In her husband's presence, the virtous one laid her
eggs in the nest. Through Hari's inconceivable powers, at the right

[1061] That is, he does not store food for a next meal.

time, the babies were born and their delicate limbs and feathers were formed. With the children born, the couple was delighted and devoted to their young. They were delighted to hear their chirping and indistinct sounds. The feathers were extremely gentle to the touch. As they chirped and made charming efforts to fly, the parents were overjoyed with them. Confounded by Vishnu's maya, their hearts were bound to each other and, inferior in intelligence, they reared their young children. Once, both of them went out to find food for the family. Pursuing this objective, they roamed around in the forest for a very long time. There was a fowler who was wandering around in the forest as he willed. He saw the young pigeons moving around in their own nest. He spread out his net and captured them. The male and female pigeons were always eager to nurture their offspring. Having gone and obtained food, they now approached their nest. The female pigeon saw that her children had been ensnared in the net. Extremely miserable, she shrieked and while shrieking, she rushed towards them. Because of Aja's maya, her intelligence was inferior and she was bound in that constant quality of affection. Having seen her children, she forgot herself and rushed forward, getting herself ensnared in the net. The male pigeon saw that his children had been ensnared. Even worse, his beloved wife, who was like his own self, had also been ensnared. Miserable and burdened with grief, he lamented. "Alas! Behold my destruction. I am limited in good deeds and am evil in intelligence. I have still not satisfied the purpose of my existence. My household, the foundation for the three objectives of existence, has been destroyed. She was just right for me. She regarded me, her husband, as a divinity. However, she has left me alone in my home now. With her sons, the virtuous one is going to heaven. I am alone and miserable in my empty house. My wife is dead. My children are dead. Why should I wish to live? Separated from them, it will be terrible to remain alive." The male pigeon saw them struggling inside the net, as if they were surrounded by death. He was miserable and flung himself into the net. The fowler was cruel. He obtained the male pigeon who was in the role of a householder, the female pigeon and the young pigeons. Having accomplished his objective, he went home. In this way, like the bird, a person with a family is not tranquil in his soul and finds pleasure in this sense of duality. Miserably, he tries to sustain the family and along with his relatives, is made to suffer. If a person has been born as a human in this world, this is like the door to liberation being opened. Nevertheless, if he is attached to a household, the learned look upon him as a bird, one who has climbed high, but has fallen down.'"

Chapter 11(8)

'The brahmana continued, "O king! Embodied beings can experience happiness of the senses in heaven or hell too. Therefore, a learned person must desire to avoid unhappiness. Like the python, a person should not make any efforts, but should eat whatever turns up on its own. This is regardless of whether the food is tasty or tasteless, large in quantity or small. Like the giant serpent, he must be content with whatever fortune brings to him. Even if there is no food, he must not make any efforts and must fast. Even if it is for many days, he must lie down. Even if he possesses energy, physical strength and mental strength, he must not make efforts to maintain the body. He must lie down, without any sleep. Even if he possesses his senses, he must not make efforts. A sage must be as tranquil and deep as the ocean, fathomless and impossible to cross. He possesses no limits. He is as calm as the water and cannot be agitated. Depending on what rivers do, an ocean does not overflow or dry up. Like that, a sage who is devoted to Narayana is not affected by the fulfilment or non-fulfilment of his wishes. A woman has been fashioned by the god's maya. On seeing her, a person who has not conquered his senses is tempted by her seductive behaviour. Like a moth headed towards a fire, he descends into blinding darkness. A foolish person's mind is allured by a woman's golden ornaments and garments and other objects fashioned out of maya. His mind is tempted by the desire to gratify the senses. With his vision destroyed, he is destroyed like a moth. A sage must follow the conduct of a bee and with each morsel, only eat a little, just enough to maintain the body. Without causing trouble, he must not tarry at any household for long.[1062] The bee collects the essence from flowers everywhere, big or small. Like that, an accomplished man gathers from all texts, great or small. "This is what I will eat when evening is over. This is what I will eat tomorrow." What has been begged must not be collected in this fashion. The hand is the vessel and the stomach is the container. One must not collect, as the bee does. A mendicant must not collect for eating at night or the next day. If a person collects the way a bee does, he and his collection are destroyed. Even with a foot, a mendicant must not touch a young woman, not even an image made out of wood. Otherwise, like a male elephant that wishes to touch the limbs of a female elephant, he will be bound. A wise person must never approach a woman. She is like his death. A male elephant which does this is killed by a stronger male elephant. An avaricious person accumulates after making efforts. He does not give it away, nor enjoy it. The wealth is stolen and enjoyed by others, just as the gatherer of honey steals honey from a honeycomb. Those who desire the life of a householder aspire to acquire riches after a great deal of effort. However, like the honey gatherer, the mendicant enjoys this before the householder. A mendicant who roams around in the forest must never listen to songs about carnal pleasures. He must learn from the deer. Captivated by the hunter's singing, it was captured. Addicted to the dancing, musical instruments and singing of vulgar women, Rishyashringa, the son of a deer, came under their subjugation and became like a puppet. If a person is bewitched by taste, the tongue becomes extremely powerful for him. His intelligence becomes wicked and he faces a futile death, like a fish through a hook. Through fasting, learned people quickly bring their senses under control, with the exception of the tongue. When one is without food, its power increases. Until this sense has been conquered, it cannot be said that a man has conquered his senses. The tongue must be defeated. When taste has been conquered, everything has been conquered.

[1062] He must not beg for too much of alms at any house, just as a bee collects little from every flower.

'"In ancient times, in the city of Videha, there used to be a courtesan named Pingala. O son of a king! Listen to what I learnt from her. Once, that svairini sought to entice a beloved into her house. At the right time, she stood outside her door, displaying her supreme beauty. O bull among men! She was greedy for money. She looked at the men who were passing along the road, considering who would pay her price. She wanted a wealthy lover. Prostitution was her means of subsistence and men came and went. She kept thinking, 'Perhaps another wealthy person will approach me and give me a lot of money.' As she waited at the door in this vain hope, she lost her sleep. Sometimes, she went out into the street. Sometimes, she again entered her house. In this way, midnight arrived. In her wish for money, her mouth dried up and her mind was distressed. As a result of her thoughts, a great sense of detachment arose in her and it brought happiness. Non-attachment is like a sword in a man's hand. It severs the bonds of desire. Her mind was full of non-attachment, and hear her song from me. O king! A person in whom non-attachment has not been generated is unable to cast aside the bonds of the body. This is just like a man without vijnana being unable to give up the notion of 'mine'.

'"Pingala said, 'Alas! Behold my pervasive delusion. I have not been able to conquer my atman. Like a foolish person, I desire pleasure, even from a worthless lover. The most beloved person, the one who can give me pleasure, is near me. He will always give me riches, but I have forsaken him. Like an ignorant person, I am serving an inferior person who cannot satisfy my desires. This gives rise to misery, fear, mental distress, grief and delusion. I have tormented my atman in vain. My occupation has been that of a courtesan. It is a censured vocation. Hankering after riches, I sell myself to pitiable men who seek women. Thereby, I hope to obtain pleasure and riches for myself. Who but me would crave for this house made out of nine gates?[1063] It is fashioned out of bones, the spine, the ribs, the bones of the hands and the feet, body hair and nails, and is covered with skin. It is full of urine and excrement that oozes out. In this

[1063] The body is the city with nine gates—the two eyes, the two nostrils, the two ears, the mouth, the genital organs and the anus.

city of Videha, I am the only person who is foolish in intelligence. I did not desire Achyuta, who gives his own atman to others. Instead, like a wicked person, I wished for others. He is the most beloved well-wisher. He is the protector. He is the atman in all embodied creatures. I will sell myself to him and like Rama, find pleasure with him. What pleasure can men provide to wives who desire pleasure? They have a beginning and an end and time separates them from their wives. This is also true of gods. I must have done some karma that makes the illustrious Vishnu favour me. I have hankered after evil desires. However, this non-attachment, the bringer of pleasure, has been generated in me. For someone as unfortunate as me, the hardship has become a cause of non-attachment. A man who desires serenity can destroy all bondage through this. I will bow my head down and accept this favour, giving up all carnal pleasure and wicked desires. I will seek shelter in the lord. I am faithful and devoted. I will survive on whatever comes to me. I will enjoy myself and find pleasure in the atman. If a person falls down into the well of samsara, his vision is destroyed by material objects. His atman is devoured by a serpent in the form of time. Apart from the supreme lord, who can save such a person? When a person is not distracted, he can see that this entire universe is being devoured by a serpent in the form of time. He realizes that his atman is his own protector and he becomes detached towards everything that is material.'"

'The brahmana said, "Having made up her mind in this way, she gave up and severed all the wicked desires for lovers. Resorting to serenity, she sat down on her bed. Hope is the greatest misery. Lack of hope is the greatest happiness. Therefore, severing all desire for lovers, Pingala slept well, in happiness."'

Chapter 11(9)

'The brahmana said, "Whatever men love to possess is the cause of their misery. A learned person who possesses nothing obtains infinite happiness. Powerful ospreys who did not have any flesh attacked an osprey that had some flesh. When it gave up that piece of meat, it obtained happiness. I have no sense of honour or dishonour. I do not have to think about my home or children. I sport with my own atman and find pleasure in my own atman. Like a child, I thus roam around this world. There are two kinds of people who are free from anxiety and are flooded with supreme bliss. There is the dumb and ignorant child and there is the person who has gone beyond the gunas. Once, a maiden had to herself receive guests who had come to her house to choose her,[1064] her relatives having gone elsewhere. She welcomed them hospitably. O king! In private, she was pounding some paddy so that she could serve them food. However, the conch shell bangles on her hands rubbed against each other and made a sound while she was pounding. She was greatly ashamed at this and embarrassed because of what they would think.[1065] One by one, she broke all the bangles, so that only two remained on each hand. However, as she pounded, these still rubbed against each other and created a sound. Therefore, she broke one from each pair so that the other one would not create a sound. O scorcher of enemies! I wandered around the world, wishing to know the truth about the world. That is how I witnessed the lesson I learnt from the maiden. When many people reside together, there are quarrels. When there are two, there is conversation. Therefore, one must reside alone, like the maiden's bangle. Having perfected the asana,[1066] one must control the breath and fix the mind. Non-attachment must be cultivated through the practice of yoga. The mind must be attentively steadied. When the mind is permanently fixed on him, the particles of karma are gradually shed off. As sattva increases, rajas and tamas are destroyed. Like a fire extinguished without kindling, one achieves nirvana. One's mind is then completely immersed in one's atman. One is no longer conscious of anything, inside or outside. This is like a maker of arrows who was so absorbed in the making of his arrow that he did not notice the king passing

---

[1064] As a possible bride.

[1065] Since she was dehusking the rice herself, they would take her to be poor.

[1066] The seating posture.

by his side. A person must move around alone, without a fixed
residence. He must not be distracted and must seek out caves.[1067]
The sage's activities must be such that he is not noticed. He must be
alone and must speak little. When a person attempts to construct a
house, this is futile and leads to misery, since his existence is itself
temporary. A snake enters a house that has been built by someone
else and enjoys happiness. Narayana is the only divinity. Earlier,
he used his own maya to create. At the end of the kalpa, using
his portion known as time, he withdraws.[1068] He is the lord of the
universe. He is absolute and without a second. He is the support
of his atman and supports everything. Everything seeks refuge in
him. Using his powers in the form of time, he brings his powers,
sattva and the others, into a state of equilibrium and remains as
the original being. He is the lord of Purusha and Pradhana. For
both superior and inferior beings, he is the supreme. He has been
described as kaivalya. He is the aggregate of pure consciousness
and bliss, and there is nothing else that can designate him. His
atman is pure consciousness. O scorcher of enemies! At the time
of the original creation, he used his own maya to agitate the three
gunas and create the thread.[1069] This thread is spoken of as the
manifestation of the three gunas and creates the universe, which
faces in all the directions. This universe is woven into that thread,
through which, humans undergo samsara. From inside its heart,
the spider expands its web through its mouth, plays for a while
and then swallows it up again. The great lord behaves like that.
If an embodied being fixes his mind and intelligence completely
in something, out of love, hatred or fear, that will certainly be the
form he obtains. O king! An insect is forced by a wasp to enter its
nest and once there, it thinks about the wasp and assumes its form,
without giving up its former form. O lord! My intelligence has
learnt from these preceptors. Now hear about what my intelligence
has learnt from my own body. I will tell you. Since it has caused

---

[1067] That is, secluded spots for dwelling in. There are obvious similarities
with a snake's behaviour.

[1068] Like a spider.

[1069] The thread of creation, known as Mahat.

non-attachment and discrimination, my body is my preceptor. Since it is subject to creation, preservation and destruction, it is a constant source of hardships. Nevertheless, I have used it to contemplate the truth. Having determined that it belongs to others,[1070] I roam around without being attached to it. It is with a desire to nourish and develop this beloved body that a person goes through great hardships to get a wife, offspring, riches, animals, servants, houses and relatives and accumulate wealth. However, at the end, it is destroyed, just as a tree follows its dharma and perishes, leaving a seed behind. The tongue drags such a person in one direction, thirst in another. The genitals drag in one direction, the stomach or the ears somewhere else. The sense of smell drags in one direction, the fickle eyes in another. The organs of action head elsewhere. These are like many co-wives who tug at the master of the household. In ancient times, using his own potencies, the one without origin created many species—trees, reptiles, animals, birds, gnats and fish. However, his heart was not satisfied with this and he fashioned humans. The divinity was delighted, because they possessed the intelligence to realize the brahman. Though it is not permanent, this birth as a human is extremely difficult to obtain and comes after many births. Before he dies, a persevering person must immediately make efforts to prevent his downfall. Indeed, the objects of the senses can be enjoyed as any kind of species. In this way, non-attachment was generated and I obtained insight about vijnana. Devoid of attachment, I roam around in this world and have no sense of ahamkara. Jnana obtained from a single preceptor is not stable and may not even be complete. Though the brahman is without a second, rishis have chanted about it in many ways."

'The illustrious one concluded, "The brahmana, profound in his intelligence, spoke to Yadu in this way and sought his leave. The king honoured and worshipped him. Happy, he went to wherever he had come from. Hearing the words of the avadhuta, the forefather of our ancestors freed himself of all his attachments and his mind became impartial towards everything."'

[1070] The parents by virtue of birth, worms, predatory creatures and so on after death.

Chapter 11(10)

'The illustrious one said, "A person must seek refuge with me and carefully follow his own dharma, as instructed by me. Without harbouring any desire, he must observe the conduct appropriate to his varna, ashrama and lineage. With his atman purified, he must think about the truth and see that embodied beings are attached to material objects. Since these are based on the gunas, all efforts will lead to calamities. While asleep, one sees material objects, thinking and wishing for them, but this is futile. Similarly, because of the gunas, the intelligence thinks of the atman as many and differentiated. Immersed in me, a person must give up acts of pravritti and engage in acts of nivritti. A person must be engaged in inquiring and must not accept acts simply because they have been sanctioned. Having immersed himself in me, a person must always accept the norms of yama and, occasionally, the norms of niyama.[1071] He must be free from pride and envy. He must be accomplished, without a sense of ownership and firm in his friendship. He must not be hasty and must seek to know the truth. He must not be jealous and must not waste his words in unnecessary talk. He must be indifferent towards a wife, offspring, a house, fields, relatives, property and other things. He must be impartial and realize that all these are for the purposes of the atman. The gross is distinct from the subtle. Similarly, he must look at his own atman and know it as distinct from the body. The fire is different from the kindling that is burnt. The fire that burns is different from the one that illuminates. Depending on the qualities of what it has entered, the fire assumes those qualities—dormant, blazing, large, small. That is the way with the atman and the attributes of the body.

'"This body is fashioned out of Purusha's gunas and is bound to this samsara. It is only through knowledge that a being can separate

---

[1071] There are issues of interpretation here. Yama means restraint or control and the five norms of yama are non-violence, patience, sincerity, obedience to a preceptor and purification. These are major ordinances, so to speak. Niyama stands for minor ordinances, such as fasting, visiting tirthas, donations, or acts of atonement.

these from the atman. Therefore, through inquiry, one must approach the pure and the supreme that is within oneself. Gradually, one must give up the perception that material objects are real. The preceptor is like the lower piece of kindling that is the support and the disciple is the upper piece of kindling. Instruction is the friction between the two and knowledge is the resulting fire that brings happiness. The pure intelligence of a disciple is refined through the intelligence of an accomplished preceptor and drives away the maya that results from the gunas. The gunas are eventually burnt and so is the intelligence itself, just as the fire is pacified when there is no kindling left. O dear one! You may think there are many agents who perform karma and many who enjoy the consequent happiness and unhappiness; you may think that all the material objects in the world are eternal, as some sacred texts say, regardless of the progress of time; you may think that all the material objects have an original existence, the intelligence perceiving them as different depending on their origin, transformations and forms; you may think that all embodied beings constantly adopt different forms, depending on their births, states and other things, but even then, the agents of karma are not noticed to be independent.[1072] What is the value of the enjoyment of joy or misery by someone who is under someone else's control? It is seen that even learned embodied beings do not enjoy even a little bit of happiness. Nor do foolish people experience unhappiness. Therefore, ahamkara is pointless. Even if people know how to achieve happiness and how to remove unhappiness, they do not know the yoga that will directly enable them to avoid the power of death. When death is at hand, what material object of desire provides happiness? When one is conveyed to a place of execution so as to be killed, this does not satisfy. We have already seen that the happiness we have heard about is contaminated by rivalry, envy, decay and death. There are many impediments in pursuing objects of desire. Like agriculture, it often

---

[1072] These shlokas, with the argument extending across several shlokas, are extremely difficult to translate. The gist is, do agents of karma and material objects have an independent and permanent existence? The answer is no, there is no free will.

fails. Even if the recommended dharma[1073] is properly performed, without any impediments, a person earns certain positions and goes to them. Hear about these. In this world, when gods are worshipped through sacrifices, the performer of the sacrifice goes to the world of heaven. He has earned this divine state for himself and, like a god, enjoys himself there. Because of his own accumulated good deeds, he is astride a vimana and is praised by gandharvas. He wears enchanting garments and is amidst celestial women. The vimana is adorned with bells, nets and garlands and can go anywhere it wills. Along with the women, he amuses himself in divine pleasures. He is content and does not know that he will fall down. He enjoys himself in heaven until his store of good deeds is exhausted. When the store of good deeds is exhausted, driven by time, he is made to unwillingly fall down. There may be a person who is addicted to adharma because of his association with wicked people or because he has not conquered his senses; he is addicted to desire, miserly and avaricious; he craves for women and causes injury to beings; he kills animals without following the injunctions; he offers sacrifices to large numbers of pretas and bhutas; such a person is helpless and goes to many hells, where he is submerged in terrible darkness. Having assumed a body, he again undertakes karma that leads to hardships in the future. Therefore, he has to assume another body there. What happiness can there be for a person who follows the dharma of mortals? The worlds and the guardians of the worlds live for a kalpa and are scared of me. Brahma, whose lifespan is for two *parardhas*,[1074] is also scared of me. The gunas create karma and the gunas create the senses. The jivatman is united with the gunas and enjoys the fruits of karma. As long as disequilibrium between the gunas exists, until then, there will be differentiated perception of the atman. As long as differentiated perception of the atman exists, until then, there will be dependence on something else. As long as dependence on something else exists, until then, there will be fear from the lord. Therefore, those who resort to the gunas and

---

[1073] Interpreted as rituals and sacrifices.

[1074] One parardha is fifty years of Brahma's life. So two parardhas is 100 years of Brahma's life.

are absorbed in them are confounded and lament. When there is imbalance in the gunas, I am addressed by different names—time, atman, agama, the world, nature, dharma and so on."

'Uddhava asked, "O lord! In the body, the jivatman is born with the gunas and exists amidst them. How can it not be covered and bound by the gunas? Alternatively, how can it be bound by them? What are the signs of it existing, amusing itself, enjoying itself, letting go, lying down, being seated, or leaving? O Achyuta! O supreme among those who can answer questions! Tell me this. How can it always be bound? How can it always be free? This is the doubt that I have."'

Chapter 11(11)

'The illustrious one said, "I am bound" or "I am free", such descriptions are for the gunas, not in reality. The gunas have their roots in maya. For me, there is no bondage or liberation. Grief, confusion, happiness, unhappiness and the state of the body result from maya. What one sees in a dream is not spoken of as real. It is the same with samsara. O Uddhava! Among embodied creatures, knowledge and ignorance have existed since the beginning and have been fashioned by my maya, leading to bondage or liberation. O immensely intelligent one! The jivatman is part of my portion, but is bound because of ignorance. The state of liberation occurs through knowledge. I will speak to you about the contrary signs of bondage and liberation. O son![1075] Though existing in the same body, these are opposite kinds of tendencies. These are like two birds which are similar and are friends.[1076] By chance, they have made their nest on the same tree. One of them eats the fruits of the *pippala* tree. The

---

[1075] The word used is *tata*.

[1076] The word used for bird is *suparna*. One of these birds is the jivatman, the other is the paramatman. The jivatman eats the fruits of the pippala (the holy fig) tree, that is, enjoys the fruits of karma. The tree is a metaphor for the body.

other one does not eat, but is stronger. The one who does not eat the fruits of the pippala tree has knowledge and knows himself, as well as the other one. However, this is not true of the one who eats the fruits of the pippala tree. He is full of ignorance and is always bound. The one who possesses knowledge is always free. Like a person waking up from sleep, the learned person knows that he is in a body, but is not the body. However, like seeing something in a dream, an evil-minded person is in the body and does not know that he is not the body. A learned person accepts the senses and the objects of the senses, knowing that these attributes are products of the gunas. He is not attached to an act as an agent. However, an ignorant person exists in this body and, driven by destiny, performs acts through the senses, which are the products of the gunas. He takes himself to be the agent and is bound. Thus, in acts of lying down, sitting, walking, bathing, seeing, touching, inhaling, eating, hearing and other things, the learned person is not bound. He knows that these are experienced by the gunas. Though he exists in the material body, he is not touched, just as the sky, the sun or the wind are not attached. His vision is accomplished and sharpened through non-attachment and his doubts are dispelled. Like a person who has woken up from sleep, he turns away from these things. When a person's breath of life, senses, mind, intelligence and conduct are devoid of desire, even though he is in a body, he is not bound by the gunas. A learned person is not affected when he is injured through violence, nor if he is worshipped by chance. He does not praise or criticize, regardless of what is done or said, good or bad. Delinked from good and evil, a sage is impartial in his outlook. He does not speak anything, or think about doing anything, good or bad. He takes pleasure in his own atman. With this kind of conduct, a sage roams around, like a dumb person. If a person is accomplished in the sacred texts about the brahman, but he is not immersed in the supreme, all his efforts bear no fruit. These are like the efforts of a person who tends to a cow that yields no milk. O dear one! If a person maintains a cow that has already been milked[1077] or maintains an unchaste wife, if his body is under

---

[1077] In the sense that the cow is old and can no longer be milked again.

someone else's control, if his offspring are wicked, if his wealth is
not used for worthy purposes, or if his words are not used to speak
about me, he is a person who moves from one misery to another
misery. O dear one! Words that speak about my deeds of creation,
preservation and destruction, my avataras, births and pastimes,
are those that purify the worlds. Words that do not speak about
these are barren and the intelligent do not accept them. Having thus
inquired, one must give up the error about the atman being many.
The mind must be immersed in the all-pervasive me and everything
else must be given up. If you are incapable of fixing your mind in
the brahman in an unwavering fashion, render all acts to me and
undertake them with indifference.[1078] O Uddhava! Listen faithfully
to extremely auspicious narrations about me. They purify the
worlds. Repeatedly chant, remember and enact my birth and deeds.
Seeking refuge in me, undertake dharma, artha and kama for my
sake. In this way, you will obtain unwavering devotion in me, the
eternal one. A person who associates with virtuous people develops
devotion towards me and worships me. Hence, he easily obtains my
abode, seen by virtuous people."

'Uddhava asked, "O Uttamashloka! O lord! In your view,
what kind of a person is virtuous? What kind of devotion towards
you is approved of by virtuous people? O controller and supreme
being! O controller of the worlds! O lord of the universe! I am
bowing down before you. I am devoted to you. I am seeking shelter
in you. Please tell me this. You are the brahman. You are the
paramatman. You are detached like the sky. You are the supreme
being. You are superior to Prakriti. O illustrious one! It is because
of your own wishes that you assume different kinds of forms and
descend."

'The illustrious one replied, "A sage is compassionate and does
not injure others. He is forgiving towards all creatures. He bases
himself only on the truth and his atman is without blemish. He is
impartial and always tries to help others. His mind is not affected
by desire. He is mild and controlled. He is pure and possesses
nothing. He is not attached to this world. He eats moderately and

[1078] Without expecting the fruits.

is serene and steady. He seeks refuge in me. He is not distracted. His intelligence is deep. He is determined and has conquered the six attributes.[1079] He is not proud, but honours others. He is willing to teach and friendly. He is merciful and wise. He knows his own dharma and what I have instructed about good and bad. However, he ignores them and worships me.[1080] Such a person is supreme. Those who worship me may or may not know my nature. However, because they single-mindedly worship me, they are regarded as the supreme among devotees. O Uddhava! Seeing, touching and worshipping my signs and people who are devoted to me; serving, praising and chanting about my qualities and deeds; devotion towards hearing about my account and meditating on me; rendering everything that has been obtained and their own selves to me; immersing themselves in accounts of my deeds and taking delight in my festivals; singing, dancing, playing musical instruments and engaging in collective festivities in my temples; going on pilgrimages and rendering me the sanctioned offerings at the time of all the annual festivals; getting initiated into methods of worshipping me through the Vedas and the tantras and observing my vows; singly, and with others, making efforts to erect my images; constructing gardens, groves, pleasure grounds, cities and temples; like a servant, rendering service at my temples without any duplicity, through sweeping, smearing, sprinkling and ornamenting; being without pride, insolence and self-praise; not using anything that is offered to me, not even the light of a lamp; rendering everything that is loved in this world, including what is most dear, to me—these are the things that make one qualified for the infinite. O fortunate one! The sun, the fire, brahmanas, cattle, Vaishnavas, the sky, the wind, the water, the earth, the atman and all creatures—these are places where I am worshipped. I am worshipped in the sun with hymns from the three Vedas. I am worshipped in the fire through the oblations that are offered. O dear one! In the best of brahmanas, I am worshipped through hospitality. I am worshipped in cattle with grass and other things. Through fraternal affection, I am worshipped

---

[1079] As in worries—hunger, thirst, grief, infatuation, old age, death.
[1080] He has transcended all injunctions.

in Vaishnavas. In the heart and in the sky, I am worshipped through faithful meditation. I am worshipped in the best of the wind through intelligence.[1081] I am worshipped in the water through various objects[1082] mixed with water. I am worshipped in the earth with various mantras. I am worshipped in one's own atman with objects of pleasure. I am worshipped in all creatures as the atman that is in their hearts. I am the kshetrajna who is there in all creatures. Those who worship me are impartial and see me everywhere. In these places of worship, one must control oneself and serenely meditate and worship me in my four-armed form, with a conch shell, chakra, mace and lotus. If a person controls himself and worships me through sacrifices and civic works, he develops devotion towards me. Through serving virtuous people, remembrance about me is generated. O Uddhava! In general, there is no means other than *bhakti yoga* and association with the virtuous. This is generally the best, because I support the virtuous."'

Chapter 11(12)

'The illustrious one said, "The control of yoga, samkhya, dharma, studying, austerities, renunciation, sacrifices, civic works, donations, vows, worshipping through mantras, tirthas, niyama and yama cannot capture me as easily as does association with the virtuous. That destroys all attachment. From one yuga to another yuga, many creatures have obtained me through association with the virtuous—daityas, yatudhanas, animals, birds, gandharvas, apsaras, nagas, Siddhas, charanas, guhyakas, vidyadharas, humans, vaishyas, shudras, women, outcastes and those who were dominated by rajas and tamas in their nature. There were Vrishaparva, Bali, Bana, Maya, Vibhishana, Sugriva, Hanuman, Riksha,[1083] the elephant, the

---

[1081] The best of the wind means the vital prana.
[1082] Like sesamum seeds and rice.
[1083] Jambavat.

eagle,[1084] Vanikpatha,[1085] the hunter,[1086] the gopis from Vraja and the wives of the brahmanas who were performing the sacrifice. They did not study large numbers of sacred texts. They did not worship great people. They did not observe vows, or torment themselves through austerities. They associated with those who were devoted to me and obtained me. It is only through devotion towards me that gopis, cattle, trees,[1087] animals and others with inferior intelligence and nagas[1088] became successful and easily obtained me. However, I cannot be obtained by making efforts through yoga, samkhya, donations, vows, austerities, sacrifices, expounding of the sacred texts, studying and sannyasa. With Rama, Shvaphalka[1089] brought me to Mathura. Because of their intense love, their[1090] hearts were devoted to me. As a result of separation from me, they suffered from great distress and could not find any happiness. I was their dearly beloved and they had spent nights with me in Vrindavana. When I was with them, they seemed to pass like half a kshana. O dear one! However, without me, it was like a kalpa. Rivers that enter the waters of the ocean no longer retain their names and forms. This is also true of sages immersed in meditation. Like that, bound in their association with me, their minds could not think of their own selves, or anything near or far. Those women desired me as a lover and did not know about my true form. However, through their association with me, hundreds and thousands of them obtained the supreme brahman. O Uddhava! Therefore, give up the primary injunctions and the secondary injunctions, pravritti and nivritti, what has been learnt and what is yet to be learnt. Seek refuge in me alone. I am in the atmans of all embodied creatures. Those who seek me with all their souls are granted freedom from fear by me."

[1084] Jatayu.

[1085] A merchant from Kashi, also known as Tuladhara. He taught dharma to the sage Jajali. This is a story from the Mahabharata.

[1086] This is Dharmavyadha from the Mahabharata, who taught dharma to the sage Koushika.

[1087] This is probably an allusion to the twin arjuna trees.

[1088] A specific example being Kaliya.

[1089] Akrura.

[1090] Specifically, the gopis. In general, the residents of Vraja.

'Uddhava said, "O lord of the lords of yoga! I have heard your words. But there is still a doubt and it does not go away. Therefore, my mind is in a whirl."

'The illustrious one replied, "He manifests himself inside the jivatman who has been given life. Through the sound of prana, he enters the cave. He assumes a subtle mental form. He is *matra*, *svara*, *varna* and *sthavishtha*.[1091] The fire exists as space in kindling. When two pieces of kindling are rubbed together with force, it is kindled by the heat and the wind acts like a friend and fans it. When a small spark has been ignited, oblations make it blaze up. That is the way I am manifested through speech. Like speech, action, locomotion, evacuation of urine and excrement, smell, taste, sight, touch, hearing, resolution, vijnana, ego, Pradhana and the transformations of sattva, rajas and tamas are my manifestations. I am the one who gives life. I am the refuge of the three gunas. I am the source of the cosmic lotus. I am unmanifest. I am alone and absolute. In the course, I divide and manifest my potencies in many different ways. I am like the seeds that appear in fields. Like a piece of cloth exists in the warp and woof of threads, I am woven into the universe and exist in it. This tree of samsara is ancient and based on karma. It yields flowers and fruits. It has two seeds, one hundred roots and three stalks.[1092] There are five major branches and these give rise to five kinds of juice.[1093] There are eleven smaller branches and two birds in the nest, with three kinds of bark.[1094] There are two fruits

[1091] There are many hidden meanings inside this shloka. For instance, the manifestation is in *muladhara chakra* and the cave is *svadhishthana chakra*. There is an implicit reference to ascending upwards, to the manipura and *vishuddha chakra*s. *Nada* is the sound of prana. Matra indicates the time taken by an akshara, svara is a vowel, varna is a letter and sthavishtha is the gross form of speech.

[1092] The two seeds are good deeds (*punya*) and bad deeds (*papa*), the roots are desires and the three stalks are sattva, rajas and tamas.

[1093] The five major branches are the five elements and the five kinds of juice are the objects of the five senses.

[1094] The eleven smaller branches are the five senses of perception, the five senses of action and the mind, the two birds are the jivatman and the paramatman and the three kinds of bark are wind, bile and phlegm.

and they enter the sun.[1095] Vultures that dwell in villages[1096] eat only one kind of fruit. There are others who reside in the forest and eat the other kind of fruit. They are the swans[1097] who worship the absolute who appears in many kinds of forms. A person who knows that all this is formed out of maya is a person who truly knows. In this way, worship the preceptor; have single-minded devotion towards me; use the sharp axe of knowledge; persevere, sever the residence of the jivatman; be without distraction; realize the atman; after that, cast aside the weapon.'"[1098]

Chapter 11(13)

'The illustrious one said, "The gunas of sattva, rajas and tamas concern the intelligence, not the atman. Using sattva, one should destroy the other two. Then, one should use sattva to subdue sattva. Through sattva, dharma is enhanced and a person develops the signs of devotion towards me. Sattva develops from the use of things that are *sattvika* in nature and dharma is furthered through this. Dharma destroys rajas and tamas and there is the excellent outcome of sattva being enhanced. When these two are destroyed, the foundation of adharma is quickly destroyed. A guna is the outcome of ten things—sacred texts, offspring, the place, time, karma, birth, meditation, mantras and samskaras. Among these, what the elders have spoken about is sattvika. What they have criticized is *tamasika*. What they are indifferent to is *rajasika*. For the enhancement of sattva, a man must cultivate things that are sattvika. That leads to dharma. That leads to jnana. That drives away loss of memory. A fire is generated from the friction of bamboos and that burns down the forest of bamboos. In that way,

---

[1095] The two fruits are joy and misery and entering the sun means going beyond samsara.

[1096] A pun indicating those addicted to vulgar pleasures.

[1097] *Hamsa*s.

[1098] The weapon of knowledge. It is no longer needed.

the body is the consequence of disequilbrium among the gunas and their interaction destroys it."

'Uddhava asked, "O Krishna! Mortal people generally know that gratification due to material objects is the cause of hardships. Nevertheless, like dogs, mules and goats, why do they pursue them?"

'The illustrious one replied, "It is ahamkara that leads to this perversion of intelligence and the heart becomes distracted. Though the mind is born from sattva, terrible rajas takes over. When the mind is full of rajas, resolutions and doubts result. In evil-minded people, this leads to thinking about the qualities of desirable things and this is impossible to resist. He is not in control of his senses and overtaken by desire, he performs corresponding acts. Though he can see the hardships this will bring about, he is confounded by the force of rajas. Even if a learned person's intelligence is agitated by rajas and tamas, with an unwavering mind, he must clearly see the taints and not get attached. Without getting distracted and distressed, he must gradually fix his mind on me, having conquered his breathing and having conquered his posture. This is the yoga that was taught to my disciples, Sanaka and the others. This is the means of withdrawing the mind and immersing it in me."

'Uddhava asked, "O Keshava! When, and in what form, did you instruct Sanaka and the others about this yoga? I wish to know about this."

'The illustrious one replied, "Sanaka and the others were born through the mental powers of Hiranyagarbha.[1099] They asked their father about the subtle yoga that leads to the supreme destination.'

'"Sanaka and the others asked, 'O lord! The mind gets attracted to the attributes of material objects and those attributes enter the mind. How can one give up the relationship between the two? How can a person who desires liberation transcend these?'"

'The illustrious one continued, "The great divinity, Svayambhu, the creator of beings, was asked in this way. However, his mind was fixed on the act of creation and he could not identify the fundamental answer. The divinity wished to know the ultimate

[1099] Brahma.

answer to the question and thought about me. I appeared before him in the form of a swan. Seeing me, with Brahma at the forefront, they approached me and worshipped my feet. They asked, 'Who are you?' The sages wished to know about the truth and asked me this. O Uddhava! Listen to what I told them. 'O brahmanas! If this differentiation and multiplicity does not exist in the atman, how can such a question arise? What is the basis for me to answer?[1100] All living beings are made out of the five elements and therefore, they are essentially the same. "Who are you?" is a question whose words mean nothing. Everything perceived by the mind, spoken about in speech, seen through the eyes, or visualized by the other senses, is nothing but me. You must understand this. O offspring! The mind gets attracted to the attributes of material objects and the attributes enter the minds. In the jivatman's body, both the attributes and the mind relate to an atman that has me as the basis. Repeatedly realizing my form, a person must give up both—the attributes of material objects that enter the mind and the material objects, which also result from the mind. Being awake, sleeping and sushupti are states of the mind caused by the gunas. As a witness, the jivatman should ascertain that he is distinct from them. Because of the functioning of the gunas, the jivatman is bound to samsara. He should immerse himself in me, the state of turiya. He should thus renounce and discard both the attributes of material objects and the mind. Ahamkara creates the bondage of the atman and leads to its hardships. Therefore, a learned person must be detached and must give up all thoughts of samsara, basing himself on the turiya state. As long as a man does not use his reasoning to free his intelligence of this notion of many kinds of diversity, he is ignorant. Even though he is awake, he is asleep, like a person who takes himself to be awake in his dreams. Any states of existence that are separate from the atman, any differences that are created by them and any such objectives and causes are not real. They are false, like things seen in a dream. In a state of wakefulness, a person who is a lord of the senses uses his senses of perception and

---

[1100] Since I am not a person who is different from you, how can you ask me the question?

action to experience all external objects, knowing that their nature is temporary; in a state of sleep, he does that mentally; and in a state of sushupti, he withdraws them. He alone understands the functioning of the three states and remembers himself. Having thus considered the gunas, the mind and the three states of consciousness, one must firmly arrive at the determination that these have been caused by my maya and are imposed on me.[1101] Inference and the words of the virtuous are the sharp sword of jnana that can be used to sever the sources of all doubts that are in the heart. Hence, worship me. One must see that this universe is an illusion caused by the working of the mind. It can be seen today, but it will be destroyed tomorrow. It is extremely evanescent, like the circle of fire caused by a firebrand. In vijnana, it exists as one. It appears in many forms because of maya. The three states of consciousness, sleeping and the others, are caused by the transformation of the gunas. They are nothing but perception. Therefore, one must withdraw one's vision and refrain from all kinds of thirst. One must be silent and experience happiness in one's own atman. For this world, one must not strive for anything. Using one's intelligence, it can be observed that nothing in this material world is real. Until the moment of death, one must remember this and give up this illusion. A person who is a Siddha has comprehended his true nature. He does not notice whether this transient body is standing, or is seated. He does not care whether this body is destroyed by destiny, or whether he obtains a new one through destiny.[1102] This is like a person intoxicated with liquor not noticing whether he is wearing clothes or not. Karma has brought this body into being and therefore, it continues to strive, remaining alive and waiting. However, it is under the control of destiny. Established in *samadhi yoga*, one must transcend these illusory manifestations. Like a

[1101] By the jivatman, they are not real.

[1102] The word *daiva* is used twice, once for the present body being destroyed, the second time for a new body being obtained. Daiva can mean the result of one's past karma, destiny, or the supreme one's will. Depending on the view one takes, different permutations and combinations of meaning are possible.

woken up from a dream, such a person does not serve the unreal. O
brahmanas! I have spoken to you about the secret of samkhya and
yoga. Know me as Yajna,[1103] who has come here with the intention
of teaching you about dharma. I am the objective of samkhya, yoga,
satyam,[1104] *ritam*, energy, prosperity, fame and self-control. O best
among brahmanas! I am the ultimate refuge. All the gunas find a
refuge in me. I am nirguna and am non-attached. I am the beloved
friend of the atman. I exist everywhere and am without any kind of
attachment. I am devoid of gunas.' Thus, the doubts of Sanaka and
the other sages were dispelled. They worshipped me with supreme
devotion. They praised me and chanted about me. Those supreme
rishis worshipped me and honoured me properly. While they and
Parameshthi[1105] looked on, I returned to my own abode."'

Chapter 11(14)

'Uddhava asked, "O Krishna! Those who know about the
brahman speak about many ways of ensuring benefit. Many
kinds of alternatives are spoken about as being important. Is there
one that is the most important? O master! You have spoken about
bhakti yoga and removing all kinds of desires and attachments,
whereby, the mind becomes immersed in you."

'The illustrious one replied, "These words of mine came to be
known as the Vedas. In the course of time, they were destroyed in
the deluge. I originally spoke about it to Brahma, the dharma of
devoting one's self to me. He spoke about it to his eldest son, Manu.
The seven brahmana rishis, Bhrigu and the others, learnt it from
him. The offspring learnt it from these ancestors—gods, danavas,
guhyakas, humans, Siddhas, gandharvas, vidyadharas, charanas,

---

[1103] The embodiment of sacrifices, Vishnu.

[1104] Satyam is truth, while ritam can be interpreted in different ways,
divine truth or divine law being one.

[1105] Brahma.

kindevas,[1106] kinnaras, nagas, rakshasas, *kimpurusha*s and others. However, their natures were affected by different combinations of sattva, rajas and tamas. These differences contributed to differences among creatures and their leaders. It is because of these differences in nature that colourful words[1107] flowed out. In this way, because of diversity in nature, there are differences in the views of men. Some of this occurred because of the nature of transmission. There were others who came to hold heretical views. O bull among men! The minds of men were confounded by my maya. Therefore, depending on their activities and their proclivities, they spoke about many kinds of ways of ensuring benefit. Some speak only of dharma.[1108] Others speak of kama. Others speak of truthfulness, self-control and serenity. Others speak of selfish ends and prosperity. Some speak of renunciation and fasting. Others speak of sacrifices, austerities, donations, vows, niyama and yama. All the worlds obtained through karma have a beginning and an end. They inevitably give rise to misery, darkness, inferiority, wretchedness and lamentation. O noble one! Those who have immersed their atmans in me do not have desire in any form. With their atmans in me, they enjoy a happiness that cannot be obtained by those who pursue material objects. He does not possess anything. He is controlled and serene. He regards everything impartially. His mind is satisfied in me. All the directions bring him happiness. With his atman immersed in me, he desires nothing other than me—not the states of Parameshthi, the great Indra, lordship, sovereignty over the earth, sovereignty over the nether regions, the siddhis of yoga, or emancipation from samsara. I do not love the self-created one,[1109] Shankara, Samkarshana, Shri or my own self as much as I love you.[1110] Such a sage is serene, without any desires. He is without enmity and is impartial in vision. I always follow such a person, so that I can be purified by the dust of his lotus feet. With his mind devoted to me, he desires nothing.

[1106] Minor gods.

[1107] As in different interpretations of the Vedas.

[1108] Interpreted in the narrow sense of the rituals of the Vedas.

[1109] Brahma.

[1110] That is, as much as I love a devotee like you.

He is tranquil. He is a great soul who is compassionate towards all creatures. His intelligence is not affected by the objects of desire he has not obtained. He is devoted to me and without any desires, experiences a happiness not obtained by anyone else. A person who is devoted to me may not have conquered his senses. Therefore, he may be agitated by the objects of desire. But because his devotion is powerful, he will not be overcome by the objects of the senses. O Uddhava! The flames of a blazing fire reduce the kindling to ashes. Just like that, devotion towards me burns down all sins. O Uddhava! What is achieved by strong devotion towards me is not achieved by yoga, samkhya, dharma, studying, austerities or renunciation. My atman can only be grasped through devotion. I am dear to the virtuous. Even if a person is born as a *svapacha*, devotion and faith towards me purifies him. Without devotion towards me, a person cannot completely purify himself through dharma, truth, compassion, learning and austerities. Without the body hair standing up, without the heart being melted, without tears of bliss flowing from the eyes, without devotion, how can the consciousness be purified? If a person is filled with devotion towards me, he purifies the universe. His speech is choked. His heart melts. He weeps repeatedly. Sometimes, he smiles. Without any shame, he sings and dances. Heated in a fire, gold gives up all its impurities and regains its pure form. When I am worshipped through bhakti yoga, the atman is cleansed from the impurities of karma. The more one hears about my sacred accounts and chants them, the atman is cleansed. Accordingly, a person perceives the subtle truth, like the eye when it is treated with medicinal collyrium. When the mind thinks about material objects, it gets attached to material objects. When the mind remembers me, it becomes absorbed in me. Therefore, like the wishes in a dream, everything material must be given up. The mind must be fixed in me and must think about me. A person who knows about his atman must keep women, and those who associate with women, far away. Fearless, he must be seated in a solitary spot, single-mindedly thinking about me. In that state, there is no hardship and no bondage that results from other associations. This is unlike a man who associate with women or associates with those who associate with them."

'Uddhava asked, "O lotus-eyed one! If a person desires to meditate on you, what is the nature of your form that he should use? You should tell me about how he should meditate."

'The illustrious one replied, "He must be comfortably seated on a level seat. He must be upright. His palms must be gathered together on his lap. He must fix his eyes on the tip of his nose. Through *puraka*, *kumbhaka* and *rechaka*, he must purify the path of prana.[1111] He must gradually reverse the process and conquer all his senses. Like the thread that runs up the stem of a lotus, he must continuously raise his prana upwards to his heart, to the sound of *omkara*, which resounds like the sound of a bell. There, prana must be merged with the vibrations of the sound. In this way, he must practise prana being united with the sound of omkara. Thrice a day, morning, noon and evening, this must be done ten times. Within a month, he will then obtain control over prana. He must contemplate that the heart inside his body is like a lotus, with the stalk facing upwards. This lotus, with eight petals, has bloomed and the pericarp faces upwards. One after another, the sun, the moon and the fire are placed in his pericarp. He must remember my auspicious form inside the fire and meditate on it. My form is serene and symmetrical, with an excellent face. My four arms are long and beautiful. His neck is charming and beautiful. I have excellent cheeks, with a pure smile. My symmetrical ears are adorned with dazzling earrings that are shaped like makaras. My garments are golden yellow and my complexion is dark blue. The shrivatsa mark is on my chest, Shri's abode. I am ornamented with a conch shell, a chakra, a mace, a lotus and a garland of wild flowers. My feet have shining anklets. Koustubha adds to my radiance. I wear a resplendent diadem, bracelets, armlets and a girdle. All my limbs are beautiful and charming. My supreme glance bestows favours.

[1111] Prana draws breath into the body, *apana* exhales it. *Ayama* means control or restraint, so pranayama is control of the breath of life. Pranayama has three components—puraka, rechaka and kumbhaka. Puraka is when the inhaled apana air fills up the exhaled prana air and temporarily stops its exit. Rechaka is when the exhaled prana air stops the entry of the inhaled apana air. Kumbhaka is when prana and apana are both controlled and the air is restrained inside the body.

He must fix his mind on all my charming limbs and meditate on them. He must withdraw his mind from the senses and the objects of the senses, which distract the mind. A persevering person will use his intelligence like the driver of a chariot. He will fix everything in me. When the consciousness has spread over all of my limbs, it must then be withdrawn and fixed on only one specific limb. All the thoughts must be gathered and fixed on my smiling and handsome face. Once that state has been attained, the consciousness must be withdrawn and fixed on the sky. Having given that up next, he ascends upwards to me and thinks of nothing else. In this way, his intelligence is controlled and immersed in me. He sees my atman in his atman. He sees me in all atmans, like a blaze of light united with other lights. The yogi's mind is thus fixed in extremely intense meditation. Perceptions and illusions about material objects and their functions quickly vanish and he achieves nirvana."'

Chapter 11(15)

'The illustrious one said, "If a yogi conquers his senses, conquers his breath and fixes his consciousness in me, the siddhis appear before him."

'Uddhava asked, "O Achyuta! What is the type of meditation and what is its form? How many siddhis are there? You are the one who bestows siddhis on yogis. Tell me about this."

'The illustrious one replied, "Those who are accomplished in the yoga of meditation have said that there are eighteen siddhis. Among these, eight are major and are in me. The other ten have the gunas as a cause.[1112] O amiable one! It is held that there are eight supernormal powers[1113] that have an origin in me—anima, mahima,

---

[1112] The major eight are bestowed by me and help to obtain me. The other ten have an origin in *sattva guna* and are for enjoying material objects.

[1113] Yoga leads to eight major siddhis or powers. These are anima (becoming as small as one desires), mahima (as large as one desires), laghima (as light as one wants), garima (as heavy as one wants), prapti (obtaining

burdening the body, laghima, using the senses for prapti, prakamya
over visible and invisible things, using powers for the sake of *ishita*
and *vashita*, so that one is not attached to the gunas. Through these,
one can get whatever one wants. Immunity from any changes in
the body; the ability to hear and see from a distance; the power to
use the mind to travel; the ability to assume any form one wants;
to enter someone else's body; to die whenever one wills; the ability
to see the gods play; the ability to play with them; the capacity to
accomplish one's resolutions; and like a king, to be unimpeded in
progress.[1114] The ability to know the past, the present and the future;
the power to transcend the opposite pairs of sentiments; the ablity
to decipher the minds of others; the power to counter the effects of
fire, sun, water and poison; the ability to remain undefeated—these
have also been described as siddhis obtained through yoga and
meditation. I will tell you which is obtained through what process
of meditation. Listen. If a person worships me as existing in the
form of the tanmatras and meditates on my subtle atman existing
in the elements, he obtains the power of anima. If a person fixes his
mind on my atman existing in pervasive form in the tattva of Mahat,
he obtains mahima. As he separately meditates on each element,
he obtains the pervasive nature of that element. If a person fixes
his mind on me being attached to the paramanus of the elements
and on me as the subtle form of time, that yogi obtains laghima.
If a person is immersed in me and meditates on me as *vaikarika
ahamkara* and on me existing in all the senses, he obtains prapti.
If a person fixes his mind and meditates on my atman existing in
the *sutra* of Mahat, an unmanifest form that cannot be perceived,
he obtains the supreme power of prakamya. Vishnu is the lord of
the three gunas, time is his personified form. If a person meditates
with me in his mind in this form, he obtains ishita over all bodies
and can urge their souls too. I am Narayana, known as turiya. I am
addressed by the name of Bhagavan. If a yogi fixes his mind on me

what one wants), prakamya (travelling where one wants), vashita (powers
to control creatures) and ishita (obtaining divine powers).

[1114] The sentence doesn't have a noun or a verb in the Sanskrit. These
are the ten minor powers.

in this form, he obtains my attributes and the power of vashita. If a person purifies his mind and meditates on me in the form of the *nirguna brahman*, he obtains the supreme state of bliss, known as *kamavasiyata*.[1115] I am pure and the lord of Shvetadvipa. I am full of dharma. If a man fixes his mind on me and meditates on me in this form, he becomes white in complexion and is freed from the six changes.[1116] I am the atman in the sky. I am the transcendental vibrations. I am prana. If a person meditates on me in this form, such a hamsa can hear the speech of all creatures. The vision must be united with the sun and the sun must be united with the vision. If a person uses his mind to meditate on me in this form, he can see anything in the universe, even from a distance. When the mind, the body and the breath of life are immersed in me and a person meditates on me, through that power, the person can transport his body to wherever the mind wants. Whatever form the mind wants to assume, whatever form the mind thinks of, a person is able to appear in that form. This happens by resorting to the strength of my yoga. If a Siddha wants to enter another person's body, he must meditate on himself in that other person's body. Just as a bee moves from a flower to another flower, his prana will then leave his body, travel through the air and then enter the other person's body. A person blocks his anus with the heel of his foot, raising the prana up from the heart to the throat, the head and the crown of the head.[1117] He propels it through the aperture in the crown of the head, leaves his body and attains the brahman. If a person wishes to amuse himself with the gods, he must meditate on me in the form of sattva. Celestial women, who are full of sattva by nature, will then arrive before him in vimanas. If a man unites his mind in me, the supreme truth, he obtains whatever resolution his intelligence has sought to achieve. I am the lord. If a man is full of me and meditates on me as the lord, how can he be frustrated in any way?

[1115] In the list of the eight major powers, garima seems to have been replaced with kamavasiyata.

[1116] White in complexion stands for purity. The six changes are hunger, thirst, old age, death, delusion and grief.

[1117] This is the description of a person who can die whenever he wills.

His command is like my own. If a yogi has become pure because of his devotion to me and if he knows about the process of meditation, he can know about the past, the present and the future and about birth and death. If a sage's body has been perfected with yoga, fire and other things cannot harm him, just as aquatic creatures are not harmed by water. Because of yoga towards me, his mind is serene. My opulent form is ornamented with shrivatsa, weapons, the standard, the umbrella and whisks. If a person meditates on this, he cannot be defeated. If a devoted sage uses yoga to meditate on me, he approaches me in every way and obtains the siddhis that have been described earlier. If a sage has conquered his senses, if he is controlled and if he has conquered his breath of life and his mind, if he is immersed in me and meditates on me, what siddhi will be impossible for him to obtain? But those who are engaged in supreme yoga say that these are nothing but impediments. For those who wish to obtain me, these are nothing but a waste of time. Birth, herbs, austerities and mantras can accomplish siddhis. But all these can be obtained through yoga and the destination obtained by yoga cannot be obtained through these other means. I am the cause and the master of all these siddhis. I am the lord of yoga, samkhya, dharma and those who speak about the brahman. I cannot be covered and am inside and outside all embodied beings. The elements exist inside and outside all beings and I am myself like that.'"

Chapter 11(16)

'Uddhava said, "You are yourself the supreme brahman. You have no beginning and no end. You are not covered. You are the source of the creation, preservation and destruction of all beings. You exist in all beings, superior and inferior. For those who have not cleansed their atmans, you are impossible to comprehend. O illustrious one! Brahmanas worship you exactly as you are. The supreme rishis have devotedly worshipped you and obtained success. What are the forms in which they have worshipped you?

Please tell me. O creator of all beings! Though you are in the atmans of all creatures, your movements are hidden. Though you see them, because they are confounded, the beings cannot see you. O one who is great in powers! What are your powers on earth, in heaven, in the nether regions and in the directions? Please explain those manifestations to me. I bow down before you. Your lotus feet are a refuge for all tirthas."

'The illustrious one replied, "O supreme among those who know how to ask questions! The question that you have asked me is exactly the question that Arjuna, wishing to fight with his rivals, asked me at the time of the destructive battle. For the sake of the kingdom, he was aware that slaying the king was reprehensible adharma. He refrained, thinking, 'They will be killed and I will be the slayer.' He thought in this worldly way. At that time, using reasoning, I made that tiger among men understand. In the field of the battle, he spoke to me in the way that you are doing now. O Uddhava! I am the atman, the controller and the well-wisher of all beings. I am in all beings and exist as the creator, the preserver and the destroyer. For those who move, I am the one who makes them move. I am time, the one who controls everyone. I am the equilibrium of the gunas. I am the attributes among those who naturally possess attributes. I am the sutra that strings together the gunas among those who possess them. Among those that are large, I am the great principle of Mahat. Among those that are subtle, I am the principle of life. Among those who cannot be conquered, I am the mind. Among the Vedas, I am Hiranyagarbha.[1118] Among mantras, I am 'Oum', consisting of three syllables. Among letters of the alphabet, I am the first letter, 'A'. Among metres, I am *gayatri*.[1119] Among all the gods, I am Indra. Among all the Vasus, I am the one who bears oblations.[1120] Among all the Adityas, I

[1118] Brahma.

[1119] Gayatri is a metre, as well as a mantra. The gayatri metre has three lines. The text refers to the gayatri metre indirectly, referring to it as one with lines.

[1120] That is, the fire god.

am Vishnu. Among all the Rudras, I am Nilalohita.[1121] Among all the brahmana rishis, I am Bhrigu. Among all the royal sages, I am Manu. Among all the devarshis, I am Narada. Among all the cows, I am the one who supplies oblations.[1122] Among all the lords of siddhis, I am Kapila. Among all the birds, I am Suparna. Among all the Prajapatis, I am Daksha. Among all the ancestors, I am Aryama. O Uddhava! Among all the daityas, know me to be Prahlada, the lord of the asuras. Among the nakshatras and the herbs, I am Soma. Among the yakshas and the rakshasas, I am the lord of riches.[1123] Among the Indras of the elephants, I am Airavata. Among aquatic creatures, I am Lord Varuna. Among those who heat and illuminate, I am Surya. Among human beings, I am the king. Among horses, I am Ucchaihshrava. Among metals, I am gold. Among those who chastise, I am Yama. Among snakes, I am Vasuki. Among Indras of the nagas, I am Ananta. Among those with horns and teeth, I am the lion. O unblemished one! I am the fourth ashrama and the first varna. Among tirthas and rivers that flow, I am Ganga. Among bodies of water, I am the ocean. Among weapons, I am the bow. Among those who wield bows, I am the destroyer of Tripura.[1124] Among all abodes, I am Meru. Among inaccessible places, I am the Himalayas. Among trees, I am the ashvattha. Among plants, I am barley. Among priests, I am Vasishtha. Among those who know about the brahman, I am Brihaspati. Among all the commanders of armies, I am Skanda. Among all the foremost ones, I am the illustrious Aja.[1125] Among sacrifices, I am sacrifices at which the Vedas are recited. Among vows, I am non-violence. Among things that purify, wind, fire, sun, water and speech, I am the power of purification. Among the different stages of yoga, I am *samadhi*. Among those who seek to conquer, I am wise counsel. Among those who seek to inquire, I am skill. Among those who engage in philosophical debate, I am diversity of views. Among women, I am

---

[1121] That is, Shiva.
[1122] That is, *kamadhenu*.
[1123] That is, Kubera.
[1124] Shiva.
[1125] Brahma.

Shatarupa. Among men, I am Svayambhuva Manu. Among sages, I am Narayana. Among *brahmacharis*, I am Kumara.[1126] Among different kinds of dharma, I am *sannyasa*. Among different kinds of assurance, I am the intelligence that exists internally. Among methods of ensuring secrecy, I am pleasant speech and silence. Among different kinds of couples, I am Aja.[1127] Among the different measures of time, I am the year. Among the seasons, I am spring. Among the months, I am Margashirsha. Among the nakshatras, I am Abhijit. Among the yugas, I am krita. Among those who are patient, I am Asita and Devala. Among all those known as Vyasa, I am Dvaipayana. Among wise ones, I am Kavya,[1128] who knew about the atman. Among illustrious ones, I am Vasudeva. Among those who are devoted to the illustrious one, I am you. Among kimpurushas, I am Hanuman. Among vidyadharas, I am Sudarshana. Among gems, I am the ruby. Among delicate and lovely objects, I am the bud of a lotus. Among different kinds of *darbha* grass, I am kusha. Among oblations, I am oblations that come from a cow's milk. Among merchants, I am Lakshmi. Among gamblers, I am the attribute of deceit. Among those who tolerate, I am the quality of tolerating. Among those who are enterprising, I am the attribute of enterprise. Among the powerful, I am physical and mental strength. Know me to be the devoted activities my devotees engage in. My devotees worship me in nine forms.[1129] Among these, I am the original and primary form.[1130] Among the gandharvas, I am Vishvavasu. Among the apsaras, I am Purvachitti. I am the stability of the mountains. In earth, I am the attribute of smell. Among liquids, I am the taste in the water. Among objects that are extremely radiant, I am the sun. I am the radiance of the sun, the moon and the stars. I am the transcendental sound in the sky. Among those who are devoted to brahmanas, I am Bali. Among those who are brave, I am Arjuna.

[1126] That is, Sanatkumara.

[1127] Brahma divided himself into man and woman.

[1128] Shukracharya.

[1129] Vasudeva, Samkarshana, Pradyumna, Aniruddha, Narayana, Hayagriva, Varaha, Narasimha and Vamana.

[1130] Vasudeva.

I am the lord of the creation, preservation and destruction of beings.[1131] I am the function of the organs of action, movement, speech, excretion, receiving and pleasure,[1132] and also that of touch, taste, hearing, sight and smell. I am the power behind all the senses. I am the subtle forms of earth, air, space, water, fire, ahamkara and Mahat. I am the transformations. I am Prakriti and Purusha. I am sattva, rajas and tamas. I am the supreme one. I am all that has been ascertained about the truth and spoken about. I am jnana. I am the quality of life in living beings. I am the gunas and the quality of these gunas. I am in all atmans. I am in everything. Nothing exists without me. Over a period of time, even if I count all the paramanus, I will not be able to count all my opulences. I create crores of cosmic eggs. Energy, prosperity, fame, affluence, modesty, renunciation, good fortune, the quality of being pleasant, valour, fortitude and knowledge—in all of these, my manifestations exist. I have briefly described all my opulences to you. These are nothing but transformations of the mind and are described in various ways through words. Control your speech. Control your mind. Control your breath of life. Control your senses. Use your atman to control yourself, so that you do not descend into material existence yet again. If a mendicant does not properly control his speech and mind through his intelligence, his vows, austerities and gifts leak out, like water from a pot that has not been baked. Therefore, with devotion towards me, control your speech, mind and breath of life. Using the intelligence to be fixed in devotion towards me, one completes the process.'"[1133]

Chapter 11(17)

'Uddhava said, "You have earlier spoken about the dharma that is characterized by bhakti, to be observed by those who

---

[1131] Alternatively, of the elements.

[1132] Respectively related to legs, mouth, anus, hands and genital organs.

[1133] That is, one ceases to be part of samsara.

follow the varnas and the ashramas and all men.[1134] O lotus-eyed one! When men are engaged in their own dharma, what can they do to increase their devotion towards you? You should tell me this. O mighty-armed one! O lord! O Madhava! Earlier, in the form of a swan, you spoke about this supreme dharma to Brahma. O destroyer of enemies! However, a long period of time has passed since then. What you had instructed earlier, is not generally witnessed in the mortal world. O Achyuta! With your exception, there is no one on earth, not even in Virinchi's assembly, which the arts attend in personified form, who can propound, act or protect that dharma. O god! O Madhusudana! You are the propounder, the performer and the protector. When you leave the surface of the earth, it will be destroyed. Who will speak about it? You know about all the forms of dharma. Therefore, speak to me about the dharma that is characterized by *bhakti* towards you. Who should practise it and in what form? O lord! Please describe this."'

Shri-Shuka said, 'Thus addressed by the foremost among his servants, the illustrious Hari was pleased. For the benefit of mortals, he spoke about this eternal dharma.

'The illustrious one replied, "Your question is about this dharma and it brings the greatest benefit to men who follow the varnas and the ashramas. O Uddhava! Listen to me. In the beginning, in *krita yuga*, there was only one varna among men and it was known as hamsa. As soon as they were born, subjects accomplished their objectives. That is the reason the learned called it krita yuga.[1135] In that first age, all the Vedas were there in 'Oum'. In the form of a bull, I held up dharma.[1136] Engaged in austerities and free of sins, the hamsas worshipped me. O immensely fortunate one! At the beginning of *treta yuga*, the three Vedas were manifested from my heart as my breath of life. From that knowledge, I was manifested as the three parts of the sacrifice.[1137] From the cosmic Purusha, four

---

[1134] The qualification 'all men' is necessary because some may be outside the varna and ashrama fold.

[1135] The etymology of the word krita means accomplished.

[1136] As a metaphor for the four feet of dharma.

[1137] A reference to the *hotri*, *udgatri* and *adhvaryu*.

categories were born—brahmanas from the mouth, kshatriyas from the arms, vaishyas from the thighs and shudras from the feet. They were characterized by their own conduct. *Garhasthya* appeared from my loins, brahmacharya from my heart, *vanaprastha* from my chest and sannyasa from the top of my head. The varnas and the ashramas followed the order in which they were created. The higher the position, the higher the order of men. The lower the position, the lower the order. The natural attributes of brahmanas are control over the mind, control over the senses, austerities, purity, contentment, fortitude, uprightness, devotion towards me, compassion and truthfulness. The natural attributes of kshatriyas are energy, strength, perseverance, valour, tolerance, generosity, enterprise, steadiness, prosperity and devotion towards brahmanas. The natural attributes of vaishyas are faith, devotion to donating, lack of hypocrisy, dissatisfaction towards wealth[1138] and service towards brahmanas. The natural attributes of shudras are lack of duplicity in serving brahmanas, cattle and gods and satisfaction with whatever has been obtained. The natural attributes of those who are outside the varna system are lack of cleanliness, dishonesty, theft, hereticism, pointless quarrelling, lust, anger and avarice. For all the varnas, dharma consists of non-violence, truth, honesty, lack of desire, anger and greed and a desire to ensure the pleasure and welfare of all beings.

'"A dvija obtains a second birth by gradually going through the investiture of the sacred thread ritual. Controlling himself, he resides in his *guru*'s household and when summoned by the preceptor, studies the sacred texts. During brahmacharya, he wears a girdle made out of munja grass and garments made out of deerskin. He carries a staff, a string of rudraksha beads, the sacred thread and a kamandalu. His hair is matted. His garments must not be washed.[1139] He must not use a polished seat. Instead, he must carry kusha grass for sitting. He must not speak while bathing, eating, offering oblations, chanting mantras and passing stool and urine. He must not clip his nails. Nor must he cut his hair, including

---

[1138] That is, there is an urge to acquire more wealth.

[1139] The sense is that they should not be washed by someone else.

that on his chest or in the pubic region. As long as he follows the vow of brahmacharya, he must never voluntarily allow the passing of semen. It is oozes out involuntarily, he must bathe, practise pranayama and chant the gayatri mantra. Pure and controlled, he must perform worship during the two sandhyas, silently chanting the mantras. He must worship the fire, the sun, the preceptor, cattle, brahmanas, seniors, the aged and the gods. He must know that the preceptor is my own form and never show him disrespect. All the gods exist in the guru. Thinking that he is a mere mortal, one must never envy him. Any alms that have been obtained in the morning and the evening through begging, must be offered to him. Controlling oneself, one must accept whatever has been permitted by the preceptor. Like an inferior person, one must always serve and worship the preceptor. When he goes out, sleeps or is seated, one must be nearby, hands joined in salutation. In this way, devoid of any material gratification, he must reside in his guru's household. Until the process of learning has been completed, he must never deviate from his vows. If he wishes to ascend to Maharloka or Brahmaloka, he must observe that great vow of celibacy throughout his life. For the sake of studying, he must offer his body to the preceptor. I am the supreme, present in the fire, the preceptor, his own atman and in all creatures. He must worship me in this undifferentiated way and resplendent with the radiance of the brahman, he will be cleansed of all sins. A person not in garhasthya must not look at women, touch them, converse with them or joke with them. Nor must he look at creatures engaged in sexual intercourse. O delight of the lineage! There are some rules that are applicable to all the ashramas. These are purity, touching water before any sacred rite, bathing, worship at the time of sandhya, worshipping me, visiting tirthas, chanting, not touching what should not be touched, not eating what should not be eaten, not speaking to those who should not be spoken to, control over mind, speech and body and visualizing me in all creatures. In this way, a brahmana who observes the great vow blazes like a fire. He burns down the store of karma through fierce austerities and devotion towards me. He becomes pure.

"'After having studied the sacred texts properly, a student may wish to enter garhasthya. He must pay his *guru dakshina* and

with the guru's permission, must bathe. He may either go to the
forest, or enter garhasthya. An excellent dvija who is not devoted
to me must always move from one ashrama to another ashrama
in the proper order and never in a contrary way.[1140] A person who
desires to become a householder must marry a wife who is his
equal. She must be younger in age. She must be from the same
varna and one progressively goes down this order.[1141] Performing
sacrifices, studying and donating are meant for all dvijas. But only
brahmanas can receive gifts, teach and officiate at sacrifices. If a
brahmana thinks that receiving gifts will diminish his austerities,
energy and fame, he can use the other two. If he sees those as
unacceptable, he can resort to *shila-unchchha*.[1142] A brahmana's
body must not be used for satisfying inferior objects of desire. It
is meant for hardships and austerities in this world. He obtains
infinite happiness after death. He must satisfy his mind with shila-
unchchha. Purified of all desire, he must observe this great dharma.
Even if he is a householder, he must offer himself to me and not be
excessively attached. He will then obtain serenity. If a brahmana is
suffering and is devoted to me, or if a person helps such a brahmana
and is devoted to me, within a short period of time, I raise them above
all sufferings, like a boat in the ocean. Like a father, a king must
protect his subjects from all hardships, like a leader of elephants
saving all elephants. He must find that perseverance within his own
self. In this way, a king is cleansed of everything inauspicious. He
enjoys himself with Indra, in a vimana that is as dazzling as the
sun. If a brahmana is in the midst of hardships, he can survive
by using the occupation of a merchant and even trade prohibited
objects.[1143] When he is afflicted, he may even earn a living using the
sword. However, he must never follow a dog's conduct.[1144] To earn

[1140] From vanaprastha, one should not return to garhasthya. However,
there is the clause that this progressive order is not binding on devotees.

[1141] This is interpreted in the following way. The first wife has to be
from the same varna. The second wife can be from a lower varna and so on.

[1142] Shila-unchchha means subsistence on the basis of collecting grains
from the ground.

[1143] There are some objects a brahmana is prohibited from trading.

[1144] That is, engage in lowly occupations, or serve inferior masters.

a living, a king may follow the occupation of a vaishya and even earn a living through hunting. He may even follow a brahmana's occupation. But he must never follow a dog's conduct. A vaishya can follow a shudra's occupation. A shudra can be an artisan or make mats. However, once a person is freed from the calamity, he must not engage in occupations that are not sanctioned. According to capacity, studying, offering oblations with *svadha*, offering oblations with *svaha*,[1145] offering food to others and worshipping gods, rishis, ancestors and creatures every day, since these are my forms.[1146] Without causing hardship to dependants and using objects that have come on their own or have been purchased with wealth obtained through legitimate means, one must perform the sacrifices. However, one should not get attached to the family. Nor should one neglect the family. A learned person sees that what cannot be seen is just as temporary as what can be seen.[1147] Sons, wives, relatives and friends are like travellers meeting. When sleep is over, what is seen in a dream is no longer there. Like that, when the body changes, there is separation from these too. Considering this, a person who has been liberated resides in his household like a guest. He is not bound to the house. He is without a sense of 'I' and 'mine'. While performing the tasks of a householder and remaining in that state, he should be devoted to me. Or, if he has had children, he can leave for vanaprastha or sannyasa. A person whose mind is attached to the household is afflicted by the desire for sons and wealth. He is attached to women and his mind becomes miserly and foolish. He is bound down by notions of 'I' and 'mine'. 'Alas! My aged parents. My wife and my infant children. Without me, they won't have a protector and will be distressed. Miserable, how will they remain alive?' Thus, the heart of a person who is attached to the household is agitated. His intelligence is foolish. Thinking

[1145] Svadha is for ancestors, svaha is for gods.
[1146] The sentence lacks a noun. These are tasks for all householders, referred to as *pancha yajna*, the five daily sacrifices for gods, rishis, ancestors, men and non-human creatures.
[1147] What is earned in heaven is as temporary as what is seen in this world.

about these, he is dissatisfied. When he dies, he enters blinding darkness."'

Chapter 11(18)

'The illustrious one said, "When a person goes to the forest, he can take his wife with him, or entrust her to the care of his sons. The third quarter of the lifespan should be spent in serenity in the forest. Subsistence must be ensured through bulbs, roots and fruits that grow in the middle of the forest. When residing in the forest, garments must be made out of bark, grass, leaves or deerskin. He must not clean his hair, body hair, beard or dirt on the body. He must not brush his teeth. He must immerse himself in the water thrice a day.[1148] He must sleep on the ground. In the summer, he must torment himself through five fires.[1149] During monsoon, he must stand in the rain. In the winter, he must submerge himself in water, up to the neck. He must perform austerities in this way. He can eat what has been cooked in the fire, or what has ripened in the course of time. The food can be ground with a pestle, or the teeth can be used as pestle and mortar. He must himself collect whatever is required for his subsistence, considering what is right for the time and the place and what he is capable of. He must not accept anything from anyone else. He can perform seasonal sacrifices by making cakes out of forest fare. However, a person in vanaprastha ashrama must not worship me through animal sacrifices mentioned in the shruti texts. While residing in the forest, aghihotra, *darsha*, *pournamasa* and *chaturmasya* sacrifices[1150] can be performed, as he used to do earlier. These are sanctioned by the sacred texts. Through the observance of such austerities, the sage

---

[1148] Morning, noon and evening. The bath must be no more than this dip in the water.

[1149] Four fires on four sides and the sun overhead.

[1150] Darsha is on the day of the new moon, pournamasa is on the day of the full moon and chaturmasya is once every four months.

seems to be covered with veins everywhere. Worshipping me with such austerities over a long period of time, he goes to the world of the rishis and obtains me. These extremely difficult austerities, performed over a long period of time, are for the sake of great benefit. Who but a fool will engage in such austerities for the sake of gratifying the senses? When his body starts to tremble and he is no longer capable of observing these rituals because of old age, he must ignite the fire within his atman. With his mind immersed in me, he must enter the fire.

'"Karma obtains various things, including worlds that are no better than hell. When a person has completely cast aside the fires[1151] he can leave for sannyasa. Having worshipped me through the instructed sacrifices, he must give everything away to the officiating priests. He must withdraw the fires within his own prana and without any attachment, must take to sannyasa. For a brahmana who wishes to take to sannyasa, the gods create impediments in the form of wives and other things, since he might surpass them and obtain the supreme. If the sage wishes to wear anything more than a *koupina*,[1152] he can wear another garment on top of this. Unless there is a calamity, he should not possess anything other than a staff and a water pot. He must place his foot on the ground only after it has been purified through his eyes.[1153] He must drink water only after he has strained it with his garment. He must only speak what is the truth. He must only do what his mind thinks is pure. O dear one! Unless one accepts the rules of maintaining silence, giving up desire for anything in this world and controlling the breath, related to speech, body and the mind, one does not become a mendicant only because one has got a staff made out of bamboo. When a person roams around searching for alms, for all the four varnas, he must shun condemned households. Without any hopes, he must go to seven houses and no more and be content with whatever has been obtained. Taking this, he must go to a body of water that is

---

[1151] The *ahavaniya*, *garhapatya* and *dakshinagni* fires that are maintained.

[1152] A loin cloth.

[1153] To make sure he does not step on insects or other living creatures.

outside.[1154] He must maintain silence. He must perform his ablutions. He must divide his food.[1155] Thus purified, he must completely[1156] eat whatever has been obtained. He must wander around the earth alone, without attachment and in control of his senses. He must find pleasure within his own atman. He must impartially look upon everything like his own self. He must reside in a solitary and safe place, cleaning his mind by being immersed in me. The sage must think of the atman alone, which is not different from me. Resorting to jnana, he must examine the atman and the nature of its bondage and liberation. The bondage occurs because of attachment to the senses and liberation is control over them. Therefore, controlling the six categories,[1157] the sage roams around, immersed in me. He is not attached to inferior desires. He obtains great happiness in the atman. He must travel the earth and go to sacred places, rivers, mountains, forests and hermitages. He must enter cities, villages, cowherd settlements and places where caravans gather only for the sake of alms. He must seek alms following the practice of those in vanaprastha ashrama,[1158] or practise shila-unchchha. He will then be quickly purified, become free of delusion and obtain success. He must never see reality in material objects. Anything visible will be destroyed. With the mind completely detached towards anything in this world or in the next world, he will not wish to do anything to pursue these. Through reasoning, he must establish that everything, the world, mind, speech, prana and everything else, is maya. Thus, basing himself on the atman, he must give up everything else and not remember them.

'"My devotee who is devoted to jnana, without attachment and without desire for anything else, can give up all attributes connected to any ashrama. He can roam around, beyond these rules. Though wise, he should play like a child. Though accomplished, he should act like one who is stupid. Though learned, he should speak like a

---

[1154] Outside the habitation.

[1155] Leaving a bit on the ground for other creatures.

[1156] Without leaving anything for the future.

[1157] The five senses and the mind. Alternatively, the six vices.

[1158] Avoiding condemned households.

mad person. Though he knows about the sacred texts, he should tend to cattle. He should not engage in debates about the Vedas. He is not a heretic. But he is not a debater either. In pointless arguments and counter-arguments, he should not take either side. Such a patient person does not agitate other people, nor is he agitated by other people. He should tolerate harsh words and must never disrespect anyone. For the sake of the body, like an animal, he must never exhibit enmity towards anyone. The supreme atman is one and is present in the atmans of all creatures, just as the moon is reflected in different bodies of water. Therefore, other creatures are no different from one's own self. At different times, he should not be distressed if he does not get food. At other times, he should not rejoice because he has obtained food. Fixed in his patience, he realizes that both these are the outcome of destiny. He must engage himself in trying to obtain food, since that is required for the sake of sustaining life. It is only through life that the truth can be contemplated. When one has discerned the truth, one is freed. A sage must accept whatever has come of its own accord, food, garments, bed, regardless of whether these are superior or inferior. I am the lord. Yet I engage in pastimes. Like that, a learned person must observe the rituals of cleanliness and bathing, not because he has been forced to do them. He has no sense of differentiation left. Having realized me, all that has been destroyed. However, as long as the body remains, sometimes, these perceptions recur. But after that, he merges into me. A person who has realized his atman knows that all objects of desire bring misery in the future. Therefore, non-attachment is generated. However, a sage who has not considered this dharma of devotion to me, must approach a guru. Until the devotee has got to realize the brahman as being nothing other than me, he must respectfully serve the guru with devotion and without any envy. A person who has not controlled the six categories, with the mind as the fierce charioteer of the senses, he is devoid of jnana and non-attachment. He resorts to the triple staff of sannyasa only as a means of subsistence. He destroys dharma and deceives the gods and his own atman. He also denies me. His impurities have still not ripened and he has destroyed this world and the next. The main dharma of a person in sannyasa is control and non-violence. The main dharma of a person in

vanaprastha is austerities and examination. The main dharma of a
person in garhasthya is protection of creatures and the performance
of sacrifices. The main dharma of a dvija in brahmacharya is serving
the preceptor. Brahmacharya,[1159] austerities, purity, satisfaction,
friendliness towards creatures and approaching the wife in season
are the duties of a householder. Everyone should worship me. In
this way, a person must follow his own dharma and worship me
and nothing else. He is conscious of me existing in all creatures
and thereby develops firm devotion towards me. O Uddhava! I am
the great lord of all the worlds. I am the brahman. I am the cause
behind the creation and destruction of everything. A person who
does not deviate from being devoted towards me obtains me. Thus,
a person must engage in his own dharma and purify himself, thus
ascertaining my nature. He becomes full of jnana and vijnana and
soon obtains me. These are the signs and conduct of the dharma of
the varnas and the ashramas. When devotion towards me is added
to this, a person obtains the greatest benefit. O virtuous one! I have
thus described to you what you had asked me about. This is the
way one follows one's own dharma and being devoted towards me,
obtains me, the supreme."'

Chapter 11(19)

'The illustrious one said, "A person who possesses learning
about the shruti texts, knows about the atman and does
not depend on inferences, possesses the jnana that everything in
the universe is only maya. Therefore, he renders everything to me.
For those who possess jnana, I am the only object of worship. It is
accepted that I am the goal and also the means of achieving that
goal. I am the cause of happiness in heaven. I am also the cause of
liberation. Therefore, other than me, nothing else is loved by him.
A person who possesses jnana and vijnana knows that my state is
the supreme object. I love a person who possesses jnana the most.

[1159] In this context, only engaging in recommended sexual intercourse.

A person who possesses jnana nurtures me. Austerities, tirthas, meditating, donations and other sacred acts do not obtain as much of success as a little bit of jnana ensures. O Uddhava! Therefore, using jnana, you should know your own atman. With jnana and vijnana and filled with devotion towards me, worship me. Earlier, sages possessed jnana and vijnana and used these to perform sacrifices to me, the atman, within their own atmans. I am the lord of sacrifices. Therefore, approaching me, they obtained success. O Uddhava! The three kinds of transformations[1160] become attached because of maya. They suddenly appear now. They didn't exist in the beginning. Nor will they exist at the end. Birth, death and other things have to do with the body. What do they have to do with you? Something that did not exist in the beginning and will not exist at the end is unreal and only seems to exist in the middle."

'Uddhava said, "O lord of the universe! O one whose form is the universe! Please explain to me the ancient, pure and extensive nature of jnana and vijnana, which ensures non-attachment. Explain the bhakti yoga that the great seek out. In this path of samsara, I am terribly tormented and afflicted by the three kinds of miseries.[1161] O lord! I do not see any shelter other than at your two feet. They are like an umbrella and also shower down amrita. O one who is immensely powerful! This person has been bitten by the snake that is time. He has fallen into a hole and is thirsting after inferior pleasures. Show him your favours and raise him up to liberation by sprinkling your words on him."

'The illustrious one replied, "In earlier times, while all of us heard, King Ajatashatru asked Bhishma, supreme among the upholders of dharma, exactly this question. When the war among those of the Bharata lineage was over, he was overwhelmed by the destruction of his well-wishers. After hearing about many kinds of dharma, he finally asked about moksha dharma. The words emerging from Devavrata's[1162] mouth spoke about jnana,

[1160] Interpreted in different ways—the three gunas; birth, existence and death; the three kinds of miseries.
[1161] Adhidaivika, adhibhoutika and adhyatmika.
[1162] Bhishma's.

non-attachment, vijnana, faith and bhakti. I will describe those to
you. I approve of the jnana through which one sees the nine, the
eleven, the five and the three attributes in all creatures[1163] and the
one that permeates everything. In that way, when one no longer
sees this differentiation, but the single one that is the cause, this is
vijnana. Such a person sees that material attributes like creation,
preservation and destruction are caused by the gunas. What is
created is destroyed. What is destroyed is created again. From one
creation to another, that which remains at the beginning, in the
middle and at the end is the only entity that is real. Through four
means—the shruti texts, direct experience, tradition and inference—
one gets evidence that the material existence is transitory. Therefore,
one becomes detached from this. Any karma leads to consequences
and is therefore subject to transformations. It is inauspicious, even
if it happens to be Virinchi's position. A learned man perceives what
is visible and what is not visible in the same way. O unblemished
one! Since you love me, I have already spoken about bhakti yoga
to you. I will again speak about bhakti towards me, the supreme
method. Faithfully listening to my immortal accounts; constant
chanting of my glories; devoted worship towards me; singing hymns
in my praise; affectionately serving me; using all the limbs to be
prostrate before me; using great devotion to worship my devotees;
the perception that I exist in all creatures; using all physical activities
for my sake; using speech to sing about my qualities; surrendering
the mind to me; shunning all objects of desire; for my sake, giving
up wealth, objects of pleasure and happiness; dedicating sacrifices,
donations, oblations, chanting, vows and austerities to me—all these
generate bhakti towards me. What other objective remains to be
attained? If a person dedicates himself to me, he is serene and is full
of sattva. He also obtains dharma, jnana, non-attachment and every
kind of opulence. When the mind is surrendered to something else,
the senses run around. Know that because of this devotion to rajas

---

[1163] The nine are Purusha, Prakriti, Mahat, ahamkara and the five
tanmatras. The eleven are the five organs of action, the five senses of
perception and the mind. The five are the five gross elements. The three are
the three gunas. The one is the paramatman.

and the unreal in the consciousness, perverse effects result. Dharma is stated to be that which leads to bhakti towards me. Jnana is that which sees only me in everything. Non-attachment is being delinked from the gunas. Opulence means anima and the other things."

'Uddhava asked, "O afflicter of enemies! How many kinds of yama are there? What is the *niyama* that is spoken about? What is *shama*? What is *dama*? O Krishna! O lord! What are *titiksha* and *dhriti*? What is *dana*? What is *tapas*? What is *shourya*? What is spoken of as satyam and ritam? What is *tyaga*? What *dhana* should one strive for? What is yajna? What is dakshina? What is a man's real *bala*? What is the best *bhaga*? O Keshava! What is *labha*? What is vidya? What is the supreme form of *hri*? What is shri? What are *sukha* and *duhkha*? Who is *pandita* and who is *murkha*? What is *pantha*? What is *utpatha*? What are *svarga* and *naraka*? Who is a *bandhu* and what is a *griha*? Who is *adhya* and who is *daridra*? Who is *kripana*? Who is *ishvara*? O lord of the virtuous! Tell me the answers to these questions. Also tell me about the opposites of these attributes."

'The illustrious one replied, "Yama[1164] consists of non-violence, truthfulness, refraining from theft, lack of attachment, modesty, refraining from accumulation, belief in the sacred texts, brahmacharya, silence, steadfastness, forgiveness and fearlessness. Niyama[1165] consists of external purity, internal purity, meditating, austerities, oblations, faith, hospitality, my worship, visiting tirthas, ensuring benefit to others, contentment and service to the preceptor. These are yama and niyama and each is said to have twelve practices. O son! A man who practises them can milk all the objects of desire. Shama[1166] is being devoted to me. Dama[1167] is the control of the senses. Titiksha[1168] is tolerance of miseries. Dhriti[1169] is the conquest of the stomach and the genital organs. The supreme

---

[1164] Self-control.
[1165] Prescribed practices.
[1166] Mental equilibrium.
[1167] Self-restraint.
[1168] Forbearance.
[1169] Fortitude.

form of dana[1170] is abstention from using the rod against others. Tapas[1171] is said to be the giving up of desire. Shourya[1172] is victory over one's own nature. Satyam[1173] is impartiality in vision. The wise have declared that pleasant speech is ritam.[1174] Not being attached to karma is *shoucha*.[1175] Tyaga[1176] is said to be renunciation. Engaging in dharma is the desirable form of dhana.[1177] I, the supreme and illustrious one, am yajna.[1178] Dakshina is instruction about jnana. Pranayama is supreme bala.[1179] Bhaga[1180] is my divine opulence. Labha[1181] is supreme devotion towards me. Vidya[1182] is negation of differentiation in the atman. Hri[1183] is disgust towards perverse karma. Shri[1184] is indifference towards the gunas. Sukha[1185] is transcending both sukha and duhkha. Duhkha[1186] is expected sukha from objects of desire. A pandita[1187] is someone who knows about liberation from bondage. A murkha[1188] is a person whose intelligence is such that he identifies himself with his body. Pantha[1189] is said to be the path that leads to me. Utpatha[1190] is that which leads to agitation of the intelligence. Svarga[1191] is the predominance of *sattva*

[1170] Donations.
[1171] Austerities.
[1172] Heroism.
[1173] Truth.
[1174] Also a variety of truth.
[1175] Purity.
[1176] Renunciation.
[1177] Wealth.
[1178] Sacrifice.
[1179] Strength.
[1180] Fortune.
[1181] Gain.
[1182] Learning.
[1183] Modesty.
[1184] Beauty, prosperity.
[1185] Happiness.
[1186] Unhappiness.
[1187] A learned person.
[1188] A fool.
[1189] Path.
[1190] Perverse path.
[1191] Heaven.

guna. Naraka[1192] is the predominance of tamas guna. O friend! I am the preceptor and the bandhu.[1193] A man's body is his griha.[1194] One who is full of qualities is said to be adhya.[1195] A daridra[1196] is a person who is not satisfied. Kripana[1197] is a person who has not conquered his senses. An ishvara[1198] is a person whose intelligence is such that he is not attached to the gunas. If there is attachment to the gunas, the opposite happens. O Uddhava! I have thus clearly determined the answers to your questions. What is the need to speak more about the attributes of what is good and what is bad? Thinking about good and bad is itself bad. Being devoid of notions of both good and bad is good."'

Chapter 11(20)

'Uddhava said, "O lotus-eyed one! You are indeed the lord and the injunctions and prohibitions of the sacred texts are therefore your commands. They do talk about good and bad acts. They talk about the different types of varnas and ashramas, birth from pratiloma and *anuloma* marriages, the attributes of objects, place, age and time and heaven and hell.[1199] Without perceiving the differenece between good and bad, which have injunctions and prohibitions, how can men undersand your words?[1200] How can they ensure what is best for them? O lord! As your words, the Vedas

---

[1192] Hell.
[1193] Relative.
[1194] House.
[1195] Wealthy.
[1196] Poor person.
[1197] A wretched person.
[1198] Controller, master.
[1199] They talk about good and bad associated with these. In an anuloma marriage, the husband has a higher varna. In a pratiloma marriage, the wife has a higher varna. Yet, you have said one should not think of good and bad.
[1200] As given in the sacred texts.

are like eyes for ancestors, gods and men. They understand what is best, the end and the means. This insight about good and bad in the sacred texts did not evolve on its own, but comes from you. If one counters the differences in the sacred texts, there will be confusion."

'The illustrious one replied, "To ensure the best for men, I have spoken about three kinds of yoga—jnana, karma and bhakti. Other than these, no other path exists. Jnana yoga is for those who are disgusted with all karma and have given it up. Those whose minds are still not disgusted and who still desire, should resort to *karma yoga*. On its own, if devotion towards me is generated in a man, because he has heard about my accounts, even if he is not disgusted, nor excessively attached, he should obtain success through bhakti yoga. As long as one is not satisfied, or until devotion towards me has been generated by hearing about my accounts, one must perform karma. O Uddhava! If a person is established in his own dharma and worships me without desiring anything, he will not go to heaven or hell, unless he does something perverse. In this world, if a person performs his own dharma and is unblemished and pure, he obtains pure jnana. Bhakti is a matter of chance. The residents of heaven and the residents of hell desire to be born in this world, because that can ensure success for both jnana and bhakti. Those two worlds can't ensure that success. A learned man should not crave for a destination in either heaven or hell. Nor should he desire to be born in this world. Attachment to the body leads to confusion. Knowing in advance that death is inevitable, he must unwaveringly act so as to achieve the goal of success, before death overtakes him. Men who are like death cut down a tree in which a bird has made its nest. Without being attached to its home, the bird goes elsewhere and finds peace. Knowing that the lifespan is being severed by the passage of nights and days, a person should tremble with fear. He must free himself of attachment and realize the supreme. Without any desire, he will find peace. He has easily obtained this human body, which is very difficult to obtain. It is like a well-designed boat and the guru is like a helmsman. I am like the favourable wind that propels it. After this, if a man does not cross the ocean of samsara, he is killing himself. When a person is disgusted with material pursuits, he must become detached and control his senses.

Through practice, the yogi must fix his fickle mind in his atman. When the mind does not remain concentrated and starts to stray, he must not get distracted. He must use the techniques and the path to bring the atman under control. A person must retain control over where the mind is going. He must conquer his prana and conquer his senses. Using an intelligence that is full of sattva, he must bring the mind under the control of the atman. This is said to be the supreme yoga for controlling the mind, knowing and watching over the inclinations of the heart and repeatedly controlling them, like a horse. He must use samkhya to understand the nature of all material objects, their generation and their withdrawal. Observing the process of creation and destruction, the mind becomes serene. On the basis of what has been said, a man becomes disgusted and non-attached. Thinking about these, the mind gives up all wicked thoughts. Using the learning, a person examines the path of yoga, yama and the others. The mind must remember that I am the one to be worshipped. Nothing else is worthwhile. Because of being distracted, if a yogi commits a reprehensible act, he must burn that sin down through yoga. Nothing else should be done.[1201] Depending on a person's respective status, a steady practice of what is good has been spoken about and niyama has been laid down. However, by its very nature, karma is impure. The norms of good and bad must be used by a person with the desire of giving up attachment. When devotion towards my accounts has been generated, a person develops disgust for all karma. Though he knows that all objects of desire give rise to unhappiness, he is unable to give them up. He must then happily worship me, filled with firm devotion and determination. Even if he pursues objects of desire, he must condemn them as being the cause of miseries. I have spoken about bhakti yoga, which a sage can use to completely worship me. This destroys all the desires in the heart and the heart becomes immersed in me. The bonds of the heart are severed and all the doubts are dispelled. When I am seen as the atman who exists everywhere, all karma is terminated. Thus, using bhakti yoga, a yogi is immersed in my atman. In general, in this world, neither jnana, nor non-attachment, is necessary for

[1201] Meaning that no other means of atonement is necessary.

obtaining benefit. All the benefit that can be obtained through karma, austerities, jnana, non-attachment, yoga, donations and dharma can be obtained easily by my devotee through bhakti yoga. If he so desires, he can obtain heaven, emancipation, or my abode. Those who are my virtuous and persevering devotees are fixed in me and desire nothing else. I give them kaivalya and freedom from being born again. It has been said that indifference is the best and greatest method for obtaining benefit. Therefore, a person who is indifferent and not attached, develops devotion. Good and bad, which arise from the gunas, do not exist in those who are single-minded in their devotion to me. Those virtuous ones are impartial in their intelligence and obtain the supreme. This path has been propounded by me. If a person follows this, he obtains peace and my abode. The learned know this as the supreme brahman."'

Chapter 11(21)

'The illustrious one said, "My path is that of bhakti, jnana and rituals I have spoken about. Those who are inferior forsake it and pursue the temporary goals of the senses and objects of desire. They become tied to samsara. Depending on a person's state, there are steady practices that have been spoken of as being good. Deviation from these is bad. This is what has been determined about them. O unblemished one! Pure and impure, good and bad, auspicious and inauspicious, can coexist in the same object.[1202] These have been laid down so that the principles can be used to investigate the pursuit of dharma, everyday conduct and the sustenance of life. I have revealed these norms for those who have to uphold dharma. Beginning with Brahma and down to immobile objects, all embodied entities result from earth, water, fire, air and space, the five elements. All of them are united with the atman. Though they are equal, the Vedas give them different names and

---

[1202] That is, an act, per se, is not pure/impure, good/bad, auspicious/inauspicious. The answer depends on the context.

forms. O Uddhava! This is so that each can accomplish its own respective objective. O excellent one! For the sake of regulating karma, I have laid down good and bad for entities, depending on the place, the time and other aspects. There are places where there are no black antelopes. Devotion towards brahmanas is missing. Such places are inauspicious. Even if there are black antelopes, these are known as Souvira and Kikata.[1203] These desolate places are not clean. Depending on the task, the availability of objects, or because it is naturally that, a specific time period is said to be good. When there are impediments towards performing karma, that is said to be bad and one should not attempt karma then. The good or the bad of an object depends on which other object it is attached to, words,[1204] whether it has been cleaned, the passage of time and whether it is large or small.[1205] Depending on a person's intelligence, prosperity, location and state, an impure object may be able to, or may not be able to, taint him. Grain, objects made out of wood, bones, thread, liquids, metals and hides can be purified, or not, through time, air, fire, water and earth, acting singly or jointly. When touched by an impure smell, a fragrant substance can remove that impure coating and make it regain its original nature. That substance is then considered to be a purifying agent. Bathing, donations, austerities and performing purifying acts, depending on age and status, are means of purifying oneself. After first remembering me, a dvija must perform these acts of purification. A mantra is pure when it is chanted by someone who possesses proper knowledge. A karma is pure when it is offered to me. An act of dharma is pure when six things are considered.[1206] Anything contrary is adharma. Sometimes, something good may turn out to be bad. Sometimes, something the norms declare as bad may turn

---

[1203] Souvira was to the north-west and west, Kikata towards the extreme east.

[1204] Based on interpretations of the sacred texts or learned people.

[1205] Through the passage of time, the purity of an object may be affected. Size can determine the extent of contamination something suffers from contact with another object.

[1206] Time, place, substance, the one undertaking the act, mantras and the nature of the act.

out to be good. These specific circumstances constrain the use of those principles to determine what is good and bad. For those who have already fallen down, the performance of a similar act is no longer a sin. Someone who is lying down on the ground cannot fall further down. In conjunction with one's natural conduct, something may turn out to be good.[1207] Whatever course of action one refrains from, one is freed from that. This is dharma for men. It leads to well-being and removes grief, delusion and fear. If a man thinks of the good qualities of objects, he becomes attached to them. Desire results from that attachment. Among men, this desire leads to conflict. Conflict leads to intolerable rage and ignorance follows. This ignorance swiftly pervades a man's intelligence. O virtuous one! Deprived of intelligence, a person is thought to be as empty as an animal. He thus deviates from what is good for him. He is like a person who has lost his consciousness or is dead. Absorbed in material objects, he does not know his atman or the supreme. His life is as futile as that of a tree. Though he breathes, he is no more than bellows. The fruits spoken about in the sacred texts do not bring benefit. They are only meant to entice attraction for the supreme. They have been spoken about with the intention of indicating the benefit, like making someone imbibe a bitter medicine. Because of birth, desire, attachment to life and attachment to relatives, the minds of mortals become attached and these act as constraints in their realizing their atmans. Ignorant people submit themselves and wander along a dangerous path, deviating from what is good for them. If a learned person has entered the darkness of ignorance, why should he again engage in those pursuits? Some who are inferior in intelligence are ignorant and do not understand the true intention[1208] and pursue the flowering fruits of the sacred texts. Those who actually know about the Vedas do not speak in that way. Those driven by desire are miserly and greedy. Their intelligence is such that they regard the flowers as the fruit. Enticed by the fire and blinded by the smoke, they do not obtain their own

[1207] For example, for people in garhasthya and sannyasa, brahmacharya may not have the same implication.
[1208] Of the sacred texts.

destinations. O dear one! They do not know me, present in all hearts and in this universe. They are content with their own lives and what has been spoken about in the sacred texts. It is as if their eyes are covered by mist. Those who are attached to material objects do not understand my views, which have been implicitly stated. Thus, they are attracted to violent sacrifices, as if these have been encouraged. Taking pleasure in violence, because they desire their own happiness, these deceitful[1209] people offer the animals that have thus been obtained at sacrifices dedicated to gods, ancestors and the lords of bhutas. In their dreams, they sketch out a world that is unreal, though it is pleasant to hear about. Because of the hope and resolution in their hearts, like a merchant, they give up their riches.[1210] Those who are full of sattva, rajas and tamas worship gods and others, Indra being the foremost, who are full of sattva, rajas and tamas. They do not worship me. 'Through sacrifices to the gods, we will enjoy ourselves in heaven. When that is over, we will again obtain large mansions and noble births in this world.' The minds of men are agitated through such flowery words. They are proud and extremely greedy and my accounts are not attractive to them. The Vedas are about three subjects—the brahman, the atman and rituals.[1211] The rishis speak about things indirectly and the indirect method also appeals to me. It is extremely difficult to understand about the brahman in words, since the vital air of speech, the sense of speaking and the perception of the mind are involved. The brahman has no limits. It is fathomless and is as deep as the ocean. I am the lord, infinite in powers. I am the brahman. I manifest myself before creatures in the form of sound and can only be perceived indirectly, like the subtle fibre in the stalk of a lotus. Through its mouth, the spider takes out strands of web from its heart. Like that, the vital air manifests itself from space as sound and touches the mind and assumes a form. The lord is full of metres, full of amrita and there are thousands of different sounds, classified

---

[1209] Because the sacrifices are a deceit. They actually love the violence.

[1210] A merchant takes a risk with existing riches in the hope of greater riches.

[1211] And about identity between the brahman and the jivatman.

as consonants, vowels, sibilants and semi-vowels. Omkara was thus embellished in different ways, expanding through colourful expressions. There were chhandas,[1212] each containing four aksharas more than the previous one. The lord, infinite and limitless, creates this large expanse and again withdraws it into himself. The metres are gayatri, *ushnik*, *anushtup*, *brihati*, *pankti*, *trishtup*, *jagati*, *atichchhanda*, *atyasti*, *atijagati* and *virat*.[1213] What is prescribed? What is indicated? What is described? What is not recommended? What is the heart of the matter? Other than me, there is no one in the world who knows this. I am the one it has injunctions about worshipping. If there are injunctions about not worshipping me, that is also me. That is the meaning of all the Vedas. Resorting to speech, it differentiates me. Having differentiated because of maya, it negates me and is finally reduced to silence."'

Chapter 11(22)

'Uddhava asked, "O lord! O lord of the universe! How many principles have the rishis enumerated? We have heard from you that there are twenty-eight—nine, eleven, five and three.[1214] Some learned ones speak of twenty-six, others mention twenty-five. Some say seven, nine or six. Others say eleven. Some speak of seventeen, others speak of sixteen or thirteen. O one with a long life! With what intention have rishis sung about these differing numbers of principles? You should explain this to us."

'The illustrious one replied, "Since everything is present everywhere, it is reasonable that brahmanas should speak in this way. They are under the grasp of my maya. That being the case, whatever they say cannot be contradicted. 'What you have said

---

[1212] Metres.

[1213] Gayatri has twenty-four aksharas, each successive metre has four aksharas more than the preceding one. Thus, anushtup has thirty-two and so on.

[1214] Those mentioned in Chapter 11(19).

is not true. Truth is what I have spoken.' Since my powers that urge them are insurmountable, they cite reasons and argue in this way. That is how those differences-à and alternatives arise when they speak about the subject. When control over the mind and the senses has been obtained, all debate subsides. O bull among men! The principles enter one another. Depending on what the speaker perceives, he categorizes them as cause and effect. All the principles are seen to be present in one principle. A principle exists within its cause and also within its effect. The principles are everywhere. Each of the disputant enumerates, depending on whether the effect is included in the cause, or whether the cause is included in the effect. He speaks as he has ascertained. We accept the reasoning and the conclusion. A man who has been covered with ignorance right from the beginning is unable to realize his own atman on his own. Therefore, there must be someone else who knows about the truth, so that he can impart knowledge to him. The slightest difference does not exist between Purusha and Ishvara.[1215] The perception about these being different is pointless and such knowledge arises because of Prakriti's gunas. Prakriti has an equilibrium of the gunas. The gunas are Prakriti's attributes, not those of the atman. Sattva, rajas and tamas are the cause of creation, preservation and destruction. The transformation of sattva is said to be jnana, the transformation of rajas is said to be karma and the transformation of tamas is said to be *ajnana*. Time is disequilibrium in the gunas, while nature is Sutra. The nine principles enumerated by me are Purusha, Prakriti, Mahat, ahamkara, space, wind, fire, water and earth. The powers of perception are hearing, touch, sight, smell and taste. O dear one! The organs of action are tongue, hands, genitals, anus and legs. The mind is used for both perception and action. The attributes of the senses that perceive are sound, what is touched, the seen, what is smelt and form. The functions of the senses of action are movement, expression, excretion[1216] and artisanship. In the beginning, at the time of creation, Prakriti assumes the form of both

---

[1215] Those who count twenty-five vis-à-vis those who count twenty-six.
[1216] Both urine and stool. Hence, two under excretion.

cause and effect. Through sattva and the other gunas, it assumes that state, while the unmanifest Purusha is only a witness. Because of the glance of Purusha, Mahat and the elements are agitated and thus obtain vigour. They are brought together by Prakriti's strength and create the cosmic egg. Those who say there are seven principles enumerate the five elements, space and the others, the jivatman and the atman. These are regarded as the basis for the evolution of the body, the senses and the breath of life. Those who speak of six principles include the five elements and the supreme Purusha as the sixth. Uniting with those, he created this universe and entered it. Some say there are only four principles, with fire, water and earth having evolved from the atman.[1217] Just as something that has been born takes a form, this universe has also originated from these. There are some who enumerate seventeen principles—the five gross elements, the five senses, the five objects of the senses, the mind and the atman as the seventeenth. In that way, when sixteen principles are enumerated, the atman is also spoken of as the mind. When thirteen are mentioned, this includes the five elements, the five senses, the mind, the jivatman and the atman. Eleven includes the atman, the five gross elements and the five senses. Eight means Mahat, ahamkara, the mind and the five elements. When it is nine, Purusha is added to this list. In this way, the rishis differ in the number of principles they have enumerated. All of them are supported by reasoning and are true. Such embellishments are worthy of the learned."

'Uddhava said, "O Krishna! Prakriti and Purusha are different in characteristics. But because they depend on each other, no difference between them is seen. Prakriti can be discerned in the atman and the atman can be discerned in Prakriti. O lotus-eyed one! In this connection, there is a grave doubt in my mind. O one who knows everything! Using your polished words and reasoning, you should dispel this. It is from you that living beings obtain knowledge. It is your power that takes the knowledge away. Barring you, no one else can comprehend the progress of your maya."

[1217] These three are thus subtracted from the list of seven principles.

'The illustrious one replied, "O bull among men! There is a difference between Purusha and Prakriti.[1218] This manifest creation results from the agitation in the gunas. O dear one! My maya creates many differences in the gunas. This leads to differences in intelligence and diversity in attributes. Creation has three kinds of transformations—adhyatmika, adhidaivika and adhibhoutika. The sense of sight is adhyatmika, the form of the sun is adhibhoutika and the part of the sun that enters through the aperture in the eye is adhidaivika. They interact with each other to show the sun, but the sun exists independently. In that way, the atman is the original cause and is separate from anything else. Through its own illumination, it illuminates other agents and they in turn illuminate everything else. This is the way touch, hearing, eyes, the tongue and the nose can also be analysed.[1219] When the gunas are agitated, with Pradhana as the basis, there is a transformation and ahamkara is generated. Created from Mahat, it is the source of delusion and differentiation. There are three kinds of ahamkara—resulting from sattva, rajas and tamas. Lack of jnana leads to debates about the atman. 'This is real.' 'That is not real.' Such arguments are based on differentiation and are pointless. Men who have turned their intelligences away from me will not be able to give these up, though I exist within their own selves."

'Uddhava said, "O lord! The intelligences of those who deviate from you are diverted by the karma of what they have themselves done. They accept and give up superior and inferior bodies. O Govinda! Tell me about this. It is extremely difficult for those who are not intelligent to understand this. Since most people are deceived, learned people are rare in this world."

'The illustrious one replied, "The minds of men are full of karma. Along with the five senses, they travel from one body to another. Though distinct, the atman also follows. The mind thinks about material objects, those that have been seen, or those that have been heard of. It dissolves and subsequently rises again, bound

---

[1218] Purusha cannot be subject to change.

[1219] Differentiating between the sense, the object of the sense and the presiding deity of the sense.

by karma. But the former memory is lost. Because of attachment towards material objects, he no longer has any memory of his former self. For a living being, this kind of loss of memory, whatever be the reason, is known as death. O generous one! Birth is said to be nothing but the complete identification of a man with a new body. This kind of acceptance is like accepting the wishes in a dream. In the present state of dreaming, a person does not remember the former dreams. In that way, unable to see the past, he thinks that he has no past. The mind, where the senses rest, identifies with the three forms of the new body,[1220] which only appears as real. Just as a good father may give birth to a wicked son, a person thus becomes the cause of external and internal differences.[1221] O dear one! The force of time is powerful, but because it is subtle, its progress is not seen. As a result of time, beings are constantly created and destroyed. Flames in a fire change, as do flows in rivers. The fruits on a tree also change. In that way, changes are brought about in age and other aspects of all creatures. Since flames change, 'This is the same light of a lamp,' is an untrue statement. Since flows change, 'This is the same water in the river,' is an untrue statement. In that way, people who say, 'This is the same man,' are wasting their time and stating what is not true. A man is not born because of the seeds of his karma. Nor does he die because of that. Just as fire appears and is extinguished because of the presence or absence of kindling, death and immortality are the result of illusion. The nine stages of the body are conception, pregnancy, birth, infancy, childhood, youth, middle age, old age and death. Superior and inferior perceptions about the body arise because of false speculations in the mind. They are accepted as a consequence of being attached to the gunas. It is only rarely that a person discards them. From a father's death, one can infer about one's own death. From a son's birth, one can infer about one's own birth. If a person understands that creation and destruction are only related to the body, he is no longer subject to duality. A tree is born from a seed and is eventually destroyed. A person who knows this

---

[1220] Such as superior birth, average birth and inferior birth.
[1221] This shloka has complicated interpretations. The idea is that the atman loses its real identity and identifies with unreal differences.

attribute about a tree's birth and death is a distinct witness. It is the same with the witness who is distinct from the body. An ordinary and ignorant man fails to distinguish his atman from the material body. Because he thinks contact with material objects is real, he returns to samsara. If he is dominated by sattva, he becomes a rishi or a god. If he is dominated by rajas, he is born as an asura or as a man. If he is dominated by tamas, he becomes a bhuta or inferior species. Thus, he is whirled around in karma. A person imitates those whom he sees acting or dancing. In that way, the atman does not act. But seeing the qualities of intelligence, it is made to follow. O Dasharha! Though they do not move, the reflections of trees in the water seem to move. When the eyes roll around, the earth is seen to be in a whirl. Mental perceptions and intelligence lead to false identifications with material objects. Like what is seen in a dream, the atman falsely identifies with samsara. Material objects do not really exist. However, like calamities that are experienced in a dream, samsara does not vanish for those who think about material objects. O Uddhava! Therefore, do not use the senses to enjoy material objects. See that this delusion is based on apparent differentiation and on an inability to grasp the nature of the atman. Even if abused, shown disrespect, defrauded, ridiculed, envied, chastised, bound, deprived of livelihood, defiled with spit, urine or excrement and troubled in many ways by those who are ignorant, a person who desires his own benefit uses his own atman to rise above these hardships."

'Uddhava said, "O supreme among eloquent ones! Please tell us how we can understand this properly. O atman of the universe! I think that even the learned find it extremely difficult to tolerate the transgressions of the wicked. Nature is too powerful. The only exceptions are those who are serene because they are engaged in dharma by seeking shelter at your feet."'

Chapter 11(23)

Badarayana's son said, 'The foremost among the Dasharhas was thus asked by Uddhava, the foremost among his devotees.

Mukunda, whose valour is worth speaking about, praised his servant's words and spoke to him.

'The illustrious one said, "O Brihaspati's disciple! When agitated by the abuse of wicked men, there is no virtuous person in this world who is capable of composing himself. A man is not tormented as much by arrows that pierce his inner organs as much as he is by the harsh words of the wicked that strike at his inner organs. O Uddhava! In this connection, there is an extremely sacred account. I will describe it to you. Control yourself and listen. A mendicant was abused by wicked people and he sung this. He regained his composure when he remembered that this was the consequence of his own karma. There was a brahmana in Avanti. He was among the most wealthy and prosperous. He earned a living through commerce. He was miserly, lascivious, avaricious and extremely prone to rage. He never honoured kin or guests, not even with words. His house was empty.[1222] At the right time, he did not even allow himself to enjoy objects of pleasure. He was so wicked in conduct and so miserly that his sons, relatives, wife, daughters and servants were disgusted with him and displayed no affection towards him. In this way, he was like a yaksha[1223] guarding riches and was deprived of both this world and the next. Deprived of dharma and kama, the five entitled to shares[1224] became angry with him. O generous one! Because of this neglect, his share of good deeds was exhausted. Indeed, all the wealth that he had accumulated with a great deal of effort was also lost. O Uddhava! Some was taken away by kin, some by bandits. Some was lost because of destiny and some was taken away by brahma-bandhus, men and kings. He was deprived of his riches and he was devoid of dharma and kama. He was ignored by his own people. He was tormented by worries and those were impossible to overcome. He thought for a long time. Having lost his riches, he was tormented. He lamented and his voice choked with tears. A great sense of renunciation arose. 'Alas! What

[1222] There were no kin or guests there. Nor were there any rituals.

[1223] Yakshas guard Kubera's treasure and do not enjoy it themselves.

[1224] The five who get shares in the five sacrifices a householder undertakes.

hardship! I have unnecessarily tormented myself. I did not strive for
dharma or kama and the artha has also been lost. In general, the
riches of misers never bring them happiness. It causes torments in
this world and, after death, leads to hell. The pure fame of those
who are famous and the praiseworthy qualities of those who are
qualified are destroyed by even the slightest bit of greed, just as
beauty is destroyed by a little bit of white leprosy. In earning wealth,
achieving it, increasing it, protecting it and spending it, men go
through a great deal of efforts, fare, anxiety and confusion. It is held
that there are fifteen kinds of hardships experienced by men that are
due to wealth—theft, violence, falsehood, duplicity, desire, anger,
confusion, intoxication, dissension, enmity, lack of trust, rivalry,
addiction to women, addiction to wine and addiction to gambling.
Therefore, though it is spoken of as desirable, wealth is actually
undesirable. If a person desires what is good for him, he should cast
it far away. Brothers, wives, fathers and well-wishers who are loved
become instant enemies because of a small coin. Birth as a human is
desired by the immortals, that too as a foremost brahmana. Having
obtained it, a person neglects it. He destroys his own benefit and
obtains an inauspicious end. A man has obtained this world, which
is the gate to both heaven and emancipation. Why should he become
attached to something that is temporary, something that is the store
of calamities? If a person does not distribute it among gods, rishis,
beings, kin, relatives and others who have shares, he is protecting
riches like a yaksha and will fall downwards. I have been distracted
and my life and strength have been squandered in the futile pursuit
of riches. An accomplished person can obtain success. What can an
aged person like me do? Why should a learned person constantly
suffer in the futile pursuit of wealth? Indeed, this entire world is
completely confounded by someone's maya. When a person is
about to be devoured by death, what will riches and those who
bestow riches accomplish? What is the purpose of kama and those
who can bestow kama? Such karma only leads to another birth. The
illustrious Hari is in all the gods and he must certainly be satisfied
with me. He has reduced me to this state, with non-attachment as
a boat to carry me across. In whatever little bit of time I have left, I
will cease to care about anything, or about my own beloved body.

Without being distracted, I will devote myself entirely to my own benefit. I will find satisfaction within my own atman. May the gods and the lords of the three worlds approve of this. In the space of a muhurta, Khatvanga was able to reach Brahma's world.'[1225] The excellent brahmana from Avanti made up his mind in this way.

'"He loosened the bonds of his heart. He became a tranquil sage and mendicant. Controlling himself, his senses and his breath of life, he roamed around the earth. Without being attached to anything, he went to cities and villages for the sake of alms and entered unnoticed. O fortunate one! Seeing that aged and unclean beggar, wicked people showed him disrespect and abused him in many ways. Some took away the staff made of bamboo. Some took away his begging bowl. Some took away his kamandalu. Some took away his seat. Some took away his string of rudraksha beads. Some took away his torn rags. They would show them to the sage. Pretending to return them to him, they would take them away again. He would sit down on the bank of a river, to eat the food that he had begged. Wicked people would spit or urinate on his head. He had a vow of silence and they would try to make him speak. If he did not speak, they would strike him. If he did speak, others would chastise him. Some said, 'He is a thief.' Others said, 'He should be bound. Bind him with ropes.' Saying this, they bound him up. Some criticized and slighted him. 'Displaying the standard of dharma, this one is a fraud. His own relatives have thrown him out. Since his riches have been destroyed, he is using this to ensure a means of livelihood.' Some said, 'This one is great in substance. He is as steady as the king of the mountains. He is using silence to achieve his goal. He is as firm in determination as a crane.' Some ridiculed him. Some broke wind against him. Some bound him. Some tied up the brahmana, like something to play with. There were hardships caused by nature, by destiny and by his own body. He tolerated all this, realizing that he was obtaining all this as a result of destiny. Thus insulted by the worst among men, who were trying to make him fall down, he sang a song. He was based in dharma. Based in sattva, he resorted to his fortitude.

[1225] This has been described in Chapter 2(1).

'"The brahmana said, 'These men are not the cause of my happiness or unhappiness. Nor are the gods, my own body, the planets, karma, or time. It is said that the mind is alone the supreme cause. That is the reason one circles around in samsara. The powerful mind makes the gunas function and that leads to the different kinds of karma—white, black and red.[1226] The different species of life are created from this. The atman is not active. It is the mind which is active. My friend is golden in enlightenment[1227] and looks down from above. But I, as jivatman, have assumed its identity with the mind and am enjoying the objects of desire. Attached to the gunas, I have bound myself down. The goal of donations, one's own dharma, niyama, yama, learning, karma and good vows is to control the mind. All of them have this characteristic. The supreme form of yoga is to immerse the mind in samadhi. When the mind is controlled and tranquil, what is the need for donations and other things? Tell me. When the mind is not controlled and is distracted, what purpose will donations and other things serve? When the mind is under control, all others, including the divinities,[1228] are under control. The mind is never under the control of anything else. The mind is a divinity who is stronger than the strongest. If a person can bring it under control, he is the god of all the divinities. The mind is an enemy impossible to vanquish. Some are tormented by it and are unable to conquer it. Therefore, they are confused and have futile conflicts with other mortals—enemies, but even friends and neutrals. The body is only a creation of the mind. With their intelligence blinded, humans identify themselves with it and have notions of "I" and "mine". They suffer from the illusion, "I am this" and "He is someone else." Hence, they wander around in a darkness that is impossible to cross. If people are the cause of my happiness and unhappiness, that has to do with the physical body. What does the atman have to do with this? If a person bites his tongue by chance, he has done this himself. Why should he be angry at someone else for the suffering? If divinities of the senses are

[1226] Respectively associated with sattva, tamas and rajas.
[1227] The atman.
[1228] The senses and the divinities who preside over the senses.

responsible for the unhappiness, what does the atman have to do with this? That has to do with transformations. If one limb in his own body chooses to attack another limb, with whom will a man get angry? If the atman is the cause for happiness and unhappiness, then nothing else can be responsible. This is just a person's own nature. If there is anything other than the atman, it cannot be real. Why should one be angry? Happiness or unhappiness don't really exist. If the planets are the cause of happiness and unhappiness, what does it have to do with the atman? One doesn't have a birth, while the other is born. It is said that planets cause suffering to other planets. Whom should a man get angry with? The atman is distinct from both a body and a planet. If karma is the cause of happiness and unhappiness, what is the role for the atman there? The body of a man is not sentient, while it is the atman which is sentient.[1229] Whom will he be angry with? There is no foundation for the notion of karma. If time is the cause of happiness and unhappiness, what is the role of the atman there? Time is a manifestation of the atman. A flame does not burn its own spark. Ice does not destroy the quality of coldness. The supreme has no notion of duality. Whom will one be angry with? There is no agency anywhere, of any variety. The atman is supreme and beyond any attachment and duality. It is ahamkara which gives rise to samsara. A person who understands this has nothing to fear from anything that has been created. That being the case, I will faithfully base myself on the paramatman. That is what the maharshis spoke about earlier. I will cross this insurmountable darkness and serve at Mukunda's feet.'"

'The illustrious one continued, "With his wealth destroyed, he was disgusted. He overcame his despondency and, becoming a mendicant, roamed all over the earth. Though he was reviled by the wicked, he remained steadfast in his own dharma. The sage sang the following chant. 'Nothing other than a man's confusion gives rise to happiness and unhappiness. Friends, neutrals and enemies are the creations of the darkness of samsara.' O son! Therefore, in every

---

[1229] Is karma based on the body or the atman? The experience of happiness or unhappiness can only be felt by the sentient and the body is insentient.

possible way, use your intelligence to control your mind. Immerse yourself in me. That is what yoga propounds. The mendicant's chant is about devotion to the brahman. If a person controls himself and meditates on it, makes others listen to it or hears it, he will never be overwhelmed by the opposite pair of sentiments."'

Chapter 11(24)

'The illustrious one said, "I will now speak to you about samkhya, the nature of which has been determined earlier.[1230] Realizing this, a man can instantly give up any confusion caused by a sense of differentiation. In the beginning, at the time of krita yuga and when there were no yugas,[1231] people were accomplished in discrimination and because of that knowledge, saw everything as one and without any differentiation. It was one and undifferentiated, beyond the reach of mind and speech. However, that great truth differentiated itself into two and became the fruits of maya and that reflected in this.[1232] Out of these two entities, one is Prakriti, with the two aspects of cause and effect. The entity that possesses jnana is spoken of as Purusha. Prakriti was agitated by my glances as Purusha and with my sanction, the gunas—sattva, rajas and tamas—were evolved. Sutra[1233] evolved from these and Mahat was created from Sutra. Together, Mahat and Sutra underwent transformations and ahamkara, which causes bewilderment, was evolved. This has three types—vaikarika, taijasa and tamasa. These have intelligent and non-intelligent forms and are the cause of the tanmatras, the senses and the mind. *Tamasa ahamkara* lead to the creation of the tanmatras and the gross elements.

[1230] By Kapila and others.

[1231] At the time of destruction. At this time, there is no question of people existing. Therefore, what is meant is that only undifferentiated consciousness existed.

[1232] The fruits of maya are interpreted as material existence and the jiva is reflected in this.

[1233] Sutra is an intervening stage between the gunas and Mahat.

Taijasa ahamkara lead to the creation of the senses.[1234] The eleven divinities were created from vaikarika ahamkara.[1235] Urged by me, all these entities came together and worked collectively. The cosmic egg was created in this way, an excellent place for me to lie down on. That cosmic egg was floating around in the water and I manifested myself inside it. A lotus known as Vishva sprouted from my navel and the self-creating one[1236] appeared inside that. Through my favours, he was endowed with rajas and performed austerities for the sake of creating. Thus, the atman of the universe created the worlds, the guardians of the worlds and the three—*bhur, bhuvar* and *svar*. Svar is the abode of the gods, bhuvar is the abode of the bhutas and bhur is the abode of mortals and others. The Siddhas reside beyond these three worlds. The lord created the regions that are below the earth for the asuras and the nagas. All the karma performed under the influence of the gunas leads to a destination in the three worlds. Through yoga, austerities and renunciation, a person obtains a destination in the unblemished worlds of *maharloka, janaloka, tapoloka* and *satyaloka*. A person who practises bhakti yoga finds a destination in me. I am the creator and, in my form as time, have linked this world to karma. In the flow of the gunas, one sometimes rises up and is sometimes submerged. All the manifestations that have been established, large or small, thin or stout, have been created by Purusha and Prakriti. Anything that exists at the beginning, the middle and the end of an entity, across all these transformations, is regarded as the real entity. This is the case with objects made out of gold or earth.[1237] But the subsequent product may have a cause which is the product of a transformation resulting from an earlier cause. That which exists at the beginning and the end of the chain is referred to as the real entity. Prakriti can be regarded as the primary cause, but the supreme Purusha is its foundation. Time manifests these and in this triad of what is real, I am established as the brahman. As long as my favourable glance

---

[1234] The five senses of perception and the five senses of action.
[1235] Presiding over the ten senses and the mind.
[1236] Brahma.
[1237] Gold is the real entity for ornaments and earth is the real entity for pots.

remains, this progressive creation, from cause to subsequent effect, continues. For the sake of creation, this great flow of the gunas also continues. This universal form, in which creation and destruction of the worlds take place, is pervaded by me. I have devised the worlds and the means of their dissolution into the five elements. Mortals are withdrawn into food.[1238] Food is withdrawn into grain. Grain is withdrawn into the earth. The earth is withdrawn into its attribute of smell. Smell is withdrawn into water. Water is withdrawn into its attribute of taste. Taste is withdrawn into fire. Fire is withdrawn into its attribute of form. Form is withdrawn into wind. Wind is withdrawn into its attribute of touch. Touch is withdrawn into space. All the senses are withdrawn into their sources. These sources are then withdrawn into their controllers. The mind is withdrawn into the controller of the mind, vaikarika ahamkara. Sound is withdrawn into tamasa ahamkara. All of ahamkara is withdrawn into Mahat. The powerful Mahat is withdrawn into the gunas that generated it. The gunas are withdrawn into the unmanifest Prakriti. Prakriti is withdrawn into time, which ceases to function. Time is withdrawn into jiva, full of maya. Jiva is withdrawn into atman, which caused it. The atman is only based on the atman and its existence can be inferred from the process of creation and destruction. When the sun rises, there is no longer any darkness in the sky. In that way, if a person examines this differentiation of the atman in his mind, all illusion is destroyed. This is known as the process of samkhya and it severs the bonds of doubt. The superior and the inferior, the process of creation and of destruction, can be clearly seen and I have spoken about this.""

Chapter 11(25)

'The illustrious one said, "O noble being! I will now tell you about a person being affected by the mixture of the gunas. Please understand. Control of the mind, control of the senses, forbearance, austerities, truthfulness, compassion, memory,

[1238] This is a description of the process of destruction.

contentment, renunciation, lack of desire, devotion, modesty, generosity and pleasure in one's own self—these are the effects of sattva.[1239] Desire, efforts, insolence, greed, pride, seeking benedictions for the sake of happiness, rashness resulting from intoxication, love of fame, laughing at others, valour, strength and enterprise— these are the effects of rajas. Anger, avarice, falsehood, violence, begging, hypocrisy, lassitude, dissension, sorrow, delusion, grief, despondency, sloth, hopes, fear and lack of enterprise—these are the effects of tamas. These, in that order, are the effects of sattva, rajas and tamas. I have generally described the effects of these attributes. Now hear about their combinations. The combination of these leads to the mindset of 'I' and 'mine'. Anything done by the mind, the organs of action, the organs of perception or the breath of life result from such combinations. If a person devotes himself to dharma, artha and kama and this leads to obtaining faith, satisfaction and wealth, this is nothing but the combination of the gunas.[1240] If a person is characterized by devotion to pravritti and is a householder, when he pursues his own dharma, this is a manifestation of the combination of the gunas.[1241] If a person exhibits attributes of self-control and similar things, it can be deduced he is full of sattva. If he has attributes of desire and similar things, he is full of rajas. If he has attributes of anger and similar things, he is full of tamas. If a person, irrespective of being a man or a woman, is engaged in his own tasks and devotedly worships me, without any desire, this should be known as a nature based on sattva. If a person is engaged in his own tasks and worships me in the hope of benedictions or wishes being satisfied, this is known as a nature based on rajas. If the hope is one of causing injury, this is based on tamas. The gunas, sattva, rajas and tamas, affect the jiva, not me. They are the outcomes of the minds of beings. Becoming attached, they are bound down. Sattva is radiant,

[1239] The text doesn't use the word sattva, it being left implicit. We have added it, as we have done for rajas and tamas, to make the meaning clear.

[1240] The pursuit of dharma is based on sattva, the pursuit of artha is based on rajas and the pursuit of kama is based on tamas.

[1241] The tasks of dharma are based on sattva, the pravritti is based on rajas and the attachment to the home is based on tamas.

pure and auspicious. When it triumphs over the other two, the man enjoys happiness, dharma, jnana and similar things. Rajas leads to attachment, differentiation and fickleness. When it triumphs over sattva and tamas, the person enjoys unhappiness and undertakes tasks for the sake of fame and prosperity. When tamas triumphs over sattva and rajas, the person loses discrimination and insight and becomes dull. He is full of misery, delusion, sloth, violence and hopes. When the intelligence is pleased and there is a retreat from the senses, without fear about the body and attachment in the mind, know that this is based on sattva and leads to a destination in me. When the intelligence is agitated by activity and the mind cannot restrain it, when the body is not healthy and the mind is awhirl, understand that these are the attributes of rajas. When the intelligence fails and the mind is incapable of controlling it, when the mind ceases to function and there is ignorance and despondency, understand that these are the attributes of tamas. When sattva guna becomes more powerful, the strength of the gods increases. It is the same with rajas for the asuras and tamas for the rakshasas. Among beings, know that wakefulness results from sattva, sleep is indicated by rajas and sushupti results from tamas. Turiya is pervaded by all three gunas. Through sattva, people who are brahmanas ascend further upwards. Tamas drags people downwards, with their faces hanging downwards. Rajas makes them roam around in an intermediary stage. Those who possess sattva at the time of death go to heaven, those who possess rajas at the time of death go to the world of men and those who possess tamas at the time of death go to hell. Those who are devoid of gunas obtain me. If a person undertakes his own tasks, offering them to me, without any desire for the fruits, this is characterized by sattva. If the resolution is because of the fruits, this is characterized by rajas. Violence is generally characterized by tamas. Kaivalya is jnana characterized by sattva. A sense of differentiation is characterized by rajas. Knowledge about material objects alone is characterized by tamas. Jnana that is based on me is said to be nirguna. Residing in the forest is characterized by sattva. Residing in a village is said to be characterized by rajas. Residing in a gambling house is characterized by tamas. Residing in my abode is nirguna. An agent who is not attached is characterized by sattva. An agent who is blinded by attachment is said to be characterized by rajas. An agent whose memory has been destroyed is characterized by tamas. A person who seeks refuge in me is nirguna. Faith in the adhyamtika is characterized by sattva. Faith in karma is characterized by rajas. Faith in adharma is characterized by tamas. Serving me is nirguna. Nourishing and pure food that is easily obtained is said to be characterized by sattva. Love for food that pander to the senses is characterized by rajas. Love for unclean food that causes affliction is characterized by tamas. Happiness from one's own atman is characterized by sattva, from material objects is characterized by rajas and from misery and delusion is characterized by tamas. Everything is based on the three gunas—the object, the place, the fruit, time, jnana, karma, the agent, faith, state of consciousness, form and destination. O bull among men! All states of existence are full of the gunas and are based on Purusha and Prakriti. This is true of everything that is seen, heard or conceived by the mind. O amiable one! These gunas lead to a man being bound in karma and samsara. The gunas are created from the mind. Firmly established in devotion to me, if a jiva conquers them through bhakti yoga, he obtains my state. Therefore, a learned person who obtains this body in this world, which can give rise to jnana and vijnana, cleanses all attachment to the gunas and worships me. A learned person is not distracted. He conquers his senses and worships me, free from attachment. Such a sage conquers rajas and tamas and only serves sattva. Thus serving sattva, he also conquers sattva and becomes indifferent to the gunas, serene in his intelligence. The jiva becomes free of the gunas. Giving up the state of jiva, he obtains me. The jiva is freed from the state of being a jiva and from the gunas, which are created in his own mind. He does not roam around inside or outside, but is complete in me, the brahman.'"

Chapter 11(26)

'The illustrious one said, "Having got this human body, if a person resorts to my dharma, he can obtain me, the bliss and the paramatman that exist in his own atman. Through faith and jnana, one can be freed from the state of being a jiva, created by the gunas. He can see that what can be seen by the eyes is not real. It is only maya, caused by the gunas. Such a person does not get entangled in unreal objects that are caused by the gunas, even though he exists amidst them. One must never be associated with those who are wicked, with those who seek to satisfy their penises and their stomachs. Like a blind person following another blind person, by following them, one falls into blinding darkness. Emperor Aila[1242] was extensive in fame. Separated from Urvashi, he was bewildered. He controlled his grief through non-attachment and chanted this song. While she was leaving him, the king lamented. Overwhelmed with grief, he was maddened. In that naked state, he rushed after her and said, 'O cruel wife! Remain.' He had passed several years with her, in the pursuit of this insignificant desire, not noticing the nights coming and going. He was unconscious because of his attraction towards her and was still not satisfied.

'"Aila said, 'Alas! My delusion is extensive. My mind has been contaminated by desire. When the queen clasped me by the neck, I did not notice that parts of my life had passed away. I was so deceived by her that I did not notice the sun rising or setting. Many days, amounting to many years, have certainly passed. Alas! I have brought this delusion on myself. Despite being an emperor and like a jewel on the crest of all the kings, I behaved like a domesticated deer in the hands of a woman. Though I am a lord, she cast me and my royal power aside, like a blade of grass. When the woman left, I followed her, like a mad man, naked and weeping. Despite my being a lord, where is my power? Where is my energy? Like a donkey, she kicked me with her foot. As the woman left, I followed her. What will one do with learning, with austerities, with yoga and with learning? What will I do with solitude, or with silence? These are of no use to a person whose mind is stolen by a woman. Shame on me. I did not know what was good for me. Though I prided myself on being learned, I was a fool. Though I obtained lordship, like a bull or a donkey, I allowed myself to be conquered

---

[1242] Ila's son, Pururava.

by a woman. I savoured the nectar of Urvashi's lips for many years. But like a fire fed with oblations, the desire in me was not satisfied. When the mind is stolen by a pumshchali,[1243] who other than the illustrious lord Adhokshaja can save a person? He is the lord of those who find bliss in the atman. Using the words of a *sukta*, the queen tried to make me come to my senses. However, I was evil-minded. The great delusion in my mind did not go away. I was unable to control myself. How has she caused me any harm? Since I had not conquered my sense, I did not know my own nature. Such was my mind that I saw a rope and took it to be a snake. What is this physical body? It is full of filth and bad smells. It is inauspicious. What are the good qualities a flower possesses? These are nothing but impositions caused by ignorance. Is the body the property of the parents, the wife, the master, the fire, dogs or vultures?[1244] Does it belong to the atman? Or does it belong to well-wishers? It is impossible to decide. One becomes attached to this abominable body which heads to an inferior destination. This is very handsome. There is an excellent one. The face is beautiful. These are the things one says about a woman's face. The body consists of skin, flesh, blood, nerves, fat, marrow, bones, urine, excrement and pus. What is the difference between those who find pleasure in it and worms? Therefore, a person who knows the true meaning should not get attached to women, or to those who associate with women. When the senses are attached to material objects, the mind is agitated. It cannot but be otherwise. If a thing is not heard about, or if it is not seen, no attachment towards it follows. If the prana is not engaged with something that is not present, the mind is calm and pacified. Therefore, one should not get attached to women, nor to those whose senses pursue women. Even learned men do not trust the six categories.[1245] What need be said about a person like me?'"

[1243] Loose woman.

[1244] Fire, dogs or vultures depends on how it is disposed of after death.

[1245] Kama (desire), *krodha* (anger), *lobha* (avarice), *moha* (delusion), *mada* (arrogance) and *matsarya* (jealousy). Alternatively, the five senses and the mind.

'The illustrious one said, "Having sung in this way, the lord of the kings gave up Urvashi's world. He obtained me in his own atman. With this jnana, he cleansed himself of his delusion. Therefore, an intelligent person must avoid association with those who are wicked and associate with those who are virtuous. It is such sages who can sever the excessive attachment of the mind through what they say. Without expecting anything, sages immerse their minds in me. They are serene and impartial in outlook. They are without a sense of ownership and without ahamkara. They possess nothing and are not affected by the opposite pair of sentiments. O immensely fortunate one! Among those immensely fortunate ones, there is always conversation about me. Men who take part in these obtain benefit for themselves and are cleansed of sins. Those who respectfully hear, chant and approve of these, become faithful and devoted towards me. They obtain devotion towards me. If a virtuous person obtains devotion towards me, what else remains to be accomplished? My qualities are infinite. I am the brahman. I am the atman, the one who confers bliss. If a person approaches the illustrious, fire, cold, fear and darkness are dispelled. Serving the virtuous is like that. They are the supreme shelter for those who are rising and falling in the terrible ocean of samsara. The sages know about the brahman. They are serene. To those who are drowning in the water, they are like a firm boat. Just as food provides life to living beings, I am the refuge for those who are afflicted. For men who die, dharma represents riches. Like that, sages represent shelter for those who are scared of falling downwards. Sages bestow vision on the eyes, just as the rising sun confers external vision.[1246] Sages are divinities and relatives. Sages are my own atman. Thus, losing all desire for the world that belonged to Urvashi, Vaitasena[1247] became free of attachment. He roamed around on earth, finding happiness in his own atman."'

[1246] Sages confer internal vision.

[1247] Pururava's name, one that occurs rarely.

Chapter 11(27)

'Uddhava asked, "O bull among the Satvatas! Tell me about the method of using *kriya yoga* to worship you. What is its form? How do those who are devoted to you use it to worship you? All the sages, Narada, the illustrious Vyasa and the preceptor who was the son of Angiras,[1248] have repeatedly said that this brings great benefit to men. It first emerged from your lotus mouth. The illustrious Aja spoke about it to his sons, Bhrigu being the foremost. The illustrious Bhava spoke about it to the goddess.[1249] This is approved of by all the varnas and ashramas. O one who grants honours! I think it brings the greatest benefit for women and shudras. O lotus-eyed one! This frees a person from the bonds of karma. You are attached to your devotees. O lord of all the lords of the universe! Tell me about this."

'The illustrious one replied, "O Uddhava! There is no end to *karmakanda*.[1250] It is without limits. Briefly, but progressively, I will describe it to you. There are three kinds of worship—following the Vedas, following the tantras, and mixed. Using whichever one a person prefers, he must follow the rituals and worship me. A man may become a dvija according to what is stated in his own sacred text. He must then worship me faithfully and devotedly. Hear about this from me. This dvija must worship me in the earth,[1251] in fire, in the sun, in water, or inside his own heart. He must be filled with devotion and then worship me, his preceptor, using various objects. He must be without any deception. He must first bathe, clean his teeth and purify his body. He must bathe himself by smearing himself with mud and other things.[1252] In the course of both kinds of bathing, he must chant mantras. He must perform sandhya and other rituals towards me that have been mentioned in the Vedas. Firm in his resolution, he must arrange for the worship, such that

---

[1248] That is, Brihaspati.
[1249] Parvati.
[1250] Karmakanda stands for ritualistic worship.
[1251] Interpreted as an image made out of earth.
[1252] The first is a physical bath. The second is a figurative bath.

the subsequent tasks are purified. It is said that the image can be of eight types—stone, wood, metal, clay,[1253] painted, made out of sand, made out of jewels, or conceived in the mind. When the lord's shrine is established, it can be of two types—mobile or immobile. O Uddhava! When the worshipped image is immovable, there is no need for *avahana* or *udvasa*.[1254] When the image is movable, the observance of these two rituals is optional. If the image is not made out of clay or is not painted, it can be bathed. In other cases, it must be sprinkled with water. When I am worshipped in the form of an image, excellent objects must be used. However, a devotee who is not deceitful can worship me with whatever is available. As long as the sentiment is there, he can even worship me inside his heart. O Uddhava! When I am worshipped in the form of an image, I love bathing and ornamenting the most. If I am worshipped in the form of an altar, the tattvas must be spread out.[1255] If I am worshipped in the form of fire, oblations of ghee must be offered. If I am worshipped in the form of the sun, I love arghya the most. If I am worshipped in the form of water, water must be offered. I love whatever a devotee offers me faithfully, even if it is some water. However, even if a lot of offerings are given to me by a person who lacks in devotion, I am not satisfied. What need be said about fragrances, incense, flowers, lamps, food and other things? After purifying himself, the worshipper must gather all the offerings together. He will devise a seat for himself, with the blades of the darbha grass pointing eastwards. He will sit down, facing the east or the north. He can also worship by facing the image directly. He must perform nyasa on his body. He must perform nyasa on the image. Using his hands, he must clean the image. As is appropriate, he must then get ready by consecrating the vessel that contains auspicious objects and the

[1253] Or sandalwood paste.

[1254] Avahana is invoking the deity's presence, udvasa/*visarjana* is bidding farewell.

[1255] This can be interpreted in different ways. For example, there are the twenty-five tattvas of samkhya—five tanmatras, five great elements, five senses of action, five senses of perception, the mind, *buddhi*, ahamkara, Prakriti and Purusha. These, or the respective divinities, are worshipped with the corresponding mantras.

vessel that contains water. He must use water from the vessel containing water to sprinkle the place where the deity is being worshipped, the objects of worship and his own self. He must then arrange for three other vessels to be filled with water,[1256] reciting respective mantras for the heart, the head and the tuft of hair on the head. After this, he must chant gayatri mantra. The body has now been purified by the air and the fire. My supreme and subtle form, the source of life, is located in its portion in the lotus in the heart and after chanting 'Oum', he must meditate on this. This is what Siddhas experience. Depending on the level of his perception, he contemplates his body to be pervaded by the atman. He thus worships me. Conceiving of the image being pervaded by me, he invokes me through the objects of worship and establishes me in the image. He then performs nyasa in the limbs and worships me. He mentally thinks of a seat for me, with dharma and the other nine powers in attendance.[1257] A lotus with eight petals is spread on that seat and the lotus has a radiant whorl and filaments. For the sake of success in this world and in the next, he follows both the Vedas and the tantras and offers me padya, arghya and achamaniya. In due order, he must then worship Sudarshana, Panchajanya, the mace, the sword, the arrows, the bow, the plough, the club, Koustubha, the garland and the shrivatsa mark. He must worship Nanda, Sunanda, Garuda, Prachanda, Chanda, Mahabala, Bala, Kumuda and Kumudekshana.[1258] In their respective places, all facing the lord, with water and other objects, he must then worship Durga, Vinayaka, Vyasa, Vishvaksena, his preceptor and the gods. If he possesses the riches, he must chant mantras and every day, offer me water for bathing, fragrant with sandalwood, *ushira*,[1259] camphor, kunkuma and aloe. He must chant *svarnagharmanuvaka*,

[1256] These three vessels contain water for washing the deity's feet (padya), washing the hands (arghya) and rinsing the mouth (achamaniya).

[1257] The nine powers are *vimala* (purity), *utkarshni* (exalted state), jnana, *kriya* (activity), yoga, *prahvi* (modesty), *satya*, ishana (sovereignty) and *anugraha* (grace).

[1258] There are eight attendants in eight directions, with Garuda standing in front.

[1259] Ushira is the root of the fragrant grass *Andropogon muricatus*.

mahapurusha vidya, purusha sukta and hymns from the Sama Veda, *rajana* and the others.[1260] As is appropriate, my devotee must lovingly decorate me with garments, the sacred thread, ornaments, decorations for parts of the body, garlands, fragrances and unguents. The worshipper must offer me padya, achamaniya, fragrances, flowers, *akshata*,[1261] incense, lamps and other objects. If it is possible, he must arrange for candy made out of molasses, payasam, ghee, *shashkuli*, sweet cakes, dumplings, *samyava*, curds, *supa* and other *naivedya*.[1262] Every day, else on days of festivals, the image must be massaged with ointments and bathed, and offered a mirror and equipment to clean the teeth. Food and other objects must be offered, with singing and dancing. A sacrificial arena must be prepared, as is recommended, with a pit and an altar and a surrounding girdle.[1263] Using the hands,[1264] a fire must be invoked and kindled on all sides. Spreading a mat of kusha grass, all sides of the fire must be sprinkled with water and following the rituals, the kindling must be placed for the fire. The objects of worship must be placed and sprinkled with water. After sprinkling with water, he must think of me in the fire. My complexion is that of molten gold. I hold a conch shell, chakra, mace and lotus. My brilliant form possesses four arms. I am serene and my garments have a complexion like that of the filament of a lotus. I wear a dazzling diadem, bracelets, a girdle and excellent armlets. The shrivatsa mark is on my chest, with the radiant Koustubha and a garland of wild flowers. Having meditated on me and worshipped me, he must soak the kindling with ghee and offer them into the fire. He must tender two

---

[1260] Svarnagharmanuvaka is from the *Taittiriya Aranyaka*, mahapurusha vidya is a specific mantra and rajana and *rouhina* are hymns from the Sama Veda.

[1261] This can mean grain of any kind. But it is specifically used for threshed and winnowed rice that has not been dehusked.

[1262] Naivedya is a general term for offerings of food. We have translated *guda* as candy made out of molasses, apupa as sweet cakes and *modaka* as dumpling. Shashkuli is a cake made out of rice or barley, supa can only be translated as soup and samyava is a kind of cake.

[1263] Interpretations explain that a sacrifice is not meant for everyone.

[1264] For the kindling.

offerings of ghee and then the other oblations that have been soaked with ghee. A learned person will offer oblations with chanting of the main mantra and then follow with the sixteen kinds of worship, ending each verse with an oblation.[1265] Beginning with Dharma,[1266] each deity is worshipped according to the appropriate mantra, ending with *agnaye svishtakrite svaha*.[1267] Having bowed down before me and worshipped me, he must tender offerings to the attendants. Using the main mantra, he meditates on the brahman, remembering that this is nothing but Narayana's atman. He must again offer me achamaniya and offer whatever is left to Vishvaksena. He must offer fragrant betel leaves to freshen the mouth. He must sing and chant loudly, also dancing and imitating my deeds. He must listen to my account and recite it, remaining in that state for a while. He must praise me with hymns, superior and inferior, from the Puranas and ordinary texts. 'O lord! May you show me your favours.' Saying this, he must prostrate himself before me, like a rod. He will place his head on my feet, clasping them with both his arms. 'O lord! I seek refuge with you. Save me. I am terrified of this ocean of samsara, with crocodiles in the form of death.' After this, he must lovingly place on his head the remnants of the worship, representing something given by me. If udvasa is meant to be performed, he must conceive of the light in the image as again merging into the light that is me. I can be worshipped in whatever form and whenever, as long as that worship is faithful. My atman exists in all beings and all atmans are in me. If a man follows the Vedas and the tantras and worships me through kriya yoga, from me, he obtains success in both the worlds and gets what he desires. He must firmly establish my worship by constructing temples and beautiful gardens of flowers. Or he can ensure this worship through pilgrimages and festivals. If a person gives land, markets, villages and cities, so that my worship is continuously ensured on general or

[1265] The main mantra is *oum namo narayanaya*. The sixteen refers to the sixteen verses of the purusha sukta. After each verse, the mantra for the corresponding deity is chanted.

[1266] Yama.

[1267] The text merely states *svishti*, we have added the mantra for clarity.

special occasions, he obtains me, with my opulence. By constructing a temple to me, one obtains sovereignty over the three worlds. Through worship and other things, a person obtains Brahma's world. However, if one does all three,[1268] one obtains serenity in me. If a person has no wishes and engages in bhakti yoga, he obtains me. If a person worships me through bhakti yoga, it is me that he obtains. If a person gives something to gods or brahmanas and then himself steals it back, he is subsequently born as a worm and survives on excrement for a hundred million years. After death, the agent, the assistant who helps the act and the person who approves of it have a share in the karma and proportionately reap the consequences.'"

Chapter 11(28)

'The illustrious one said, "One should not praise or reprimand the nature or deeds of someone else, considering that the universe is formed out of Purusha and Prakriti, based on a single atman. If a person praises or reprimands the nature or deeds of someone else, he soon deviates from his own objective and becomes attached to something unreal. The senses are formed out of taijasa ahamkara. When a man is asleep, the consciousness is lost and the atman is in a shell.[1269] Overcome by maya, a man is like a person who is dead. It is the same for a person who finds reality in material objects. When this duality of material objects is unreal, what is good and what is bad? Anything that is spoken about with words, or anything that is thought of through the mind, is unreal. Shadows, echoes and illusions are unreal and lead to similar effects. But these conceptions are based on the body and give rise to fear, right up to the moment of death. The lord is the atman of the universe. He is the creator and the object of creation. He is the atman of the universe. He is the protector and the object of protection. The lord is the one

---

[1268] Donations, constructing temples and performing worship.
[1269] Of the body.

who withdraws and he is the object of withdrawal. Therefore, no object other than the atman can be distinctly discerned. The three kinds of appearance[1270] in his atman are without foundation. Know that these are the outcome of the three kinds of gunas and are the result of maya. If a person understands what I have expounded, he becomes accomplished in jnana and vijnana. He does not criticize or praise. He roams around in the world like the sun.[1271] Through perception, inference, the sacred texts and realization of the atman, one should know that since this world has a beginning and an end, it is unreal. Hence, one must roam around without attachment."

'Uddhava asked, "O lord! The atman is the seer. The body, which is not the atman, is what is seen. Samsara is experienced by neither the atman, nor the body. In that case, who experiences samsara? The atman is without decay. It is without gunas and is pure. It is self-luminous and is not covered by anything. It is like the fire, while the body is like kindling. Who experiences samsara in this world?"[1272]

'The illustrious one replied, 'Samsara is without meaning. But as long as the atman lacks discrimination, it is attracted to the senses and to prana. Till then, it has to experience the fruits. As long as one thinks about material objects, like experiencing disagreeable things in a dream, samsara, though it does not truly exist, is not withdrawn. If a person is asleep and has not woken up, he experiences many disagreeable things. On waking up, this can no longer confuse him. Grief, joy, fear, anger, avarice, confusion, desire and other things, as well as birth and death, are seen to be related to ahamkara, not to the atman. Because of the identification with the body, the senses, prana, the mind and ahamkara, the atman who is inside the body assumes the form of jiva, with gunas and karma.[1273] Strung in this great thread,

[1270] Creation, preservation and destruction.
[1271] The sun is impartial.
[1272] Who goes through the cycle of birth and death?
[1273] There are many complicated intepretations here. Stated simply, the jivatman, in the absence of knowledge, suffers from ahamkara and goes through samsara, suffering the consequences of karma.

he is chanted about in many ways. Under the control of time, he revolves around in samsara. This has no foundation and is perceived in many different forms—the mind, speech, prana, the body and karma. Using worship and the sharp sword of jnana to sever this, sages roam around on this earth, free from all desire. Jnana and discrimination result from the sacred texts, austerities, direct perception, instruction and inference. The absolute is time and the cause, existing at the beginning, the end and the middle of this creation. Everything made out of gold was gold before the object was fashioned out of its own self and continues to be gold afterwards. In the middle, in the process of manufacture, though described with different names, it continues to be gold. I am exactly like that. O dear one! This vijnana exists in three states.[1274] The three gunas manifest themselves as the senses, the gross elements and the agent, collectively and separately. What is manifested in the state of turiya is the truth. That which had no existence earlier, and will have no existence in the future, has an existence in the middle only because of its name.[1275] It is my view that an entity which exists merely because someone else gives it an appellation does not really exist. Though this universe appears to be manifest, it does not really exist. This is a modification caused by rajas. The brahman is manifest in its own illumination. The senses, the objects of the senses, and the mind are but wonderful transformations brought about by the brahman. In this way, an accomplished person uses discrimination and refutation to clearly differentiate the brahman from something else. Thus, one severs any doubts about the nature of the atman. One desists from all objects of desire and is satisfied in one's own bliss. The atman is not the physical body. Nor is it the senses, the divinities of the senses, the breath of life, wind, water, fire, space, earth, mind, objects of the senses, ahamkara, or the equilibrium between the gunas. The senses are manifestations of the gunas. If a person has controlled himself and has properly ascertained me as the lord,

[1274] Wakefulness, sleeping and sushupti.

[1275] Therefore, this body does not make an existence merely because it is called a body.

why will such a virtuous person get agitated by these? Irrespective
of whether the sun is covered by clouds or the clouds have
dispersed, why should the sun be blamed? The sky is not affected
by the qualities of the wind, the fire, the water and the earth. Nor
is it affected by the coming and going of the seasons. In that way,
the truth is not contaminated by the impurities of sattva, rajas
and tamas. It is beyond ahamkara and is the supreme cause of
samsara. Rajas contaminates the mind because of attachment to
material objects. Therefore, until it has been eliminated through
firm bhakti yoga towards me, all association with objects of the
senses, devised by maya, must be avoided. A disease that has not
been properly treated recurs again and repeatedly causes distress
to men. In this way, a mind that has not been purified suffers from
the contamination of karma and an imperfect yogi is tormented
by all kinds of attachment. An imperfect yogi suffers from
impediments caused by men, other creatures and those created by
the gods. Based on the strength of former practices,[1276] he engages
in yoga again and is not entangled in the path of karma. Urged by
something else,[1277] till the time of death, a being undertakes karma
and is acted upon.[1278] However, though a learned person remains
in Prakriti's domain, he experiences his own happiness, having
cast aside all desires. Regardless of whether he is standing, seated,
walking, lying down, urinating, eating food or doing anything else
that is natural, his consciousness is based in his atman and he does
not recognize the body. Even if a learned person sees the many
objects of the senses, he uses his inference to think of them as
unreal and as being other than the atman. He is like a person who
has woken up, to see that what he has seen in a dream has vanished.
O dear one! Earlier, because of ignorance, it was accepted that
this body, wrought by the gunas and colourful with karma, was
no different from the atman and was identical. However, with
re-examination, that view no longer exists. The atman cannot be
perceived. Nor can its existence be rejected. When the sun rises,

---

[1276] In an earlier life.
[1277] Past karma, or destiny.
[1278] That karma works on him.

it destroys darkness from the eyes of men. But the objects that
are seen already existed. Thus, accomplished examination sees
the truth in me and destroys the darkness that covers a person's
intelligence. This is self-luminous. It is unborn. It is impossible to
measure it. It is great in consciousness and can perceive everything.
It is one, without a second. It is beyond the conception of words.
It makes speech and the breath of life move. Any sense of duality
about the absolute is the result of delusion. There is nothing other
than the atman. There is no support other than one's own atman.
There are some, proud of their learning, who hold that these
names and forms, constituted by the five elements, are undeniable.
However, this duality, based on debates about what is real, has
no basis. If a yogi has not perfected himself in yoga, many kinds
of things will rise up in the body and try to engage his attention.
There is a recommended procedure whereby these disturbances
can be repulsed. Some of these disturbances can be repulsed
through the process of yoga, some through asana, some through
dharana,[1279] some through austerities, some through mantras and
some through herbs. Some can be countered by meditating on me,
chanting my name and doing similar things. These inauspicious
aspects can be gradually destroyed by following the lords of yoga.
Some persevering people keep their body fit and maintain their
youth by using different kinds of techniques. They engage in yoga
for siddhis. However, those who are accomplished do not have
any respect for these efforts and regard them as useless. Like the
fruits of a tree, this body is destructible. If a person constantly
engages in yoga, his body will become fit, but an intelligent person
will not attach any importance to this. He will give up this kind
of yoga and immerse himself in me. A yogi who seeks refuge in
me and observes the process of yoga is not obstructed by any
impediments. He is without desire and experiences happiness
within himself.'"

[1279] Yoga has eight elements—yama (restraint), niyama (rituals), asana
(posture), pranayama (breathing), pratyahara (withdrawal), dharana
(retention), dhyana (meditation) and samadhi (liberation). That's the
reason the expression ashtanga (eight-formed) yoga is used.

Chapter 11(29)

'Uddhava said, "O Achyuta! If a person is not in control of his mind, I think that this yoga is extremely difficult to practise. Tell me about a method whereby a man can easily obtain success. O Pundarikaksha! Often, yogis who try to control their minds are unable to control their minds and become frustrated, fatigued and despondent. O lotus-eyed one! Therefore, hamsas happily resort to your feet, which are the source of bliss. O lord of the universe! However, proud people[1280] who use yoga and karma are confounded by your maya. O Achyuta! It is not surprising that you are a friend to all those who are your servants and seek refuge with you, with their atmans devoted to you. The lords of the worlds seek the refuge of your feet, with the edges of their shining diadems touching them. But you were affectionate towards animals.[1281] You are in all atmans. You are the beloved lord of all those who seek refuge with you. You are all the objectives. Knowing this, who can reject you? Who will forget you and worship other beings? What can not be obtained by us, those who serve the dust of your feet? O lord! Wise ones happily remember you for your generous deeds and are incapable of repaying their debt, even if they possess Brahma's lifespan. You exist inside and outside embodied beings, as a preceptor and as consciousness,[1282] to destroy everything that is inauspicious and to show them their objective."'

Shri-Shuka said, 'Uddhava's heart was extremely devoted to him. He spoke to the lord of the lords, who had used his own potencies to play with the universe and had assumed three forms,[1283] in this way and asked him. He[1284] addressed him with a charming smile that was full of love.

[1280] Who are therefore not devoted to you.

[1281] Like those in the Ramayana.

[1282] As a preceptor outside the body and as consciousness inside the body.

[1283] Brahma, Vishnu and Shiva. Alternatively, this can also be interpreted as sattva, rajas and tamas.

[1284] Krishna.

'The illustrious one replied, "I will tell you about the extremely auspicious dharma of devotion to me. If a mortal person follows this faithfully, he defeats death, which is extremely difficult to vanquish. Remembering me, all tasks must be gradually undertaken for my sake. The mind and the intelligence must be immersed in me. There must be attraction towards the dharma of being devoted to me. Such a person must frequent sacred places that are frequented by virtuous people who are devoted to me. He must follow the conduct of gods, asuras and men who are devoted to me. Alone, or collectively, he must celebrate auspicious days, pilgrimages[1285] or great festivities that are dedicated to me, making arrangements for singing, dancing and other signs of opulence deserving of kings. He must see me inside and outside all beings, like the sky. With an unblemished heart, he must see me in his own atman. O immensely radiant one! Thus, thinking that all creatures are full of my presence, he must show them respect, establishing himself in pure jnana. If a person is impartial towards brahmanas, *pukkasas*,[1286] thieves, those who are devoted to brahmanas, the sun, a spark of fire, a cruel person and a compassionate person, it is held that he is learned. If a man looks at all men and thinks that they are full of me, all feelings of rivalry, jealousy, censure and ahamkara are quickly dispelled. Ignoring the ridiculing laughs of one's relatives, one should abandon the view that one should be ashamed of anything connected with the body. Like a staff, he must prostrate himself on the ground before a horse, a chandala, a cow or an ass. Until the sense of me being in all creatures has been generated, he must continue to worship me through all acts of speech, mind and body. Through knowledge that the brahman is everywhere and by realizing the atman, he is dispelled of doubts and can cease from everything else. It is my view that this process is the most appropriate, using acts of speech, mind and body to see me in all creatures. O Uddhava! This perfect dharma is devoid of gunas and has been established by me. It is not

---

[1285] Or journeys.

[1286] Pedantically, a chandala is the son of a brahmana mother and a shudra father. A *pulkasa* (equivalently pukkasa) is the son of a *nishada* father and a shudra mother.

driven by wishes. Therefore, even if a beginning is made, the effort is not wasted. O excellent one! This supreme dharma of devotion towards me has been fashioned to free onself of the fruits of karma, which are futile efforts to free oneself of fear and other things. This is the most intelligent thing that an intelligent person can do. This is the most learned thing that a learned person can do. Using a mortal body in this unreal world, one can obtain truth and immortality. I have told you about the entire collection of teachings about the brahman, in brief and in detail. Even the gods find this extremely difficult to comprehend. I have repeatedly spoken to you about this jnana, with clear reasoning. If a man knows this, his doubts are destroyed and he is freed. These are extremely well-articulated answers to your questions, given by me. They are about the eternal, supreme and mysterious brahman. If a person nurtures this, he obtains the brahman. If a person bestows all of this knowledge on my devotees, he is like one who gives the brahman and I give my atman to him. It is sacred and supremely auspicious. If a person recites this every day, he is purified and uses the lamp of knowledge to reveal me to others. If a man constantly listens to this, without being distracted, he develops supreme devotion towards me and is not bound by any karma that he undertakes. O friend! O Uddhava! Have you now understood the brahman? Have the delusion and sorrow that arose in your mind been dispelled? This knowledge must not be given to those who are insolent, heretics, deceitful, lacking in servitude, lacking in devotion or lacking in humility. This must be spoken about to pure and virtuous people, those who are devoid of such defects and those who are devoted to brahmanas and are loved by them, even if they happen to be shudras and women, as long as they possess devotion. Once a curious person comprehends this, there is nothing else left for him to know. When one has drunk the nectar of amrita, there is nothing else that remains to be drunk. O son! Men pursue the four kinds of objectives[1287] through jnana, karma, yoga, trade and the wielding of the staff.[1288] But through me, all these objectives exist in you. If a mortal person gives up all

---

[1287] Dharma, artha, kama and moksha.
[1288] By kings.

other tasks and devotes himself to me, I regard him as special. He
is worthy of obtaining immortality and uniting himself with my
potencies."'

Shri-Shuka said, 'He heard the words of Uttamashloka, which
instructed him about the path of yoga. He joined his hands in
salutation and his voice choked with love. Tears flowed from his
eyes and he was incapable of saying anything. O king! His mind
was awhirl with love. Using his fortitude, he steadied himself.
Taking himself to be extremely respected, he joined his hand in
salutation. He bowed his head down and touched the lotus feet
of the foremost one among the Yadus. He said, "I was submerged
in the great confusion of darkness, but that has been driven away,
since I sought shelter in your presence. O original one! O one
without birth! If a person approaches the sun, how can he be scared
of cold or darkness? You have been compassionate. In return, you
have given me, your servant, the lamp of vijnana. What person,
devoted to you, will give up your feet and seek shelter with someone
else? My bonds of affection towards the Dasharhas, the Vrishnis,
the Andhakas and the Satvatas were extremely firm. For the reason
of expanding your creation, you are the one who extended these,
using your own maya. However, using the weapon of knowledge
about the atman, you are the one who has now cut them asunder.
O great yogi! I bow down to you. I am seeking shelter with you.
Instruct me. May my affection towards your lotus feet remain."
The illustrious one replied, "O Uddhava! Commanded by me, go to
my hermitage, known as Badari. Bathe in the waters of that tirtha,
purified by touching my feet.[1289] Cleanse yourself of the remaining
taints by seeing the Alakananda. O dear one! Use garments made
out of bark. Eat wild fare. Without any desires, be happy. Tolerate
the opposite pairs of sentiments that arise from material objects.
Control your senses and be good in conduct. Be tranquil and in
control of your intelligence. Be full of jnana and vijnana. Use your
discrimination to think about what you have learnt from me. Let
your speech and intelligence be immersed in me. Always observe the
dharma of being devoted to me. Very soon, you will transcend the

---

[1289] A reference to the Ganga.

three[1290] and obtain me, the supreme one." Uddhava was addressed
by the intelligent Hari in this way. At the time of departure, he
circumambulated him, bending his head down and touching his feet,
sprinkling them with his tears. His heart was melting, though he had
transcended the opposite pairs of sentiments. He was bound to him
in a love that was extremely difficult to give up and was suffering
on account of the separation. He was afflicted and was incapable of
tolerating the separation. With a great deal of difficulty, he placed
his master's sandals on his head. As he left, he repeatedly bowed
down again and again. Placing the infinite one in his heart, the one
who was greatly devoted to the illustrious one went to Vishala.[1291]
He observed what the only friend of the universe had instructed
him. Engaging in austerities, he obtained the destination with Hari.
This jnana, the immortal ocean of bliss, was spoken about by the
illustrious Krishna to his devotees. The lords of yoga serve his feet
and if a person serves them faithfully, he is liberated from this
world. I bow down before the one who is known as Krishna. He
is the original one, a bull among men. He is the composer of the
sacred texts and like a bee, he gathered the essence of the Vedas, the
substance of jnana and vijnana, for destroying the fear of samsara
among his large number of servants. This is like amrita churned
from the ocean and they can drink it.'

Chapter 11(30)

The king asked, 'Uddhava, the great devotee of the illustrious
one, left for the forest. What did the illustrious one, the creator
of all beings, do in Dvaravati? The bull among the Yadava lineage
saw that his own lineage would be destroyed because of the curse
of the brahmanas. His body was loved by all eyes. How did he give
that up? Once the eyes of women were fixed on his form, they were
unable to withdraw their eyes. When his form entered the hearts

---

[1290] Sattva, rajas and tamas.
[1291] Badarikashrama.

of virtuous people through the ears, it no longer left. His beautiful words generated attraction, not to speak of the respect shown to them by wise people. In the battle, Jishnu saw that form astride the chariot and obtained equanimity.'

Shri-Shuka replied, 'Krishna saw many great and evil portents arise in the sky, on earth and in the space between them. He spoke to the Yadus who were seated in Sudharma. The illustrious one said, "O bulls among the Yadus! These are great and evil portents in Dvaravati. These are Yama's standards. We should not remain here, not even for an instant. Let the women, the old and children go to Shankhodvara.[1292] Let us go to Prabhasa, where the Sarasvati flows in a western direction. We must bathe there, purify ourselves, fast and control ourselves. We must bathe and worship the gods and offer them unguents and other objects. Let us receive the benedictions of the immensely fortunate brahmanas and give them cows, land, gold, garments, elephants, horses, chariots and houses. This is the supremely auspicious rite for warding off impediments. For this world and for the next, gods, brahmanas and cattle must be worshipped." All the Yadu elders heard the words spoken by Madhu's slayer. They agreed. Having crossed the water on boats, they left for Prabhasa on chariots. There, as instructed by the illustrious one, the divinity of the Yadus, the Yadavas, with supreme devotion, performed all the auspicious rites that would ensure them benefit.

'Because of destiny, their judgement was confused. There, they had a great bout of drinking the liquor *maireya*.[1293] That liquor destroyed their reasoning. As a result of that great bout of drinking, those brave ones became insolent. Their minds turned arrogant. Confused because of Krishna's maya, a great conflict arose among them. On the shores of the ocean, intolerant because of their rage, they attacked each other with bows, swords, broadheaded arrows, clubs, bludgeons and javelins. Flags fluttered atop their chariots and elephants. They were astride donkeys, camels,

[1292] This is the place where Krishna killed Shankhasura/Shankhachuda, now known as Bet Dwarka.

[1293] Maireya is made from molasses or grain.

bulls, buffaloes, mules and men. Extremely insolent, they struck each other, like elephants charging against each other in the forest. With enmity aroused, Pradyumna fought against Samba, Akrura against Bhoja, Aniruddha against Satyaki, Subhadra[1294] against Samgramjit, Sumitra against Suratha and Gada against Gada.[1295] It was an extremely terrible encounter. Others, Nishatha, Ulmuka, Sahasrajit, Shatajit and Bhanu being the most prominent, attacked each other, blind with intoxication. They were severely bewildered by Mukunda. Dasharhas, Vrishnis, Andhakas, Bhojas, Satvatas, Madhus, Arbudas, Mathuras, Shurasenas, Visarjanas, Kukuras and Kuntis forgot their friendly relations and fought against each other. Filled with folly, sons fought against fathers, brothers with brothers, nephews with maternal uncles, nephews with paternal uncles, maternal grandfathers with grandsons, paternal grandfathers with grandsons, friends with friends and well-wishers with well-wishers. Kin killed kin. The arrows were exhausted and their bows were shattered. When their weapons were exhausted, they grasped stalks of eraka grass in their hands. As soon as they held them in their fists, these turned into clubs that were as firm as the vajra. They attacked their adversaries with these. When Krishna tried to restrain them, they attacked him too. O king! They were so bewildered that they thought Balabhadra was an adversary. Having made up their minds to kill them, they attacked them like assassins. O descendant of the Kuru lineage! At this, they[1296] also became angry. They moved around in the field of battle, holding the eraka grass, turned into clubs, in their hands. Their[1297] rage and rivalry was caused by the curse of the brahmanas and they were enveloped in Krishna's maya. Like a fire that starts in a forest of bamboo, they brought destruction on themselves.

'When all the members of his lineage had been destroyed, Keshava thought that the remaining burden of the earth had been

---

[1294] Not to be confused with Subhadraa.

[1295] One of these Gadas was Krishna's brother, the other one was Krishna's son.

[1296] Krishna and Balarama.

[1297] Meaning the Yadavas.

removed. Rama went to the shores of the ocean. Using yoga, he immersed himself in Purusha. Uniting his atman with the atman, he left the world of humans. Devaki's illustrious son witnessed Rama's departure. He silently sat down under a pippala tree. He showed his radiant four-armed form, dazzling because of its own brilliance. Like a fire without smoke, this dispelled the darkness of the directions. He wore the shrivatsa mark. His complexion was dark blue, but his radiance was like that of molten gold. He was attired in silken garments and bore the auspicious signs. His lotus face had a charming smile and the locks of his hair were dark. His eyes were like lotuses and he wore brilliant earrings shaped like makaras. He was ornamented with a girdle, a sacred thread, crown, armlets, bangles, a necklace, anklets, his signs, Koustubha and a garland of wild flowers. The personified forms of his weapons were around him. He was seated with his left foot, as red as a lotus, placed on his right thigh.

'A hunter named Jara had fashioned an arrow from the remaining bit of the club.[1298] He arrived there on a hunt. Taking the foot to be a deer, he pierced it and saw the four-armed person. Having committed a sin, he was scared. He prostrated himself and touched the feet of the enemy of the asuras with his head. "O Madhusudana! I have committed this sin in my ignorance. O Uttamashloka! O unblemished one! You should pardon this sinner. O Vishnu! O lord! It is said that if men remember you, their ignorance is destroyed. I have committed a wicked act. O Vaikuntha! Therefore, quickly slay this evil hunter who desired deer, so that he does not commit such transgressions against virtuous people again. Even those whose atmans are immersed in yoga, Virinchi, Rudra and the others, their offspring and the lords of speech do not comprehend your maya, since their vision is clouded. What can I say about those like us, born as inferior beings?" The illustrious one replied, "Do not be frightened. Get up. What you have done is my wish. With my permission, go to heaven, the destination obtained by those who are virtuous." The illustrious Krishna can assume any

---

[1298] The bit that was swallowed by the fish, mentioned in Chapter 11(1).

form at will.[1299] Thus addressed, he circumambulated him thrice and was conveyed to heaven in a vimana.

'Following Krishna's footprints, Daruka arrived there, searching for him, heading in the direction from which the wind bore the fragrance of tulasi. He saw his master seated at the foot of the ashvattha tree, surrounded by the personified and shining forms of his weapons. His heart overflowing with love, he leapt down from the chariot and fell at his feet. His eyes were full of tears. "O lord! Since I could not see your lotus feet, it was as if I had entered darkness, with my vision destroyed. I could not see the directions, nor could I find peace. I was like a person in the night, when there is no moon." O Indra among kings! As the charioteer was saying this, while he looked on, the chariot with Garuda on the standard, along with the horses and the standard, rose up into the sky. Vishnu's divine weapons followed it. The charioteer was surprised to see this and Janardana spoke to him. "O charioteer! Go to Dvaravati and tell the relatives about the mutual destruction of the kin, Samkarshana's departure and my state. You and your own relatives should no longer reside in Dvaraka. When I leave it, the city of the Yadus will be flooded by the ocean. Let everyone take their families. Take my parents. All of you leave for Indraprastha, protected by Arjuna. You are immersed in my dharma. You are fixed in jnana. Therefore, remain indifferent. Know that these things have been created by my maya. Therefore, find peace." Thus addressed, he circumambulated and bowed down repeatedly, placing his feet on his head. Distressed in his mind, he left for the city.'

Chapter 11(31)

Shri-Shuka said, 'Brahma, Bhava, along with Bhavani, the gods, with the great Indra at the forefront, the sages and the lords of subjects arrived there. There were the ancestors, the Siddhas, the gandharvas, the vidyadharas, the giant serpents, the charanas, the

[1299] Suggesting that Krishna gave up his four-armed form.

yakshas, the rakshasas, the kinnaras, the apsaras and the brahmanas.
They were extremely eager to witness the departure of the illustrious
one. They chanted and sang about Shouri's birth and deeds. O king!
Filled with great devotion, they were in a large number of vimanas
that gathered in the sky. From these, they showered down a large
number of flowers. The illustrious lord saw the grandfather and the
others, who were manifestations of his own atman. He fixed his
atman in his own atman and closed his lotus eyes. In transcendental
meditation, he fixed himself in yoga. However, he did not use
agneyi to burn down his auspicious body, which is a delight to the
worlds.[1300] Instead, he entered his own abode. The drums of the
gods were sounded. Flowers were showered down from the sky.
Truth, dharma, fortitude, fame and prosperity left the earth and
followed him. The gods, with Brahma at the forefront, returned
to their own abodes. Since Krishna's movements could not be
discerned, though they had watched, they were extremely surprised.
In the sky, when a flash of lightning leaves the circle of the clouds,
mortals cannot notice its movement. It was the same with Krishna
and the gods. However, a few, Brahma, Rudra and some others,
noticed Hari's movements of yoga. They were astounded and
praised them. They left for their own respective worlds. O king!
Know that his birth, disappearance and activities in this world were
the result of his maya, since like an actor, he imitated the behaviour
of embodied creatures. He creates this universe out of his atman
and enters it. Having played with it, at the end, he withdraws it into
the greatness of his atman. After this, he alone remains. As a mortal,
he brought his preceptor's son back from Yama's world. When you
were being scorched by the great weapon, he accorded you shelter.
He conquered Isha, the one who is like death to the attendants of
Death. He conveyed the hunter[1301] to heaven in his physical body.
How could the lord not have protected himself? He is the only cause

---

[1300] Agneyi is a process used by yogis to destroy the physical body,
which they then leave. In this, a process of yoga is used to make the body
burst out in spontaneous flames, so that it is destroyed. However, Krishna
did not use this technique.

[1301] Jara.

behind creation, preservation and destruction. He is the possessor
of infinite potencies. However, he no longer desired to maintain his
body in this mortal world, after having demonstrated the ultimate
state of welfare. If a person gets up in the morning, controls himself
and chants devotedly about Krishna's supreme state, he obtains a
position that is unmatched.

'Daruka reached Dvaraka. He felt down at the feet of Vasudeva
and Ugrasena and drenched their feet with his tears, telling them
about the separation from Krishna. O king! He told them about
the complete destruction of the Vrishnis. Hearing this, the hearts
of the people were anxious. Because of their sorrow, they lost their
senses. They were distressed at being separated from Krishna. They
beat their own faces and quickly rushed to the spot where their
dead relatives were lying down. Devaki, Rohini and Vasudeva
could not see their sons, Krishna and Rama. They were afflicted by
grief and lost their senses. Tormented because of their separation
from the illustrious one, they gave up their lives at the spot. O
son! The women embraced their husbands and climbed on to their
funeral pyres. Rama's wives embraced his body and entered the
fire. Vasudeva's[1302] wives embraced his body. Hari's daughters-in-
law did that for Pradyumna and the others. With their hearts fixed
on him, Krishna's wives, Rukmini and the others, entered the fire.
At being separated from his beloved friend, Krishna, Arjuna was
afflicted by grief. He comforted himself with the excellent words
that Krishna had sung.[1303] Arjuna ensured that the funeral rites were
performed for the relatives whose gotras had been destroyed.[1304]
According to age, he did this progressively for everyone who had
been killed. O great king! Since Hari had left Dvaraka, the ocean
immediately flooded it. It only spared the illustrious one's splendid
residence. However, the illustrious Madhusudana is always present
there. It is the most auspicious among all auspicious places and even
remembering it, quickly destroys all sins. Dhananjaya collected the

[1302] Krishna's father.
[1303] Such as the Bhagavat Gita.
[1304] Those who had no descendants who could perform the funeral
rites.

remaining women, children and aged people. He gathered them in Indraprastha and instated Vajra[1305] as the king there. O king! Learning about the death of their well-wisher from Arjuna, your grandfathers instated you as the successor of their lineage.[1306] All of them left on the great journey. Vishnu is the god of the gods. If a mortal person faithfully hears about his birth and deeds and chants about them, he is freed from all sins. This is the beautiful account of the illustrious Hari's avatara, his valour and his childhood pastimes. They are stated here. It is extremely sacred. If a person hears them and chants them, he obtains great devotion and obtains the destination obtained by paramahamsas.'

This ends the Eleventh Skandha.

[1305] Aniruddha's son.
[1306] In Hastinapura.

Twelfth Skandha

Chapter 12(1)

The king asked, 'Krishna, the ornament of the Yadu lineage, returned to his own abode. O sage! Which lineage existed on earth? Please tell me this.'

Shri-Shuka said, 'The king named Puranjaya,[1307] the last king of the Brihadratha dynasty, will be born. His adviser, Shunaka, will kill his master and instate his son, known as Pradyota, as the king.[1308] Pradyota's son will be Palaka, Palaka's son will be Vishakhayupa and Vishakhayupa's son will be Rajaka. Rajaka's son will be Nandivardhana. These five kings from the Pradyota

---

[1307] In Chapter 9(22), he has been referred to as Ripunjaya.

[1308] Pradyota established a dynasty in Avanti and was a contemporary of Bimbisara, who established the Magadhan empire (the Shishunaga dynasty), after the end of the Brihadratha dynasty.

lineage will enjoy the earth for one hundred and thirty-eight years. Shishunaga will be born[1309] and his son will be Kakavarna. Kakavarna's son will be Kshemadharma and Kshemadharma's son will be Kshetrajna. His son will be Vidhisara and Vidhisara's son will be Ajatashatru. Ajatashatru's son will be Darbhaka and it is said that Darbhaka's son will be Ajaya. Ajaya's son will be Nandivardhana and Nandivardhana's son will be Mahanandi. O best among the Kuru lineage! In kali yuga, the ten kings of the Shishunaga dynasty will enjoy the earth for three hundred and sixty years. O king! Mahanandi's powerful son will be born from the womb of a shudra woman. He will be one named Nanda and he will be the lord of a great amount of treasure.[1310] He will be the destroyer of kshatriyas. Thus, the kings will generally be like shudras and will be the followers of adharma. Mahapadma will be the solitary emperor of the earth and no one will transgress his commands. He will be like a second Bhargava.[1311] He will have eight sons, Sumalya being the chief. These kings will enjoy the earth for one hundred years. A brahmana, whom the nine Nandas will trust, will uproot them.[1312] In their absence, during kali yuga, the Mouryas will enjoy the world. The brahmana will instate Chandragupta in the kingdom. Chandragupta's son will be Varisara and Varisara's son will be Ashokavardhana. Ashokavardhana's son will be Suyasha and Suyasha's son will be Sangata. Sangata's son will be Shalishuka and Shalishuka's son will be Somasharma. Somasharma's son will be Shatadhanva and Shatadhanva's son will be Brihadratha. O extender of the Kuru lineage! During kali yuga, the ten kings of the Mourya dynasty will enjoy the earth for more than one hundred and thirty-seven years. O extender of the Kuru lineage! Thereafter, there will be Agnimitra and Agnimitra's son will be

[1309] The text does not suggest that Nandivardhana's son will be Shishunaga.

[1310] A great amount of treasure is *mahapadma* and this is thus Mahapadma Nanda.

[1311] The allusion is to Bhargava Parashurama destroying kshatriyas.

[1312] This brahmana should be Chanakya/Koutilya, but there was no question of the Nandas having trusted him. Alternatively, this brahmana might mean Rakshasa, Nanda's minister.

Sujyeshtha.[1313] Sujyeshtha's son will be Vasumitra, Vasumitra's son will be Bhadraka and Bhadraka's son will be Pulinda. Pulinda's son will be Ghosha and Ghosha's son will be Vajramitra. Thereafter, there will be Bhagavata and Bhagavata's son will be Devabhuti. The ten kings of the Shunga dynasty will enjoy the earth for more than one hundred years. O king! After this, the Kanva dynasty will rule over the earth and it will possess limited qualities. The Shunga Devabhuti will be addicted to desire. His adviser, the immensely intelligent Vasudeva from the Kanva lineage, will kill him and rule over the kingdom himself. Vasudeva's son will be Bhumitra and Bhumitra's son will be Narayana. During kali yuga, the kings of the Kanva dynasty will enjoy the earth for three hundred and forty-five years. The last Kanva, Susharma, will be killed by his servant, the *vrishala*[1314] Bali of the Andhra race.[1315] This wretched one will enjoy the earth for some time. His brother, Krishna, will be the lord of the earth. Krishna's son will be Shrishantakarna and Shrishantakarna's son will be Pournamasu. Pournamasu's son will be Lambodara and Lambodara's son will be King Chibilaka. Chibilaka's son will be Meghasvati and Meghasvati's son will be Atamana. His son will be Anishtakarma and Anishtakarma's son will be Haleya. Haleya's son will be Talaka. Talaka's son will be Purishabhiru and Purishabhiru's son will be King Sunandana. Sunandana's son will be Chakora and his sons will be the Bahus, Shivasvati, the scorcher of enemies, being one of them. Shivasvati's son will be Gomati and Gomati's son will be Puriman. After this, there will be Medhashira and Shivaskanda. Shivaskanda's son will be Yajnashri. Yajnashri's son will be Vijaya. Thereafter, there will be Chandravijna and Lomadhi. O descendant of the Kuru lineage! These thirty kings[1316] will enjoy the earth for

[1313] The name of Agnimitra's father, Pushyamitra, is missing in the text. Hence, the text mentions ten kings of the Shunga dynasty, but only names nine. Pushyamitra killed Brihadratha and established the Shunga dynasty.

[1314] While this means shudra, it also means outcast.

[1315] The text uses Bali as a proper name. Other Puranas use Bali as an adjective, meaning powerful, and state the name as Simuka.

[1316] The names listed actually fall short of thirty. But thirty is the number also cited in other Puranas.

four hundred and fifty-six years. After this, seven Abhira kings and ten Gardhabhi kings will rule from Avabhriti. There will be sixteen kings from the Kanka lineage and they will be exceedingly greedy. Thereafter, there will be eight Yavanas, fourteen Turushkas, ten Gurundas and eleven Mounas. These[1317] will enjoy the earth for one thousand and ninety-nine years. The eleven Mounas will enjoy the earth for three hundred years. O dear one! After this, from Kilkila, the kings Bhutananda, Vangiri, Shishunandi, his brother Yashonandi, Pravirika and others will rule for more than one hundred and six years. They will be followed by their thirteen sons, the Bahlikas. Pushpamitra will be the king and his son, Dumitra. At the same time, these kings will rule over parts of the earth— seven Andhras, seven Kosalas, the kings of Vidura and the Nishadhas. There will be a king named Vishvasphurji in Magadha, also known as Puranjaya. He will reduce all varnas to the status of Pulindas, Yadus and Madrakas. The evil-minded king will turn most subjects against brahmanas.[1318] The valiant one will exterminate kshatriyas. From his city of Padmavati, he will protect and rule over the earth, from Gangadvara[1319] to Prayaga. The brahmanas in Sourashtra, Avanti, Abhira, Shura, Arbuda and Malava will become *vratyas*[1320] and the kings will generally be like shudras. Shudras, vratyas and others, mlechchhas and brahmanas bereft of radiance will rule along the banks of the Sindhu and the Chandrabhaga, in Kounti and the region of Kashmira. O king! At the same time, there will be kings who will be just like mlechchhas. They will be devoted to adharma and falsehood. They will be limited in generosity, fierce and prone to anger. They will kill women, children, cows and brahmanas. They will seize the wives and wealth of others. They will be subject to sudden rises and sudden downfalls. Their spirits and lifespan will be limited. They will not be refined and will be devoid of rituals. They will be enveloped by rajas and tamas. In the disguise of kings, they will be mlechchhas who will devour their subjects. With these

---

[1317] Abhiras, Gardabhis, Kankas, Yavanas, Turushkas and Gurundas.
[1318] Or, against the Vedas.
[1319] Gangadvara usually refers to Har ki Pauri in Haridvara/Haridwar.
[1320] Outcastes, deviants from the varna system.

as kings, the citizens of those countries will imitate their conduct, behaviour and speech. They will oppress each other and will be oppressed by their kings. In this way, they will face hardships and destruction.'

Chapter 12(2)

Shri-Shuka said, 'O king! Thereafter, because of the force of time, day after day, dharma, truth, purity, forgiveness, compassion, lifespan, strength and memory will decay. In kali yuga, wealth will connote nobility of birth, good conduct and all the qualities for men. The determinant of dharma and rule of law will be strength. The reason for a couple to live together will be mutual liking alone. Deceit will be the foundation of business. Masculinity and femininity will be decided on the basis of sexual dexterity. The test of being a brahmana will only be the sacred thread. External signs will be the only indications of following an ashrama and that will be the basis for mutual exchanges. For those without a means of subsistence, the delivery of justice will be weak. Garrulity in speech will be an indicator of learning. A person without wealth will be regarded as one without virtue. Insolence will become an indicator of virtue. Mutual consent will be sufficient for marriage. Adornments will become a substitute for bathing. A distant place with water will be regarded as a tirtha. Long hair will become a sign of beauty. The filling of the stomach will be the only selfish pursuit. Audacity will become a substitute for veracity. A person who can maintain his family will be regarded as accomplished. Dharma will only be followed for the purpose of establishing one's fame. The surface of the earth will thus be filled with wicked subjects. The strongest among brahmanas, kshatriyas, vaishyas and shudras will become the king. The subjects will be deprived of their wives and wealth by avaricious and merciless kings who will be like bandits who follow adharma. They will flee to mountains and forests and survive on leaves, roots, meat, wild honey, fruits, flowers and seeds. They will be devastated by drought and famine, suffering from taxes. Suffering from cold, wind, heat, rain, ice, hunger, thirst and tormented by thoughts, subjects will quarrel with each other. In kali yuga, the human lifespan will be fifty years. Because of the sins of kali, the bodies of embodied beings will become emaciated. The dharma of varnas and ashramas will become lost and men will deviate from the path of the Vedas. In the name of dharma, there will be many heretics. The kings will generally be like bandits. Men will earn many kinds of living through theft, falsehood and pointless violence. All the varnas will be like shudras. The cows will be like goats. All the ashramas will be reduced to garhasthya. Relatives will mean those connected through marriage. Medicinal herbs will generally be reduced in size. Trees will become as small as *shami* trees. Clouds will only yield lightning. The houses will generally be empty.

'Vishnu is the lord and preceptor of all mobile and immobile objects. He is the atman of everything. He takes birth for the protection of dharma and the virtuous and for the cessation of karma. In the house of the great-souled and foremost brahmana, Vishnuyasha, in the village of Shambhala, Kalki will manifest himself. The lord of the universe will mount his swift steed, Devadatta. He will possess the eight potencies and the eight qualities.[1321] The immensely radiant one will quickly travel around the earth on his horse, wielding his sword and chastising the wicked. He will slaughter crores of bandits who have disguised themselves as kings. After all the bandits have been killed, the inhabitants of the cities and the countryside will have their minds purified, as the extremely sacred fragrance from the decorations on Vasudeva's body is borne along by the wind and touches them. When the illustrious Vasudeva is based in their hearts in the form of sattva, an abundance of subjects will be created. When the illustrious Hari descends as Kalki, the lord of dharma, there will be krita yuga and the offspring who are born will be inclined towards sattva. Krita yuga will commence when Chandra,

---

[1321] Compassion, forgiveness, cleanliness, lack of jealousy, altruism, lack of greed, purity and self-control are the eight potencies and the eight qualities are the eight siddhis.

Surya and Brihaspati are simultaneously in the nakshatra Tishya.[1322] The kings of the past and the future, belonging to the solar and the lunar dynasties, have been briefly mentioned to you. One thousand one hundred and fifteen years will elapse between your birth and the coronation of Nanda.

'Among the saptarshis, two are first seen to rise in the eastern sky.[1323] If a straight line is drawn between them, in the night, a nakshatra is seen at the midpoint. Those two rishis will be associated with that nakshatra for one hundred human years. Right now, at the present time, those two brahmanas are in Magha nakshatra. The illustrious Vishnu, as radiant as the sun and known by the name of Krishna, went to heaven. At that time, Kali entered the world and people started to take delight in evil. As long as the lotus feet of Rama's consort touched the earth, Kali was incapable of overcoming her. When the saptarshis enter Magha nakshatra, Kali will commence and will last for twelve hundred years.[1324] When these great rishis proceed from Magha to Purvashadha, starting with Nanda's dynasty, Kali will become more powerful. Those who know about the ancient accounts state that kali yuga commenced on the precise day and the exact time that Krishna left for heaven. When the fourth yuga of one thousand divine years is over, krita yuga will commence again.[1325] At that time, the minds of men will reveal the atman. I have thus enumerated Manu's lineage on earth. In the same way, from one yuga to another yuga, brahmanas, vaishyas and shudras can also be understood. The names are the only means of remembering these great-souled ones. Only some parts of their accounts remain, but their deeds are established on earth. Shantanu's brother, Devapi, and Maru are descended from the Ikshvaku lineage. They are powerful and great yogis and

---

[1322] Tishya is the same as Pushya.

[1323] In the constellation of the Big Dipper (part of Ursa Major), these are Pulaha and Kratu. Pulaha is Merak and Kratu is Dubhe.

[1324] This is interpreted as 1200 years of the gods, though the text doesn't explicitly state that. This is equivalent to 432,000 human years. However, the text states this clearly later.

[1325] The missing 200 years is explained as 100 between dvapara and kali and 100 between kali and krita. These are intervening periods.

reside in the village of Kalapa. At the end of kali yuga, they will be instructed by Vasudeva and will re-establish the dharma of varnas and ashramas, just as it had existed earlier. Beings on earth progressively exist in accordance with the four yugas—krita, treta, dvapara and kali. O king! The kings that I have spoken about, and others, will claim ownership over the earth. But at the end, they will be killed and depart, giving this up. Even if a person is known as a king, it will be known as worms, excrement or ashes. One is selfish for the sake of this physical body. Does one not know that one is going to hell? "This unrestricted earth was earlier ruled over by my forefathers.[1326] It now belongs to me and will subsequently belong to my son and my grandson, those from my lineage." The ignorant accept the view that their physical bodies, made out of heat, water and food, is "mine" and think of the earth as "mine". However, at the end, they must give up both and disappear from sight. O king! There were kings who used their energy to enjoy the earth. However, because of time, all of them have only become accounts that are spoken about.'

Chapter 12(3)

Shri-Shuka said, 'Seeing that the kings were eager to conquer her, the earth laughed. "These kings are puppets before Death, but they wish to conquer me. Despite being learned, because of their desire, these Indras among men fail. The kings have a lot of trust in their own physical bodies, but are like bubbles in foam. 'I will first vanquish the six.[1327] I will then conquer the royal ministers, the advisers, the citizens, relatives, the elephant keepers[1328] and other thorns. In this way, I will gradually conquer the earth, right up to the girdle of the ocean.' With such hopes in their hearts, they

---

[1326] These are the thoughts of foolish kings.

[1327] These are the thoughts of the kings. The five senses and the mind constitute the six.

[1328] Belonging to rival kings.

do not perceive that Death is near. After conquering me, bounded
by the ocean, they use their energy to enter the ocean. Where is
their victory over their own selves? Victory over one's own self is
for the fruit of emancipation." O extender of the Kuru lineage!
"In the past, humans and their sons have left, just as they had
come.[1329] The ignorant ones fight in an attempt to conquer me.
For my sake, fathers and sons fight and so do brothers. There is
a sense of ownership in the unreal kingdom and their minds are
attached to this. Those foolish ones say, 'This entire earth belongs
to me.' For my sake, the kings rival each other. They kill and are
killed. There were Prithu, Pururava, Gadhi, Nahusha, Bharata,
Arjuna,[1330] Mandhata, Sagara, Rama, Khatvanga, Dhundhumara,
Raghu, Trinabindu, Yayati, Sharyati, Shantanu, Gaya, Bhagiratha,
Kuvalayashva, Kakutstha, Naishadha,[1331] Nriga, Hiranyakashipu,
Vritra, Ravana, the one who made the worlds scream, Namuchi,
Shambara, Bhouma,[1332] Hiranyaksha, Taraka, many other daityas
and great lords among kings. All of them possessed knowledge. All
of them were brave. All of them conquered everything and were
unvanquished. They followed the dharma of mortals. However,
because of a sense of ownership, they tried to excessively possess
me." O king! They were unsuccessful in their objectives. Due to the
progress of time, they have only remained as accounts. O lord! I
have spoken to you about these great ones. Their fame was spread
throughout the world, but they have departed. I have spoken to
you about them with a desire to impart vijnana and *vairagya* to
you. These words represent the power of the supreme objective. A
person who desires unblemished devotion to Krishna should always
hear Uttamashloka's qualities being chanted and sung. They destroy
everything that is inauspicious.'

The king asked, 'O illustrious one! How can people who live in
kali yuga destroy the accumulated contamination of kali yuga?[1333]

[1329] This is the earth speaking again.

[1330] Kartavirya Arjuna.

[1331] Nala.

[1332] Naraka.

[1333] Parikshit deduces that the age prevents devotion towards Krishna.

Tell me about the yugas and the dharma of the yugas. What are the dimensions of creation and destruction? What is the nature of time? What is the progress and form of the great-souled Vishnu?'

Shri-Shuka continued, 'O king! In the beginning, during krita yuga, dharma is nurtured by people and possesses its four legs. The four legs of truth, compassion, austerities and donations represent its power. The people are generally satisfied, compassionate, friendly, serene, self-controlled, tolerant, impartial in attitude and enterprising and find happiness in their atmans. During treta, a fourth part of each of the legs of dharma is gradually destroyed by each of the four legs of adharma—falsehood, violence, discontentment and dissension. O king! The people are devoted to rituals and austerities. They are not exceedingly violent or lascivious. They pursue three objectives[1334] and obtain prosperity through the three.[1335] Among varnas, brahmanas are regarded as superior. During dvapara, austerities, truth, compassion and donations are reduced by half. This happens because of the attributes of adharma—violence, discontentment, falsehood and hatred. People are great in conduct, but strive for fame. They are devoted to studying and teaching. They are happy and possess large families. Among varnas, brahmanas and kshatriyas are regarded as superior. Because of increase of adharma, during kali, each of dharma's feet is reduced by one-fourth and only one-fourth remains. Towards the end, whatever remains will also be diminished and eventually destroyed. Subjects are avaricious, wicked in conduct, cruel and quarrel without any reason. They are unfortunate and preoccupied with many kinds of desires. Shudras and dasas[1336] are regarded as superior. The gunas of sattva, rajas and tamas are seen among men. Urged by time, their influence over a person varies. When the mind, intelligence and senses are under the influence of sattva, that should be known as a sign of krita yuga. Knowledge and austerities bring pleasure. O intelligent one! When the conduct of embodied beings is based on karma,

---

[1334] Dharma, artha and kama.
[1335] The first three Vedas.
[1336] Servants, inferior varnas.

desire and liking for fame, know that under the influence of rajas, this is treta. When one desires to undertake tasks because of greed, discontentment, pride, insolence and jealousy, that is dvapara, under the influence of rajas and tamas. When there is maya, falsehood, lassitude, sleep, violence, depression, sorrow, delusion, fear and misery, this is said to be kali, under the influence of tamas. Therefore, mortals become short-sighted, unfortunate, given to eating, addicted to desire and devoid of riches. The women are unchaste and svairinis. The countryside is infested with bandits. The Vedas are polluted by heretics. The kings devour subjects. Brahmanas love their penises and their stomachs. Brahmacharis do not observe their vows and are unclean. Householders become beggars. Ascetics reside in villages. Sannyasis become greedy for wealth. The women are short in stature, but eat a lot. They lose their shame and have a lot of offspring. They are always harsh in speech. They are thieves, deceitful and full of excessive rashness. Inferior people become traders. Merchants are fraudulent. Even when there is no calamity, people consider it virtuous to earn a living from condemned pursuits. Even if a master is excellent in every possible way, when he is without wealth, servants abandon him. Masters abandon distressed servants who have worked for the family for a long time and cows that no longer yield milk. Because of friendships based on sex, people abandon fathers, brothers, well-wishers and kin. Consulting sisters-in-law and brothers-in-law,[1337] people are wretched. During kali, men are attached to women. Shudras accept donations and earn a living in the disguise of ascetics. Those who know about adharma speak about dharma and ascend the best of seats. Minds are always agitated, suffering from famines and taxes. O king! No food can be found on the surface of the earth. People suffer from drought and fear. They are devoid of garments, food, drink, beds, sexual satisfaction, bathing and ornaments. During kali, people are like pishachas. During kali, people abandon and fight with their

---

[1337] Respectively, sisters of husbands and brothers of wives. Wives consult the former and husbands the latter.

friends even for a few measly coins.[1338] For this, they will even kill
their own relatives, or give up their own beloved lives. Men do not
protect their aged parents, sons or wives. Even if they are born in
noble lineages, they are inferior and only interested in satisfying
the penis and the stomach. O king! During kali, people generally
do not worship the illustrious Achyuta, the supreme preceptor of
the universe, whose lotus feet are worshipped by the guardians of
the three worlds. Instead, with their intelligence perverted, they
offer sacrifices to heretics. During kali, a man will not chant his
name or worship him even when he is dying, distressed, falling
down, faltering or helpless, though this frees him from the fetters
of karma and secures a supreme destination for him. Because of
kali, men, objects, regions and innate nature are contaminated.
However, if the mind is immersed in the illustrious Purushottama,
all this can be dispelled. The illustrious one is in the heart. If a man
hears about him, chants about him, meditates on him, worships
him, or even shows him respect, everything inauspicious that has
been accumulated over tens of thousands of births, is destroyed.
This is like fire destroying impurities resulting from other metals
which are inside gold, robbing it of its lustre. In that way,
Vishnu is in the atman of yogis and swiftly destroys everything
inauspicious. Learning, austerities, control of prana, friendliness,
bathing in tirthas, vows, donations and meditation do not grant
as much purification of the inner atman as does the illustrious
Ananta who is inside the heart. O king! Therefore, with all your
soul, concentrate and place Keshava in your heart. Thus, even at
the time of death, you will obtain the supreme destination. O dear
one! He is in all atmans and is the refuge for everyone. Those
who are about to die must meditate on the supreme and illustrious
lord and he will lead them to his own atman. O king! There is an
ocean of taints in kali, but there is one great quality. Even if one
chants Krishna's name, one is freed from attachment and goes to
the supreme destination. What is achieved in krita by meditating
on Vishnu, what is achieved in treta by performing sacrifices and

---

[1338] *Kakini* or *kakinika*, equal to twenty cowries or a quarter of a *pana*.

what is achieved in dvapara through serving him, can be obtained
in kali by chanting Hari's name.'

Chapter 12(4)

Shri-Shuka said, 'O king! The measurement of time, beginning
with paramanu and ending with twice a parardha have been
described to you and so has the measurement of yugas. Now hear
about kalpa and *laya*. One thousand cycles of the four yugas is said
to constitute Brahma's day. O lord of the earth! This is kalpa, within
which, there are fourteen Manus. After this, there is Brahma's night,
which is said to be of the same duration. This is *pralaya*.[1339] At the
end of the kalpa, these three worlds are destroyed. This is said to
be *naimittika pralaya*. During this, the creator of the universe lies
down on Ananta,[1340] withdrawing the universe and the self-created
one[1341] into his atman. When the two parardhas are over, the seven
elements of Prakriti[1342] and Parameshthi Brahma are destroyed.
This has been thought of as *prakritika pralaya*.[1343] O king! When
there is prakritika pralaya, the cosmic egg also faces destruction,
since the primordial matter that has led to its creation is destroyed.
O king! Parjanya does not shower down on the earth for one
hundred years. There is lack of food. Subjects suffer from hunger
and devour each other. Thus, afflicted by time, they gradually head
towards destruction. The samvartaka[1344] sun's rays are fierce and
drink up all the water in the ocean and the moisture in the earth
and within embodied beings, releasing nothing in return.[1345] The
samvartaka fire arises from Samkarshana's mouth. Aided by the
force of the wind, it burns down the worlds and the intervening

[1339] Laya and pralaya are synonymous, meaning destruction.
[1340] Shesha.
[1341] Brahma.
[1342] Mahat, ahamkara and the five tanmatras.
[1343] The primordial matter is destroyed.
[1344] At the time of universal destruction.
[1345] There is no rain.

space, which have already been emptied. The flames of the fire and
the sun scorch from every direction, above and below. The cosmic
egg is burnt like a ball of cow dung. A terrible storm rages for more
than one hundred years. This samvartaka storm envelopes the sky
in smoke and dust. O dear one! After this, many masses of clouds
gather and they are multicoloured. They thunder with a terrible
roar and shower down for one hundred years. The universe, inside
the shell of the cosmic egg, becomes a single deluge of water. The
flood of water takes away the quality of smell from the earth.[1346]
When the quality of smell has been taken away, the earth ceases to
exist. The fire takes away the quality of taste from water. Without
the quality of taste, water ceases to exist. The wind takes away the
quality of form from fire. Without the quality of form, fire ceases
to exist. Space takes away the quality of touch from the wind. O
king! Without the quality of touch, the wind ceases to exist and
merges into space. Tamasika ahamkara takes away the quality of
sound from space and space ceases to exist. O dear one! Taijasa
ahamkara absorbs the senses and vaikarika ahamkara absorbs the
divinities who preside over the senses. Mahat absorbs ahamkara
and sattva and the other gunas absorb Mahat. O king! Thereafter,
urged by time, the unmanifest Prakriti absorbs the gunas. Pradhana
has no form. It is not subject to the modifications of time and does
not have any attributes. It is without beginning and without end. It
is not manifest and is eternal. It is without decay and is the cause
behind everything. There is no speech and no mind. Sattva, rajas,
tamas and Mahat and the others do not exist. Prana, intelligence,
the senses and their presiding deities do not exist. Indeed, there is
no structure there that can be called the world. There is no state of
remaining awake, sleeping or in sushupti. The sky, space, water,
earth, fire and the sun do not exist. The emptiness is somewhat
similar to the state of sushupti. But it is a state that cannot be
thought about. It is said that this state is the root cause behind
creation. Urged by time, the potencies of Purusha and Prakriti are
disabled and merge into each other. This is said to be prakritika

[1346] In these sections, we have expanded on the text a bit, so that the
meaning becomes clear.

pralaya. Jnana is manifest as the only form of intelligence, the senses and the objects of the senses. Anything with a beginning and an end no longer has any meaning, since whatever is perceived can no longer be distinguished from its cause. Light, the eye that sees the light and the form of the light are not different from the original element of fire. In that way, intelligence, the senses and the objects of the senses are not distinct from the brahman, which however is distinct from them.[1347] The three states of intelligence are said to be wakefulness, sleep and sushupti. O king! However, these are based on maya and are not experienced by the pure atman. Sometimes, clouds exist in the sky and sometimes, they do not. In that way, the appearance and disappearance of different parts of the universe occur within the brahman. O dear one! Even if a piece of cloth does not exist, its potential existence can be inferred from the existence of threads that make it up. In that way, the potential existence of all the forms in the world can be inferred from the truth that is the foundation. Anything generally perceived as cause or effect is an illusion, since the two are linked. Anything with a beginning or an end is actually unreal. Without reference to the pure atman, all apparent transformations are inexplicable. For even an *anu* to be identified as real, it must be like the atman.[1348] Truth has no diversity. It is only the ignorant person who thinks otherwise. That is like two skies, two suns or two winds.[1349] Depending on what they want to do with it and the way in which it is used, men use different names for gold. In that way, the illustrious Adhokshaja is addressed in different ways by ordinary people and those who know about the Vedas. The cloud is created by the powers of the sun[1350] and is made visible by the sun. But it can lead to darkness

[1347] Their root cause is the brahman. However, the brahman is distinct because it continues to exist.

[1348] That is, it must be eternal and not subject to change. Anu is a small particle.

[1349] These are apparent and not real, such as the sky outside and the sky inside an enclosed space, the sun and its image reflected somewhere, and the wind outside the body and inside the body.

[1350] Since the sun evaporates water to form clouds. It is made visible by the sun's light.

and prevent the eye, which is a portion of the sun, from seeing the sun. In that way, ahamkara evolves from the brahman's attributes and obtains its powers from the brahman. However, this portion of the brahman can also lead to bonds and prevent the jivatman from perceiving the brahman. When clouds, created by the powers of the sun, are dispersed, the eye can see the sun, which is its own form. In that way, when the jivatman investigates and destroys the covering of ahamkara, it regains its memory. In this way, the sword of discrimination can be used to sever the maya of ahamkara, the bond created for the jivatman. One is then firmly established in realizing the atman. O dear one! This is said to be the ultimate[1351] destruction. O scorcher of enemies! Those who know about subtle matters have averred that there is always a continuous creation and destruction of living beings, beginning with Brahma. Anything with transformation is always subject to being quickly taken away by the speedy flow of time. That is the cause behind creation and destruction. This time is without beginning and without end and is the lord's form. Its momentary movements are imperceptible, like the movement of stellar bodies in the sky. The progress of time has been described in terms of these kinds of laya—*nitya*,[1352] naimittika, prakritika and *atyantika*. O best among the Kuru lineage! Narayana is the reservoir of all kinds of existence. He is the creator of the universe. I have briefly described the account of his pastimes to you. Even the lord Aja[1353] is incapable of describing all of them. The ocean of samsara is extremely difficult to cross. If a person desires to cross it, no boat other than the illustrious Purushottama is appropriate. One must constantly serve him and listen to the account of his pastimes. That is the way for a man who is suffering because of many kinds of misery and affliction. In ancient times, the undecaying rishi Narayana told Narada about this Purana *samhita*[1354] and Narada told Krishna Dvaipayana about it. O great

---

[1351] The word used is atyantika.

[1352] Constant.

[1353] Brahma.

[1354] Samhita means collection. This specifically means the Bhagavata Purana. However, in Chapter 2(9), we were told Brahma recounted this to

king! The illustrious Badarayana was pleased with me and taught
me this Bhagavata samhita, as revered as the Vedas. O best among
the Kuru lineage! When the rishis undertake a great sacrifice in the
forest of Naimisha and Shounaka and the others ask him about it,
this Suta will narrate it to them.'

Chapter 12(5)

Shri-Shuka said, 'The illustrious Hari is the atman of the universe.
Brahma was created through his favours and Rudra arose out
of his rage. He has been repeatedly described in this text. O king!
Conquer this animal-like notion that you are going to die. Earlier,
there never was a time when you did not exist. Unlike your physical
body, you will not be destroyed. Like a sprout resulting from a
seed, you will not be born in the form of your sons and grandsons.
Like fire is distinct from kindling, you are more than your physical
body. In a dream, one can see one's head being severed and one's
own self dying as a consequence. The atman, which is without birth
and is immortal, looks at the physical body in that way. When a
pot is broken, the bit of sky that was inside the pot becomes the
sky, as it used to be earlier. In that way, when the physical body
dies, the jivatman again merges with the brahman. The mind
creates the physical body, the qualities and the karma the atman
must undertake. But maya creates the mind and this leads to the
jivatman resorting to samsara. A lamp possesses the characteristics
of being a lamp as long as there is a combination of oil, a vessel,
a wick and fire. The material existence of the body is like that.[1355]
Enveloped in sattva, rajas and tamas, it is born and is destroyed.
But this is not true of the self-luminous atman, which is distinct
from the gross and the subtle body. It is eternal and without an end.
As a foundation, it can be compared to the sky. O lord! Use the

---

Narada.

[1355] In interpretations, karma is the oil, the mind is the vessel, the body
is the wick and the jivatman is the fire.

base of your intelligence and reasoning to think about Vasudeva. Thus, consider the atman that is inside your own self. Urged by the words of the brahmana, Takshaka won't be able to burn you.[1356] Death cannot burn the lord, who is Death to the agents of Death. "I am the brahman. I am the supreme abode. I am the brahman, the supreme destination." Thinking in this way, immerse yourself in the atman, which is free from every possible limit. Your atman is distinct from your body and when Takshaka bites you in the feet with his flickering tongue and mouth full of poison, you will not even notice him, or the world. O son! O king! In accordance with everything that you asked me about the activities of Hari, the atman of the universe, I have told you. What else do you wish to hear?'

Chapter 12(6)

Suta said, 'Vyasa's son was impartial in vision and had insight about the one who is the atman of everything. Hearing what this sage had narrated, Parikshit Vishnurata approached him. He joined his hands in salution, bowing his head down and touching his feet. The king said, "Your soul is full of compassion and since I have obtained your favours, I am successful. I have heard from you about how I can directly obtain Hari, who is without beginning and without end. I do not think this is extraordinary. Great ones who have Achyuta in their hearts do show their favours to ignorant creatures who are tormented. We have heard about this Purana samhita from you and it describes the illustrious Uttamashloka. O illustrious one! I am not scared of death, because of Takshaka or because of anything else. You have shown me freedom from fear. I will enter the brahman, free of everything material. O brahmana! Grant me leave. I will control my speech[1357] and immerse myself in Adhokshaja. My mind is free of all wishes and desires. I will immerse myself and give up my breath of life. You have destroyed

[1356] Since you are immersed in Vasudeva.
[1357] And other senses.

my ignorance and have shown me jnana, vijnana and devotion, and the illustrious, supreme and auspicious destination." Thus addressed, Badarayana's illustrious son granted him permission. Worshipped by the kings and the mendicants, he departed.

'The royal sage, Parikshit, used his atman to immerse himself in the atman. He meditated on the supreme. He controlled his breath of life and was as motionless as a tree. He sat on a seat of *barhi* grass, with the tips of the blades facing the east. He was seated on the banks of the Ganga, with his face facing the north. Without attachment and with all his doubts dispelled, the great yogi immersed himself in the brahman. O brahmanas! Takshaka was sent by the angry son of the brahmana. Wishing to kill him, he headed towards the king. Along the way, he saw Kashyapa. He[1358] satisfied him with riches and made him return. Since he could assume any form at will, he disguised himself as a brahmana and went and bit the king. The royal sage was immersed in the brahman and the fiery poison from the snake instantly reduced his body to ashes, while all the embodied beings looked on. Great lamentations arose everywhere on earth, the sky and the directions. Everyone among gods, asuras, humans and others, was astonished. The drums of the gods were sounded. Gandharvas and apsaras sang. The gods uttered words of praise and showered down flowers. Janamejaya heard that his own father had been bitten by Takshaka. Along with brahmanas, he undertook a sacrifice and angrily offered nagas as oblations. In that snake sacrifice, giant serpents were offered as oblations into the fire and were burnt. Seeing this, Takshaka was scared and anxious and sought refuge with Indra. The king who was Parikshit's son did not see Takshaka there. He asked the brahmanas, "Where is Takshaka, worst among serpents? Why is he not being burnt?" "O Indra among kings! He has gone to Shakra for refuge and is being protected by him. Since the snake has been held back there, he is not falling into the fire." Extensive in his intelligence, Parikshit's son heard this. He told the officiating priests, "O brahmanas! Along with Takshaka, why not make Indra fall down into the fire?"

[1358] Kashyapa. Kashyapa was capable of countering poison. Therefore, Takshaka dissuaded Kashyapa from going to Parikshit.

Hearing this, in that sacrifice, the brahmanas invoked Indra as an oblation, along with Takshaka. "O Takshaka! Along with Indra, the lord of the Maruts, quickly fall down." The words spoken by the brahmanas dislodged Indra from his position, along with his vimana and along with Takshaka. His mind was agitated. Along with his vimana and Takshaka, he fell down from the sky. On seeing this, Brihaspati, of the Angiras lineage, spoke to the king. "O Indra among men! It is not appropriate that you should kill the king of the snakes. This one has drunk amrita. He is immortal and does not suffer from old age. A creature's life, death and destination are determined by his own karma. O king! There is no one else who should bestow joy or misery on him. O king! When a living being experiences death through snakes, thieves, fire, lightning, hunger, thirst, physical disease or mental ailment, this is because of his own *arabdha* karma.[1359] O king! Therefore, you should stop this sacrifice. It is being undertaken with the objective of harming others. The snakes are innocent. Every being must enjoy its destiny." Thus addressed, he honoured the maharshi's words and agreed. He stopped the snake sacrifice and worshipped the lord of speech.[1360]

'This is Vishnu's great maya. It is not discernible and cannot be countered. Though the atman is inside all creatures, creatures are confounded because of the working of the gunas. When one realizes the atman, the maya of insolence or fear is not visible.[1361] When one completely realizes the atman, there is no scope for many differing kinds of arguments, which are based on maya. The mind, which resorts to decisions and doubts, does not exist. Both created material objects and their causes do not exist. In that supreme state of bliss, the jivatman, along with its three attributes[1362] and ahamkara are non-existent. There is no obstruction and nothing that can create obstructions. With the waves[1363] contained, the sage is in a state

[1359] There are different types of karma. Arabdha karma is that karma which has matured and is ready to yield fruit.

[1360] Brihaspati.

[1361] There are four shlokas here, subject to differing interpretations.

[1362] Sattva, rajas and tamas.

[1363] Of everything—material objects, the senses, the objects of the senses, the mind, ahamkara.

of delight. This is described as Vishnu's supreme state, which can only be described as "neti", "neti". Those who give up everything evil in their souls resort to nothing else. With love in their hearts, they control themselves and embrace him, and he dwells with them. Those who have given up notions of "I" and "mine" are the only ones who can go to Vishnu's supreme state. These degradations arise from associations with the body and the house. A person must tolerate disparaging words and never show anyone disrespect. Avoiding any identification with the body, he must never harbour enmity towards anyone. I bow down before the illustrious Krishna, infinite in his intelligence. I have been able to assimilate this samhita by meditating on his lotus feet.'

Shounaka said, 'O amiable one! Paila and the others[1364] were the disciples of the great-souled preceptor of the Vedas. Into how many branches did they, the expounders of the Vedas, divide them? Please tell us that.'

Suta continued, 'O brahmana! Parameshthi Brahma controlled his atman. A sound arose from the space inside his heart. When the functioning of the ears is stopped,[1365] it is this sound that can be heard. O brahmana! By meditating on this, yogis cleanse the impurities of their atmans. Having cleansed what is known as substances, activities and agents,[1366] they go to the place from which there is no return. The three syllables of omkara arose from the powers of the unmanifest, the self-ruling one. This is a sign of the illustrious brahman, the paramatman. He[1367] hears this subtle sound even when the sense of hearing is dormant and even when sight and the other senses are non-existent. It[1368] manifests itself inside the cavity of the atman and the Vedas are its elaboration. The brahman is its source and it directly expresses the paramatman. It is the eternal seed of all the mantras, Upanishads and Vedas. O

[1364] Vaishampayana, Jaimini, Sumantu, Shuka.

[1365] When the ears are covered.

[1366] Respectively, the elements constituting the body, the activities performed and the agent who performs action. By not returning, what is meant is that they don't return to samsara.

[1367] This can mean either Brahma, or the brahman.

[1368] Omkara.

extender of the Bhrigu lineage! It has the three sounds—"O", "U" and "M". These sustain the three states—gunas, names, objectives and consciousness.[1369] Using this, the illustrious Aja[1370] created the aggregate of the aksharas, the semi-vowels, the aspirants, the vowels and the consonants, classified into the short and the long. Using these, the illustrious one created the four Vedas out of his four mouths, the *vyahritis*[1371] and omkara. He desired to describe the tasks of the four kinds of officiating priests.[1372] He taught these to his sons, the brahmana rishis who were accomplished about the brahman. They became instructors of dharma and in turn, taught these to their own sons. In this way, from one generation to another, disciples who were firm in their vows obtained these. In the course of the four yugas, at the beginning of dvapara, maharshis classified them.[1373] With the passage of time, brahmana rishis saw that people were limited in lifespans, limited in spirit and evil in intelligence. Urged by the Achyuta in their hearts, they classified the Vedas.

'O brahmana! In this manvantara too, Brahma, Isha and the other guardians of the worlds requested the illustrious creator of the worlds to protect dharma. Therefore, using a portion of his portion, the lord was born as the son of Parashara and Satyavati. O immensely fortunate one! Having descended, he divided the Vedas into four parts. Like heaps of jewels, he divided the mass of mantras into four categories of samhitas—Rig, Sama, Yajur and Atharva. The immensely intelligent one summoned four disciples.

[1369] The three gunas are sattva, rajas and tamas, the three names are Rig Veda, Sama Veda and Atharva Veda, the three objectives are *bhur*, *bhuvah* and *svah,* and the three kinds of consciousness are wakefulness, sleep and deep sleep.

[1370] Brahma.

[1371] Vyahriti means the words bhuh, bhuvah and svah, uttered after Oum.

[1372] There are four types of officiating priests—*hotar* (one who recites from the Rig Veda), *udgatar* (one who recites from the Sama Veda), adhvaryu (one who recites from the Yajur Veda) and brahman (one who recites from the Atharva Veda). This brahman is not to be confused with the supreme soul (brahman or paramatman).

[1373] Maharshis known as Vedavyasa (or Vyasadeva) classified the Vedas into different branches. There is an inconsistency though. This should read at the end of every dvapara yuga, not at the beginning of every dvapara yuga.

O brahmana! The lord gave each of them one samhita. He spoke about the first samhita, known as *bahvrich*, to Paila.[1374] To the one known as Vaishampayana, he imparted the collection known as Nigada or Yajur Veda. He spoke about Sama Veda, the samhita composed according to metres, to Jaimini. The one known as Atharva-Anigrasi[1375] was taught to Sumantu, his disciple. The sage Paila taught his own samhita to Indrapramiti and Bashkala. O Bhargava! Bashkala divided the samhita that he had received into four branches and taught one to each of his disciples—Bodhya, Yajnavalkya, Parashara and Agnimitra. Indrapramiti was in control of his atman. He taught his samhita to the wise rishi Mandukeya, his son. His disciple, Devamitra, taught it to Soubhari and others. Shakalya, Mandukeya's son, divided his samhita into five parts and gave it to Vatsya, Mudgala, Shaliya, Gokhalya and Shishira. Shakalya's disciple, the sage Jatukarna, divided his samhita into three parts and adding nirukta,[1376] gave it to Balaka, Paija, Vaitala and Viraja. Bashkali[1377] used all the sub-branches and reclassified them as *Valakhilya* samhita, taught to Balayani, Bhajya and Kashara. The brahmana rishis maintained bahvrich samhita in this way. If a person listens to the classification of these verses, he is freed from all sins.

'Vaishampayana's disciples were known as Charakadhvaryus.[1378] For their preceptor's sake, they undertook a vow to atone for the sin of killing a brahmana.[1379] Yajnavalkya, his disciple, told him, "O

[1374] This is the Rig Veda, known as bahvrich because it had the most number of mantras.

[1375] Atharva Veda.

[1376] Etymological dictionary, explaining the words used in the Vedas.

[1377] Bashkala's son.

[1378] Vaishampayana was taught the Yajur Veda and adhvaryus are priests who recite verses from the Yajur Veda. Charakadhvaryus means Charakas who became adhvaryus or adhvaryus who were known as Charakas. Charakas are those who undertake specific vows.

[1379] Vaishampayana did not actually kill a brahmana. There was a sacrifice and it was decreed that anyone who absented himself from this sacrifice would perform a sin that was tantamount to that from killing a brahmana. Because he had to perform his father's funeral ceremony, Vaishampayana couldn't be present and incurred the sin. Yajnavalkya offered to atone for it alone.

illustrious one! These ones are limited in substance. What can be gained from anything they undertake? I alone will perform extremely difficult austerities." Thus addressed, the preceptor became angry and said, "Enough! You have insulted the brahmanas. Give up everything that you have been taught by me." At this, Devarata's son[1380] vomited out the collection from the Yajur Veda. When he left, the sages saw the collection from the Yajur Veda. They looked at them greedily and assuming the form of *tittira* birds,[1381] gathered them up. This beautiful branch of the Yajur Veda came to be known as *Taittiriya*. O brahmana! Yajnavalkya wished to search out verses that were not known even to his preceptor. Therefore, he worshipped the lord, the sun god. Yajnavalkya said, "Oum! I bow down before the illustrious Aditya. In the form of the atman, he is present in the entire universe. He is in the form of time. He is inside the hearts of the four kinds of living creatures, beginning with Brahma and ending with clumps of grass. Like the sky, he covers everything that has a name from the outside, but is himself not covered. He gathers up the waters and gives them back for the sustenance of the worlds. He alone is the fragments of kshana, lava, nimesha and *samvatsara*. O bull among the gods! O Savita! O glowing one! Following the rituals of the sacred texts, we worship you thrice a day.[1382] You are the one who burns down the seeds of all sins and the resultant sufferings. O illustrious one! We meditate on your glowing orb. You are inside all mobile and immobile objects and they depend on you for refuge. You are the atman inside them, inspiring the aggregate of their minds, senses and breaths of life, which are distinct from the atman. This world has been swallowed up by a python and is unconscious, as if it is dead. The python's terrible mouth is known as darkness. O extremely compassionate one! Glance favourably towards it, so that thrice a day, the virtuous engage in ensuring what is beneficial. Urge their atmans towards what is known as their own dharma. Like a king on earth, you travel around everywhere, generating fear among the wicked. You

---

[1380] Yajnavalkya.
[1381] Pheasants.
[1382] Morning, noon and evening.

are surrounded by the guardians of the directions. In their cupped hands, which are like lotus buds, they bring you offerings. O lord! Therefore, I have approached and am worshipping your lotus feet, which are revered by the preceptors of the three worlds. I desire that part of the Yajur Veda that is not known to anyone else." Thus addressed, the illustrious sun god was pleased and assuming the form of a horse, taught the sage parts of the Yajur Veda that were not known to anyone else. The lord used these to classify fifteen branches of the Yajur Veda, known as *vajasanya*.[1383] He taught these to Kanva, Madhyadina and others.

'Jaimini possessed knowledge about the Sama Veda and Sumantu was his son. The sage[1384] taught the samhita to each of his sons. Jaimini's disciple, Sukarma, was a great brahmana and divided the great tree of the Sama Veda, with the Sama hymns, into one thousand samhitas. Sukarma's disciples were Hiranyanabha from Kosala, Poushyanji and Avantya,[1385] supreme in knowledge of the brahman, and they learnt this. Poushyanji and Avantya had five hundred disciples each. They were known as the northern reciters of the Sama hymns, though some among them came to be known as the eastern reciters. Poushyanji's disciples, Lougakshi, Mangali, Kulya, Kushida and Kukshi, received one hundred samhitas each. Hiranyanabha's disciple, Krita, taught his own disciples twenty-four samhitas. The rest were taught by Avantya, who was in control of his atman.'

Chapter 12(7)

Suta said, 'Sumantu, who knew about the Atharva Veda, taught it to his own disciple,[1386] who in turn spoke about the samhita to

[1383] Literally, from the mane of a horse.

[1384] Jaimini. At least, that is what the text seems to suggest. But it might also mean Sumantu.

[1385] Literally, resident of Avanti.

[1386] From the Vishnu Purana, it is known that this disciple's name was Kabandha.

his own disciples, Pathya and Vedadarsha. Vedadarsha's disciples were Shouklayani, Brahmabali, Modosha and Pippalayani. O brahmana! Hear about Pathya's disciples. They were Kumuda, Shunaka, descended from the Angiras lineage, and Jajali, who knew about the Atharva Veda. Shunaka's disciples, Babhru and Saindhavayana, studied the two samhitas. Savarnya and others also did this. Nakshatrakalpa, Shanti, Kashyapa, Angiras and others were teachers of the Atharva Veda.

'O sage! Now hear about the teachers of the Puranas. There were six who were teachers of the Puranas—Trayaruna, Kashyapa, Savarni, Akritavarna, Vaishampayana and Harita. From the mouth of my father,[1387] Vyasa's disciple, each of them learnt one part of the samhita. I became a disciple to each of them and learnt all of it. I, Kashyapa, Savarni and Akritavarna, Rama's[1388] disciple, learnt the four original samhitas from Vyasa's disciple. O brahmana! Using their intelligence and following the sacred texts of the Vedas, the brahmana rishis have determined the characteristics of the Puranas. Hear that. O brahmana! The learned have said that there are ten characteristics associated a Purana — sarga, visarga, vritti, raksha, antara, vamsha, vamshanucharita, samstha, hetu and apashraya.[1389] Some say there are only five and that this distinguishes the major ones from the minor ones. Sarga is about the generation of Mahat from the agitation of the gunas of the umanifest, the three kinds of ahamkara, the gross and the subtle and the senses and the objects of the senses. Through the favours of Purusha, visarga is the aggregation of desires of mobile and immobile objects, just as a seed is created from another seed.[1390] Vritti is the means whereby mobile and immobile

---

[1387] Romaharshana.

[1388] Parashurama's.

[1389] These characteristics are known as the *lakshana* of a Purana. Sarga is subtle creation, visarga is gross destruction, vritti is sustenance, raksha is protection, antara means the manvantaras, vamsha is lineage (usually of gods and rishis), vamshanucharita is lineage and conduct (of kings), samstha is destruction, hetu is cause (for karma) and apashraya is refuge (the ultimate one).

[1390] An allusion to karma.

creatures sustain themselves on other creatures. Goaded by desire and the injunctions, men create this for themselves. From one yuga to another yuga, for the protection of the universe and the destruction of those who hate the three,[1391] Achyuta descends. This is raksha. In each manvantara, there are said to be six kinds of appearances—Manu himself, the set of gods, Manu's sons, the lord of the gods,[1392] the rishis and Hari's descent through his portion. Through Brahma, vamsha is about the lineage of kings, progressing through the three phases of time.[1393] Vamshanucharita is about the conduct of their descendants. The wise have said that there are intrinsically four kinds of layas—naimittika, prakritika, nitya and atyantika. When all of these happen, that is samstha. The brahman is the ultimate apashraya, present in the three states of living creatures, wakefulness, sleeping and sushupti, covered in maya, but also distinct from them. The substance of a material object is the basis for its existence and assumes different names and forms.[1394] That original seed is present, both separate and joined in all states, ending with death. When the mind is regulated, or when one transcends the three states,[1395] through yoga, one retreats from this world and realizes the atman. Thus, sages who know about the ancient accounts have spoken about the major and minor Puranas as being eighteen, depending on their characteristics. The names of the eighteen are known as Brahma, Padma, Vishnu, Shiva, Linga, Garuda, Narada, Bhagavata, Agni, Skanda, Bhavishya, Brahmavaivarta, Markandeya, Vamana, Varaha, Matsya, Kurma and Brahmanda.[1396] O brahmana! I have described to you the various branches expounded by the sage,[1397] his disciples and the disciples of his disciples. These extend the brahman's glory.'

[1391] The three Vedas.

[1392] Indra.

[1393] The past, the present and the future.

[1394] Like the clay in an earthen pot.

[1395] Wakefulness, sleep and sushupti.

[1396] Since Bhavishya Purana has been included, Vayu Purana is missing from the list.

[1397] Vedavyasa.

Chapter 12(8)

Shounaka said, 'O Suta! O virtuous one! O supreme among
speakers! May you live for a long time. Men are roaming around
in darkness and you are the one who can show them the way to
the other shore. Tell us this. People say that the rishi who was
Mrikandu's son had a long lifespan. At the end of the kalpa, when
this universe was destroyed, he was the only one left. In this kalpa,
the bull among the Bhargava lineage was born in our lineage.[1398]
No one born now has witnessed living beings destroyed through a
deluge. When he was whirled around on that single ocean, he saw
Purusha, in the wonderful form of an infant who was lying down
inside a banyan leaf. O Suta! Among us, this generates curiosity and
a doubt. You are revered as a great yogi and someone who knows
about the Puranas. Please dispel this.'

Suta replied, 'O maharshi! The question you have asked will
remove a confusion among people. This will lead to Narayana's
account being sung and will destroy the impurities of kali yuga. In
the course of time, from his father, Markandeya obtained the sacred
thread, as is done for dvijas. Following dharma, he studied the
hymns and came to possess austerities and learning. He observed
great vows. He was tranquil. With matted hair, his garments were
made out of bark. He carried a water pot and a staff and wore a
sacred thread and girdle. He was attired in black antelope skin and
held a bead of rudrakshas and some kusha grass, so that the rituals
were followed. At the time of the morning and evening sandhyas,
he worshipped Hari in the form of the fire, the sun, preceptors,
brahmanas and his own atman. Controlling his speech, he begged
in the morning and the evening and gave whatever he got to his
preceptor. He ate only once a day, when he had been granted
permission by his preceptor. Otherwise, he fasted. In this way,
engaged in austerities and studying, he spent one hundred million
years.[1399] He worshipped Hrishikesha and conquered death, which

---

[1398] These are things people say about Markandeya.
[1399] Meaning a large number of years.

is impossible to vanquish. Brahma, Bhrigu, Bhava, Daksha, the other sons of Brahma, humans, gods, ancestors and other beings were extremely astounded at this. Thus, the yogi worshipped Adhokshaja through great vows, austerities, studying and control. Withdrawing into this inner atman, he destroyed all hardships. The yogi fixed his mind in this great yoga. A long period of time passed, extending across six manvantaras.

'O brahmana! In the current seventh manvantara, Purandara got to know about this. He was scared of the austerities and started to create impediments. He sent gandharvas, apsaras, desire, the pleasant breeze of the spring and, from Mount Malaya, the children of rajas and intoxication to the sage. O lord! They went to his hermitage, on the northern slopes of the Himalaya mountains, where the River Pushpabhadra flows near the stone known as Chitra. The sacred hermitage was adorned with sacred trees and creepers. It was full of flocks of sacred birds. There were sacred and spotless bodies of water. There was the singing of intoxicated bees. Maddened cuckoos called. Crazy peacocks danced in ecstasy. It was full of flocks of crazy birds. The breeze entered, bearing with it the cool spray from waterfalls in the mountains, embraced by the fragrance of flowers. As it blew, it ignited desire. The moon arose, as if it was the face of the night. Rows of sprouts and blossoms covered the trees and the creepers in a net. Spring manifested itself. Followed by the songs of gandharvas and the playing of musical instruments, the god of love was seen, the lord of a bevy of women, and with a bow and arrow in his hand. Shakra's servants saw him seated there, having offered oblations into the fire. His eyes were closed and he was impossible to assail. He was like the fire personified. The women danced in front of him and the singers sang. Delightful music was played from drums, veenas and cymbals. Kama fixed the five-headed weapon to his own bow.[1400] Spring, the children of rajas and Indra's servants tried to make his mind waver. Punjikasthali[1401] played with balls, her heavy breasts weighing down on her slender

---

[1400] Kama's arrow has five heads, each head standing for one of the senses.

[1401] An apsara.

waist. The garlands were dislodged from the braids of her hair. Her eyes darted around here and there. As she ran after the balls, the string of her girdle loosened and the wind blew her garment away. Thinking that he was ready to be vanquished, the god of love released his arrow. But like all the efforts of those who do not believe in the lord, the attempt was unsuccessful. O sage! When they tried to harm him, the sage's energy burnt them down and they stopped, like children who have awoken a snake. O brahmana! Thus, though he was afflicted by Indra's followers, the great sage did not succumb to ahamkara. Among those who are great, this is not surprising. The illustrious lord of heaven saw and heard that the god of love and his companions had lost their energy. Perceiving the brahmana rishi's powers, he was filled with great surprise. While his[1402] mind was immersed in austerities, studying and control, Hari Nara-Narayana desired to show him his favours and manifested himself. One was fair and the other was dark. Their eyes were like freshly bloomed lotuses. They were four-armed and were clad in garments made out of bark and the skin of ruru antelopes. Their purifying hands held a sacred thread made out of three strings, a kamandalu, an upright staff made out of bamboo, a garland made out of lotus seeds and a broom to brush away insects.[1403] They were the personified forms of the Vedas and austerities. Their yellowish radiance possessed the complexion of lightning. They were tall in stature and the bulls among the gods worshipped them. On seeing the illustrious one's form as the Nara and Narayana rishis, he stood up with great respect. Like a staff, he bent down and prostrated himself. The bliss of seeing them satisfied his body, his mind and his senses. His body hair stood up and his eyes were full of tears. He was incapable of looking at them. He arose and humbly joined his hands in salutation. In his eagerness, it was almost as if he was embracing them. In faltering words, he said, "I bow down. I bow down." He gave them seats to sit on and washed their feet. He worshipped them with offerings, unguents, incense and garlands. When they were comfortably seated and ready to shower their

---

[1402] Markandeya's.
[1403] So that the insects are not harmed or killed.

favours on him, he again bowed down at the feet of the two sages. He spoke to the revered ones.

'Markandeya said, "O lord! How can I describe you? It is through your urging that the breath of life pulsates. It is through your urging that speech, mind and the senses pulsate. This is for all living beings, Aja and Sharva included. That is also true of me. However, you are a friend to those who worship you. O illustrious one! These two forms of the illustrious one are for the welfare of the three worlds, the cessation of torments and the conquest of death. For the sake of protection, you assume many transcendental forms like this. Like a spider, you create and withdraw everything. I seek refuge at the feet of the protector and controller of mobile and immobile beings, where one is not touched by the impurities of karma, gunas and time. Sages who have grasped the essence of the Vedas praise you, bow down to you, constantly worship you and meditate on you. You are the personified form of liberation. O lord! From all sides, people are subjected to fear and we do not know of any refuge other than your feet. Brahma's lordship is for a period of two parardhas and therefore, he is also extremely scared of you, in the form of time. What need be said about beings who are created by him? Therefore, I worship the feet of the one whose intelligence represents the truth. I give up the body and other things that are useless, unreal and temporary. They are coverings for the atman and are thought of as different from you, the atman's preceptor. I will thereby obtain all the desired objects. O lord! O friend of the atman! Sattva, rajas and tamas are the result of maya. These causes behind creation, preservation and destruction are the result of your pastimes. Full of sattva, you alone lead to serenity. The other two do not free men from delusion.[1404] O illustrious one! Therefore, accomplished devotees worship your pure form, so loved by those who are your own. Great devotees can see the form of Purusha that is based on sattva. That is what grants people freedom from fear and joy in realization of the atman, nothing else. I bow down to the illustrious one, the pervasive Purusha. The universe is your form.

[1404] The two are interpreted as Brahma and Shiva, but might mean rajas and tamas too.

You are the preceptor of the universe. You are the supreme divinity. You are Narayana rishi and Nara, supreme among humans. You are hamsa, the controller of speech and the propounder of the sacred texts. You are established within a person's own breath of life, heart and the objects of the senses that he can see. However, his intelligence is enveloped in maya and his mind follows the misguided path of the senses. Therefore, he does not know you. However, when a person directly realizes you, the preceptor of everything, he knows you, the origin of everything. The vision of the sacred texts illuminates the mysterious nature of your atman. However, even though they try, wise ones, Aja being the foremost, are confounded. Depending on whichever school of thought is being debated, you present your nature in an appropriate form. I worship the great being, the comprehension about whose atman is concealed."

Chapter 12(9)

Suta said, 'Praised in this way by the intelligent Markandeya, the illustrious Narayana, Nara's friend, was pleased and spoke to the descendant of the Bhrigu lineage. The illustrious one said, "O noble brahmana rishi! You are supreme among those who have meditated on the atman. Your devotion towards me is unwavering. You are controlled and have performed austerities and have studied. We are satisfied with the great vow you have observed. O fortunate one! I confer boons. I wish to confer a boon on you. Ask whatever you desire." The rishi replied, "O lord of the lord of the gods! May you be victorious. O Achyuta! You remove the afflictions of those who seek shelter with you. This is enough of a boon that you have shown yourself to me. After ripening their minds through yoga, Aja and the others see your lotus feet and obtain all their opulences. However, you are in front of my eyes. O one with eyes like the petals of a lotus! O jewel on the crest of everyone who is praised! Because of your maya, the worlds and the guardians of the worlds take everything to be differentiated. I want to witness that." O sage! Praised and worshipped in this way, the illustrious one agreed to the rishi's wish. The lord smiled and returned to his hermitage in Badarika.

'The rishi remained in his hermitage and continued to think about his objective. He meditated on Hari everywhere—fire, the sun, the moon, water, the earth, the wind, the sky and within his own atman. He worshipped him with mental objects.[1405] Sometimes, he was so overwhelmed in the deluge of love that he forgot to worship him at all. O best among the Bhrigu lineage! O brahmana! Once, during sandhya, the sage was seated on the banks of the River Pushpabhadra and was meditating. A giant storm arose, generating a terrible roar. Fierce clouds followed it and showered down rain that was as heavy as the wheels of chariots. There was lightning and the loud roar of thunder. The oceans were seen in the four directions. They advanced and swallowed up the surface of the earth. The force of the wind stirred up waves, full of extremely fierce aquatic creatures. There was the terrible sound of whirlpools. All the four kinds of creatures, and he himself, suffered inside and outside. The water rose up into the sky. The wind was fierce and there was thunder and lightning. The world was scorched. The earth was deluged with water. On seeing this, the sage's mind was distressed and he was scared. As he looked on, the fierce waves rose up still higher and the great ocean was whirled around by the turbulent storm. Everything was filled by the wind and the clouds. The earth, the dvipas, the varshas and the mountains were deluged. The earth, the sky, heaven, the stellar bodies and their inhabitants, the three worlds and the directions were submerged in that deluge and the great sage was the only one who remained. He wandered around, as if he was blind and dumb, with his matted hair dishevelled. He was afflicted by hunger and thirst. He was oppressed by makaras and timingilas. He was struck by the storm and the wind. He descended into a fathomless darkness and roamed around. He could not determine the directions, the sky or the earth and was exhausted. Sometimes, he was dragged into a gigantic whirlpool. Sometimes, he was tossed by the waves. Sometimes, he was bitten by aquatic monsters. While trying to seize him, they fought against each other.

[1405] These were objects he thought of in his mind, not physical offerings.

Sometimes, he was filled with grief. Sometimes, he was filled with delusion. Sometimes, he experienced misery, happiness or fear. Sometimes, he thought he was about to die. Sometimes, he suffered from physical ailments, mental ailments and the wind. Hundreds, thousands and billions of years passed in this way. With his atman shrouded in Vishnu's maya, he wandered around there.

'While wandering around, on one occasion, the brahmana saw a bit of ground that jutted out. There was a young nyagrodha tree there and it was adorned with fruits and foliage. He saw an infant boy lying down on a branch towards the north-east, within the cup of a leaf. His radiance swallowed up the darkness. His complexion was dark blue, like a giant emerald. His face was as beautiful as a lotus. His neck was like a conch shell. His chest was broad. His nose was excellent and his eyebrows were handsome. Because of his breathing, his radiant locks trembled. His beautiful ears were like conch shells. His lips had the radiance of coral. There was a sweet smile on his reddened lips. The ends of his eyes were red, like the whorls of a lotus. His looks and glances were enchanting. His deep navel was like a leaf, and as he breathed, the lines on his stomach moved. The Indra among brahmanas was amazed to see him pick up one of his lotus feet with the beautiful fingers of his hand, place it in his mouth, and suck it. On seeing this, his exhaustion vanished. He was so delighted that the lotus in his heart and the lotuses in his eyes blossomed. His body hair stood up in joy. Confused about who this extraordinary child in front of him was, he approached and asked. At that moment, along with the breathing, Bhargava was drawn inside the infant's body, like a mosquito. When he entered, he saw everything laid out exactly as it had been earlier.[1406] He was extremely surprised. He saw the entire universe manifested there, as if it was real—the sky, the heaven, the earth, the large number of stellar bodies, the dvipas, the varshas, the directions, the gods, the asuras, the forests, the countries, the rivers, the cities, the mines, the villages, the settlements of cattle, the ashramas, the varnas, the occupations, the gross elements, the gross manifestations, time, the

---

[1406] The entire universe was inside the stomach, exactly as it had been before the destruction and deluge.

many yugas, the kalpas, everything that regulates and everything else that can be regarded as a cause. The rishi saw the Himalayas, the River Pushpavaha[1407] and his own hermitage. As he gazed at the universe, the child exhaled him with his breathing and he fell down into the ocean of deluge. He again saw the elevated ground with the banyan tree and the infant lying down, inside the cup of a leaf. The child cast sweet and sidelong glances full of love towards him. As he glanced back, he was extremely agitated and rushed forward to embrace Adhokshaja. But the child entered his heart through his eyes and stationed himself there. The illustrious one is the lord of yoga himself and resides inside hearts. Like the undertakings of a person who is without a lord,[1408] the child vanished from the rishi's vision. O brahmana! Following him, the banyan tree and the water that deluged the worlds also vanished in an instant. He found himself in his own hermitage, as he had been earlier.'

Chapter 12(10)

Suta said, 'He thus experienced the powers of the yoga maya created by Narayana and sought refuge with him again. Markandeya said, "O Hari! I have sought shelter at your feet, which grant freedom from fear. Your maya appears in the form of jnana, but confounds even the gods." He had thus withdrawn himself completely inside his atman. The illustrious Rudra was travelling through the sky on his bull, along with Rudrani, and surrounded by his own companions. He saw him. On seeing the rishi, Uma spoke to Girisha. "O illustrious one! Look at the brahmana. His body, his mind and his heart have been controlled. He is like an ocean, when the schools of fish in the water are still and there is no wind. You are the one who ensures the success of austerities. Please confer success on him." The illustrious one[1409] said, "This brahmana rishi

---

[1407] The same as Pushpabhadra.
[1408] That is, a godless person.
[1409] Shiva.

does not wish for any benedictions, moksha, or anything at all. He has obtained supreme devotion in the illustrious and undecaying Purusha. O Bhavani! However, let us converse with this virtuous person. The greatest gain for men is to be associated with virtuous people." The illustrious Ishana is the lord of all kinds of knowledge. He is inside all embodied beings and is the destination of the virtuous. Having said this, he approached him. However, he had withdrawn his intelligence and his conduct and was not aware on his own self, or the universe. Therefore, he did not perceive that the two lords and atmans of the universe had themselves arrived. Understanding this, the illustrious Girisha used yoga maya to enter his heart. The lord entered, just as the wind enters through an opening. He perceived that Shiva had entered inside him, like a flash of lightning. His hair was matted. He was three-eyed and possessed ten arms. He was tall and as radiant as the rising sun. His garments were made out of tiger skin. He held a trident, a bow, a sword and a shield. He held a garland of rudrakshas, a drum, a skull and an axe. On seeing this sudden manifestation appear inside his heart, he was amazed. Ceasing his meditation, the sage wondered, "Who is this and where has he come from?" He opened his eyes and saw that Uma and the companions had also arrived. The sage bowed his head down before Rudra, the preceptor of the three worlds. He worshipped him, Uma and the companions with offerings. Having welcomed them, he gave them seats, padya, arghya, fragrances, garlands, incense and lamps. He said, "O lord! All your wishes are satisfied within your own self. O Ishana! You are the one who satisfies this universe. What can I do for you? I bow down to Shiva, the serene one. As the personficatin of sattva, you bestow pleasure. You are the personification of rajas. As the personification of tamas, you are terrible. I bow down before you." The illustrious one is the destination of the virtuous. Thus praised, the original god was pleased.

'Delighted, the original god smiled and spoke to him. The illustrious one said, "We three[1410] are the ones who bestow boons. Ask for the boon you wish. Our vision cannot be futile. A mortal

[1410] Brahma, Vishnu and Shiva.

person who sees us obtains immortality. I, the illustorius Brahma, the lord Hari himself, the worlds and the guardians of the worlds revere, worship and serve brahmanas who are virtuous, serene, without attachment, affectionate towards beings, without hatred, impartial in outlook and single-minded in devotion towards us. They do not perceive any difference between me, Achyuta and Aja, nor between themselves and others. That is the reason we worship those like you. Places with water are not tirthas. Images without life are not gods. These purify after a long period of time, but the sight of those like you purifies instantly. We bow down before brahmanas. They are our forms and are full of the three.[1411] Meditating on the atman, they control themselves and undertake studying and austerities. Seeing you and hearing you, the perpetrators of great sins are purified, even those who are outcastes. What need be said about those who converse with you?" He is the one who is decorated with the moon and his words were full of the mysteries of dharma. They were like a reservoir of amrita and the rishi was not satisfied at drinking them in with his ears. Because of Vishnu's maya, he had been whirled around for a long time and had suffered greatly. But Shiva's amrita-like words dispelled all his piles of hardship. He spoke these words. Markandeya said, "It is impossible for those with bodies to comprehend the lord's pastimes. The lords of the universe are controlled by him and worship him. To make embodied creatures accept dharma, those who propound it also generally practise it and praise those who perform the approved acts. The conduct of the illustrious one is not affected by his own maya, nor are his powers tainted by this. He is like a conjurer exhibiting tricks. I bow down to the illustrious one. The gunas are in his atman and he uses these gunas to create. He is absolute and without a second. He is the preceptor and the one who is the personified form of the brahman. O supreme lord! Your sight is itself a boon. What superior boon can I ask for? From the mere act of seeing you, a man accomplishes all his wishes and all his desires come true. However, you are capable of showering down all the cherished wishes. Therefore, I do ask for a boon from you. May I have devotion towards the illustrious

[1411] The three Vedas.

Achyuta and towards those like you who are devoted to him." The
illustrious Sharva was thus worshipped and praised by the sage in
sweet words that were approved of by Sharvaya.[1412] He said, "O
maharshi! Since you are devoted to Adhokshaja, all your wishes
will be fulfilled. Till the end of the kalpa, you will obtain pious
fame and will not suffer from old age or death. O brahmana! You
possess the radiance of the brahman. You will have knowledge
about the three phases of time,[1413] transcendental knowledge and
non-attachment. You will also be a propounder of a Purana."[1414]
Having bestowed this boon on the sage, the three-eyed lord left. He
told the goddess about his[1415] deeds about what he had experienced
earlier. The supreme one from the Bhargava lineage obtained the
greatness of the great yoga. He roams around even now, immersing
himself single-mindedly in Hari. I have described to you how the
intelligent Markandeya experienced the illustrious one's maya and
extraordinary powers. Some ignorant men say this is like the maya
of samsara created from his atman, which men have been whirling
around in since the beginning.[1416] O noble one from the Bhrigu
lineage! What has been described is full of the powers of the one
who wields a chakra in his hand. If a person hears this, or makes
it heard, he does not have to experience samsara, the result of his
past karma.'

Chapter 12(11)

Sounaka said, 'You are diverse in your learning. You know
everything about the conclusions of the sacred texts and the

[1412] Sharva's consort, Uma.

[1413] Past, present and future.

[1414] Markandeya Purana.

[1415] Markandeya's.

[1416] This requires explanation. The illustrious one's atman creates the
maya of samsara. Some ignorant people compare Markandeya's experience
with this and suggest it was all maya, and not real. But Markandeya actually
experienced it.

tantras. You are devoted to the illustrious one and know the truth. Therefore, I am asking you about the following. Shri's consort is pure consciousness. However, those who follow the principles of tantra conceive him and worship him as one with limbs, companions, weapons and accoutrements. O fortunate one! Therefore, describe to us these techinques of kriya yoga. We are eager to know the principles of kriya, whereby mortals become accomplished and achieve immortality.'

Suta replied, 'Having bowed down to my preceptors, I will tell you about Vishnu's glory. The one who was born from the lotus and other preceptors of the Vedas and the tantras have spoken about this. His Virat form begins with maya and includes the nine principles and transformations.[1417] When these have been created and infused with consciousness, the three worlds become visible. This is his cosmic or Purusha form. His feet are the earth. Heaven is his head. The sky is his navel. His eyes are the sun. His nostrils are the wind. The directions are the lord's ears. His genitals are Prajapati. The lord's anus is death. The guardians of the world are his arms. The moon is his mind. His eyebrows are Yama. Modesty is his upper lip. Greed is his lower lip. Moonlight is his teeth. His smile is delusion. The lord's body hair is the trees. The clouds are the hair on Purusha's head. Any person's dimensions can be gauged by measuring his limbs and their positions. In a similar way, the great Purusha can be gauged from the positions of the worlds. The unborn one wears Koustubha and that is the radiance of the self-luminous atman. The effulgence spreading from this is directly the shrivatsa mark the lord has on his chest. He wears his own maya as the garland of wild flowers, consisting of many different kinds of gunas. The hymns of the Vedas constitute his yellow garments. The three syllables are his sacred thread.[1418] The god wears two earrings shaped like makaras and these are samkhya and yoga. His diadem

---

[1417] There are diverse interpretations of this. For instance, the nine principles are Prakriti, Mahat, sutra (the active principle of Mahat), ahamkara and the five tanmatras. The transformations are the ten senses, the mind and the five gross elements.

[1418] O, U and M, making up Oum.

bestows freedom from fear to all the worlds and is the supreme place for Parameshthi.[1419] The seat on which he lies down is known as Ananta and is the unmanifest.[1420] The lotus throne on which he sits is said to be sattva, consisting of dharma, jnana and the others.[1421] The mace that he wields is the main form of prana, consisting of energy, fortitude and strength. His supreme conch shell is the principle of water, the Sudarshana chakra is the principle of fire, his sparkling sword is like the sky and is the principle of space and the shield is the priniciple of tamas or ignorance. His Sharnga bow is the form of time and the quiver represents the principle of karma. The senses are said to be his arrows and the mind, which can control them, are his chariot. The objects of the senses are the external appearance of the chariot. His *mudra*s are the purpose of activity.[1422] One must consecrate oneself and that destroys all the sins of the atman. The illustrious one can then be worshipped and the solar disc is the place for worshipping the divinity. He is Bhagavan and playfully carries a lotus, signifying the implicit potencies in the word "bhaga".[1423] The illustrious one is worshipped with two whisks, representing dharma and fame. O brahmanas! The umbrella held over his head signifies his abode of Vaikuntha, with freedom from fear. The one known as Suparna[1424] represents the three Vedas and bears Purusha, the personified form of a sacrifice. The illustrious Shri does not leave him and directly represents Hari's atman. Vishvaksena, foremost among his attendants, is known as the personified form of the tantras.[1425] Nanda and the others, his eight gatekeepers are Hari's attributes, anima and the others. O brahmana! Vasudeva, Samkarshana,

---

[1419] Brahma.

[1420] Prakriti.

[1421] The others are vairagya and so on.

[1422] Mudras are the positions and gestures of the fingers and the hands, such as one that confers boons (*barada*) and one that grants freedom from fear (*abhaya*).

[1423] In this context, the word bhaga means potency and Bhagavan is one with these potencies. The relevant potencies are rulership, virtue, glory, affluence, wisdom and non-attachment.

[1424] Garuda.

[1425] Intepreted as the pancharatra texts.

Pradyumna and Aniruddha are designated as direct manifestations of Purusha himself. The illustrious one is conceived as *vishva*, guiding external objects; taijasa, guiding the senses; *prajna*, guiding the mind; and turiya, guiding transcendental consciousness.[1426] The illustrious lord Hari thus manifests himself in four forms, each with separate limbs, attendants, weapons and ornaments, but all four are his own expansions. O bull among brahmanas! He is the source of the Vedas. He is the one who illuminates himself. He is complete in his own glory. It is through his own maya that he creates, preserves and destroys, and is accordingly addressed. He is described as differentiated. However, those who are devoted to him can uncover his transcendental nature and realize him as their own atmans. O Shrikrishna! O Krishna's friend![1427] O bull in the lineage of the Vrishnis! O one who scorched the lineages of the kings on earth! O one whose valour does not diminish! O Govinda! O one whose glory is sung by the women of Vraja and by your servants! O one whose fame is like a tirtha! O one whose deeds are auspicious to hear! Save your servants. If a person rises at the right time, controls himself and immerses his mind in these attributes of the great Purusha and meditates, he realizes him within his heart.'

Shounaka said, 'Vishnurata was listening and the illustrious Shuka spoke to him about the seven different categories that reside in each of the solar months. We are faithful ones who wish to hear. Please tell us about their names, their tasks, about how they are engaged and about the manifestations of Surya, who is nothing but Hari's manifestation.'

Suta replied, 'Vishnu is in the atmans of all beings. He is without a beginning and his maya has fashioned Surya, who travels through the worlds and creates these worlds. Hari is the original atman who is one and is the creator of everything. For the worlds, it is he who

---

[1426] Vishva is the state of wakefulness, guiding the functioning of external objects (artha) and the divinity is Pradyumna; taijasa is the state of dreaming, guiding the functioning of the senses (*indriya*) and the divinity is Samkarshana; prajna is the state of dreamless and deep sleep, guiding the functioning of the mind (*manas*) and the divinity is Aniruddha; turiya is the state of transcental self-realization (jnana) and the divinity is Vasudeva.

[1427] This Krishna means Arjuna.

is Surya. He is the foundation of all the rites of the Vedas and the rishis have designated him by different names. O brahmana! Hari's maya is without origin and it is this that leads him to be described according to nine categories—the time, the place, the ritual, the agent, the instrument, the task, the sacred text, the objects and the fruits. In his form of time, beginning with Madhu,[1428] the illustrious one travels along twelve months, regulating the worlds and with twelve different sets of associates. In the month of Madhu, the controllers are Dhata, Kritasthali, Heti, Vasuki, Rathakrit, Pulastya as the sage and Tumburu.[1429] In the month of Madhava,[1430] the controllers are Aryama, Punjikasthali, Praheti, Kachchhanira, Athouja, Pulaha and Narada. In the month of Shukramasa,[1431] the controllers are Mitra, Menaka, Pourusheya, Takshaka, Rathasvana, Atri and Haha. In the month of Shuchimasa,[1432] the controllers are Varuna, Rambha, Sahajanya, Shukra, Chitrasvana, Vasishtha and Huhu. In the month of Nabhomasa,[1433] the controllers are Indra, Pramlocha, Varya, Elapatra, Shrota, Angira and Vishvavasu. In the month of Nabhasya,[1434] the controllers are Vivasvan, Anumlocha, Vyaghra, Shankhapala, Asarana, Bhrigu and Ugrasena. In the month of Tapomasa,[1435] the controllers are Pusha, Ghritachi, Vata, Dhananjaya, Suruchi, Goutama and Sushena. In the month of Tapasya,[1436] the controllers are Parjanya, Senajit, Varcha, Airavata, Kratu, Bharadvaja and Vishva. In the month of Sahomasa,[1437] the controllers are Amshu, Urvashi, Vidyuchchhatru, Mahashankha,

---

[1428] Chaitra.

[1429] Dhata is the form of Surya, Kritasthali is the apsara, Heti is the rakshasa, Vasuki is the naga, Rathakrit is the yaksha, Pulastya is the rishi and Tumburu is the gandharava. For the other eleven months, this exact order is followed. Therefore, there is no need to add additional notes.

[1430] Vaishakha.

[1431] Jyeshtha.

[1432] Ashadha.

[1433] Shravana.

[1434] Bhadrapada.

[1435] Magha.

[1436] Phalguna.

[1437] Margashirsha.

Tarkshya, Kashyapa and Ritasena. In the month of Pushyamasa,[1438] the controllers are Bhaga, Purvachitti, Sphurja, Karkotaka, Urna, Ayu and Arishtanemi. In the month of Ishambhara,[1439] the controllers are Tvashta, Tilottama, Brahmapeta, Kambala, Shatajit, Jamadagni and Dhritarashtra. In the month of Urjamasa,[1440] the controllers are Vishnu, Rambha, Makhapeta, Ashvatara, Satyajit, Vishvamitra and Suryavarcha. These are the opulences of the illustrious Vishnu, in the form of Aditya. If men remember them at the time of the sandhyas, from one day to another day, their sins are taken away. Through each of the twelve months, the divinity travels along with six sets of associates, spreading virtuous intelligence everywhere, for this world and for the next. Rishis chant his glories through hymns from the Sama, Rig and Yajur Vedas. Gandharvas chant his praise and the best of apsaras dance before him. The nagas yoke his chariot and the yakshas drive the chariot from the front. The extremely powerful rakshasas push the chariot from the rear. There are sixty thousand unblemished brahmana rishis known as *valakhilya*s. They advance in front of him, praising and worshipping the lord. The illustrious lord Hari is without a beginning and without an end. He is without birth. In this way, from one kalpa to another kalpa, he divides his own atman and protects the worlds.'

Chapter 12(12)

Suta said, 'I bow down to great dharma. I bow down before Krishna, the creator. I bow down to brahmanas. It is after this that I will speak about eternal dharma. O brahmanas! I have spoken to you about Vishnu's extraordinary conduct. You had asked me about this. If a man is truly a man, he should hear about it. Hari, who himself destroys all sins, has been extolled here. He is the illustrious Narayana Hrishikesha, the lord of the Satvatas. It

[1438] Pousha.
[1439] Ashvina.
[1440] Kartika.

describes the mysterious supreme brahman, whose power causes the creation and destruction of the universe. It has discussions about achieving vijnana. It has spoken about bhakti yoga, with the objective of non-attachment. It has the account of Parikshit and the account of Narada. Because of the curse of the brahmana, the royal sage, Parikshit, engaged in *praya*[1441] and there was a conversation between Parikshit and Shuka, bull among brahmanas. There is a description of how one can use yoga to free oneself at the time of death, the conversation between Narada and Aja, a recital of avataras and the original creation through Pradhana. There is a conversation between Vidura and Uddhava, a conversation between Kshatta[1442] and Maitreya, a question about Purana samhitas and the dormant state of the great being. There is a description of the creation from Prakriti, the seven kinds of transformation and the generation of the cosmic egg, from which, Virat Purusha evolved. There is the gross and subtle progress of time, the generation of the lotus and the slaying of Hiranyaksha, to raise the earth up from the ocean. There is a description of the creation of superior species, inferior species and nether regions, Rudra's creation and the appearance of Svayambhuva Manu from the half-man and half-woman form. As a wife, he obtained Shatarupa, supreme among women. Through virtuous wives, Kardama Prajapati had sons. The illustrious one's avatara was the great-souled Kapila. There is a conversation between the intelligent Kapila and Devahuti. There is the account of the nine sons of Brahma, the destruction of Daksha's sacrifice and the conduct of Dhruva, followed by that of Prithu and Prachinabarhi. O brahmanas! There is the conversation with Narada and the accounts of Priyavrata, Nabhi, Rishabha and Bharata. There is a description of dvipas, varshas, oceans, mountains, rivers, the position of stellar bodies and the arrangements of patala and hell. There is the birth of Daksha as the son of Prachetas and the offspring of his daughters—gods, asuras, humans, inferior species, trees, birds and others. O brahmanas! There is the birth and death of Tvashta's son,[1443] two

---

[1441] Act of giving up one's life by fasting to death.
[1442] Vidura.
[1443] Vritra.

of Diti's sons, the lords among the daityas, and the conduct of the great-souled Prahlada. There is a recital of the manvantaras and the freeing of the Indra among elephants. There is a description of Vishnu's avataras in different manvantaras, Hayashira and the others. The lord of the universe appeared as a tortoise, a fish, narasimha and as a vamana, so that the residents of heaven could obtain amrita through the churning of the ocean. The great battle between gods and asuras and the lineages of the kings have been described. There is Ikshvaku's birth and his lineage and that of the great-souled Sudyumna. Ila's account has been narrated and Tara's account has also been narrated. There is a description of the kings of the solar dynasty, Shashada, Nriga and others. There are accounts of Sukanya, Sharyati's daughter, the intelligent Kakutstha, Khatvanga, Mandhata, Soubhari and Sagara. There is the conduct of Rama, Indra among Kosalas, and it destroys all sins. There is the account of Nimi giving up his body and the birth of Janaka's lineage. Rama, Indra among Bhargavas, exterminated kshatriyas from earth. Through Ila, there is an account of the lunar dynasty, Yayati and Nahusha. There are accounts of Bharata, Dushyanta's son, Shantanu and his son.

'The lineage of Yadu, Yayati's eldest son, has been described. The illustrious lord of the universe descended there and was known by the name of Krishna. He was born in Vasudeva's house, but grew up in Gokula. The innumerable deeds of the enemy of the asuras has been described. As a child, he sucked out Putana's life with the milk, broke the cart, crushed Trinavarta, Baka and Vatsa, Dhenuka and his brother and slaughtered Pralamba. He protected the gopas from the forest conflagration that encircled them. He subdued Kaliya, the great serpent, and saved Nanda. The maidens observed a vow and Achyuta was pleased through this vow. He bestowed his favours on the wives of the brahmanas who were performing sacrifices and the brahmanas repented. He held up Govardhana and Shakra and Surabhi worshipped him, consecrating him at a sacrifice. For several nights, Krishna sported with the women. He killed the evil-minded Shankhachuda, Arishta and Keshi. After Akrura arrived, Rama and Krishna departed, while the women of Vraja lamented. They went and saw Mathura. There was the death of the elephant,

Mushtika, Chanura, Kamsa and others. He brought back from the land of the dead the son of Sandipani, his preceptor. O brahmanas! While residing in Mathura with Uddhava and Rama, Hari did what would bring pleasure to the Yadus. On several occasions, there was the destruction of Jarasandha's army. There was the slaying of the Indra among the Yavanas and the establishment of Kushasthali. From the world of the gods, there was the bringing of Parijata and Sudharma. Crushing the enemies in a battle, Hari abducted Rukmini. Hara was made to yawn in a battle and Bana's arms were severed. He killed the lord of Pragjyotisha and rescued the maidens who had been abducted there. The greatness and destruction of Chedi, Poundraka, Shalva, the evil-minded Dantavakra, Shambara, Dvivida, Pitha, Mura, Panchajana and others have been described. Varanavata was burnt down and the Pandavas were engaged for reducing the earth's burden. Using the pretext of the curse of the brahmanas, he arranged for the destruction of his own lineage. There is the wonderful conversation between Uddhava and Vasudeva. All the knowledge about the atman is described there and the determination of dharma is spoken about. Using the powers of his own yoga, he gave up the mortal world.

'There is a description of the conduct and attributes of yugas and the disturbances men face during kali yuga. There are the four kinds of pralaya and the three kinds of creation. The royal sage, the intelligent Vishnurata, gave up his body. There is a description of how the different branches were composed[1444] and the virtuous Markandeya's account. He is the atman of the universe and there is a description of the great being's expanse and of his form as the sun. O best among the brahmanas! In this way, I have told you everything that you had asked me about here, about his pastimes, avataras and deeds. I have recounted everything to you here. When a person is falling down, is stumbling, is afflicted or is sneezing, even if involuntarily chants, "I bow down to Hari", he is freed from all sins. If men chant about the infinite and illustrious one or hear about his powers, he enters their hearts and completely cleans all hardships, just as the sun destroys darkness, or the wind drives

---

[1444] By Vedavyasa.

away the clouds. Those who do not speak about the illustrious
Adhokshaja, speak about unreal and temporary things instead.
He alone is truth. He alone is auspicious. He alone is sacred. All
qualities arise from the illustrious one. He alone is beautiful and
attractive, appearing in newer and newer forms. His accounts
are always like a great festivity in the mind. If men chant about
Uttamashloka's glory, that is what dries up the ocean of grief. Even
if they are not composed in perfect metres and verses, if words are
chanted about Hari's glory, they purify the universe. Otherwise,
they are like tirthas frequented by crows and not by swans. Spotless
and virtuous people only exist where Achyuta exists. Even if words
are imperfectly created and composed, as long as they depict the
infinite Utttamashloka's names and fame, they free people from this
deluge of sin. Virtuous ones hear them, sing them and chant them. If
naishkarma is devoid of devotion towards Achyuta, it is not bright
enough. That jnana is not devoid of impurities and taints. Karma
that is not rendered to the lord is always inferior and inauspicious.
How can that purify? Supreme efforts, the conduct of the varnas
and the ashramas, austerities, learning and other things may be
for fame and prosperity. However, if one respectfully hears the
chanting of his qualities and does similar things, one never fails to
remember Sridhara's lotus feet.[1445] Remembrance of Krishna's lotus
feet destroys everything inauspicious and evil. It enhances sattva,
purification and devotion towards the paramatman. It is full of
jnana, vijnana and non-attachment. O foremost among brahmanas!
You are extremely fortunate. He is in the atmans of all beings and
you have him in your hearts. He is the divinity Narayana, the lord
of all the gods. Love him constantly. Immerse yourselves in him
and worship him. When King Parikshit was engaged in praya, in
the assembly of the great rishis, from the mouth of the supreme
rishi, I had formerly heard the truth about the atman and I have
now been reminded about it. O brahmanas! I have described
the greatness of Urukrama Vasudeva to you. It swiftly destroys
all that is inauspicious. If a person hears this continuously, with
single-minded devotion, for one yama or even for one kshana, if

[1445] Shridhara, the one who holds Shri, is Vishnu's name.

a person hears one shloka, half a shloka, a quarter of a shloka, or even one-eighth of a shloka, as long as he hears it faithfully, he purifies his atman. A person who hears it on the eleventh or twelfth lunar day has a long life. If a person is attentive and hears it while fasting, he is purified of sins. If a person controls himself, fasts and reads this samhita in Pushkara, Mathura or Dvaravati, he is freed from fear. Those who sing it, hear it or chant it obtain all their objects of desire from gods, sages, Siddhas, ancestors, Manus and kings. By studying the Rig Veda, the Yajur Veda and the Sama Veda, brahmanas obtain rivers of honey, rivers of ghee and rivers of milk. Those fruits can be obtained by studying this. Brahmanas who control themselves and study this Purana samhita go to the supreme destination the illustrious one spoke about. A brahmana who studies this obtains wisdom, a king obtains sovereignty up to the girdle of the ocean, a vaishya becomes the lord of riches and a shudra is purified from sins. The lord of everything, Hari, destroys all the impurities of kali yuga brought about by time. However, he is not chanted about as much elsewhere.[1446] The illustrious one, infinite in his forms, is extolled here. He is directly described here, in every verse and in connection with every account. He is without birth. He is infinite. He is the truth about the atman. It is through his powers that he creates, preserves and destroys the universe. Aja, Shakra, Shankara and the other lords of heaven find it impossible to comprehend him. I bow down before Achyuta. Through his own atman, he has evolved the nine potencies.[1447] Within himself, he has laid out the abodes of mobile and immobile beings. The illustrious one's state is that of pure consciousness. I bow down to the eternal one, the bull among the gods. I bow down before Vyasa's son, the one who destroys everything inauspicious. His heart was attracted towards the pastimes and activities of the unvanquished one. For the sake of that divine bliss, he lived alone, immersing himself in that consciousness and giving up everything else. Out of his compassion, he expounded on this Purana, which is like a lamp towards the truth.'

[1446] In other Puranas.
[1447] Purusha, Prakriti, Mahat, ahamkara and the five tanmatras.

Chapter 12(13)

Suta said, 'Brahma, Varuna, Indra, Rudra and the Maruts praise him through divine hymns. He is chanted about in the Vedas, the Vedangas and the Upanishads, in duly arranged lines, and by those who recite the Sama hymns. When yogis meditate with their minds fixed on him, they see him. The large number of gods and asuras cannot comprehend his limits. I bow down to that god. The illustrious one appeared in the form of a tortoise and when it was rotated, the sharp points of Mount Mandara scratched his back, making him sleepy. May the wind from his breathing protect you. As a legacy of that, the waters of the ocean beat against the shoreline, ebbing and flowing and imitating his breathing. Even now, the ocean ceaselessly continues and does not stop.

'Now hear about the total number of verses in each Purana and the main theme and objective of each, the greateness of giving them as gifts, the gifts they must be given with, and about teaching them. Brahma has ten thousand verses, Padma fifty thousand, Vishnu twenty-three thousand and Shiva twenty-four thousand. Bhagavata has eighteen thousand, Narada twenty-five thousand, Markandeya nine thousand and Agni fifteen thousand and four hundred. Bhavishya has fourteen thousand and five hundred, Brahmavaivarta has eighteen thousand and Linga has eleven thousand. Varaha has twenty-four thousand, Skanda has eighty-one thousand and one hundred and Vamana is said to have eleven thousand. Kurma is said to have seventeen thousand, Matsya fourteen thousand, Garuda[1448] nineteen thousand and Brahmanda twelve thousand. Thus, the total number of verses in all the Puranas is said to be four hundred thousand. Of these, Bhagavata is said to have eighteen thousand. Earlier, when Brahma was seated on the lotus in his navel and was scared of samsara, out of compassion towards him, the illustrious one revealed it completely to him. Its beginning, middle and end is full of accounts about non-attachment. It has the amrita of accounts about Hari's pastimes and delights virtuous people and gods. It has the essence of all of Vedanta.

[1448] Referred to as Suparna in the text.

It possesses the attribute of oneness between the brahman and the atman. It is second to none and its only purpose is kaivalya. On a full moon night in the month of Prosthapada, if a person places the Bhagavata Purana on a golden throne and donates it, he goes to the supreme destination. In the midst of an assembly of the virtuous, all the other Puranas shine only as long as the Bhagavata Purana, the ocean of amrita, is not heard. The Bhagavata Purana is said to be the essence of all Vedanta. If a person is satisfied with the sap of its amrita, he will never be attracted to anything else. Just as Ganga is the best among rivers, Achyuta the best among gods and Shambhu the best among all those who are devoted to Vishnu, this is the best among all the Puranas. O brahmanas! Just as the supreme Kashi is the best among all kshetras, Bhagavata is the best among all the Puranas. The unblemished Bhagavata Purana is loved by all those who are devoted to Vishnu. It has chanted about that supreme and pure jnana that can only be obtained by paramahamsas. It is full of jnana, non-attachment and devotion and about freedom from all karma. If a man hears it, reads it properly and thinks about it devotedly, he is freed. He is unmatched. In ancient times, he illuminated Brahma[1449] with this lamp of jnana. Brahma passed it on to the sage Narada and Narada passed it on to Krishna.[1450] Vedavyasa passed it on to his son, Indra among yogis.[1451] Out of compassion, Shuka passed it on to Bhagavadrata.[1452] He is pure and spotless. He is the amrita that is without sorrow. We meditate on that supreme truth. I bow down to the illustrious Vasudeva who is the witness. Kah desired liberation and out of compassion, he told him about this. I bow down to Shuka, the Indra among yogis who was a personified form of the brahman. He freed Vishnurata, who was bitten by the snake of samsara. O lord of the gods! Act so that in life after life, devotion towards your feet is generated in me. O lord! You are our protector. Chanting his name destroys all kinds of sins. I prostrate myself before the one who destroys all misery. I bow down before the supreme Hari.'

This ends the Twelfth Skandha and the Bhagavata Purana.

[1449] The word used is Ka.
[1450] Vedavyasa.
[1451] Shuka.
[1452] That is, Vishnurata or Parikshit.

CONTENT

This edition published in 2011

King Edward High School for Girls
Edgbaston Park Road
Birmingham
B15 2UB
UK

Printed by Lion F·P·G

ACKNOWLEDGEMENTS

Writing this book became an unexpected and fascinating adventure as I gathered material and set out to tell a rather neglected story.

Thanks are due to everyone who contributed in any way but especially to:

Sarah Evans, whose idea this first was, thus giving me an 'introduction' to Florence George and the original book and challenging me to find out more; my husband, Marcus, for his encouragement and helpful proofreading; my son, Thomas, for IT assistance; Fred Rogers for both layout and typesetting plus friendly advice; Alison Wheatley, King Edward Foundation Archivist, for her diligent searching of many volumes of Governors' Orders and Cas Britton for items from the KEHS archive.

I am indebted to the many Old Edwardians who supplied recipes and anecdotes, not to mention several lovingly preserved school exercise books, present day colleagues who produced favourite recipes in the face of constant cajoling and KEHS girls and their families who kindly provided recipes and fascinating stories.

I am grateful too to our School Caterer, Peter Webber, for sharing some top secret school recipes.

It was a privilege to meet Old Edwardians from the New Street days and hear their reminiscences of a quite different era.

The recipes speak for themselves.

PHOTOGRAPHS

I am grateful to the following for use of archive photographs:

Mrs Claire Hewitt, Headmistress, Manchester High School for Girls and Dr Christine Joy, School Archivist;

Ray Marjoram, Belper Historical Society;

Kings College London Archive;

Graham Renshaw, Headteacher, Pentyrch Primary School, Cardiff.

THE
ART
OF
COOKERY,

Made PLAIN and EASY;

Which far exceeds any THING of the Kind ever yet Publiſhed.

CONTAINING,

I. Of Roaſting, Boiling, &c.
II. Of Made-Diſhes.
III. Read this Chapter, and you will find how Expenſive a *French* Cook's Sauce is.
IV. To make a Number of pretty little Diſhes fit for a Supper, or Side-Diſh, and little Corner-Diſhes for a great Table; and the reſt you have in the Chapter for *Lent*.
V. To dreſs Fiſh.
VI. Of Soops and Broths.
VII. Of Puddings.
VIII. Of Pies.
IX. For a Faſt-Dinner, a Number of good Diſhes, which you may make uſe for a Table at any other Time.
X. Directions for the Sick.
XI. For Captains of Ships.
XII. Of Hog's Puddings, Sauſages, &c.

XIII. To Pot and Make Hams, &c.
XIV. Of Pickling.
XV. Of Making Cakes, &c.
XVI. Of Cheeſecakes, Creams, Jellies, Whip Syllabubs, &c.
XVII. Of Made Wines, Brewing, *French* Bread, Muffins, &c.
XVIII. Jarring Cherries, and Preſerves, &c.
XIX. To Make Anchovies, Vermicella, Ketchup, Vinegar, and to keep Artichokes, French-Beans, &c.
XX. Of Diſtilling.
XXI. How to Market, and the Seaſons of the Year for Butcher's Meat, Poultry, Fiſh, Herbs, Roots, &c. and Fruit.
XXII. A certain Cure for the Bite of a Mad Dog. By Dr. *Mead*.

BY A LADY.

LONDON:

Printed for the AUTHOR; and ſold at Mrs. *Aſhburn*'s, a China-Shop, the Corner of *Fleet-Ditch*. MDCCXLVII.

[*Price* 3 s. ſstitch'd, *and* 5 s. *bound.*]

d at Mrs. Wharton's, at the Blue-coat Boy, near the Royal Exchange

INTRODUCTION

'If I have not wrote in the high polite stile, I hope I shall be forgiven; for my Intention is to instruct the lower sort... In many ways the great Cooks have such a high way of expressing themselves that the poor Girls are at a loss to know what they mean; and in all Recipt books yet printed there are such an odd jumble of things as would quite spoil a good dish. I have heard of a Cook that will use six pounds of butter to fry a dozen eggs, when every baby knows that understands cooking that half a pound is full enough....'

So wrote Hannah Glasse in the mid eighteenth century in the preface to her book *The Art of Cookery, Made Plain and Easy, which far exceeds anything of the kind ever yet published.* Not an immediately catchy title, but a sentiment with which Florence George, author of the *King Edward's Cookery Book* would have surely concurred, as she felt a similar need to both simplify and instruct in her book, which is both a text book and a cookery book. As Miss George explains in the preface, there was no suitable book available to help her pupils when she was teaching them, so she decided to write one herself. Teachers of the subject have always adopted a pragmatic 'can do' approach to most difficulties!

When King Edward VI High School for Girls (KEHS) was founded in Birmingham in 1883, its first headmistress, Miss Creak, was determined that the girls should enjoy as broad an education as possible. By any standards, Miss Creak was a remarkable woman, gaining this, her second headship, at the age of only twenty seven. So, as well as Science in up-to-date laboratories, Needlework was taught from the start and by 1894 theoretical lessons in Cookery were being taught by Florence George, Mistress of Cookery. This soon became a practical reality when a purpose-built Cookery room was completed in 1896.

Miss George will have been one of the first fully trained Cookery teachers to be employed in secondary education and this school must have been very unusual, if not unique, to have included Cookery in its curriculum, as it was usually regarded as a subject suitable only for working class girls in Elementary Schools.

In the following chapters I hope to explore how Cookery developed at KEHS, from Miss George's pioneering example and leadership to the present day. Central to this aim is a closer look at her Cookery Book and its contents plus recollections from former pupils and teachers of Cookery lessons. Of course, no research on such a subject would be complete without a practical element and so there is a substantial collection of varied recipes contributed by Old Edwardians, KEHS girls and their families and KEHS staff along with some current recipes from the Food Studies Department.

I hope that Miss George would have approved!

THE BOOK

OF

HOUSEHOLD MANAGEMENT.

CHAPTER I.

THE MISTRESS.

"Strength and honour are her clothing; and she shall rejoice in time to come. She openeth her mouth with wisdom; and in her tongue is the law of kindness. She looketh well to the ways of her household; and eateth not the bread of idleness. Her children arise up, and call her blessed; her husband also, and he praiseth her."—*Proverbs*, xxxi. 25—28.

1. As WITH THE COMMANDER OF AN ARMY, or the leader of any enterprise, so is it with the mistress of a house. Her spirit will be seen through the whole establishment; and just in proportion as she performs her duties intelligently and thoroughly, so will her domestics follow in her path. Of all those acquirements, which more particularly belong to the feminine character, there are none which take a higher rank, in our estimation, than such as enter into a knowledge of household duties; for on these are perpetually dependent the happiness, comfort, and well-being of a family. In this opinion we are borne out by the author of "The Vicar of Wakefield," who says: "The modest virgin, the prudent wife, and the careful matron, are much more serviceable in life than petticoated philosophers, blustering heroines, or virago queens. She who makes her husband and her children happy, who reclaims the one from vice and trains up the other to virtue, is a much greater character than ladies described in romances, whose whole occupation is to murder mankind with shafts from their quiver, or their eyes."

2. PURSUING THIS PICTURE, we may add, that to be a good housewife does not necessarily imply an abandonment of proper pleasures or amusing recreation; and we think it the more necessary to express this, as the performance of the duties of a mistress may, to some minds, perhaps seem to be

B

PUDDINGS & PASTRY.

Mrs Beeton's Introduction

CHAPTER 1

COOKERY BOOKS IN THE 19TH CENTURY

The first book which usually comes to mind when thinking of 19th Century cookery books is, of course, *Mrs. Beeton's Book of Household Management*, written in 1861.

The original work was a guide to running a home for the upwardly mobile and rapidly expanding middle classes – a marketing opportunity if ever there was one! Recipes were certainly a major part of the book, but almost as important was advice ranging from the management of servants to writing a will. Some of Isabella Beeton's recipes were provided by friends and correspondents to her publication, *Englishwoman's Domestic Magazine* – she was an educated woman and journalist and not fond of cooking - and were of variable quality. Others were, doubtless, taken from existing cookery books. It is generally believed that she had no practical involvement in testing the recipes and it is doubtful whether any were tested at all.

Contrary to popular belief she never began any recipe with 'first catch your hare' and she certainly didn't have the time to experiment with them, dying in 1865 (the year of Florence George's birth) at the tragically young age of 28. Nevertheless, her publisher husband spotted a profitable opportunity, as the book had instantly become popular because it was the first such book to be presented in such a logical and readable form, and so he kept quiet about her death, which allowed for several reprints. Lacking his late wife's management skills, however, Samuel Beeton soon got into financial difficulties and sold the copyright to Ward Lock in 1867. The book quickly moved away from its original format and by the end of the century contained elaborate dishes from professional chefs. These are the recipes often cited to illustrate the extravagance of Victorian cuisine – 'take a dozen eggs and two pints of cream...' but had little connection with Isabella Beeton. Many of her original recipes were, in fact, quite plain.

Her real (and stated) aim was to improve domestic harmony and comfort through practical knowledge. She said, 'I have always thought that there is no more fruitful source of family discontent than a housewife's badly cooked dinners and untidy ways'.

Florence George expresses a similar sentiment in her preface: 'I believe all will agree that the ignorance of the art (of cookery) in the young housewife has been not seldom the cause of a good deal of misery in the home'.

Isabella Beeton's influence on domestic life lasted well into the twentieth century and, to some extent, will have influenced Florence George when she compiled her book.

Another pioneer of straightforward cookery writing was Eliza Acton, whose *Modern Cookery for Private Families* (1845) was a

Eliza Acton
MODERN COOKERY

for
private families

with an Introduction by Elizabeth Ray

successful attempt at clear, informative detail. Until this time cookery books had had a reputation for vagueness

PUDDINGS AND PASTRY. 667

RAISINS.—Raisins are grapes, prepared by suffering them to remain on the vine until they are perfectly ripe, and then drying them in the sun or by the heat of an oven. The sun-dried grapes are sweet, the oven-dried of an acid flavour. The common way of drying grapes for raisins is to tie the two or three bunches of them together, whilst yet on the vine, and dip them into a hot lixivium of wood-ashes mixed with a little of the oil of olives; this disposes them to shrink and wrinkle, after which they are left on the vine three or four days, separated, on sticks in a horizontal situation, and then dried in the sun at leisure, after being cut from the tree.

CHRISTMAS PLUM-PUDDING.
(*Very Good.*)

1328. INGREDIENTS.—1½ lb. of raisins, ½ lb. of currants, ½ lb. of mixed peel, ¾ lb. of bread crumbs, ¾ lb. of suet, 8 eggs, 1 wineglassful of brandy.

Mode.—Stone and cut the raisins in halves, but do not chop them; wash, pick, and dry the currants, and mince the suet finely; cut the candied peel into thin slices, and grate down the bread into fine crumbs. When all these dry ingredients are prepared, mix them well together; then moisten the mixture with the eggs, which should be well beaten, and the brandy; stir well, that everything may be very thoroughly blended, and *press* the pudding into a buttered mould; tie it down tightly with a floured cloth, and boil for 5 or 6 hours.

CHRISTMAS PLUM-PUDDING IN MOULD

It may be boiled in a cloth without a mould, and will require the same time allowed for cooking. As Christmas puddings are usually made a few days before they are required for table, when the pudding is taken out of the pot, hang it up immediately, and put a plate or saucer underneath to catch the water that may drain from it. The day it is to be eaten, plunge it into boiling water, and keep it boiling for at least 2 hours; then turn it out of the mould, and serve with brandy-sauce. On Christmas-day a sprig of holly is usually placed in the middle of the pudding, and about a wineglassful of brandy poured round it, which, at the moment of serving, is lighted, and the pudding thus brought to table encircled in flame.

Time.—5 or 6 hours the first time of boiling; 2 hours the day it is to be served.

Average cost, 4s.

Sufficient for a quart mould for 7 or 8 persons.

Seasonable on the 25th of December, and on various festive occasions till March.

Note.—Five or six of these puddings should be made at one time, as they

Recipe from original 'Mrs Beeton'

8

haddocks, smelts, dory, gurnet, herrings, sprats, oysters, mussels, cockles, lobsters, crabs, and shell-fish in general, perch, carp, eels, dace, ling.

Vegetables.—Cabbages, broccoli, savoys, Brussels sprouts, Scotch kale, sea-kale, spinach, endive, cardoons, lettuces, skirret, salsify, scorzonera, sorrel, potatoes, turnips, parsnips, carrots, beetroot, Jerusalem artichokes, celery, peas, haricot beans, leeks, onions, shallots, mushrooms, horse-radish, parsley, thyme, tarragon, chervil, mint, sage, small salads. Garden herbs,

or pot herbs, which are chiefly used for stuffings, in soups, and for flavouring dishes, or for garnishing, are always in season, and can be procured at any time, either green or dried.

Fruits.—Apples, pears, medlars, grapes, figs, chestnuts, almonds, filberts, nuts, walnuts, raisins, currants, prunes, and all sorts of preserved and dried fruits, jams, marmalades, and fruit jellies.

Especially in Season in December.—Haddocks, tench, dace, cod, dory, ling, skate, turbot, capons, pea-fowl, turkeys.

C.—GLOSSARY OF TERMS USED IN COOKERY.

ASPIC.—A savoury jelly.

ASSIETTE.—Small entrées not more than a plate will contain.

ATELET.—A small silver skewer.

AU BLEU.—Applied to fish so dressed as to have a bluish appearance.

AU GRAS.—Dressed with meat gravy.

AU JUS.—In the natural juice, or gravy.

AU NATUREL.—Plain, simple cookery.

BABA.—Very light plum-cake, or sweet French yeast cake.

BAIN-MARIE.—An open vessel which has a loose bottom for the reception of hot water. It is used to keep sauces nearly at the boiling-point without reduction or burning.

BARDE.—A thin slice of bacon fat placed over any substance specially requiring the assistance of fat without larding.

BATTERIE DE CUISINE.—Complete set of cooking apparatus.

BAVAROISE À L'EAU.—Tea sweetened with syrup of capillaire, and flavoured with a little orange-flower water.

BAVAROISE AU LAIT.—Made in the same way as the above, but with equal quantities of milk and tea.

BÉCHAMEL.—A rich white French sauce.

BEIGNET, OR FRITTER (*see* Fritter).

BISQUE.—A soup made of shell-fish.

BLANC.—White broth used to give a more delicate appearance to the flesh of fowl, lamb, &c.

BLANCH.—Placing anything on the fire in cold water until it boils, and after straining it off, plunging it into cold water for the purpose of rendering it white. Used to whiten poultry, vegetables, &c.

BLANQUETTE.—A fricassée usually made of thin slices of white meat, with white sauce thickened with egg yolk.

BLIGNET.—To fritter anything enveloped in butter or egg and fried.

BOUDIN.—A rich compound of various meats.

BOUILLI.—Beef very much boiled, and served with sauce.

BOUILLIE.—A French dish resembling that called hasty pudding.

BOUILLON.—The common soup of France.

BOUQUET OF HERBS.—Parsley, thyme, and green onions tied together.

BOUQUET GARNI.—The same, with the addition of cloves or aromatic herbs.

BOURGUIGNOTE.—A ragoût of truffles.

BRAISE.—Meat cooked in a closely-covered stewpan to prevent evaporation, so that the meat retains not only its own juices, but those of any other articles, such as bacon, herbs, roots, and spice put with it.

BRAISIÈRE.—A saucepan with ledges to the lid, so that it will contain firing.

BRIDER.—To truss fowls with a needle and thread.

BRIOCHE.—A sponge cake similar to Bath buns.

BUISSON.—A cluster or bush of small pastry piled on a dish.

CALLIPASH.—The glutinous portion of the turtle found in the upper shell.

CALLIPEE.—The glutinous meat of the turtle's under shell.

CANNELONS.—Small rolls or collars of mince-meat, or of rice and pastry with fruit.

CAPILOTADE.—A hash of poultry.

CASSEROLE.—The form of rice to be filled with a fricassée of white meat or a purée of game; also a stewpan.

CIVET.—A dark, thickish stew of hare or venison.

COMPEIGNE.—Sweet French yeast cake, with fruit.

COMPÔTE.—Stewed fruits served with syrup. There are also compôtes of small birds.

CONFITURES.—Sweetmeats of sugars, fruits, syrups, and essences.

Cassell's Dictionary of Cookery

and were, therefore, of little use to the average cook. There was a great need for more precision, both in quantities specified and instructions. Eliza Acton had proven literary skill as a published poet and her book was well organised, clear and useful, becoming a model of its type and, as with Mrs Beeton soon after, her books found a ready market in the emerging middle classes.

The successes of Eliza Acton and Mrs Beeton encouraged many more writers of cookery books, with varying degrees of success. The market was unprecedented as cookery in its many forms became an attainable notion domestically. New books included *A New System of Domestic Cookery* by Mrs Maria Rundell (1860s), which was a modest but

practical best seller, while *Cassell's Dictionary of Cookery* (1875) was still on sale well into the 20th century and contained around 10,000 recipes. T F Garrett's *Encyclopaedia of Practical Cookery* (1892) in several volumes was an important indicator of the new importance of the genre and is still regarded as an important reference work today.

Florence George was probably less influenced by Mrs A B Marshall's *Cookery Book* (1888).

Mrs Agnes Marshall was very popular, running her own cookery school in London, where she marketed her own ingredients and equipment (not unlike Jamie Oliver, except hers were Marshall Brand). Her recipes were intended for the mistress of the house to direct her Cook to provide fashionable food from very

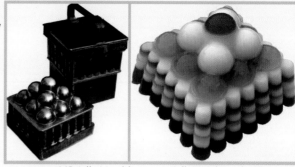

MB Jelly Mould   Jelly made with MB Mould

elaborate recipes, many of which required the use of Marshall Brand equipment! Nevertheless, she did claim to have tested all her recipes and so they probably did work.

Miss George bemoaned the lack of a suitable textbook for the girls she taught, although some had been written earlier in the 19th century, once literacy had become more widespread. C M Buckton's *Food and Home Cooking* and J Stoker's *Home Comforts and Helping Hands* all served to instruct girls in their domestic responsibilities. Even middle class girls were now expected to move beyond a little French, natural science, embroidery and music and learn something of domestic activities. They were helped by the *Little Girls' Cookery Book* by C F Benton and the *Girls' Own Cookery Book* sponsored by the *Girls' Own Paper*. M M Mitchell's *Polytechnic Cookery Book* was written for trainee teachers.

Cookery books of the time soon diversified to satisfy their increasing and eclectic readership. Books specialising in a particular theme proliferated: dinner parties, breakfast and luncheon received attention, followed by many books on individual foods such as Eliza Acton's *The English Bread Book*, J Massey's *Biscuit, Ice and Compote Book* and O Green's *How to Cook Fish*.

Many Victorian young women found themselves accompanying their husbands on lengthy postings to the Indian sub-continent, which created a market for

books on English cookery adapted to local ingredients. W H Dawes' *Wife's Help to Indian Cookery* and *The Indian Cookery Book* would have probably been a welcome gift, although I imagine much of the information would have been equally useful for both mistress and her cook.

French cuisine was already held in high esteem and an emerging taste for Italian food was popularised by several writers at the turn of the twentieth century. The USA led the way in many aspects of cookery publications, especially the scientific study of food and its relation to health.

Some promotional but, nevertheless, sound offerings

Fannie Farmer

include Fannie Farmer's *Boston Cooking-School Cookbook* (1896), a classic of its type. As can be seen, she was a firm believer in the connection between personal knowledge of nutrition and cookery and good health.

M J Lincoln's *Boston School Kitchen Textbook for Schoolgirls* and E E Kellogg's *Healthful Cookery* of 1894 were both notable. Mrs Dr E E Kellogg combined her roles of Superintendent of the Sanitarium School of Cookery in Battle Creek, Michigan with oversight of the cuisine of the Sanitarium hospital and so was in a good position to practise

PREFACE.

"But for life the universe were nothing; and all that has life requires nourishment."

With the progress of knowledge the needs of the human body have not been forgotten. During the last decade much time has been given by scientists to the study of foods and their dietetic value, and it is a subject which rightfully should demand much consideration from all. I certainly feel that the time is not far distant when a knowledge of the principles of diet will be an essential part of one's education. Then mankind will eat to live, will be able to do better mental and physical work, and disease will be less frequent.

At the earnest solicitation of educators, pupils, and friends, I have been urged to prepare this book, and I trust it may be a help to many who need its aid. It is my wish that it may not only be looked upon as a compilation of tried and tested recipes, but that it may awaken an interest through its condensed scientific knowledge which will lead to deeper thought and broader study of what to eat.

F. M. F.

her culinary ideas on the inmates, apparently with success. Her recipes were vegetarian, a concept which gained steady ground in the UK and US during the latter half of the 19th century.

The Vegetarian Society had been formed in 1847 but books of recipes were rare before 1890. Florence George

PLEASURES OF VEGETARIANISM.
"OH, GRACIOUS, MISS LEGUME! I FEAR I HAVE TASTED ANIMAL FOOD. I HAVE EATEN A WHOLE EARWIG IN MY SALAD!"

Vegetarianism was viewed with some suspicion at the time!

published her *Vegetarian Cookery* in 1908 with such success that it ran to several re-prints. Her recipes were regarded as rather more interesting than some of her contemporaries, as she made full use of flavourings

Mention must also be made of Invalid Cookery, which had had its own section in most cookery books throughout the 19th century and which progressed to being the subject of whole books, e g *The Art of Feeding the Invalid* by A B Crust, and *Sickroom Cookery* by M Earle. One can surmise that the prevalence of illness made this a popular topic. Whether the suggested recipes were tempting is a matter of opinion - raw beef tea, served in a coloured glass so that the patient wouldn't notice the red colour (!) makes one wonder - but much of the general advice is certainly sound.

Despite this plethora of available cookery books, still there was none which combined information suitable for teaching intelligent girls with practical recipes.

There was an obvious opening for Florence George.

CHAPTER VI

CURRIES, STEWS, AND SCALLOPS

Curried Eggs.

¾ oz. butter.	1½ tablespoonfuls flour.
2 oz. chopped onion.	½ tablespoonful chutney.
3 oz. chopped apple.	¼ tablespoonful sugar.
1 oz. sliced tomato.	½ tablespoonful lemon-juice.
½ tablespoonful curry-powder.	1½ gills milk.
1 tablespoonful curry-paste.	2 hard-boiled eggs.

FRY the onion to a golden brown in the butter ; add the apple and tomato. Mix the curry-powder, paste, flour, chutney, and sugar together, and add them to the onion, etc. Put on the lid of the saucepan, and cook for three minutes. Add the lemon-juice and milk. Simmer for one hour. Add the eggs (cutting each egg into eight pieces). Let them get hot through. Serve with boiled rice, or in timbales of rice (see below), in which case the curry that will not go into the cases should be served in a boat.

Vegetarian Cookery: Florence George

1   Steamed Fillets of Sole, Fairy Toast, Beef Tea, Baked Custard, Barley Water.
2 —Toast, Fried Soles and Potato Straws, Beef Tea, Lemonade, Jelly.
3   Clear Soup, Lamb Cutlet, Mashed Potato and Spinach, Milanaise Soufflé, Lemonade, Tomato Sauce.

CHAPTER 2

THE NATIONAL TRAINING SCHOOL
AND TEACHER TRAINING (DOMESTIC SUBJECTS)

Although Florence George called her book a text book, it is in many ways similar to many books of the time, not least Mrs Beeton, and there is a noticeable similarity with the published cookery books of the National Training School.

Miss George, who was born in Gloucestershire in 1865, gained a First Class Diploma from the National Training School of Cookery, Kensington and was possibly one of its first fully trained teachers. Acceptable occupations for (unmarried) 'respectable women of some intelligence' in late Victorian England were rather circumscribed. However, Cookery Instruction and/or a teaching course were, happily, deemed acceptable, nursing, music teaching and dressmaking being others in a short list.

The National Training School of Cookery developed from the 1873 International Exhibition in South Kensington (visited by half a million people), where the cookery section caught the public imagination. (Queen Victoria attended a demonstration, which she later recorded as 'rather tiresome'.)

Sir Henry Cole, Secretary to the Department of Science and Art and influential figure in the founding of the Victoria and Albert Museum, assessed the public response to the cookery lectures and felt something should be done to exploit this growing interest for the benefit of the nation. There was an interest in food and cookery, a realisation of the need for qualified teachers and a growing awareness of the need for social and domestic happiness. He persuaded the committee responsible for the lectures that a national training school for cookery should be set up. Such was his influence that this was agreed, with the far-sighted condition

Cookery Demonstration at the 1873 International Exhibition

that the school should be in alliance with the School Boards and Training Schools throughout the country. The 'National' aspect was emphasised from the beginning and it attracted students from the rest of the country.

Initially the National Training School operated in a rather formal and class-conscious manner, whereby ladies were encouraged to attend cookery demonstrations with their cooks for a fortnight's course. Plain or High Class Cookery courses were available. The mornings were spent on cleaning and learning to manage ovens and flues with some basic cookery to, presumably, relieve the tedium, while the afternoons comprised lecture demonstrations of more advanced dishes. One could avoid the cleaning sessions by paying an extra guinea. However, this made the pupil ineligible for the certificate!

An extensive range of recipes was assembled for the various classes of cookery and these later formed the basis of several cookery books published by the school.

Afternoon Lecture on Practical Cookery

The following is a fairly modest example of the rather extravagant dishes in the High - Class book.

Soon a written examination was devised

HIGH-CLASS COOKERY. 35

Boiled Turbot and Lobster Sauce.

Ingredients.

One small Turbot.
One Lobster.
Two ounces of Butter.
One ounce of Flour.
Half a pint of Water.
One tablespoonful of Cream.
Half a teaspoonful of Lemon-juice.
Salt and Cayenne.

Put sufficient water in the fish-kettle to cover the fish. Add as much salt as will make the water taste salt. When the water boils, put in the turbot and let it boil slowly for twenty or thirty minutes.

Lobster sauce. Remove the flesh from the tail and claws and cut it up into dice. Take the coral and wash and dry it, pound it with one ounce of butter and rub it through a hair-sieve. Put into a stewpan one ounce of butter and the flour. Mix these over the fire and add half a pint of water, stir well, and boil the sauce a few minutes. Then add the coral butter, the pieces of lobster, the seasoning, and the cream. Mix and warm thoroughly, and the sauce is ready. Dish the turbot on a hot dish, garnished with coral and slices of lemon, and hand the sauce in a sauce-boat.

3 *

Mark Sheet – National Training School

and this had also to include an assessment of practical skill, although marks were awarded for attendance and so the chances of failure were low.

By 1875 a wider range of classes was devised, targeting women and households with different incomes so that there was an Artisans' Cookery course, a Cooks' course, one for Ladies' maids and, crucially, a course for trainee teachers.

A First Class Diploma (which Miss George proudly announces) required a mark of eighty per cent and she would have taken courses in High Class, Household and Artisan Cookery, in which she would have had to demonstrate theoretical as well as practical knowledge.

The demand for teachers was soon great and those from 'The National' soon gained a reputation as being the best. This would chime with Miss Creak's aim to employ the highest quality staff.

Many of these first teachers worked long hours for little pay, but were imbued with an almost missionary zeal to 'spread the gospel' and teach the domestic arts to a whole generation.

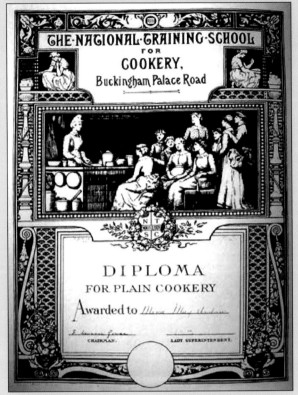

THE·NATIONAL·TRAINING·SCHOOL
FOR
COOKERY,
Buckingham Palace Road

DIPLOMA
FOR PLAIN COOKERY

Awarded to

CHAIRMAN.   LADY SUPERINTENDENT.

t. Ultimately they are "examined," and receive a Kensington "certificate of proficiency." In this school young ladies of gentle birth, young matrons who had no idea kitchen work could be so 'nice,' rosy-checked country girls about to take their first place, and cooks anxious to improve themselves, may all be seen working together with a will, and vying with each other as to who shall turn out the most brilliant copper-lid or the most resplendently clean saucepan. The certificate is much coveted." Of that fact I have not the slightest doubt. To judge from the ridiculous questions propounded in the official examination papers, the "certificates" will afford about as accurate an index to the culinary "proficiency" of the examinee as to her proficiency in Hindustani or Mr. Dickens' "Chinese metaphysics."—*Belgravia.*

Quote from the New York Times 1874 –
luckily this was not taken seriously by the National Training School founders!

The first principal of the school advocated the teaching of cookery to boys, who, she said, 'made even more apt pupils than girls'.

This advice has still not been fully implemented.

Training teachers was soon to be the main aim of the 'National', and admission requirements said that:

'She should not be under twenty one years of age. She must be sufficiently educated to be able to perform the duties of a teacher after the special training, to speak aloud, also to write from dictation and keep accounts.'

Applicants were carefully selected for their maturity and experience.

Teaching experience was gained by lecturing in the Learners' Kitchen in the early days. To obtain a Teachers' Diploma, the student had to go through all the classes offered in the school (Scullery, Artisan, Middle Class and Demonstration) and then practise teaching what had been learned, under supervision. However, when compared with the teacher training of their elementary school counterparts, future teachers of domestic subjects received an inferior experience, which left them in an often vulnerable position within a school, especially where working conditions were concerned.

Children's Cookery Class 1892

In 1874 the London School Board proposed a motion declaring:

'that it is desirable to promote a knowledge of plain cookery and of the household operations connected therewith as part of the elementary education of girls'.

This was a far-sighted move as it paved the way for the teaching of Cookery or Domestic Economy in many parts of the country. The National Training School was at the forefront of instructing children from Board Schools, producing teachers for these. Children initially came to the NT School, but then certain schools had a Cookery department built for the use of many surrounding schools. Instruction of working class girls being the main objective, wider educational principles were probably not a priority. The NT School was requested by the School Board for London to produce a *Scholars' Handbook of Household Management and Cookery* (1876), which had an appendix of recipes used by the teachers at the National Training School. This was the blueprint for the *Official Handbook*, which was first published in the following decade.

Inevitably money was a prime consideration and many school boards were against spending any money on the subject, but in 1882 the government made a grant available of 4 shillings per girl per year. This obviously paved the way for more cookery teachers to be trained and more training schools were opened around the UK, but the National refused to become involved in moderating minimum national standards, declaring that only teachers trained at its school could hold its Diploma. This seems slightly short-sighted in retrospect, as it took until 1919 for a uniform standard to be recognised.

By this time the demand for teachers was great and records show how the policy of hand-picking the best paid off, with a recurring theme of non-stop toil and significant results (see further information on Miss George). By the time that Florence George graduated from the National Training School, Nutrition and Food Science were well established components of the course and she was, therefore, in a good position to educate and instruct bright girls in both the practical and theoretical aspects of the subject.

No doubt Miss Creak realised this too.

London County Council Cookery Scholars 1905

CHAPTER 3

DOMESTIC SUBJECTS TEACHING AND FLORENCE GEORGE'S APPOINTMENT AND CAREER

F lorence George was appointed Cookery Mistress in 1894 when the school was still in Congreve Street, central Birmingham, and it had no practical cookery room. The lessons were theoretical with demonstrations but the girls could not cook themselves. Happily this was soon resolved when the school moved to nearby New Street, complete with a new practical cookery room.

Children's cookery class 1908

There was evidently some initial tension with the governors, who, unlike Miss Creak, did not approve of Cookery being part of the curriculum and consequently allocated insufficient funds.

At this time domestic subjects were considered to belong firmly in the domain of Board Schools, their main objective being to instruct working class girls in basic cookery, laundry and household management. This would also have been of use if they (as was likely) entered domestic service. When other similar girls' schools were modelling themselves on boys' schools and rejecting anything that smacked of domesticity, it now seems almost radical that Miss Creak should be so convinced that girls should have as broad an experience as possible. The prevailing view was that such girls would not need these skills, which were, besides, for the academically inferior – a view which recurred throughout the 20th Century in English education.

Domestic Subjects teachers usually had different social origins from those of an elementary school teacher, the latter position being an aspiration of working class girls. Florence George's father was a canal manager, a position of some responsibility and she would have considered herself middle class. As has been mentioned, cookery teaching (later expanded into other 'domestic' areas) was considered suitable for a girl of more genteel origins and who may well have seen a social need to improve the lot of the more impoverished in society. Whether she had direct knowledge of such people is another matter.

By the 1890s, when Florence George's career started, a more realistic approach was growing with an acknowledgement that pay and conditions were a concern and that the physical toll of such work was significant. The Education Department (regrettably) regarded Domestic Subjects teaching with indifference long after it granted financial aid for its practical teaching. Teachers qualified from 'The National' within a year, rather than the two years it took to train an elementary school teacher, and the academic side of their education was doubtless inferior. An accusation that the many cookery schools were more interested in fees than education was, unfortunately, probably true.

This situation meant that a Domestic Subjects teacher was often regarded as having inferior status by her colleagues due to the lack of regulation and uniformity in her education. It was not until 1905 that the Board of Education began to pay grants to students studying on approved courses and it took until 1918 for the best institutions to receive funding as training colleges, producing fully trained and certificated teachers. This had implications for sick pay and pensions, as they were not included in any state scheme. At least Miss George was luckier than many in having purpose-built facilities (eventually), as many teachers had to make do with ordinary classrooms with randomly placed cookers and boilers. Accident reports were frequent. On the plus side, the lack of regulation meant that some domestic subjects teachers could be more enterprising than most, earning tidy sums for outside engagements if they wished, though few full time teachers would have had the time or energy.

The subject was affected by the prevailing notion that many women could teach practical skills without special training, it being merely common sense and of no academic merit. Thus, the teachers were often held in lowly regard as not 'proper teachers', a notion which often extended to pupils, and this lingered long after they had gained fully qualified status. It was not unusual to find a Domestic Subjects teacher in charge of school meals and unofficial caterer for school events as well as her teaching - the former until the 1940s and 1950s and the latter much later than that.

Happily, Florence George seems to have been regarded with esteem and affection during most of her career, though she obviously had occasional tensions with the Governors.

Cookery Lesson: Pentyrch School near Cardiff.
This has been set up in an ordinary classroom, requiring excellent organisational and management skills from the teacher.

Cookery Lesson: South Western Polytechnic Day School for Girls, London
This appears to be a purpose built cookery room with much more working space and a large cooking range in the background.

Once the new Cookery room was built all girls had their turn, finally, to take part in real, practical cookery.

Article by Miss George for The Phoenix 1896

Cooking.

COOKING is a science which every girl should study, it is a necessary element of every day life; yet there are some girls who are so clever, they could work out any imaginable Euclid proposition, do any amount of Greek, and could not make a rice pudding. It is certain this won't be the case now, since cooking lessons have been introduced into the school. I am sure all the girls who have had any experience will agree with me that the cooking lessons are charming; of course the preliminaries are not so delightful as they will be, on account of not having the proper ranges, etc., but when we have the new kitchen they are certain to be more charming still. The girls arrive in the kitchen at half-past eleven, arrayed in large white aprons, eager to begin; perhaps one tiresome girl happens to be half a minute late, and keeps the others waiting, and the frowns and pinches she receives on taking her place, make her firmly resolve never to repeat her sad mistake. They sit in two rows before the table, taking it in turns to have the front row, and they take down notes about whatever is being made, which are neatly written out, and are to be handed down to their great grandchildren and posterity. They are told that soon they will begin to cook joints of meat and make pastry; one plaintive little voice asks: "Oh, shan't we be getting to cakes soon?" and is told that there are more important things first, but it will all come in good time. I strongly advise the parents of the girls to lay in a stock of pills, in case any of the girls happen to experiment at home.

Clarified fat was the first thing attempted, which was very exciting, as different girls were called out to experiment on the boiling liquid; someone mischievously pinched the gas tube which sent the light out, causing great amusement and making the fat splutter about.

The consequence of learning how to clarify fat was, the following week, small jars of beautiful white fat were constantly brought to school by different girls, to be inspected, showing how interested and anxious to learn they were. One girl had the misfortune to upset her jar in her school bag, greatly improving the appearance of her books.

The following is an example of how the girls enjoy the cooking lessons. I said to one small girl, "Do the girls in your class enjoy the cooking lessons?" she said, "I should think they do; you should see the number of girls who come back on Friday, which is our cooking day, after having been away all the rest of the week, and I wouldn't stop away on Friday for anything." I heard another say, "I like Wednesday better than any other day in the school week now," on being asked why, she said "Because it is our cooking day." Soup was the next thing taught, and there was great fun over the peeling and chopping of the vegetables, which was done by two of the girls, one had to stir it, another to skim it; and nearly everyone had a turn in putting it though the sieve.

I daresay someone will quote the old proverb, "Too many cooks spoil the broth," but I think this must have been an exception to the case, as it turned out to be remarkably good. Every day girls swarmed to the kitchen at recess, like so many bees to a hive, to taste the result of their yesterday's labour which could be had, nice and hot for a half-penny a plate. Soup of a different kind was tried the next week, and was, if possible, a still greater success. One girl said she made some soup at home for dinner, and everyone enjoyed it very much. I did not hear that the pills were required after it, so perhaps my advice is not so urgent after all.

Soon pancakes are going to be made, and I am sure it will be great fun to watch the girls toss them, and I have no doubt that the girls of the K.E.G.H.S. will soon turn out the best cooks in Birmingham.

As well as teaching the High School girls in the morning, Miss George initially spent her afternoons teaching girls from the four KE grammar schools (who travelled to New Street), whilst also supervising the provision of over 200 dinners daily. It was stated that she gave lessons to 240 girls per week, half of these being from the High School. She was employed from '9am – 6pm five days a week and a few hours on the sixth day'. She also provided 'elevenses' each morning which appears to have been a substantial snack including soup and cakes, and she did apparently comment that she wished more staff would have a better breakfast before they came to school! She also provided refreshments for meetings and functions.

Gas stove

As she had only one scullery maid as an assistant, it is not surprising to read in the Governors' Orders of 1897 that Miss George was feeling the need of extra assistance. A temporary assistant, Miss Britten, was appointed at £16 3s 4d per term and a separate room was fitted out for the dinner preparation. At the same time, more money was approved for the general teaching of the subject, including providing an extra gas stove and so, presumably, Miss George had already made a positive impact which was being recognised.

Cookery lesson Herbert Strutt School, Belper.
The teacher in the picture is Miss N Symons who had a Diploma in Cookery at the time.

Nº 1192 — "Girls' High School — Cookery.

"The Committee have received a report from the
"Chairmen from which it appears desirable that some
"steps should be taken to relieve Miss George, the
"Cookery Mistress, of a portion of her work. From
"the particulars supplied to them the Committee learn
"that Miss George is engaged usually from 9 a.m.
"to 6 p.m. on five days in the week, and for some
"hours on the sixth day, in preparing for lessons,
"giving demonstrations, or superintending the
"preparation of the pupils dinners; and in the
"course of each week gives lessons to 240 girls,
"half of them from the Girls' High School and the
"the remainder from the four Girls' Grammar Schools;
"and she also prepares on the average over 200
"dinners for pupils of the Girls' High School. With
"a view to giving the Cookery Mistress some relief
"the Committee therefore recommend that the Governors
"sanction a payment of Ten Guineas to Miss Britten
"for the May Term for assistance rendered to Miss
"George with the approval of the Chairman of the
"Committee; and that a similar payment to Miss

By 1898 it was recommended by the governors that two student teachers should be engaged for two years with a possibility of a third year. Subsequently there was a third student teacher. They had to pay a fee and were to be at least 16 years old but were not obliged to take up teaching as a profession, though what alternative career they might have in mind is not suggested. Miss George would have had to teach them and supervise their progress, but they would have been a useful addition to the department eventually.

In 1899 there is a report (in the Governors' Orders) of Miss George's extended absence through illness and Miss Creak's statement that the work was too much for one mistress. At this time she was in charge of the production of pupil dinners at both the Boys' and Girls' Schools as well as her teaching. This led to more assistance being provided in the form of a permanent assistant mistress (Miss Smith), who took temporary charge (at £50 per annum) and a further two student teachers. At least the high regard which FG and the subject now enjoyed was stated when the Governors' Orders of October 1899 recognised that there had been a great increase in the work of the department since it opened 'and its popularity and good work among the pupils' were to be celebrated.

Florence George must have had enviable micro-management skills to organise and run the department, teach the children, supervise / teach student teachers and write five meticulously detailed books, all of which were published. The only photograph I have seen shows a rather slight woman and it seems fairly clear that the job did, in part, account for the decline in her health. An account of her by her sister recounts how frail and delicate-looking she was, but that, as well as her obvious capabilities, she had a clear mind, good memory and amazing grasp of detail, which she could readily translate into action. Furthermore she rarely complained and would never refuse an extra task. Whilst laudable in its way, the long term consequences were rather predictable.

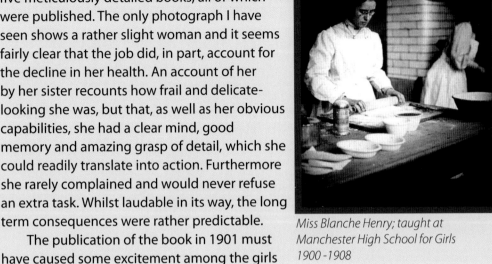

Miss Blanche Henry; taught at Manchester High School for Girls 1900-1908

The publication of the book in 1901 must have caused some excitement among the girls and it appears to have been an instant success. As the publisher Edward Arnold's promotion clearly states, it took nothing for granted.

Mr. Edward Arnold's New and Popular Books, December, 1901

KING EDWARD'S COOKERY BOOK.

By FLORENCE A. GEORGE,
TEACHER OF COOKERY IN KING EDWARD'S SCHOOLS, BIRMINGHAM.

Crown 8vo. 3s. 6d.

This little volume is designed to give practical instruction in simple cookery. It takes nothing for granted, and gives sensible notes and rules for every phase of culinary work.

The chief part of the book is occupied with recipes suitable for ordinary English households under economical management. It will be found equally useful in Schools of Cookery and for domestic purposes.

The period from 1900 to 1913 must have passed unremarkably and successfully. In 1912 Miss M E Wolverson replaced Miss M Bishop as Assistant Cookery Mistress at £100 pa and in 1914 another Assistant Cookery Mistress,

9 Miss Major and Staff, 1913
Top row—Student, Student, Miss Byrne, Miss Earl, Miss M. Ravenhill, Miss Archibald, Miss Bromhead
Miss Keeling, Miss G. Ravenhill, Miss Whalley, Miss Dunlop
Middle row—Miss George, Miss Baugh, Miss Davison, Miss Major, Miss Slater, Miss Ward
Front row—Miss Hooke, Miss Brock, Miss Aston, Miss Nicholas, Miss Bock, Miss Rattey

Miss Keeling, was given three months' notice owing to absence through ill-health. Miss George was obviously immersed in her teaching and writing books – the publication of *Vegetarian Cookery* in 1908 seems to have met with general approval.

By 1913 some of the grammar schools had their own cookery rooms, which must have eased the burden a little, but the routine of teaching and supervising lunches continued. In 1917 a *Wartime Cookery Book* was produced and Miss George was evidently instrumental in encouraging and organising cookery in the form of morale-boosting jam, Christmas cakes and sweets for the Services and Bournbrook Hospital, as well as supplying jellies and cakes to the ambulance trains and the Hospital. The 610lbs of jam and 58 Christmas cakes recorded for 1915 conjures up an image of a 'permanent flame' of jam-making, bubbling pans of hot fruit never far from Miss George's expert eye.

By 1917 there are further remarks in the Governors' Orders of Miss George's extended absence owing to ill-health, with the recommendation that she be served with 3 months' notice, that Miss D Featherstone should be appointed in her absence and that Miss George should pay half her successor's salary for three months!! This prompted a letter from Miss Major, now headmistress, to the governors, who backtracked a little, withdrawing the notice and granting leave of absence until the following July, but still insisting on FG paying the salary of Miss Featherstone. Perhaps the payment to her substitute was standard procedure, but it does seem a little severe from this distance.

On 21st April 1918 Miss George resigned because of illness, and an expression of the governors' gratitude for her 23 years' service was to be conveyed to her. They 'especially recognise the ability Miss George has shown in organising and conducting the School's Cookery Department ... and they sincerely hope that in relief from her responsibilities she may find complete restoration to health'.

> 6586. IT IS ORDERED that the Governors have received with great regret the resignation of Miss Florence A. George and desire to record their appreciation of the fidelity and efficiency with which she has discharged her duties during her 23 years' connection with King Edward's High School for Girls. They especially recognise the ability Miss George has shown in organising and conducting the School's Cookery Department, of which she was the first Mistress, and which under her direction achieved and maintained a high standard of efficiency; and they sincerely hope that in relief from her responsibilities she may find complete restoration to health.

This was a forlorn hope, as Florence George died on 3rd July 1918 aged 54. Her death certificate states Sarcoma of the right hip which had been diagnosed two years earlier as the primary cause, with 'exhaustion' as the second . Whether her extraordinary workload and unstinting effort contributed in any way one can only speculate.

She was obviously held in high regard by staff, pupils and former pupils, and there were touching tributes describing both the perfectionism in her work and her readiness to help others. Although this is a sad conclusion, her legacy is the solid foundation that she laid for the continuation of Food Studies and Cookery teaching throughout the existence of KEHS, and her groundbreaking books.

CERTIFIED COPY OF AN ENTRY OF DEATH

GIVEN AT THE **GENERAL REGISTER OFFICE**

Application Number 1588432-1

	REGISTRATION DISTRICT				STROUD			
1918	DEATH in the Sub-district of Minchinhampton				in the County of Gloucester			

Columns:	1	2	3	4	5	6	7	8	9
No.	When and where died	Name and surname	Sex	Age	Occupation	Cause of death	Signature, description and residence of informant	When registered	Signature of registrar
32	Third July 1918 Woodside Amberley Minchinhampton R D	Florence Annie George	Female	54 years	Spinster Teacher-Domestic Science + Cookery daughter of William Denyer George Canal Manager	Sarcoma of the Right Hip Bone (2 years) 2 Exhaustion Certified by C Lionel Goode M D	William D George Father in attendance Woodside Amberley Stroud	Fourth July 1918	Annie Simmonds Deputy Registrar.

CERTIFIED to be a true copy of an entry in the certified copy of a Register of Deaths in the District above mentioned.

Chapter 4

Social and Economic Background

From about 1896 to the beginning of World War 1 (the period in which Florence George was writing), a distinct economic period existed in England. The country was apparently affluent and powerful with low income tax, but distribution of income was still as unequal as it had been earlier in the 19th Century – 1 ½ million 'Upper Class' received 1/3rd of the National Income, as did 29 million Working Class (calculated by occupation). The cost of living began to rise but not in line with wages so that the purchasing power of the pound fell from 20 shillings in 1896 to 16s 3d in 1912 (20 shillings to £1, 12 pence in each shilling). This checked the previously steady growth in consumption and created some social unrest. Nevertheless, during this period food was relatively cheaper than it had been and there was a wider variety, as long as you had enough income.

Between a quarter and a third of the population lived in poverty – defined as 'earnings insufficient to obtain the minimum necessaries for the maintenance of mere physical efficiency' (*Rowntree – Survey of York 1899*)

Booth had reached a similar conclusion in London a few years earlier in *Life and Labour of the People in London* (1886 -1902), noting that many people could not afford enough food to sustain them and their families, and that inmates of jails and workhouses had a better diet. (NB Contrary to popular belief, the Workhouse diet by this time was carefully controlled nutritionally and bore no resemblance to that of Oliver Twist.) Both *Rowntree and Booth* calculated that at least half the children of the working classes were underweight and undernourished. Food was the major item of working class expenditure, though, as income grew, that proportion declined.

Between these two extremes sat a rapidly expanding Middle Class, many of whom had working class origins and had prospered in the industrial and technological explosion of the mid to late 19th Century.

The late 19th Century was a period of changing food habits in England, some of which were systematically documented. In 1881 a committee appointed by BAAS (*British Association for the Advancement of Science*) considered how much the population spent per head on food. Though not perfect, the figures indicate that, for example, more money was being spent on meat than bread – 1 ¾ lb per head per week. This compares closely with more recent figures (DEFRA 2007) of 2 ¼ lbs per head per week. Until this time bread was an important staple food, particularly amongst those on low incomes, and potatoes were the most important vegetable averaging 6lbs per head per week, although this was likely to be substantially more where families had a plot of land on which to grow their own. Meat was a small part of the poorest people's diets but, as the relative standard of living improved, so meat consumption increased as bread decreased. This was not unconnected with a change in prices as meat and meat products became cheaper.

Potatoes remained an important part of the diet, providing a regular, if low, source of vitamin C (in a diet which traditionally was always low in fruit and vegetables), as well as carbohydrates, a little protein and some fibre. More money was being spent on milk and eggs than potatoes and sugar, while tea and butter (considered luxury foods) were featuring much more in people's weekly expenditure. Beer and Spirits were disproportionately represented in many households, although, until the advent of a reliably clean domestic water supply, small beer and porter were a safer option, having been made with boiling water and containing a relatively low quantity of bacteria-inhibiting alcohol, and they were commonly drunk, even by children. The popularity of tea was probably a good thing, as it was a safe drink without the alcohol!

By 1909 -1913 meat consumption had risen to present day levels and potato consumption had fallen by about a third compared to 25 years previously. The general trend was away from cheap carbohydrate foods to dearer protein foods and thus more variety. This is always a noticeable trend in any society which becomes more affluent.

Tea and coffee consumption saw a spectacular rise, before coffee tailed off as tea established its place as the national drink, partly due to cheaper imports from India and Ceylon (now Sri Lanka). Cocoa went from insignificance at the beginning of the 19th century to 22 million lbs imported in 1894, mostly for drinking.

These two drinks (tea and cocoa) may have accounted, in part, for the rather alarming sugar consumption of 80lbs per head per annum (compared with 14lbs in 2007).

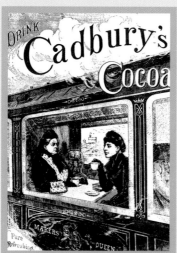

In general and of necessity, there was a habit of buying food little and often. Thanks to the general industrial expansion, rail links, refrigeration (in ships and trawlers as well as in the domestic food industry) and other forms of preservation, there was an ever increasing variety of foods available to those who could afford it.

The middle classes were in a position to use these foods and prepare them in a variety of ways. The term 'middle class' as applied at the beginning of the twentieth century is always going to be a

generalisation. One definition in use at the time was any household that could afford one servant. This put them on the lowest rung. It was certainly not a homogeneous unit, ranging as it did from wealthy industrialists to small shopkeepers and clerks. The distinguishing feature as far as food was concerned was the ability to provide more than bare necessities, with some choice.

Miss George was primarily aiming her book at this group when she states that the book 'will be as useful to those who have £200 per year at their disposal as to those who have £1,000.' £200 in 1900 would have been just about enough to qualify for a middle class lifestyle. Clerks and schoolteachers could earn this and this roughly translates as £14,500 now - so not a great deal - but relative costs would also need to be compared. As they were neither poor nor destitute, the analysis of middle class expenditure was less common, as they were not in need of extra assistance, so weren't of that much interest and less is therefore on record.

As an aspirational force, the middle classes looked to the upper class for 'guidance' in matters gastronomical. They particularly liked to copy the tradition of the Dinner Party, though less frequently and with plainer food. An opportunity to entertain and maybe impress was the usual aim, with a little matchmaking not

	1871	1888
Sugar	6d	2d
Bread	9d	5½d
Leg of Mutton (all per pound)	1s 1d	7½d (from New Zealand)

unknown. Books began to appear to cater for this with menus and costings and general advice on food selection.

J E Panton's *From Kitchen to Garret (1888)* was aimed at those with an income of £300 - £500 a year, and pointed out the relative cheapness

Grand Dinner Table

of food compared with just a few years previously. Fish and Game were also cheaper.

He calculated that £2 10s per week would keep two adults and a maid, with spending as follows:

Meat 12s, bread and flour 4s, eggs 2s, milk 4s, ½ lb tea 2s 6d, 1lb coffee 1s 7d, sugar 6d, butter (2lb) 3s, and the rest for fruit, vegetables, chicken and washing.

Typical meals might include:

Breakfast – fruit, eggs, curried kidneys, bacon, coffee

Lunch – cold meat, pudding

Dinner – soup or fish, meat (often a joint), vegetables, pudding

A more detailed picture of a week's diet of a family of five adults and three children in York in May 1901 is shown here.

COLD DISHES—1 Pigeon Pie. 2 Raised Game Pie. 3 Cutlets and Peas. 4 Prawns en Bouquet. 5 Crème Chicken. 6 Plovers' Eggs. 7 Lamb Cutlets. 8 Larks Farcie. 9 Piped Ham. 10 Boned Capon.

Day	Breakfast	Dinner	Tea	Supper
Friday	Porridge, fried bacon and eggs, toast, white and brown bread, butter, marmalade, tea, coffee, milk, cream	Haricot mutton, carrots, potatoes, tapioca pudding	Brown and white bread, butter, cake, tea, milk	Boiled chicken, white sauce, bacon, potato chips, stewed rhubarb, bread, butter, cocoa
Saturday	Porridge, fried bacon and eggs, toast, white and brown bread, butter, marmalade, tea, coffee, milk, cream	Haricot mutton, cold chicken, sausages, boiled rice, stewed rhubarb	Bread, butter, tea-cake, cake, tea, milk, cream	Chicken, cheese, potatoes, bread, butter milk
Sunday	Porridge, eggs, bread, butter, milk, coffee, tea, cream	Mutton, cauliflower, bread sauce, potatoes, rhubarb, custard, blancmange, oranges, biscuits, tea	Potted meat sandwiches, bread, butter, cake, marmalade, tea, milk	Potted meat cornflour mould, bread, butter, cake, rhubarb custard, cheese, hot milk
Monday	Porridge, fried bacon and bread, toast, bread, butter, marmalade, treacle, tea, coffee, milk, cream	Boiled mutton, carrots, turnips, potatoes, caper sauce, roly-poly pudding, rice pudding, oranges, tea	Bread, butter, tea-cake, cake, milk, tea	Fish, bread, butter, biscuits, cake, oranges, cocoa
Tuesday	Porridge, fried bacon and eggs, bread, butter, toast, marmalade, coffee, tea, milk, cream	Mutton, carrots, turnips, caper sauce, potatoes, hayrick pudding, lemon sauce, tapioca pudding, tea	Bread, butter, Frame food, marmalade, milk, cream, tea	Cutlets, stewed plums, bread, biscuits, cheese, cocoa
Wednesday	Frame food, fried eggs, bacon and bread, toast, white and brown bread, butter, marmalade, coffee, tea, milk, cream	Rissoles, poached eggs, potatoes, bread pudding, bread, butter, tea	Bread, butter, tea-cake, Frame food, milk, tea	Baked haddock, stewed plums, biscuits, hot milk
Thursday	Frame food, bacon, eggs, toast, white and brown bread, butter, marmalade, tea, coffee, milk, cream	Roast mutton, greens, potatoes, chocolate mould, rhubarb and orange tart, bananas, coffee, cream	Bread, butter, tea-cake, seed-cake, Frame food, marmalade, milk, tea	Fish cakes, stewed rhubarb, biscuits, bread, butter, hot milk

From R Seebohm Rowntree - Poverty: A Study of Town Life 1901

Frame Food was a patent cereal dish similar to *Benger's Food*, and *Farola* and was thought to have health giving properties.

The food in Rowntree's chart cost £2 10s 6d so would have needed a middle class income to provide it. This is quite nutritious, although lacking many fresh fruits and vegetables, a common feature recurring throughout the history of the British Isles.

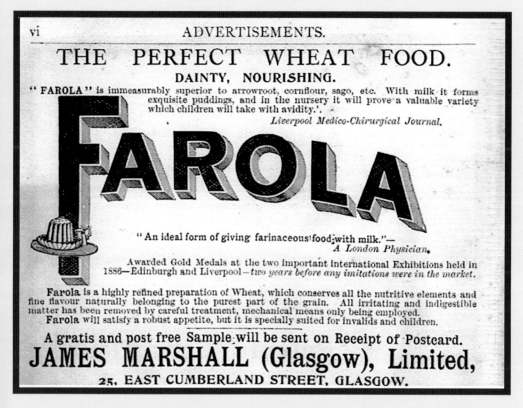

All essential nutrients are present and calories are above the minimum required but it is fair to say that most people led generally more active lives, so would use more calories.

The meals are a little repetitive, showing the use of the same ingredients at many meals, mutton being especially popular. This may have been from one large piece and was a cheap cut of meat. Meat was especially popular at this time among the English and, to an extent, the frequency of its consumption could indicate one's social status.

At least eating between meals (much frowned upon) would have been less tempting with this substantial fare!

CHAPTER 5

THE BOOK

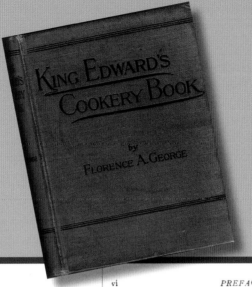

PREFACE

I HAVE been induced to write this book because, from my experience as mistress of cookery in King Edward's High School for Girls, Birmingham, I have felt the great need of a suitable text-book. My aim has been to write a clear, concise, and methodical manual, which will contain everything that the ordinary Englishwoman of the middle class need know about cookery. It has a wide range, insomuch as it includes artisan, household, and a little high-class cookery, so that I believe the book will be as useful to those who have £200 a year at their disposal as to those who have £1,000.

The lack of such a text-book is no doubt due to the tardiness with which the advantages of including cookery in the modern high-school curriculum have been realized.

Surely the art of cookery is an important one both for its own sake and as a training for other things. If arranged so as to come in the school course when girls are between the ages of twelve and sixteen years, every girl will acquire much necessary and useful knowledge ; she will receive a special kind of training in thoroughness, dexterity, accuracy, neatness, method, and order, which will be of great service to her in her years.

art in the young housewife has been not seldom the cause of a good deal of misery in the home.

As regards the special points of the book, I have sought in my arrangement, as far as possible, to educate readers to think for themselves by giving them principles and rules by which to work. With this object in view, I have given the foundations in most cases separately, and in cakes the principal methods of mixing also. If these are thoroughly learnt, all cake-making will be much simplified. This applies also in the case of soups and sauces.

I think the appendices will be found useful, and also the chapter on afternoon teas, especially now that this form of entertainment is such a favourite one.

In recipes where wine or alcohol of any kind is given as an ingredient, it may be omitted, and the equivalent amount of liquid of a suitable kind, such as cream, milk, or syrup used instead. In some cases, such as Christmas puddings and mincemeat, the alcohol serves as a preservative. If omitted, it is better not to make these mixtures too long beforehand.

Although written in the first instance for my pupils here, I have every reason for hoping that this book will find its way, not only into many other secondary schools where cookery is taught, but into domestic circles, where a simple and practical manual is always welcome.

FLORENCE A. GEORGE.

KING EDWARD VI.'s HIGH SCHOOL FOR GIRLS,
BIRMINGHAM.

I n her quest to produce a *'clear, concise and methodical manual'*, Florence George appears to have succeeded, as generations of OEs refer to its usefulness, even today.

The book was published circa 1901 and is an impressively comprehensive guide in 316 pages, in which she is faithful in her aim of giving the girls a lifetime's culinary knowledge. All sections are admirably concise and illustrate the emphasis Miss George put on basic techniques. It is very much in the style of those produced by her *alma mater*, the National Training School, from which she probably drew inspiration, with just a hint of 'Mrs Beeton'. I haven't, though, been able to discover just how much it was used in lessons and in what way. Was it used just to refer to recipes or for note taking or to copy out the recipes? Maybe all of these tasks. As some OEs still have the book – and use it – I'm guessing each girl had her own copy, at least during certain periods of the school's existence.

Although much of the first few pages can seem almost comical through modern eyes, discussing scullery work and the finer points of gas stoves and ranges, this was a potentially ground-breaking enterprise – a practical, informative textbook / recipe book specifically aimed at schoolgirls and young women from a middle class background, speaking directly to them rather than as a conduit for servants. Florence George had education as a specific aim, and she wanted her girls to understand why recipes are so ordered, how to select the right ingredients and what to look for when preparing dishes. In other words how to have the confidence to make an independent judgement - sentiments which would still find favour today.

The book is divided into the following chapters:-
Stocks and Soups, Fish, Meat Dishes, Cold Meat Cookery, Poultry and Game, Vegetables and Salad, Small

APPENDIX II
COMPLETE LIST OF COOKING UTENSILS REQUIRED FOR A LARGE KITCHEN.

1 copper stewpan, for fruit and jelly (2½-qt. size).
2 copper stewpans, for sauces (1-qt. size).
1 copper preserving-pan.
1 stock-pot.
1 oval boiling-pot, for hams, etc. (5-gal. size).
1 oval boiling-pot, for roly-polys, galantines, etc. (1½-gal. size.).
4 iron saucepans (from 1½ to 5 qts.).
1 potato-steamer (to fit one of the iron saucepans).
2 steel stewpans (1½ qts. and 2 qts.)
Fish-kettle (tin).
Frying-basket and iron stewpan to fit.
1 tin saucepan (small).
2 frying-pans (6 in. and 9 in. diameter), for pancakes and omelettes.
1 frying-pan (oval, for cutlets).
1 enamelled colander.
1 enamelled handbowl.
1 meat-mincing machine ('Enterprise,' No. 5).
1 bread, suet, and almond grating-machine.
1 raisin-stoner.
1 coffee-mill.
1 percolating coffee-pot (1½ pts.)
1 pestle and mortar (8 in. diameter).
1 potato-masher (No. 3 size).
1 iron kettle (3 qts.).
1 tin kettle (1 qt.).
1 Dutch-oven with loose pan (11 in.).
1 iron gridiron.
1 double meat-tin with grid.
1 girdle (11 in. diameter).
1 Yorkshire pudding-tin.
3 flat baking-sheets (14½ × 10 × ⅞ in.).
2 flat baking-sheets (small, 12 × 7 × ⅞ in.).
2 round sandwich-tins (8 in. diameter).
2 sandwich-tins (12 × 6 × 1½ in.).
1 cake-tin, Genoa (8 × 8 × 3 in.).
1 set of 3 cake-tins (4 in., 5 in., 6 in. diameter).
1 doz. dariole-moulds.
1 doz. custard-cups (tin).
1 doz. patty-pans.
1 doz. queen-cake tins.
1 box plain cutters.
1 box fluted cutters.
2 vegetable-cutters of different patterns.
2 tin moulds (best tin, copper tops, 1 pt., 1½ pts.).
1 tin border-mould (best tin, 1½ pts.).
1 spice-box (6 boxes in stand).
1 grater.
1 fish-slice.
1 flour-dredger.
1 sugar-sifter.
1 pepper-castor.
1 gravy-strainers (1 fine, 1 coarse).
3 measures (gill, ¼ pt., 1 pt.).
1 tin funnel.
... scales and weights.

1 salt-box.
1 hair sieve.
2 wire sieves (2 sizes).
1 chopping-board.
2 saucepan-trivets.
1 rolling-pin.
1 pastry-board.
1 porkpie block (8½ in.)
1 knife-board.
1 flour-tub.
1 steel.
1 pair scissors.
1 cutlet-bat.
1 meat-saw.
1 meat-chopper.
1 palette knife (9 in.).
1 basting-spoon.
1 set of skewers.
2 or 3 trussing-needles.
2 larding-needles.
½ doz. kitchen forks.
½ doz. kitchen knives.
3 cook's knives.
1 cook's fork. ,
½ doz. teaspoons.
3 iron spoons.
½ doz. wooden spoons.
1 toasting-fork.
1 egg-whisk.
1 corkscrew.
1 tin-opener ('Never-slip').
1 apple-corer.
1 potato-peeler.
1 oyster-knife.
Set of icing tools.
1 knife-box.
1 saucepan-brush.
1 pastry-brush.
3 scrubbing-brushes (set).
2 butter and egg brushes.
Leathers for tins.
2 jug-mops.
1 bottle-brush.
1 zinc washing-up bath.
2 buckets.
Clock.
1 lemon-squeezer (glass).
12 store jars.
3 china moulds.
½ doz. pudding-basins.
4 pie-dishes.
2 mixing-bowls (large).
1 salt-cellar.
1 doz. cups and saucers.
1 teapot.
1 doz. soup-plates.
6 dishes (in sizes).
3 jugs (set).
Oven-cloths.
Knife-cloths.
Tea-towels.
Glass-cloths.
Pudding-cloths.
House-flannels.

35

Savoury Dishes, Sauces, Forcemeats, Flavourings and Butters, Omlets and Soufflés, Puddings and Sweets, Bread and Pastry, Cakes, Icings, Invalid Cookery (including Convalescent), Preserves and Pickles, Beverages, Afternoon Teas, Menus and their compilation, Notes on Cheese; plus a Vocabulary (of culinary terms), Seasonal Lists and Cooking Utensils.

Instructions for looking after and stoking the Range Oven make the Gas stove seem very desirable, while her advice to invest in an oven thermometer is practical and she stresses the importance of correct temperatures to ensure success. The list of equipment for a large kitchen underlines how few labour-saving devices were available then and how much physical work cooking often entailed, despite the extensive list.

This will have been a sufficiently broad collection of information to fulfil her desire that the girls would want to use it long after their school days. It is also an insight into the sorts of dishes eaten or aspired to in late Victorian / early Edwardian England.

There is a recurring theme at the beginning of each chapter where she meticulously begins with rules, explanations and descriptions before any recipes.

Her recipes, though similar in style to those of the National Training School, have obviously been carefully

Victoria Sandwich Mixture.

4 eggs ; their weight in
Butter,
Sugar,
Flour.
Pinch of salt.

1 oz. rice flour.
1 teaspoonful baking-powder.
Flavouring : 3 drops essence of almonds or ½ teaspoonful vanilla.

Method No. 2 (c). Bake the mixture in a buttered and papered tin for about thirty minutes—size of tin 12 by 6 by 1½ inches. When baked leave until the next day before cutting up. This mixture is suitable for small fancy cakes, jam sandwiches, etc., by simply cutting the cake into various shapes, which may be iced and decorated ad lib.

N.B.—If the cake is coloured, two teaspoonfuls of cochineal will be required to make it a pretty pink.

considered so that a schoolgirl would not become confused. Her recipes and methods are generally both refreshingly easy to follow and surprisingly varied, and many would not be out of place today.

There are, of course, some which stand out as being rather unusual for schoolgirls to be considering, the most obvious being Chaudfroid of Larks. Chaudfroids were rather popular as entrées to a formal dinner, being some sort of bird / poultry glazed with aspic jelly and arranged decoratively on a bed of chopped aspic and salad.

Gooseberry Fool.

2 lb. gooseberries.
½ lb. sugar.

1 gill water.
½ pint custard or cream.

(Enough for 7 or 8 persons.)

Boil the sugar and water together for a few minutes, pu the gooseberries, and cook until tender. Rub through a si mix with the cream or custard, pour into a glass dish, serve cold.

Dessert Normandy Pippins.

½ lb. Normandy pippins.
Pinch of cinnamon.
Pinch of ground ginger.

½ lb. moist sugar.
1 lemon.
1½ pints water.

(Enough for 8 or 9 persons.)

Well wash the pippins and put them into a basin with water, cinnamon, and ginger ; soak all night. Peel the le very thinly and cut it in slices, removing all the white add this to the pippins and half of the sugar. Turn all i stewpan and cook gently for an hour, then add the rest o sugar, and cook until tender. When cold arrange in dishes.

Chaudfroid of Larks.

12 larks.
1 jar foie gras.
1 lb. quenelle meat.
2 truffles.

Macédoine (mixed vegetables).
1 pint aspic jelly.
Glaze.

(Enough for 12 persons.)

Bone the larks and stuff with the foie gras. Mix the truffles (chopped) with the quenelle meat, butter some small moulds and line with this mixture, put a lark in each and press the meat round, making them a nice shape at the top (not covering up all the lark). Put these into a sauté-pan with enough water to come halfway up the moulds, cover with buttered paper, and put in the oven to cook for twenty minutes. Turn out, and when cold glaze. Arrange on rounds of aspic jelly, decorate with aspic and macédoine. The glaze may be made by cooking the bones in butter, adding some brown sauce, and leaving it to simmer. Strain, and add a little melted aspic jelly to it.

N.B.—This can be made into a hot entrée by omitting the aspic and serving with sauce.

Unsurprisingly (to me), this dish appears in *The National Training School Cookery Book*. I think it was something to aspire to, with its foie gras, quenelle meat and truffles – hardly an economical or practical dish. In modern terms rather as

we might be keen to try out an exotic 'Nigella' recipe or Gordon Ramsay.

The book's penultimate chapter has a selection of menus consisting mostly of formal dinners and all the courses with an explanation of the formal terms, in French as was the fashion. This can only have been aimed at future hostesses and certainly of use to OEs promoted to greatness.

Many of the recipes are fairly time–consuming, and I think it is reasonable to assume that people generally spent more time on food preparation. Most food was prepared from fresh ingredients - although tinned meat and fish were now widely available and jam, biscuit and chocolate manufacturers were producing their goods on an industrial scale. Also, the much greater variety of foods in the shops meant that meals could be made much more interesting.

Economical use of ingredients was much more common than today so that all parts of the animal seem to feature in the sections on Meat cookery. So we find '*interesting*' recipes using pigs' trotters, sweetbread, calf head, tongue, heart and kidneys but also fillet of beef. Such ingredients (apart from the fillet) were cheap and nutritious and produced many meat products and staple dishes – brawn, polony, haslet and black pudding, for example, probably being the cheapest. Cheaper cuts of meat gave rise to such favourites as Steak and Kidney Pie (and Pudding), Hot Pot, Cottage Pie, Cornish Pasties, Pork Pie, Liver and Bacon etc.

The more economical cuts are certainly in evidence here with some quite imaginative recipes – Beef Roll (p55), Curried Veal and Beef à la Mode – although some seem distinctly less appealing – Brain Balls (p89), Calf's Head with Egg Sauce and Pigs' Feet (p74), for example.

She was, though, being realistic about what was available to those of ordinary means.

As was the habit in a less wasteful society, there are plenty of recipes and advice on the use of leftovers. In fact, some of the cold meat recipes sound tastier than the hot offerings – Croquettes of Meat, Curry of Cold Meat , Mutton and Mushrooms (enlivened with sherry) and Pastry Rissoles all have an appealing mix of ingredients.

It was a peculiarity of recipe books at this time –

Brain Balls.

Calf's brains.	½ teaspoonful salt.
Stock.	¼ teaspoonful pepper.
1 oz. butter.	1 egg.
1 teaspoonful chopped parsley.	A little mace.
A pinch of chopped lemon-rind.	4 oz. breadcrumbs.

(Enough for 12 balls.)

Well wash the brains, tie them in muslin, and cook in stock for ten minutes. Chop them up, mix with 2 oz. of the crumbs, add seasoning and parsley. Mix with the yolk of the egg, divide into equal portions, make into balls; whip up the white of the egg, brush over the balls, roll well in breadcrumbs; fry in deep fat, drain on kitchen-paper. Serve with a calf's head.

Croquettes of Meat.

	Sauce
½ lb. cooked meat.	½ shallot.
Pinch of sweet herbs.	¾ oz. butter.
1 egg.	¾ oz. flour.
6 tablespoonfuls breadcrumbs.	¾ gill stock.
Fat for frying.	Pepper and salt.
A few sprigs of parsley.	

(Enough for 8 croquettes.)

Chop the meat finely or pass it through a mincing-machine. Make the sauce as in Recipe (see p. 84). Add the meat and herbs, mix well. When cool divide into eight portions, make into cork shapes, egg and crumb. Fry in deep fat. Fry the parsley. Dish on a d'oyley, garnish with fried parsley.

and into the first half of the century - that Invalid / Convalescent cookery and advice were always included, and Miss George does not disappoint,

presumably reflecting a time when illness was common and palliative care was the most available option for many ailments. It would be hard to imagine Jamie Oliver or Nigella Lawson even giving it a moment's thought. As well as devoting

KING EDWARD'S COOKERY BOOK

Curry of Cold Meat.

1 lb. meat.	2 teaspoonful curry-paste.
1½ oz. butter.	3 teaspoonfuls flour.
½ Spanish onion (chopped finely).	1 teaspoonful chutney.
	½ teaspoonful sugar.
1 apple (chopped).	1 teaspoonful lemon-juice.
1 tomato (sliced).	3 gills stock.
1 teaspoonful curry-powder.	6 oz. boiled rice.

(Enough for 6 or 7 persons.)

Cut the meat into small pieces, fry the onion in the butter, add the apple and tomato. Mix the curry-powder, paste, flour, chutney and sugar together, and add them to the butter, etc. Put on the lid of the saucepan, and cook for three minutes, moving the saucepan gently to prevent the contents from burning; add the lemon-juice and stock. Bring to boiling-point, skim, and simmer slowly for one hour. Add the meat, and let it remain in the sauce for an hour or longer before serving. Dish on a hot dish with a border of rice.

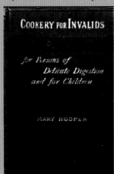

almost 20 pages to this topic, the contents section, rather helpfully, includes a long list of other suitable dishes so that the overworked 'nurse' is relieved of the perennial problem of what to make.

Much sensible advice is dispensed about dainty portions and attractive presentation and some of the recipes sound quite tempting – Apple Soufflé, Chicken Broth, Invalid Ice which includes sherry or brandy of unspecified quantity, Scalloped Oysters and Orange Pudding. Less tempting, I feel, would be Tea made with Milk (½ pt of milk!), Bread and Milk, Calf's Foot Jelly made with milk, and Toast Water. Toast Water was made by putting not quite burnt toast into a jug of boiling water, leaving it until cold, straining it and then, obviously, drinking it.

Its comforting properties seem not to have been recorded.

'For a Cough.'

| 1 gill whisky. | 2 oz. glycerine. |
| ¼ lb. honey. | Juice of 2½ lemons. |

Mix all well together, and take a little when the cough is troublesome.

Egg and Milk.

| 1 new-laid egg. | 1 gill milk. |
| 1 teaspoonful sugar. | Nutmeg. |

Beat up the egg, add the sugar, pour into a tumbler, add the boiling milk, grate a little nutmeg on the top. Serve with a biscuit.

Egg and Port-wine.

| 1 new-laid egg. | ½ gill hot water. |
| Sugar. | ½ wineglass port-wine. |

Beat up the egg, pour it into a tumbler, add a little sugar, the hot water and wine. Serve with a plain biscuit.

---

7. If beef-tea is required to set in a jelly when cold, stew a little shin of beef separately to mix with it afterwards, or add some isinglass.

8. When cooked, strain and remove all fat with tissue or blotting paper.

9. If allowed, add a little cayenne and celery salt before serving.

10. Dip a teacup in hot water, pour in the beef-tea, and serve at once.

11. In warming up beef-tea, put it in a jar and stand it in boiling water until hot.

Beef-tea No. 1.

¼ lb. lean juicy steak.
½ pint water.
Pinch of salt.

(Enough for 2 cupfuls.)

Prepare the meat, soak in a basin, then turn into a saucepan and heat very slowly, stirring all the time, and pressing the meat against the sides of the pan; cook until the liquor turns a rich red brown. Strain into a cup and remove any fat with a piece of paper.

Beef-tea No. 2.

⅔ lb. beefsteak.	
¼ lb. shin of beef.	Pinch of salt.
	1 pint water.

Prepare meat, put into a jar with the water and salt, cover closely, and stand in a saucepan of water; put on the lid, cook slowly for three hours, stirring from time to time. Strain, and when cold remove the fat.

N.B.—The shin of beef is used to improve the flavour.

A sizeable minority of recipes include wine and spirits, which were thought to have medicinal properties or possibly just lifted a rather dull recipe. However the *sine qua non* of any sickroom was, undoubtedly, Beef Tea. Miss George devotes almost three pages to the subject, including some precise notes on preparation. Beef Tea gained a reputation for being especially palatable for the invalid and was believed to stimulate the appetite. It was to be made from steak without fat plus water and a little salt. The meat was first soaked and then slowly boiled and strained, and the liquid served immediately.

Probably less tempting was the Raw Beef Tea, for which the steak was merely soaked in cold water for 2 hours then served in a coloured glass to disguise the red colour! Such was the popularity of Beef Tea that both Oxo and, later, Bovril were developed as an easier way to make it.

Another staple of recipe books at this time was Afternoon Tea. Given that there were plenty of suitable recipes already in the book, Miss George merely mentions possibilities in her brief chapter which stresses the daintiness of all food served and how to make the tea (three minutes maximum infusion time) plus a few tips on the best bread for sandwiches (one day old, less likely to crumble). Her assumption that cream would be served with the tea might be something of a surprise nowadays, but was standard then.

She makes alternative suggestions for winter and summer - tomato and cucumber sandwiches plus iced tea for a refreshing summer snack and small scones and potato cakes for colder weather. Miss George was obviously attuned to both her audience's and society's needs regarding food at the turn of the 20th Century.

When I first saw this book, I thought that it might be rather quaint and

Afternoon tea

unnecessarily flowery in the approach to recipes. However, on reading it, I find it still stands its ground as a useful recipe book. Most of the recipes are straightforward and easy for a cook with some experience to follow, and many dishes are still popular – Shepherd's Pie, Victoria Sandwich cake and Cornish Pasties, for example. Considering the lack of modern aids at her disposal, Florence George demonstrated her skill in choosing both standard, popular dishes as well as more challenging recipes, thus encouraging her pupils to return to the book throughout their lives. Her ability to marshal all this information into a logical, readable whole obviously says much about this remarkable woman.

CHAPTER 6

FLORENCE GEORGE'S OTHER PUBLICATIONS

As well as her, arguably, most famous book, Florence George wrote several others which were also popular at the time. Her *Vegetarian Cookery* was widely admired in contemporary reviews and still gets a mention in discussions of vegetarian dishes today.

'*Florence George, a cookery teacher in Birmingham, UK published "Vegetarian Cookery" in 1908, and included recipes for a stuffed Roast Chicken made from butter beans and Roast Goose made from lentils. A woman surely well ahead of her time!'*

The case for excluding all animal products seems to be recognised only in terms of easy digestion, but certainly by 1908, Florence George lists such an exclusion as one of the forms of vegetarianism. Many of the recipes are made simply with vegetables, such as Spinach with Peas and Tomatoes, or vegetables served with bread in the form of toast or crumbs, such as Herb Soup thickened with breadcrumbs. Special efforts are made, such as an Omelet without Eggs or Butter, a mould made with macaroni, and by the turn of the 20th century vegan butter substitutes appear in the recipes, as do various brands of 'nut meat'.

"*...Affording a good clean nourishment*"

This is quoted from *Turnip Tops and Nettles on Toast – A taste of Victorian Vegetarian Cookery*, a discussion on early vegetarian cookery writers.

In *A Heretic's Feast – a history of Vegetarianism (Colin Spencer 1996)*, Miss George receives criticism for imitating meat products, but redeems herself a little by producing tasty recipes with a good range of flavourings, and her Nut Cutlet is said to sound delicious. Vegetarianism has always provoked strong feelings in some!

The book is as thorough as the *KE Cookery Book*, with plenty of explanation and menus.

ANNOUNCEMENTS OF NEW YORK BOOKS

Fewer Books of Fiction as Holidays Draw Near—Some Important History and Biography Promised.

THE approaching 'Lincoln centenary is naturally actin-- as a stimulus to the output of books dealing with every aspect of the career of the great American President. The latest publication which is promised on the subject is one from the pen of David M. De Witt, author of "The Impeachment and Trial of Andrew Johnson," who has just written a historical monograph on "The Assassination of Abraham Lincoln," which will be published between now and Lincoln's Birthday by the Macmillan Company.

For Vegetarians.

A number of books are published this week by Longmans, Green & Co., among them a volume on "Vegetarian Cookery," by Florence A. George, author of "King Edward's Cookery Book." From her new vegetarian book Miss George does not exclude all animal food, since eggs, butter, milk, and cheese form a large part of her dishes. The various chapters deal with soups, sauces, pastes, pies, curries, stews, salads, &c., the author furnishing under each head recipes for vegetarian dishes. Another volume is called "Known to the Police" and consists, as its sub-title explains, of "Memories of a Police Court Missionary." The writer is Thomas Holmes, who describes from the first hand experiences of one whose whole life is spent among that class of London's population generally known as "the submerged tenth."

Other books for the week are: "Old and Odd Memories," by the Hon. Lionel Tollemache, in which is given a collection of reminiscences of Harrow, Oxford, and the political and social side of London life during the middle half of the last century; an anthology of love-lyrics, in which special prominence is given to the Elizabethan and Jacobean poets, called

The New York Times

Published: November 21, 1908
Copyright © The New York Times

George's fame even went Transatlantic.

Her introduction is typical and, although this was written before vitamins had even been isolated, she was keen to promote the benefits of fruits and vegetables in a healthy diet. Some of the recipes are repeats of earlier ones, some new, and there is little suggestion of dullness. The extended menu section has something for everyone so that Asparagus Soufflé and Coffee cream would be more special than Baked Potatoes, Salad and Rice Pudding.

In 1917 a wartime cookery book was published entitled *Economical Dishes for Wartime* with suitably adapted recipes, some more appealing than others. There is much sound advice about making the most of food and not wasting food or fuel – e g steaming vegetables, cooking in skins and conservative boiling. Though food shortages were not as potentially serious as during the Second World War, rationing did happen towards the end of the war, when ships importing food from the US and Canada were sunk by German U Boats.

As the country relied on these supplies, malnutrition increased in poor communities and rationing was a fairer way of feeding the whole population.

Wheat and therefore flour – was a particular problem, as much of it was imported and, although more land was turned over to agricultural use, it was often a case of making the best of what you could get hold of as far as flour and baking were

---

CASEROLES, GÂTEAUX, PATTIES, PIES, ETC.   63

Broad Bean and Tomato Pudding.

1 lb. cooked broad beans.	¼ teaspoonful pepper.
½ lb. tomatoes.	Boiled crust (see p. 39).
½ teaspoonful chopped parsley.	½ pint white sauce or parsley
1 teaspoonful salt.	sauce.

Skin the beans; skin the tomatoes, and cut them into sixths. Butter a pint basin, and line it with the pastry. Put in a layer of beans and tomatoes; sprinkle over the pepper, salt, and parsley. Fill up the basin in this way; cover over with pastry; put a piece of buttered paper on top; tie up in a pudding-cloth. Boil for one and a half hours. Turn the pudding on to a hot dish, put the sauce in a sauce-boat, and serve at once.

(Enough for 4 or 5 persons.)

NOTE ON VEGETARIAN FOODS AND MENUS   3

SIMPLE MENUS FOR A WEEK.

Sunday.

Breakfast.—Porridge, boiled eggs, wholemeal bread, milk rolls, butter, marmalade, fresh fruit.
Dinner.—Mushroom pie (No. 1), cauliflower, macaroni cheese, black-currant sponge.
Supper.—Stewed butter beans, stewed fruit, wheat crystal mould cheese and biscuits.

Monday.

Breakfast.—Eggs with tomatoes, dry toast, scones, butter, honey.
Dinner.—Curried vegetables, boiled rice, potatoes, boiled fruit pudding.
Supper.—Boiled Spanish onions, brown bread and butter, semolina cakes.

Tuesday.

Breakfast.—Porridge, baked mushrooms, wholemeal bread and butter, marmalade, stewed fruit.
Dinner.—Roast chicken, bread sauce, potatoes, Brussels sprouts, junket and cream.
Supper.—Potato and cauliflower pie, tartlets, baked custard.

Wednesday.

Breakfast.—Porridge, baked tomatoes, toast, wholemeal bread, butter, marmalade, fresh fruit.
Dinner.—Celery soup, casserole of colcannon, wholemeal pudding.
Supper.—Vegetable Irish stew, cabinet pudding.

Thursday.

Breakfast.—Porridge, Swiss eggs, wholemeal bread and butter, oat cakes, marmalade.
Dinner.—Stewed macaroni and celery, potatoes, cabbage, fruit pudding and cream.
Supper.—Baked potatoes, salad, rice pudding.

1—2

Oatmeal Pudding.

Ingredients:—2 ozs. Oatmeal; 1 pint Milk; Pinch of Salt.

Method:—Spread 1¼ pint pie dish with margarine. Put in the oatmeal, milk and salt. Stir together. Bake very slowly for 2 hours. Serve with sugar.

2. As above adding 3 ozs. dates. The dates should be scalded, stoned and cut up. Serve with sugar and lemon juice.

3. As above adding 3 ozs. apple rings. The apple rings should be washed, soaked all night and cut across. Serve with sugar and whipped cream.

4. As above adding 3 ozs. prunes. The prunes should be washed, soaked all night and stoned. Serve with sugar and whipped cream.

Rice Dumpling.

Ingredients:—8 ozs. Rice; 8 ozs. Dates or 4 ozs. Raisins; 2 tablespoonfuls Treacle.

Method:—Wash the Rice. Scald and stone the dates and cut them in pieces. Raisins may be left whole.

Tie the rice and dates in a cloth or double muslin, not too tightly. Boil for 1¼ hours. Turn out on to a hot dish. Pour the treacle over.

17

Cakes made with very little or entirely without Flour.

Ingredients (1):—¼ lb. Maizemeal; 6 ozs. Barley Flour and 2 ozs. Flour (or 8 ozs. Barley Flour); ⅛ teaspoonful Salt; 1 teaspoonful Cream of Tartar; ½ teaspoonful Bi-carbonate of Soda; 5 ozs. of Margarine; 6 ozs. of Dates; ½ the rind of a lemon (grated); 1 teaspoonful treacle; 1¼ gills Water; 2 teaspoonfuls Nestlés Condensed Milk.

Ingredients (2):—6 ozs. fine Oatmeal; 2 ozs. Cornflour; 4 ozs. Rice Flour; ⅛ teaspoonful salt; 3 teaspoonfuls Egg Powder; 5 ozs. Margarine; 6 ozs. Raisins; ½ teaspoonful lemon rind (grated); 2 tablespoonfuls Treacle; 1 gill of Water; 2 teaspoonfuls Nestlés Condensed Milk.

Ingredients (3):—4 ozs. Maizemeal; 4 ozs. Flour; 4 ozs. Oatmeal; ⅛ teaspoonful Salt; 1 teaspoonful Cream of Tartar; ½ teaspoonful Bi-carbonate of Soda; 5 ozs. Margarine; 6 ozs. Dates; ½ the rind of a small lemon (grated); 2 tablespoonfuls Treacle; ¾ gill Water; 2 teaspoonfuls Nestlés Condensed Milk; 1 Egg.

Method:—Prepare the cake tins. The quantity given in the recipe will make about 24 small cakes, or one 2 lb. tin.

Prepare the fruit. Raisins should be stoned and torn in halves. Dates scalded, stoned and cut into small pieces.

Pass the flour substitutes through a sieve with the salt and egg powder or cream of tartar and bi-carbonate of soda according to recipe.

Rub in the margarine.

Add the fruit, lemon rind or spice and mix well together.

Dissolve the treacle and milk in a little boiling water, and

concerned. A recipe for 'Cakes made with very little or entirely without Flour' fits the bill perfectly. As can be seen, Maize, Barley, Oatmeal, Cornflour, Rice flour and Wheat flour are all used in various combinations.

There are two recipes for bread. Unfermented bread, without yeast, using Barley flour and bicarbonate of soda / cream of tartar, must have been rather similar to Irish Soda Bread. Fermented bread is only recommended if sufficient wheat flour is available. Again, in typical Florence George style, there is helpful explanation and instruction with each recipe.

A Manual of Cookery was published in 1921, three years after her death and is the longest of her books at 430 pages. In the introduction by the publisher he explains that she had been engaged on it for several years and that the *King Edward's Cookery Book* had been 'appreciated by thousands of readers' (so evidently not just a school text book); further, that this book was an extension and re-writing of the original.

War Time Bread (Fermented.)

Ingredients:— 2lbs. Flour; ½ lb. Barley Flour; ½ lb. Maizemeal Flour; 1½ ozs. Yeast; 1 teaspoonful Sugar; 1¾ pints Tepid Water (barely); ½ oz. salt.

Method:—Pass the flours through a sieve into a warm basin. Make a hole in the centre. Break up the yeast, add the sugar and cream together until liquid. Pour into the flour, add the water and stir in enough flour to form a batter. Sprinkle with flour, put the salt round the sides, cover with a cloth and put in a warm place for 1 hour. Knead into a smooth dough. Cover over and leave in a warm place until it has risen to more than double its size. Turn on to a floured board, divide into two, and put into buttered bread tins. Leave in a warm place for 10 minutes. Bake for 1 hour 20 minutes.

N.B. The oven must be very hot when the bread goes in and then be allowed to cool down a little. To get the water the right heat take rather more than ½ pint quite boiling water and the rest cold. The water in which rice has been boiled may be used for mixing the bread instead of plain water, and will improve the colour and flavour.

Despite being unable to finish it herself, she had got it to a stage where little more had to be done. The few gaps were filled in by former pupil Miss Kate Lackland as a tribute to her memory, while Miss Irene Davidson (Editor of *Home Cookery*) saw it through the press and suggested improvements. It seems to have disappeared into obscurity, which is a shame, as her handy tips for kitchen care and food storage are a lesson to any of us tempted to moan about meal preparation. Boiling up milk, putting the jug into cold water and keeping the muslin cover damp, not to mention wiping meat each day, dusting with pepper and vinegar to drive away flies and wrapping it in muslin should mean no fridge is ever taken for granted again! The fashion for cleaning calves' heads, removing the brains and then slowly boiling the head seems to have, unaccountably, died.

There is much more about household routine, food storage, shopping and cooking methods and, reflecting changes in technology, how to cook with electricity.

PUDDINGS 291

Champagne Jelly.

1½ pints calf's foot stock.	1 inch stick cinnamon.
½ oz. gelatine.	1 clove.
¼ oz. isinglass.	Whites and shells of 2 eggs.
½ lb. loaf sugar.	1 gill sherry.
Rind and juice of 1 lemon.	A small bottle of champagne
Rind and juice of 1 orange.	(¾ pint).

Remove every particle of fat from the stock, put it into a perfectly clean saucepan with the gelatine and sugar. Stir over the fire until the gelatine has dissolved, then add the rind and juice of the lemon and orange, the piece of cinnamon, the clove, the sherry, the shells (crushed), and the whites, slightly whipped. Whisk vigorously till it comes to boiling point. Let it boil up, put it by the side of the fire, add the champagne, and let it stand for ten minutes. Then strain through a teacloth.

Coronation Mould.

½ pint champagne jelly (for the border mould).
¼ pint champagne jelly (for the crown mould).

Mixture for the Plain Mould :
½ pint cream.
2 crystallised oranges.
1½ oz. glacé cherries.
¼ oz. pistachios.
1 teaspoonful sugar.
2 oz. praline {4 oz. sugar.
{5 oz. almonds, browned and pounded.
¼ oz. gelatine, dissolved in 2 tablespoonfuls milk.
1 tablespoonful orange liqueur.
4 tablespoonfuls liquid jelly.
(Enough for 5 or 6 persons.)

Decorate seven small crown moulds and fill with jelly. Mask a soufflé tin (size one pint) with jelly. Cut the oranges in quarters, the cherries in halves, and the nuts. Whip the cream, mix all the ingredients together, and pour into the tin. When set, turn on to a border of jelly (mould, half-pint size), arrange the small crowns round the sides and one on top. Decorate with cherries and strawberry leaves of marzipan.

The recipes and menus cover a wide range from Champagne Jelly and Chaudfroids of Partridges (perhaps the Lark supply was now extinct!) to Pig's Cheek and Calf's Brain in Cases.

Dinner becomes a rather grand French affair each day after fairly ordinary suggestions for the other meals – but at least all the recipes are in the book. Invalid Cookery is still there, but with fewer recipes, while Beef Tea is nowhere to be found, perhaps seen off by Bovril.

It is a pity that the book didn't have more success, as it has many good recipes, but perhaps the market was already saturated and Florence George was no longer around to promote it, or else people were happy enough with the original book. The only copy I could find was in the Bodleian Library.

Veal and Ham Pie.

Make as for Pork Pie, substituting 1 lb. of veal and 6 oz. of ham for the pork, and omitting the powdered sage. A sliced hard-boiled egg may be arranged on top of the meat before the crust is put on.

Game Pie (1).

- ½ hare (the hind part).
- ¼ lb. lean Wiltshire ham.
- 1 onion, stuck with a clove.
- 12 peppercorns.
- ½ lemon.
- Small piece of bay leaf.
- Good stock (jellied) to cover.
- 1 gill port.
- 1 teaspoonful red currant jelly.
- 1 pheasant (roasted).
- ¼ oz. gelatine to each pint of stock.
- Spiced pepper and salt.
- Aspic jelly.

(*Enough for* 10—12 *persons.*)

Cut the hare into joints and put it into a jar with the ham (cut up), cover with good stock, and cook slowly in the oven. When boiling, add the onion, peppercorns, bay leaf, and lemon. When nearly cooked, add the port, red currant jelly, spiced pepper, and a little salt. When tender, remove the meat from the bones and cut it into neat pieces. Measure the liquid, add the right proportion of gelatine, dissolve it, and strain; add more seasoning, if necessary. Remove the meat from the pheasant and arrange it loosely in a game pie dish with the pieces of hare. Fill up to the top with the liquor. When cold, remove the fat, pour over a little liquid aspic. When set, decorate with finely chopped aspic round the edge and aspic leaves in the middle of the pie, with a tiny bunch of small cress in the centre.

The bones and trimmings from the pheasant and the hare should be put on with some good stock and cooked for one or two hours, then use it for making the aspic (see page 235).

Note.—This pie will be more satisfactory if it is finished off as soon as the hare is cooked and the pheasant roasted, while the meat is still hot. It requires much pepper and salt.

A MANUAL OF COOKERY

MENUS FOR THREE DAYS (WINTER).

Four Persons.

SUNDAY.

	Quantity.		Quantity.
Breakfast.		*Tea.*	
Finnan Haddock	2 lbs.	Scones, No. 1	½lb. flour, etc.
Grilled Sausages	1lb.	Swiss Roll	2 eggs, etc.
Stewed Figs	¾lb.	Fancy Cakes	Set 2, ¼ quant.
Toast. White Bread			
Tea. Coffee		*Supper.*	
		Chicken in Jelly	½ quant.
Lunch.		Celery Salad	1 head celery
Tomato Soup	1½ pints	Chartreuse of Bananas	Using 4 bananas
Roast Sirloin of Beef	3lbs. + 1lb. fillet for entrée on Tuesday	Cheese and Biscuits	
Potatoes	2lbs.		
Cauliflower	1. ¾pt. sauce		
Horseradish Sauce	½ pint		
Yorkshire Pudding	½ pint batter		
Richemont Pudding	1 pint milk, etc.		

MONDAY.

	Quantity.		Quantity.
Breakfast.		*Tea.*	
Porridge	3 pints	Girdle Scones	½lb flour, etc.
Kedgeree	3oz. rice and using up haddock from Sunday.	Guernsey Cake	½ quant.
		Fancy Cakes	Remains from Sunday
		Dinner.	
Kidney Omelet	Quant. given	Consommé à la Julienne	1½ pints
Rolls. Marmalade. Brown Bread	1lb. flour for rolls	Crême de Volaille à la Suprême	Using other half of fowl
Lunch.		Faisan au Cresson	2 pheasants
Stuffed Plaice	1 plaice (1½ lbs.)	Pommes Pailles	1lb.
		Salade à la Francaise	Quant. given
Beef Roll	¾lb. cooked beef, etc.		
Potatoes (Mashed)	2lbs.	Pouding au Chocolat	¾ pint milk, 3 eggs. Bake in a ramakin dish
Brussels Sprouts	1lb.		
Apple Charlotte	1½lbs. apples, etc.		

CHAPTER 7

MEMORIES OF COOKERY LESSONS GONE BY

After the unfortunate demise of Miss George in the summer of 1918, her successor, Miss French, was appointed. She had been a student teacher of Miss George and wrote of her '*unparalleled standard and genius*', with Miss Major adding that she had been a '*true artist*'. She was obviously much loved and had set exacting standards in her quest to promote the teaching of Cookery, not only at KEHS, but in all girls' secondary schools. This must have been a little daunting for Miss French, but she continued a line unbroken to the present day.

There is sparse information about subsequent teachers, although a few Old Edwardians (OEs) have shared some of their particular memories. Mrs M Devonshire attended the New Street school from 1925 and she remembers the Cookery Room being at the top of three flights of stairs. This was probably during Miss French's tenure. She has vivid memories of long benches, basic equipment and large gas cookers. She remembers making mainly straightforward dishes – bread, cakes, pastry, sauces etc. The girls were possibly not challenged enough, as she was keen to recount how, because the Cookery Room overlooked the Boys' School playground, she and her friends would throw 'bits and pieces but especially soap' out of the window for the boys to slip on!

She recalled making and icing a Christmas Cake – a perennial stalwart until recent years, and using the *King Edward's Cookery Book* only indirectly whilst at school. However, she has kept and used her copy throughout her life and is still using it (producing her copy to prove it).

A little later, in 1931, OE Margery Elliot entered the New Street school and was taught Cookery by Miss Donovan, whom she remembers as kind. Her repertoire included Rock buns, Queen cakes, Shortbread, steamed puddings (cooked in teacups), Irish Stew, fried fish, Macaroni Cheese and Scotch Eggs. At this time Cookery lessons spanned two periods of approximately one hour each and were taught to the middle school (13 - 15 yrs) with a demonstration one week and a practical the next. Girls worked in pairs, all the ingredients were supplied and the girls paid for the finished dish. All the food would have been bought in and provided at cost price for the girls to buy if they wished. Miss George's article of 1896 suggests that dishes produced in lessons were then sold in the tuck shop or dining room. Funding would have been too tight to allow this food to be given to the girls without payment, a recurring problem in the teaching of practical cookery in schools generally.

She recalled a calamity in a cookery exam when her sausagemeat mixture (for Scotch Eggs) was too wet and would not stick to the hardboiled egg. Luckily, Miss Donovan quietly told her to add more flour and she passed.

Invalid cookery was practised as well as preached, and all girls had to produce an attractive tray for an invalid which was then to be scrutinised by Miss Barrie (by now Headmistress). Mrs Devonshire's recollection of Miss Barrie was of a rather 'dour' figure.

Happily, both women appreciated the usefulness of their lessons in later years and found the cookery book a continuing source of information.

Ruth Naish, who entered school in 1932, remembered 'dear, gentle Mrs Hopkins', who was a wonderful and unique character. Cookery at that time was taught to LIV and UIV on alternate weeks with Science. She remembers an exam which involved laying a tray (probably for the invalid) - complete with nosegay - and making a junket and taking it home in her basket on the tram. The transporting of the finished product has always exercised minds!

A few OEs' memories have been stirred by mention of Cookery lessons and it was a pleasant surprise to receive some anecdotes and a few old exercise books, lovingly preserved.

Eileen Vaughton's exercise book from 1940, (when Cookery was taught by Mrs Hopkins, for a long time the only married woman on the staff, though widowed) has solid information and very neat handwriting. From cakemaking to information about preservation, soup and cooking methods, the progression to more complex skills and knowledge is quite impressively contained in what amounts to a few pages. In 1940 there is no evidence of impact of wartime rationing.

Incidentally, I was amused by her own notes in the back detailing suitable wine choices, especially the drinking of claret. I suspect this was added in later years and became the sort of book

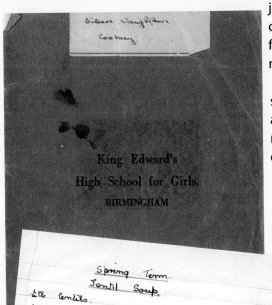

ileen Vaughton

many of us have in the house with a disparate, yet vital, collection of scribbled down recipes and advice. Impossible to replicate!

By 1942 it would seem that less practical cookery was taking place and I would guess that more demonstration work was happening, especially as the timetable was somewhat disrupted by the War. An exercise book belonging to *Audrey Sutton* from the same period begins as a 'Hygiene' book and continues as 'Cookery'. This could, of course, have been necessitated by a lack of exercise books, but the human biology information in the first section seamlessly complements the nutrition information and recipes. The effect of the war is also reflected in the recipes where dried egg becomes increasingly common and there is also a recipe for 'Pre-War Biscuits'. Fresh egg would certainly have been too precious for biscuits.

Margaret Gosney (née Vicary) who was in U4 in 1941 shares her school recipe book from the 1940s which was used by the teachers and, possibly, pupils.

This is the ATDS (Association of Teachers of Domestic Subjects) - the professional body for all DS teachers and active in promoting nutrition and cookery information and education - Cookery Book, which is typically thorough in all matters related to food. It is in the 'Miss George' tradition – clearly set out chapters beginning with cookery terms

Cookery 1942 October 8
Scones
Ingredients:-
½ lb Self-raising flour.
Large pinch of salt.
2 teasp. baking powder.
1 or 1½ oz fat (lard or marg).
2 teasp. sugar.
1 tablesp. sultanas (if liked)
¼ pt (about) milk (sour or fresh.
Method
1. Light oven.
2. Wash hands.
3. Get out utensils.
4. Weigh ingredients.
5. Sieve flour, salt and Baking P.
6. Clean fruit.
7. Rub in fat (grease Tin).
8. Add fruit.
9. Pour in Milk all at once & mix quickly with a wooden

Recipe for Pre-War Biscuits.
Ingredients :-
4 oz Plain Flour.
2 oz marg or butter
2 oz castor sugar
¼ beaten egg.
(use flavouring if marg is used
Method :-
As for Oatmeal Biscuits only leaving out milk and water and using egg instead.

Steamed Sponge Pudding.
(Jam)
Ingredients:-
3 oz Self Raising Flour
1 oz Margarine or book. Fat.
Pinch Salt   1 oz Sugar
1 teasp dried egg or ½ egg powd
2 teasp jam ½ gill milk.

THE

A. T. D. S.
COOKERY BOOK

To be obtained from the Secretary,
Association of Teachers of Domestic Subjects,
29 Gordon Square, London, W.C.1.

PRICE 1/2 net   Postage 2½d.

1940-1

and nutrition, moving on to invaluable information such as:

'homely measures'

- ½ oz breadcrumbs = 1 tablespoon,

-1 gill = 1 teacupful etc.

- 8oz golden syrup = 1 teacupful

-1oz fat = a piece the size of a small hen's egg

All the usual dishes are present and invalids are still catered for – minced tripe is one of the less enticing recipes - but we now have Camp Cookery which includes useful advice about what sort of fire to make and the range of dishes possible, encouraging the cook to be more adventurous than stew.

Recipes which would rarely feature in a modern recipe book indicate the sorts of dishes which made use of available ingredients and which would not have been remarkable in those days.

Stewed Rabbit (white or brown), Rabbit Soup, Fried Sweetbreads, Stewed Ox Kidney and Rice and Boiled Mutton are just a few suggested meat offerings.

There is a whole section devoted to preservation.

Bottling fruit, jam making, pulping fruit, drying fruit (in an oven), jellymaking, marmalade and pickling a wide variety of fruits and vegetables were part of the yearly cycle for many families well into the twentieth century.

All produce – home

17.—RABBIT SOUP

1 rabbit.	1 oz. flour.
A bacon bone.	½ pt. milk.
Onion, celery.	2 qts. water.
Small bunch of herbs.	Salt and pepper.
1 oz. fat.	

Soak the rabbit 15 minutes in salted water. Wash thoroughly and cut in joints. Place in a saucepan with the bacon bone and water. Bring slowly to the boil and skim. Add the vegetables, and simmer gently for 2 to 3 hours. Strain, and lift out the herbs. Remove the meat from the bones and rub the vegetables through a sieve, or break down with the back of a wooden spoon. Melt the fat, add the flour, and blend carefully. Add the milk and boil up. Add to this the strained soup, sieved vegetables, and pieces of rabbit. Season and serve. If liked, a little nutmeg or chopped parsley may be added.

N.B.—1. If an old rabbit is used it should first be blanched to remove the strong flavour.

2. The best joints of the rabbit may be served as a separate course.

23

grown or gathered from hedgerows or given by friends and neighbours - would have been used over the subsequent months to give interest and flavour to many a meal.

The list of ATDS publications in the front lists *Hard Time Cookery, Meat Dishes at Small Cost* and *Guide to School Dinners in War-Time* amongst others.

A few OEs still retain vivid memories of Food Studies staff or incidents many years later. Pat McGowan still has her exercise book with recipes for Macaroni Cheese, Scones, Stuffed Herring and Meat Rolls to mention a few. She speaks of her enjoyment of Mrs Hopkins' practical lessons - sadly curtailed by wartime rationing.

Elizabeth Taylor remembers her Cookery lessons just after the war, especially Cheese Dreams (deep-fried cheese sandwiches). They had to make a raised hard crust pie (used for Pork Pies) but, as pork was still rationed, they used a mixture of fish and aspic jelly. 'I can't say our families enjoyed the results!' she comments. 'I also remember taking a brown stew home in a jam jar, which was a risk to other bus passengers as it was very liquid.'

320.—BLACK CURRANT JAM

4 lb. black currants.
3¼ pts. water.
6 lb. sugar.

Prepare the fruit and put it into a preserving pan with the water and simmer gently until it is quite tender and the skins thoroughly soft. Add the sugar, continue to stir until all is dissolved. Boil rapidly from 15 to 20 minutes. Test, remove scum, pour into pots and tie down when cold.

321.—MARROW JAM

By using the following recipe it has been found that the squares of marrow, as a result of steaming, are very soft and tender. Marrow is treated rather differently from other fruits, as it is almost entirely lacking in pectin and acid, and whatever method is used the result is always more of a conserve than a jam.

4 lb. marrow (after peeling).
2 oz. root ginger.
Juice of 2 lemons and rind of ½ lemon.
3½ lb. sugar.

Peel the marrow, remove the seeds and pulp, and cut into large squares. Place the squares of marrow in a colander over a pan of boiling water and steam until the marrow looks cooked and is just tender. Remove the marrow, and place it in an earthenware basin, cover with the weighed quantity of sugar, add the lemon juice and the peel cut very finely. Leave overnight. On the following morning add the crushed ginger tied in muslin and transfer the jam to a preserving pan. Cook slowly until the squares are transparent and until the syrup is fairly thick. When the marrow has been previously steamed the cooking process usually takes from one hour to one and a half hours. Remove the ginger, pour into pots, and tie down when cold.

4. PICKLES

324.—BENGAL CHUTNEY

6 large apples.
6 tomatoes.
4 oz. shallots or onions.
8 oz. tamarinds.
4 oz. garlic.
8 oz. raisins.
4 oz. loaf sugar.
4 oz. mustard seed.
½ oz. ground ginger.
2 tbsps. salt.
¼ oz. Cayenne pepper.
3 pts. vinegar.

Prepare and chop the first six ingredients finely. Put all the dry ingredients in a saucepan with the vinegar. Boil all together for 1 hour, or until quite soft, stirring well. Bottle and tie down.

325.—RHUBARB CHUTNEY

4 lb. rhubarb.
6 medium-size onions.
1 lb. sugar.
½ lb. raisins.
2 oz. curry powder.
4 tbsps. salt.
1 tsp. pepper.
1 pt. vinegar.

Prepare the rhubarb and onions and boil with the sugar and vinegar till soft. Stone and chop the raisins and mix with the other ingredients. Add them to the rhubarb and onion. Boil all together for 1 hour or until quite soft, stirring well. Put into jars and tie down.

326.—GREEN TOMATO CHUTNEY

6 lb. green tomatoes.
3 lb. green apples.
1 tsp. ground ginger.
1 tsp. ground mace.
12 cloves.
½ lb. brown sugar.
6 pickling onions.
½ lb. raisins.
1 tbsp. salt.
½ tsp. red pepper.
½ tsp. ordinary pepper.
3 pts. vinegar.

Bake the apples, steam the tomatoes and sieve them. Chop the onions. Stone and chop the raisins. Put all the ingredients into a large stew-pan and add the vinegar. Stir well and cook gently in the oven for 5 or 6 hours until the mixture becomes mellow and red. Allow it to get cold, and then bottle and tie down.

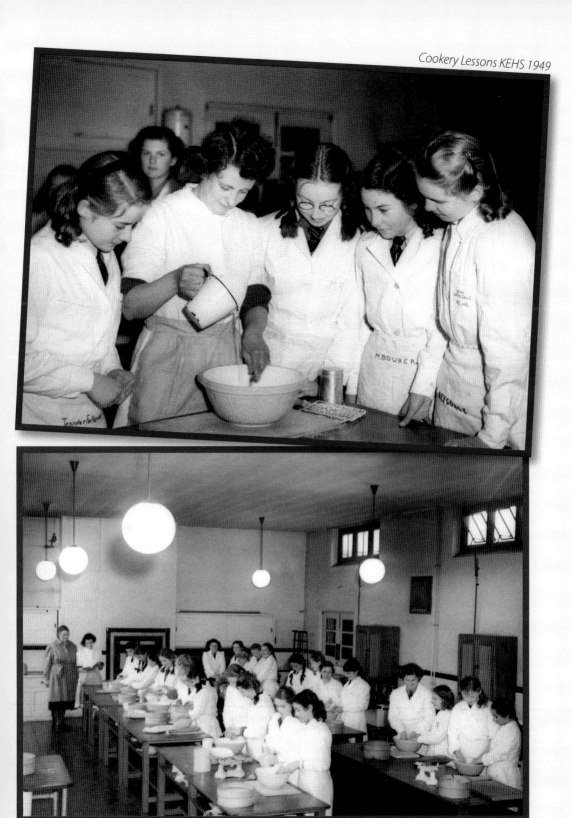

Christine Hutchinson (née Johnson) kindly produced her exercise book from 1955-56 (see right) and recalls the 'much loved Mrs Carmalt' (married women now being allowed in) and her Macaroni Cheese recipe is still in use. It also contains a variety of information and recipes and the tradition of a 'theory' lesson followed by a 'practical' is evident from her notes.

There are suggestions for picnics and salads and puddings, but I am a little puzzled about a lesson which coupled batters with cabbages. Use of leftovers is, again, included here and would have been unremarkable then, and so it must cause some amusement to older OEs that the nation has recently had this notion promoted by so many newspaper and magazine columns. Economising was once second nature.

Mrs Carmalt was succeeded by Mrs Etheridge, after whom Mrs Geraldine Mutlow took over the department in 1976.

Alison Fairchild (née de Reybekill) remembers making cheese scones and also being amazed that the Christmas Pudding recipe contained grated carrot.

Debbie Hayes (née King) (1967-75) also still has her exercise book and Mrs Etheridge was the teacher.

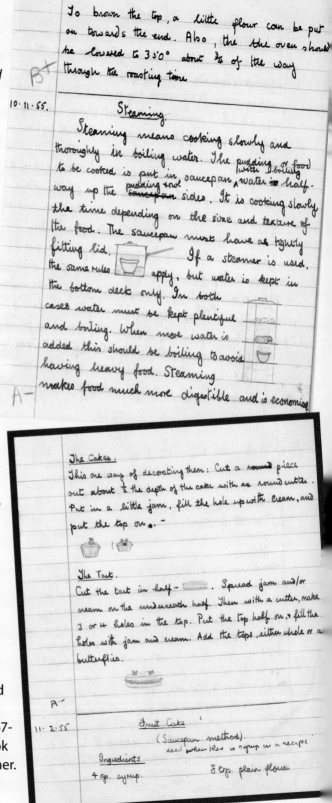

52

1957 Practical

She remembers making bread and some dough was 'saved' and taken to the next lesson (French) where it was thrown around when Madame's back was turned. They thought this hilarious. This may indicate that standards of behaviour have, in fact, improved!!

On a more conformist note, her recollection of Christmas Puddings and Cakes is positive and she did enjoy the lessons – and presumably was not in the habit of smuggling out mixtures.

More detailed memories of Mrs. Etheridge's lessons have been kindly provided below by current KEHS staff member Mrs Chris Hosty, who as KEHS pupil *Christine Forsyth* experienced Home Economics (as it now was) as life-enhancing .

Cooking with Mrs Etheridge

I was asked to write these memories down as a result of a casual comment one lunchtime to the effect that Old Edwardians who had been taught to cook by Mrs Etheridge still find themselves, as middle age catches up with them, making crumble with one hand only, so as to be able to answer the door.

In the Old Edwardians' Report for 1976-1977 Miss Stevens records that "the school was much saddened by the sudden death of Mrs Etheridge at the start of the summer term. She is especially remembered for her guidance with catering for parties held for deprived children and the elderly."

I especially remember her for teaching me how to plan a meal, for introducing me to the pleasure of cooking for other people, for her lessons in how to manage on a student grant and for her trademark bright red lipstick.

When I was in the U4th we had the luxury of triple cookery, recess until lunch, once a week for the whole year. My old exercise book shows that the first term was devoted to basic skills; Bread Rolls (Quick Method) cost 1s 2d, Hot Dogs 10d. On 29th October we made our Christmas puddings.

I actually remember none of this; all my memories are of cooking lunches. This apparently began in term two. We worked in pairs, one girl went to the library and browsed through recipe books, planning a menu complete with nutritive analysis and detailed timetable. Meanwhile her partner cooked lunch for two. Although my mother was a good cook, meals at home were very traditional with only the occasional Vesta packet meal to add an international dimension, so the Chicken Biscaienne with rice I chose to make at school was quite an adventure. ("Good but an expensive meal" commented Mrs Etheridge.)

Once we had proved reasonably proficient (apparently by March 11th for Annegret and me), we were allowed to invite two other girls and a member of staff. This was real entertaining; a three course meal for five, the best crockery, seersucker table cloth and napkins, water jug and polite conversation. (Interestingly the scheme was still in place when I returned eighteen years later as a member of staff and I found it quite a treat to be the invited guest, too.)

Each meal had to be followed by a detailed account of how our planning had worked or not, just like the write up after a science experiment. We were expected to be cost-conscious (this was, after all, "Home Economics").

Our guidelines included, as Rule 6, "Consider the amount of fuel you will use, make full use of whatever part of the cooker is alight".

In the 6th form I chose to return to the delights of cookery as one of my Friday blocks and spent happy winter afternoons making bread and

---

7th Jan. 1970. **Meal Planning.**

1. Provide well balanced meals, i.e. meals with all the nutrients the body requires in the correct proportions.
2. Consider the number in the family, and their ages, sex, and occupations.
3. Consider how much money is available to be spent on food.
4. Consider the season of the year, both for temperature and foods available.
5. Consider the time available for preparation and cooking.
6. Consider the amount of fuel you will use, make full use of whatever part of the cooker is alight.
7. Consider bite, colour and flavour.

cakes, sometimes to take home, sometimes to be ferried straight over to KES for the appreciative boys and teachers at Anagnostics.

Mrs Etheridge also contributed money management sessions to our General Studies programme, and offered wise advice on the perils of rented accommodation, including landlords who fixed gas and electricity meters in order to profiteer from innocent students. Her own daughter (Caroline, I think?) was at the post grad stage and this helped us to imagine ourselves in a world beyond school, particularly as many of our parents had not had the chance to go to university.

Sometimes scary, frequently wickedly funny, always wise, I know Mrs Etheridge played a big part in sending me out into the world able to look after myself and keen to cook.

Annette Duffy (née Glennon) (1976–1983) still remembers Mrs. Mutlow's golden rule – Add a sprig of parsley.

Jenny Douglas (née Buckley) (1982-89) is now a professional chef in Canada and has fond memories of Friday Afternoon Cookery in the sixth form with Mrs Mutlow and members of KES. That was bound to be memorable!

Hannah Brown (1981–88) has clear memories of Mrs Mutlow's lessons and her influence. In those days the girls had more lessons than is now the case and the first year was devoted to nutrition and food without any practical work.

She continues – 'In the third year we were finally allowed to cook' and she proudly brought her ingredients in her basket. 'I remember we all got more attention from the boys on the bus home after Cookery - my Mum never got to taste my chocolate éclairs.'

She goes on to recount how she and three others won the regional final of the Country Life and British Gas competition, earning a day out to London and returning with a Microwave oven. She also remembers the tradition of inviting teachers to lunch.

In 1992 Mrs Jenny Kerridge took over the department. Throughout this time all KEHS girls have had some Food Studies and Cookery teaching as a compulsory part of their timetable, thus maintaining Miss Creak's initial wish that Cookery was important as a skill and as part of a balanced curriculum

Mrs. Mutlow writes:

When I joined the school in 1976, Home Economics was a non-examination subject so it was important to make the subject challenging to all students.

A nutrition course in the second year, followed by a triple period of mostly practical work in the third year, ensured that knowledge and skills developed together. At the end of those two years every student was able to plan, prepare and serve balanced meals with due regard to nutritional value, cost and good practice of food hygiene. Students worked together in small groups, which developed social interaction and group responsibility. They entertained each other in a formal manner at meals they had prepared and staff were often invited.

Almost every year students entered National Competitions in various aspects of food and nutrition. They were often rewarded with success in National Finals, which led to press coverage and several television appearances.

Parallel with food technology, a textiles course was taken in the first year, when students gained confidence in using the sewing machine and had pleasure and satisfaction in developing their craft skills making kimonos, pictures, bags and cushions, which they were able to personalise.

The option courses in food technology and textiles in the Upper School were always well subscribed. Students became confident and creative, producing work of a very high standard which helped them towards goals for the Duke of Edinburgh Award.

The curriculum within an academic environment recognised the value of Home Economics and Textiles in equipping students with life skills.

Geraldine Mutlow
1976-1992

Mrs Jenny Kerridge followed Mrs Mutlow and recalls how the subject progressed:

I joined the school in September 1992. The position was full-time and temporary for the first year and then a permanent part-time job was offered as the time for the subject was reduced.

The subject was still a non-examination, very practical course with the practical aspect being concentrated in the L4th & U4th. The pupils could opt in for Food Technology in the L5th and it was part of General Studies in the 6th Form. Textiles was still taken in the 3rds, where creativity and design became very important. The use of hand and machine skills were emphasised and projects lasting a term were undertaken. Textiles Technology was eventually incorporated into the Arts & Design department, where a contribution could be made to GCSE Art.

At this time, Technology was the modern development of all the practical subjects, when designing, making, evaluation and working in groups became very important. In order for the pupils to experience this, the U4ths were able to go to the Technology Department of KES and work with plastic and wood materials. They produced very attractive results and enjoyed the courses greatly.

The L4ths also took part in a day course run by Abbas Shah, an architect, where design and construction ideas were introduced. Using canes and rubber bands, building skills based on tetrahedron structures became a fun project. They also had to make an item strong enough to sit on, using tightly rolled-up newspaper.

At this time, KES 6th Form boys were able to take a two-year practical Food Studies course. Lacking many skills at the start, they were quick to learn and seemed to enjoy the course, mainly because they could eat the results!

However both the girls and boys were unable to continue with these courses, owing to the constraints of the timetable.

The chance to enter competitions had also been reduced, but one competition in which we were successful was run by Creda. Twice the girls got through to the area final at the College of Food, where they won a prize for themselves and a cooker for the Food Technology room.

By 1999 it was felt that other practical subjects should be introduced and so Creative Living was developed. The aim of this course was to give the student skills in many areas, combining modern technology with traditional crafts. The practical skills would also have relevance to adult life, being of value in both leisure time and careers.

The subject comprised short courses in video, ceramics, electronics, food, photography and drama and was for all pupils in years 7-9. Food Studies was still offered as an option in the L5th & 6th Forms, where practical skills could be developed further.

Thus the Subject moved into the 21st century, equipping the students to become creative and practical.

J. Kerridge
1992 - 2004

Food Studies Today at KEHS

Fortunately, the teaching of practical cookery and wider aspects of food and nutrition continues at KEHS. In 2009 the Food Studies room was significantly updated and provided me with an exciting opportunity to design a space suited to today's needs. There are 'mini kitchens' per two girls and a set of lightweight tables which can easily be moved to suit different types of lessons. An array of electrical gadgets is available for use in lessons and a ceiling projector links to a computer and so illustrations, recipes and the vast scope of the Internet are at our fingertips. Within the wider school community the department gets involved in summer schools, coffee mornings hosted by the girls, helps with parties for the elderly and recently enjoyed having Old Edwardian and journalist, Huma Qureshi, spend the day in Food Studies, which she subsequently wrote about in The Times. For our 1883 day we transported ourselves back in time - and dress - and produced some delicious cakes for visitors' afternoon tea. Florence George would surely have approved.

From the Thirds to Upper Fourth all girls spend part of each year in Food Studies and may also choose it as a non-exam option for the entire Lower Fifth year and as part of the Sixth Form Friday Block for one term. All lessons are double periods. Basic skills and traditional methods are combined with a realistic approach to using time-saving equipment, some commercial products and a firm belief that relevance to today's lifestyles and cultural backgrounds should underpin much of what happens in the department.

Thirds learn to use all parts of the cooker, knife skills, some basic methods and general safe practice through a variety of dishes. These will typically be Scones / Jam Buns, Fruit Salad, Flapjack, Bread Shapes, Pasta Salad and Pizza. They begin to learn about Healthy Eating and Meal Planning and, when time permits, enjoy preparing and eating a breakfast together at a properly laid table. Essential to all this is learning about planning and time management and co-operative team work.

In Lower Fourth a greater emphasis is placed on nutritional knowledge and its application and how to adapt a recipe to suit individual needs e g add more fibre, reduce sugar, improve flavour etc. We also introduce Sensory Analysis of foods so that girls can begin to compare aspects of taste and texture of similar products, in the hope of developing some of their critical faculties. We taste and compare a wide variety of cheeses, find out about cheese production and nutrient content and follow this up by using it in recipes such as mini quiches and cheese and potato bake. Girls also increase their repertoire of basic skills to include shortcrust pastry; will adapt a fruit crumble to make it 'healthier', may compare different types of commercially produced soup and then make their own vegetable soup. On a more creative / fun side they also enjoy producing a Swiss Roll and we usually find time to include some seasonal items, e g sweets at Christmas or marzipan models.

Upper Fourth continue with further Sensory Analysis and will make some main meal dishes which are versatile and adaptable, whilst underpinning some essential skills, eg bolognaise sauce, stir fry, savoury/ sweet uses of bought flaky pastry. They also participate in a national award 'Active Kids Get Cooking' run by Sainsbury's, Food Standards Agency and the British Nutrition Foundation, which involves their independently researching, planning and making their own choice of dish and presenting supporting written work - by which time their confidence in their own practical skills is well established.

Lower Fifth have more time and freedom to diversify and they produce a wide variety of dishes, learn new techniques (modelling with icing is always popular) and enjoy challenges such as Ready Steady Cook! (KEHS version). They all sit the CIEH Basic Safety in Catering award and venture further afield to the BBC Good Food Show and the Three Counties Show.

Sixth Form have the flexibility to improve basic skills or hone advanced ones and Friday afternoons will see them making a wide range of dishes from quiches to cheesecakes, ragu sauces to Chelsea buns. We include Student Cookery and try to ensure that they will be able to feed themselves wisely and budget carefully when released from parental scrutiny.

The teaching of practical cookery at KEHS has come a long way since Florence George first made her mark but all her successors have remained faithful to her ideals. As the 21st Century continues I would hope that further generations of Edwardians gain enough confidence in handling food to make their own informed choices - whether in using fresh ingredients or ready-made products. Above all, the enjoyment of food can never be understated, and we owe a debt of gratitude to Florence George and Miss Creak that their determination to include Cookery within an academic curriculum is still bearing fruit (!) more than a century later.

*Thirds preparing and eating breakfast in re-designed Food Studies room.
Can you spot any similarities with the 1949 photo on page 51?*

Various activities in the Food Studies room

Never a dull moment in Food Studies

Jpper Fourth - 'Food Around the World' practical dishes

The Recipes

The recipes are a diverse collection of tried and tested favourites ranging from very simple to more challenging with a few surprises too. Staff, girls' families and Old Edwardians have all contributed and there are plenty of recipes which are used in Food Studies lessons. Some recipes have a little background explanation – where the recipe came from; why it is a family favourite; who passed the recipe on plus a few particular tips. There are a couple to improve the reader's grasp of modern foreign languages and a couple to be taken with 'a pinch of salt' (even though we are told to cut down on our salt intake these days). There is even one for the family dog!

Old or familiar recipes are treasured in many families, especially when they are passed down through the generations, and even an ordinary dish acquires its own particular 'personality' with specific instructions about flavourings, cooking times, how it should look and what to serve it with. We can feel quite possessive about such recipes, but it's always good to share a new food idea, especially when looking for inspiration.

Most of these recipes are in both imperial and metric measures with 30g being used for one ounce, so it is important to stick to one version when trying the recipe. There is also an American conversion chart.

The recipes used in Food Studies lessons are obvious as they are not 'signed', and range from the simple and familiar to the more challenging. Miss George would have recognised a few and I'm sure that she would have approved of the many technological advances and the explosion of interest in cookery nowadays.

Soups, Salads and Savoury Snacks

CREAM OF MUSHROOM SOUP

INGREDIENTS

8oz/240g	mushrooms, chopped
1oz/30g	onion, chopped
2pts/1ltr	stock
2oz/60g	butter
1oz/30g	flour
8fl oz/250ml	single cream
	salt / pepper

METHOD

1   Put mushrooms and onion into stock and simmer 20 minutes. Sieve or blend in blender. Reheat.
2   Work butter and flour together to form a paste and whisk into soup to thicken it
3   Season with salt and pepper, add cream.

Do not allow to boil.

CRUSTY BREAD PIZZA

INGREDIENTS

1 small ciabatta loaf/thick french stick or similar

TOPPING

1 –2tbsps	tomato purée
100-150g / 4-6 oz	grated cheese

Optional

1	small can chopped tomatoes
OR	
1 –2	sliced tomatoes
	a little finely chopped onion / spring onions

Plus herbs, salt, pepper

METHOD

1   Prepare all topping ingredients
2   Slice bread in half lengthways.
3   Spread tomato purée thinly on bread
4   Arrange any other ingredients evenly on top finishing with cheese and herbs
5   Put on baking tray. Place in oven 200°c/ Gas 6 for 10 –15 minutes

Serve immediately

FENNEL AND ORANGE SALAD
FROM ITALY

I've been living in Rome for the last five years and so have included a very simple recipe for a starter that I often make. It only takes a couple of minutes and is so refreshing in the hot weather that we have here.

SERVES 4

2	medium fennel bulbs
3-4	oranges, in season
100g	shelled fresh walnuts, roughly chopped,
	extra virgin olive oil
	salt and freshly ground pepper

METHOD

1 Chop the fennel.
2 Using a sharp knife, cut the rinds off the oranges, removing all the white pith. Thinly slice the oranges crosswise.
3 On individual plates, arrange the orange and fennel.
4 Sprinkle with walnuts.
5 Drizzle with olive oil and season with salt and pepper.

Fiona Talbot (Old Edwardian)

MANGO & AVOCADO SALAD WITH STICKY BALSAMIC VINEGAR

Use fresh or dried mango for this recipe

SERVES 4

INGREDIENTS

	generous handful of pine nuts
	olive oil for toasting
2	small avocados (not too ripe)
3	small or medium, ripe mangoes
1	ripe lime
	good quality balsamic vinegar

METHOD

1 Mix the pine nuts with a little olive oil and place in the oven on a baking tray to toast for five minutes, or until nicely golden.
2 Meanwhile, peel the avocados and mangoes and slice them lengthways into generous pieces. Mix and arrange them on a plate — but avoid damaging the delicate fruit.
3 Add a generous squeeze of lime juice, a drizzle of the stickiest balsamic vinegar you can get your hands on, and scatter the toasted pine nuts on the top.

This recipe is reproduced with the kind permission of Joanne Harris.

Liz Cummings

KASHK-E-BADEMJAN –
IRANIAN
AUBERGINE DIP

SERVES 4

INGREDIENTS

3	large aubergines
2	large onions, sliced
2	garlic cloves, minced
¼	vegetable oil (or olive oil)
½	cup kashk (Iranian whey)
	teaspoon salt
¼	teaspoon pepper
¼	teaspoon turmeric
½	cup walnuts, coarsely chopped
1	tomato, chopped
½	cup water
1	tablespoon dried mint

METHOD

1 Wash and peel aubergines. Cut the aubergines in lengthwise slices.
2 Dry aubergines with a paper towel and sprinkle them with salt.
3 In a pan, heat oil and fry the onions until it starts to brown.
4 Add the garlic. Continue to cook, frequently stirring until the onions and garlic become brown and crispy. Set aside.
5 Heat oil in another frying pan and lay the slices of aubergine in the pan over medium heat. Fry on both sides.
6 Add water, tomatoes, salt, pepper, turmeric, half the fried onions and garlic, and half the Kashk to the aubergine in the pan.
Simmer over low heat for about 10 minutes, or until tomato and aubergine become soft.
7 Mash the contents in the pan with a fork.
8 Add the walnuts and the remainder of the Kashk. Simmer a few minutes.
9 Season to taste with salt and Kashk.
10 Garnish with Kashk, the remainder of the onions and garlic, and mint.
11 Serve with naan lavash, taftoon, pitta bread, or pitta chips.

Alternative Aubergine Cooking

12 Line a baking sheet with foil and spray with cooking spray.
13 Lay the sliced aubergine on the foil and spray each side with the cooking spray.
14 Put under the grill for 5 - 6 minutes, or until each side is browned and begins to fall apart.

Donya Ghorbani

QUICK AND HEARTY MEXICAN BEAN SOUP

INGREDIENTS

1	large onion
4	sticks celery
2	cloves garlic
2	cans tomatoes
2	cans kidney beans
1	fresh chili pepper or chili powder to taste
	salt and pepper

METHOD

1. Chop and sauté first 3 ingredients until soft.
2. Stir in chili powder/fresh chili.
3. Add tomatoes and beans and simmer for 20 mins - 2 hours (it doesn't really matter - the longer it is the more the flavours will infuse).
4. Puree, reheat, season and serve, topped with crème fraiche and chopped coriander leaves.

Jenny Douglas (Buckley) OE

OLIVIEH SALAD
– TRADITIONAL PERSIAN SALAD STARTER

SERVES 4

INGREDIENTS

6	(well) boiled eggs
500g	new potatoes
100g	carrots
150g	garden peas
500g	chicken breast
200g	mayonnaise
150g	gherkins
50g	olives
3	tablespoons of fresh lemon juice salt and pepper (for flavouring)

METHOD

1. Firstly, prepare the chicken breast: before cooking/steaming it, chop into small pieces.
2. Peel and boil the new potatoes and then chop into small pieces.
3. Crack and boil eggs really well. They are then to be grated.
4. Carrots to be boiled and chopped into small pieces. Garden peas boiled for a few moments (if frozen).
5. Chop gherkins and olives.
6. Mix all ingredients. Add mayonnaise, lemon juice, salt and pepper, tasting until desired flavour is acquired.
7. Decorate with pieces of chicken, fresh tomato, olives and gherkins

Donya Ghorbani

PASTA SALAD

BASIC INGREDIENTS

225g   pasta shells (or other dried pasta)
4   tablespoons mayonnaise or small pot natural yogurt, adjust quantities to suit
1   tablespoon lemon / lime juice (fresh or bottled)

Suggested additions – any combination (you may think of others)

    small can sweetcorn
2-3   spring onions (washed)
    small tin kidney beans/ chick peas
    medium tin tuna
100g *approx*
    chopped ham / cooked chicken
    diced cucumber
    diced tomato
    salt & pepper
    herbs

METHOD

1   1/3 fill saucepan with boiling water.
2   Carefully add pasta, return to boil and stir with wooden spoon. Simmer with lid off approx. 6 -10 minutes until 'al dente'
3   When pasta is cooked drain in colander and rinse under cold running water. Leave to cool.
4   Meanwhile prepare other ingredients and put in large mixing bowl:

    'top and tail' onions and chop finely
    drain tuna and flake with fork
    drain sweetcorn etc.

5   Mix mayonnaise, yogurt, lemon juice and salt / pepper
6   Add cooked, cooled pasta to mixing bowl and stir in dressing
7   Transfer to serving dish

Delicious as light lunchtime dish

PASTA WITH APPLES AND NUTS (POLISH)

INGREDIENTS

400g   short pasta *
2-3   sour apples
3   spoons chopped walnuts and hazelnuts
100g   raisins
2   spoons honey
1   spoon butter
3   spoons single cream
    the juice from half a lemon
2   spoons sugar

* Butterflies and Pasta Shells work best

METHOD

1   Soak the raisins in water. Peel the apples and cut them into cubes, then sprinkle them with lemon juice.
2   Melt the honey and sugar in a pan, add butter, and when it's boiled, add the apples.
3   Heat for two to three minutes, throw in the nuts, and stir thoroughly.
4   Drain the raisins.
5   Cook the pasta in lightly salted and sweetened water; mix with oil and cream, with apples, with honey-roasted nuts and with raisins.

Serve hot.

Given and translated by the Czepiel family

PIZZA WHEELS

INGREDIENTS

BASE
150g   self raising flour
25g   butter/ margarine.
1   egg (beaten)
50ml   *(approx)* milk

TOPPING
25g   tomato purée
1   small onion
3   mushrooms (washed)
1   tomato (washed)
50 – 75g cheddar cheese (grated)
1tsp   mixed herbs

Variations : chopped ham, tuna, chopped cooked sausage, sweetcorn

METHOD

1 Oven 200ºc / gas 6. Line baking tray with baking parchment.
2 Put flour & butter in mixing bowl. Rub in.
3 Mix egg & milk together. Stir most of it into bowl to form firm dough.
4 On chopping board slice tomato into small pieces, chop mushrooms & chop onion finely.
5 Roll out base on floured surface to form a rectangle.
6 Spread with tomato purée leaving a 2cm margin.
7 Spread chopped vegetables. on top, then sprinkle with grated cheese & herbs.
8 Roll up from the long end sealing filling inside.
9 Cut into 4 cm slices & place flat side onto tray.
10 Bake approx. 10 minutes

Cool on wire rack

POTATO WEDGES

SERVES 2

INGREDIENTS

500g potatoes (esp. Maris Piper or King Edwards)
1tbsp olive oil
       salt and ground black pepper

For a spicier version toss in ground cumin/ paprika/chilli powder/oregano etc.

Also crush garlic clove & add sprig of rosemary

METHOD

1 Oven 210º c / Gas 7.
2 Scrub potatoes. Halve lengthways. Cut each half into thirds lengthways. Rinse in cold water and dry.
3 Put in bowl, toss in oil and any other flavourings / seasonings
4 Spread out on baking tray
5 Cook 20 – 30 minutes until crisp and golden

TOMATO SOUP

INGREDIENTS

8-10	ripe tomatoes
2	vegetable stock cubes
	pinch of sugar
	fresh basil
1	medium onion
	knob of butter
	grated cheddar cheese
	salt and pepper

METHOD

1. Sauté the onions in the butter.
2. Add half of the basil and chopped tomatoes. (if preferred peeled tomatoes - pour over hot water, leave for a few minutes and peel)
3. Add sugar and stock cubes.
4. Leave for 30 minutes to cook through
5. Add remaining basil and blend until smooth
6. Add hot water to required thickness and add salt and pepper to taste
7. Garnish with basil and grated cheddar cheese.

Susan Bhagi

VEGETABLE COUSCOUS SALAD

INGREDIENTS

200g	couscous
1	red onion
1	red pepper
50g	almond flakes
50g	raisins
100g	chickpeas (canned)
2 x 15ml	spoons chopped parsley
360ml	water
1	stock cube

METHOD

1. Make up the stock with boiling water.
2. Pour stock over couscous in a large bowl.
3. Fluff with fork and leave 5 minutes.
4. Chop onion and (washed) pepper finely.
5. Toast almonds – dry fry in non-stick pan for 1 – 2 minutes.
6. Drain chickpeas
7. Mix the onion, pepper, raisins, almonds and chickpeas with the couscous.
8. Sprinkle parsley on top and serve

Serves 4

VARIATIONS

- Vary the vegetables, e.g. celery, spring onion, sweetcorn, peas, olives, mushrooms
- Replace chickpeas with cooked chicken, ham, tuna, feta cheese
- Omit raisins & almonds. Add chopped dried apricots

VEGETABLE STICKS AND CHEESE DIP (CRUDITÉS)

INGREDIENTS

½	small carrot
¼	cucumber
	small stick celery
	piece pepper
¼	small pot plain yogurt / 1 tbsp crème fraiche
30g	cream cheese
	herbs / spices for flavouring
	e.g. chopped chives, parsley, basil, etc
	paprika, cumin, garlic powder, etc

METHOD

1 Wash and dry all vegetables.
2 Peel carrot. Cut all vegetables into equal sized pieces on chopping board.
3 Arrange on a plate.
4 Soften cream cheese in small basin with a fork.
5 Add yogurt gradually, mixing well. Thin with milk, if necessary.
6 Add any flavourings to dip and stir in. Taste (hygienically) and adjust, if needed.
7 Put dip into a container.
8 Serve crudités.

SIMPLE VEGETABLE SOUP

INGREDIENTS

1	onion
1	carrot
1	potato

OPTIONAL

3	mushrooms
2	celery sticks
	small tin chopped tomatoes
1	pepper
1	leek (cleaned)

PLUS

1	vegetable stock cube
25g	butter/vegetable oil
250 –500ml	water

METHOD

1 Clean all vegetables except onion.
2 Peel carrot & potato. Dice & put on plate.
3 Chop other vegetables, leaving onion until last.
4 Heat butter / oil in medium / large saucepan. Add onion & stir with wooden spoon for 2 minutes.
5 Add rest of vegetables & cook over medium heat for 10mins, stirring frequently.
6 Sprinkle stock cube in and stir in cold water.
7 Bring soup slowly to boil, stirring well, then reduce heat to low , put lid on and simmer 10- 15 minutes. Stir occasionally.

Serve

WARM POTATO SALAD

INGREDIENTS

500g (approx) small new potatoes (skins on, washed)
2 sprigs fresh mint (optional)

DRESSING

grated lemon zest
1 - 2 tablespoons lemon juice
2 tablespoons olive oil
1 clove garlic
salt & pepper

GARNISH

3 spring onions, cleaned
1 tablespoon chopped chives

METHOD

1 Put potatoes in saucepan, just cover with boiling water, add mint, bring to boil and simmer 15 – 20 minutes until tender.
2 Crush garlic, add salt and gradually add other dressing ingredients. Mix well.
Chop spring onions finely.
3 Drain potatoes. Put in serving dish. Pour vinaigrette dressing over, coat well and garnish with chopped chives and chopped spring onions.

Serve

WINTER SALAD

This a versatile recipe which lends itself to a number of alternative ingredients

INGREDIENTS

1 eating apple
1 carrot
1 stick celery
few nuts e.g. walnuts, hazelnuts etc./ or sesame seeds

VARIATIONS

¼ red onion
¼ pepper
small tin red kidney beans
3 mushrooms
small amount red cabbage

DRESSING

2 tablespoons olive oil
1 tablespoon white wine vinegar / lemon juice
herbs/crushed garlic/salt/pepper

METHOD

1 Wash and dry all ingredients.
Have a large mixing bowl ready.
2 Peel and grate carrot. Chop celery finely.
3 Quarter, core and chop apple. Chop nuts.
4 Mix all ingredients together.
5 Variations: chop onion / pepper finely; slice mushrooms thinly; drain beans and add to salad.

DRESSING

Put all ingredients in a sealed container e.g. jam jar etc.
Shake / mix well and pour over salad.
Toss lightly

Vegetarian Dishes

AALOO (POTATO) CURRY

SERVES 6-8

Served with chapatti or rice pulav

INGREDIENTS

I	large tin of tomatoes, puréed
4	medium sized potatoes
200g	frozen peas
250g	fried paneer (Indian cheese)
5 tbsp	oil

Curry Preparation - To be ground into a paste

1	large Spanish onion
2"	ginger
2	green chillies
1	peeled potato

Dry Masalas

1 tsp	cumin seeds
1 tsp	garam masala
2 tsp	salt
1 tsp	red chilli powder

METHOD

In a deep pan heat the vegetable oil. Add the cumin seeds and watch them sizzle, followed by the ground onion paste. On a medium heat roast the onion paste until golden brown. This takes about five minutes by continually stirring the mix. When the oil separates from the roasted paste it is time to add the pureed tomato and roast again.

In the meantime prepare the potatoes by peeling them and cut them in halves or quarters. Prick the potatoes with a fork or knife to reduce the cooking time.
We know the tomatoes are cooked when the oil separates and is visible at the top.

Now it is time to add the dry ingredients. Cook the curry preparation for another 2 minutes to allow the Masalas to roast in the curry.

Add the cut and pierced potatoes to the curry with 2 cups of water and bring to boil.

Once boiling, simmer down the flame and cook for half an hour, until the potatoes are thoroughly cooked.

Add the defrosted peas once the potatoes are cooked and the fried Paneer and cook for another 10 minutes.

Garnish with fresh cut coriander and serve hot over a bed of rice pulay.

ENJOY!

(My grandad's recipe! – Prem Prakash Jain)
Aayushi Jain

BAKED OMELETTE
OMELETTA STO FOURNO

I've always been fond of eggs in any shape or form, but I also love cooking with eggs. Not necessarily a major feature in Greek cuisine, I've nonetheless created a real Greek version of the classic omelette. It's always really popular in my household (perhaps that's because I always end up eating far too much myself!).

The other great thing about it is that it requires very little effort; ideal to throw together in minutes after a tiring day at work, and perfect with a simple tomato and onion salad, some lovely fresh bread, and a tablespoon or three of thick Greek yogurt on the side ...... a heavenly combination. The added benefit is that it looks like you've spent a lot longer in preparing it but we can keep that our secret.... just take the praise for this all round (pardon the pun) winner.

SERVES 5 or 6 -
or far less depending on the portions you prefer to serve!

INGREDIENTS

4	tablespoons extra virgin olive oil
2	large onions, finely chopped
150g	bag of watercress, spinach and rocket salad (I prefer this combination, but you could use any of these greens on their own)
10	large eggs, beaten
1	heaped tablespoon Greek yogurt
200g	feta cheese, crumbled
1	tablespoon dried oregano
1	tablespoon dried mint
	Salt and freshly ground black pepper

METHOD

You will need a greased 10 inch non-stick (preferably round) cake tin.

Pre-heat your oven to 160ºc.

Begin by heating the olive oil in a large frying pan over a low/ medium heat.

Add the onions and fry until soft but not brown.

Now add the bag of salad and fry gently until it begins to wilt down and soften and then remove from the heat.

Next, gently whisk the yogurt into the beaten eggs with a hand whisk.

Stir in the feta cheese, oregano and mint and season with only a little salt (as the feta is quite salty) and plenty of freshly ground black pepper.

Finally add the contents of the frying pan and give it all a really good stir.

Pour the mixture into your cake tin and bake in the centre of the oven for about 40 — 45 minutes until the eggs have just about set and turned golden.

Let it stand for about 10 minutes (if you can possibly resist!) before inverting onto a large serving dish.

As an alternative, try replacing the greens with mushrooms.

Ira Phedon (Christy)

BEAN RISSOLES

INGREDIENTS

	Make up about 250 grams (dried weight) of pulses (can be a mixture or either red kidney bean, butter bean, mung bean, yellow lentils etc.)
	fresh garlic - several cloves
2	fresh chillies
1	large onion
1	green pepper
	herbs to taste (various)
4cm	slice wholemeal bread - made into breadcrumbs
1	egg - beaten
	seasoning
	wholemeal flour
	cooking oil for frying

METHOD

1 Soak pulses overnight or for one hour in boiling water.
2 Cook in fresh water with clove of garlic and 1 chilli for one hour or in pressure cooker for 20 minutes.
3 Drain and put in bowl.
4 Chop onion and green pepper and fry in oil. Add these to bowl with cooked pulses.
5 Add chopped garlic and other chopped chilli plus other herbs to taste.
   Season to taste.
6 Add breadcrumbs and mix all together.
7 Add beaten egg to create thick wet mixture.
8 Shape into burgers and roll in flour.
9 Fry in oil in frying pan until outside is crisp.

RED WINE SAUCE
(To serve with Bean Rissoles)

INGREDIENTS

25g	butter or margarine
1	medium -sized onion
30g	wholemeal flour (2 tbsp)
3	chopped ripe tomatoes
300ml	dry red wine
150ml	vegetable stock
	vegetable stock concentrate or yeast extract to taste
	salt and pepper
30g	parsley, chopped (2 tbsp)

METHOD

1 Melt the butter and sauté onion until brown.
2 Stir in flour and cook for one minute.
3 Add tomatoes, wine and stock and simmer covered for 20 minutes.
4 Add stock concentrate and seasoning to taste.
5 Stir in chopped parsley before serving.

For a thicker consistency simmer for longer, uncovered

Sharon Wall

CATALAN BEAN CASSEROLE

INGREDIENTS

8oz	white haricot or borlotti or black -eyed beans (soaked overnight and boiled for half an hour).
8oz	haricots verts
2lb	fresh tomatoes with skins removed (soak in boiling water 2 minutes, remove from bowl and carefully peel)
1lb	onions (I use red and white) garlic if liked bunch of parsley olive oil stock and seasoning

METHOD

1 In a casserole dish such as Le Creuset (ie for use on top of hob), heat oil and cook chopped onions until transparent.
2 Add finely chopped garlic and tomatoes skinned and chopped.
3 Cook for further ten minutes and add haricots verts about halfway through.
4 Add parsley chopped coarsely.
5 Add beans at end and heat for ten minutes.

Serve with garlic bread and/or rice.

Liz Cummings

CHEESE AND ONION TARTS (MINI QUICHES)

INGREDIENTS

150g / 6 oz	plain flour
75g / 3oz	butter / block margarine
1½ - 2 tbsp	(approx) cold water
1	egg
100ml	milk
75g	cheese
3	spring onions, finely chopped

METHOD

1 Oven on 200°c / Gas 6. Flour a tartlet tin.
2 Make shortcrust pastry – rub fat into flour until it looks like breadcrumbs
3 Add 2-3 tablespoons cold water. Stir in with knife to form stiff dough.
4 Roll out on floured surface.
5 Cut out 12 bases and line tartlet tins.
6 Beat egg in jug, add milk .
7 Divide cheese and onions between pastry cases. Top up with egg mixture.
8 Bake approx 15 minutes until set and golden brown

Cool on wire rack

Try alternative filling ingredients
e g finely chopped tomatoes, pepper, cooked broccoli etc.

CHICKPEA CASSEROLE WITH SPINACH

(not using anything particularly fair trade but veggie and therefore avoiding use of land for cattle rearing and producing our beef steaks!)

INGREDIENTS

500 g	chickpeas soaked overnight
2½ lbs	onions diced.
100g/4oz	tomatoes
100ml/4fl oz	olive oil
2	cloves garlic, finely chopped
2	tsps ground coriander
1	tsp ground cumin
2	bay leaves
1	tbsp paprika
200g (7oz)	new potatoes cut into chunks
250g (8oz)	carrots in chunks
1	small piece of ginger root, sliced
250g / 8oz	fresh spinach washed and with stalks removed
	salt and freshly ground black pepper

METHOD

1   Cook the soaked chickpeas in a pan of simmering water until they are tender. Do not add any salt at this stage
2   Meanwhile fry the diced onion in olive oil until transparent.
Add the garlic and all the herbs and spices and continue to fry, adding some water just before the garlic browns.
3   Simmer gently for five minutes or more until all water is absorbed and you are left with a thick sauce.
4   Add the potatoes, carrots and chilli and ginger and enough water to cover and cover with a lid. Stir regularly, adding more water if necessary until the potatoes and carrots are tender.
5   Add the chickpeas and continue to cook for a further 15 minutes.
6   At the last minute stir in the spinach so that it just wilts. Add more salt and pepper to taste.

Liz Cummings

CHICK PEA CROQUETTES

INGREDIENTS

1½lb	cooked chick peas
2	cloves garlic, finely chopped
2	tbspns chopped parsley
I	medium potato, cooked
1	tbspn soy sauce
	squeeze lemon juice
	seasoning
	flour for coating
	vegetable oil for frying

METHOD

1 Mash chick peas with garlic and potato.
2 Add parsley. Add soy sauce, lemon juice, seasoning. Mix well.
3 Roll mixture into croquette shapes in flour. Leave in refrigerator for one hour if possible.
4 Cook under grill until brown (we rolled them in breadcrumbs previously).

Serve with spinach, onion gravy and wholemeal bread.

Liz Cummings

FILLED BAKED POTATO

INGREDIENTS

1	large potato
60-90g/2-3oz	grated cheese
1	spring onion, chopped finely & softened in pan with butter
1	tsp mustard
	a little butter/margarine
1	medium egg (optional)

METHOD

1 Wash and dry potato. Prick with fork. Place directly on oven shelf, bake approx 1 hour until soft 200°c/ gas 6. Alternatively microwave.
2 Split in half, scoop out middle & add all other ingredients. Mix well.
3 Pile filling back in potato, place on baking sheet and return to oven for 10-15 minutes until golden

Serve on its own or with salad / baked beans etc.

Vary filling with chopped, cooked meat, tomato, mushroom etc.

GINGERED MOROCCAN VEGETABLE STEW WITH APRICOTS

INGREDIENTS

3	onions, peeled and finely chopped
3	red onions (ditto)
3	sticks of celery finely chopped
4	carrots
2	parsnips
2 oz/ 60g	root ginger, peeled and finely chopped
4 oz / 120g	dried apricots soaked overnight in orange juice
1	jar mango chutney
2	tins chopped tomatoes freshly ground black and red pepper (& cinnamon, optionally)

To serve: Basmati rice

METHOD

1 Peel and chop onions, wash and chop celery. Put olive oil into large skillet pan and heat.
2 Add onions, celery, carrots, ginger oot and swede and cook for a few minutes until vegetables start to soften.
3 Add two tins tomato and slowly braise vegetables in juices. Add two jars good quality mango chutney.
3 Add apricots chopped into small pieces, seasoning and a little water to return to simmer for half an hour.

Liz Cummings and Nigella!

GOUGÈRE WITH CHEESE
– SAVOURY CHOUX PASTRY RING

INGREDIENTS - CHOUX PASTRY

150ml (5fl oz)	cold water
50g/2oz	butter
60g (2½oz)	strong plain flour)
2	medium eggs, well beaten

METHOD

1 Oven 200ºc / Gas 6. Line baking sheet.
2. Fold sheet greaseproof to make a crease, open it out and sieve flour onto it.
3 Put water & butter in med. saucepan. Place over moderate heat , stir with wooden spoon.
4 As soon as butter melts and water comes to boil, switch off heat.
5 Tip all flour in quickly whilst beating the mixture.
6 Beat until mixture leaves sides of pan (may need to turn heat back on) and you have a smooth ball of paste. Cool the mixture slightly.
7 Gradually beat in eggs, mixing thoroughly before adding more until you have a smooth, glossy paste. Use electric whisk if necessary.

INGREDIENTS - GOUGÈRE

60g/2½oz	grated cheddar cheese
½	teaspoon mustard powder pinch cayenne pepper
1	egg , beaten salt and black pepper

METHOD

1 Oven 200ºc / Gas 6. Make Choux pastry BUT add 50g of the cheese, mustard & cayenne pepper immediately after eggs have been beaten in.
2 Grease & dampen baking sheet. Spoon dessertspoons of mixture onto baking sheet, so that they touch, each other in a circle approx. 18cm / 7".
3 Brush circle with beaten egg & sprinkle remaining cheese round top.
4 Bake 10 minutes. then raise oven to 210ºc / Gas 7 and bake further 20 minutes.

Serve hot.

MACARONI CHEESE

INGREDIENTS

Sauce :   30g flour
             30g butter / margarine
             325 ml milk
                  salt/pepper/mustard to taste

             175g macaroni (or other pasta)
             150g grated cheese (add extra if desired)

Optional : 50g chopped ham / cooked chicken/ chopped

             50g   tomato / sweetcorn
                  tomato slices for top
                  small chopped onion (red / white)
             50g   mushrooms (washed & chopped)

             15g   butter / ½ tbsp vegetable oil

                  medium / large ovenproof dish

METHOD

1   Boil water in pan - approx ⅓rd to ½ full
2   Carefully add macaroni, stir and reduce heat to medium
3   Cook 10 -12 minutes until tender, drain and put lid on pan
4   Grate cheese.
5   If using onion / mushrooms soften in pan on medium heat (remove)
6   Put butter, flour and milk in saucepan. Stir continuously with
     small balloon whisk over a LOW heat until thick and bubbling.
7   Switch heat off. Remove pan and stir in ¾ of cheese (save some for top)
8   Put macaroni into pan with sauce (if big enough) and stir well
9   Pour into ovenproof dish. Sprinkle with remaining cheese. Decorate with tomato slices,
     if used. Grill 4-5 minutes until golden brown.
10 Flash under a hot grill.

Serve.

Mushroom and Mixed Vegetable Curry with Cashew nuts
(Indian dish - Sha nam Karl)

INGREDIENTS

I	red onion finely sliced
½	packet frozen mixed vegetables (or fresh vegetables of choice)
2	cloves
1	tbsp raisins or sultanas
2	cups sliced mushrooms
4	tbsps Greek Yoghurt
2	tbsps cream (optional)
½	cup water
2	tbsps margarine
	handful of chopped cashew nuts

For the paste

5	cloves (stalks discarded)
½	teasp fresh ginger grated
2	tbsps cashew nuts
2	tbsps poppy seeds (or mustard seeds)
	seeds from 2 cardamom pods
I	green chilli chopped
	salt and pepper to taste

METHOD

1 Boil the frozen mixed vegetables or steam your choice of fresh mixed vegetables. for a few minutes until just tender.
2 While they are cooking prepare the paste. Put the cloves , ginger, cashew nuts, poppy seeds, cardamom seeds and chilli into a blender, adding few tsps water as necessary to make a smooth paste. Set aside.
3 Returning to the main ingredients, beat margarine in pan and sauté onion until soft. Add the cloves and cook for a few moments before spooning in the blended paste, raisins or sultanas. Stir and cook for three minutes.
4 Add mixed vegetables, mushrooms, yoghurt and cream and some water and salt. Cook gently for 5 minx before serving with cashew nuts scattered on top and on a bed of brown basmati rice.

Liz Cummings

MUSHROOM, TOMATO AND BROCCOLI RISOTTO

INGREDIENTS

1	onion, finely chopped
1	clove garlic or 1 tsp garlic paste
240g/8oz	mushrooms (washed)
1	small can chopped tomatoes
180g/6oz	broccoli – washed and chopped into small pieces
240g/8oz	risotto or long grain rice
1-2	stock cubes
1½	pts/ 900 ml water
1	tablespoon oil
2	tablespoons grated parmesan - optional
2	tablespoons chopped parsley
15g/½oz	butter

METHOD

1 Wash and chop broccoli into very small pieces.
2 Wash and slice mushrooms.
3 Heat oil in a large pan and gently fry onion and garlic 3 -5 mins. Stir in mushrooms, broccoli and chopped tomatoes.
4 Stir in rice and 1 pint of water (may need more) plus stock cubes. Stir well and gradually bring to boil.
5 Cook over moderate heat (ie not too low). Stir frequently and add remaining water as rice absorbs liquid.

   NB Risotto should be creamy, not dry

6 After approx. 20 minutes remove from heat and stir in butter, parmesan and parsley.

Serve immediately.

Substitute different vegetables, herbs or add chopped cold meat. Add a glass of wine in place of some of the stock

NUT ROAST

SERVES 4 - 6

INGREDIENTS

1	medium - sized onion
25g	butter or margarine
225g	mixed nuts (I prefer a mixture of cashew and pine)
100g	wholemeal bread
300ml	vegetable stock or water
10ml	yeast extract (2 tsp)
5ml	mixed herbs (1 tsp)
	salt and pepper

METHOD

1   Chop onions and sauté in butter until transparent. Grind nuts and bread until fine.
2   Heat stock and yeast extract to boiling point.
3   Combine all the ingredients together. Turn into a greased shallow baking dish, level the surface, sprinkle with breadcrumbs and bake in oven at 180°c /Gas Mark 4 for 30 minutes. until golden brown.

Sharon Wall

NUT ROAST

This simple recipe has long been part of the Christmas repertoire in our family, not that there is anything particularly Christmassy about it! We tend to have big family Christmases - it's not unusual for 20 or more of us to sit down together for lunch on Christmas Day. Because there are a few vegetarians in the extended family, we have always made the nut roast as the veggie alternative to roast turkey, but we've found over the years that we have to make several because the meat eaters like it too, and they will eat it at that meal and over the next few days.

INGREDIENTS

8oz/240g	chopped onions
8oz/240g	chopped mushrooms
8oz/240g	chopped mixed nuts
2	teaspoons marmite
4oz/120g	breadcrumbs
1	large beaten egg
	salt and pepper
2oz/60g	butter

METHOD

1   Heat oven to gas mark 4 / 180°c. Grease and line a 1lb loaf tin.
2   Mix the onions with the mushrooms.
3   Melt the butter in a saucepan and cook the onions and mushrooms.
4   Add the nuts, breadcrumbs, salt, pepper, marmite and egg. Stir well.
5   Put the mixture into the loaf tin and cook in the centre of the oven for 1hour.
6   When slightly cool, remove from the tin and the lining paper. The loaf can, if you wish, be garnished with lemon, tomato and parsley.

Pam Rutter

CHEESE AND POTATO PIE

This was one of the first dishes we were taught in Home Economics - as it was called when I was at KEHS!

I still make it and think it is the ultimate in comfort food and can be easily adapted to suit all palates!

SERVES 4 (adapt to suit)

INGREDIENTS

1kg	potatoes
100g	cheese (mature is best for taste!)
	milk
	butter
250g	mushrooms
1	onion

METHOD

1   Peel and chop the potatoes.
    Place in saucepan with water and bring to the boil. Simmer until soft.
2   Peel and chop onion and mushrooms. Fry in a little oil until soft and place in an oven proof dish.
3   Drain potatoes and mash with butter and milk and most of the cheese until creamy. Spoon over the mushrooms and onion, sprinkle remaining cheese on top and place under grill until cheese melts.
4   Add a sprig of parsley to garnish - Mrs Mutlow's golden rule!!

Annette Duffy (née Glennon)
(at school 1976 -1983)

QUORN LASAGNE

INGREDIENTS

8oz	Quorn
1	onion
2	cloves garlic
1	stick celery
½	red pepper & ½ green pepper
2oz	mushrooms
2	tablespoons tomato purée
16oz	tin chopped tomatoes
1	tablespoon mixed herbs
1	bay leaf
	salt & pepper
2	tablespoons olive oil

BÉCHAMEL SAUCE

2oz	margarine
2oz	plain flour
2	pints milk
	seasoning

METHOD

1   Sauté onion, garlic, celery in oil until soft. Add quorn. Sauté till brown.
2   Add peppers, mushrooms, mixed herbs. Sauté for 5 minutes.
3   Add purée, chopped tomatoes, bay leaf and seasoning.
4   Simmer gently for 30 minutes.

SAUCE

5   Melt margarine till foaming. Add flour. Mix till sandy.
    Add hot milk, slowly whisking till smooth. Season.
6   Put a layer of sauce in dish. Cover with lasagne.
7   Add a layer of quorn mix.
8   Add another layer of lasagne and quorn mix and lasagne and white sauce.
9   Sprinkle with cheese.

Bake in oven 130ºc for 1 hour.

School Kitchen

VEGETARIAN MOUSSAKA

I have copied below the recipe for vegetarian moussaka that I got from my Home Economics lessons all those years ago. I'm ashamed to say that I haven't made it in twenty years, but my mum makes it on a regular basis and it's become a family favourite, even for my meat eating father!

INGREDIENTS

MOUSSAKA

225g	brown lentils
2	medium aubergines (approx weight 500g)
	salt
6	tablespoons oil
1	onion peeled and chopped
1	can of tomatoes (do not use all the juice unless the mixture dries out)
1	garlic clove
1	tablespoon tomato puree
½	teaspoon cinnamon powder
3-4	tablespoons red wine (optional)
	black pepper
3oz	mature cheddar cheese

CHEESE SAUCE

45g	butter
45g	plain flour
85g	cheddar cheese 425ml of milk
1	egg
	salt and pepper

METHOD

1   Cover the dry lentils with water, bring to the boil then simmer for 40-50 minutes. Drain.

2   Slice the aubergines into thin rounds, sprinkle with salt and leave for 30 minutes.

3   Rinse and dry the pieces of aubergine. Fry them lightly in oil. Pat with kitchen paper to remove excess oil.

4   Fry onion in remaining oil, add garlic and cook for a further 5 minutes. Remove from the heat and stir in the tomatoes, tomato puree, lentils, cinnamon, wine, salt and paper.

5   Make the sauce- put milk, butter and flour in saucepan and stir continuously with small balloon whisk over low heat until bubbling and thickened. Remove from heat, add half the cheese and add the egg last.

6   Layer aubergines, lentil mixture and cheese sauce ending with the sauce. Sprinkle with the remaining cheese and bake at Gas mark 4 (180°c) for 1 hour.

OE Fiona Talbot KEHS 1983-90

A DISH FOR ALL REASONS

For cooking in a microwave oven.

This dish can be used as a vegetable accompaniment to any meal or as a supper dish with parmesan cheese sprinkled over and accompanied by crusty bread.
OR as a vegetarian dish served with pasta.

Serves 4 as an accompaniment dish, or 3 as a supper (2 if very hungry).

INGREDIENTS

1   medium sized aubergine, cut in half and thinly sliced, sprinkle with salt and leave during the preparation of the other ingredients.
1   large onion sliced and cut into small pieces.
1   red pepper cut into strips then into small pieces.
1   large cooking apple or 2 smaller apples to make 450 g (1lb) in weight.
1   can 397gms(14oz) chopped tomatoes (this can be plain or with herbs, or garlic according to your taste)

If a bulkier dish is required add 1 small courgette sliced and chopped.

METHOD

1   Place the aubergine, onion, pepper (and courgette, if used) into a microwavable covered dish and cook on high for 3 minutes.
2   Add the apple(s) and cook for 5 minutes
3   Add the chopped tomatoes and cook for 10 minutes. Season and stir.
4   Stand for a minute and serve.

This dish may be cooked in advance and frozen.

For those without a microwave.

Fry the aubergine, onion and pepper (and courgette) until soft, put all the ingredients, seasoned and stirred together into a covered, ovenproof dish, and put into a heated oven at 170ºc/gas 3 for approximately 40 minutes.

Please check this as ovens vary. The dish should be piping hot and all ingredients soft.

OE Magazine

TOMATO SAUCE
(RAGU)

INGREDIENTS

1	large tin chopped tomatoes
1	onion
1-2	cloves garlic
	dried or fresh herbs – basil, mixed herbs etc.
	salt and black pepper
1tbsp	oil

METHOD

1. Chop onion and crush garlic
2. Heat oil in medium pan. Soften onion and garlic.
3. Add tomatoes, herbs, salt and pepper. Bring slowly to boil & reduce heat immediately.
4. Cover pan with lid and simmer for 20 minutes, stirring occasionally.

VARIATIONS

- For hot sauce add ½ a finely chopped red chilli
- For simple veggie sauce add 75g chopped mushrooms and 1 chopped courgette with onion
- Add 2 tablespoons crème fraiche for a smooth, creamy sauce
- Add 200g minced meat with onion for a simple meat sauce (cook both first – i.e. fry in a little oil)
- Add chopped black olives and tuna
- A combination of these – plus others you can think of – would be suitable

Can be served with pasta, rice, garlic bread, crusty bread, baked potatoes etc. etc.

GARLIC/HERB LOAF

INGREDIENTS

1	small French stick (baguette)
2	cloves of garlic
1tbsp	chopped parsley or similar
50g	butter
	foil

METHOD

1. Crush garlic , blend into butter with parsley
2. Cut baguette into slices without going through bottom.
3. Spread each section with butter mixture
4. Wrap loosely in foil. Bake 10 -12 minutes on baking tray 200°c / gas 6.

RATATOUILLE

INGREDIENTS:

1	onion (red or white)
1-2	cloves garlic
1-2	peppers
1	aubergine
2-3	courgettes
100g	mushrooms
6	medium tomatoes (skinned)

OR

1 tin chopped tomatoes
(small or medium)
mixed herbs / torn basil leaves
(optional)
a little oil / butter

METHOD

1   Wash vegetables (except onion).
    (Skin tomatoes in boiling water)
2   De-seed pepper and slice into
    small chunks.
3   Trim ends of courgettes and slice.
4   Slice aubergine into quarters then
    into 1 -2 cm chunks
5   Chop mushrooms, then onion.
6   Heat oil / butter in large pan, add
    aubergine and cook 5 minutes until
    soft. Remove from pan.
7   Add onion and crushed garlic to pan.
    Cook 2-3 minutes until soft.
8   Add peppers and courgettes followed
    by mushrooms. Return aubergine to
    pan.
9   Cook over med. heat, stirring
    frequently for approx. 5 minutes.
10 Add chopped tomatoes and herbs
    and simmer, with lid on, for 10-15
    minutes.

Crusty bread and grated cheese make a
good accompaniment or serve as a side
dish.

ROOT VEGETABLE & NUT CRUMBLE

SERVES 6

INGREDIENTS

175g	peeled and seeded butternut squash
175g	peeled carrots
175g	peeled parsnips cut into 2cm chunks
175g	peeled potatoes
175g	peeled swede
25g	butter
2	leeks, cleaned and sliced
50g	plain flour
300ml	vegetable stock
400g	tin chopped tomatoes
	seasoning

CRUMBLE

200g	plain flour
100g	butter
100g	grated cheese
100g	coarsely chopped cashews

METHOD

1   Pre-heat oven to 190°c.
2   Melt butter in a large pan, add root
    vegetables, cover and cook gently for
    10 minutes.
3   Add the leeks and cook for a further
    5 minutes.
4   Stir in the flour and cook for
    2 minutes. Add stock and tomatoes.
    Cover and simmer till the vegetables
    are just tender (about 10 minutes
    more).
5   For the crumble, rub the butter into
    the flour and then stir in the cheese
    and nuts.
6   Spoon the vegetables into a shallow
    ovenproof dish and spoon over the
    topping.
7   Bake in the oven for 30 minutes till
    golden.

Chris Pollard

ALOO PARATHA
(flatbread stuffed with potatoes)

Many children have a very special relationship with their grandmothers (this must have been so 125 years ago also when the school was founded) and this is certainly true of my three children.

My mother was present when they came into the world. She dressed in the same Indian suit for the births which came to be known as the midwife's uniform. She nurtured them in their early years as only grandmothers can and rejoiced when all three of them thankfully gained entry to KEHS or KES. The children delight most in their nannima's cooking, a highlight in every school holiday.

Aloo Parathas (enriched flatbread stuffed with potatoes) are a favourite for all the family. It is traditional food originating from the Punjab state in north India and is relished throughout the world as we Punjabis travel the globe. I would guess that the early 20th Century KEHS cookery book must have had recipes which included potatoes but none quite like this.

125 years ago agricultural productivity was rising and there was an increase in the use of root crops and potatoes. The Victorians even began to compete in potato growing competitions. It was in the 1880's that Mr Walker started making Walker's crisps in nearby Leicester. Apparently there are over 5,000 different varieties of cultivated potatoes in the world (3,000 of which can be found in the Andes). Today, as food prices rise people are returning to the classic staples such as potatoes. 2008 was the United Nations' International Year of the Potato. It was intended that this should bring focus on the importance of the potato in providing food security and alleviating poverty.

Here is the recipe for Aloo Parathas although we always say that the special ingredient is nannima's love which is added in abundance to every meal she cooks for her grandchildren. Also, whilst I am giving an indication of the necessary measurements for the ingredients, nannima just uses her hand or a spoon and neither imperial or metric measurements come into her consideration.

INGREDIENTS

STUFFING

4	large boiled potatoes (aloos)
1	small finely chopped onion
	a handful of coriander leaves finely chopped
1	green chilli finely chopped
½	teaspoon jeera (cumin seeds)
½	teaspoon citric acid or dry mango powder
	salt and red chilli powder to taste

▷

DOUGH

3   cups wheat flour
½   teaspoon ajwain (carom) seeds
    pinch of salt
    enough water to make dough
    (keep dough fairly firm so that it is easier to roll out).
    Also keep a little flour for dusting and some butter
    for pan frying the Parathas.

METHOD

1   Mash the potatoes and add all the stuffing ingredients to the potatoes and mix well.
2   Add salt and jewan seeds to the flour and then add a little water at a time whilst kneading this dough. Knead the dough for about 5 minutes and leave to settle for about 30 minutes.
3   Divide the dough and stuffing (separately) into balls of about equal size.
4   Roll out one ball of dough at a time using a little dry flour to stop any sticking.
5   Put a portion of stuffing on the rolled out dough and encase the stuffing with the dough by closing it in from all sides.
6   Gently put the stuffed dough in the palms and then roll it out gently into a round shape again using some of the dry flour.
7   Cook on a tava (skillet) or frying pan on the cooker hob. Allow both sides to cook until the colour is light brown. Then drizzle a little butter and cook further on each side until ready (rich golden brown).
8   Serve with plain yoghurt.

Aloo Parathas are delicious for breakfast, lunch or dinner and are easy to make.

Enjoy!

Neeraj Sharma (Mother of Kiran and Shivani)

TROPICAL SPICED RICE

INGREDIENTS

25g / 1oz	creamed coconut
225g	can pineapple pieces (in natural juice)
225g / 8oz	long grain or basmati rice or basmati and wild rice
8	spring onions
50g / 2oz	frozen peas (thawed)
25g / 1oz	sultanas
¼	tsp ground turmeric
¼	tsp ground coriander
	salt and pepper
1	tablespoon vegetable oil

METHOD

1. Cut coconut into cubes and put in jug. Pour 600ml/1pt boiling water over and stir to dissolve all pieces.
2. Drain pineapple in sieve over bowl. Save juice.
3. Pour coconut liquid and pineapple juice into large pan, add turmeric + ½tsp salt. Bring pan to boil.
4. Add rice to pan, stir and bring back to boil.
5. Turn heat down, put lid on and simmer for 15 - 20 minutes, stirring occasionally.
6. Wash, top and tail; spring onions. Chop into 2cm/1" pieces.
7. Heat oil in frying pan, add onions and cook for approx. 4 minutes, stirring occasionally. Stir in coriander.
8. When rice is cooked add pineapple, peas, onions, sultanas and pepper. Cook for 1 minute.

Serve

CHEESE BAKE

SERVES 4

INGREDIENTS

2	onions chopped
50g	margarine
50g	rolled oats
150g	grated cheese
2 tsp	yeast extract
2 tsp	mixed herbs
2	eggs, separated
	seasoning

METHOD

1. Pre-heat oven to 190°c.
2. Soften the onion in the margarine and stir in the oats.
3. Mix till well coated.
4. Add cheese, herbs and yeast extract.
5. Stir in beaten egg yolks and season.
6. Fold in stiffly beaten egg whites and spoon into an ovenproof dish.
7. Cook for about 25 minutes until set.
8. Allow to cool in the dish for about 10 minutes.

Serve sliced warm or cold.

Good with roast vegetables or salad.

Chris Pollard

Main Courses

ANNA'S LASAGNE

No recipe book would be complete without lasagne as it seems to be every child's favourite meal. You might think all lasagnes are the same but they are not. When I begged this recipe for lasagne from my friend Anna - who makes the best lasagne I have ever had - it literally changed my life. Now I try to make this regularly and make at least two, one to eat and one to freeze. I always hope for some leftovers because it is even nicer the next day - but there are hardly ever any in our house!

Leftovers can also be frozen in individual portions for a quick lunch. You must try it and see what I mean. It can be made with any type of mince - chicken, turkey, beef and even quorn is still delicious. Go to a proper butcher and ask them to mince the meat for you. It is so much nicer than buying the ready made ones in the supermarket. Anna is an expert caterer and makes large quantities which she freezes and always has at the ready for people who drop in for lunch. If you have enough room in your freezer you can make the meat mixture in bulk, simply buy 5lb of mince and multiply everything by 5, but use only 1 bottle of wine. You will need a really big pan and might need to cook it for a little longer. It freezes really well.

Serves 6 (depending on how much you eat - it can be cut into 8 pieces but usually these get eaten as second helpings!)

INGREDIENTS

1	packet of pre-cooked dry lasagne (you will use about half the packet)
1lb	mince
1	tin plum tomatoes, chopped, in natural juice
2	large onions
5	cloves garlic
2	tablespoons tomato puree
1	dessert spoon of mixed herbs
1	tsp of a nutmeg, freshly grated
2	teaspoons of dried red chilli flakes, if liked
1	500ml tub half-fat crème fraiche
1	tablespoon grated parmesan
50g	grated mozzarella
100 g	grated strong cheddar (or substitute an extra 50g strong cheddar for the mozzarella)
250ml	red wine (only use the cheap cooking type)
2	tablespoons of olive oil
	salt and pepper

ovenproof dish 8" x 12" or equivalent

▷

METHOD

1   Preheat oven on 200°c.

2   Peel onion and garlic and cut into chunks. Place in the food mixer and pulse until it is finely chopped, (not puréed). Warm the olive oil in a large casserole pan. Add the onion and garlic and sauté gently on a medium heat until soft and golden brown and almost caramelized. This step may take quite a long time since the onion will give off a bit of water, but don't be tempted to rush it. It might take up to 30 mins but you can leave it to simmer gently and just give the odd stir.

3   Next add the mince and brown it off too. Continue sautéeing until it is all well browned and coated with the oil and onion mixture. Then add the red wine and let it bubble up for a few seconds, but do not reduce. Then add the tin of tomatoes and mix well, stirring vigorously to ensure you break up any clumps of mince. Add the tomato puree, mixed herbs and chilli flakes if using. Season with salt and pepper. Now, bring the whole thing to the boil, put the lid on and turn down the heat, simmer for 30 minutes, stirring occasionally until you have a thick rich sauce.

4   Meanwhile prepare the crème fraiche. Tip the crème fraiche into a large bowl and beat gently for a moment until smooth. Add salt, pepper and ½ tsp of a grated nutmeg. Mix well.

5   When the meat mixture is ready, spoon half of it into your oven proof dish. Take the lasagne sheets and if you have a dish with slightly rounded corners as most of them are, simply break off a small corner of each lasagne sheet before placing it with the broken off corner next to the corner of your dish. This ensures a better fit in the dish and means that the slices come out evenly. Layer over one layer of lasagne sheets this way. Then, layer over half of the crème fraiche mixture. Repeat the process with the other half of the meat, another layer of lasagne, followed by the crème fraiche.

6   Finally sprinkle over the cheese until you have a good thick layer of grated cheese and bake in the oven for 30 minutes or until golden brown and bubbling.

Maclean Family

BOLOGNAISE SAUCE

INGREDIENTS

250 - 500g	minced beef (or lamb, pork, turkey, quorn)
1	onion
	large tin chopped tomatoes
2-3	tablespoons tomato puree
1	tablespoon vegetable oil

Optional

1-2	cloves garlic
	grated carrot (med - large)
	worcester sauce (½ - 1 tbsp)
	dried herbs (1 tsp)
	chopped mushrooms (50g approx)
	stock cube (any)
	chopped celery (50g approx)
	chopped bacon (100g approx)
½	pepper

METHOD

1 Chop onion finely. Peel and chop / crush garlic (if used). Open tomatoes. Prepare any other ingredients.
2 Heat oil in large saucepan. Add onion and stir over medium heat until partially soft.
3 Add garlic + carrot / mushrooms/ celery/ bacon if used.
4 Add mince, break up and stir thoroughly until browned.
5 Pour chopped tomatoes in and add tomato puree.
6 Add any other ingredients.
7 Bring to the boil slowly, stirring all the time.
8 Turn heat to low, put lid on pan & simmer for 10 – 15 mins stirring occasionally
9 Switch off heat.

CHEESEY LAMB CRUMBLE

INGREDIENTS

90g/3oz	butter / margarine
180g/6oz	plain flour
90g/3oz	grated cheese
1	tsp mixed herbs

480g/1lb	minced lamb (or turkey)
1	medium onion
1	large tin chopped tomatoes
1	stock cube
1	dessertspoon worcester sauce
	herbs
½	level tablespoon cornflour
1	tablespoon oil

METHOD

1 Oven on 180°c / gas 4 –5. Chop onion finely. Cook 2 – 3 mins. in oil
2 Add mince and cook until brown
3 Add tomatoes, worcester sauce, stock cube, herbs and cornflour and simmer five minutes with lid on pan. Stir.
4 Rub butter into flour. Add cheese and herbs.
5 Place meat in ovenproof dish and cover with crumble mix.
6 Bake for 30 – 40 minutes

Serve with a selection of vegetables

BREAKFASTS

In our family breakfast is very important. It really sets you up for the day and we get up early to make and eat a proper breakfast, usually made by our father who is an expert breakfast maker. Eating a good breakfast helps you concentrate all day and stops you wanting to snack at 11 on unhealthy things like chocolate!

Here are some of our favourite breakfasts.

KAISERSHMARM

We first came across this recipe while trekking across the Austrian alps and ate it in a mountain hut high up in the hills on a sunny terrace looking out over a spectacular view of the pass we had just struggled over. It was just what we needed after an 8 hour walk in the baking heat - and is just as good at 7 am on a wet Thursday morning in Birmingham. It is a traditional Austrian recipe and can be made with ready made pancakes, or if you like, you can use home made ones. The original recipe has rum in which can be used if you are making it for a dessert for over 18s. If not, just substitute apple juice for the rum.

SERVES 4

INGREDIENTS

6	ready made thin pancakes (not more than 20cm in diameter)
2	tablespoons dark rum (or apple juice if not using rum)
110g	dried cherries, or raisins
50g	unsalted butter
110g	ready toasted flaked almonds
2	tablespoons icing sugar
1	teaspoon ground cinnamon

METHOD

1   Warm the rum in a small pan then add the dried cherries or raisins and turn off the heat. If using apple juice soak the fruit in it. Leave to soak for 15 mins.

2   Meanwhile stack the pancakes and using a sharp knife cut them all up into strips lengthways and then across so you end up with small squares.

3   Next, pre heat the grill to its hottest setting.

4   Now melt the butter in a large frying pan and when it starts to foam add the pieces of pancake and the cherry or raisin mixture, followed by the almonds.

5   Cook over a medium heat for 3-4 minutes, tossing and turning the mixture until it is hot and golden.

6   Then sift the icing sugar and cinnamon over the top.

7   Place under the grill for a few minutes until the sugar starts to caramelize and serve immediately. You can pour cream or ice cream over if you like.

Maclean Family

BREAKFAST TORTILLAS

This is a great and very easy recipe. Tortillas keep for ages in the breadbox and can be used for many different meals. Lots and lots of filling can be used; find your favourite!

SERVES 6

INGREDIENTS

3   ready made wholegrain tortillas
sweet chilli sauce from a bottle
parma ham or other good quality thin cut ham
a few basil leaves
a few thinly sliced pieces of strong mature cheddar

METHOD

1 Start by warming a large non stick frying pan over a medium heat.
2 Place one tortilla in the pan and arrange the cheese over it. Tear over the parma ham and basil leaves and then drizzle over some sweet chilli sauce.
3 Top with the next tortilla. Then carefully turn the whole thing over and repeat with another layer of ham, basil and cheese and another tortilla.
4 Cook for a further minute or so, pressing down gently with your spatula until the cheese is melting and oozing and the underside is crisp and brown.
5 Turn over the sandwich carefully and cook the other side for a minute or so.
6 Turn out onto a plate and slice into six wedges.

Maclean Family

BREAKFAST TOMATOES

This is a very easy way to have breakfast ready as soon as you come down in the morning without any fuss. Simply put the tomatoes in the oven the night before on a low heat. When you get them out they will be soft and richly flavoured and perfect with crisp buttered toast and crispy bacon or sausages

SERVES 6

INGREDIENTS

6   large tomatoes
olive oil - approx 2 tablespoons
dried red chilli flakes (to taste)
grated parmesan cheese
mixed herbs
salt and pepper

METHOD

1 Cut the top off each tomato and make a small hollow in the top. Place in an ovenproof dish which is just large enough for the tomatoes to stand snugly in altogether. Drizzle over the olive oil and sprinkle over the chilli to taste, plus the herbs.
2 Season with salt and pepper.
3 Place in the oven at 120ºc and cook for approx 8 hours.
4 In the morning, sprinkle over some parmesan cheese and put the whole dish under a preheated grill for 5 minutes until the cheese is golden.
5 Toast some slices of wholemeal bread until brown and crispy, then give each person a slice of toast topped with a tomato.

Maclean Family

CHICKEN AND MUSHROOM CURRY

INGREDIENTS

2	onions (chopped)
	small can chopped tomatoes
	olive oil
2	tsp cumin seeds
2	chillies (green)
2	tsp turmeric powder
	mushrooms (cleaned)
	double cream
2	tsp garam masala
4	tsp curry powder
4	tsp paprika
2	tsp salt
3-4	chicken breasts (diced)
	table spoon of ginger
	a clove of garlic (crushed)

METHOD

1 Add cumin to heated oil
2 Add chopped onions, chillies, ginger and garlic and fry until brown. Add tin tomatoes and cook for a further 5 minutes.
3 Using a hand blender, blend into a smooth paste (the smoother the paste the smoother the curry)
4. Add all the spices and salt.
5 Leave for 5-10 minutes cooking on low heat until the oil comes out of the masala.
6 Add 50-100ml of double cream and mix.
7 Add diced chicken and a chopped mushrooms to masala.
8 Cook meat thoroughly on a low to medium heat for about 30-45 minutes.
9 Add hot water (100ml at a time) to create a sauce if need be.
10 Cook for a further 20-30 minutes

Add coriander leaves and serve.

Susan Bhagi

CHICKEN AND MUSHROOM PASTA

INGREDIENTS

250g/8oz	pasta e.g. penne, spiralli
175g/6oz	mushrooms (washed)
1	onion
½	pepper (optional)
1 or 2	garlic cloves
2	chicken breasts
400ml / ¾pt	milk
30g/1oz	plain flour
30g/1oz	butter
180g/6oz	mature cheddar, grated

METHOD

1 Cook pasta in boiling water 8 - 10 minutes. Drain well and replace lid
2 Cut chicken into thin strips, put on plate and clean board.
3 Chop onion and slice mushrooms and pepper (if using)
4 Heat oil in wok or large pan. Add chicken, onion , pepper and crushed garlic. Stir fry for 3 -4 minutes. Remove from pan and set aside.
5 Cook mushrooms in same pan and add to chicken
6 Add butter to pan, melt and add flour to form a roux.
7 Take off heat and gradually add milk. Return to heat and stir until thickened
8 Take off heat and stir in ½ the cheese. Season well
9 Preheat grill. Mix chicken mixture into sauce, add pasta and heat for 1 - 2 minutes, stirring well.
10 Transfer to ovenproof dish, sprinkle with remaining cheese and grill until golden brown.

CHICKEN DIVAN

Quick & Easy

INGREDIENTS

1	medium cooked chicken
250gm	broccoli
1 x 295gm	tin condensed cream of chicken soup
1 x 200ml	tub of half fat crème fraiche
3	heaped tbsp mayonnaise
2	teaspoons lemon juice
1	heaped teaspoon curry powder
110gm	fresh breadcrumbs
50gm	butter
50gm	grated mature cheddar cheese shallow, oven-proof baking dish, lightly greased

METHOD

1 Oven at gas 3, 180°c, 160°c fan oven.
1 Trim broccoli, separate into florets and cook for 2 minutes.; drain
2 Cut cooked chicken into bite-sized pieces
3 Mix soup, crème fraiche, mayonnaise, curry powder and lemon juice; season with black pepper
4 Melt butter, stir in breadcrumbs
5 Mix chicken with sauce, place in dish
6 Top with breadcrumbs, then grated cheese
7 Bake for 40 minutes.

Serve with green salad

Jenny Kerridge

CHICKEN STIR FRY

INGREDIENTS

1	boneless chicken breast
1	onion – red or white
1	pepper
1	carrot
50g	mushrooms
50g	bean sprouts
50g	sweetcorn / baby corn
	optional:
	small tin pineapple pieces
	1 courgette
50g	water chestnuts
50g	bamboo shoots
50g	baby corn
	mange tout
1	tablespoon oil

STIR FRY SAUCE

1	tsp cornflour
1	stock cube
1	tablespoon soy sauce
½	tsp 5 spice powder/ paste
50 - 75ml water	

METHOD

1 Mix sauce. Mix soy sauce and cornflour, blend smoothly. Add stock cube + 5 spice and water
2 Cut chicken into thin strips.
3 Slice onion. De-seed and slice pepper thinly. Grate carrot
4 Slice mushrooms. Trim and slice courgettes.
   Prepare all other vegetables*
5 Put oil in wok / large pan. Heat and immediately add chicken. Cook on medium heat, stirring with wooden spoon.
6 Add all other ingredients EXCEPT pineapple, if used
7 Cook 10 -12 minutes, stirring frequently.
8 Add pineapple.
9 Stir in sauce and mix well. Cook for a further 1-2 minutes then turn off heat.

Serve with rice or noodles

CEVICHE DE CAMARONES (ECUADOR)
(MARINATED SHRIMPS IN LIME SAUCE)

Una de mis recetas favoritas ya que no hay mucho que cocinar.

PARA 4 personas

INGREDIENTES

1	libra de camarones grandes
2	tomates pequenos
2	aji jalapeno
2	limas
2	naranjas
1	cebolla
	sal
	pimenta
	taza de culantro picado

Optional

1 aguacate Cangil
*chifles

PREPARACION

1   Cortar la cebolla por la mitad y rebanarlas a la juliana muy finamente. Poner sal y refrejar las cebollas, luego enjaguarlas en agua fria, escurrir el agua y ponerlas en el 1 jugo de una lima. Dejarlas reposar mientras se preparan los otros ingredientes.
2   Poner los camarones en agua hirviendo por 2-3 minutos guardar un poco de agua.
3   Sacar el jugo de la lima y las naranjas.
4   Pelar los tomates y cortarlos en trocitos pequenos
5   Cortar el aji, descartar las semillas y cortar el resto muy finamente
6   Cortar el culantro muy finno
Poner todos los ingredientes juntos y sasonar con sal, pimienta, aceite y salsa de tomate.

Servir en pozuelos pequenos con aguacate, canguil o chifles*

Marcia Atkins

CEVICHE DE CAMARONES (ECUADOR)
(MARINATED PRAWNS IN LIME SAUCE)

One of my favourite recipes as it requires very little cooking.

SERVES 4

INGREDIENTS

1 lb/450g large prawns	
2	tomatoes
2	jalapeno chillies
	juice of 2 limes
	juice of 2 oranges
1	onion
	salt and pepper
	fresh coriander
	tomato ketchup

PREPARATION

1   Slice the onion finely. Sprinkle with salt and rub the salt into the onion. Rinse in cold water, then drain. Place the onions in the lime juice, and leave while preparing other ingredients.
2   Cook the prawns in boiling water for 2-3 minutes. Remove from the water, retaining a little of the water for later use.
3   Skin the tomatoes and cut into small chunks.
4   Cut the chillies, discarding all seeds and white stuff from inside. Slice the chillies very finely.
5   Chop the coriander finely.
6   Put together all the ingredients, including a little of the retained prawn water.
7   Season with salt and pepper. Add a little oil and a tablespoonful of tomato ketchup.

Serve at room temperature in small bowls with avocado, salted popcorn or chifles (green plantain thinly sliced and fried).

Marcia Atkins

EVERYDAY ROAST MEAL

Many people find the timing and organisation of a traditional 'roast meal' a challenge. This recipe allows a little practice.

INGREDIENTS

Choose from: 1 chop – lamb / pork
              1 chicken piece – MUST
              contain the bone
              eg chicken quarter

1 large or 3 – 4 small potatoes

FRESH vegetables:

	1	carrot
2 from	50g	broccoli
	50g	green beans
	50g	cauliflower

1tbsp   bisto granules
½tbsp   vegetable oil

METHOD

1 Oven on 200ºc / gas 6.
2 Put ⅓ pan water to boil. Put meat in small roasting tin with oil. Place in oven.
3 Wash, peel, scrape potatoes. Chop medium size.
4 Either – Add to roasting tin OR put in pan of boiling water and boil on medium.
5 Wash, peel, chop vegetables as necessary.
6 Warm plate. Prepare table.
7 Add vegetables. to pan
8 Put meat (and roast potatoes) on plate. Keep warm (inside of small oven)
9 Put roasting tin on hob. Carefully drain vegetable water into jug. Pour approx. 200ml vegetables water into roasting tin, stir in bisto and bring to boil stirring with wooden spoon.
10 Switch off cooker.
11 Pour gravy into jug.
    Serve meal.

FISH CAKES

INGREDIENTS

200 - 400g	white fish (cod, haddock, coley - fresh or frozen)
500 - 700g	floury potatoes
25g	butter (optional)
10g	flat leaf / curly parsley, chopped (or I tsp dried)
	salt and pepper
	small chopped onion (optional)
1	egg

COATING

3 - 4tbsp	fine breadcrumbs
1 egg	beaten, in small bowl.
2-3tbsp	oil

METHOD

1 Peel, quarter and place potatoes in pan, cover with cold water and bring to boil.
2 Place washed fish on metal plate above pan, cover with pan lid or another plate. Simmer until fish flakes and has set.
3 Remove fish & plate, leave to cool slightly. (Sauté onion lightly in oil or butter for 2-3 minutes.)
4 Cook potatoes until soft, drain and mash. Add butter, if used, egg , salt and pepper, chopped onion and parsley to potato. Mix well.
5 Flake fish and mash slightly. Stir into potato mixture. Shape mixture into even-sized cakes. Ideally, cover and put in fridge for 1 hour.
6 Dip in egg and then onto plate of breadcrumbs.
7 Heat oil in frying pan, put fishcakes in pan, fry gently 3-4 minutes each side until golden brown.
8 Remove from pan and drain on kitchen paper and put on a warm plate.

FISH IN CHEESE & MUSHROOM SAUCE

INGREDIENTS

250g	white fish (cod, haddock coley etc.)
	small packet instant potato
100-150g	mushrooms
15g	butter/marg.
1	tomato

SAUCE

250ml/½ pt milk	
25g	plain flour
25g	butter / marg.
125g	cheese
	salt & pepper
	parsley (optional)

Medium ovenproof dish

METHOD

1   Wash and skin fish (if necessary). Place between 2 plates and steam over pan simmering water approx. 15 minutes until just firm
2   Make up instant potato. Grate cheese. Wash & slice mushrooms and cook in 15g butter until soft. Remove from pan
3   Put all sauce ingredients in a pan and bring slowly to boil, gently whisking with small whisk, until mixture thickens
4   Remove from heat, stir in ¾ cheese, mushrooms and seasoning
5   Flake fish gently and stir carefully into sauce, Pour into dish
6   Sprinkle remaining cheese on top, garnish with sliced tomato.
7   Pipe potato round edge of dish.
8   Flash under grill and add sprig of parsley

Serve

FLORIDA CHICKEN CASSEROLE

INGREDIENTS

	chicken breasts
1 lb/459g	onions
2tsps	paprika in 1 oz flour for dipping chicken into
2 oz/60g	margarine
	grated rind and juice of one large orange
	orange juice
½	pint of stock
	pineapple (tinned or fresh)
	salt and freshly ground black pepper

METHOD

1   In a heavy based casserole dish melt margarine and add onions to brown.
2   Coat diced chicken breasts in flour and paprika mixture and add salt and pepper.
3   Remove onions from pan and add diced chicken. Cook for ten minute until sealed.
4   Return onions to casserole dish and add orange juice and grated rind, stock and orange juice and flesh of two oranges.
5   Season to taste.
6   Cook for further half hour until tender.

Serve with slices of fresh orange on top and sprinkle with parsley. Goes well with Traidcraft brown rice.

Liz Cummings

KHORESHTE KARAFS
(CELERY STEW)

SERVES 4

INGREDIENTS

½kg	lamb or beef
2	bunches celery
1	bunch fresh mint
1	bunch fresh parsley
3	medium onions
1	cup fresh lime juice
2	tablespoons sugar
¼	cup cooking oil
½	teaspoon salt
1	teaspoon turmeric
	black pepper

METHOD

1 Fry the thinly sliced onions in oil until slightly golden.
2 Cut the meat and fry in onions with ½tsp turmeric and ½tsp black pepper until colour changes.
   Add 2-3 glasses of hot water and bring to boil.
3 Cook over medium heat for about 45 or more minutes, adding more hot water during cooking if needed.
4 Wash celery and cut into 3 cm pieces.
5 Finely chop mint and parsley and fry slightly in oil.
6 Add celery, mint, parsley, salt to the meat and continue cooking for about 20 minutes (celery should not become too soft).
7 Add lime juice and sugar to taste and cook for another 3-4 minutes. Taste the juice and adjust to your taste.

Serve with plain rice.

Donya Ghorbani

MAGRETS DE CANARD AU POIVRE VERT
(DUCK BREASTS WITH GREEN PEPPERCORNS)

1 Grillez sans couper la peau "au début". Ensuite fendre sur côté peau seulement en croisillons. Faire cuire sur feu pas trop fort. Servir pas trop cuit.

Sauce poivre vert

2 Base Béchamel (beurre, farine, eau): faire bouillir.
3 Ensuite colorer avec arôme. Saler, poivrer avec poivre vert (une bonne cuillerée à café bien pleine).
4 Au dernier moment 2 bonnes cuillerées de crème fraîche.

Servir chaud.

1 Grill the breasts intact to start with. Then cut into the skin-side only in a criss-cross pattern. Cook at not too high a temperature. Serve lightly done.

GREEN PEPPERCORN SAUCE

2 Basic Béchamel sauce: butter, flour, water (bring to the boil)
3 Then add arome flavouring. Add salt and a heaped teaspoonful of green peppercorns.
4 At the last minute add 2 good spoonfuls of crème fraîche.

Serve hot.

Adèle Lerouge's grandmère

CHICKEN, MUSHROOM AND BACON RISOTTO

INGREDIENTS

1	tbsp olive oil
3	shallots or 1 medium onion
1	chicken breast
4	rashers bacon
240g/8oz	mushrooms - washed
1	red pepper
	(other colour if preferred)
240g/8oz	long grain rice / risotto rice
1 - 2	chicken stock cubes
2	tbsp tomato purée
1	tsp dried marjoram
1	tsp mixed herbs

METHOD

1   Chop bacon and dice chicken.
2   Finely chop shallots and slice mushrooms. De-seed and chop pepper.
3   Cook meat and onions in the oil for a few minutes until lightly browned
4   Add mushrooms and pepper and cook a further 5 minutes, stirring frequently.
5   Stir in rice . Make up stock with approx. 1½ pt/750ml water
6   Add ¾ of this stock and all remaining ingredients. Stir well and bring to boil
7   Lower heat and simmer gently 20 - 25 minutes or until rice is tender and has absorbed liquid. Add remaining stock as necessary.

RECIPE FOR ALL ...
BUT PARTICULARLY FOR THOSE WHO ARE AWAY FROM HOME WITH LIMITED EQUIPMENT

UTENSILS NEEDED

a tin opener
a wooden spoon
a frying pan or saucepan

All these recipes can be spread over a bed of pasta or rice. Use pasta of your choice, and long grain rice.

Cook according to the instructions on the packets.

Quantities given are for one person and should be multiplied up for the number of people being catered for.

INGREDIENTS

4oz/120g minced beef or lamb,

I	large onion.
2	tomatoes with skin taken off, or (just remove skins from mixture when cooked)
I	large mushroom, or 2 small. Salt and pepper to taste. A dash of mixed herbs. half a crushed garlic clove

METHOD

1   Chop all the ingredients up into small pieces and fry in a small amount of olive oil.
2   Add half a pint of chicken stock (made with boiling water and a chicken stock cube) and simmer until the meat is cooked.

Alternatively, diced chicken, or prawns, can be substituted for the minced beef or lamb. Also substitute jar of 'cook in sauce" for the chicken stock, and a green or red pepper may be added to the mixture.

OE Magazine

PORK THE JAVA WAY

I still have my cookery exercise book with information on stewing and steaming etc and recipes for macaroni cheese, scones, stuffed herring, meat rolls and other tasty dishes.

I remember with great enjoyment my cookery lessons with Mrs Hopkins, sadly curtailed by rationing during the war. If you ask my family about my cooking I am sure the thing they would all say is McGowan Specials--born of necessity and developed into a skill for using up the most unlikely combinations of ingredients left over in the fridge. We have had the most exciting dishes never to be repeated because we never had the same leftovers together again. (We've also had a few we should never wish to repeat!)

I should like to offer the following recipe:

INGREDIENTS

4	pork steaks
2	onions
	celery
	curry powder
	butter
	a little orange peel
1	cup stock
½	cup milk
	juices/2 lemon
	cream

METHOD

1 Brown pork steaks lightly on both sides by frying them in butter. Salt and put on one side in a saucepan while you brown onions, celery and orange peel chopped very finely.

2 When these are golden mix in a soup - spoonful of flour and then, stirring all the time, add a cupful of stock to which you have added a cofee - spoonful of curry powder.

3 Add milk. Pour mixture on to pork and simmer not less than ½ hour and not more than 1 hour

4 Lastly stir in lemon juice and 2 tbsp cream.

OE Ann Wright

ONE-PAN CHICKEN DINNER

A super recipe which uses any Mediterranean vegetables and has a great herby flavour. I have used any vegetables according to the season — carrots, swede and parsnip in the winter months. If it needs stretching to feed extra mouths serve with crusty bread and steamed vegetables. I remove the skin from the chicken pieces to reduce the fat content.

INGREDIENTS

500g	old waxy potatoes - cut into 2cm chunks
1	red onion - cut into wedges
1	aubergine - sliced into l cm slices
5	unpeeled garlic cloves
	chicken thighs or drumsticks - 2 each depending upon appetite
1	tbsp balsamic vinegar
2	tbsp olive oil
150ml	hot stock - vegetable or chicken
	a few basil leaves to garnish

METHOD

1 Parboil potatoes for 5 minutes. Drain well

2 Preheat oven to 200°c/gas 6

3 Arrange vegetables in large roasting tin and add unpeeled garlic cloves

4 Tuck chicken around the vegetables.

5 Add seasoning

6 Mix vinegar, oil and stock in a jug. Pour over the chicken and vegetables

7 Roast for l hr - 1 hr 10 minutes, basting once or twice with the cooking juices

8 When cooked sprinkle with basil and serve.

Sue Ralph
(Laura Ralph)

ORANGE AND BASIL CHICKEN

INGREDIENTS

125g/4oz marmalade
        juice of 2 oranges
        juice of 2 lemons
3tbsp   freshly chopped basil
        salt and freshly ground black
        pepper
8   skinless, boneless chicken
        breasts

METHOD

1   Preheat oven to Gas Mark 6/200°c (fan ovens 180°c)
2   Blend the marmalade with the orange and lemon juices, basil and seasoning and pour over the chicken breasts in an oven proof dish.
3   Place the dish in the oven and cook for 20 minutes, basting the chicken with the sauce half way through.
4   Serve on warmed plates with new potatoes, green beans and carrots for a quick and easy dinner party dish.

OE Annette Duffy

PASTA WITH PINE NUTS

This is a quick and tasty number. It originates from the need for a high carbohydrate diet that has ingredients readily available in the cupboard or fridge.

As an ex - international hockey player we used to consume many pasta dishes in between training sessions.

INGREDIENTS

Pasta -   as much as required for number of people

Pesto sauce - a jar is fine, quick and easy (although you can make your own)

Smoked bacon - streaky is best, but any bacon would be fine even unsmoked.

Pine nuts

Now as far as quantities are concerned it's up to you!

Basic guidelines are:

enough pesto to coat the pasta. Yum! (a table spoon per person),

at least three strips of (streaky) bacon per person, cut up into small bite - size pieces and dry fried.

A handful of pine nuts per person.

Dry fry these off in the frying pan at the end until they're golden brown, (about 2 minutes).

Bang it all in the drained pasta pan, mix up and serve.

Lovely jubbly!

Ready in about 10 -12 mins

Sarah Blanks

PERSIAN CHICKEN BREASTS

INGREDIENTS

4	large boneless skinless chicken breasts
1	lemon, juice of
4	seedless oranges
½	teaspoon salt
½	teaspoon pepper
¼	teaspoon turmeric
½	cup onion, chopped
5	tablespoons butter, divided
¼	cup vinegar
6	tablespoons sugar

METHOD

1. Cut chicken into 1" cubes.
2. Marinate chicken in lemon juice for 1 hour.
3. Peel short, very thin strips of orange zest with a vegetable peeler, set aside.
4. Peel the oranges, remove as much of the white pith as possible, divide into sections.
5. Put orange sections, salt, pepper and turmeric in a saucepan.
6. Sauté onions in 1 tbsp. butter until browned (about 10 minutes).
7. Add orange peel to onions, cook, stirring, about 1-2 minutes.
8. Add onion mixture to saucepan with orange sections.
9. Add vinegar and sugar, cook 15 minutes stirring gently so orange sections remain intact.
10. Remove chicken from marinade, sauté in remaining butter until browned.
11. To serve: place chicken pieces on plate and spoon orange mixture on top.

Donya Ghorbani

POCO DE GALLO & MEXICAN PRAWN SALAD

POCO DE GALLO

This Mexican dish is the base for many recipes. A Mexican friend taught me to make it as a way of improving her English conversation.

INGREDIENTS

2	fresh tomatoes
½	onion
	fresh coriander
1	chilli (optional)
	lemon juice or lime juice

METHOD

Dice the tomatoes and onion (and chilli) very finely. Tear some coriander leaves into pieces. Mix together with a sprinkling of lemon or lime juice.

MEXICAN PRAWN SALAD

2	fresh tomatoes
½	onion
	fresh coriander
	1 chilli (optional)
	lemon juice or lime juice
½	a cup approx ready –to-eat prawns ketchup (Heinz)
½	avocado (diced)

METHOD

The Mexican version involves mixing all the above ingredients. I am not a great lover of ketchup (although it appears to be a staple for many Mexicans) and so I leave it out. Instead, sprinkle more lime juice over the avocado before adding it to stop it turning brown.

These dishes are both very popular for buffets etc.

Stephanie Hayton

PRAWN AND PEPPER PILAFF

INGREDIENTS

200g/7oz	peeled prawns
1	medium onion
1	clove garlic
1	red or yellow pepper
2	tablespoons oil
15g/½oz	butter
1	teaspoon mild curry powder
200g/7oz	basmati or long grain rice
50g/2oz	creamed coconut
100g/4oz	peas
1	teaspoon salt
	black pepper
400ml	water

METHOD

1. Spread prawns out on plate, if frozen. Drain.
2. Dice onion. Peel garlic. De-seed pepper and slice finely, cut into small pieces. Cut coconut into chunks.
3. Heat oil and butter in large pan, add vegetables, including crushed garlic and cook medium heat approx. 7 minutes.
4. Stir in curry powder rice, coconut and water and salt.
5. Bring to boil and simmer, covered 10 minutes
6. Remove lid, stir in prawns and peas, cook for further 2 - 3 minutes.
7. Remove from heat, stir well and serve.

QUICHE LORRAINE

INGREDIENTS

SHORTCRUST PASTRY

150g/6oz	plain flour
75g/3 oz	butter/margarine
6-8 tsp	cold water

OR

½ pkt	ready-made shortcrust pastry

FILLING

2	eggs , large
200ml / ⅓pt	milk *
50 - 100g	cheddar cheese
1	small/ medium onion
2	rashers bacon
1	tomato

20-22cm / 8-9" flan dish

OPTIONAL VARIATIONS

- Omit bacon. Add canned tuna or salmon; cooked, flaked salmon; chopped cooked asparagus
- Sweetcorn, broccoli, mixed vegetables (all canned or cooked)
- Try goats cheese, sliced red pepper etc.

METHOD

1. Oven 190°c/ gas 5. Lightly grease flan dish.
2. Prepare shortcrust pastry. Rub fat into flour until like breadcrumbs. Add enough cold water until it binds together.
3. Roll out and line flan dish. Bake 'blind' (10 – 15 minutes) with greaseproof and rice / 'baking beans' or similar.
4. Chop onion , cut up bacon, slice mushrooms, grate cheese.
5. Remove pastry from oven. Add bacon etc. and cheese to flan.
6. Beat eggs , add milk and pour over pastry base.
7. Slice tomato and place over top.
8. Bake approx. 20 minutes until firm.

Serve hot or cold

* NB If using a smaller flan dish reduce milk to 125ml + 1 rasher bacon

QUICK PIZZA

INGREDIENTS

BASE

240g/8oz	strong plain flour (bread flour)
1	sachet easy blend yeast
½	teaspoon salt
125ml	approx warm water

TOPPING

100 - 150g/4 - 6oz	grated cheese or sliced mozzarella
¼	jar pizza topping fresh or dried herbs

PLUS own choice of additional toppings, e.g:

50g/2oz	chopped ham / chicken / tuna
1 - 2	sliced tomatoes (washed)
30g/1oz	sliced mushrooms
30g/1oz	sweetcorn

METHOD

Oven on 200ºc / Gas 6. Line baking sheet.

1 Mix flour, salt, yeast and olive oil and then add enough warm water to form an easy dough.
2 Knead on lightly floured surface for 5 minutes.
3 Shape and roll dough. Lift onto baking sheet and pinch edges to form small wall.
4 Spread pizza topping evenly over surface, leaving 1 cm margin.
5 Arrange other ingredients evenly and sprinkle with herbs, if liked.
6 Bake for approx. 15-20 minutes until golden brown and risen.
7 Lift carefully from baking sheet.

Alternatively – make individual pizzas

SAUSAGE & BACON TOAD-IN-THE-HOLE

SERVES 8

INGREDIENTS

16	good quality pork sausages
8	rashers unsmoked back bacon
4	tablespoons cooking oil

For the batter:

12oz	plain flour
4	eggs
12fl oz	semi-skimmed milk
8fl oz	water
	salt & milled black pepper

METHOD

1 Begin by making the batter, and, to do this, sieve the flour into a large bowl, holding the sieve up high to give the flour a good airing.
2 Now with the back of a spoon make a well in the centre, break the eggs into it and add some salt and pepper.
3 Measure the milk and water. Then, using an electric hand whisk on a slow speed, begin to whisk the eggs into the flour. As you whisk the flour around, the edges will slowly be incorporated.
4 Then add the liquid gradually, stopping to scrape the flour into the mixture. Whisk till the batter is smooth.
5 Divide the sausages into twos and wrap each pair with a rasher of bacon. Arrange sausages in a roasting tin and place in the oven for 10 mins at 150º.
6 Remove from oven and place tin over direct heat. Add the oil and, when the oil starts to shimmer, add the batter, making sure the sausages are coated.
7 Place in the oven on 180ºc for 25-30 minutes. When the toad is ready, it should be puffed brown and crisp and the centre should look cooked and not too squidgy.

Serve with onion gravy and creamed mashed potato.

School Kitchen

SAUSAGE CASSEROLE

INGREDIENTS

1	tbsp oil
8	sausages
1	onion peeled and chopped
2	carrots, peeled and chopped
2	rashers bacon
1	tbsp plain flour
2	tbsp Worcester sauce
2	tbsp tomato puree
1	pint stock (beef or chicken stock cube)
1	tin mixed beans / or baked beans

METHOD

1 Turn on oven - 190ºc/Gas 5
2 Heat oil in a large pan, fry sausage over a medium heat until brown, transfer to a casserole dish
3 Add the onion, carrot and bacon to the pan and cook gently over medium heat for about 5 mins
4 Stir in the flour, then add the Worcester Sauce, tomato puree, stock and beans. Stir thoroughly and bring to the boil.
5 Pour over the sausages, cover and cook in the oven for 30 mins. (Transfer to casserole dish, if necessary)
6 Remove the lid and cook for a further 15 mins.

SAUSAGE, ONION AND TOMATO PLAIT

INGREDIENTS

1	pack flaky/puff pastry (approx. 425g)

FILLING

450g/1lb	sausagemeat
1	teaspoon mixed herbs
1	small to medium onion
2	medium tomatoes
	salt & pepper
1	egg

VEGETARIAN ALTERNATIVE

250g +	cheese (eg mature cheddar)
1	onion
3	medium tomatoes
1	teaspoon mixed herbs
1	egg

METHOD

1 Oven 200°c / Gas 6. Line baking tray with silicone paper. Break egg into small bowl and mix with fork.
2 Prepare filling. Put sausagemeat in large bowl. Chop onion finely and add to sausagemeat. (For Vegetarian Plait grate cheese and continue)
3 Add herbs and salt and pepper
4 Slice tomatoes thinly on the board
5 Roll pastry on floured surface to rectangle approx 30cm x 20cm
6 Fold into 1/3rds and open out again
7 Place filling down middle section.
8 Cut diagonal 2.5cm (approx) strips each side of filling. Damp ends of strips
9 Take each strip separately and lay across each side.
10 Tuck in ends and neaten. Glaze thoroughly with beaten egg.
11 Place on baking sheet & bake 25 - 30 minutes.

Serve hot or cold. Alternatively - make 2 smaller plaits or other shapes.

SOUR CREAM CHICKEN ENCHILADAS

This is an adaptation of Paula Jackson's recipe in 'The Kitchen Window' (a collection of recipes from the Parents' Association of The Hockaday School, Dallas, Texas).

I organised the first KEHS cultural exchange with The Hockaday School in 1993 and we had three exchange visits with the school during the 1990s. We had a wonderful time visiting Dallas, Fort Worth, Austen and San Antonio. The concert hall in Dallas was designed by the same architects as designed Symphony Hall in Birmingham and it looks almost identical, so we felt quite at home in some respects, but the culture was very different - it might have been the Stetsons and gun holsters that unnerved me!

The Tex Mex cuisine was an instant winner with the whole family and we have continued to prepare the following on a regular basis – usually on a Friday evening. I would serve this either on its own, or alongside chilli and rice with guacamole, sour cream and salsa as accompaniments (and a good bottled beer with lime wedges for authenticity). Whilst the enchiladas are bubbling in the oven, dip into some nachos with home made salsa or sour cream and, if you're over18 and haven't got school the next day, I'd recommend a margherita - lime juice, tequila, triple sec and crushed ice (use Cointreau if you can't find triple sec).

INGREDIENTS

4	boneless chicken breasts cooked and cut into pieces
200ml	sour cream
1	can mushroom soup
1/3	jar jalapeno chillies (chopped)
8	chopped black olives (optional)
1	onion chopped and sautéed
125g	matured cheddar cheese (grated)
½	tsp ground cumin (or more)
	salt and pepper
8	flour tortillas

METHOD

1   Mix sour cream, soup, chillies, onion, seasonings.
2   Fill each tortilla with chicken, a little sauce and a sprinkling of cheese and then roll.
3   Place rolled tortillas in a greased baking dish.
4   Cover with remaining sauce, cheese and olives (if desired)
5   Bake uncovered for 30 minutes at 180ºc until bubbling and browned on top.

This will serve 4 as a main course or more if you are serving chilli as well. It keeps warm without ruining, can be prepared in advance and can be frozen and re-heated!

Alison Warne

TORTSFI
REGIONAL DUMPLINGS (POLISH)

100g = 180 kcal

INGREDIENTS

Dough

350g	flour
	an egg
	salt
	cup water

Filling

700g	potatoes
300g	ewe's cheese or `twarog' (tva-rog)
2	fairly small onions
	salt
	ground black pepper
50g	lard or smoked bacon

METHOD

1 Peel and cook the potatoes and, along with the onions, put in the food processor.
Once the mixture has cooled down, mix thoroughly with the ewe's cheese.
(In Polish shops, you can buy white cheese called twarog *(tva-rog)* and twarog is the
best for these dumplings.)
2 Season with salt and pepper.
3 Fold the egg into the flour, add a pinch of salt and the water, knead the dough
until soft and then flatten using a rolling pin.
4 From the dough, cut circles of about 5cm in diameter - you can use a glass,
cup or round biscuit cutter if you wish.
5 Put the filling on each circle, then fold the dough in half and - using your fingers - press
down the edges making sure the filling is not caught in them, or the dumpling will split
whilst being cooked.
6 Put the dumplings into boiling, slightly salted water and cook until they rise to the
surface adding two minutes to be sure they're ready.
7 When they float to the top take them out of the water using a strainer, drain
them and put them in a bowl.
8 Pour melted lard on top or sprinkle smoked bacon over your dumplings.

Czepiel family

VENISON CASSEROLE

INGREDIENTS

500 - 600g	venison (cubed)
1	onion
2	cloves garlic
1	tbsp olive oil
60g	plain flour
250ml	red wine
	bay leaf
3	tbsps dried cranberries
	small handful juniper berries
2	allspice berries
1tbsp	sweet paprika (not regular paprika)
	salt
	black pepper

METHOD

1 Oven 120°c / gas 1-2
2 Mix flour, paprika, salt and pepper in bowl and add cubed venison.
   Mix thoroughly and remove meat.
3 Pour oil in large casserole-type pan (ovenproof), heat and add meat , chopped onion
   and crushed garlic.
4 Brown for 5 minutes, pour in wine and add all other ingredients.
5 Stir thoroughly and bring slowly to the boil
6 Stir well, put lid on pan and transfer to the middle of the oven and cook for
   approximately 2½ hours until venison is tender.
7. Check periodically and add some water if it is a little dry.

Serve with crusty bread and green salad

Heather Neal

Puddings and Desserts

APPLE BAR CAKE

This is a variation of Dutch Apple Cake and is very easy and versatile. Other fruits and flavourings work well. Very popular with the Sixth Form!

INGREDIENTS

120g/4oz	soft margarine
120g/4oz	caster sugar
120g/4oz	self raising flour
2	eggs
1 - 2	medium cooking apples
60g	brown sugar
1	teaspoon ground cinnamon
	handful of raisins - optional
	grated lemon rind - optional

METHOD

1   Oven on 180°c/ Gas 4-5. Grease a tin 18cm/7" round or small swiss roll tin or equivalent. Line with greaseproof if non-stick.
2   Peel, core and thinly slice apples. Lay in bottom of tin & sprinkle with brown sugar and cinnamon.
3.   Beat eggs. Put margarine, sugar, flour and eggs in mixing bowl and beat with wooden spoon for 2 - 3 minutes until combined. (alternatively, use an electric whisk)
4.   Spread cake mixture on top of apples and bake 20 - 25 minutes until risen and golden brown.
     NB A wider tin will bake the cake more quickly.
5.   Leave in tin to cool. Cut into squares.

This cake is delicious hot or cold.

APPLE AND LEMON LAYER PUDDING

SERVES 3

INGREDIENTS

60g/2oz	margarine / butter
1	lemon
150g/5oz	caster sugar
2	eggs
60g/2oz	self raising flour
275ml/½	pint milk
480g/1lb	cooking apples

METHOD

1   Beat margarine and lemon rind.
2   Stir in 120g/4oz sugar then egg yolks and flour
3   Beat well, then stir in milk and lemon juice (it will look curdled!)
4   Slice apples into a deep dish, sprinkle with the rest of the sugar.
5   Whisk egg whites and fold into mixture, pour over apples and bake at Gas 5/190°c for approx 40 minutes.

(It produces a spongy top layer and a tangy sauce beneath)

Serve with ice cream.

OE Annette Duffy (Grace Duffy)

APPLE CRUMBLE

When we moved to our house over ten years ago we discovered that it had an apple tree in the garden.. The first year we were there, my mum made an apple pie and all the family seemed to love it so she made lots of them and gave them away on the condition that we would get our casserole dishes back! It was a deal.

After about four years the family started to get bored with apple pie so my mum converted to crumble. She would agree that she isn't actually a big fan of crumble and that she makes so many just to avoid having to pick up decomposing apples from the lawn in the autumn. I love that time of year as it means I get to see more of my (wider) family – and I also think she likes it too for the very same reason.

I hope that you like her crumble recipe; it's easy to make and good fun for children to join in too!

INGREDIENTS

FOR THE FILLING

500g   (approx) cooking apples
50g   sultanas
       pinch ground cinnamon
       sugar – enough to sweeten apples

FOR THE TOPPING

175g   plain flour
75g   butter
75g   brown sugar

METHOD

1   Peel and cut apples into thick slices. Cook on medium heat (saucepan) or microwave 2 - 3 minutes until just tender. Add sugar, cinnamon and sultanas.
2   Put in ovenproof dish.
3   Make topping: Rub butter into flour until like breadcrumbs, stir in the sugar and cover the apples with this mixture. Optional - sprinkle 1 teaspoon sugar over the top
4   Bake 25 - 30 minutes Gas 6/200°c.

Nimmie Nijjar, written by Siman Nijjar

APPLE (AND OTHER FRUIT) CRUMBLE

I have a recipe for apple crumble- it's something my mum always makes for us on special occasions - particularly Jewish festivals or for Shabbat sometimes. Both my sister and I love it and cook it lots!! We all have varieties on the theme!

This is my favourite at the moment.

INGREDIENTS

	lots of apples
	some plums
12oz	flour
12oz	sugar
	dash of cinnamon
6oz	butter
	lots of raisins
	a bit of muesli

METHOD

1   Peel and chop apples and plums and put in saucepan on low heat with a bit of water to become delicious and mushy. Leave to cool.
2   While you're waiting, make the crumble. Mix any amount of flour and sugar (but the same measure of each) to half the amount of butter and add a dash or two of cinnamon. Then use fingers to make the crumbly texture. It helps if you chop up the butter into small pieces before you pop it in the bowl. Get stuck in!
3   Layer a rectangular oven proof dish with one layer of crumble, then fruit, then raisins, until you have lots of layers.
4   On the top add a sprinkling of muesli.
5   Put in the oven (Gas 5 / 190ºc) to cook until it looks brown and smells delicious: approx 15 - 20 minutes

Don't leave it in too long or it will burn!

Natalie White

124

APRICOTS WITH BRANDY & ORANGE

INGREDIENTS

1	packet dried apricots or Hunza apricots (wild apricots that are sun-dried whole)
	juice of 6 oranges or orange juice carton
6	cardamom seeds
2	tbsps brandy (optional 2 tbsps brown sugar)
1	carton Greek yoghurt (optional) or fresh cream

METHOD

1   Put fruit in a pan with orange and. if you prefer sweeter fruit, sugar. Cover fruit with water and stir.
2   Leave to soak overnight covered in cling film or lid.
3   After soaking, add cardamom pods and bring to boil, cover and simmer for 30-40 minutes, making sure there is plenty of liquid in pan
4   Leave to cool
5   Add brandy and serve with yoghurt or fresh cream

Liz Cummings

AUTUMN FRUIT JALOUSIE

INGREDIENTS

1	packet flaky / puff pastry (fresh or frozen)
1	egg

FILLING

500 -750g	cooking apples
OR	
500-750g	plums / cooking apples totalling 750g
150g	sugar
	cinnamon

METHOD

1 Oven 200°c/Gas 6. Line large baking tray with silicone paper
2 Wash and peel apples/wash, halve and stone plums. Quarter if large plums.
3 Slice apples very thinly.
4. Cut pastry in half. Roll out first half pastry approx. 15cm x 10cm on floured surface. Fold into thirds and open out again.
5 Roll second piece of pastry, fold in half and open out.
6 Damp pastry edges with water, then arrange fruit in centre of pastry. Cut diagonal strips down each side of pastry 1 and inner lines across other half of pastry 2.
7 Spread sugar and a little cinnamon evenly over fruit, leaving 2 tsp sugar for top
8 Fold pastry over, seal well and brush with beaten egg. Sprinkle remaining sugar over top.
9 Bake approx. 20 minutes until brown and well risen.
10 Cool on cooling tray

Soft fruits such as raspberries and strawberries can be mixed with apples for a summer version, and mincemeat and apples combine for a variation on Mince Pies.

UPSIDE DOWN CAKE

INGREDIENTS

90g/3oz	self raising flour
60g/2oz	soft margarine
60g/2oz	caster sugar
1	egg
1	tablespoon golden syrup
1	small tin pineapple rings/sliced peaches/apricots
2 - 4	glacé cherries

METHOD

1 Grease and line 17cm/7" sandwich tin. Oven 180°c/gas 4 - 5
2 Beat margarine and sugar with wooden spoon until soft. Add egg and flour and mix until smooth
3 Put syrup in cake tin. Arrange fruit neatly on top. Halve cherries and place upside down with fruit
4 Carefully spoon cake mixture in tin, smooth top.
5 Bake 25 - 30 minutes until golden brown and springy
6 Loosen sides and turn out.
7 Cool

303 PHYSICS AND COOKING
PART 4
BAKED ALASKA

Baked Alaska is a hot ice cream dessert. It is made of ice cream, sponge cake and soft meringue (Figure 8).It is baked in a hot oven until the peaks of the meringue are golden. But why doesn't the ice cream melt?
Try it yourself and find out.
The recipe given below is very easy.

RECIPE

INGREDIENTS

Sponge cake, 180 mm diameter approximately
(buy one or use the recipe in Part 3 to make your own)
Note - Unless you own this textbook a
2 egg sponge cake or a Victoria Sandwich Cake recipe is fine (Ed)
family size block of vanilla ice cream
raspberry sauce or jam
3- 4 egg whites
0.1 kg caster sugar (about 4 ounces)

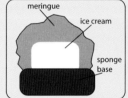

Cross-section through a Baked Alaska

METHOD

1   Preheat the oven to 230°c (450°f, gas mark 8).
2   Place the sponge cake on a flat, heatproof dish.
3   Spread the raspberry sauce or jam on top of the sponge
4   Make the meringue by whisking the egg whites until they are stiff (electric mixer if you have one). Add the sugar and whisk again.
5   Place the ice cream on the sponge cake and spread the meringue mixture carefully over it. Make sure there are no gaps.
6   Bake in a hot oven for three minutes until the outside of the meringue just begins to turn golden brown.
7   Serve immediately.

QUESTIONS

13   Both meringue and sponge cake are good insulators. Explain why.
14   Explain why the ice cream doesn't melt.
15   The secret of success is to cook this dish in a very hot oven. Explain why.
16   Why is it not possible to prepare this dish in individual portions?

Physics Department

BREAD AND BUTTER PUDDING

INGREDIENTS

6 - 8	slices bread (removal of crusts optional)
60g/2oz	butter
90g/3oz	dried fruit (any)
45g/1½oz	sugar
425ml/¾pt	milk
3	eggs

OPTIONAL

	grated rind of lemon or orange little grated nutmeg or mixed spice
2tbsp	marmalade

METHOD

1. Oven on 180ºc/gas 4
2. Spread butter (and marmalade, if using) on bread. Cut into fingers or triangles
3. Arrange half in base of an ovenproof dish.
4. Sprinkle with half sugar and fruit (plus grated rind)
5. Add remaining bread – butter side up -, fruit and sugar.
6. Beat eggs and add milk. Mix thoroughly.
7. Pour slowly and evenly over bread. Sprinkle nutmeg, spice over top (if using)
8. Bake 35 - 45 minutes until top is golden brown and crisp

CHOCOLATE UPSIDE DOWN PUDDING

SERVES 6

INGREDIENTS

¾	cup sugar
2tbsp	margarine
½	cup milk
1¼	cups plain flour
½	cup chopped nuts (optional)
1tsp	vanilla extract
2tsp	baking powder
1oz/30g	cocoa/drinking chocolate

METHOD

1. Mix dry ingredients together.
2. Melt margarine and cocoa/drinking chocolate together.
3. Add to dry ingredients along with milk and vanilla essence and mix together.
4. Pour into a greased dish.

TOPPING

1. Mix ½ cup sugar, ½ cup brown sugar and 1 tbsp cocoa/drinking chocolate.
2. Sprinkle over the mixture in the dish and pour 1 cup of boiling water over.

Cook at Gas 6/200ºc for 45 minutes.

Sponge rises, leaving a chocolate sauce underneath.

Chris Pollard

CHOCOLATE, REDCURRANT AND PEAR TART

INGREDIENTS

1½lb/675g	shortcrust pastry
4oz/120g	ground almonds
2	fresh eggs
3½oz/95g	caster sugar
6oz/185g	chocolate (a mixture of plain and milk - or whatever combination preferred)
8oz/240g	frozen redcurrants or raspberries
5	conference pears peeled, cored and each cut into eight

METHOD

1 Preheat oven to 180ºc/gas 4 - 5.
2 Make pastry in normal way (I add 1oz icing sugar and half an egg to this quantity).
3 Roll out and line a well greased fluted flan tin with removable base.
4 Prick base with a fork and put in fridge for 20 minutes to help prevent base rising in blind baking.
5 Blind bake (I put baking parchment in the flan case and fill it with split peas).
6 Bake for 10 minutes, remove and set aside.
7 Mix almonds, eggs, sugar together in a bowl. Stir in melted chocolate while still warm. Add frozen berries and mix again.
8 Pour the mixture into flan case and sink strips of pear into mixture as wheel-like decoration and bake for 40 - 45 minutes in oven - watch and test to ensure top is cooked. The inside will be a little gooey. Alternatively cook a little longer to achieve cake like texture.
9 Remove from oven and cool in tin.

Serve with Greek Yoghurt or crème fraiche

Liz Cummings (with a few ideas from Jamie Oliver!)

COCONUT STRAWBERRY TART

SERVES 6 - 8

INGREDIENTS

BASE

4oz/120g	ground almonds
4oz/120g	desiccated coconut
2oz/60g	margarine
1oz/30g	raw cane sugar.

FILLING

	cream cheese or low fat cream cheese
2tbsps	soured cream
1oz	raw brown sugar
	grated rind of 1 small lemon + tsp lemon juice
8oz/250g	strawberries
4tbsps	strawberry jam or similar jam

METHOD

1 Mix together the almonds, coconut, melted margarine and sugar. Press into tin.
2 Bake at 170ºc for fifteen minutes - be careful that it does not brown too quickly.
3 Beat the softened cream cheese, soured cream, sugar, lemon rind and juice until smooth.
4 Spread evenly over the coconut base. Hull and slice the strawberries and lay over the cream cheese.
5 Cover with warmed strawberry jam.

Liz Cummings

COCONUT TREACLE TART

INGREDIENTS

150g/5oz	white breadcrumbs
90g/3oz	desiccated coconut
	grated rind and juice of 1 lemon
½tsp	ground ginger
5tbsp	golden syrup

FOR SHORTCRUST PASTRY

180g/6oz	plain flour
90g/3oz	butter

METHOD

1   Rub fat into flour, add about 1 tbsp cold water and stir it in with a knife till the mixture starts to stick together.
2   Gather into a ball, wrap in cling film and leave for half an hour.
3   Roll out pastry and line an 8 inch flan ring.
4   Pre-heat oven to 190°c.
5   Measure golden syrup into a saucepan (using a spoon dipped in hot water). Stir in the lemon rind and juice and ginger and warm till liquid.
6   Stir in the breadcrumbs and coconut and leave the mixture to stand for 10 mins. If the mixture is too stiff, add a little more warmed syrup. If too sloppy, add more crumbs or coconut.
7   Spoon into the pastry case and bake for about 25 minutes until lightly browned.

Leave to cool 15 minutes before serving with vanilla ice cream or crème fraîche.

Chris Pollard

FANTASTIC HEALTHIER & EASY CHRISTMAS PUDDING

INGREDIENTS

125g	demarara sugar
50g	muscovado sugar
100g	wholemeal bread crumbs
100g	wholemeal flour
50ml	sunflower oil
200g	seedless raisins
100g	sultanas
100g	currants
250ml	unsweetened orange juice
	a little alcohol, eg Cointreau (optional)
	a spoonful of black treacle (optional)
1	beaten egg
¼tsp	ground ginger
¼tsp	nutmeg
¼tsp	cinnamon
25g	almonds
1tsp	baking powder

METHOD

1   Soak fruit in ½ the juice for 1-2 hours
2   In a separate bowl mix together the dry ingredients
3   Add the egg, soaked fruit and oil. Mix thoroughly adding the remaining juice until a dropping consistency is obtained. Mix in the almonds.
4   Pour mixture into a 2 pint or 2 smaller greased basins. Cover and steam for as long as possible - say 5 hours, this does not have to be done in one session. The longer the steaming time the better to develop a nice dark, rich flavour and colour.
5   Best matured for as long as possible, wrap in waxed paper in a plastic box.
6   Do not store in contact with metal if keeping for a long time, e.g. more than 3 months.

Pat Brown, retired Head of Technology Department, King Edward VI Handsworth School

FRENCH APPLE FLAN

INGREDIENTS

PÂTE SUCRÉE (RICH SHORTCRUST PASTRY)

180g/6oz   plain flour
90g/3oz   butter
30g/1oz   caster sugar
2   egg yolks
½ - 1tbsp   water (as required)

FILLING

500g-750g/
1 - 1½lb   cooking apples
2   dessert apples
30g/1oz   butter
120g/4oz   caster sugar
1tbsp   apricot jam
1   lemon

20-24cm/8-9" Flan dish

METHOD

1   Oven 190°-200°c/gas 5 –6.
2   Make pastry. Rub butter into flour until like breadcrumbs. Add 30g sugar.
3   Stir in egg yolk plus enough water to bind to a fairly stiff dough.
4   Cover and rest dough in fridge.
5   Peel, core and slice cooking apples. Microwave, with butter, until soft (5- 6 minutes).
6   Add sugar and leave to cool.
7   Roll out pastry and line lightly greased (with butter/margarine) flan dish. Lightly fork bottom.
8   Quarter, core and thinly slice dessert apples. Sprinkle with a little lemon juice. Spoon apple purée in flan case. Arrange apple slices, slightly overlapping on top.
9   Put jam, lemon juice and 50g sugar in pan & dissolve slowly then bring to boil. Brush half over apples.
10   Bake flan 25 –35 minutes. Cover with foil if apples brown too quickly.
11   Remove flan and brush with remaining glaze.

FRENCH 'FONDANT AU CHOCOLAT'

If you are looking for a recipe that always works:

INGREDIENTS

4   eggs
200g   dark chocolate
200g   sugar
3   level tablespoons of flour
125g   butter
        a touch of milk!

METHOD

1   Separate the eggs
2   Beat the egg whites until stiff peaks form.
3   Melt the chocolate 'au bain-marie' and then add the butter
4   In a salad bowl, mix the chocolate and butter melted with the yellow part of the eggs and a bit of milk. Then add the sugar and the flour.
5   It is very important that the sugar and the flour are incorporated together!
6   Then with a wooden spoon, incorporate the egg whites with delicacy!
7.   It's ready!
8   Cook at 170°c for about 25 minutes

It's delicious and so tasty!!!!!

DELICIEUX!

Ludovine – French Assistante

FRESH FRUIT SALAD

INGREDIENTS

1   apple
1   orange
1   banana

PLUS any of the following ingredients:

100g   seedless grapes
100g   strawberries, raspberries/kiwi
        fruit/ clementine, satsuma/pear/
        melon/pineapple etc
25g   sugar
2-3   teaspoons fresh lemon/lime/
        orange juice
150ml water

METHOD

1   Wash and dry all fruit. Remove any
     stalks.
2   Prepare syrup. Put sugar and water in
     medium size pan. Stir continuously
     over medium heat with wooden spoon
     until water begins to boil . Switch
     heat off . Put pan to cool.
3   Prepare fruit in this order: citrus fruits
     (oranges, clementines etc.) grapes,
     berries, kiwi fruit. Then apples, pears,
     bananas.
4   Peel and segment orange. Remove any
     pith. Slice into small pieces.
5   Cut grapes/ strawberries. in half / peel
     and slice kiwi fruit in rings
6   Peel and slice banana
7   Apples/Pears – cut into quarters,
     remove core. Dice.
8   Put all fruit in dish / container. Add fruit
     juice to pan . Pour cool syrup over.

Store in fridge for up to 24 hours.

FRUIT PIE

INGREDIENTS

FOR SHORTCRUST PASTRY

240g/8oz   plain flour
120g/4oz   butter/block margarine
3-4tbsp   cold water (approx)

FILLING

3 - 4   med/large cooking apples
         (700g/1.5lb approx.)
         (Can be made using plums,
         rhubarb - same weight.
         Also can mix other fruits in,
         eg blackberries, strawberries,
         raspberries etc - 100g)
90 -110g/4oz sugar (more may be required)

1 deep pie dish - approx 23cm / 9"

METHOD

1   Oven 200°c/gas 6.
2   Put flour in large mixing bowl, cut
     fat into small pieces and rub in until
     like breadcrumbs.
3   Stir in water with table knife until
     dough just holds together. Leave
     pastry in bowl.
4   Prepare fruit. Wash then peel apples,
     core and slice thinly/slice rhubarb
     finely/quarter and stone plums.
5   Cut pastry in half. Roll out on floured
     surface to fit bottom of pie dish plus
     small margin.
6   Line pie dish carefully. Trim edges.
7   Fill with fruit and sprinkle sugar on top.
     Add cinnamon if desired.
8   Roll out pastry for top - put loosely
     over dish, trim slightly and seal edges
     neatly.
9   Brush top with water, sprinkle with
     a little sugar, make 2 air holes, place on
     baking tray and bake - middle shelf for
     25 - 35 minutes.

Serve hot or cold.

KEHS SPECIAL CHOCOLATE CRUNCH RECIPE

We have had this recipe for at least 25 years (but it could be longer). No one can remember where it came from, but we believe it was given over the telephone by a dinner lady from another school to one of the team here, way back in the early 1980s.

This is the very first time we have ever let anyone have a copy, so be assured you have got yourself a valuable piece of KEHS history!!

As you may well guess, we usually make 200 plus portions at a time, so making it on a small scale may lose a little in translation. But I'm sure any accomplished budding 'Delia', with a little perseverance will get it to their liking (eventually).

So here it is, after 25 years!!

You will need:

> an electric mixer, with a beater attachment;
> stainless steel baking tray - 34cm x 24cm;
> preheat the oven to 145°c fan assisted - (add 25°c for non fan assisted).

INGREDIENTS

17oz	self raising flour
14oz	caster sugar
1½ oz	sieved cocoa
14oz	melted butter or margarine
1	extra, extra large egg

METHOD

1. Put all dry ingredients into the mixing bowl and briefly combine (flour, sugar, cocoa) Pour in melted margarine. And again mix briefly.

Two points to note here:

- Don't get the margarine / butter too hot.
- Don't over mix the margarine/butter in to the dry ingredients, only enough to bring it together.

2. Then add the beaten egg and mix well (but again, not for very long, just until it leaves the side of the bowl and looks shiny).
3. Place in to a greased tin and flatten down firmly.
4. Bake for 45 minutes.
5. Remove from oven and sprinkle with caster sugar.
6. Portion and serve with custard (preferably lumpy for an authentic finish!)

ENJOY

School Kitchen (Peter Webber – Head Caterer)

LAVENDER AND CHOCOLATE CHIP ICE CREAM

Jenny always enjoyed cooking - particularly the memorable Friday afternoon option sessions with Mrs Mutlow that included members of KES - but she had never considered it as a possible career. After a period teaching in the UK, she and her husband emigrated to Canada in 2000. There, the first available jobs were casual ones in restaurants. Jenny's talents were soon spotted and she was offered the opportunity to train as a professional Chef whilst also being employed at 'Cannery Row' a specialist fish restaurant.

Jenny qualified as a Chef in 2003 having been awarded two scholarships, being selected to compete in a number of competitions and chosen as Alberta Apprentice of the Year (Cook). She was quickly snapped up by The Petroleum Club, an exclusive gentlemen's club in Calgary which insists on never repeating the same potato dish and lately, she has moved to Route 40 Soup Company, a renowned organic food restaurant whose homemade soups have become THE Calgary businessman's gourmet gift. Jenny is particularly known for her nourishing soups and innovative desserts and owns a collection of countless cookery books! Her other occupation is as a specialist backpacking and camping advisor and she has recently devised her own "wild camping" recipes, including drying the food to minimise carriage.

Angela Buckley – sister

THE RECIPE

I will reveal my most precious and secret recipe for lavender ice cream. I don't normally write my recipes down for people. It looks much more fiddly than it actually is so people sometimes have to be encouraged to try it but then they think it's fantastic. Have a go — it's worth it!

INGREDIENTS

500ml milk
500ml whipping cream
1 tablespoon dried lavender (fairly fresh is good!)
12 egg yolks
300g sugar
1 dessert spoon vanilla extract
250g dark chocolate pieces (more interesting and usually better quality than boring chocolate chips. They need to be quite small though)

METHOD

1 Heat milk and cream in pan with lavender. Once it starts to boil remove from heat and leave to steep, covered (to prevent a skin from forming) for 15 minutes.
2 Meanwhile, whisk egg yolks and sugar together until thick. Strain milk/cream into this and mix thoroughly.
3 Return to pan (give it a quick rinse first) and bring to boil, STIRRING ALL THE TIME. As it starts to boil it should thicken.
4 Remove from heat and leave to cool, stirring often. Stir in vanilla.
  Leave to cool completely, then place in freezer.
5 After 1 hour, remove from freezer and whisk vigorously.
6 Repeat this twice more. On the last go, add chocolate - add more or less pieces according to what looks good for you!
7 Leave to freeze overnight before serving.

TOP TIP

If your custard (that's what it is when you're boiling it) really starts to curdle, remove from heat and whisk like hell. It should mend it - works for me!

If the phone goes or something while you're at the 'bring to the boil' stage, ignore it! Or at least remove pan from heat and carry on again when you've finished!

Jenny Douglas (née Buckley) KEHS 1982-1989); professional chef

LEMON AND CHOCOLATE MOUSSE

INGREDIENTS

5oz/150g	white chocolate, broken into pieces
3½oz/100g	plain chocolate, broken into pieces
2	medium eggs, separated grated rind and juice of one lemon
8	tablespoons fromage frais
1 - 2	tablespoons brandy (optional) cocoa powder, to dust

METHOD

1   Melt chocolate in separate bowls either in microwave or over a pan of simmering water.
2   Add one egg yolk, lemon juice and rind and half fromage frais to the white chocolate and beat until smooth.
3   Add other yolk, remaining fromage frais and brandy to plain chocolate and beat until smooth.
4.   Whisk egg whites until stiff and fold half into each chocolate mixture.
5.   Layer mixtures into 6 small glasses and chill.
6.   Dust with cocoa powder or a twist of lemon rind.

OE Annette Duffy (née Glennon)

LEMON TIRAMISU

INGREDIENTS

240g/8oz	0% fat Greek yoghurt
100g/3½oz	low fat soft cheese
5	tablespoons lemon curd
1½	tablespoons icing sugar – sifted
18	sponge fingers
4 - 5	tablespoons lemon liqueur

METHOD

1   Mix together the yoghurt, soft cheese, icing sugar and lemon curd. (I find this best to do by hand as an electric mixer tends to make it runny)
2   Dip the sponge fingers into the liqueur and arrange in a shallow dish. Spread a third of the yoghurt mixture over the fingers. Repeat, finishing with the yoghurt mixture. Drizzle any remaining liqueur over the top.
3   Chill for at least an hour in the fridge.
4   Decorate with strips of lemon rind or grated rind over the top.

OE Annette Duffy (née Glennon)

MAHALLEBI

If you're of Cypriot descent then don't turn the page ... this is not the traditional Mahallebi desert made with only sugar, cornflour and water, which once set, is served with a generous amount of rosewater. Although it may be very refreshing, it is a little too bland for my palate!

This creamy version of Mahallebi is far more interesting and delicious, so much so it seems inappropriate that it has the same name as its Cypriot relation. In terms of what it is - well, I can't think of a translation for this dessert other than just to say it has a wonderful texture, and the combination of flavours are not only sensational but remarkably comforting too (you'll know exactly what I mean when you try it)!

It was during a holiday in Cyprus a couple of years ago that I tried this in a renowned Lebanese restaurant which I always insist on revisiting during every trip to Cyprus. Obviously, I tried to find out how they made it, but understandably, they weren't giving anything away. So it then became my mission to re-create this modern day traditional sweet with my own little Greek spin on it, and I'm pleased to say that two years on, I think I've mastered it!

SERVES 6-8

INGREDIENTS

1300ml	full cream milk
80g	demerara sugar
80g	golden caster sugar
150g	blanched almonds, very finely ground
¼	teaspoon ground all-spice
5	tablespoons ground rice
5	tablespoons cornflour
2	teaspoons vanilla extract
150ml	rosewater
	a really good handful of chopped almonds or pistachios for decoration

METHOD

1   I find this recipe works best be mixing the ground rice and the cornflour with the milk from the start. Admittedly, you'll have a bit of a sore arm, but just think of it as good exercise!
2   Pour the milk into a large saucepan and add the sugars, almonds and the all-spice and stir.
3   Now add the ground rice and cornflour, stirring continuously; don't worry about any lumps at this stage, as they will dissolve with the heat.
4   Place the saucepan over a medium heat and stir continuously with a balloon whisk until the custard heats up and thickens (about 15 minutes).
5   Remove from the heat and stir in the vanilla extract and the rosewater.
6   Pour into a wide, shallow serving bowl or individual ramekins, sprinkle with the nuts and refrigerate for at least two hours, or overnight.

Ira Phedon (Christy)

MANDARIN / PINEAPPLE PUDDING

INGREDIENTS

1	medium tin mandarin oranges / pineapple
2	eggs
30g/1oz	plain flour
30g/1oz	butter / margarine
90g/3oz	sugar
200ml	milk
1	lemon
1	medium ovenproof dish

METHOD

1. Oven 170°c / Gas 4. Drain fruit and chop. Reserve juice.
2. Make roux using butter and flour. (Melt butter & add flour. Cook 1 min. Remove from heat)
3. Gradually add milk and juice to a maximum of 250ml.
4. Bring to boil stirring continuously. Remove from heat and add 30g sugar.
5. Separate eggs carefully. Add yolks to sauce.
6. Add juice of ½ lemon plus fruit. Pour into dish.
7. Whisk egg whites until stiff. Add ½ sugar with and whisk again. Fold in rest of sugar with thin spoon or spatula.
8. Pile meringue on top of pudding, sealing edges well.
9. Bake 20 - 25 minutes until golden brown

MANGO MOUSSE (COURTESY OF TRAIDCRAFT RECIPE LEAFLET)

INGREDIENTS

2oz/60g	dried mango *
1	cup orange juice
2tsps	gelatine
8oz/200ml	creamy yoghurt
1	egg white

METHOD

1. Soak mango overnight in three quarters of the orange juice. Blend in food processor to reduce to a puree.
2. Sprinkle the gelatine onto a generous tablespoon of cold water and, when dissolved, heat slightly with the remaining orange juice.
3. Add the gelatine mixture to the mango puree.
4. Add the yoghurt and process lightly.
5. Refrigerate the mixture until sufficiently thickened to add the egg white. You could add a little sugar to egg white if mango tastes too sharp.
6. Spoon the mousse into individual glasses and refrigerate for 3-4 hours.

*Apricot mousse.
Using dried apricots as a substitute for the mango

Liz Cummings

"MAZUREK"
WITH FRUIT AND NUTS
(POLISH)

100g = 320 kcal

INGREDIENTS

	wafers
250g	almonds
50g	dates
250g	raisins
150g	bitter chocolate
250g	icing sugar
8	egg whites
	a pinch of salt

METHOD

1. Steam the almonds, then peel and chop them into fairly big pieces.
2. Cut the dates, wash the raisins and then leave them to dry on a tea towel.
3. Beat the egg whites till stiff, adding a pinch of salt in the process, and towards the end - the sugar, in two parts.
4. Using a wooden spoon, delicately mix the egg whites with all the dried fruit and nuts and with grated chocolate.
5. Delicately spread the mixture on the wafers.
6. Bake on a low gas mark (e.g., gas mark 3) for 40 minutes.
7. Decorate with icing sugar once cool.

Czepiel Family

COLD BUTTERMILK
SOUP
(KAERNEMAELKSKOLDSKALL)
WITH APPLE PUDDING

This is a Danish recipe that I learned at school and have used often since. It's lovely, and the buttermilk soup makes a refreshing change from cream or custard.

SERVES 4

INGREDIENTS

10fl oz	buttermilk
2	eggs
4	tbsp sugar
1	tsp vanilla extract Juice of 1 lemon
4	cooking apples
	sugar to taste
	oatflakes
	grated dark chocolate

METHOD

1. Beat the eggs, sugar, lemon juice and vanilla together in a bowl.
2. Beat the buttermilk and fold in a little at a time. Chill.
3. Peel and chop up the cooking apples.
4. Cook in a pan with sugar, to taste. When soft, but not too mushy, put in a baking dish. Top with sufficient oatflakes to cover and make a crunchy topping.
5. Dot with butter. Scatter the grated chocolate over.
6. Cook in a medium oven for 10 - 15 minutes, until golden and chocolatey. Serve the apple pudding hot, with cold buttermilk soup.

Delicious!

OE Ann Wright

MOUSSE AU CHOCOLAT

Time needed: 30 minutes (to be made the previous day)

INGREDIENTS

4	bars of dark cooking chocolate (or 150g)
4	eggs
3	heaped dessert spoons of sugar

100ml thick cream

OPTIONAL

thimbleful of your favourite liqueur (e g rum, cointreau, amaretto, kahlua)

4   ramekins

METHOD

1   Separate the eggs. Mix the yolks with the sugar until foamy and white. Melt the chocolate in a bain-marie and, after adding the cream (and liqueur) add it to the yolks and sugar.
2   Beat the whites till stiff with a pinch of salt. Carefully add the whites to the other mixture, ensuring the whites maintain their stiff consistency.
3   Pour into ramekins and refrigerate for serving the following day.

Before serving, sprinkle 'hundreds and thousands' on the top (or Smarties for children!).

Bon Appétit!

Aurore Marquette

EASY MOUSSE PUDDING

INGREDIENTS

200g	low fat soft cheese
100g	Greek yoghurt
25g	sugar free jelly (any flavour)

METHOD

1   Pour 300m1 boiling water into a jug. Sprinkle the sugar free jelly into the water and stir well to dissolve. Allow to cool slightly.
2   Beat the cheese and yoghurt together until smooth and then gradually beat in the cooled jelly.
3   Either pour into individual ramekins or a large bowl and leave to set in the fridge - should take approximately 1½ hours.

If using a lemon and lime jelly, try adding the juice of a lemon to the jelly at the first stage of the recipe.

OE Annette Duffy

CHOCOLATE DELIGHTS FOR EASTER!

Chocomallow Mousse

INGREDIENTS

100g/4oz	crushed ratafia or digestive biscuits
200g/7oz	plain chocolate broken
75g/3oz	miniature marshmallows
15ml/1tbsp	almond liqueur
300ml/½ pint	fresh double cream
90ml/3fl oz	fresh single cream chocolate shapes and cream to decorate

METHOD

1 Grease with vegetable oil 4 - 6 ramekins. Divide half the crushed biscuits into the bases of the ramekins.
2 Melt the chocolate, 50g of marshmallows and almond liqueur in a bowl over hot water.
3 Remove from heat and cool for 5 minutes. Whip the creams together and carefully fold into the chocolate mixture.
4 Put 2tbsp of the mixture into each ramekin and then layer remain: biscuits, marshmallows and chocolate mixture.
5 Place in freezer for 30 minutes.
6 Decorate with whipped cream and chocolate shapes.

OE Magazine

MICROWAVED SPONGE PUDDING

INGREDIENTS

60g/2oz	butter or margarine
60g/2oz	caster sugar
60g/2oz	self-raising flour
1	egg
2tbsp	cocoa

METHOD

1 Sift cocoa into flour. Mix butter, sugar, egg, flour and cocoa in a bowl and beat thoroughly.
2 Place mixture in a greased 1.5 litre/2 pint pudding basin and cook on full power for 4 minutes.
3 Leave pudding to stand in basin for 4 - 5 minutes and then turn out.
4 Serve with custard, ice-cream or Chocolate Toffee Sauce - break 2 Mars bars in a basin and microwave on full power for 2 minutes. Beat well and stir in 2 tbsp milk.

Serve at once.

If you have had enough of chocolate, this recipe can be adapted to:

jam sponge pudding - omit cocoa and place 100g/4oz jam in pudding basin before adding sponge mixture, cook as before;

fruit pudding - add 50g/2oz dried mixed fruit to pudding mixture, cook as before.

OE Magazine

BORTH BROWNIES

`A Level Biologists' Favourite Pudding'

Here's a recipe for Brownies from the youth hostel at Borth. It would be lovely to give the youth hostel some free publicity as they are so wonderful to the biologists and they are constantly worried about whether the hostel is to remain open.

'A level biologists and biology staff have enjoyed excellent food at the youth hostel in Borth for a number of years during their field course. This is the best pudding at the youth hostel and it is delicious!'

`A LEVEL BIOLOGISTS' FAVOURITE PUDDING'

METHOD
(For ingredients and quantities see table)

BROWNIE

1   Preheat the oven to 180°c / 350°f/gas 4. Grease tin. Stir the dry ingredients together in a bowl.
2   Melt the chocolate carefully in bain-marie or in bowl over a pan of gently simmering water.
3   Add the butter and the golden syrup and stir until blended. Leave to cool to lukewarm, then stir in the eggs any vanilla essence.
4   Fold in the dry ingredients and stir quickly until smooth.
5   Fold in the nuts, and pour into the tin. Bake in a preheated oven for 30-45 minutes. The top and edges will be crusty. The inside will be slightly gooey but not runny.
6   Cut into individual squares

DARK CHOCOLATE SAUCE

1   Heat the water and sugar in a pan, stirring constantly to dissolve the sugar. Bring to the boil and continue to stir until all the sugar has been dissolved.
2   Break the chocolate into small pieces and cut the butter into small chunks. Add to the pan of water and sugar and stir.
3   Remove the pan from the heat and stir the sauce until the chocolate and butter have melted and all the ingredients have blended together. Stir in the cream and vanilla essence.

RECIPE CARD

Hot Chocolate Brownie with Vanilla Ice Cream & Dark Chocolate Sauce

BROWNIE

plain flour,
icing Sugar
cocoa powder
plain chocolate
butter
eggs
syrup
hazelnuts
vanilla essence

CHOCOLATE SAUCE

dark chocolate
water
butter
cream
sugar
vanilla essence
components

Serve poured over the warmed Brownie with (optional) vanilla ice cream.

Biology Department

Hot Chocolate Brownie with Chocolate Ice Cream   BORTH YOUTH HOSTEL

Difficulty 2	Menu (Children Menu Day 4)			Dessert

Ingredients	Measure	10 Portions	30 Portions	Tip
Plain flour	grams	180	540	
Icing sugar	grams	300	900	
Cocoa powder	grams	40	120	
Plain chocolate	grams	300	900	
Unsalted butter melted	grams	180	540	
Golden syrup	tbsp	4	12	
eggs	each	4	12	Omit hazelnuts for larger groups to avoid nut allergies
Vanilla essence	tsp	3	9	
Hazelnuts, roasted, skinned and chopped	grams	80	240	
Chocolate sauce				
Dark chocolate	grams	340	1 kilo 20 grams	
water	ml	230	690	
butter	grams	60	180	
cream	tbsp	12	36	
sugar	tbsp	6	18	
Vanilla essence	tsp	1	3	
Keep for	Fridge	5 days		
	Freezer	2 months		

Notes / Quality Points				
Prep Levels	Low	Medium	High
Small Hostel			
Medium Hostel			
Large Hostel			

ORANGE / LEMON CHEESCAKE

INGREDIENTS

BASE

225g/8 oz	ginger biscuits/ digestive biscuits/ chocolate digestives
1	dessertspoon golden syrup
100 -125g/3-4 oz	butter

(1 -2 tsp ground ginger adds to the flavour)

FILLING

1	small orange, washed
1	small lemon, washed
225g/8 oz	cream cheese – mascarpone is good
125ml/¼ pt	double cream - not UHT (longlife)
½tbsp	caster sugar
½ sachet/½tbsp	gelatine/vege gel + 2 tbsp hot water, made up as instructed
	grated chocolate/crumbled flake/grated orange or lemon rind to decorate
20cm/8"	flan dish or tin

METHOD

1 Crush biscuits well. Melt ¾ of butter with golden syrup in pan , add biscuits and stir well until mixture will stick together. If necessary, add remaining butter.
2 Press into flan dish and chill in fridge.
3 Add gelatine to hot water & stir briskly until dissolved. Cool slightly.
4 Soften cream cheese in large bowl, grate lemon and orange rind and add to cream cheese.
5 Whisk cream CAREFULLY until just thick. Mix into cream cheese. Stir in juice of fruit and sugar thoroughly.
6 NB If fruit is very juicy add only enough so that the mixture remains fairly thick
7 Stir reasonably cool gelatine into cheesecake mixture.
8 Pour into biscuit base and chill in fridge until set.
9 Decorate with chocolate, grated rind etc.

Lemon and Lime is a good alternative

PANCAKES

INGREDIENTS

125g	plain flour
250 - 300 ml	milk
1	egg
2tbsp	vegetable oil

METHOD

1. Put flour, egg and half the milk in mixing bowl.
2. Mix together smoothly with hand whisk until it looks blended.
3. Gradually add the rest of milk so that it is a smooth liquid consistency.
4. Pour into jug.
5. Heat ½ tablespoon. oil in frying pan. Test with drop of batter - if it sizzles it is ready.
6. Pour enough batter to cover bottom of pan . Cook 1 - 2 minutes.
   Turn pancake over quickly & cook until golden brown.
   Turn heat off.

Eat immediately or keep warm

IDEAS

Basic pancakes can then be used as a savoury or sweet dish.

Roll up with cooked vegetables and pour a cheese sauce over, flash under grill for a main meal dish.

Add sweetened, hot stewed apple etc (or a tin of pie filling), roll up

PROFITEROLES

INGREDIENTS

CHOUX PASTRY

150ml/5fl oz	cold water
60g/2oz	butter
75g/2½oz	strong plain flour
2	medium eggs (or 1 large), well beaten

FILLING/TOPPING

5fl oz/125ml	double/whipping cream
30g/1oz	icing sugar
120g/4oz	chocolate

METHOD

CHOUX PASTRY

1. Oven 200ºc / Gas 6. Line baking sheet.
2. Fold sheet greaseproof to make a crease, open it out and sieve flour onto it.
3. Put water & butter in med. saucepan. Place over moderate heat , stir with a wooden spoon.
4. As soon as butter melts and water comes to boil, switch off heat.
5. Tip all flour in quickly whilst beating the mixture.
6. Beat until mixture leaves sides of pan (may need to turn heat back on) and you have a smooth ball of paste which leaves the side of the pan.
   Cool mixture slightly.
7. Gradually beat in eggs, mixing thoroughly before adding more until you have a smooth, glossy paste. Use electric whisk if necessary.
8. Make the pastry into any finished choux recipe.

PROFITEROLES

1. Place teaspoons of mixture on baking tray. Put in oven for 10 minutes. Raise heat to 210ºc/Gas 7 & bake further 15 - 20 minutes until risen, crisp & golden. Slit sides & cool.
2. Melt chocolate in microwave - 1 minute - stir, then 15 seconds until melted
3. Whisk cream (& icing sugar if used).
4. Split buns in half & spoon in cream. Arrange on dish / plate & pour chocolate over
5. Serve immediately or refrigerate.

PEASANT PUDDING

This recipe came to us from an Aunt and I think she had it from a friend, but before that its provenance is unknown. It is probably the number one pudding at our house. It is a good alternative to apple crumble, especially for people who are not great pastry chefs! It is simple and quick to make and always seems to go down well with everyone. We prefer it chilled in the Walmsley household but a friend of ours assembles it as per the recipe and then, rather than chilling, heats it through in a moderate oven and serves it warm — each to their own...

INGREDIENTS

480g/1lb cooking apples, peeled, cored, sliced.

90g/3oz margarine or buttery spread (anything suitable for baking)

90g/3oz Demerara sugar (or soft brown sugar will do)

180g/6oz rolled oats (jumbo whole rolled oats taste best and the mixture will take a generous 6oz)

METHOD

1 Cook the fruit in a pan on a gentle/moderate heat, with a dash of water, until just stewed. Add a little sugar to taste. When the fruit is ready leave it to one side.

2 Put the rest of the sugar and margarine in a pan on a moderate heat and stir continuously until completely blended.

3 Remove from the heat and add the oats, stirring well, so that all the oats get soaked in the melted mixture.

4 In a serving bowl, layer the oat mixture alternately with the cooked fruit, starting with fruit and finishing with oats. These quantities will probably give you four layers in all.

5 Leave to cool & then refrigerate.

6 Serve with nothing, cream, yoghurt, creme fraiche, ice cream or anything else you fancy!

Vary the recipe by adding a pinch of cinnamon to the stewed apple or using any other fruit which will stew in the same way as apples e.g. blackcurrants, plums, rhubarb, or combinations such as blackberry & apple. Blackberry & apple is especially good!

We often make increased quantities as it keeps overnight very well in the fridge: simply scale the ingredients in proportion.

Walmsley Family

QUICK CHOCOLATE MOUSSE

SERVES 4

INGREDIENTS

100g   plain chocolate
250g   carton mascarpone cheese
2tbsp sifted icing sugar

METHOD

1   Melt chocolate in microwave.
2   Quickly beat in icing sugar and mascarpone.
3   Spoon into dishes and chill to set.

Chris Pollard

STRAWBERRY MOUSSE

This recipe uses a food processor

INGREDIENTS

400g   fresh or frozen strawberries (thawed)
60g   caster sugar
110ml   cold water
1   sachet gelatine
250 ml   double cream
2   egg whites

METHOD

1   Put water in a pan, sprinkle gelatine over. Heat v gently, stirring until dissolved. Do not boil.
2   Whisk egg whites until stiff
3   Put strawberries and sugar in a food processor and purée
4   Pour gelatine through food tube, machine running. Then pour in cream and blend well
5   Lift lid, add egg whites and blend on medium.

Immediately pour into serving dish or individual moulds. Chill until set.

TIRAMISU

I have been making this recipe for many years but have only tasted it on one occasion!!! Every time I make this for a 'do', there is never any left by the time I get to it!! On one occasion, about 10 years ago, I had made this dessert for a neighbour's party and one of the guests said "Oh have you tried the Tiramisu over there? It is absolutely delicious." She smiled when I said I had made it. I finally got to taste it last year when my son-in-law, Stephen made a bee-line for the "pudding queue" at the same neighbour's barbecue party and grabbed me a portion. It was definitely worth the wait.

INGREDIENTS

200g (8oz)   trifle sponges
300ml (10floz) strong black coffee
8 tbsp   marsala wine or tia maria
400g   carton fresh custard
250g (10oz)   mascarpone cheese
140ml (5floz)   whipping cream
2 tbsp   cocoa powder
                a few amaretti biscuits for decoration (optional)

METHOD

1   Pour the black coffee and liqueur into a glass jug and stir. Arrange half of the trifle sponges in the bottom of a deep glass dish, pour over half of the coffee and liqueur and leave to stand for about 10 minutes.
2   In another bowl, beat together the fresh custard and mascarpone cheese until smooth. Spread half of this mixture over the soaked sponges.
3   Dip the remaining sponge fingers into the coffee and liqueur mixture and layer on top followed by the rest of the custard mixture. Chill for 2-3 hours.
4   Lightly whip the cream and spread over the top of the custard mixture.
5   Dust with cocoa powder and place Amaretti biscuits on the top if desired.
6   Chill for 1 hour.

Mrs Rhona Davis, Maternal Grandmother of Jessica Andrews

SATSUMA
CREAM ICES

A recipe found by Liz Cummings in Family Circle (1984), and used almost every Christmas since!

SERVES

6 or more.

Store up to three months in a freezer.

INGREDIENTS

6oz/180g	caster sugar
½ pint/280ml	of water
8	medium sized satsumas (I use 3-4 more)
½	lemon
2	egg whites
1	small carton of fresh double cream.

METHOD

1. Place the sugar and water in a saucepan over a low heat. Stir until the sugar dissolves then increase the heat and boil for ten minutes. Leave to cool.
2. Wash the satsumas.
3. Slice off the tops of six of them. Take care not to damage the skins, use a teaspoon to scoop the flesh into a sieve standing over a bowl. Press the satsuma flesh to squeeze as much juice as possible into the bowl.
4. Take the remaining two satsumas and finely grate the rind into the cool sugar syrup.
5. Measure the satsuma juice in the bowl, making it up to half a pint with juice from the grated satsumas if necessary.
6. Squeeze the juice from the lemon half and add, with the ½ pint of satsuma juice, to the sugar syrup. Pour into a plastic container. Cover and freeze until slushy.
7. Whisk the egg whites stiffly, mash down the slushy fruit ice and mix in the whisked egg whites. Freeze until semi-frozen.
8. Whip the cream until softly thick, mash down the fruit ice again, then mix in the cream until all is evenly mixed. Freeze until solid.
9. Make sure the insides of the satsuma cups are well cleaned out then fill them to the brim with orange ice cream. There should be some ice cream left over which is why I use more satsumas than the recipe recommends.

To FREEZE

Place the lids on the satsumas. Store in a polythene box for future use.

NB Allow 20 minutes defrost time before serving.

Liz Cummings

SIMPLE CHOCOLATE GATEAU

INGREDIENTS

BASE

3	eggs
90g (3 oz)	caster sugar
75g (2½oz)	self raising flour
15g	cocoa powder
2 - 3tbsp	fruit jam
1tsp	extra caster sugar

FILLING

Choose from the following:

- 150ml double/whipping cream
- 150g fresh fruit (e.g. sliced strawberries) or 1 tin fruit
- Chocolate buttercream :

  60g (2oz) butter
  100-150g icing sugar
  15g cocoa powder
  blend ingredients thoroughly

  NB Buttercream can be vanilla (few drops, no cocoa)
  orange/lemon/lime (add zest & juice of 1 fruit)
  or coffee (add 2 teaspoons instant coffee mixed with
  2 teaspoons hot water)

TOPPING

120g (4oz) milk cooking chocolate + 30g (1oz) white cooking
chocolate

METHOD

1. Grease & line large swiss roll tin. Oven 200°c/gas 5-6.
2. Whisk eggs and sugar until thick and creamy (ribbon stage)
3. Sieve flour and cocoa in to mixture. Fold in gently with spatula / metal spoon.
4. Pour evenly into tin
5. Bake approx. 8 - 10 minutes
6. Turn out onto greaseproof paper sprinkled with 1 tsp caster sugar.
7. Remove lining paper from sponge and divide sponge into 3
8. Prepare fillings and melt chocolate in 2 bowls in microwave*
9. Sandwich together with choice of filling leaving top plain
10. Spread milk chocolate over top. Immediately pour very thin lines of white choc. over top then pull a thin skewer through top to create a feather pattern. Put on plate and refrigerate.

Melt chocolate on high for 1 minute max. Stir and then melt for 15 sec intervals. Chocolate can burn in a microwave.

SPONGE FRUIT FLAN

INGREDIENTS

SPONGE

2	eggs
60g/2oz	caster sugar
60g/2oz	SR flour

FILLING

250g/8oz	fruit (strawberries, raspberries , tin fruit etc.)
2tsp	sugar
1tsp	lemon juice
2tsp	arrowroot
125ml/¼pt	water

METHOD

1 Grease, line & flour sponge flan tin. Oven 200°c/gas 6
2 Whisk eggs and sugar until thick & creamy (ribbon stage)
3 Fold in sieved flour. Pour into tin.
4 Bake until golden brown & springs back to touch (approx 10 mins)
5 Remove carefully from tin
6 Arrange fruit in flan attractively
7 Put arrowroot , sugar, lemon juice & water in pan (if using tin fruit use juice from can instead)
8 Stir over medium heat until it thickens. Cool slightly and pour evenly over fruit.

SAUCY LEMON PUDDING

INGREDIENTS

Grated rind and juice of 1 lemon	
60g/2oz	butter
120g/4oz	caster sugar
2	eggs, separated
60g/2oz	SR flour
275ml/½	pt milk

Medium size ovenproof dish
Shallow roasting tin or similar

METHOD

Oven on 200°c / Gas 6

1 Cream butter and sugar until fluffy, add lemon rind.
2 Mix in egg yolks and flour. Beat well.
3 Stir in milk and lemon juice to form a smooth batter.
4 Whisk egg whites until stiff, mix carefully into mixture.
   NB a small, balloon whisk may help, but use gently.
5. Pour mixture into ovenproof dish
6. Stand dish in tin and pour in warm water to just cover bottom of tin (bain marie).
7. Cook 45 mins approx until the top is golden brown and spongy to touch. There will be a lemony, soft custard layer at the bottom.

SUMMER FRUIT TARTLETS

INGREDIENTS

RICH SHORTCRUST PASTRY

180g/6oz	plain flour
90g/3oz	butter
60g/2oz	caster sugar
2	egg yolks

FILLING

500g/1lb strawberries/raspberries or other soft fruit
e.g. sliced nectarines/peaches, blueberries,
mandarin oranges, grapes – in any suitable
combination

Plus - 180g/6oz redcurrant jelly – for lining and glaze.

OR

1	med. cooking apple + 60g/2oz caster sugar
2 tsp	arrowroot for lining and glaze
30g/1oz	caster sugar
150ml	water

METHOD

1   Oven 190°c/gas 5-6. Flour medium - large size tartlet tins.
2.   Rub in butter & flour. Add egg yolks to form a smooth dough (use cold water if too stiff)
3   Roll pastry fairly thinly - handle carefully. Cut out and line tins.
4   Line with greaseproof & baking beans & bake blind for approx 15 minutes.
5   Wash and slice fruit as necessary.
6   Remove greaseproof etc. from pastry and return to oven 5 minutes until pale brown. Cool.
7   **Apple filling:** Peel, core & chop apple. Microwave (covered) 4 - 5 minutes until soft. Press through sieve to purée. Add sugar. Spoon this in pastry cases.
8.   Put arrowroot, water & sugar in pan. Bring SLOWLY to boil, stirring well until thickened. Switch off.
9.   **Redcurrant Jelly:** Heat gently in pan until melted. Spoon some in pastry cases.
10   Arrange fruit tastefully in cases.
11   Spoon *warm* glaze over top to give even glossy finish.

TRIFLE
SCHOOL KITCHEN SPECIAL

INGREDIENTS

1	madeira cake
1	pack frozen raspberries
	raspberry sauce/coulis

PASTRY CREAM
(makes approx 500ml/17 fl oz)

4	eggs yolks
75g/3ozs	caster Sugar
	salt - pinch
25qrm/1oz	cornflour
300ml/½ pt	milk
1-2	vanilla pods, split and scraped

OR

2 - 3 tsp/35ml/1¼ fl oz vanilla essence
double cream
| 25g/1oz | unsalted Butter |

METHOD

Break up the Madeira cake, put into the serving bowl. Add the frozen raspberries and the raspberry sauce. Cover the bowl and put in the fridge over night.

Make the pastry cream next day:

1   Cream together the eggs yolks and caster sugar in a bowl.
2   Add a small pinch of salt and the cornflour.
3   Bring the milk to the boil with the split and scraped vanilla pod (or essence) and pour carefully onto the egg yolk mixture.
4   Return the mixture to the pan, slowly simmer, stirring all the time and cook until it thickens.
5   Stir in butter (If sauce is lumpy then pass through sieve)
6   Pour pastry cream over the cake and raspberries whilst still hot.
    Press a piece of greaseproof paper or cling film onto the surface to prevent a skin from forming. Leave to cool.
7   Decorate with double cream and chocolate shapes.

Note: Try using custard powder instead of cornflour for an even more intense flavour.

Cakes, Bars and Cookies

ALL- IN -ONE CAKES AND PUDDINGS

BASIC MIXTURE

INGREDIENTS FOR 1 QUANTITY

150g caster sugar
150g butter / soft margarine
150g self raising flour
3   eggs
1   level tsp baking powder (optional)

Options and additional ingredients
(each option uses 1 quantity of basic recipe):

CAKE   Victoria sandwich – 2 tablespoons jam,
        1 tablespoon icing sugar
        chocolate – 30g cocoa powder + 1tablespooon water
        coffee - 2 teaspoons instant coffee dissolved in 10ml water
        (coffee and walnut – as above plus 50g chopped walnuts)
        lemon/orange – grated rind of 1 lemon / orange

BUTTERCREAM ICING   75g butter/ soft margarine
                      150g icing sugar (plus extra 50g)

FLAVOURINGS   (depending on cake)
                   1 tablespoon juice of orange/lemon juice
                   1 tablespoon cocoa
                   ½ tsp coffee in 1 tsp water
                   (plus 50g of whole walnuts)

                   or other suitable
                   flavourings/decorationss

TRAYBAKE   Add 100g fresh blueberries OR 2 tablespoon
                 chopped glace cherries.

BUTTERFLY CAKES   18 cake cases + flavourings + buttercream

EVE's PUDDING   2 - 3 cooking apples + 2 tbsp sugar + ovenproof
                 dish (med. - large)

CHOCOLATE PUDDLE PUDDING   30g cocoa (for cake mixture)
                 PLUS 30g cocoa + 30g soft brown sugar + 170g
                 evaporated milk (makes a rich chocolate sauce on
                 bottom of pudding). Ovenproof dish

NB All the above to be made from basic mixture plus additions

BASIC METHOD

1   Heat oven 180 ºc / gas 4.
2   Prepare tins according to type of dish (see below).
3   Place all ingredients in large mixing bowl .
4   Mix well with hand mixer or wooden spoon to form a 'soft
    dropping' consistency (may require 1-2 tsp extra water / fruit juice).
5   Divide mixture.
6   Bake.

VARIATIONS

VICTORIA SANDWICH   Grease and line 2 x 18cm sandwich tins.
                    Bake 20 – 25 minutes approx.
                    Remove from tins and cool.
                    Sandwich together with softened jam.
                    Sieve icing sugar over top.

OTHER CAKES   Add flavourings to mixture.. Bake as above and
                    cool.

BUTTERCREAM   Soften butter with fork + add icing sugar gradually.
                    Add flavourings

TRAYBAKE   Add blueberries / cherries to mixture. Grease and
                    line shallow 21x 30 (approx) rectangular tin.

BUTTERFLY CAKES   Divide between cases. Cool. Slice tops off carefully
                    and cut in half. Add a little buttercream to each
                    bun. Place 'wings' on top.

EVE'S PUDDING   Peel and slice apples VERY thinly. Put on bottom of
                    dish with 2 tbsp sugar. Put mixture on top.
                    Bake 35 - 40 minutes.

CHOCOLATE PUDDLE PUDDING   Add 30g cocoa to mixture. Put in dish.
                    Mix cocoa, sugar and evaporated milk. Pour onto
                    mixture. Bake 30- 40 minutes or until well risen.

AUNTIE DORIS'S CHOCOLATE CAKE

INGREDIENTS

4 oz/120g	margarine
4oz/120g	caster sugar (or muscovado sugar)
3	eggs
4oz/120g	SR Flour
2 oz/60g	ground almonds - or ground hazelnuts
1tbsp	drinking chocolate or cocoa powder
1tbsp	or more of milk to ease mixture

METHOD

1   Grease and line an 8"/18cm round cake tin.
    Oven 170ºc/gas 3 - 4.
2   Beat margarine and sugar until light and creamy.
3   Add eggs and beat further.
4   Fold in flour mixed with drinking chocolate/cocoa powder.
5   Add ground almonds.
6   Add milk to ease mixture.
7   Spoon into cake tin and bake for approx 20 minutes.
    Test by pressing centre gently to check that it springs back to touch.

To serve, decorate with your favourite topping - try melting some chocolate and mix with a little cream to make a runnier consistency.

Can be frozen.

Liz Cummings

BANANA CAKE (ORGANIC)

INGREDIENTS

250g/8oz	organic white self-raising flour
¼	of an organic nutmeg, ground (a challenge to find, but it does exist, honest!)
1 tsp	organic cinnamon (also can be a challenge to find)
125g/4oz	organic butter
125g/4oz	organic caster sugar grated rind of an organic lemon
2	organic free range eggs
3	medium bananas, mashed with a fork (it is better if they are a bit old and squashy)
1	handful of organic sultanas
6	heaped tablespoons organic set honey
1	whole firm banana (optional)

METHOD

1   Heat oven to 180ºc/Gas Mark 4.
2   Sieve the flour, nutmeg and cinnamon into a bowl, and rub in the margarine.
3   Using a wooden spoon, fold in the sugar, eggs, lemon rind, sultanas, mashed bananas and honey.
4   Pour half of the mixture in the tin, drop in the whole firm banana and add the rest of the mixture.
5   Bake for 1¼ to 1½ hours or until a skewer pushed into the cake comes out clean (avoid pushing into the whole banana!).
6   Leave to cool in the tin for at least ten minutes before turning out onto a rack to cool.

Slice, spread with organic butter, eat.

NB This will work with non-organic ingredients!

Liz Cummings

BANANA MUFFINS

INGREDIENTS

285g/10oz	self raising flour
1tsp	baking powder
½tsp	salt
3	large, ripe bananas (weighing approx. 450g/1lb total including skins)
85-110g/3-4 oz caster sugar	
1	egg (beaten)
60ml	milk (or buttermilk if you can get it)
90ml	vegetable oil
or	
85g/3oz	melted butter
60g	chocolate chips (optional)
12	muffin cases

METHOD

1   Prepare 12 muffin tin.
    Oven 190ºc/gas 5-6
2   In large bowl sieve flour, baking
    powder & salt. Add choc. chips if using.
3   In another bowl mash bananas
    thoroughly. Add sugar, beaten egg,
    milk/water and oil/melted butter.
    Stir well.
4   Pour all wet ingredients into dry ones
    and mix thoroughly until fairly smooth
5   Immediately spoon or pour carefully
    into muffin cases.
6   Bake 20 - 25 minutes until tops are
    lightly browned and spring back to
    touch.
7   Cool on cooling tray.

BROWNIES

Brownies were unheard of in Florence George's Birmingham, yet they probably owe their popularity to the 1896 Boston Cooking-School Cook Book (as mentioned in chapter 1) which contained the first printed Brownie recipe. This, however, did not contain chocolate, a glaring omission which was put right in the 1906 edition. Thus the Boston Brownie was born.

I had always had problems finding a good Brownie recipe; one which was chocolatey and rich and gooey enough, yet with body. So, on a recent trip to New England, I thought this was as good an opportunity as I was going to get to find the definitive chocolate Brownie recipe. We were staying with a family in Connecticut who took up my cause with enthusiasm and, before I knew it, Brownie recipes were coming my way via friends and neighbours.

I quickly learned that there is no such thing as the definitive recipe, everyone swearing theirs is the one! The local pastor's wife – a truly excellent cook – told me that her husband's family make a version to be reckoned with and so she phoned her mother-in-law back in Illinois for a dictated recipe, which is reproduced verbatim. I kept being told that unsweetened chocolate is 'a must' for Brownies but this is fairly hard to find in the UK (and expensive) so I would suggest good quality plain chocolate with a cocoa mass of at least 70%.

I did have some fun trying out the different recipes though!

Sally Huxley

JIM LEMLER'S MOM'S BROWNIES

INGREDIENTS

4	squares (120g) unsweetened chocolate, melted
2/3	cup shortening
2	cups sugar
4	eggs
1½	cups flour
1	tsp baking powder
1 tsp	salt
1	cup chopped walnuts or pecans

METHOD

1 Mix shortening with sugar.
2 Add eggs and mix well. Add chocolate.
3 Blend dry ingredients then add to mixture.
4 Bake in a greased 9 x 13" pan at 180ºc/gas 4 25 - 30 minutes.

Don't overbake!

CONVERSIONS*

1 cup rice	U.S =	225g rice
1 cup flour	U.S =	115g flour
1 cup butter	U.S =	225g butter
1 stick butter	U.S =	115g butter
1 cup dried fruit	U.S =	225g dried fruit
1 cup brown sugar	U.S =	180g brown sugar
1 cup granulated sugar	U.S =	225g granulated sugar

NOTES

Flour is plain.
*These conversions vary according to source but are consistent.
Shortening = butter, margarine, cooking fat.

Maggie's Brownies

INGREDIENTS

4	squares (120g) unsweetened chocolate
¾	cup butter or margarine
2	cups sugar
3	eggs
1	cup flour
1	cup chopped walnuts or pecans (NB These may be omitted)

METHOD

1 Line 13 x 9" baking pan with greaseproof. Oven on 180ºc/gas 4.
2 Melt chocolate and butter in microwave - 1 min then stir then max 30 seconds until melted.
3 Stir in sugar and eggs, then add flour and nuts. Mix well.
4 Put in baking pan and bake for 30 - 35 minutes until just set.

Allow to cool in tin (very important) and cut into squares.

Chocca Mocca Brownies

INGREDIENTS

60g/2oz	butter
120g/4oz	plain chocolate
180g/6oz	muscovado sugar
2	eggs
2tbs	strong coffee, cooled
90g/3oz	plain flour
½tsp	baking powder
60g/2oz	chopped walnuts/pecans (optional)

METHOD

1 Grease and line 8" / 20cm square tin.
2 Melt butter and chocolate in heatproof bowl either in microwave - 1 min then stir, then max 30 seconds until melted. or over pan of simmering water. Stir well
3 Beat eggs and sugar well until pale and thick. Stir in chocolate mixture and coffee. Mix well.
4 Sieve flour and baking powder into mixture, fold in and add nuts, if using.
5 Spread into tin and bake 20 - 25 minutes.

Cool in tin and cut into squares.

Nutty Chocolate and Coffee Brownies with Frosting

INGREDIENTS
Makes about 12 brownies

50g	dark chocolate, roughly broken up
110g	butter
2	eggs, beaten
225g	unrefined (golden) sugar
50g	plain flour
1tsp	baking powder
	pinch of salt
100g	hazelnuts (chopped in half)

For the frosting

100g	butter, softened to room temperature
100g	icing sugar
100g	cream cheese
1tbsp	strong black coffee

METHOD

1 Pre-heat oven to 180°c / 350°F/gas mark 4.
2 Grease a tin measuring approximately 27cm x 18cm and line with baking parchment, allowing paper to rise 3cm above the tin.
3 Toast hazelnuts in oven for 10 minutes (maximum) until lightly browned.
4 Melt chocolate and butter in a bowl over a pan of simmering water.
5 Sieve flour, baking powder and salt into a bowl.
6 Stir in sugar.
7 Beat in eggs and chocolate mixture until well-mixed.
8 Stir in hazelnuts.
9 Pour mixture into the tin and bake for 30 - 40 minutes until centre springs back when lightly pressed.
10 Remove from oven and allow to cool completely in tin.

To make frosting

11 Beat butter and icing sugar together until pale and fluffy.
12 Beat in cream cheese and coffee.
13 Spread frosting on cooled Brownies.

Chill in fridge for 30 minutes. Cut into squares.

Liz Cummings

CHELSEA BUNS

INGREDIENTS

DOUGH

240g/8oz	strong plain flour
1	sachet easyblend yeast
½tsp	salt
30g/1oz	butter / margerine
1	egg , beaten
125ml/¼pt	milk (warmed slightly)
40g/1½ oz	melted butter
150g/5oz	dried fruit (any combination)
60g/2oz	sugar
¼tsp	ground cinnamon

GLAZE

30g/1oz	sugar
50ml	water

METHOD

1 Oven 200ºc / gas 6 - 7.
2 Make dough. Put flour, yeast, salt and 30g butter in mixing bowl. Rub in.
3 Mix beaten egg and milk. Stir into flour mixture. Beat well.
4 Turn onto floured surface and knead for 5 minutes until dough is smooth.
5 Roll out into rectangle approx 30 x 23cm/12" x 9"
6 Brush with melted butter. Cover with dried fruit, sugar & cinnamon.
7 Roll up dough like a swiss roll & cut into 9 pieces.
8 Place , cut side down, on baking tray just touching each other. Cover loosely and rise in warm place for 15 - 20 minutes and bake 15 - 20 minutes.
9 Check buns are cooked in centre
10 Make glaze by boiling water and sugar. Brush over buns immediately after baking.

Cool.

CHOCOLATE CAKE

INGREDIENTS

10oz/300g	caster sugar
6 oz/180g	margarine
3	eggs
1tsp	vanilla essence
6 oz/180ml	low fat natural yoghurt
8 oz/240g	self raising flour
2 oz/60g	cocoa
1tsp	bicarbonate of soda

METHOD

1 Prepare 8"/18cm cake tin or muffin tins.
2 Cream the margarine and sugar together.
3 Add the other ingredients as listed.
4 Put into tin (s)
5 Bake 160°c/gas 3, for 40 - 45 minutes.

(Muffins, or small cakes take about 25 minutes.)

Beth Ashfield

CHOCOLATE CHIP COOKIES

INGREDIENTS

125g butter/margarine
125g caster Sugar
1   egg (beaten)
200g SR Flour
125g choc chips (substitute any small
      dried fruit)
50g   chopped nuts (optional)

NB It is important to weigh ingredients accurately. If egg is large only add ¾.

METHOD

1   Oven 190ºc/Gas 4 - 5. Line baking sheet with silicone paper.
2   Cream butter and sugar with wooden spoon until light and fluffy.
3   Add egg a little at a time.
4   Mix in flour thoroughly. Stir in chocolate chips
5   Place heaped teaspoonfuls (approx. 8) on baking sheet and flatten slightly.
6   Bake 10 - 12 minutes until just golden brown.

Cool on a wire rack

CHRISTMAS CAKE (LIGHTER VERSION)

INGREDIENTS

250g butter
200g light brown muscovado sugar
5   medium eggs, lightly mixed in jug
300g plain flour
200g walnut pieces
500g sultanas
250g raisins
250g dried apricots, quartered
200g cut mixed peel
200g glacé cherries, halved
100g dried prunes, roughly chopped
1   orange
100ml brandy

METHOD

1   Prepare cake tin - 23cm round/9". Grease and line with double thickness parchment. (This mixture can also be divided between 2 x 20cm/8" tins)
2   Chop and place all fruit in large bowl. Add grated zest and juice of orange and pour brandy over. Mix well, cover with cling film and leave to stand up to 24 hrs.
3   Oven 150ºc/gas 2.
4   In large mixing bowl cream butter and sugar until pale. Gradually add eggs, beating well each time. If mixture begins to separate add some flour.
5   Add the fruit, any liquid from fruit and nuts. Mix well.
6   Fold in the flour carefully and thoroughly until mixture is totally blended.
7   Spoon the mixture into the tin(s) and level top gently.
8   Bake middle shelf 3½ - 4 hrs. A thin skewer should come out clean when gently inserted into middle of cake.

Cool in tin, wrap in foil and cling film and store for at least 2 -3 weeks if possible.

NB   If top of cake starts to brown too quickly, cover with double circle of parchment.

CHRISTMAS CAKE

INGREDIENTS

(for 8"/ 20cm round or 7" /18cm square tin)
(for 6"/ 16cm square or 7"/18cm round tin use ¾ of this recipe)

8oz/240g	butter/margarine
8oz/240g	soft dark brown sugar (preferably Muscovado/Molasses)
4	eggs - beaten
2lb/900g	dried fruit - currants 8oz/240g
	sultanas 8oz/240g
	raisins 8oz/240g
	chopped glace cherries 4oz/120g
	chopped peel 4oz/120g
4oz/120g	ground almonds
8oz/240g	plain flour + 1 tsp mixed spice
	grated rind & juice of 1 - 2 lemons/oranges
1 - 2	tablespoons sherry/brandy

METHOD

NB If possible, soak fruit in juice/rind/sherry etc. overnight.

1   Grease & line tin with double layer silicone paper. Oven on 150°c - 160°c/Gas 2 - 3
2   Cream butter and sugar until soft. Gradually add beaten egg, using some of the flour/ground almonds with 2nd half of egg (to prevent 'curdling').
3   Stir in remaining ground almonds.
4   Sieve in flour and spice.
5   Carefully fold in fruit and mix thoroughly (add rind and juice/sherry if not already in fruit).
6   Put mixture in tin. Smooth top & cover with greaseproof/silicone circle
    Bake 150°c - 160°c/Gas 2 - 3 for 2 - 3 hours.(this depends on the density of the cake plus individual oven).
7   Test centre of cake with fine skewer. If it comes out almost clean, cake is cooked.

Cool in tin and then wrap cake in foil and cling film. Keep in cool, dry place.

DATE AND WALNUT LOAF

INGREDIENTS

180g/6oz	plain flour
½tsp	bicarbonate of soda
120g/4oz	sugar
60g/2oz	butter/ margarine.
1	egg
90g/3oz	chopped dates
90g/3oz	chopped walnuts
150ml/¼pt	warm milk

METHOD

1 Prepare a 1lb loaf tin (grease and line with silicone/parchment).
    Oven 180°c/gas 4
2 Put all ingredients in a bowl, beat well for 2 - 3 minutes with wooden spoon.
3. Put mixture in tin.
4. Bake approx 45 minutes.

Cool in tin. Wrap in foil/cling film and keep for at least a day before eating. This improves the flavour and moistness.

DECORATED CAKES (SIMILAR TO CUPCAKES)

INGREDIENTS

150g/6oz	soft margarine
150g/6oz	caster sugar
150g/6oz	S.R. flour
1level tsp	baking powder
3	large eggs + 1 - 2 tablespoons water
1	dessertspoon cocoa (for chocolate cakes only)
	paper cases – to make larger cakes use muffin cases

METHOD

1 Oven 190°c/Gas 5. Place all ingredients in mixing bowl. Use electric mixer to blend to smooth mixture . Add a little cold water if mixture seems stiff
2 Divide between paper cases.
    Bake 12 - 15 minutes. Cool on wire rack.

DECORATION

Buttercream – 120g/4oz butter/margarine
350g/8 - 10oz icing sugar

Soften butter with fork in large bowl. Gradually add icing sugar until soft peaks form. Use as desired.

Glacé Icing - 350g/8 - 10oz icing sugar
Water/lemon juice/orange juice etc.
Stir in gradually just enough to form stiff but fluid consistency.

The following can also be used for decoration:

food colourings
cake decorations (from packets)
small sweets
glacé cherries etc. etc.

EFFIE'S BISCUIT CAKE

This simple recipe has been passed down from my mother-in-law, Effie Hunter.

INGREDIENTS

120g/4oz	margarine
300g/10oz	digestive biscuits
120g/4oz	sultanas
3tbsp	golden syrup
30g/1oz	cocoa powder

METHOD

1   Grease and line a shallow baking tray (11" x 7"/28cm x 17cm).
2   Melt margarine and syrup together.
3   Crush the biscuits, add all other ingredients and mix well.
    Pour into the tin.
4   When set, cover with melted chocolate (or, if preferred, while still warm, sprinkle with chocolate vermicelli or desiccated coconut).

Cut into slices.

Sue Hunter (Louise)

FRUITY FLAPJACKS

INGREDIENTS

250g/8oz	porridge oats (supermarket own brand are often the most successful!)
125g/4oz	butter/margarine.
60g/2oz	sugar – any type
1	(heaped) tbsp golden syrup
90g	dried fruit : eg raisins
	chopped apricots
	chopped prunes
	dried cranberries

optional : 60g/2oz chopped nuts

METHOD

1   Oven 180ºc/gas 4. Grease shallow, oblong tin or swiss roll tin or line with silicone paper.
2   Put butter, sugar and syrup in pan. Stir on low heat using wooden spoon until ingredients are melted.
3   Switch heat off & take pan off cooker. Stir in oats, fruit (& nuts if using). Mix well.
4   Pour mixture in tin, press down and bake approx. 20 minutes until light brown and firm on top.
5   Cut mixture into squares,allow to cool in tin if possible.
6   Lift out using palette knife.

GINGER BISCUITS

INGREDIENTS

120g/4oz SR Flour
1   rounded teaspoon ginger
1tsp   bicarbonate of soda.
45g/1½oz granulated sugar
60g/2oz   butter/margarine.
2tbsp   golden syrup

METHOD

1 Oven gas 4 - 5/180ºc
2 Line 1 large or 2 small baking
   sheets with silicone/greaseproof paper.
3 Sieve flour, ginger & bicarbonate.
4 Add sugar and rub in butter
5 Mix in syrup to form stiff paste.
6 Divide into approx. 16 pieces.
7 Roll each into ball, place on baking
   sheet and flatten slightly.
8 Bake 10 - 15 minutes until pale golden
   and well spread.
9 Allow to cool on baking sheet 5 - 10
   minutes then transfer to cooling tray.

GINGERBREAD MEN (NO CUTTERS REQUIRED)

INGREDIENTS

240g/8oz plain flour
120g/4oz butter or margarine
120g   sugar
2 - 3tps ground ginger
1   level teaspoon bicarbonate of
          soda
2tbsp   golden syrup
          few currants / raisins

METHOD

1 Oven 160ºc/Gas 3-4
2 Line 2 baking sheets with silicone /
   greaseproof paper.
3 Rub butter into flour using fingertips
   until like breadcrumbs.
4 Add sugar, ginger and bicarbonate. Stir.
5 Add syrup & mix with wooden spoon
   to form stiff dough.
6 Flour hands. Divide mixture into
   12 - 18 pieces (depending on number
   & size wanted)
7 Shape into 1 large (body) & 1 small
   (head) rounds with palm of hand.
8 Place on greased baking tray. Decorate
   with currants/raisins.
9 Bake 10 - 15 minutes until pale golden
   brown and slightly risen.
   (May need a little longer)
10 Cool on tray for minute then lift off
   with palette knife or spatula.
11 Leave to cool.

GINGERBREAD

Though this is called Gingerbread it is actually a moist dark ginger cake, which after a day or two develops a delicious sticky top. It is a recipe from Rosemary and Joanna's maternal grandfather's mother! She lived in East Lancashire around Clitheroe and Chipping. Grandad remembers it first being made for him as a child in the 1930s but it was already an old family recipe dating back into the 1800s. He has baked it all his life and we hope to carry on the tradition. Obviously it has evolved slightly over time to include golden syrup and margarine and the cooking time in today's efficient fan ovens may need to be slightly reduced. Interestingly our original handwritten recipe includes notes about it being a good recipe to use up any sour milk; thrifty housekeeping in a farming family and in the war-time days. In our house we particularly enjoy it for supper with a glass of cold milk.

INGREDIENTS

8oz	margarine
8oz	soft brown sugar
8oz	black treacle and golden syrup (we use 4oz of each)
12oz	plain flour
4	level teaspoons ground ginger
3	level teaspoons ground cinnamon
2	beaten eggs
½pt	milk
2	level teaspoons bicarbonate of soda

a roasting tin or deep baking tray measuring approx 7" by 11" or equivalent.

METHOD

1   Line the tin with greaseproof paper or line the bottom and grease the sides.
2   Melt the margarine, soft brown sugar, treacle and golden syrup together in a pan, stir until they are melted and blended together. Turn off heat.
3   Sift the flour, ground ginger and ground cinnamon together. Add the beaten eggs and the melted mixture and stir well.
4   Warm the milk to 'blood' heat and pour it onto the bicarbonate. Stir and add to the other mixture.
5   Stir all the ingredients together until blended (a balloon whisk works well for this) and pour into the tin.
6   Bake in the middle of a slow oven, Gas Mark 2 or 150°c or 310°f, for between 45 minutes and 1 hour depending on efficiency of your oven! Check after 30 minutes and if the top is browning too much, cover with greaseproof. Test after 45 minutes using usual knife technique.
7   When cooked remove from tin and leave to cool. The cake keeps really well wrapped in greaseproof in an airtight tin and is actually even more delicious after a couple of days. Vary the amounts of ginger and cinnamon and the ratios of treacle to golden syrup to suit personal taste.

Walmsley Family

GINGERBREAD SHAPES: FOR BISCUITS, STARS, TREE DECORATIONS ETC.

INGREDIENTS

225g/8oz	plain flour
½	level teaspoon baking powder
1 - 2tsp	ground ginger
75g/3oz	butter/margarine
50g/2oz	caster sugar
1tbsp	golden syrup
1 - 2tbsp	milk

DECORATIONS

Royal Icing Sugar	150g/6oz (made up as instructed)
Fondant/Roll-Out icing	150g/6oz

Colourings/decorations of choice.

METHOD

1   Oven 160°c/gas 4. Mix flour, ginger & baking powder in large bowl.
2   Rub fat into flour. Stir in sugar, golden syrup and, if necessary, milk so that a fairly stiff dough is formed.
3   Knead until smooth.
4   Roll out thinly on floured surface and cut into shapes. (Put small hole at top for tree decorations).
5   Place on lined baking trays and bake 10 - 12 minutes until pale golden.
6   Lift onto cooling tray and leave to harden.
7   Prepare icings according to instructions on packs. Colour, if desired
8   Decorate imaginatively and leave to set.

HEALTHIER SMALL CAKES

INGREDIENTS

BASIC RECIPE

120g/4oz	butter/margarine
120g/4oz	caster sugar
120g/4 oz	SR flour
2	eggs
12	paper cake cases

MODIFICATIONS/ADAPTATIONS

To add more fibre/give different texture/ change the flavour:

- use all wholemeal SR flour or ½ white & ½ wholemeal
- raisins (50g), lemon/orange rind and juice, chopped mixed nuts, desiccated coconut,
- mixed dried fruit, All Bran, finely chopped cooking apple, (all 50g)
- 1 dessertspoon cocoa

METHOD

1   Oven on 190°c/Gas 5. Organise equipment.
2   Prepare tin with paper cases. Break eggs into small basin and mix with fork.
3   Put butter and sugar in mixing bowl and mix with wooden spoon.
4   Add eggs and flour. Mix thoroughly. Alternatively - mix all cake ingredients with electric mixer until smooth
5   Add all other extra ingredients. Add a little water if mixture seems stiff.
6   Divide mixture evenly between cake cases.
7.   Bake 10 - 15 minutes or until well risen and springy to touch.
8   Cool on cooling tray.

JAM BUNS

For many, their introduction to cooking at school. A foolproof recipe which Florence George includes in her book - and which is still going strong!

INGREDIENTS

240g/8oz	SR flour
90g/3oz	caster sugar
90g/3oz	butter/margarine (block not tub)
125ml/¼pt	milk
1tbsp	jam

METHOD

1   Oven on 180°c/Gas 5. Put silicone paper on a baking tray.
2   Put flour and butter in mixing bowl. Rub in until like breadcrumbs.
3   Stir in sugar. Stir in just enough milk with fork to form a stiff dough.
4   Flour table lightly. Shape dough into an oblong and divide into 10 - 12 pieces, roll into balls and flatten slightly. Put buns on baking tray
5   Make a small 'hole' in centre of each bun and put jam in this.
6   Bake until golden brown - approx. 15 minutes.
7   Remove from tray with palette knife and cool.

LEMON CAKE

INGREDIENTS

4oz/120g	soft margarine
5oz/150g	self raising flour
3½oz/105g	caster sugar
2	eggs
2tbsp	lemon curd
	rind of 1 lemon
	syrup
optional:	juice of 1 lemon
	2 tbsp caster sugar

METHOD

1   Beat all cake ingredients together.
2   Place in lined 2lb loaf tin.
3   Bake gas mark 4 (350°f, 180°c) for 1 hour.
4   Mix lemon juice and sugar.
5   Remove cake and cool slightly.
6   Turn out and leave to cool thoroughly.
7   Pour syrup over, if used.

Jill Oldfield

MAIDS OF HONOUR

INGREDIENTS

150g/6oz	plain flour
75g/3oz	butter/block margarine
1½ - 2tbsp	cold water (approx)

FILLING

60g/2oz	butter/soft margarine
60g/2oz	caster sugar
60g/2oz *	SR Flour
1	egg
1	tablespoon jam, softened

* (Remove 1 dessertspoon flour and replace with 1 dessertspoon ground almonds/desiccated coconut if preferred)

METHOD

1 Oven on 190°c/gas 5. Flour a tartlet tin.
2 Make shortcrust pastry - rub fat into flour until like breadcrumbs.
3 Add water to form stiff dough. Roll out on floured surface.
4 Cut into 12 rounds and line tin. Put 1/3rd teaspoon jam in bottom.
5 Make topping. Soften butter/margarine with wooden spoon then add all other ingredients. Mix thoroughly until smooth.
6 Divide mixture evenly between pastry cases.
7 Bake approx. 15 minutes until sponge is just golden brown and springy to touch.
8 Cool on wire rack.

MILLIONAIRE'S SHORTBREAD

INGREDIENTS

BASE

6oz/180g	self raising flour (I often find you need to add a little more!)
6oz/180g	margarine or butter
3oz/90g	sugar

METHOD

1 Rub margarine into flour and then add sugar.
2 Press into a deep baking tray.
3 Bake gas no 4, 180°c, 350°f for 15 minutes.

FILLING

1	tin of condensed milk
6oz	sugar
6oz	margarine
4tbsp	golden syrup

METHOD

1 Melt in pan with constant stirring.
2 Bring to the boil and simmer for 3 minutes.
3 Cover cooled base with toffee mixture.
4 Place in fridge to set.

CHOCOLATE

1	large bar cooking chocolate

METHOD

1 Melt chocolate and cover toffee with chocolate.
2. Chill in fridge.

Can be frozen (best frozen on tray before cutting).

Jill Oldfield

MINCE PIES

INGREDIENTS

240g/8oz plain flour
120g/4oz butter/block margarine
          cold water
1   jar mincemeat (sweet)

METHOD

1 Oven on 200°c/gas 6. Flour a tartlet tin.
2 Make shortcrust pastry - rub fat into
   flour until it looks like breadcrumbs.
3 Add 2 - 3 tablespoons cold water. Stir in
   with knife to form stiff dough.
4 Divide into 1/3rd and 2/3rds. Roll out
   larger piece on floured surface.
5 Cut out 12 bases and line tartlet tins.
6 Put 1 heaped teaspoon mincemeat in
   each base.
7 Roll out remaining pastry and cut out
   tops*. Wet edges of bases to help tops
   to stick.
8 Position tops and brush with milk or
   water. Make 3 scissor snips on tops (
   only if it covers base completely).
9 Bake 15 - 20 minutes until golden
   brown..

Cool on wire rack. Dust with icing sugar, if
liked.

* Use star/bell etc. shaped cutter for variety.

MINCEMEAT PARCELS

MAKES 8

INGREDIENTS

1pkt   Filo pastry - defrosted
411g/14.5oz   jar mincemeat
              grated rind of 1 orange
15g/½ oz   butter, melted
1tbsp   icing sugar

METHOD

1 Trim the pastry sheets and cut into 24
   squares, approx. 15cm (6 ins)
2 Place 3 filo pastry squares on top of
   each other at a slight angle to form a
   12 pointed star.
3 Place a heaped tablespoon of the
   mincemeat in the centre and add a
   little grated orange rind. Carefully pick
   up the pastry corners to enclose the
   filling and press together to form a
   parcel.
4 Repeat with the remaining pastry and
   mincemeat to make 8 parcels. Arrange
   on a baking tray and lightly brush with
   melted butter.
5 Place in a pre-heated oven 190°c/Gas
   mark 5 for 10 - 15 minutes until crisp
   and golden.
6 Dust with icing sugar. Serve hot or cold.

Delicious with ice cream.

THE BASIC MUFFIN

INGREDIENTS

240g/8oz	SR Flour (white or wholemeal)
1tsp	baking powder
¼tsp	salt
110g/3 - 4 oz	caster sugar
1	egg
250ml/8 fl. oz	milk
90ml/3 fl. oz	vegetable oil

PLUS 12 muffin cases

METHOD

1   Oven 190 - 200°c / gas 5-6. Put muffin cases in tin.
2   In large bowl sieve flour, salt, baking powder and stir in sugar.
3   In separate bowl , beat egg with fork, stir in milk and oil.
4   Pour liquid mixture into dry mixture. Combine thoroughly for approx. 30 seconds until a
     batter is formed.
5   Fill muffin cases three quarters full. Bake 20 - 25 minutes until tops are lightly browned
     and spring back to touch.
6   Allow to cool before removing them.

VARIATIONS

CHOCOLATE CHIIP Also add 90g/3 oz choc chips to dry ingredients.
                 For double Choc Chip add 1 dessertspoon cocoa to dry ingredients too.
                 Add 90g/3oz chopped nuts for Nutty Choc Chip

DRIED FRUIT   Add 90 - 120g/3 - 4oz any dried fruit.
              Try some more unusual varieties: e g pineapple, mango, bananas or
               the more usual raisins, chopped cherries etc.

              OR

              you could try a combination of grated cheese and apple/grated carrot and
              raisin or invent your own combination of fillings and flavourings.

LEMON AND COCONUT DRIZZLE CAKE

INGREDIENTS

3tbsp	freshly squeezed lemon juice
	finely grated zest of 2 lemons
50g	desiccated coconut
175g	self raising flour
175g	caster sugar
175g	margarine
3	medium eggs
½tsp	baking powder

FOR THE ICING

1½tbsp	freshly squeezed lemon juice
7tbsp	caster sugar
2tbsp	desiccated coconut

METHOD

1   Preheat the oven to 180ºc/350ºf/Gas Mark 4. Lightly oil and base-line a 900g/2lb loaf tin.
2   Put lemon juice and zest into a bowl, stir in coconut and set aside for 5 minutes.
3   Place the flour, sugar, margarine, eggs and baking powder in a food processor or mix together with a wooden spoon.
4   Add the lemon and coconut mixture and mix again until smooth.
5   Spoon into the prepared tin and bake for 40 - 45 minutes until well risen and firm to the touch - if the cake is browning too much cover loosely with foil for the last 15 minutes.
6   Cool in the tin for 5 minutes and then turn out and cool on a wire rack for 30 minutes.
7   For the icing, mix the lemon juice with the sugar and spread over the cake allowing the icing to drizzle down the sides. Sprinkle with coconut and leave for 30 minutes to set.

If you prefer glace icing you can use icing sugar instead - but I don't think it "drizzles" so well!!

OE Annette Duffy (née Glennon)

LOW FAT BLUEBERRY MUFFINS

INGREDIENTS

200g	self raising flour
½tsp	bicarbonate of soda
2tsp	baking powder
75g	caster sugar
1	pinch of salt
75g	polyunsaturated margarine, melted
100ml	natural low fat yoghurt
100ml	skimmed milk
1	medium egg
200g	blueberries (fresh or dried)

METHOD

1   Preheat the oven to Gas mark 6/200cº. Line a cake or muffin tray with 12 muffin cases.
2   Combine all the dry ingredients in a bowl.
3   In another bowl mix together the melted margarine, yoghurt, milk and egg.
4   Pour the wet ingredients into the dry and combine quickly but gently so as not to overwork the mixture.
5   Add the blueberries and gently stir to mix them in.
6   Spoon into the muffin cases and bake for 20 minutes until risen and golden on top.

Transfer to a wire rack to cool or eat warm - they are hard to resist!!

OE Annette Duffy (née Glennon)

A "VERY GOOD CAKE" RECIPE

INGREDIENTS

150g/5oz	castor sugar
120g/4oz	margarine
2	soft bananas
2	eggs - beaten
240g/8oz	self raising flour
1½oz	good drinking chocolate
1tsp	baking powder
4tbsp	milk

METHOD

1   Mix all the ingredients together. Place in prepared tin eg 8 x 21 cm loaf tin.
2   Bake on gas mark 4/180°c.
3   Cool and cover with chocolate melted with butter.

Susan Powell
OE Magazine

ORANGE CAKE (NO FLOUR)

INGREDIENTS

2	big oranges
½lb/240g	ground almonds
½lb/240g	sugar
1tsp	bicarbonate of soda
6	eggs

METHOD

1   Boil the oranges for 2 hours, topping up the water if necessary, then remove the pips and liquidise the rest of the oranges.
2   Beat the eggs together then add the rest of the ingredients.
3   Pour into an 8" tin and cook for 1 hour at 200°c (400°f)/Gas 6
(It's done if a skewer inserted into the cake comes out clean.)

Beth Ashfield

PARKIN

My grandmother, born in the last year of the nineteenth century, baked. When as a child I used to visit her in Oldham, Lancashire, the culinary highlight was Sunday lunch which was a Lancashire hotpot followed by apple pie.

It was undoubtedly such a treat because my mother, who left Oldham at 18 never to return except for short stays, to go to London University, rather disliked all forms of cookery. She was of that generation of educated women who believed it was rather a waste of time to cook when you could be changing the world. She was thrilled by timesaving devices such as the pressure cooker and until I went to a fashionable southern university where other students had been brought up by parents who used Elizabeth David, my idea of a dinner was potatoes, carrots and stewing steak all cooked together, for the same time, in the pressure cooker. In later years, my friends whom I had brought home to stay with us, would look back nostalgically with a stunned fascination on my mother's pressure cooker vegetable stew which she always provided the evening of their arrival because `it didn't matter how late the train was'.

For as long as I can remember my grandmother baked a tray of parkin every week. She came to live with us when she was in her sixties and continued to provide us with this delight until just before she died in her mid eighties. Friends visiting always asked eagerly if my grandmother had been baking. My mother took over after my grandmother's death and my son and three nephews all continued to enjoy this simple and relatively wholesome recipe until she died. To my shame, I have not continued the tradition, but perhaps there will be more time in the future to revive this delicious and very easy cake.

The recipe I have, is written in my grandmother's handwriting with the odd note added by my mother.

INGREDIENTS

½lb   flour (my mother has written ½ lb self raising flour)
1tsp   bicarbonate of soda
½lb   fine oatmeal
½oz   ginger

Put in a pan:

¼lb   margarine / butter
½lb   syrup or treacle (2 tbsp syrup writes my mother)
½lb   brown sugar

METHOD

1   Melt the above but do not let it boil.
2   Pour over dry ingredients.
3   Add a little milk (my mother added, one beaten egg). Put in a shallow greased baking tin and cook for 1 hour in a slow oven, maybe a little over the hour. (My mother added 35 minutes at 140ºc.)

On the few occasions when I have made this, I have followed my mother's additions. It is wonderful eaten straightaway and also keeps very well. It has been a particular favourite on long walks.

Sarah Evans

PICNIC SLICE

INGREDIENTS

½   large bock of cooking chocolate
         e.g. Kake Brand
2oz/60g   margarine
4oz/130g sugar
1   egg
4oz/120g coconut
2oz/60g   sultanas
2oz/60g   cherries

METHOD

1   Melt chocolate and spread evenly over base of baking tray, previously lined with aluminium foil. Place in fridge to set.
2   Cream together margarine and sugar.
3   Beat in egg.
4   Add coconut, sultanas and cherries.
5   Press mixture onto hard chocolate and spread evenly.
6   Bake at Gas 5, 190°c or 375°f for about 20 minutes. Centre of tray will still appear slightly runny but will set on cooling.
7   Leave to fully cool, remove foil and cut into slices.

Jill Oldfield

CHOCOLATE CAKE

My mother has been baking this cake for the whole family for the last 40 years. We all think it is absolutely delicious.

My mother apparently came across the recipe in a church parish magazine many years ago!

INGREDIENTS

7oz/210g self raising flour
8oz/240g caster sugar
¾tsp   salt
2tbsp   cocoa powder
4oz/120g margarine
2   eggs
5tbsp   evaporated milk
5tbsp   warm water

METHOD

1   Cream the margarine and sugar together.
2   Beat the egg and the milk together
3   Add in to the margarine and sugar small quantities of the egg and milk mixture, followed by quantities of the flour and the cocoa.
4   When all the ingredients have been mixed together add the warm water.
5   Then divide the mixture into 2 sandwich tins (7"/18cm).
6   Bake gas mark 3/4 (180°c) for between 15 - 20 minutes.
7   Use margarine, icing sugar and cocoa powder to create a butter cream centre.

Susan Pallister

SCONE RECIPES

INGREDIENTS

BASIC SCONE

240g   SR flour
60g   butter/margarine
125ml (approx) milk
60g   sugar

WHOLEMEAL FRUIT SCONES

240g   wholemeal SR flour
60g   butter/margarine
125ml (approx) milk
60g   sugar
50g   raisins

FRUIT SCONES

240g   SR flour
60g   butter/margarine
125ml (approx) milk
60g   sugar
50g   raisins/mixed fruit

APPLE AND NUT SCONES

240g   SR flour
60g   butter/margarine
125ml (approx) milk
60g   sugar
50g   chopped apple
25g c hopped nuts

HERB AND CHEESE SCONES

240g   SR flour
60g   butter/margarine
125ml (approx) milk
60g   grated cheese
1 teaspoon mixed herbs

BANANA

240g   SR flour
60g   butter/margarine
125ml (approx) milk
60g   sugar
1   mashed banana

BACON AND ONION

240g   SR Flour
60g   butter/margarine
125ml (approx) milk
50g   chopped cooked
       bacon
50g   chopped cooked
       onion

CHOC CHIP

240g   SR Flour
60g   butter/margarine
125ml (approx) milk
60g   sugar
75g   chocolate chips

METHOD

1   Oven 200°c/Gas 6. Flour baking sheet
    or line with baking parchment.
2   Rub butter into flour. Add sugar/raisins/
    cheese & herbs etc. etc. as required in
    your recipe.
3   Stir in enough milk to make a stiff-ish
    dough.
4   Knead gently to smooth dough and
    flatten to 2 - 3 cm thick on floured
    surface.
5   Cut into rounds using cutter.
6   Place on baking sheet & brush tops
    with milk.
7   Bake 10 - 15 minutes until well risen
    and golden brown.
8   Cool immediately on cooling tray.

SHORTBREAD

INGREDIENTS
(accurate weighing essential)

180g/6oz   plain flour
120g/4oz   butter
60g/2oz   caster sugar

METHOD

1   Oven 160°c -170°c/Gas 4. Flour baking sheet.
2   Cream butter and sugar with wooden spoon until soft and creamy.
3   Gradually add all flour stirring well as you do so.
4   Bring mixture together with hands and place on lightly floured surface.
5   Roll out lightly, remembering to move the dough so that it doesn't stick, to a thickness of approx 0.5 cm / ¼ inch.
6   Cut out biscuits & place on lightly floured baking sheet.
7   Bake 10 - 15 minutes until pale golden.
8   Cool on cooling tray.
9   Sprinkle with caster sugar, if liked

SWISS ROLL

INGREDIENTS

3   eggs
90g/3oz   caster sugar
90g/3oz   SR flour

accurate weighing essential

FILLING

2 - 3tbsp jam (or lemon curd, chocolate spread etc.)
1   dessertspoon caster sugar

METHOD

1   Prepare swiss roll tin (30cm x 20cm - 12"x8") and turn oven on 200°c/gas 6.
2   Put eggs and sugar in mixing bowl and whisk until thick and creamy (ribbon stage).
3   Sieve flour into mixture. Carefully fold in with plastic scraper or metal spoon until ALL flour has disappeared.
4   Pour mixture into centre of tin and spread to corners quickly.
5   Put in oven for approx. 10 minutes.
6   Clear table and put sheet of greaseproof sprinkled with caster sugar ready. Soften jam/spread etc.
7   Remove sponge when just golden brown and springy to touch.
8   Turn upside down onto prepared paper. Remove greaseproof quickly, trim ends with sharp knife if necessary and carefully spread filling onto sponge.
9   Roll up immediately, rolling carefully away from you.
10 Put on a plate or cooling tray.

Alternatives: replace 1 dessertspoon flour with 1 dessertspoon cocoa powder and sieve in with flour.

SWEDISH
TEA RING

INGREDIENTS

DOUGH

1	sachet easy blend yeast
75g/3oz	brown sugar and 2 tsp ground cinnamon mixed together
125ml/¼pt	milk (warmed)
250g/8oz	strong plain flour

FILLING

15g/½oz	butter- melted
½tsp	salt

ICING

2tsp	sugar
250g/7oz	icing sugar
30g/1oz	butter/margarine
1 - 2tbsp	hot water
1	egg - beaten
few glacé cherries - mixed colours ideally	

METHOD

1. Oven 200ºc/gas 6. Put silicone paper on baking sheet.
2. Mix flour, salt, 2 tsp sugar & yeast. Rub in butter.
3. Mix beaten egg & warm milk.
4. Stir into flour to make soft dough.
5. Turn onto floured surface. Knead 5 minutes until smooth, not sticky.
6. Roll to rectangle approx. 25 x 37cm/ 10" x 15".
7. Brush with melted butter. Sprinkle with cinnamon sugar.
8. Roll up loosely like a long Swiss Roll.
9. Form into a circle on baking sheet. Moisten ends & firmly join. Place on baking sheet/silicone paper.
10. Clip dough with scissors on outside edge at 2.5cm/1" intervals almost cutting right through . Turn corners backwards + bend downwards so that they fan out slightly
11. Rise in warm place 15 minutes or until doubled in size.
12. Bake 20 - 25 minutes. Until light brown on top and bubbling sugar round edges. Put on cooling tray.
13. Slice cherries .
14. Make fairly thick icing. Pour over cooled tea ring & decorate with cut cherries.

TEA LOAF

INGREDIENTS

4oz/120g	margarine
½pt/280ml	tea
6oz/180g	mixed fruit
4oz/120g	sugar
9oz/270g	SR flour
1 level tsp	bicarbonate
½tsp	mixed spice

METHOD

1 Place margarine, tea, fruit and sugar in a pan.
2 Stir over a low heat, bring to boil and simmer for 4 minutes.
3 Allow to cool.
4 Mix together with dry ingredients.
5 Place in greased loaf tin and cook for 1 - 1¼ hrs. at Mark 4.
6 Leave to cool in tin for 10 minutes before turning out.

Chris Pollard

WHOLEFOOD MINCEMEAT SLICES

These are a good alternative to Mince Pies

INGREDIENTS

6oz/180g	butter/margarine
3oz/90g	soft brown sugar
8oz/240g	wholemeal flour
4oz/120g	porridge oats/muesli
8oz/240g	mincemeat (sweet)

METHOD

1 Line base of 11"x 7" (28 x 18cm) tin with silicone paper.
2 Pre-heat oven 200°c/Gas Mark 6
3 Mix flour and oats together.
4 Melt butter/margarine and sugar over a gentle heat.
5 Add this to flour and oats in a bowl.
6 Spoon half the mixture into tin pressing firmly into the corners.
7 Spread mincemeat evenly over this and cover with remaining mixture, pressing firmly.
8 Bake for 20 minutes or until lightly browned.
9 Cut into 12 squares and leave in tin to cool.

VICTORIA SANDWICH CAKE

INGREDIENTS

180g/6oz caster sugar
180g/6oz butter/soft margarine
180g/6oz self raising flour
3   large eggs
2 - 3tbsp jam
½tbsp   icing sugar

OR

180g   icing sugar
90g   butter/margarine (for buttercream)

METHOD

1   Oven 180°c/gas 4. Grease & line 2 x 18cm/7" sandwich cake tins.
2. Cream butter & sugar until pale & creamy (wooden spoon or electric mixer).
3   Beat eggs in small bowl. Add gradually to mixture. Use a little flour with last bit of egg.
4   Add flour and fold in carefully with spatula or metal spoon. Add a little cold water if necessary to form a soft mixture.
5   Divide mixture between tins. Smooth tops lightly.
6   Bake approx. 15-20 minutes or until well risen and golden.
7   Turn out carefully and cool on wire tray

FLAVOURS

        grated orange/lemon rind/juice
2   dessertspoons cocoa to filling+ 1 tablespoon water
1   dessertspoon instant coffee mixed with 1 tablespoon warm water

BUTTERCREAM

1   Soften butter in bowl and gradually add sieved icing sugar.
2   Add cocoa powder/strong (dissolved) coffee/grated lemon rind, juice etc. - for flavouring as desired.

FINISH CAKE
Soften jam and spread on base of one cake.

IF USING BUTTERCREAM

1   Spread on base of other cake.
2   Sandwich cakes together.
3   Sieve a little icing sugar over top.

Place on plate.

Sweets and Treats

CHOCOLATE FUDGE SAUCE

INGREDIENTS

90g/3oz plain chocolate, broken
30g/1oz butter
1 small can evaporated milk
60g soft brown sugar

METHOD

Put all ingredients in saucepan, stir over low heat until sugar has dissolved and chocolate melted.

Serve hot

HOT BLUEBERRY SAUCE

INGREDIENTS

240g/8oz fresh or frozen blueberries
75g/2½ oz sugar
1tsp cornflour
½ lemon – zest and juice
180g/6oz redcurrant jelly

METHOD

1 Mix cornflour, water, sugar and lemon thoroughly.
2 Put in saucepan, stir continuously over medium heat until boiling.
3 Reduce heat, add redcurrant jelly and simmer 5 minutes
4 Add blueberries, bring to boil, simmer over low heat 15 - 20 minutes or until thick.

Serve with ice cream, crepes, cheesecake, etc.

PEPPERMINT CREAMS

INGREDIENTS

350g icing Sugar + some extra
1 small egg white

OR

This can also be made using a box of Fondant Icing Powder. Omit egg white and follow instructions on packet.

½tsp peppermint essence/oil
small bar chocolate
green food colouring -
optional

METHOD

1 Separate egg. Beat white slightly.
2 Add peppermint. Stir in icing sugar until stiff (similar to playdough).
3 Colour half the mixture.
4 Roll out in icing sugar on a little icing sugar or cornflour. Cut out.
5 Melt chocolate (microwave or over hot water)
6 Dip ½ of peppermint cream in chocolate. Dry on waxed or greaseproof paper
7 Put in paper cases and box.

Will keep several weeks in fridge.

TRUFFLES

INGREDIENTS

60g/2oz	trifle sponges or cake crumbs
175g/6oz	plain chocolate
60g/2oz	butter
1tbsp	brandy

OR

	few drops brandy/rum essence
60g/2oz	sieved icing sugar
2tbsp	cocoa or chocolate strands/vermicelli
	plus extra icing sugar in case mixture needs more

METHOD

1 Break up trifle sponge cakes in crumbs.
2 Break up chocolate and place in a basin with butter. Melt by: [i] stand over a saucepan of hot water or [ii] Microwave on medium power for 1 min and stir , then 20 seconds at a time.
3 Stir in brandy; add sieved icing sugar and cake crumbs to form stiff mixture.
4 Leave mixture until cool enough to handle. Take spoonfuls of the mixture and roll in palms of hands into small balls.
5 Coat truffles with cocoa or vermicelli and place each one in paper sweet case or presentation box.

CHOCOLATE CHERRIES/NUTS

INGREDIENTS

glacé/Maraschino cherries (can be soaked in brandy/sherry etc)
nuts (Brazil, Hazelnuts etc - not soaked)
small bar of chocolate
paper sweet cases

METHOD

1 Melt chocolate (Microwave or over hot water)
2 Put a little in each case.
3 Place cherries or nuts on top.
4 Cover with chocolate. Leave to set.

MARZIPAN FRUITS

INGREDIENTS

¼ to ½lb	marzipan + a little icing sugar or cornflour (for kneading)
	cloves and food colouring
1tbsp	caster sugar
	sweet cases plus box or tin

METHOD

1 Divide marzipan and knead in colours.
2 Shape into fruits. Be creative!
3 Roll in caster sugar. Add cloves where necessary.
4 Place in sweet cases.

CREAMY TOFFEE

INGREDIENTS

240g/8oz	butter/margarine
480g/1lb	sugar
480g/1lb	golden syrup
1	medium tin condensed milk
1tsp	vinegar

METHOD

1 Melt butter. Add sugar, syrup and condensed milk
2 Bring to the boil, stirring with a long wooden spoon
3 Boil fairly fast for approx 20 minutes, stirring continuously. Add vinegar
4 Pour into shallow tin lined with silicone paper/baking parchment

Fill pan with warm water!!

NB Toffee is ready when it reaches 150ºc (using a sugar thermometer) or hardens quickly when a drop is put into cold water.

CAUTION - toffee is very hot and needs a strong, thick, large pan and careful supervision.

FUDGE

INGREDIENTS

275ml/½pt	milk
240g/8oz	butter
960g/2lb	sugar
2tbsp	golden syrup
1	can condensed milk

(Vary with additional chopped cherries, raisins, nuts etc)

METHOD

1 Lightly grease tin 30cm/12". Heat milk, butter and sugar in a large heavy-based pan until sugar dissolves.
2 Add syrup and condensed milk, bring to boil and boil lightly, stirring gently for 30 - 40 minutes until fudge reaches soft ball/240ºc. Test by dropping into cold water and it should be pliable.
3 Remove from heat, add any extra flavourings and beat with wooden spoon until thick and slightly grainy. NB This can be tiring!
4 Pour into tin and smooth.
5 Cool and cut into squares

CAUTION - fudge is very hot and needs a strong, thick, large pan and careful supervision.

ROCKY ROAD
SLICE

INGREDIENTS

200g	good quality milk chocolate
90g	dark chocolate
30g	butter
60g	mixed pink & white marshmallows, cut with scissors into small pieces
60g	shortbread or amaretti biscuits, chopped into bite-sized pieces
120g	roughly chopped nuts eg hazelnuts, pecan, almonds, macadamia
30g	raisins or glacé cherries (chopped)

METHOD

1   Line a 3cm deep, 8 x 25cm shallow baking tray with baking parchment/ greaseproof paper. Put the chocolates and butter in a heatproof bowl over a pan of simmering water (don't let the bowl touch the water) and stir, or on medium power in microwave, until melted.
2   Stir marshmallows into chocolate with remaining ingredients.
3   Spread into tray, chill in fridge for 2 hours or until hard.
4   Slice in the tray.

NUTTY CHOCOLATE
WHIRLS

INGREDIENTS

240g/½lb	marzipan - divide into 3 and colour 1 block green and 1 block chocolate brown
120g/4oz	glacé cherries, quartered
120g/4oz	flaked almonds
120g/4oz	chocolate, melted

METHOD

1   Roll marzipan into long, rectangular strips - put plain at bottom, green centre, brown on top (sandwich).
2   Place cherries along top and roll up like a swiss roll.
3   Cover with melted chocolate, sprinkle thickly with flaked almonds.
4   Put in fridge for chocolate to set.
5   Cut into slices.

TREACLE TOFFEE

INGREDIENTS

480g/1lb	brown sugar
60g/2oz	butter
120g/4oz	black treacle
120g/4oz	golden syrup
150ml/¼pt	water
1tsp	lemon juice

METHOD

1   Dissolve sugar in water, add lemon juice, butter, treacle and golden syrup.
2   Bring to boil to reach temperature of 140ºc, stir occasionally.
3   Pour into shallow tin lined with silicone paper / baking parchment.

CAUTION - toffee is very hot and needs a strong, thick, large pan and careful supervision.

TOFFEE APPLES

INGREDIENTS

360g/12oz	sugar
150ml/¼pt	water
60g/2oz	butter
120g/4oz	treacle/golden syrup
1tsp	vinegar
4	eating apples

METHOD

1 Put apples on wooden skewers.
2 Put all toffee ingredients in a heavy based pan.
3 Heat until dissolved, stirring occasionally.
4 Bring to the boil and boil rapidly until 145°c - or until a little will set in a cup of cold water.
5 Switch off and when bubbles die down lower apples carefully into toffee and coat.
6 Stand apples on waxed or silicone paper and leave to set.

CAUTION - the toffee reaches a very high temperature so careful supervision may be required.

UNCOOKED FUDGE

INGREDIENTS

240g/8oz	plain chocolate
120g/¼lb	butter
1	egg
480g/1lb	caster sugar
2	level tbsp condensed milk
60g/2oz	chopped nuts

METHOD

1 Melt chocolate and butter in heatproof bowl.
2 Mix egg, sugar and condensed milk together.
3 Blend in chocolate and butter.
4 Stir in nuts and pour into lightly greased 17cm/7" tin
5 Chill in fridge for several hours until set.

Miscellaneous

APPLE CHUTNEY

INGREDIENTS

1½kg/3lbs	cooking apples
480g/1lb	onions
275ml/½pt	vinegar
1dstsp	salt
½tsp	cayenne pepper
240g/8oz	sultanas
700g/1½lbs	sugar

METHOD

1 Peel, core and chop apples.
2 Peel onions. Chop finely.
3 Put all ingredients except sugar in large pan, bring to the boil, cover and simmer. Stir occasionally. Cook for 30 - 45 minutes until apples are soft.
4 Add sugar and simmer uncovered for further 30 - 45 minutes or until chutney is thick.
5 Spoon into warm, clean jars and seal with airtight covers.

BANANA AND ORANGE SMOOTHIES

INGREDIENTS

1	large banana (ripe)
	juice of 2 oranges (about 150ml)
200ml	white grape juice/apple juice
	juice of 2 limes (1 tablespoon)
2 - 3	ice cubes

METHOD

1 Put all ingredients in a blender and whiz until smooth.

Tip: Freeze peeled, chopped bananas and blend straight from frozen in a powerful blender. You will not need the ice cubes and the drink will be ice-cold with a creamy texture.

Liz Cummings

BASIC BREAD

INGREDIENTS

250g	strong plain flour/bread flour
1	packet easy blend yeast
½tsp	salt
125ml	(approx) hand hot water
50g	extra flour (for adjustments if necessary)

optional

½tbsp	vegetable. oil
1	beaten egg
	poppy seeds/sesame seeds/ cracked wheat (for toppings)

METHOD

1 Oven on 200ºc/Gas 6. Silicone paper on baking sheet. Organise ingredients.
2 Put flour, yeast and salt (and oil if using) in mixing bowl. Stir well with wooden spoon.
3 Make a well in centre and stir in enough water to form a fairly soft dough.
4 Bring the mixture together so that dough is smooth.
5 Flour surface well, put dough on and knead evenly for at least 5 minutes.
6 Shape the dough either into rolls/ shapes or a single loaf, put on baking tray, cover and prove in a warm place until doubled in size.
7 If using, brush tops with beaten egg and sprinkle with topping(s).
8. Bake for 10 - 15 minutes until lightly browned. (20 minutes for loaf)

Cool on cooling tray before packing in airtight container.

Optional adaptations: chopped sun-dried tomatoes; crushed garlic; grated cheese; herbs. Add to flour and yeast before water.

CHEF FIDO DOG BISCUITS
(ALL THE WAY FROM USA)

Makes about 27 small or 12 large biscuits.

INGREDIENTS

¾	cup of hot water or meat juices (or add Oxo or chicken stock cube)
⅓	cup of margarine
½	cup powdered milk
½tsp	salt (unless you are using a stock cube)
1	beaten egg
3	cups wholemeal flour

METHOD

1. Using a large bowl, pour the hot liquid over the margarine. Stir in the milk powder, salt and beaten egg. Add ½ cup of flour at a time and knead well. Add a little more flour if necessary.
2. Roll out the dough to ½ inch thickness. Cut out - with a bone-shaped cutter if possible.
3. Bake for 50 minutes at 80ºC.

Dogs love them and you can use up your odds and ends.

Melanie Sackett

FRUIT SMOOTHIE

INGREDIENTS
(for 1 Smoothie)

Fruit:	a mixture or one single fruit allow 200g + per person (but be flexible) e.g. banana, strawberries (fresh, frozen or tinned), mango (ripe), peaches, apricots, nectarines, passion fruit, raspberries, blueberries NB a mixture of fresh, tinned or frozen fruit is equally acceptable
125ml	apple juice - optional for non-dairy smoothie

Optional

1	yogurt - plain or flavoured
125 ml/¼	pt milk
1	scoop ice cream ice
100ml	fruit juice

METHOD

1. Wash and peel fruit as necessary.
2. Put all fruit in blender (with a little fruit juice). Fit lid tightly.
3. Blend until smooth.
4. Add any other ingredients. Blend.
5. Serve immediately.

LEMON CURD

INGREDIENTS

3	lemons (or limes)
120g/¼lb	butter
240g/8oz	granulated sugar
2	large eggs (beaten)

Small, clean, warmed jars + jam pot covers

METHOD

1 Wash lemons and finely grate. Squeeze juice.
2 Melt butter in basin over hot water on a low heat.
3 Add juice , rind, sugar and eggs, keep stirring until mixture thickens.
4 Pour carefully into jars and cover.

Keeps in a refrigerator for 2 - 3 weeks.

MINCEMEAT

INGREDIENTS

1lb/450g	mixed dried fruit
½tsp	nutmeg
2	large baking apples
½tsp	cinnamon
¼lb/125g	shredded suet
½lb/250g	soft brown sugar
	juice and rind of lemon
1tbsp	sherry/brandy

METHOD

1 Mix dried fruit ,suet, sugar & spices in large bowl.
2 Peel & grate apples onto fruit mixture. Grate lemon rind ,squeeze juice & add to mixture with sherry/brandy.
3 Pack tightly into clean jars and cover.

NB For best flavour allow it to mature for a couple of weeks.

CINNAMON TOAST

INGREDIENTS

5	eggs, beaten
3	tablespoons milk
1	pinch of salt
I	tablespoon butter
5	rounds white bread sliced. Adjust the amount of mixture according to the number of slices of bread.
2	tablespoons caster sugar with ¼ to ½ teaspoon of cinnamon powder. Adjust the cinnamon to your own taste.

METHOD

1 Beat eggs, milk and sugar in a large bowl.
2 Heat the butter gently in a non-stick frying pan. (Don't let it brown.)
3 Immerse a slice of bread into the egg mixture, then fry on a low heat on both sides until golden brown.
4 Sprinkle the toast generously with the sugar and cinnamon mixture. Repeat with all slices of bread

OE Magazine

OVEN SODA BREAD

INGREDIENTS

700g/1.5lb	plain flour
10ml/2tsp	sugar
7.5ml/1.5tsp	bicarbonate of soda
7.5ml/1.5tsp	cream of tarter
5ml/1tsp	salt
450ml/15floz	buttermilk (if you cannot get buttermilk soured or fresh milk will do)

METHOD

1 Preheat the oven to 200°c/Gas Mark 6.
2 Lightly flour a baking sheet.
3 Sift the dry ingredients together and mix in just enough buttermilk to make a fairly stiff dough.
4 Turn the dough out onto a floured surface and knead lightly until the dough has a smooth texture and shape into a round.
5 Place on the baking sheet and cut a slash or a cross in the top.
6 Bake for 50 - 60 minutes.
7 Leave to cool wrapped in a clean tea towel.

Best eaten spread liberally with butter and jam!!

OE Annette Duffy (née Glennon)

OLD FASHIONED LEMONADE

INGREDIENTS

1 - 2	lemons*
½ - 1tbsp	sugar
275ml/½pt water	
	a few mint leaves

METHOD

1 Wash lemon. Pare off rind, minus pith, with a parer or vegetable peeler.
2 Put water and rind in saucepan, bring slowly to the boil.
3 Switch off and leave to infuse (at least ½ an hour if possible). Add sugar to own taste.
4 Squeeze lemon(s), strain cooled syrup and add juice.
5 Serve in glasses with slice of lemon, mint leaf and ice.

* Try a mixture of citrus fruits in this recipe.

THE MAYONNAISE JAR
AND COFFEE
(TONGUE IN CHEEK)

When things in your life seem almost too much to handle, when 24 hours in a day are not enough, remember the mayonnaise jar ... and the coffee.

A professor stood before his philosophy class and had some items in front of him. When the class began, wordlessly, he picked up a very fat, large and empty mayonnaise jar and proceeded to fill it with golf balls. He then asked the students if the jar was full. They agreed that it was.

The professor then picked up a box of pebbles and poured them into the jar. He shook the jar lightly, the pebbles rolled into the open areas between the golf balls. He then asked the students again if the jar was full. They agreed it was.

The professor next picked up a box of sand and poured it into the jar. Of course, the sand filled up everything else. He asked once more if the jar was full. The students responded with a unanimous "yes".

The professor then produced two cups of coffee from under the table and poured the entire contents into the jar, effectively filling the empty space between the sand. The students laughed.

"Now" said the professor, as the laughter subsided, "I want you to recognise that this jar represents your life. The golf balls are the important things - your family, your children, your health, your friends and your favourite passions - things that if everything else was lost and only they remained, your life would still be full. The pebbles are the other things that matter like your job, your house and your car. The sand is everything else - the small stuff.

"If you put the sand into the jar first," he continued "there is no room for the pebbles or the golf balls. The same goes for life. If you spend all your time and energy on the small stuff, you will never have room for the things that are important to you.

Pay attention to the things that are important to your happiness. Play with your children. Take time to get medical checkups. Take your partner out to dinner. Read a book, take some leisure time with family and friends.

There will always be time to clean the house and do the chores.

Take care of the golf balls first, the things that really matter. Set your priorities. The rest is just sand."

One of the students raised her hand and inquired what the coffee represented. The professor smiled, "I'm glad you asked. It just goes to show you that, no matter how full your life may seem, there's always room for a couple of cups of coffee with a friend."

OE Magazine

SPECIAL DIET TO HELP WOMEN COPE WITH THE STRESS THAT BUILDS UP DURING THE DAY

BREAKFAST

1   grapefruit
1   slice whole-wheat toast
1   cup skimmed milk

LUNCH

1   small portion lean, steamed chicken
     with a cup of spinach
1   cup herbal tea
1   Tim Tam (Chocolate biscuit)

AFTERNOON TEA

The rest of the Tim Tams from the packet.
1   tub of Gino Ginelli ice cream with
     chocolate topping.

DINNER

4   bottles of wine (red or white)
2   loaves garlic bread
1   family size Supreme pizza
3   Snickers bars.

LATE NIGHT SNACK

1   whole cheesecake (eaten directly
     from the freezer!).

OE Magazine 2007
Passed from Kate Cary (At School 1979-86)

RASPBERRY AND APPLE JAM

INGREDIENTS

1.5 kg/3lbs   cooking apples
1kg/2lbs   raspberries
2   lemons
600ml/1pt   water
1.75kg/4 lbs preserving sugar

Clean, warm jars + covers
Large wooden spoon required

METHOD

1   Peel, core and slice apples. Grate lemon
     rind and juice. Save skins and pips.
2   Put apples in large pan (preferably
     jam pan but otherwise a heavy pan
     with capacity of at least 5 litres. Add
     lemon rind, juice and water. If possible,
     tie apple cores, pips and lemon skins in
     muslin/cotton and add to pan.
3   Heat gently, bring to boil and simmer
     for approx 15 minutes or until apples
     are soft. Add raspberries and simmer
     for 15 minutes. Stir occasionally
4   Remove muslin bag - squeeze juice
     back into pan.
5   Add sugar, heat gently, stirring until
     sugar dissolves. Bring to boil, do not
     stir.
6   Boil rapidly until setting point is
     reached
7   Switch off. Add a little butter to
     disperse any scum.
8   Cool slightly and ladle into jars. Cover
     and label

To test setting point of jam – pour a little
onto a very cold plate, put in fridge/freezer
to cool then push jam with finger. If it
wrinkles, it is ready.

Take care not to overboil jam.

PLAYDOUGH RECIPE

For Playing with – Not Eating!

Useful and easy to make for busy mums to
keep children busy modelling.

INGREDIENTS

2tsp	cream of tartar
1	cup of plain flour
½	cup of cooking salt
1	cup of water
1tbsp	cooking oil (be careful not to be too generous with the oil)
	food colouring
	almond essence

METHOD

1   Place all ingredients in a saucepan
    (non-stick is best).
2   Mix well together, then cook slowly
    stirring all the time, until the mixture
    comes away from the pan sides.
3   Add food colouring gradually as you
    stir and almond essence drops, just to
    make it smell pleasant for children's
    play.
4   Allow to cool.
5   Knead together for a while, then leave
    to go completely cold.

It will keep 3 - 4 weeks (or even longer) if
kept in cling film or polythene bag and
then in a plastic box in the fridge.

Jill Oldfield

Index

LIST OF SOURCES / BIBLIOGRAPHY

'**The Book of Household Management**' – Mrs Isabella Beeton *1861*

'**Scholars Handbook of Household Management and Cookery**' - compiled for the **School Board for London** by WB Tegetmeier (author of *'A Manual of Domestic Economy'*) and The National Training School *1876*

'**Occupations Accessible to Women – subs. Cookery Instructor**' *1879* www.victorianlondon.org

New York Times article - '**Beef Tea ; Some advice to those persons who use it**' *1880*

Victorian Advertising *'VICTORIAN BABY FOOD '* - www.sensationpress.com

KEGHS Chronicle (Phoenix Magazine) Article by Miss George entitled *'COOKING' 1896*

Extracts from King Edward Foundation Governors' Orders (various) *1897 -1918*

'**King Edward's Cookery Book**' - Florence A George *1901*

'**Gloucestershire School of Domestic Science Recipe Book**' *1902*

'**Poverty: a study of town life**' by Benjamin Seebohm Rowntree *1902*

'**The Official Handbook of the National Training School of Cookery**' – *1905 edition*

'**Mrs Beeton's Cookery Book** ' - 'One Shilling' - Ward Lock *1908*

'**Vegetarian Cookery** ' - Florence A George *1908*

'**Wartime Cookery**' - Florence A George *1917*

'**Manual of Cookery**' - Florence A George *1921*

'**Home Economics**' journal - '**Domestic Subjects Review**'. March 1959 - Article on '**Cookery Reformers Before Mrs Beeton**' - M Schofield

'**Plenty and Want**' John Burnett *1966*

'**King Edward VI High School for Girls – Birmingham Part 1 1883 -1925**' WI Candler (Winifred Vardy) *1971*

'**The National**' - The story of the National Training College of Domestic Subjects Dorothy Stone *1973*

'**Housecraft**' journal *Aug/Sept 1975* '**Triple Centenary Celebrations**'

Dissertation - **' Is Home Economics a justifiable subject in the Secondary School Curriculum?' -** sections 1 & 2 SA Bamforth *June 1979*

'Housecraft' - journal. Article **' Those Were the Days'** Muriel Grimwade *June 1981*

'Seven Hundred Years of English Cooking' Maxime McEndry *1983*

'Childhood transformed: working-class children in nineteenth-century England' by Eric Hopkins *1994* Manchester University Press

'An isolated missionary: the domestic subjects teacher in England 1870 -1914' Annmarie Turnbull - Women's History Review *March 1994*

Article - **'Women and Victorian Values 1837 -1910'** Ed. C. Anne Wilson (Brotherton and Bodleian Libraries)

'Fluid pleasures: a social history of drinks in modern Britain' John Burnett *1999* Routledge

'Britain in 1900' Asa Briggs - **History Today Magazine** (article) *December 2000*

'From plain fare to fusion food: British diet from the 1890s to the 1990s' Derek J. Oddy *2003* Boydell Press

'The working class in Britain, 1850-1939' John Benson *2003* IB Tauris & co

'Changes in Carcase Meat & Offal Consumption ' DEFRA Report *2007*

'Facts about bread in the UK' (article) Bread Consumption Changes – Flour Advisory Bureau/Federation of Bakers *2007*

'Please, sir, I want some more' Comparison of the Workhouse Diet with that of Oliver Twist Article in BMJ *Dec 2008*

'The Workhouse Cookbook' Peter Higginbotham *2008*

Cook School - Food Education magazine of the' Focus on Food' campaign - **'Cooking the Books'** Vol 7 Issue *June 2008* (Design Dimension Educational Trust)

Purchasing Power of British Pounds from 1264 to Present measuringworth.com (article and tool)

'Victorian Britain: The Cookery Book as Source Material' by Lynn Abrams BBC *2009*

'Turnip Tops and Nettles on Toast - A taste of Victorian Vegetarian Cookery' - (article) Anne O'Connell (author of *Early Vegetarian Recipes* and an Old Edwardian!) *2009*